ISBN 978-1-332-75376-5
PIBN 10438528

FB &c Ltd, Dalton House, 60 Windsor Avenue, London, SW19 2RR.
Company number 08720141. Registered in England and Wales.

For support please visit www.forgottenbooks.com

WHITNEY'S

"CHOICE OF EMBLEMES."

A FAC-SIMILE REPRINT.

EDITED BY

HENRY GREEN, M.A.

WITH

AN INTRODUCTORY DISSERTATION,
ESSAYS LITERARY AND BIBLIOGRAPHICAL,
AND EXPLANATORY NOTES.

LONDON: Lovell Reeve & Co.
CHESTER: Minshull & Hughes. NANTWICH: E. H. Griffiths.
M.DCCC.LXVI.

"nd sothely he hathe taken vpon hym," the reprint "of this present Boke neyther for hope of rewarde nor lawde of man: but onely for the holsome instruccion commodyte and doctryne of wysdome."

Alexander Barclay, A.D. 1509.

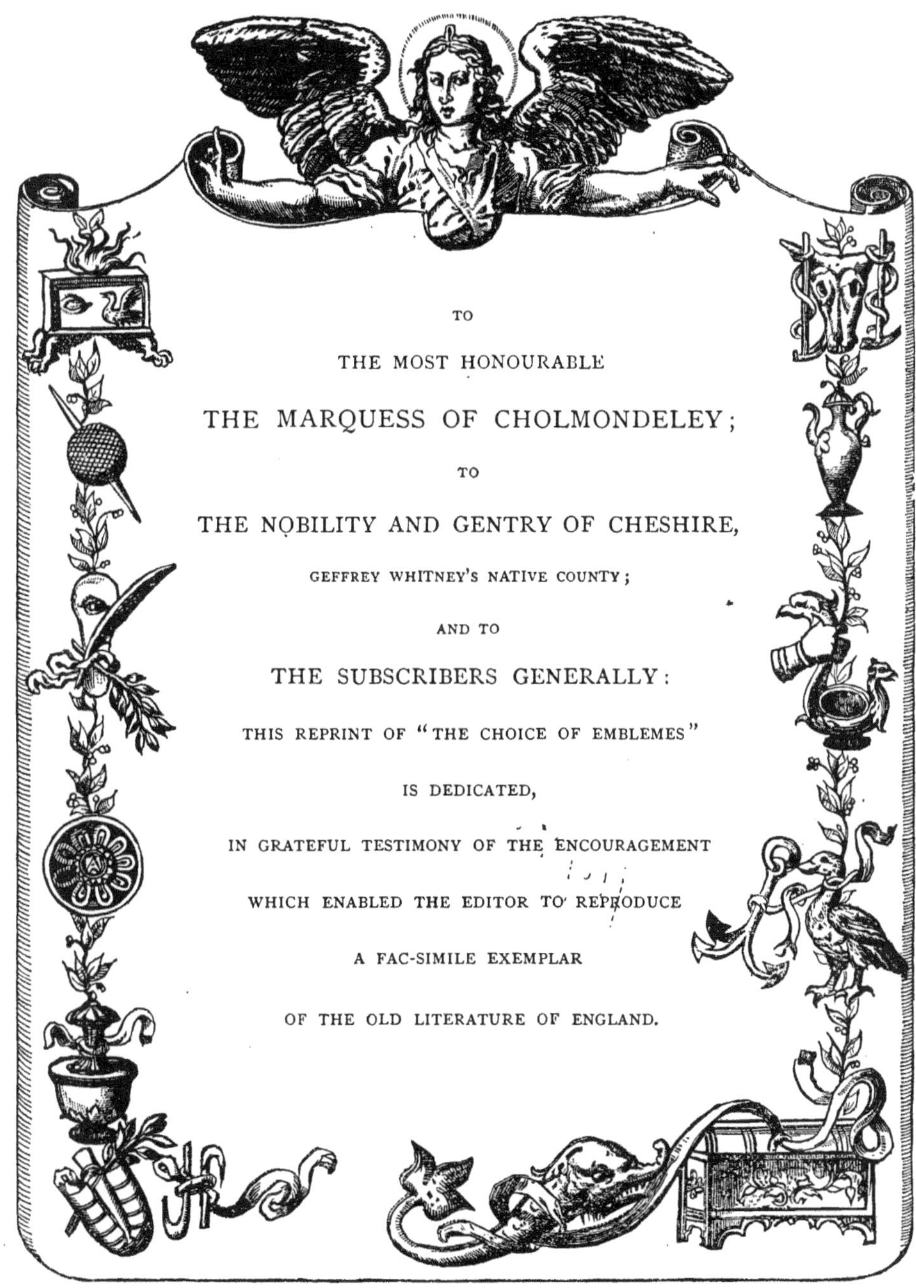

TO

THE MOST HONOURABLE

THE MARQUESS OF CHOLMONDELEY;

TO

THE NOBILITY AND GENTRY OF CHESHIRE,

GEFFREY WHITNEY'S NATIVE COUNTY;

AND TO

THE SUBSCRIBERS GENERALLY:

THIS REPRINT OF "THE CHOICE OF EMBLEMES"

IS DEDICATED,

IN GRATEFUL TESTIMONY OF THE ENCOURAGEMENT

WHICH ENABLED THE EDITOR TO REPRODUCE

A FAC-SIMILE EXEMPLAR

OF THE OLD LITERATURE OF ENGLAND.

VICTORIA EX LABORE
HONESTA, ET VTILIS.

"Victory, achieved by Labour, honourable and useful."

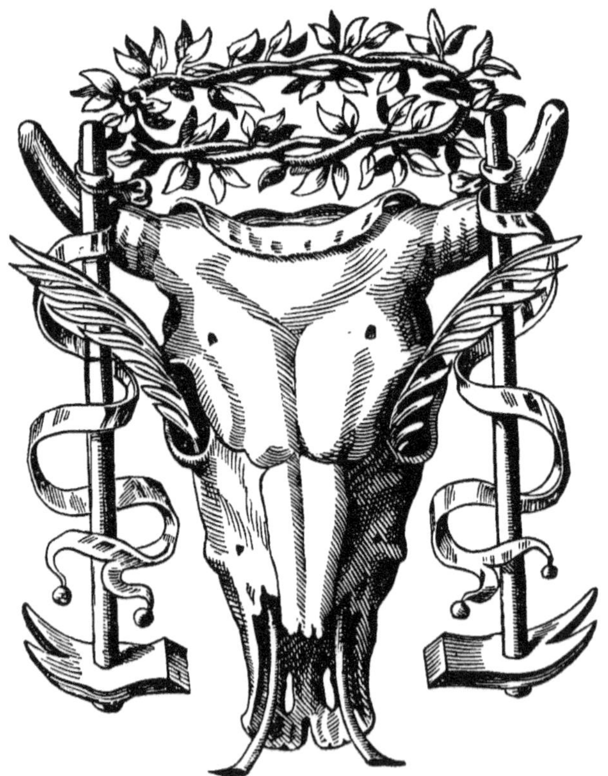

Constanter et syncere.

THE BADGE, MOTTO AND AUTOGRAPH OF GEFFREY WHITNEY.

TO THE READER.

EMORIALS of the Elizabethan culture, like mansions in the style of the Elizabethan architecture, would soon be passing away, were it not that they are reproduced from time to time, and reinstated in the interest and perchance in the regard of the literary world. When a work curious and instructive, if not of high value, has almost perished from the ravages of age, no disservice can it be to literature to rescue it from impending oblivion and offer it again to public notice. The inheritance which has come to us from a renowned ancestry is thus maintained in honour, and a restoration though it be only of a summer-house in a pleasure-garden, or of an oratory where by succeeding generations prayer was wont to be made, betokens as much reverence and love towards the illustrious dead, as if we had power to inscribe their names in the world's pantheon or to raise some monument of grandeur that would endure for ages. Whitney's own ideas are in fact so carried out:

"For writinges last when wee bee gonne, and doe preserue our name."

The work of restoration and of illustration now attempted for Whitney's Emblems was entered upon with a love for it, as well as from a desire to make the emblem literature of the sixteenth century more known; and it may be that such love may have covered a multitude of sins in the Author's style and mode both of thought and expression; but in stating the simple fact that his labours have been lightened and repaid by the liking which he had for them, the editor does not wish a single fault to be condoned. The themes here pursued have seldom if ever been treated of to the same extent or in the manner adopted,—and the probability is that some errors have been fallen into which further researches will rectify, and that inquiries have been left unattempted which are needed for the true appreciation of the subject. To place his readers as far as he can on the vantage ground both for judging his labours and for following them out to greater perfectness, the editor presents a full general Index as well as several special Indices, and has in most cases been scrupulous to name and quote his authorities. This apparatus will render the work of greater service to literary men.

So far as is ascertained no similar work exists, and though very incomplete as a history outside of the period which it embraces and of the special object to which it is devoted, it will supply the student and the general reader with information respecting emblem books and authors not easily accessible, and will enable him, if so disposed, to arrive at other stores of knowledge on the same subject. Some of the volumes consulted are of great rarity and to be found only in choice and richly-furnished libraries. For this reason, instead of a simple reference the titles themselves are photo-lithographically exhibited, and one or more pages of the devices in each emblem-book which Whitney adopted are also given in fac-simile. This feature of the work the editor trusts will be very useful to those readers who have not opportunities for consulting the old emblematists, or who may desire to see what they really are.

Philothei Symb. Christ. A writer of the sixteenth century, Hachtenburg of Francfort, 1577, assures us with much positiveness of expression, "Not one in a hundred can produce a really good emblem; not one in a thousand is competent to pass judgment upon the emblems of others." This sentiment is repeated not in depreciation of any opinion on the editor's share in this reprint and on the essays and notes with which it is accompanied, — but as an occasion to remind readers that a fac-simile by the photo-lithographic process is very different from that by the engraver's art and skill. The burin can retouch what is defective in the original, — can heighten the beauty and conceal the blemishes and yet preserve an identity of outline and character, — but the sun-light, the lens, and the camera reproduce without correction or adornment; if the original be worn and faded, — worn and faded is the copy; as the presses of Rome, Venice, Paris, Lyons, Basle, and Antwerp left their work three centuries since, — exactly so does it reappear; and this constitutes the defect as well as the excellence of photo-lithography in the printing of books.

The skill and pains bestowed by the various artists on the volume now in the reader's hands call for the editor's expression of approval. The stone has been made to give back the images, the letters and forms which the sunlight had drawn from the old pages set before it. To Mr. BROTHERS are due the photographs and their preparation, and to Mr. HARRISON the impressions themselves; the embellished capitals and other woodcuts are by Mr. MORTON, and the letter-press printing is the work of Messrs. CHARLES SIMMS & Co.

No more need I say than to express the hope that the study of the Emblem literature may be revived,— and other similar works find a similar republication.

These lines, the last as I imagined of this work, had been written and printed, and the proof awaited only revision ere my editorial labours would be ended, when, on the 14th of February 1866, I received some further information of high interest respecting the author, to which I ought at least to allude, especially as it comes from an American branch of the family, which under their ancestor, John Whitney, settled in New England so long ago as April 1635. His descendant, Henry Austin Whitney esq., of Boston, U. S. A., writes to me from the Hague, February 5th, 1866:

"I was exceedingly gratified and surprised to-day, during a visit to Leyden, to find that you had carried into effect what has for several years been one of my *dreams*, — the re-production of Whitney's emblems in fac-simile. My only regret is that the work has probably so far progressed that you will not be able to make use of one or two items relating to our author which it is in my power to furnish." "The most important of my collections is the *Will of Geffrey Whitney*, of which I have a copy in Boston. It is quite curious and important as settling the date of the writer's death, 1603 or 4, I think. In the testament, if I recollect rightly, he gives his library of Latin books to his nephew the son of his brother Brooke Whitney, 'on condition that he become a scholar.'"

Compare with Intro. Diss. pp. liv. and lv. Also p. lxxxiii.

See Emb. p. 88, and Intro. Diss. xlv. and xlvii.

Mr. H. A. Whitney then informs me that he has a large collection of materials relating to the Whitneys of different counties, some portion of which would explain who Robert Whitney is, referred to by me, and would also give data relating to Geffrey Whitney, our author's cousin, "Merchant Tailor of London." He sought out what escaped my inquiries in July last, — the original manuscript Catalogue of the Students at the University of Leyden, and in the General Index found "*Godf. Whitneus,*" with reference to p. 187 of the same volume, "where appears this

See Introd. Diss. pp. xxxviii.

Emb. p. 181; Intro. Diss. p. xlvii.

Vol. i. 1575-1616.

Compare with Intro. Diss p liv.

entry: '*Anno* 1586, *Martii* 1. *Godfridus Whitneus, Junior, Anglus*.'" This undoubtedly refers to our author, who, for several pages, is the only Englishman recorded.

The same letter also remarks: "On a trip of pleasure through Amsterdam to Paris, I resolved to make a brief visit to Leyden, not only as a place of peculiar interest to a native of New England, but in order to satisfy myself on one or two points relating to the author of the Emblems. In pursuance of my purpose I sought the University, and on making known the object of my inquiries, the librarian, M. Du Rieu, stated that Mr. Green was in Leyden about July last in quest of similar information. He at once kindly showed me the specimen sheets of your new edition, and I had just time to glimpse at the interesting and satisfactory essay read before the Cheshire Archæological Society. I was, I assure you, pleased to find that I have been so ably and *thoroughly* anticipated, and can now only regret that I had not known of your undertaking in October last, before leaving home, as it would have been my pleasure to have placed at your disposal whatever material was at my command."

So courteous and valuable an expression of regard for the labours I have been engaged in and brought to a conclusion, I acknowledge with the highest respect and under a deep sense of obligation, for the true liberality of feeling which dictated it; and I stop the press to add that should Mr. Henry Austin Whitney resolve on offering to the world the information respecting Geffrey Whitney which is in his possession, I shall most cheerfully give him every facility in my power for communicating with my subscribers. Possibly an Appendix to this fac-simile reprint might satisfy the conditions of the case and supply the admirers of emblem literature with the additional materials. I regret if my own labours interfere with those of one who by position and kinsmanship to the author had a superior claim over mine to be editor of "The Choice of Emblemes." He will not however object that in the breast of a stranger there has been kindled the admiration which in himself was a natural feeling of affection towards a writer who nearly three hundred years ago bore and adorned the Whitney name.

February 19*th*, 1866.

TABLE OF CONTENTS.

"*Per cæcum videt omnia punctum.*"

INTRODUCTORY DISSERTATION.

CHAPTER I.

EMBLEM LITERATURE.

SECTION I. — Nature of Emblems.

GEFFREY WHITNEY, in defining, as he does very accurately, the nature of Emblems, assigns to them almost their strictly literal meaning, as ornaments placed upon any surface, or inlaid, so as to form a pattern or device. He says: "The worde being in Greeke ἐμβάλλεσθαι, vel ἐπεμβλῆσθαι, is as muche to saye in Englishe as *To set in*, or *To put in:* properlie ment by suche figures or workes, as are wroughte in plate, or in stones in the pauementes, or on the waules, or suche like, for the adorning of the place: hauinge some wittie deuise expressed with cunning woorkemanship, somethinge obscure to be perceiued at the first, whereby, when with further consideration it is vnderstood, it maie the greater delighte the behoulder." So, the article Emblema, by James Yates, M.A., defines the word as denoting "an inlaid ornament," and applies it to works resembling "our marquetry, buhl, and Florentine mosaics," and to "those in which crusts (*crustæ*) exquisitely wrought in relief and of precious metals, such as gold, silver, and amber, were fastened upon the surface of vessels or other pieces of furniture."

See his Address to the Reader.

Smith's Dict. Gk. and Rom. Ant. 2nd ed. p. 456.

Spenser appears to have such work in view, when he describes "a throne of gold full bright and sheene:"

Faerie Queene, v. 9. 27.

> "Adorned all with gemmes of endlesse price,
> As either might for wealth have gotten beene,
> Or could be fram'd by workman's rare device;
> And all embost with lyons and with flourdelice."

And when Shakespeare sets forth the coronation of "The goodliest woman," Anne Bullen, he avers:

Hen. VIII. act iv. sc. i. l 87.

> "She had all the royal makings of a queen;
> As holy oil, Edward Confessor's crown,
> The rod, and bird of peace, and all such emblems
> Laid nobly on her."

Syntagma de Symbolis: per Clavdivm Minoem. Antv. 1581, p. 13.

An early commentator on Emblem-books, Claude Mignault, in 1574, endeavours to establish a distinction between *emblems* and *symbols*, which "many persons," he affirms, "rashly and ignorantly confound together. The force of the emblem depends upon the symbol, but they differ as man and animal; the latter has a more general meaning, the former a more special. All men are animals, but all animals are not men; so all emblems are symbols, tokens, or signs, but all symbols are not emblems: the two possess affinity indeed, but not identity."

We shall form, however, a sufficiently correct notion on this subject, if we conclude, that any figure engraven, embossed, or drawn,—any moulding, or picture, the implied meaning of which is something additional to what the actual delineation represents, is an emblem. Some thought or fancy, some sentiment or saying is portrayed, and the portraiture constitutes an emblem. Thus hieroglyphics, heraldic badges, significant carvings, and picture writings, are emblems; besides the forms, or devices, visibly delineated, they possess secret meanings, and shadow forth, or *line* forth sentiments, feelings, or proverbial truths.

Naturally and easily the term emblem became applicable to any painting, drawing, or print that was representative of an action, of a quality of mind, or of any peculiarity or attribute of character. Emblems in fact were, and are, a species of hieroglyphics, in which the figures or pictures, besides denoting the natural objects to which they bear resemblances, were employed to express properties of the mind, virtues and abstract ideas, and all the operations of the soul.

Excepting in the Sacred Scriptures, the earliest account we have of a work of emblematic art is the description which Homer gives, so graphically, of the forging by Vulcan of a shield for Achilles. It is solid and large, decorated all over; round it is a shining rim, triple, like marble bright, and from it a silver belt: on the shield itself there were five tablets, and for it many figures of skilful workmanship. Hesiod also, though not with equal beauty, gives a similar description of the shield of Hercules; and the two find imitators in Virgil, when the shield of Æneas is spoken of as a specimen of artistic power.

Iliad, xviii. 478-607.

Eoeæ of Hesiod, iv. 141-317.

Æneid, viii. 615-731.

But a work, truly emblematical, is presented so early as about 400 years B.C.: it is *The Tablet of Cebes*, a disciple of Socrates. Of the numerous editions, between 1497 and our own day, we give the title-page of one, which to the original Greek adds a translation both into Latin and Arabic, and which also contains a pretty emblematical device of the printer, "Fac et spera," *Work and hope.* The *Tablet* itself is a philosophical description of a picture which, it is said, was set up in the temple of Kronos at Athens or at Thebes, and which presents a symbolical view of Human Life—of its temptations and dangers, and of the course to be persevered in to attain the mansions of blessedness. The persons, characters and circumstances are drawn in so clear and lively a manner as to have furnished to the celebrated Dutch designer and engraver, Romyn de Hooghe, sufficient guidance for delineating the whole story of Human Life as narrated to the Grecian sage.

See Plate I.

Plate III.

Of Cebes himself we need only say that he was cotemporary with Parrhasius the painter, Euclid of Megara, and Lysias the orator. Xenophon ranks him among the few intimate friends of Socrates who excelled the rest in the innocency of their lives; and Plato names him as "intimate and friendly with us all," and characterizes him in the *Phædon* as a sagacious investigator of truth, never yielding his assent without convincing reasons.

Memorabilia, i, 2.

Epistle 13.

The Hieroglyphics of Horapollo, or *Horus Apollo*, of which the title-page to the Paris edition of 1551 is given in Plate II., is professedly written in the language of ancient Egypt, and was translated into Greek towards the end of the fifth century, in the time of the emperor Zeno. It is certainly a book of emblems, and probably the most ancient we possess. With the emblem writers of the fifteenth and sixteenth centuries it obtained high authority, and undoubtedly served them for guidance; but very

Plate II.

b 2

contradictory opinions are entertained of the work in the present day: some maintaining that the writer "was a native of Egypt," and that he was "a person who knew the monuments well, and had studied them with care;" others averring that "his authority as an interpreter is in itself worth nothing," and "that the power of reading a hieroglyphical inscription was not possessed by him, if it existed in his time." *

Smith's Dict. Gk. and Rom. Biog. vol. ii. pp. 517-518.

Kenrick's Anc. Egypt, vol. i. pp. 288-290.

It may here be observed that the symbols on the dedication-page of this fac-simile reprint of *Whitney* are taken from one of the emblems of Achilles Bocchius, edition 1574, who names them Egyptian letters; but on Samuel Sharpe's very competent authority I learn, they may be *Gipsy* marks, but are not true Egyptian signs. Taking them for what they are worth, I nevertheless find the *eye* symbolical of Deity; the *lamp-burning*, of life; the *lamp-extinguished*, of the soul freed from the body; the *ox's-head*, of labour; and the *spindle*, of the thread of life. A *feather* and a *laurel-branch*, also occurring in the dedication-page, are hieroglyphics, according to Horapollo, and have a meaning. The others, which remain unexplained, doubtless were significant to Achilles Bocchius, and would be to ourselves could we but obtain his key.

Plate XXIII.

Horapollo, ed. 1551, pp. 219-222.

Horapollo, bk. ii. 81 and 46, ed. 1551, pp. 178 and 143.

Whitney (as at p. 126) and the other emblematists not unfrequently had recourse to the descriptions in *Horapollo*. One of his hieroglyphics we have had figured; it is the swan,—to symbolize old age loving music,—the reason assigned being, "because this bird when it is old sends forth its sweetest melody."

Plate II.

Horapollo, bk. ii. 39, ed. 1551, p. 136.

Coins and medals, the crests and cognizances of heraldry, the flower-language of Persian and Hindoo maidens, the picture-writing of the Mexicans, and the tree-and-tomahawk newspapers of the North American Indians,—all would require full notice as instances of emblem art, were we attempting more than a sketch.

Eschenberg's Manual, by Fiske, pp. 313, 349, 375.

A very brief statement will suffice to point out how they fur-

* "The only ancient author who has left us a correct and full account of the principle of the Egyptian writing is the learned Alexandrian father, Clemens, who wrote towards the end of the second century after Christ." So testifies John Kenrick. And whoever desires to read a brief yet admirably clear account of modern discoveries respecting the meaning of the Egyptian hieroglyphics is advised to consult his work, *Ancient Egypt under the Pharaohs*, two volumes 8vo, London 1850.

Kenrick's Anc. Egypt, vol. i. p. 291.

nish examples of the nature of emblems. On Grecian coins, the owl, to use heraldic language, is the crest of Athens; a wolf's head, that of Argos; and a tortoise, that of the Peloponnesus: and on Roman coins, the figure of a woman seated on a globe is the emblem of Italy; that of a woman solitary and weeping beneath a palm-tree, of Judea, fulfilling the prophecy—"she being desolate shall sit upon the ground." An eagle grasping Isaiah iii. 26.
the thunderbolt of Jove is symbolical of Rome; and Ceres dispensing plenty from her horn of abundance, is typical of the peace which under Decius the empire enjoyed.

So at much greater length might the nature of emblems be set forth with abundant illustrations; but whoso cannot now comprehend something respecting them would still be ignorant though the heavens became his scroll and all the visions of prophecy and the fancies of poets were painted upon them, and with his divining rod an angel touched each device in its order and said, "See, and understand."

SECTION II.—Early Emblem-books, and their Introduction into English Literature.

ARLY emblem-books, from 1481 to 1522, are soon counted. We nearly exhaust the list when we name Gerard Leeu, Sebastian Brant, and Andrew Alciat—a Dutchman, a German and an Italian.

The closing in of the fifteenth century saw the rise of a species of literature in which the graving tool was very extensively employed to illustrate, as well the proverbs and terse sayings prevalent in the world, as works of greater pretensions, in which genius took a higher flight, and accomplished more important aims. These illustrations may not have been introduced as profusely as in modern times; but, I dare to say, they were often marked by superiority of artistic power.

Dante's *Inferno*, published at Florence in 1481, was one of the first books thus to be embellished; and in the same year, in Holland, as a prelude to the emblem-book *Operas*, which followed, that most odd of all odd books made its appearance—"**Twygs-spraeck der creaturen**," or *Dialogues of the Creatures*, by

Gerard Leeu, of Gouda, near Rotterdam. The copy we consulted, in the Bibliotheca Hulthemiana at Brussels, is a small folio in Gothic characters, the pages and folios unnumbered, and with a considerable apparatus of rather coarsely-executed wood engravings. The dialogues are 122: the first is between the Sun and the Moon; the second, between "**costeliken ghestienten,**" *costly stones;* the one hundred and seventh, between the Wolf and the Ass, the picture representing the two creatures sawing wood with a vertical saw; the one hundred and twenty-first, between a Man and his Wife; and the one hundred and twenty-second, between Man and Death. The last page is almost entirely occupied by a coat of arms, and the work thus concludes: "**En is volmaeckt ter goude in hollant bi me gheraert leeu prēter ter goude optē vierden dach van april Int iaer** MCCCCLXXXI.," *i.e. Here is finished at Gouda in Holland by me Gerard Leeu printer at Gouda upon the fourth day of April in the year* 1481.

The next work to be mentioned opens a direct communication in emblem literature between England and the Continental nations, inasmuch as it was soon translated, or rather paraphrased, into English by Alexander Barclay, and printed first by Wynkyn de Worde in 1508, then by Richard Pynson in 1509, and afterwards in 1570 by J. Cawood. Before the end of the fifteenth century, in 1494, the original, by Sebastian Brant, appeared in German, and is usually referred to as "THE SHIP OF FOOLS." A copy is in the British Museum; the woodcuts are rather small, but spirited, and the designs are the same with those of some subsequent editions in Latin and French. The Latin translation, bearing the title, "**Stultifera Nauis,**" or *Fool-freighted Ship*, by James Locher, is a quarto volume of 156 folios, with 115 woodcuts, and underwent the revision of Brant himself. It was published at Basle, "that city of Germany most worthy of praise," by John Bergmande Olpe, "in the year of our salvation M.CCCCXCVII." The Plates, IV. and V., are from the title-page and twenty-ninth folio of the fine and perfect copy in the very choice emblem library collected by the late Joseph Brooks Yates of Liverpool, and now the property of his grandson Henry Yates Thompson.* Plate V., "**Servire duobus,**"

Pict. Hist. Eng. vol. iii. p. 826. Dibdin's Typ. Antiq. vol. ii. p. 431.

Plates IV. and V.

Stult. N. fol. 156.

* I take this opportunity of expressing my great obligations to the family of Samuel

To serve two masters, well illustrates the saying which Whitney adopted, "*Nemo potest duobus dominis seruire*," and embellished with the device of a man dragging the decalogue by his right foot, and attempting to carry the globe on his left shoulder. Brant presents the example of a hunter blowing his horn, and seeking with one dog to catch two hares at the same time. Whitney p. 223. Plate V.

Alexander Barclay's work, "**The Shyp of Folys of the Worlde**,"* was in part only a translation of Brant's *Stultifera Nauis;* in part it was simply an imitation. And thus, perhaps, it may be regarded as the very first attempt in our language at emblem-book art. Some may be inclined to contest the accuracy of this conclusion; and when Brant's and his translator's works are compared with the perfected emblems of Alciat and of Giovio, the doubt may rise into a certainty: but in the progress of any branch of literature, as in other things, "there is first the blade, then the ear, and after that the full and ripe corn in the ear."

The translator gives the following account of himself: that his book "was translated ĩ the College of Saynt Mary Otery in the counte of Deuonshyre, out of Laten, Frenche and Doche into Englysshe tonge by Alexander Barclay Preste, and at that tyme Chaplen in the sayde College." He was educated at Oriel College, Oxford, about 1495, and died in 1552 rector of All Hallows, Lombard-street, London. The memoir of him in the *Penny Cyclopædia* gives the titles of nine of his works, and shows him to have been a voluminous writer: it declares also that "he was one of the refiners of the English language, and left many testimonies behind him of his wit and learning." Penny Cycl. vol. iii. p. 440.

Barclay's *Shyp of Folys of the Worlde* contains many curious woodcuts. A good idea of them may be gained from the first in the series which "represents several vessels loaded with fools of various denominations." This is taken from the French translation, "**La grãt nef des folz du mõde**," and has appended to it in full the title of the Latin translation, "**Stultifera Nauis.**" Dibdin. See Plates IV. and XXVIII.

Thompson, Esq., at Thingwall, near Liverpool, for the extreme generosity and courtesy with which they have granted access to and free use of their emblem treasures.

* The full title is: "The Shyp of Folys of the Worlde. Inprentyd in the Cyte of London in Fletestre[te] at the signe of Saynt George By Richard Pynson to hys Coste and charge. Ended the yere of our Sauiour m.d.ix. the xiiii day of Decembre." Folio. Dibdin's Typ. Antiq. vol. ii. p. 431.

At the beginning of the sixteenth century the art of pictorial illustration, either from brass or from wood, was carried to a very high degree of excellence. Italy might boast of Marc Antonio, who died in 1527; Germany, of Albert Durer, down to 1528; and Holland, of Lucas Jacobs, better known as Lucas van Leyden, until his death in 1533. These "skilled artisans" left pupils, followers and worthy compeers, who did not allow their "glorious mystery" to retrograde; and the touch, the turn, the soul-inspired power of their hand, survive in many a page of that eventful era.

Herbert's ed. p. 1570.

If the recording line in Ames' *Antiquities of Printing* be correct, namely "1551, Alciat's *Emblems*, Lugduni 1551, octavo," there was an English version of "honest Alciat" at this early date. As far as I have discovered, no other trace exists of such a translation. Grant that it was made, it would, almost of a certainty, have been a very small volume similar to Wechel's edition of Paris 1534, or to the Aldine at Venice in 1546, the one contained in 120 pages, the other in 48 leaves.

Plates VI. and XVI.

See Transact. Liverpool L. and P. Society, No. 5, 1849, pp. 22, 23.

A manuscript translation of *Alciat* into English, which, though incomplete, evidently was prepared for publication, with the devices drawn and coloured, is in the possession of Henry Yates Thompson, and "appears to be of the time of James the First." The manuscript thus translates Alciat's thirtieth emblem, imitated by Whitney, p. 73:

"The stork, which is well noted for her love,
In lofty nest hir naked birds doth feed;
And hopes that she the like kindness shall prove,
When she, being olde, shall stand thereof in need.
The gratefvl babes do not hir hope defeate,
They bear their dam, and give unto hir meate."

Sketch of Books of Emb. by J. B. Yates, 1849, p. 23.

Sir Thomas Wyatt, the elder, who died in 1541, and Henry Howard earl of Surrey, who was beheaded in 1547,—"the two chieftains," as they are named, of the courtly poets,—were well acquainted with the literature of Southern Europe, and probably with the emblem writers of the nations dwelling there; but it appears to have been Spenser who, in 1579, in *The Shepheard's Calender*, "entitled to the noble and vertuous Gentleman, most worthie of all titles both of learning and chivalry, Maister Philip Sidney," was so far acquainted with emblem writings as to give emblem-mottoes without devices, like songs without words. We

Moxon's ed. 1856, p. 360.

find these mottoes, termed emblems, in Italian, English, Latin, French, and even Greek, and after Spenser's death, the folio edition of his works issued in 1616 gives a woodcut emblematical of each month in the year, and thus renders the *Shepherd's Calendar* a near approach to the emblem-books of a former century.

We may add that Spenser's *Visions of Bellay*, composed about the year 1569, were derived* from Joachim du Bellay, "the Ovid of France," and needed only the designer and engraver to make them as perfectly emblem pictures as were the publications of Alciatus, Sambucus and Whitney. Those visions portray in words the world's vanity, which an artist might express in drawings. Take the description of the "pillers of iuorie," of "the chapters alabaster," of "a victorie with golden wings," and of "the triumphing chaire, the auncient glorie of the Romane lordes;" and of the whole representation might be wrought a most lively and cunning emblem.

Moxon's ed. 1856, p. 437.

See Les Œuvres Fr. Ed. à Rouen, 1592, p. 436.

Moxon's ed. p. 438, iv.

Whether William de la Perriere's *Théâtre des Bons Engins*, Paris 1539, was rendered into English at so early a date, is doubtful; but William Stirling, esq., of Keir, informs me that he possesses "a fragment of an English translation" of this author, without the title. From this copy therefore the date cannot be determined, but by the cast of the type and of the rude woodcuts "it *might* be of the sixteenth century, and probably as early as Daniell's *Jovius.*"

See Plate XXX.

Letter, 3rd June, 1865.

The next immediate link between our own country, Britain, and the emblem writers of Italy, France, Spain, Germany and the Netherlands is supplied by Beza's *Portraits and Emblems.* This work, published at Geneva in 1580, is dedicated to James VI., king of Scotland, and contains, as its frontispiece, the earliest known likeness of that monarch, when in his fourteenth year. Such a portrait would probably secure attention to the book in this island, and its well-executed devices would serve to foster among us a taste for emblem literature. No translation however of *Beza* into English appeared, and his emblems still remain in their original Latin only.

Plate VIII.

Plates XLI. and LIX.

The Italians gave the name *Imprese, i.e.* Imprints, to such

* Verified in Leiden by direct reference to Du Bellay's works, as "*Je vy haut esleué sur colomnes d'yuoire,*" &c.

"ornamentation-books" as other people indicated by the word emblem. Paolo Giovio, bishop of Nocera, wrote a discourse on the subject and entitled it, *Ragionamento di Paolo Giovio sopra i motti e designi d'armi e d'amore volgormente chiamati imprese,* Venice 1556, in 8vo, "A Discourse by Paulus Jovius on Mottoes and Designs of Arms and of Love, commonly called Imprints." The work went through several editions, and in 1561 was translated into French by Vasquin Filleul. An English translation was issued in 1585, the year before Whitney's *Choice of Emblems:* it is not indeed embellished with woodcuts or engravings, but in other respects is an emblem-book in English. The translator was the poet-laureat and historian, Samuel Daniel of Taunton, who was born in 1562 and died in 1619. He entitles his work, *The Worthy Tract of Paulus Jovius, containing a Discourse of Rare Inventions . . . called Imprese, with a Preface:*" by Samuel Daniell, London 1585, 8vo. But for the want of devices, or engravings, this may be regarded as an English emblem-book equally with Whitney's, which it preceded as a printed work, though probably not as a composition.

Still, with the modifications that have been adverted to, the praise may be accorded to Geffrey Whitney of having, in 1586, been the first to present to the English public an emblem-book complete in all its parts, and showing by the union of learning and of the engraver's art how, among the nations of continental Europe, a literature had been raised up and had grown into popularity which a century before had no recognised existence. Whitney however is to be the special theme of the next chapter, and we pass on to complete, as far as is really needed, our sketch of the steps by which emblem-books were brought into Britain.

To the Rev. Thomas Corser, rector of Stand, near Manchester, I am indebted, among other favours, for the loan of a copy of the rare translation into English of Claude Paradin's *Devises* Plate VII. *Héroiqves.* The volume is in 16mo, containing 368 pages, and ornamented with many woodcuts of considerable excellence. See Append. Plate LVI. The initials only of the translator (P. S.) are given, and the date is 1591. A curiously-worded dedication follows the title-page: "To the Right Worshipfvll the Renowmed Capteine Christopher Carleill Esquier, chiefe Commander of her Maiesties forces in the Prouince of Vlster in the Realme of Ireland, and Seneshall there of the Countries of Clandsboy, the Rowte, the Glens, the Duffre, and Kylultaugh." The prose of Paradin is given in English prose; and there are a few specimens of very inferior verses, as at p. 28:

"These Dartes are peace to humble men,
but wane to proud in deed.
For why? both life and death also
from our woundes do proceed."

SECTION III. — ENGLISH EMBLEM-BOOKS, A.D. 1586–1686.

FROM what sources Emblem-books were first introduced into English literature has just been shown, and there is no absolute necessity of following the subject to a later date; but to render our view more complete we will take a rapid glance at the English books of emblems for a century after *Whitney*. Along with Whitney are recorded the names of Willet and Combe, as worthy to be matched with Alciatus, Reusnerus and Sambucus. Of Thomas Combe's writings nothing is known now to exist; neither the British Museum nor the emblem collection of the marquis of Blandford possesses them, and they are unknown to Mr. J. Brooks Yates and to William Stirling, esq., of Keir: they take rank therefore with the lost one of the *Pleiades*, and no longer offer even a point of light to the literary world. The praise of Andrew Willet is celebrated by Thomas Fuller. His father, Thomas Willet, was prebendary of Ely, where Andrew was born in 1560, and where, probably, he died in 1621. He was a copious writer, according to the Bodleian catalogue. His emblem-book, printed at Cambridge by John Legate, probably in 1598, is dedicated to the earl of Essex: it is a 4to, without cuts, and contains 84 pages. The title is a very long one, beginning with *Sacrorvm Emblematvm Centvria vna*, &c., "A Century of Sacred Emblems," &c. As a specimen of his style we add the English to his sixty-seventh emblem in Latin; subject — "Puerorum educatio," *The education of boys:*

Censura Lit. ix. p. 39.

Worthies, vol. i. p. 238.

Athenæ Cantabrigienses.

"A Scholler must in youth be taught,
And three things keepe in minde ful sure,

God's worship that it first be saught,
And manners then with knowledge pure ;
In Church, in scoole, at table must he
Deuout, attent, and handsome be."

In these days of acrostics it may be not unacceptable to our readers to possess Willet's ingenious conceit, constituting his first emblem, "Boni Principis encomium," *The praise of a good Prince.* It is in Latin verses, arranged, like the curious fancies of Simias the Rhodian, in the form of a tree. The sentence on which the Latin lines turn is "Elizabetham Reginam Div nobis servet Iesvs incolvmem. Amen"—*Elizabeth Queen, long may Jesus keep for us safe. Amen.*

See the Theocritus of Heinsius, ed. 1604, p. 209.

"Ecce beato S.
Lux nos dedisse maximE,
Illustris illa credituR,
Sẽpiterno quæ celebrãda cultV,
Anglia, insigni generata stirpE,
Beata virgo cum regnare cæperaT ;
Eam parem patulæ dixeris arborI ;
Tempestate gravi subito ruentE
Huius se foliis tegunt volucreS,
Adeuntq. bruta procubitV
Magnũ iuvamen omnibuS
Regina princeps: profugI
Eius celebrãt nomeN :
Gentibus ipsa laC,
Inclyta, virgO,
Non negat, iis simuL
Alma nutrix manV
Miserit auxiliuM.
Det deus itaquE
Impleat annuM.
Vivat & integrA,
Nullibi vnquam deficiens supremuM
Omnibus auxilium, quæ exhibuit piE
BIS locupletur ô patriæ columeN."

Generally each of Willet's emblems has a motto, a text from Scripture, some Latin verses, and the same rendered into English.

Censura Lit. i. p. 311.

Samuel Egerton Brydges informs us he was also the author of *An Epithalamium* in English, and says of him: "I shall only cite the practical character at the end of the life and death of Dr. Andrew Willet:

"See here a true Nathaniel, in whose breast
A careful conscience kept her lasting feast;
Whose simple heart could never lodge a guile
In a soft word, nor malice in a smile.
He was a faithful labourer, whose pains
Was pleasure; and another's good, his gains:
The height of whose ambition was to grow
More ripe in knowledge, to make others know;
Whose lamp was ever shining, never hid;
And when his tongue preach'd not, his actions did.
The world was least his care; he fought for heav'n;
And what he had, he held not earn'd, but given:
The dearest wealth he own'd, the world ne'er gave;
Nor owes he ought but house-rent for a grave."

Contemporary also with Whitney was Abraham Fraunce, whose work, in 4to, was printed in London in 1588, *Insignium Armorum Emblematum Hieroglyphicorum et Symbolorum, quæ ab Italis Imprese nominantur Explicatio.** There are no plates to the work; otherwise it is similar in character to Valerian's *Hieroglyphica, sive de sacris Egyptiorum aliarumque gentium literis Commentarii;*† folio, Basle 1556 and 1567, which abounds in woodcuts. These two works, however, are rather books of heraldry, of coins, inscriptions and sacred signs, than books of emblems.

Peacham's *Minerva Britanna*, a very close imitation of *Whitney*, even to the dividing of it into two parts, appeared in 1612, and is dedicated "to Henry Prince of Wales." In 1618 was issued *The Mirrour of Majestie*, of which no more than two copies are said to exist, the only perfect one being in the choice library of Mr. Corser, of Stand. Quarle's *Emblems, Divine and Moral*, the most popular of any in English, were published in 1635; and the same year George Withers gave to the world, with 200 fine copperplates by Crispin de Pass, *A Collection of*

See Plates IX. and X.

* "An Explanation of Badges, Arms, Emblems, Hieroglyphics and Symbols, which are named by the Italians Imprints."

† "Hieroglyphics, or Commentaries on the Sacred Literature of the Egyptians and other Nations," by John P. Valerian, of Belluno.

Emblems Antient and Moderne, quickened with Metrical Illustrations both Moral and Divine, disposed into Lotteries, folio, London. The year 1641 first saw Thomas Stirry's satire against Archbishop Laud, *A Rot amongst the Bishops, or a terrible Tempest in the Sea of Canterbury, set forth in lively Emblems to please the judicious Reader;* and we may again name Mr. Corser as possessing an original copy of the work almost unique. A second edition, 4to, was issued in 1655 of *The Art of making Devices, treating of Hieroglyphicks, Symboles, Emblemes, Enigmas, &c.*, by Thomas Blount; and in 1665, without an author's name, but with 9 copperplate engravings, was set forth in 12mo, *Astrea, or the Grove of Beatitude represented in Emblemes with Meditations.* Philip Ayres, in 1683, was author of a small 4to, *Emblemata Amatoria*, "Emblems of Love," in four languages, dedicated "to the Ladies," with 44 copperplates. Hugo Hermann's *Pia Desideria, Gemitus, Vota, Suspiria animæ pœnitentis*, &c.* was published at Antwerp in 1628 with woodcuts; and again in 1632 with Bolswert's beautiful copperplates. "It was Englished by Edmund Arwaker, M.A., in 1686, and illustrated with 47 copperplates; but the omissions and alterations of the original render it scarcely deserving the name of a translation. In 1680 and in 1686 also was issued a work, now of extreme rarity, *The Protestant's Vade Mecum, or Popery displayed in its proper colors in 30 Emblems.* This date is exactly a century after *Whitney*, and it is unnecessary to name any works of a later time.†

From Peacham to Ayres were published in London.

London.

Britain can advance no early claims to originality in the production of emblem-books, and scarcely improved the works of this kind which she touched upon and translated, yet she took no inconsiderable interest in emblem literature; and during the

* "Pious Aspirations, Groans, Vows and Sighs of a Penitent Soul," &c.

† There are also during the seventeenth century ten or twelve other books of emblems in English, which I have had no opportunity of examining. These are: Montenay's *Book of Armes with* 100 *godly Emblems*, 1619; *The Soule's Solace, or* 31 *Spirituall Emblemes*, by Thomas Jennes, 1631; Colman's *Death's Duel;* Heywood's *Pleasant Dialogues, &c., extracted from Jacob Catsius*, 1637; Quarle's *Hieroglyphics of yᵉ Life of Man*, 1638; Hall's *Emblems*, 1648; *A Work for none but Angels and Men*, 1650; *Wonderful and strange Punishments inflicted on the Breakers of the* 10 *Commandments*, 1650; Castanoza's *Spiritual Conflict*, 1652; and Miller's *Emblems, Divine, Moral, &c.*, by a Person of Quality, 1673. Probably several others might be added to the list.

List of English Books of Emblems in Notes and Queries.

century, beginning with Whitney and ending with Arwaker—if we except James or Jacob Catz,* who died in 1660 in his eighty-third year, and who to this day is spoken of familiarly yet affectionately in Holland, as "Vader Catz"—our country may be said to have marched at least with equal steps by the side of other European nations. We write, however, not to contest the palm of superiority, but simply to give a connected though brief view of the earlier emblem literature among ourselves. That attempt probably is not perfect in its parts, every emblem work not being included; there may be others who will correct our deficiencies, and present to the public a fuller and more accurate history. The materials exist, and knowledge and power in one I could name: but public patronage as yet flows in a scanty stream towards the editors of old emblem writers, and turns aside to support newer fancies; or perchance the ore we dig has not enough of sterling metal in it to make it worth the working.

Penny Cycl. vol. vi. p. 377.

SECTION IV.—Extent and Decline of Emblem Literature.

OR how many years the Emblem literature bore an illustrious name, and to what extent over the nations of Europe it prevailed, a sentence or two will serve to point out. With Alciat, in 1522, we may date the rise of its popularity; with Paolo Giovio, Bocchius and Sambucus, its continuance; with Jacob Cats, a glory that still shines and has lately been renewed. All countries of Europe—except "Muscovie," which was Tartar, not Teutonic nor Roman—participated in the *furore* for emblems. The peninsulas of Spain and Italy, the distant Hungary, the *Mediterranean* Germany and France, Holland, Belgium, Britain, swelled the throng of votaries and contributed to emblem art.†

* A splendid tribute to his excellence has lately been supplied by the publication of *Moral Emblems, from Jacob Catz and Robert Farlie*, 4to, London 1862. The beautiful illustrations, by John Leighton, F.S.A., and the translations by the editor, Richard Pigot, are contributions in all respects worthy of emblem art, and deserve the admiration of all lovers of the old proverbial philosophy and literature.

† The extent of the emblem literature will be treated of in our Appendix, where we propose to show the sources and the authors from whom Whitney made his *Choice*.

What are the causes, we may ask with some misgiving as to the exact reason, that a literature has almost become forgotten, which only three centuries ago was thus popular and flourishing throughout civilised Europe? It seems to have passed away from men's knowledge: it is studied as a branch of antiquities rather than of learning, — as inscriptions disinterred from the catacombs of by-gone ages, and not as the memorials of the wit and wisdom of some of the foremost scholars of Italy, France, Spain, Germany and the Netherlands.

We have here a perplexity which at first we find it difficult to unravel. The early emblem-books delighted the literati of their age; they were patronised by popes, emperors and kings; they were illustrated with a superabundance of artistic skill, and remain unsurpassed even in modern times for beauty of execution. Their spirit became so diffused among all ranks of the people as to call for translations into six or eight languages, and for imitations wherever they were known. Now, though some of them within a century numbered more than fifty editions, and nearly all of them were reprinted, they awaken a simple stare of wonder if perchance a student of typographical antiquities ventures to name them even to well-educated men.

Paolo Giovio, Freitag.

Sketch of Emb. Lit., by J. B. Yates, p. 22.

The tide of modern thought bears onward freightages of a very different kind: they are the cargoes of useful knowledge, scientific or statistical it is called, — available for competitive examinations, — rich in illustrations of history and the economic calculus for the senate or the courts of law, and "studiisque asperrima belli," bristling with whatever can advance the pursuits of war. But our great-grandfather's literary recreations, like our great-grandfather's portraits, are consigned to darker shades than even Dante's limbos of oblivion; and all persons are looked upon as dreamers of inutilities, and consequently of vanities, who endeavour again to bring into light works which Sidney did not despise, which Spenser imitated, and which Shakespeare applied to the purposes of dramatic art.

Æneid i. l. 14.

Whitney, p. 197. Merchant of Venice, Pericles, &c.

Without any invidious comparisons, however, we have not far to seek for a sufficient reason why the old emblem writers have

It will then be seen that he laid nearly the whole circle of emblem writers under contribution, and that the *History* of his *foray* is a biographical notice of themselves and their works.

been almost forgotten. The best of them, the founders and early masters in this school of poetry wedded to pictorial embellishments, excelled as Latinists, and sometimes ran wild amidst the conceits which Latin is so fitted to express. Their later imitators in the modern languages, without generally possessing their depth or their brilliancy, have followed them especially in quaint fancies, and thus have repeated and magnified their faults. Hence, as Latin was more and more disused among scholars, and as the modern languages, under skilled and vigorous cultivators, threw aside mere witticisms and affectations, men's minds grew beyond the pleasures of tracing out resemblances between pictures and mottoes; and, with a truth laid down or a proverb uttered, gave the preference to seeing it illustrated from examples within their own knowledge to having it decked out in an obsolescent language, with imaginative parallels between emblem or symbol and the actual thoughts they were intended to shadow forth.

I do not suppose that, among the most enthusiastic lovers of the old literature, there are any who desire a restoration of the very ideas and modes of expressing them, of the very fancies and fanciful delineations which characterised the sixteenth century. We could not endure to have even a second Chaucer or a second Spenser. Dante risen from the dead, or Petrarch revivified by the smiles and graces of the veritable Laura, would be repellent to the modern culture. We honour them and value them as they are and were, and their memorials we would not allow to perish; but Cœur de Lion would have been as out of place on the plains of Waterloo, or Miles Standish "the brave soldier of Plymouth" as incongruous at Wilmington or at Richmond, as Alciat in the literary saloons of Paris, or our own Whitney at some meeting of the Camden Society, or amid excursionists peregrinating to glorify scientific archæology.

We admit that each age has its literary leaders, who seldom indeed retain the leadership for ages in succession; but we do not add, Let them utterly fade out of men's thoughts. They did the work of their own day, and for that work we honour them: if we do not observe for them festivals of remembrance, as for the worthies of the Christian year, still, as occasion demands, what they did shall be rescued from Time's ravages, and live through another period of human regard.

CHAPTER II.

MEMOIR AND WRITINGS OF GEFFREY WHITNEY.

SECTION I. — Estimation in which he was held — Notices and Criticisms.

ENOWN wide and large enough to fill a nation's praise, it were vain to seek for Whitney's name and work; he possessed genius and learning, but has not left results that justify a very high eulogium.

It is from his native county more especially that his labours may obtain recognition, and from others, who delight in "holsome preceptes, shadowed with pleasant deuises," they may receive the approving word. During a reign remarkable for the great statesmen, warriors, and men of letters, whom it produced, and by whom it was adorned, there were many to surpass our author, but only a few who were of purer minds or of more extensive learning. His education and attainments, however, the friendships which he formed and the estimation in which he was held, entitle him to rank among the band that lend authority to the saying: "Cheshire, chief of men;" and his principal work, *A Choice of Emblemes*, though not the very earliest in our literature, was the *first* of its kind to present an adequate example of the emblem-books that had issued from the presses of Paris, Lyons, Basle and Antwerp; and it remains the *first* in point of intrinsic value. It may therefore, even on the ground of comparative merit, deserve reproduction, and be adduced in proof both of the author's power and of the diligence and effectiveness with which that power had been cultivated and applied.

Whitney's title-page.

With one of his earlier admirers we shall not be able so heartily to proclaim his excellencies as to say:* John Allen of Baliol, Oxford.

> "Begone rare worke; what though thy Author bee
> Nor lord nor knight, Yet comprehendeth more
> In vertuous deeds, than titles as wee see,
> Which better is, than with all Midas store.
> Tell Momus and old Homer's chatterers all,
> Till world's end thy name shall never fall:"

Nevertheless we have something to boast of in his behalf; and it is, that in an age by no means fastidious, either in manners or in language, there is not above one passage which might not be read aloud in any circle of listeners, and not more than two or three expressions, if there are so many, to which our modern taste can legitimately object.

The estimation in which an author's writings and character were held is indeed reflected by a very flattering mirror when they come to us from the judgment of his immediate friends, and especially from the commendatory stanzas which, in the sixteenth and seventeenth centuries, were attached, as well to a ponderous folio edition of Plato's works as to a thin duodecimo of Alciat from the press of Christian Wechel. The affection, not to name it the fondness, which his contemporaries expressed for Whitney, informs us of the regard felt for the man as well as for the author; and names of such eminence as those of Dousa, Bonaventura Vulcanius, Limbert, and Colvius, were warrants against mere adulation. Their testimony supports Anthony Wood in affirming "he was in great esteem" at Leyden "among his countrymen for his ingenuity." By M. Ficinus, Francfort, 1602. Parisiis, Anno M.D.XXXIIII. Ath. Oxonienses, vol. i. p. 230, ed. 1721.

Jan Dousa, whom for learning and patriotism William the Silent appointed governor of Leyden and curator of its university, writes to the following purport "On the Emblems of Geffrey Whitney:" Introduction to Whitney's Emblems.

* Lines in manuscript from major Egerton Leigh's copy of *Whitney*, which also contains similar stanzas by the same writer. This copy belonged to a John White "Anno Domini 1683," and then passed into the possession of a William White, to whom there are two manuscript memorials: On pages 112 and 173.

> "William White his hand
> So veri a roge as ani in the Land," and
>
> "William White His Name and Pen,
> God bless king William and all his men."

"Here EMBLEMS by their charms o'ercome writings of every kind,
And here EUPHROSYNE has mingled useful things with sweet;
So when on floors of marquetry the various figures meet,
They hold the eyes entranced, and discipline the mind.
Thus witnesses SAMBUCUS, — thus JUNIUS testifies,
And ALCIATUS, who hath borne the palm in this emprise.
Now Emblems, here out-traced by hands of finest skill,
In their rich lures all writings else outvie;
And as Sambucus, Junius, Alciatus never die,
So thou, thy work, O Whitney, shalt with growing honours fill."*

Introduction to Whitney's Emblems, translation.

The name Geffrey, common to Whitney and to Chaucer, naturally suggested a comparison, especially at a time which preceded the full light of Spenser's genius, and when in reality no one else had arisen among our poets who had his native language more under command, or who could with equal grace express in it the sentiments which had first of all been clothed in a foreign garb. Hence we have the stanzas of Bonaventura Vulcanius of Bruges, "*On the Emblems of* GEFFREY WHITNEY, *who bore the name of England's great poet in the old time,* GEFFREY CHAUCER:" †

"One ENGLAND bore two GEFFREYS, — poets both by name;
And equals too in PHŒBUS' power and art;
One as his country's HOMER hailed by fame, —
The English HESIOD is the other's part.
And as once Victory stood with doubtful wings
Between the MŒONIAN and old HESIOD's song;
So, when of worthy sons glad Britain sings,
The palm between the GEFFREYS poises long.
Rare CHAUCER's lines of gold erst Britons knew,
But WHITNEY kept concealed his pen's rich ore, —
Until at LEYCESTER's word the EMBLEMS flew
Honours to gain, and honours to restore.
As shines some Indian gem encased in gold,
And graven by the workman's skill-taught hand, —

Ed. Roterodami M.DCCIV.

* In the *Poems* of Jan Dousa the younger, edited by "Gulielmo Rabo, J.U.D.," the above ode, numbered XXXIV, p. 205, is entitled "In Gulfridi Whitnei Emblemata nomine Patris;" it is therefore the son's and not the father's.

See Hofmann Peerkamp's book on the Latin poets of the Netherlands; Haarlem 1817

† Vulcanius was professor of Greek in the university of Leyden for thirty-two years. A fine original portrait of him exists among those of other eminent men at the foundation of the university and since to the present day. He died in 1614 at the age of 76.

Pursue, O Whitney, titles yet untold,—
  Raise to the stars thyself and native land."

A full fruition to this wish may not have been expected, but Peter Colvius,* also of Bruges, takes up the same strain:

Introduction to Whitney's Emblems, translation.

"As Emblems twine themselves within our eyes,
  Traced curiously around some splendid dome;
By art adorned, they shine in various guise,
  Till 'mid the image lost, the mind doth roam;
So, Geffrey, thou, within thy little book,
  With many an image symbols dost express;
On traceries by thy verse we gladly look,
  Old sayings read, and deep thy genius bless.
The immortal deeds of heroes far shall sound,
  And virtues, it is joy to bear in mind,—
Horatian hearts, and Curtius' soul renowned;—
  Fabrician faith, thou, Pyrrhus! firm didst find;
The Decii, Junii, and Metelli brave,
  Curius, and Fabius the Cunctator's fame,—
The Scipios,—bolts of war where laurels wave,—
  And whom thy mind unequal is to name,
A countless host,—in virtue's brightening day,
  Light for our light, thy conscious muse reveals,—
For why? A chieftain, LEYCESTER, doth display
  Beneath his care the wealth thy verse unseals:
'Tis he who here heroic gifts hath shown,
  Each held by mighty princes forth to praise;
These we admire; and future times shall own,
  A DUDLEY's deeds deserve the choicest lays.
So shall this book on happy pinions rise,
  Through lips of learned men its course to fly;
My augury such:—high fame herself outvies,
  That never WHYTNEY's praise may fade and die."

We must remember that when the foregoing stanzas were penned, Vulcanius and Colvius were in the immediate presence of Leicester's greatness at its proudest height, and perceived in it only the promise of their country's deliverance from Spanish tyranny; we may therefore pardon them something in the ex-

* One of the literati whose labours adorned the Leyden press of Rapheleng. He was born in 1567 and died 1594.

Jöcher's Gelehrten-Lex. vol. i. col. 2027.

travagance of their eulogy. Seeing only with an Englishman's eyes, Whitney's old tutor at Cambridge speaks of his pupil's labour as one scholar in that day was accustomed to speak of another, and puts forth, "*A Ten-lined Ode on Geffrey Whitney's Emblems*, by STEPHEN LIMBERT, *an Englishman, Master of Norwich School:*"

Cooper's Athen. Cantab. vol. ii. p. 61.

Introduction to Whitney's Emblems, translation.

" Virtue's fair form and graces excellent
Would God permit his children to behold,
How great the passions kindled in our breasts
For her whose beauties far outshine the gold.
Not Venus' self, nor Dian, thrice a queen,
Could match such glories, conquering where they shine ;
But Whitney's Emblems paint her image pure,
Apelles-like, or Zeuxis' art divine.
Thus our great Author doth for good provide,
And from his hand choice gifts with men abide."

Such are some of the praises bestowed upon Whitney by men of his own day. Following the order of time we notice, before the end of the century, that he is considered worthy of being matched with the foremost of the emblem writers; for, in *A Comparative Discourse of our English Poets with the Greeke, Latine, and Italian Poets*, thus is it maintained: "As the Latines have these emblematists, Andreas Alciatus, Reusnerus and Sambucus, so we have these, Geffrey Whitney, Andrew Willet and Thomas Combe." We have here a record which was given to the public within a few years after the *Choice of Emblemes* had been written. In 1612 Peacham's *Minerva Britanna* "was sent abroad;" and the author avers it to be, "whether for greatnes of the chardge, or that the Invention is not ordinarie: a Subiect very rare." He goes on to say: "For except the collections of Master *Whitney* and the translations of some one or two else beside, I know not an *Englishman* in our age that hath published any worke of this kind: they being (I doubt not) as ingenious, and happy in their invention, as the best French or Italian of them all." His defence of his country sounds very like a commendation of Whitney: "They terme vs *Tramontani Sempii*, Simple and of dull conceipt, when the fault is neether in the Climate, nor as they would have it, in the constitution of our bodies, but truely in the cold and frozen respect of Learning and artes,

Wit's Commonwealth, by Tho. Meres.

Cens. Literaria, by S. Egerton Brydges, vol. ix. p. 39, and Wood's Fasti Oxon. p. 146.

Plate IX. gives the title of the 2nd part.

Peacham's Address to the Reader.

generally amongst us; comming far shorte of them in the iust valewing of well-deseruing qualities."

Probably the next notice of Whitney, though without a date, is in some manuscript stanzas in major Egerton Leigh's copy* of the *Emblems*, to which reference has already been made, p. xxvii.

John Allen of Baliol, Oxford.

"Geffry thy name subscribed with thy pen,
Extractinge honor from the noblest men;
ffor by thy Emblems thou dost moralize
fram'd Poems, fitted for all human eyes,
Reflectinge on the naturall state of man,
Enviinge at none, assistinge whome he cann;
Yealdinge such frutfull rarityes that all
Which Whitney knew may wittely him call
Honor'd of men; what can theare more be said
In givinge due, wheare due ought to be paid."
"Whearfore like momus 'gainst him do not cry,
Though WHITNEY's dedd His name shall never dye.
Sic cecinit Joh'es Allen."

A long oblivion however rested on the author for whom such renown had been prophesied. For nearly two centuries, except to a very few, his name was so little known that it does not occur in some of the larger biographical dictionaries, nor in the common literary histories of Elizabeth's reign; but from the evidence adduced it is certain he was regarded by his contemporaries as an author of considerable attainments and genius. His *Emblems* are not often to be met with entirely perfect, and his *Fables and Epigrams*, if ever they existed, are not found, I believe, in the most curious and extensive of libraries. In Belgium, the country where its printer (Plantin) lived, it is more rare than even in England.†

As, Aiken's Biog. Dict.

* The words, "thy name subscribed with thy pen," seem to intimate that this was a presentation copy; unfortunately the copy is imperfect, so that the fact cannot be verified.

† During the summer of 1863 I diligently inquired in the public libraries of Brussels, Ghent, Bruges and Antwerp, and did not meet with a single copy. And in the present summer of 1865 I have renewed my researches through the public, and some valuable private, libraries in Rotterdam, the Hague, Leyden, Haarlem and Amsterdam: but, though I found emblem-books of great rarity, as the German edition of Sebastian Brant's *Fool-freighted Ship*, in the Royal Library of the Hague, no copy of Whitney's

Censur. Lit. v. p. 233.

Gen. Hist. of Printing, p. 1695.

An eminent critic of the emblem literature, Samuel Egerton Brydges, remarks: "I have every reason to suppose that this curious work is of the *greatest rarity*, which may be accounted for in some degree by its having been printed abroad; and it is very rarely (from what cause I am unable to conjecture) that a perfect copy is to be met with in this country. I refer the reader to Herbert's *Ames* for some account of it; in addition to which I beg to observe, that many of the woodcuts, with which each page is adorned, display considerable ingenuity in design, and great excellence in point of execution."

The ingenuity and excellence thus praised are comparative, not in reference to the triumphs of higher art, but when placed beside the other emblem publications of the age: and being thus judged, there are none which surpass Whitney in typographical merit, or which give a truer representation of that school of literature to which he belongs.

Retrospective Review, vol. p. 124.

One at least of our modern writers very prettily sets forth the estimation which he entertained for Whitney: "We have known," he says, "those whose boyish days have been made more agreeable by the emblems of Whitney, who could recollect the different prints, their situation, the details, the whole, to their then delighted minds, beautiful pictures, which adorn that most ancient preceptor in emblematic art. But the emblems of Whitney and of Quarles have given place to meaner efforts of art, both of the pen and pencil; gaudy silly prints, and sillier illustrative verses, now occupy the juvenile library. Alas! emblems have faded,

Emblems was forthcoming; to not more than two persons was his name known, and only one had ever seen his work. A similar statement may be made respecting the cities in Belgium before mentioned; and in addition, respecting the University Library of Louvain, — the fine old library "de l'Abbaye du Parc" near Louvain, — the extensive and curious collection made by M. Van der Haeghen of Ghent, — and that richly-stored treasure-room "du Grand Seminaire" at Bruges, where but for the depredators of the French revolution would now be found in greater number the choice specimens of the skill and loving labour which was bestowed on classic and christian books. Here was shown me an emblem-book in manuscript, excellently illuminated, and in workmanship probably of the thirteenth century, "**De Volucribus, sive de tribus Columbis,**" *i.e. Concerning Birds or the three Doves*, by Hugo de Foliato, prior of Saint Laurence at Amiens. Many birds of many kinds are depicted, as the Hawk, the Sparrow, the Pelican and the Ostrich — their properties supposed or real pointed out, and their emblematical significations given. One of the more curious illustrations is the Cedar-tree, where, as the expression runs, the birds "nidificant" in the branches.

and their poetry decayed; and, as we have no hopes to resuscitate them, all we can do is to embalm their memory, and adorn them with a wreath of their own flowers."

The reviewer then weaves his garland for Alciatus, Whitney and Withers. The whole of the fine fable of Cupid and Death exchanging arrows is presented as "at once beautiful and simple;" and the writer adds: "We shall extract a few emblems from this rare book, not, however, on account of its rarity, but the intrinsic merit of the compositions. There is a freshness about the early writers of our country, not so much, however, in the thought itself, as in the simple manner in which it is conveyed; an almost child-like simplicity of expression, as appropriate as it is artless, which has an irresistible charm for us. Their's seems the language in which Nature herself would unfold her beauties and her verities. It gives even the appearance of novelty, as well as strength and propriety, to the thought, and never bears the marks of effort, or constraint."

Retrospective Review, vol. ix. pp. 124, 128. Whitney's Emb pp. 132, 133

A few selections are then made by the reviewer; one, addressed to MILES HOBART, *Esq.*, "*The sound conscience is a brazen wall;*" one, to *Sir* WILLIAM RUSSELL, *Knight*, "*The name of the brave is immortal;*" and a third, "to EDWARDE PASTON, *Esquier,*" "*The mind not the wealth.*" Of this last, for its general excellence, we subjoin the first stanza:

Whitney's Emb. pp. 67, 193 and 198.

> "IN christall towers, and turrets richlie sette
> With glittering gemmes, that shine against the sonne:
> In regall roomes of Jasper, and of Jette,
> Contente of minde, not alwaies likes to wonne:
> But often times, it pleaseth her to staye
> In simple cotes, clos'de in with walles of claye."

Dibdin's notice of our author is in close union of sentiment with the *Retrospective Review*. "Why has my Philemon," he asks, "forgotten to mention the 'Choice of Emblems' of Geffrey Whitney? Had he seen the delectable copy of that amusing book in the possession of my friend Mr. Bolland, it would have made an impression upon his mind, at least of no quickly-perishable nature. Whitney printed his copious quarto in 1586 at Leyden '*In the House of Christopher Plantyn,*' by his son-in-law Raphelengius; and this is probably '*the only English book* which

Dibdin's Bibliog. Decam. vol. i. p. 272.

owes its existence to the matrices and puncheons of the immortal Plantyn.* I wish it were better executed—for the love I bear towards the memory of that great typographer: but the embellishments are generally indifferent, and almost all of them are copies of what had appeared in previous publications, especially in *Paradin.*"

See Appendix, chap. i.

As will afterwards be shown, this last statement is far from being correct. Indeed there is occasionally a superficialness in Dibdin which detracts considerably from our entire trust to his authority. He is a perfect bibliolater of old books, especially if they be beautiful as well as rare, and describes them as if he would have his hearers under the same enchantment with himself; but he does not always discriminate the materials out of which the worshipped idols are made, nor remember that an exact judgment is of far greater value than an admiring veneration.

History of Cheshire, vol. iii. p. 230.

Ormerod's account of *Whitney* is chiefly taken from Anthony Wood's *Athenæ Oxonienses* and from Dibdin's *Decameron.* He decides that "*the Choice of Emblemes* is indebted for its celebrity more to the beauty of its embellishments than to its matter." "The subjects," he adds, "are chiefly treated in couples of stanzas (but the form and length of the verses is varied occasionally), and some of them are inscribed to his relatives and friends."

Proceedings of Liverpool Phil. Society, 1849, p 33.

Our choice of remarks upon *Whitney* we will terminate with those of the late Joseph Brooks Yates, esq. "It was only towards the close of the sixteenth century that any English writers turned their attention to the class of composition now under

See "Annales de l'Imprimerie Plantinienne par MM De Backer et Ch. Ruelens," première partie, Christophe Plantin, 1555-1589, pp. 287, 288. Bruxelles 1865.

* In this conjecture Dibdin and Mr. J. B. Yates are slightly mistaken; for in the year 1585, the year before Whitney's *Emblems* appeared, the following work was issued from the same press: and when the treasures of the Plantin Library at Antwerp, so long hidden, shall be revealed, as probably they will be during the next year, then other English works may become known as printed by Plantin: "*The Explanation of the true and lawfull Right and Tytle of Anthonie, the most excellent prince, the first of that name King of Portugall, concerning his warres againste Phillip, king of Castile for the recouerie of his Kingdom. Translated into English, and conferred with the French and latine copies. Leyden, in the printing house of Christopher Plantyn.* 1585."†

In the absence of contrary evidence there is some probability that this translation was Whitney's work. The Latin edition was printed in 1583, and 1585 marks the time when Whitney's connection with Plantin and Rapheleng existed, or was commenced.

† "Br. in-4°. De 54 pages, plus: *A Pedigree, or table of genealogie, etc.* (Cat. etc. of the British Museum; Lowndes, Bibliogr. Manual, i. 49.)"

review. In the year 1586 Geoffrey Whitney, a native of Namptwich in Cheshire, published at Leyden (where he was then residing) his '*Choice of Emblems*,' printed by Christopher Plantyn, and probably the only English book which owes its existence to the types of that celebrated printer. Its merit is derived more from its being the first publication of a Book of Emblems which had appeared in our language, than from the excellence of the verses, which are for the most part translations from the Latin authors whose works we have been considering. Most of the engravings also are from the same Blocks as they had employed.* The Book is inscribed to the Earl of Leycester, lately made Governor of the Low Countries, and many of the Emblems are dedicated† to Cheshire Gentlemen."

Having set forth the opinions of various writers respecting Whitney and his works, I reserve, in some degree, my own, until I have told what I have to tell respecting his family and himself.

SECTION II. — THE WHITNEYS OF HEREFORDSHIRE AND CHESHIRE.

EVERY question as to the ancient pedigrees of families, especially when decay has followed comparative wealth and distinction, is generally accompanied by doubts remaining to be solved, and by inaccuracies almost unavoidable. Such there are, and probably ever will be, in any memoir of Geffrey Whitney or of the members of his race.

The name itself, as applicable to a family, like a vast number

* Through researches made in various libraries, I have been enabled to show fully, if not completely, from what authors and from what editions of their works the engravings in *Whitney* have been borrowed. This subject will be found treated of in my Appendix, chap. i., with some brief notice of the artists by whom the woodcuts were produced.

† Also to members of the Universities of Oxford and Cambridge, to various clergymen and preachers, and to other persons of station and repute, whom Whitney counted among his patrons or friends. Several of his Leyden friends are also introduced. Ames remarks: "*Many of the very neat wooden cuts, and verses, are inscribed to the greatest men of the age, both here and abroad.*" Typogr. Antiq. p. 554, ed. 1749.

Duncumb's Collections; Herefordshire, vol. i. p. 61.

of other proper names, was first given to a place. The *Domesday-book* mentions *Witenie*, *i.e.* Whitney, as being in *Elsedune* hundred in the county of Hereford. Other places in other counties bear the same name; but it does not follow that the resident owners of the land, though bearing that name, are of the slightest affinity in blood.

Duncumb, vol. ii. p. 153. Lysons' Cheshire, vol. ii. p. 473.

Of the *gens*, or family, to which Geffrey Whitney belonged, there appear to have been two principal branches: the elder settled at Whitney in Herefordshire, and possessing other estates within the county; and the younger having their homestead at Coole Pilate in the parish of Acton, near Nantwich, in Cheshire. Both branches however are of considerable antiquity, and intermarried with the leading families of their respective neighbourhoods.

Athenæ Oxon.

Anthony Wood favours the notion that Geffrey Whitney, the emblematist, was closely allied to the Herefordshire family; but, if by close alliance be meant immediate relationship, this notion is unsupported by adequate testimony. General tradition, historical evidence, and family pedigrees show the Cheshire Whitneys to have been of an independent stock for several generations.

Duncumb's Herefordshire, vol. ii. p 153.

The original Whitneys derived their name from their place of residence: they were — Eustace de Whitney, or Roger, or Baldwin de Whitney, as the christian name might be. On the confines of Herefordshire, a little north of the point where the county touches upon Radnor and Brecknock, — that was their cradle. Here the lovely Wye enters into England, and its first work is to flow between the parishes of Whitney and Clifford. On the bank to the north was formerly the castle of Whitney, one of the Welsh border strongholds, now represented by a group of mounds and also by Whitney-court, the residence of the present proprietors.

Pict. History of England, vol. iii. p. 425.

27 Henry VIII.

The parish church of Whitney is about four miles from the Hay in Brecon, and seventeen miles from Hereford. The parish contains nearly 1500 acres, the chief owners being Tomkyns Drew, esq., and the Rev. Spenser Phillips. In the old time it was a portion of the long-stretching debatable ground, within which were one hundred and forty-one little lordships, often at war with each other, and "amenable only to their several feudal chiefs." It was not included in either of the three adjoining counties, until in 1535 — by act of parliament for the incorporation of England and Wales — Huntington, Clifford, Winforton, Eardesley, and Whitney were united into the hundred of Huntington. That act serves to designate both the situation of the parish and the condition of the family. As a parish Whitney was protected and oppressed by one of those castles, like Grosmont, Skeafrith and White-castle, not to mention Ragland, which in their pride of state were of far more importance than the border peels or towers in the north of England.* As a family the Whitneys were a superior class of Wat Tinlings, doing perpetual battle in their own behalf, and, except when it suited their purposes, bidding defiance to right and law.

Penny Cyclop vol. xii. p. 153.

In the earlier times, when Bohuns, Mortimers, and the bishops of Hereford convulsed the whole country, and overshadowed even the royal sovereignty, little trace of the Whitneys appears upon record; yet, in A.D. 1306, a Eustacius de Whyteneye was knighted at the same time with a Corbet, a Lacy, and a Marmyon; and previous to that the same Eustace, in 1277 and 1280, acted as patron of the living of Pencomb, and in the latter year presented a Roger de Whitney. In 1342 W. D. de Witenie was the incumbent; in 1353 Baldwin de Whitney; and after 1378 Eustacius Whitney. The patrons of this living at various times, from 1353 to 1590, were, Robert de Whitney, 1353; Baldwin de Whitney, 1357; Robert Whitney, knt., 1419 and 1428; Robert Whitney, 1539; then the Crown, during the minority of a Robert Whitney; and again in 1567, a Robert Whitney, knt.; and lastly James Whitney, knt., in 1590.

34 Edward I.

Duncumb's Herefordshire, vol. i. p. 79.

Duncumb, vol. ii. p. 153.

In the offices of sheriffs of their county, knights of the shire in parliament, and justices in the commission of the peace, the name Whitney may be traced in Herefordshire from Henry V. (1413) to George III. (1799).

Thus of Sheriffs of Herefordshire there have been:

Henry V. 1413.
 1. Robert Whitney.
Henry VI. 1422.
 6. Robert Whitney, knt.
 11. Robert Whitney, knt.
 15. Robert Whitney.
Edward VI. 1461.
 15. Robert Whitney.

Duncumb's Herefordshire, vol. i. pp. 139-149.

* For opening to me the sources of information respecting the Herefordshire Whitneys, I here confess my obligations to Thomas Heywood esq., F.S.A., Hope End, Ledbury.

Elizabeth. 1558.	38. Eustace Whitney.
16. James Whitney, knt.	Charles I. 1625.
28. James Whitney, knt.*	14. Robert Whitney, knt.

Of Knights of the Shire in parliament:

Duncumb's Herefordshire, vol. i. pp. 150-157.

Edward II. 1307.	3. Robert de Whitteney, knt.
6. Eustace de Whitney.	Henry VI. 1422.
25. Eustace de Whitney.	1. Robert Whitteney.
Edward III. 1327.	Edward IV. 1461.
51. Robert Whitteney.	7. Eustace Whitney.
Richard II. 1377.	Elizabeth, 1558.
2. Robert de Whitteney.	1. Robert Whitney, knt.

British Museum, Bibl. Cotton. Claudius c. iii. Plut. xxi. F.

The Robert Whitney of the parliament of 1 Elizabeth had "receaued the honorable Ordre of Knighthode in the tyme of the reigne of Queene Mary," and his crest, we are informed, was the head of an ox; but another sir Robert Whitney, with the same crest, is recorded to have been "dubbed at wynesore" after 1566 and before 1570. From there being a sir James Whitney, knt., of Herefordshire, in 1574 (16 Elizabeth), it may be conjectured that the second of the two sir Robert Whitneys, "dubbed" so near together, was of the Cheshire family, and brother to the "Master John Whitney" on whose death Roger Ascham wrote a lamentation, "which was afterwards translated by Kendall, and published in his *Flowers of Epigrammes* (12mo 1577, fol. iii. *b*)." "This was, perhaps, our author's (Geffrey Whitney's) uncle," so Philip Bliss supposes, "as Ascham, or rather his translator, speaks of his dying young:"

Athenæ Oxon. ed. 1813, vol. i. p. 527.

"Yong yeres to yeeld suche fruite in courte
Where seede of vice is sowne,
Is some tyme redde, in some place seen,
Amongst vs seldome knowne."

It must however be remembered that we possess nothing of certainty on this point. We know that our author was of Cheshire birth, and if "Master John Whitney" was Geffrey's uncle, he probably was also Cheshire born, and so would the second sir Robert Whitney his brother be.

As a matter of course the name Whitney occurs in the lists of

Gent. Mag. 1847, p. 484.

* It may be mentioned that this sir James Whitney, knt., in 1584 and 1585 sought in marriage the hand of Barbara countess of Leicester.

gentlemen in the commission of the peace for Herefordshire; as *temp.* Elizabeth, Eustace Whitney; about 1673 Thomas Whitney of Whitney;* in 1799 James Whitney of Norton Canon, related to the family of Whitney-court. Duncumb's Herefordshire, vol. i. pp. 102, 113, 114, 116, 119.

The sir Robert Whitney, knt., of king James's and of Charles's reign, had four sons who all died without issue, and four daughters to whom the estate descended. They all married and enjoyed shares in the property. Robert Rodd, the only son and heir to Thomas Rodd, married Hannah Whitney, one of the four daughters, and conveyed her share to Robert Price of Foxley, by whom it was sold to William Wardour.

William Wardour acquired the rest of the estate, and built the present Whitney-court, and also in 1740 Whitney church. The former church had been swept away by an overwhelming flood of the river Wye, and of the old monuments only one was spared, that to the memory of Williams of Cabalva in the neighbourhood, who married into the Whitney family.

Mrs. Bourne held the property from William Wardour, and left it to her godson, the grandfather of the present owner Tomkyns Drew, esq., and of his brother the Rev. Henry Drew, rector of the parish.

In passing from the Whitneys of Herefordshire to those of Cheshire, we may refer again to the two sir Robert Whitneys of Mary's and of Elizabeth's reigns. According to "*Armes in Cheshire after the maner of the Alphabeth,*" we do not ascertain what the Whitney's crest was, only their shield; neither have we evidence that the Hereford and Chester branches of the same stem bore different cognizances; the argument therefore is inconclusive which maintains that, because the same crest is assigned King's Vale Royal, p. 111.

* Probably to the same family is to be assigned John Whitney, the author of a very rare book; *Genteel Recreation, or the Pleasure of Angling, a Poem, with a Dialogue between Piscator and Corydon.* 12mo. 1700. There was a rev. George Whitney, instituted in 1807 to the rectory of Stretford, Herefordshire, who died in 1836. I have read somewhere that a captain Whitney was a companion of sir Walter Raleigh, and of the name a lieutenant fought at Worcester on the royalists' side. If Whitney the highwayman was a member of the family, it would be but an outbreak of the old spirit of the border chieftains. His exploits are narrated in "*The Jacobite robber. Account of the famous life and memorable actions of captain J. Whitney.*" London 1693, 4to. Gent. Mag. 1836, p. 438.

to each of the sir Robert Whitneys in question,—they were both of the Herefordshire family. Besides the christian names of the heads of the Hereford Whitneys, except at the very beginning of Elizabeth's reign, are James and Eustace, James being a knight; and among the Cheshire Whitneys of the same period we find one Robert, if not two; namely, Robert Whitney of Coole, mentioned in the Visitation of Chester in 1580, and by the *Emblems*, p. 91, in 1586,—and Robert Whitney, returned to parliament in 1585 as member for Thetford, when Geffrey Whitney was at Yarmouth in the same county. The probability then is, that the knight Robert of Mary's reign was of Herefordshire, and the knight Robert of Elizabeth's reign of Cheshire; in fact of the same family as that to which our emblematist belonged—the brother of one Geffrey, the father of another, and the uncle of a third.

British Museum MS. 1424, Plut. 56. I.

Blomefield's Norfolk, vol. i. pp. 467, 468.

The head of an ox, as in our frontispiece, being assigned to the two knights Robert Whitney, it may be considered as the recognised badge of the families, and therefore is appropriately introduced,* as the emblem of steady and honourable industry, to symbolize our author's genius and labours. The autograph below the print was furnished me by an eminent investigator of old documents, Mr. T. W. Jones of Nantwich, with the assurance that it is authentic and genuine,† from a signature of the same date with the *Emblems*, but by which of the three cotemporaneous Geffrey Whitneys of Nantwich is not ascertained.

At length we come to treat more particularly of the Cheshire Whitneys; they were established in the county, and at Coole Pilate, a township in the wide-spread parish of Acton near Nant-

* It is adopted from one of the emblem writers, Achilles Bocchius, A.D. 1573, and the original was engraved on copper by Agostino Caracci. In this connection it may be noted that the symbols on our title-page are also from Achilles Bocchius, who names them Egyptian characters. They have been re-arranged to suit a title-page, and are merely a fancy of the editor's.

Bocchius Embl. 147, p. 344.

† Of Whitney's autographs we present an unquestioned one from a book which once belonged to him, Paradin's *Devises Héroïques*. A curious paper in *Notes and Queries*, "Autographs in Books," signed H. C. W., gives the following: "2. Oclandii *Anglorum Prælia*. London 1582, 12mo. At the bottom of the title-page occurs (in MS.) 'G. Whytney, Cestrensis;' at the top the motto, 'Constanter et syn . . . .' (the rest is missing)." "I never saw his handwriting before. It would seem from this specimen that he was a native of Chester." On this Dr. Edward F. Rimbault remarks, "This old poet was certainly a native of Cheshire," and cites Whitney's *Emblems*, p. 177.

Plate VII.

Second series, vol. ii. p. 286.

Notes and Queries, second series, vol. ii. p. 357.

wich, almost as soon as those of Herefordshire were upon the Welsh border. "The manor" of Coole Pilate, say the Lysons, writing in 1810, "which was anciently parcel of the barony of Wich-Malbank, is now the property of Lord Kilmorey: in this township were two halls, with considerable estates annexed, one of which belonged to the Whitneys, who became possessed of it in the reign of Richard II. and had a seat there for many generations: this estate was purchased in 1744 of Mr. Hugh Whitney, by whose death the family is supposed to have become extinct.* The purchaser was Mr. John Darlington, whose daughter brought it in marriage to Henry Tomkinson esq. of Dorfold, the present proprietor: the hall is occupied by a farmer."

Magna Brit. vol. ii. Cheshire, p. 473.

A.D. 1377–1399.

The *Vale Royal of England* testifies to the fact which the Lysons record. It describes where the brook *Combrus*, from which *Combermere* has its name, "meeteth shortly with the Water of *Weever*, about Broomhall a great Township," "near whereunto is scituate a Demean of the *Whitneys*, called the Mannour of *Cole Pilate*."

King's ed. 1656, pt. ii. p. 65.

This manor, in the parish of Acton, was the homestead of the family; and here or in the neighbourhood they long dwelt. Their alliances show them to have been of consideration in Cheshire in the old time. About the reign of Henry VII. Anne, daughter of John Brooke of Leighton, in Nantwich hundred, became the wife of Thomas Whitney of Coole. She was the aunt to the Richard Brooke, esq., who "Purchased from the King the Mannor of Norton with its Members and Appurtenances." †

Ormerod's Cheshire, vol. iii. p. 241.

Sir P. Leycester, Hist. and Antiq. p. 32.

37 Hen. VIII. 1545.

Hugh Massey, of Denfield and Audlem, also in Nantwich

* In speaking of the extinction of the Cheshire Whitneys, the Lysons are not entirely correct. Towards the end of last century, Mr. Silas Whitney, also a poet, or writer of verse, from the neighbourhood of Nantwich, carried on business in Knutsford as a cotton manufacturer. He was reputed to be descended from the Whitneys of Coole Pilate, and a relative of the celebrated Josiah Wedgwood. When political feeling ran high and fierce about the *first* French revolution, he is said to have emigrated to the United States of North America, then in their rising glory. There the name is borne by many families, among whom very probably are to be found the lineal representatives of the Cheshire Whitneys. In the county at the present time there are few persons of the same name, but their relationship, if any, to the emblematist is not claimed by them, nor ascertained.

† Among the Cheshire Records of Mr. T. W. Jones occur "the following members of the Whitney (or Whytney) family":—

Sir P. Leycester, Hist. and Antiq. p. 371.

Ormerod's Cheshire, vol. iii. p. 247.

hundred, son and heir of William Massey (who came of age 3 Edward VI., A.D. 1550, and was descended from sir Geoffrey Massey of Tatton, near Knutsford, "who died 4 *die* Octobris 1457"), married "Elizabeth, sister of Hugh Whitney of Coolane in Wrenbury." He died in 1646, and was buried at Audlem.*

The manor-house of Coole Pilate is pleasantly situated on the bank of the river Weever at a short distance from the stream, and is now occupied by a farmer. Of the old structure little remains, except on the side looking towards the river. This side or wing is in the usual style of ancient Cheshire houses,—a frame-work of timber painted externally black, and filled in with whitened plaster or brick. Between the house and the river is an old brine spring of at least one hundred and fifty feet deep, the brine rising to the surface. In former times salt was made

Letters dated May 19, 1862, and June 3, 1865.

The name Whitney, in the 4th of Henry VI., A.D. 1428, relating to estates in Nantwich and in the neighbourhood of Coole Pilate;
A Hugh [Whytney] of Coole Pilate in the reign of king Henry VIII.;
A Thomas Whytney, "no doubt an ancestor of Geoff. Whitney, the Poet," in the first year of queen Mary's reign, A.D. 1553;
A Richard Whytney in 1562;
Also the Geffrey Whytney whose autograph is given on the frontispiece to this work;
A Hugh Whytney in the 20th of king James, A.D. 1623; and lastly,
Thomas Whitney, esq[re], who died at Malpas in March 1792, aged 80.

Index to the Wills.

In the Probate Court at Chester are found the names of:
Whitney Thomas, of Barthomley, Adm[n] 1598;
Whitney Hugh, of Coole, gent., Inventory 1611;
Whitney Michael, of Newhall, Inventory 1617.

Lanc. and Chesh. Wills, vol. ii. pp. 126-128.

Other instances also occur, as: In the time of Elizabeth, 11th January 1592, "Mrs. Margaret Whitney;" she is named in the will of "Richard Bradshaw, servante at armes" to the queen. He was of the family of "Bradshaigh of Haigh," "now represented by the Earl of Crawford and Balcarres;" and acknowledges himself indebted "to Mrs. Margaret Whitney widow" in the sum "of xxvj[li] xiii[s] iiii[d]."

Will in the Probate court, 1598.

Thomas Whitney of Barthomley, husbandman, 39 Elizabeth left three sons, Edward, Thomas and James, and a daughter Elizabeth, to whom 45*l.* was bequeathed.

Ormerod's Cheshire, vol. ii. p. 345.

The Thomas Whitney of Malpas, gentleman, who died in 1792, lost his wife Elizabeth in the 20th year of her age, December 1740. There is, or was, a monument to her memory in Malpas church.

Ormerod, vol. iii. pp. 95, 247.

Mr. T. W. Jones, 3rd June 1865.

* Four daughters were the issue of this marriage: Elizabeth, wife to John Page, esq., of Eardshaw, living in 1666; Jane, to Edward Gregge, esq., of Bradley; Anne, to Cholmondeley Salmon, esq., of Coolane; and Maria, to John Millington, esq., of Millington. The son, William Massey, who died in 1668, married Dorothy, daughter of George Cotton of Combermere, esq. Thus some of the Whitney blood must be flowing in the veins of very many of the gentry of Cheshire.

here, and traces of the fuel employed are often found in the soil, but the spring has not been worked in living memory. The opposite bank of the river is elevated and covered with wood, and the whole valley is undulating, and at some distance, at Combermere, very picturesque. Here and there, by the rough road-side to the manor-house and close to it, are a few oaks, each of which numbers up centuries of life; and they are the only unquestionable relics of the age when Whitney the poet, in the boyhood of which he writes so tenderly, played and rambled with his brother Brooke, and his sisters Isabella a poetess, and Mary and Ann, in the fields and pretty country around.*

See Plate XIV.

This homestead, or some other in the neighbourhood, it is most probable was the birthplace of our Geffrey Whitney; though some lines in the *Poems* of his sister Isabella, published in 1573, intimate that his father at one time of his married life lived in London, for she writes in her fantastical will:†

> "To Smithfeilde I must something leaue,
> my Parents there did dwell." ‡

There are, however, undeniable proofs that the poet's younger years were passed at Coole Pilate or the immediate neighbourhood. The ancient grammar school at Audlem, a small country town about three miles from Coole Pilate, was of a certainty the place of his early education. He addresses the youth of that school —

> "Watche, write, and reade, and spend, no idle hower;"

Emblems, p. 172.

and expressly affirms it to be the place

> "wheare I my prime did spende."

The motto, "*Patria cuique chara,*" His native land to every one is dear, he illustrates from

* The Rev. Robert S. Redfern, vicar of Acton, of whose large parish Coole Pilate is a part, most courteously pointed out these localities to me, and I here most cordially acknowledge my obligations to him.

† Not an actual will and testament, but a work of mere fancy.

‡ It may be that the poet's mother was a Cartwright, sister to the Geffrey Cartwrighte owned as an uncle in the *Emblems;* for, before 1600 there certainly were Cartwrights at Sheppenhall in Wrenbury, a neighbouring parish to Acton and Audlem. "A Nycholas Cartwright of Nantwich" is recorded in 1592; William Cartwright, apothecary of London, was also a freeholder of Nantwich in 1596; and a John Cartwright is named in a post-mortem inquisition in 1635.

Emblems, p. 166.

Letter Mr. Jones of Nantwich, June 3rd 1865.

Plate XIV.

"CVMBERMAIRE that fame so far commendes;
A stately seate, whose like is harde to finde;"

This mansion of the Cottons,* now viscounts Combermere, has been superseded by a nobler edifice; it is in the immediate neighbourhood of Coole Pilate, and is spoken of by Whitney with fond affection:

Emblems, p. 200.

"So, thoughe some men doe linger longe away,
Yet loue they best their natiue countries ground.
And from the same, the more they absent bee
With more desire, they wishe the same to see."

He then adds, as if to certify of his youthful home:

"Euen so my selfe, throughe absence manie a yeere,
A straunger meere, where I did spend my prime.
Now, parentes loue dothe hale me by the eare,
And sayeth, come home, deferre no longer time:
Wherefore, when happe, some goulden honie bringes:
I will retorne, and rest my wearie wings."

The lines addressed to "THOMAS WILBRAHAM, *Esquier*," of Woodhey, in the same parish of Acton with Coole Pilate, imply familiarity with that "old English gentleman's" character, which residence in the same neighbourhood only could in that day produce. The poet says of him:

Emblems, p. 199.

"——— by proofe I knowe, you hourde not vp your store;
Whose gate, is open to your frende: and purce, vnto the pore:"
"Whose daily studie is, your countrie to adorne:
And for to keepe a worthie house, in place where you weare borne."

The restoration of Nantwich from its state of ruin, consequent on the terrible fire of 1583, gave Whitney occasion for stating more explicitly the neighbourhood, if not the exact place, of his birth. The device of the phœnix, rising from its ashes, is devoted "*To my countrimen of the* Namptwiche *in Chesshire.*" We may note that he says his *countrimen*, not his *townsmen*. In his autographs he styles himself, "*Gulfridus Whytney Cestreshir*," and "*G. Whytney, Cestrensis.*"

Emblems, p. 177. Plate VII.; and Notes and Queries, 2nd ser vol. ii. p. 286.

The registers of Acton parish, within the ample boundaries of

Ormerod, vol iii. p. 211.

* It is through the permission of George Ormerod, esq., LL.D., the historian of Cheshire, that the illustrative plate (XIV.) is given.

which Whitney most probably was born, are of too recent a date to furnish evidence of his birth or of his baptism; and those of Nantwich, which is a town and territory cut out of the middle of the ancient Acton, and intervening between it and Coole Pilate, though beginning "*the first Day of Januarie in the Yeare of our Lord God one thousand, fiue hundred seuenty & tow*," are also not sufficiently remote.* There exists however most satisfactory testimony, that in 1573 the family, of which Geffrey Whitney was the eldest, numbered two brothers, himself and Brooke, and four sisters, Ann Borron (married), Isabella (the poetess), and two younger "seruinge in London." "*Certain familier Epistles and friendly Letters by the Auctor*," Isabella Whitney, are addressed to various of her relatives; as—"To her Brother, G. W.," *i.e.* Geffrey Whitney.

See MS. "Register of the Parishe of Wiche Malbanke."

"Sweet Nosgay," published 20th Oct. 1573.

"Good Brother whē a vacāt time
doth cause you hence to ryde:
And that the fertyl feelds do make
you from the Cittie byde." &c.
"But styll to friends I must appeale
(and next our Parentes deare)
You are and must be chiefest staffe,
that I shall stay on heare." &c.
"Your louyng (though luck lesse)
Sister. Is. W."

It would thus appear that Geffrey at this time (1573) was residing in London, probably pursuing the study of the law, or following his profession of a jurisconsult.

Isabella also endites a familiar letter "*To her Brother*, B. W.," and enables us to identify him with "M. BR. WHITNEY," of the *Emblems*:

Emblems, p. 88.

"Good Brother *Brooke* I often looke
to heare of your returne:
But none can tell, if you be well
nor where you do soiourne:
Which makes me feare that I shall heare
your health appaired is:
And oft I dread, that you are dead
or somthyng goeth amys." &c.
"*Your louing Sister*, Is. W."

* To the registers of Nantwich I had access through the kindness of the Rev. Andrew F. Chater, the rector of the parish.

There is too, what is especially note-worthy from its genuine sisterly goodness and quaint simplicity, presenting quite a picture of private life in the sixteenth century, "**An order prescribed by** Is. W. *to two of her* yonger Sisters seruinge in London;" one
Emblems, p. 93. probably being in after-life M. D. Colley: *

> "**Good Sisters mine, when I**
> **shal further from you dwell:**
> **Peruse these lines, obserue the rules**
> **which in the same I tell.**
> **So shall you wealth posses,**
> **and quietness of mynde:**
> **And al your friends to se the same,**
> **a treble ioy shall fynde.**"

Then follow six curiously-conceived, though sensible and most sisterly admonitions, in six stanzas, of from twelve to twenty lines: 1°. To obserue morning prayer; 2°. "All wanton toyes, good sisters now, exile out of your minde;" 3°. To attend to despatch of business; 4°. To be faithful in keeping secrets; 5°. To be guided by virtue; and 6°. "When master's gon to bed, your Mistresses at rest"—

> "**See that their Plate be safe,**
> **and that no Spoone do lacke,**
> **See Doores & Windowes bolted fast**
> **for feare of any wrack.**"

The advice ends with enjoining prayer:

> "**Good Sisters when you pray**
> **let me remembred be;**
> **So wyll I you, and thus I cease**
> **till I your selues do see.**"

There is besides an epistle in seven stanzas, of six lines each,
Emblems, p. 191. "To her sister Misteris A. B." *i.e.* Ann Borron:

> "Because I to my Brethern wrote,
> and to my Sisters two;
> Good Sister Anne, you this might note,
> yf so I should not doo
> To you, or ere I parted hence
> you vainely had bestowed expence."

Chester Archæological Journal, vol. ii. pp. 397, 398 and 273. * The mother doubtless of Mr. William Colley of Eccleston, near Chester, to whom on "the first day of December, Ao 1643," Arthur lord Capell granted a safe conduct, and from whom the present Dr. Davies of Chester is descended.

This epistle contains a notice of her sister's children:

> "Your Husband with your prety Boyes
> God keep them free from all annoyes."

Now in 1586, when the *Choice of Emblemes* was published, one of these "prety Boyes" was our Geffrey's nephew, RO. BORRON; one of the "yonger Sisters" was M. D. COLLEY, to whom is devoted the device on the virtues of a wife; and "good Brother *Brooke*" was the person whom Geffrey names "*my brother* M. BR. WHITNEY," and whom he instructs in the apologue of a great heap arising from "manie little thinges."

Emblems, p. 191.
Emblems, p. 93.
Emblems, p. 88.

And how do we know that "IS. W." is Isabella Whitney? In THO. BIR'S "commendation of the Authour," the writer of the "Sweet Nosgay" is expressly named:

> "*and sure my great good wyll must neuer slake*
> *From* WHITNEY: loe, herein some partie take,
> *For in her worke is plainly to be seene*
> *why Ladies place in Garlands Laurell greene.*"

She is also acknowledged as a near kinswoman "by one: to whom shee had written her infortunate state," whatever that may have been, — probably some heart-disappointment:

> "*Your Letters (Cosin) scarsley seene,*
> *I catcht into my hand*:
> *In hope thereby some happy newes*
> *from you to vnderstand.*
> *But whē I had suruaid the same, and waid the tenor well*
> A heuy heap of soroues did, mi former ioyes expel;"

and so on, for nearly fifty more lines, ending with —

> "*For;* he doth yll deserue yᵉ sweet, yᵗ tasteth not yᵉ tarte.
> Your most louyng Cosyn, G. W."

This G. W., no doubt, was the same whom the very graphic lines, "*In occasionem*," on Fortune, designate, "*my Kinsman* M. GEFFREY WHITNEY."

Emblems, p. 181.

Such were the Whitneys of Coole Pilate in 1573; they all survived until 1586, when others of the family connections are presented to our notice. In the *Choice of Emblemes* a device is dedicated "*Ad Agnatum suum* R. W. *Coolensem*," *i.e.* To his kinsman Robert Whitney of Coole; another, "*Ad D. H. Wh.*

Emblems, p. 191.
Emblems, p. 92.

patruelis mei F.," *i.e.* To Hugh Whitney son of my father's brother; Emblems, p. 94. a third, "*Ad Ra. W.*," and may mean to Ralph Whitney; also a Emblems, p. 166. fourth, "*To my vncle* GEFFREY CARTWRIGHTE," and may name his mother's brother, and so the mother of our poet would be a Cartwright.

We have thus in some measure ascertained who were the kinsfolk of our Geffrey Whitney, emblematist, in 1573 and in 1586. We may now endeavour to inform ourselves of his probable age at either of these dates.

Sir Philip Sidney, after leaving Shrewsbury school, entered Christ church college, Oxford, in 1569, and quitted it in 1571. It would be two or three years at least previous to this, when Athenæ Oxonienses, vol. i. p. 230, ed. 1721. Whitney, "born at Namptwich in *Cheshire*, spent some time in this University;" for he was longer a student at Magdalen college, Cambridge, Athenæ Cantab. vol. ii. p. 23. "where he had for his tutor Stephen Limbert, afterwards master of Norwich school." Now, according to information from the Rev. Augustus Jessop, head master of king Edward VI.'s school, Norwich, Limbert was appointed master in 1570: consequently Whitney must have been a member of Magdalen two or three years previously, suppose in 1567. We thus dispose of the supposition I once made, that he was a fellow student with sir Philip Sidney, and ascertain nearly the time when he entered Cambridge. In 1567, according to the usage of that day in going up to the universities, he would be not more than twenty years of age; and thus we may consider him to have been born in 1548, or a little earlier,* near the beginning of "the happy reigne of Kinge Edward the sixt."

Athenæ Cantab. vol. ii. p. 24. What studies and pursuits Whitney engaged in on leaving Cambridge are not recorded; but from the office he once held in the corporate town of Great Yarmouth they were probably such as qualified him for the profession of the law, in which, as men of eminence, ranked several of his friends and patrons. And singular it is, that of the early emblem writers several were

History of Cheshire, vol. iii. p. 230. * This conclusion almost coincides with the conjecture of Ormerod, who says: "Here," in Nantwich, "also in 1545 was born *John Gerarde* the herbalist, most probably a collateral descendant of some of the great Cheshire families of his name; and here also about the same time GEOFFREY WHITNEY, an English poet of the reign of Elizabeth."

jurisconsults or of kindred callings. Alciat in his twenty-second year graduated as doctor of laws; Mignault, his commentator, in early manhood explained the Greek and Roman authors; John Sambucus deserved the praise of being "physician, historian, antiquary and poet;" Hadrian Junius excelled both as an able physician and a learned philologist; and Barthelemi Aneau was jurisconsult and orator.

In 1573, when Whitney had attained his twenty-fifth year, or according to Ormerod his twenty-eighth, he was no longer resident in Cheshire; nor does it appear that he had returned to his "natiue countries grounde" by 1586. The interval of thirteen years must have had a considerable portion of it devoted to various studies; for his familiarity with classic authors, with fathers of the church, and with the poets and emblem writers of the age in which he lived, and of that which preceded him, declares how diligently his life had been spent. He may not have taken a degree at Cambridge, but if not "Mr of Artes," as Peacham was, he could have been no dilatory student; each day left its line on the dial-plate of his life, and marked an onward course.

Is. W.'s Epistle.

Emblems, p. 201

Minerva Britan'a.

The preparation for a work like "the Emblemes" must have occupied the leisure of several years. There is about it a polish, a roundness of metre and of rhyme, which indicate, with as much certainty as if other writings of his were before us, that these are not the only verses which have flowed from his pen. Poetry no more than history can be written at one stretching forth of the hand; there are of necessity attempts and exercises, touches and re-touches, before anything of mastership is attained, and certainly before such power of translation as Whitney evinces can be put forth and upheld.

One of the emblem-books, from which Whitney made selections and of which he adopted some of the woodcuts, was printed by Plantin in 1583, but the copy of an earlier edition in French, bearing our author's autograph, is dated 1562; and we may reasonably conclude that his name was written in it before the issuing of Plantin's edition. The devices he borrowed from *Paradin* may therefore have had their illustrative verses composed as early as 1580, or even 1575. The verses "*vppon Video & taceo, Her Maiesties poësie, at the great Lotterie in* LONDON

Symbola Heroica M. Cl. Paradini.

Plate VII.

Emblems, p. 61.

begon M.D.LXVIII, *and ended* M.D.LXIX," may have been written in 1568, and probably had their origin near to that date. Sir Philip Sidney's *Arcadia* had received its full form, if not its completion, before 1582, and at any time afterwards the lines may have been penned:

Emblems, p. 197.

"What volumes hath hee writte, that rest among his frendes,
Which needes no other praise at all, eche worke it selfe comendes."

Emblems, pp. 121 and 122.

Foss's Judges, vol. v. pp. 407, 409, 421.

Baron Flowerdewe died in April 1586, about three weeks before the *Emblems* were published, but the *Devises* to him and to Francis Windham must have been composed some time before, and perhaps earlier than 1584, when Flowerdewe was appointed one of the barons of the exchequer, for he was an early friend, if not patron, of Whitney. So, if we pursued the subject it might appear that several of the emblems had been written and laid aside, and dedications added as the occasion served.

Plates VII. XXIV. XIX. XXI. and XXVII.

Once more, as a very large number of Whitney's devices and woodcuts are borrowed from Plantin's editions of *Paradin* (1562), of *Sambucus* (1564 and 1584), of *Junius* (1564 and 1585), of *Alciat* (1551 and 1581) and of *Faerni* (1583), many of his translations and accommodations from those writers may have taken place successively as these editions appeared, and the stanzas have been modified, added to or shortened, as taste or inclination prompted. The laws which rule other writers of selections would govern Whitney; his "Choice" would be made gradually, following out the advice of one of his own emblems:

"Althovghe thy store be small, for to beginne,
Yet guide it well, and soone it is increaste;"

and so he found

"——— in time abundance springes,
And heapes are made, of manie little thinges."

For diversion or for improvement he studied the emblem writers; and it is probably but a portion of what he "englished and moralized" that appeared in print "in the house of Christopher Plantyn."

Athenæ Cantab. vol ii. p. 23.

The first trace we have discovered of any special employment for our poet is as under-bailiff of Great Yarmouth, in Norfolk, an office similar in several respects to that of recorder in the present day. His connection with the corporation of that borough existed in 1580, but how much earlier is not evident. It was doubtless brought about either by the earl of Leicester or by some one of the various Cambridge and East Anglian friends of our author, and it continued until the year 1586.

See the Yarmouth Rolls.

Sergeant Flowerdewe, in 1580, became under-steward of the borough, and Whitney probably acted as his deputy. On Flowerdewe's resignation, in 1584, the poet for a time occupied the vacant office. Pending the election of a successor, "it was ordered, in assembly, that Mr. Whitney should receive the fees of the Court for the steward, and haue the room at the Grey Friars rent free; but upon the appointment of Mr. Stubbs, in 1585, he was required to leave the room, unless Mr. Stubbs chose to retain him as his clerk." Whitney not unjustly resented this treatment, and went to law with the corporation, but the dispute was at last settled by a payment to him of 45*l.* sterling.

Manship's Yarmouth, by Palmer, vol. ii. p. 339.

Mr. Palmer's Letter, June 2, 1865.

The earl of Leicester, who as a commoner in 1553 represented the county of Norfolk, and had been high-steward of Great Yarmouth since the year 1572, introduced Whitney to the corporation, and endeavoured to procure for him the appointment of under-steward which Flowerdewe had held,—an office nearly corresponding to that of judge of the local courts both civil and criminal. Great dissensions were the result; the earl applied to Mr. Le Grys, member of parliament for the borough and a man of great influence, to favour Whitney, which to a certain extent he did, but at the cost of his own position; for Le Grys was accused to his constituents of having promised the office, and his faithful services to the borough for five successive parliaments being forgotten, he failed to regain his seat at the next election.

Manship, vol. i. p. 65.

Le Grys' Letter, Feb 28, 1586. Manship's Yarmouth.

The fine old church of St. Nicholas, and the Elizabethan mansion* on the south quay, were doubtless often entered by

* The interior of this residence furnishes illustrations to a handsome volume, printed for private distribution by the present owner, Charles John Palmer, esq., the editor of "*Manship's History of Great Yarmouth.*" "Domestic Architecture in England, during the reign of queen Elizabeth" is the title of the work. To its author, and to those who acted with him, we are indebted for the preservation of the town-rolls and other valuable documents. Their spirited exertions rescued the corporation a few years ago from the disgrace of selling their old records, and induced the building of a suitable muniment room for their safe keeping, where they are arranged in excellent order for reference.

In Gothic characters, and in Whitneian phrase, there are inscribed on the four

Whitney; and though "The Yarmouth Hutch," or "TOWN CHEST," was "The Gift of Alice Bartlemew" to the corporation only in 1601, yet *there* probably reposed for many a year A Parchment Sheet of the Rolls of Great Yarmouth, dated 2 Aug. 1580, which was drawn up or indited by Whitney himself, and which is the earliest of his known compositions. Some have dignified it with the name of a work, as if it were a book or treatise; but a single long and narrow folio is the extent of this offspring of our poet's pen. It describes in Latin prose a scene in his life which may be characterized as the pic-nic of the borough officers and of their friends.

See Plates XII. and XIII.

Manship, writing not later than 1612 or 1614, and speaking of this *Parchment Sheet*, testifies to the "careful skillfulness, and skillful carefulness of Mr. Jeffry Whitney, (sometime the under Bailiff of this Incorporation,) to set down" "touching the said sand called Scratby Sand;" "in Latin learnedly recorded, beginning '*porro secundo die*,' &c. Thus in English: **Moreover,** on the second day of August this present year," 1580, &c.

Palmer's Manship, vol. i. pp. 105, 106.

It appears that about the 20th year of Elizabeth (1578) one of the sand-banks off Yarmouth became dry land, which from a small village on the shore received the name of Scratby Island. It "was so much elevated above high-water mark that grass and other vegetables grew and sea-fowls built thereon; and in the summer season many of the inhabitants of Yarmouth usually went thither for recreation; some feasting, bowling and using other pastimes there, according to their different inclinations. But on the Second Day of August 1580, a very elegant entertainment was prepared by the bailiffs for a select company of gentlemen, whose names are inserted in the court-roll of that year, with an account of the place and transactions of that day, by the learned and ingenious Mr. Jeffery Whitney, sub-steward to the corporation at that time."

Swinden's Hist. Great Yarmouth, pp. 685, 689.

The historian of Norfolk tells us "the bailiffs, with a respect-

Blomefield's Norfolk, vol. v. p. 1694.

divisions of the ceiling of one of the principal rooms of Mr. Palmer's house the following lines:

The Rich that liue in Wealthy state,
By Learning doo their Wealth mainteyne;
The Poore that liue in Needie rate
By Learning doo great Richesse gayne.

able company of gentlemen, burgesses, mariners, &c., went down to take formal possession of this spot by the name of *Yarmouth Island,* where they all dined and spent the day in festivity."* The excursion doubtless was pleasant enough, with knights and men learned in the law of the company, and "some odd quirks and remnants of wit" were broken at the joyous time. "But behold, exclaims Swinden, "the instability and uncertainty of all earthly acquisitions!" In 1582, when the lord of the adjoining manor, sir Edward Clere, had put in his claim, and he and the corporation of Yarmouth had commenced a law-suit in support of their respective rights, "the sea put in a more powerful claim," and "by a strong easterly wind and tide" swept the island away, "and the place became main sea" and "left not a wreck behind" whereby "to keep alive the foolish contest." †

Blomefield, vol. v. p. 1694. Swinden, p. 690.

Great Yarmouth was excellently well situated for intercourse with Holland and Belgium, then as now great centres of emblem art; and during the eight or ten years of his connection with the East Anglian borough, Whitney would have frequent opportunities of holding correspondence with, or even of visiting, the learned men who distinguished Antwerp or Leyden by their residence. We may not be able to determine how early his acquaintance with the literati of the Netherlands commenced, nor to what date it was continued; but it certainly, from the very nature of the case, must have been of some years standing when his *Emblems* were published. In reward of the bravery and fidelity of its citizens, during the memorable siege of 1573, Leyden obtained from William the Silent the establishment of its university in 1575. A fast friend of Whitney, Jan Dousa the elder, was the first who presided over the newly-founded academy; another friend, Bonaventura Vulcanius, was the Greek

Motley's Dutch Republic, vol ii. pp. 483-485.

* The names recorded are forty-five in number. Among them, the bailiffs Ralph Woolhouse and John Giles, sir R. Woodhouse, knt., Edmund Flowerdewe, esq., sergeant at law, Mr. Charles Colthorpe, steward of Yarm, Mr. William Harebome, Mr. Jeffery Whitney, &c. The whole account of the visit, as if it had been a very solemn festivity, concludes with a doxology: "*Soli Deo honor et gloria in æva sempiterna.* Amen."

See the Rolls of Great Yarmouth, year 1580.

† In a note from R. H. Inglis Palgrave, esq., of Great Yarmouth, I am informed that about a week before, the sandbank which once constituted Yarmouth or Scratby Island was again for a day or two raised to the surface of high water. Were the upheaval permanent would the lawsuit be revived that has lain dormant for 285 years?

June 3, 1865.

P. Hofmanni Peerkamp Liber. pp. 202, 239, 248, 251, and 151.

professor at the same time; and Justus Lipsius for thirteen years, until 1590, filled the chair of history. Raphalengius too, by whom the *Choice of Emblems* was imprinted, had taught Greek in Cambridge when Whitney was a student, or shortly before; and thus we have all the elements of the acquaintance and friendship between our poet and several of the eminent men by whom Leyden was adorned.

See Annales de l' Imprimerie Plantinienne, Bruxelles, 1865.

In the year 1555 Plantin established his printing-house in Antwerp, and from 1562 when "*Les Devises de Claude Paradin*" were published by him down to 1590, there was a continual succession of emblem works in Latin, French and Flemish. Four editions of *Paradin* appeared, five of *Sambucus*, four of *Faerni*, one of *Freitag*, eight of *Hadrian Junius*, and five of *Alciatus*. Out of all these Whitney had taken his "Choice;" so that it was but natural, considering what relations he had established with Leyden, that his *Emblems* should be printed in that city.

At the end of November 1585 Whitney was in London, where he penned "the Epistle Dedicatorie" to his patron, but on the 4th of May 1586 he is found "at Leyden in Hollande" commending the *Emblems* to his readers. May be we have no absolute authority for the assertion; but here it seems that he busied himself in literary pursuits, and passing out of the immediate knowledge of his countrymen formed one in the bands of the learned whom the new university and the new printing-office of Plantin had gathered together.

If the conjecture were established, that "G. W.," the initials of the author of "AVRELIA," mean Geffrey Whitney, we could present evidence that he was writing and publishing in London in 1593; otherwise we meet with no certain mention of him as living beyond the conclusion of the sixteenth century, except it be the notice in Peacham's *Minerva Britanna*, p. 172. This we may interpret as implying that Whitney personally* gave consent to Peacham's use of the device of Love and Death. If this be a sound conjecture, then Whitney was surviving in the year 1612, at the age of 64; it depends however on the words, "cum illius veniâ Ab Authore." Should we understand them as merely

See Plate X.

* "Hoc idem habet Whitnæus, quod bene cum illius veniâ Ab Authore etiam mutatus sum."

the idiom for "begging his pardon," the evidence is inconclusive; but if we give the full meaning, "with permission for it from the author," then doubtless Whitney was living in the year 1612.

The year of his death equally with the year of his birth remains unsolved. His writings are his only monument, and neither stone nor line is known to record his passage to the immortality in which he believed.

SECTION III.—THE WRITINGS OF WHITNEY—SOME ESTIMATE OF THEIR WORTH.

EARS, as they flow, have often brought to light other writings of an author than those originally ascribed to him; but in Whitney's case there are only trifling additions by Philip Bliss and the Coopers of Cambridge to the works catalogued by Anthony Wood. We will take them in their order as they are presented in the *Athenæ Cantabrigienses* and *Athenæ Oxonienses:*

See vol. ii. pp. 23, 24. See vol. i. p. 230 ed. 1721.

"1. Account in Latin of a visit to Scratby Island, off Great Yarmouth 2 August 1580. Translated in Manship's History of Great Yarmouth, 106."

Aided by Mr. C. J. Palmer, I referred to this "Account in Latin," and found it simply an entry, on a single scroll, in the Town Records. The names of the company who were present at the festivity are appended. Swinden's *History* gives the original Latin, which we reproduce in photo-lithography.

Plates XII. and XIII.

"2. A Choice of Emblemes, and other Devises, for the most part gathered out of sundrie writers, Englished and Moralized, and divers newly devised, by Geffrey Whitney. A worke adorned with varietie of matter, both pleasant and profitable: wherein those that please, maye finde to fit their fancies: Because herein, by the office of the eie, and the eare, the minde may reape dooble delighte through holsome preceptes, shadowed with pleasant devises: both fit for the vertuous, to their incoraging: and for the wicked, for their admonishing and amendment. Leyden (Plantyn), 4to, 1586.* Dedicated to Robert earl of Leycester from London 28 Nov. 1585, with an epistle to the reader dated Leyden, 4th May 1586. The author speaks as if this were a second edition; if so, no other is now known. A writer in the *Encyclopædia Metropolitana* terms this work a remarkable imitation of Alciati."

Whitney's Address to the Reader.

The Collection of Emblems "presented in writinge vnto my Lorde," constituted, I conceive, the "firste edition" of which Whitney makes mention; it was not a printed but a written edition, set forth among his friends. He afterwards added to the manuscript that had been "*offred vp to so honorable a suruaighe*" as that of his lordship, but he declares, "*licence* being obtained for the publishing thereof, I offer it heare (good Reader) to thy viewe, in the same sorte as I presented it before. Onelie this excepte: That I haue now in diuerse places, quoted in the margent some sentẽces in Latin, and such verses as I thoughte did beste fit the seuerall matters I wratte of. And also haue written somme of the Emblemes, to certaine of my frendes, to whom either in dutie or frendship, I am diuers waies bounde: which both weare wantinge in my firste edition, and nowe added herevnto."

The manuscript submitted to lord Leicester and the additional notes and Latin sentences, together with some emblems to his friends, were now set up in type and constitute the printed edition. No prior printed edition was made, and no other printed edition is known to exist besides the one which is now again set forth by the photo-lithographic process.

Athen. Oxon. vol i. p. 230, ed. 1721.

"3. Fables or Epigrams," "printed," says Anthony Wood, "much about the same time as the former, in qu. and every page hath a picture wrought from a wooden cut."

No trace has been discovered of such a work; if it exists it will probably be found in the Bibliotheca Plantiniana at Antwerp, which it is said is about to be reduced out of chaos into order by

* The title and dedication, &c., occupy twenty pages, unfigured; the emblems themselves, with a device to each, are two hundred and forty seven, contained in two parts on two hundred and thirty pages, numbered consecutively.

its present proprietor, M. Edward Moretus, and then to be opened to the public.* It is not unlikely that Anthony Wood has confounded the *two parts* of Whitney's *Emblems*, and treated them as separate works. Both parts contain Fables, especially from Faerni, and both parts have nearly every page ornamented with a woodcut.

Or possibly, except that Wood names the *Fables and Epigrams* as a 4to book, and the work about to be mentioned is a 12mo, Whitney was engaged in correcting the press for "*Centum Fabvlæ ex Antiqvis Avctoribvs delectæ, et A. Gabriele Faerno Cremonensi Carminibus explicata*," "Antuerpæ apud Christophorum Plantinum M.D.LXXXV." It has 100 plates from wooden blocks, many of them the very same as are used in Whitney's *Emblems;* and so what he simply edited may have been regarded or spoken of as his own. This however is mere conjecture.

"4. Ninety English verses in commendation of his friend Dousa's *Odæ Britannicæ.* 1586."

The odes were printed at Antwerp† by Plantin, in the same year with Whitney's *Emblems.* The commendatory English verses are interesting, from the stanza being the same as in the greater part of the *Emblems.* Thus:

"There needes no bushe, wheare nectar is to drinke;
Nor helpes by arte, wheare bewtie freshe doth bloome;
Wheare sonne doth shine, in vayne wee lighte the linke;
Wheare sea dothe swell, the brookes do loose their roome;
Let Progne cease, wheare Philomela singes,
And oaten pipe, wheare Fame her trompet ringes."

Athenæ Oxonienses, Bliss's ed. vol. i. pp. 527, 528.

"5. Translation of some complimentary verses to the Earl of Leycester 1586, occurring at page 53 of Dousa's *Odæ Britannicæ.*"

Bliss, vol i. pp 527, 528.

The degree of adulation offered to Leicester may be judged

* I must here acknowledge the very polite attention of M. baron de Borrekens, of Antwerp, a near relative of the Moretus family, in endeavouring to obtain admission for me into the library; but M. E. Moretus was absent from home and I could not await his return.

† The "*Odæ Britannicæ*," however, are not named in "*Annales de l'Imprimerie Plantinienne, par MM. A. De Backer et Ch. Ruelens.*" 1865.

from the fact that when in December 1585 he removed from Delft to the Hague a series of twelve engravings was published with the title, "*Delineatio pompæ triumphalis quâ Robertus Dudlæus comes Leicestrensis Hagæ Comitiis fuit receptus.*"

So closes the brief catalogue of Whitney's works,—meagre in comparison of his attainments and powers, but showing how a lawyer's leisure might be bestowed, or the time of a literary man employed.

Conjecture guesses, and at present it is only a guess, that another work may be attributed to our author: it is "AVRELIA: The Paragon of pleasure and Princely delights: Contayning the seuen dayes Solace (in Christmas Holydayes) of Madona Aurelia, Queen of the Christmas Pastimes, and sundry other well courted Gentlemen and Gentlewomen, in a noble Gentleman's Pallace, &c. By G. W." Device, a sweet-william, &c., as in the frontispiece. "Printed by R. Johnes,* at the Rose and Crowne, neare Holburne Bridge, 1593," 4to.

We may here, not inappropriately, subjoin a notice of the published writings of Isabella Whitney, Geffrey's eldest sister; not that they possess much literary merit or poetical beauty, but are just the outpourings of a country maiden's spirit when brought into contact with the London society of Elizabeth's reign, and will serve to carry our remarks nearer to completion.

See Plate XI.

Her principal work is entitled "**A sweet Nosgay, or pleasant Posye: contayning a hundred and ten Phylosophicall Flowers, &c.**" After the *Nosgay* follow "Familyar and friendly Epistles, by the Auctor, with Replyes," all in verse. The last poem in the volume is "The Auctors (feyned) Testament before her departing;" in which she mentions the several professions and trades of London to whom the fictitious legacies are bequeathed, and the localities where they were stationed. The date of these poems is 1573.†

For extracts, see pp. xlv. *et seq.* of this Introductory Dissertation.

Notes and Queries, 3rd series, vol. i. p. 32.

* Richard Jones, or Jhones, or Johnes, was admitted a member of the Stationers' Company 7th August 1564; and books of his printing are found down to 1600. He printed the books of Whitney's sister Isabella, and through her may have been brought into contact with him.

† The Rev. Thomas Corser, the rector of Stand near Manchester, possesses a copy, perhaps unique, of this curious work.

Sir Egerton Brydges, bart., gives the title of another work attributed to the Cheshire poetess: it is, "*The copy of a letter lately written in meeter, by a yonge Gentilwoman to her vnconstant lover; with an admonition to al yong Gentilwomen, and to all other Mayds in general to beware of mennes flattery. By Is. W. Newly joined to* a Love letter sent by a Bacheler, (a most faithfull Lover,) *to an unconstent and faithless Mayden. Impr. at London, by Rd. Jhones, dwelling in the upper end of Fleet lane, at the signe of the Spred Egle.*" 12mo. Restituta, vol. i. pp. 234, 235.

The bachelor's verses thus terminate:

> "Farewell, *a dieu* ten thousand times,
> To God I thee commend,
> Beseeching Him His heavenly grace
> Unto thee styll to send.
>
> Thy friend in wealth, thy friend in woe,
> Thy friend while life shall flyth me froe;
> And whilst that you enjoy your breath,
> Leave not your friend unto the death;
> For greater praise cannot be wonne
> Then to observe true love begonne."

To another work from the same press Isabella Whitney contributed some commendatory verses. This is the title: "*A Plaine and Easie Introduction to practicall Musicke, Set down in forme of a dialogue, &c. By Tho. Morley, Batcheler of Musick and one of the gen. of her Maiesties Royall Chappell. Imprinted &c.* 1597." "Commendatory verses by Ant. Halborne, A.B., and I. W.," folio. See Ames and Herbert's Typ Ant. vol. ii. pp 1039, 1051 and 1206

To estimate the writings of Whitney by those of his contemporaries among literary men, as Sidney, Spensér and Shakespeare, would at the first view be considered a proper method of judgment; but his style, his subject, the extent of his works, are all so different from theirs, that a comparison between them would be out of place, and the conclusions we might draw wanting some of the elements of justice. It is rather by selection than by comparison that we are to look at his labours; we shall thus perceive what his power as an author really was, and have the results foreshadowed, if he had left behind more abundant evidences of a poet's work.

His dedication to Leicester, though characterized by all the diffuseness and wildness of illustration which belong to his age, nevertheless possesses much of earnestness and clear appreciation of the kind of patronage which learning then required. A passage from it will give an idea of the stately roll of the author's ideas, as a ship well laden, but needing more press of sail to Dedication, p. 12. urge it onward. "*There be three thinges,*" he says, "*greatlie desired in this life, that is healthe, wealthe, and fame. and some haue made question which of these is the chiefe: the sick, saieth health. the couetous, comendeth wealthe. and bothe these place good name laste of all. But they be bothe partiall iudges; for he that is of sincere and vprighte iudgement, is of contrarie opinion: Bicause that healthe, and wealthe, though they bee neuer so good, and so great, determine with the bodie, and are subiecte vnto time; But honour, fame, renowme, and good reporte, doe triumphe ouer deathe, and make men liue for euer: where otherwise the greatest Princes, in shorte time are worne out of memorie, and cleane forgotten. For, what is man in this worlde? without fame to leaue behinde him, but like a bubble of water, that now riseth, & anon is not knowne where it was.*"

Another quotation from his address, TO THE READER, will, I think, confirm the opinion that Whitney had power to become a most interesting writer of prose. If *Homer*, if *Marcus Varro*, if *Cicero*, if *Virgil*, "and diuers others whose workes weare most singuler, if they coulde not escape the bites of such Basiliskes broode: Then howe maye I thinke, in this time which is so blessed, generallie with most rare and exquisite perfection in all knowledge, and iudgement: that this slender assaye of my barren muse, should passe the pikes without pusshing at: where thousandes are so quicke sighted, they will at the first, behoulde the least iote, or tittle, that is not rightly placed." "For the nature of man is alwaies delighted in nouelties, & too much corrupte with curiousnes and newfanglenes. The fairest garden, wherein is greate varietie bothe of goodlie coulors, and sweete smelles, can not like all mennes fancies: but some gallant coulours are misliked, and some pleasant smelles not regarded. No cooke, can fitte all mennes tastes, nor anie orator, please all mennes humors: but wheare the tastes are too daintie, his cookerie shalbe controlled: and wheare the auditors are to rashe and careles in regarding, his Rethoricke shalbe condempned: and no worke so absolute perfecte, but some are resolute to reprehende."

The paraphrase of the Ode of Horace, "Sæpius ventis agitatur ingens," is equal to the best in our language: Carm. 2, Od. 10.

"THE loftie Pine, that one the mountaine growes, Emblems, p. 59.
And spreades her armes, with braunches freshe, & greene,
The raginge windes, on sodaine ouerthrowes,
And makes her stoope, that longe a farre was seene:
So they, that truste to much in fortunes smiles,
Thoughe worlde do laughe, and wealthe doe moste abounde,
When leste they thinke, are often snar'de with wyles,
And from alofte, doo hedlonge fall to grounde:
Then put no truste, in anie worldlie thinges,
For frowninge fate, throwes downe the mightie kinges."

The verse is full of power, — not a weak expression in it; the meaning is admirably brought out, and with a polish of tone in the rhymes that indicate a most musical ear.

So from *Ovid* he commences one of the finest of his poems, Metamorph. lib. i.

"Without justice, confusion:"

"WHEN Fire, and Aire, and Earthe, and Water, all weare one: Emblems, p. 122
Before that worke deuine was wroughte, which nowe wee looke vppon,
There was no forme of thinges, but a confused masse:
A lumpe, which CHAOS men did call: wherein no order was.
The Coulde, and Heate, did striue: the Heauie thinges, and Lighte.
The Harde, and Softe. the Wette and Drye. for none had shape arighte.
But when they weare dispos'd, eache one into his roome:
The Fire, had Heate: the Aire, had Lighte: the Earthe, with fruites did bloome.
The Sea, had his increase: which thinges, to passe thus broughte:
Behoulde, of this vnperfecte masse, the goodly worlde was wroughte.
Then all thinges did abounde, that seru'd the vse of man:
The Riuers greate, with wyne, and oyle, and milke, and honie, ranne."

Of Anacreon's celebrated ode, which we may name *The Power of Beauty*, he gives a very excellent translation:

Emblems, p. 182 "WHEN creatures firste weare form'd, they had by natures lawes,
The bulles, their hornes: the horses, hoofes: the lions, teeth and pawes.
To hares, shee swiftenes gaue: to fishes, finnes assign'de:
To birdes, their winges: so no defence was lefte for woman kinde.
But, to supplie that wante, shee gaue her suche a face:
Which makes the boulde, the fierce, the swifte, to stoope, and pleade for grace."

But the exactness of his translation, when occasion demanded, may be seen in the rendering which is given to these two lines of Alciat:

Emblems, p 133. *"Quid me vexatis rami? Sum Palladis arbor,*
Auferte hinc botros, virgo fugit Bromium."
"Why vexe yee mee yee boughes? since I am Pallas tree;
Remoue awaie your clusters hence, the virgin wine doth flee."

His power of adaptation, of taking up the thoughts of others, and of amplifying them, if not of absolutely improving them, is no less conspicuous. From Joachim Bellay's beautiful tale* we

* See "IOACHIMI BELLAII *Andini Poematvm* LIBRI QVATVOR: Qvibvs continentvr, Elegiae, Amores. Varia Epigr. Tvmvli." "PARISIIS *Apud Fredericum Morellum, in uico Bellouaco ad vrbanam Morum* M.D.LVIII." 4to, folios 62. The printer's emblem, a mulberry tree on the title-page, with "ΠΑΝ ΔΕΝΔΡΟΝ ΑΓΑΘΟΝ ΚΑΡΠΟΥΣ ΚΑΛΟΥΣ ΠΟΙΕΙ," Every good tree brings forth fine fruit. At folio 50 are the lines:

"CVIVSDAM IVVENIS.
Mutarunt arma inter se Mors, atq. Cupido:
Hic falcem gestat, gestat at illa facem.
Afficit hæc animum, corpus sed conficit ille:
Sic moritur iuuenis, sic moribundus amat.
Vt secat hic iugulos, oculos excæcat & illa:
Illa ut amare docet, sic iubet iste mori,
Disce hinc, humanæ quæ sint ludibria uitæ:
Mors thalamum sternit, sternit Amor tumulum.
Tu quoque disce tuas, Natura, inuertere leges:
Si pereunt iuuenes, depereuntque senes."

Folio 48, ibid. We could not quit the *Bibliothèque de l'Université à Gand* without noting down the exceedingly neat epigram in the same volume of Bellay's;

CVIVSDAM CANIS.
"*Latratu fures excepi, mutus amantes:*
Sic placui domino, sic placui dominæ."
"With barking the thieves I receive, with silence the lovers:
So have I pleased the master, so have I pleased the mistress."

have an instance; the subject is *Cupid and Death;* how graphically, with what simplicity, with what exquisite grace are the lines of the "French Ovid" rendered and extended: Emblems, p. 132.

"WHILE furious Mors, from place, to place did flie,
And here, and there, her fatall dartes did throwe:
At lengthe shee mette, with Cupid passing by,
Who likewise had, bene busie with his bowe:
Within one Inne, they bothe togeather stay'd,
And for one nighte, awaie theire shooting lay'd.
The morrowe next, they bothe awaie doe haste,
And eache by chaunce, the others quiuer takes:
The frozen dartes, on Cupiddes backe weare plac'd,
The fierie dartes, the leane virago shakes:
Whereby ensued, suche alteration straunge,
As all the worlde, did wonder at the chaunge.
For gallant youthes, whome Cupid thoughte to wounde,
Of loue, and life, did make an ende at once.
And aged men, whome deathe woulde bringe to grounde:
Beganne againe to loue, with sighes and grones;
Thus natures lawes, this chaunce infringed soe:
That age did loue, and youthe to graue did goe.
Till at the laste, as Cupid drewe his bowe,
Before he shotte: a younglinge thus did crye,
Oh Venus sonne, thy dartes thou doste not knowe,
They pierce too deepe: for all thou hittes, doe die:
O spare our age, who honored thee of oulde,
Theise dartes are bone, take thou the dartes of goulde.
Which beinge saide, a while did Cupid staye,
And sawe, how youthe was almoste cleane extinct
And age did doate, with garlandes freshe, and gaye,
And heades all balde, weare newe in wedlocke linckt.
Wherefore he shewed, this error vnto Mors,
Who miscontent, did chaunge againe perforce.
Yet so, as bothe some dartes awaie conuay'd,
Which weare not theirs: yet vnto neither knowne,
Some bonie dartes, in Cupiddes quiuer stay'd,
Some goulden dartes, had Mors amongst her owne.
Then, when we see, vntimelie deathe appeare:
Or wanton age: it was this chaunce you heare." *

* It is supposed that this tale was imitated from the CLIV emblem of Alciatus,

These examples of happy translations into simple and expressive English it would be easy to extend, but we turn to the opportunity which the treatment of the same subject gives us for comparing Whitney with his great contemporary, Spenser. The two poets were probably acquainted through their mutual friends, Leicester and Sidney. One subject which they have ventured on in common is the pretty tale from Theocritus and Anacreon, in which Cupid is described as being stung by a bee, and as flying to Venus for comfort. The superiority in point of truth, grace and simplicity of expression is, I think, decidedly with Whitney. Thus Spenser:

Spenser's Poems, Moxon's edition, p. 481.

"Nathelesse, the cruell boy, not so content,
Would needs the fly pursue;
And in his hand, with heedlesse hardiment,
Him caught for to subdue.
But when on it he hasty hand did lay,
The Bee him stung therefore:
'Now out alas, he cryde, and welaway
I wounded am full sore;
The fly, that I so much did scorne,
Hath hurt me with his little horne.'
Unto his mother straight he weeping came,
And of his griefe complayned;
Who could not chuse but laugh at his fond game,
Though sad to see him pained.
'Think now (quoth she) my son, how great the smart
Of those whom thou dost wound:
Full many thou hast pricked to the heart,
That pitty never found:
Therefore, henceforth some pitty take,
When thou doest spoyle of Lovers make.'"

Whitney gives the following neat and compact version:

Emblems, p. 148.

"As VENVS sonne within the roses play'd,
An angrie bee that crept therein vnseene,
The wanton wagge with poysoned stinge asay'd:
Whereat, aloude he cri'de, throughe smarte, and teene.

Retrospective Review, vol. ix. p. 126.

Alciati Emblem. 154.

which was written by him, according to the note by Claude Mignault, on occasion of a pestilence in Italy, when many young men died and the old generally escaped safe and uninjured. Whitney has combined thoughts both from Alciat and from Bellay.

And sought about, his mother for to finde:
To whome, with griefe he vttered all his minde.
And say'd, behoulde, a little creature wilde,
Whome husbandmen (I heare) do call a bee,
Hath prick'd mee sore alas: whereat she smil'de,
And say'd: my childe, if this be griefe to thee,
Remember then, althoughe thou little arte?
What greeuous wounde, thou makest with thy darte."

Some peculiar expressions in their poems show that the two poets had read each other's works, at least in manuscript; but as the expressions alluded to occur in the *Faerie Queene*, of which three books were published in 1590 and three in 1596, the probability is that Spenser had read Whitney's *Emblems* printed in 1586, the year before Spenser took up his residence at Kilcolman in Ireland. The *first* passage of the kind from *Whitney* is,

Moxon's Spenser, pp xxix. and xliv.

Moxon, p. xxiv.

"Lo, Time dothe cut vs of, amid our carke: and care;"

Emblems, p. 199.

thus paralleled by Spenser:

He, "downe did lay
His heavie head, devoide of careful carke."

F. Queene, I. c. i. s. 44

The *second* is the following:

"They, doe but make a sporte,
His subiectes poore, to shaue, to pill and poll."

Emblems, p. 151.

Of this there are two imitations by Spenser:

"Thereto he hath a Groome of euil guize,
Whose scalp is bare, that bondage doth bewray,
Which pols and pils the poore in piteous wize;"

F. Queene, V. c. ii. s. 6.

and

"So did he good to none, to manie ill,
So did he all the kingdome rob and pill."

M. Hubberd's Tale, l. 1197.

And the *third* passage is:

"AN vserer, whose Idol was his goulde,
Within his house, a peeuishe ape retain'd:
A seruaunt fitte, for suche a miser oulde,
Of whome both mockes, and apishe mowes, he gain'd."

Emblems, p. 169.

Of which the idea is thus given by Spenser:

"And other whiles with bitter mockes and mowes
He would him scorne."

F. Queene, VI. c. viii. s. 49.

Another bond between Whitney and Spenser is in the use of emblems; which, as far as mottoes go and the adopting of the word, were inserted by Spenser in his first work, "*The Shepheards Calender,*" published in 1579. The poem is divided into twelve parts, according to the months of the year, and to each month there is added a *Poesie, i.e.* a short proverb or saying, supposed to be descriptive of a person and adopted by him as his device;—such *Poesies* Spenser named Emblems: they had not at first any pictorial illustration, but are as much intended for it as if the pictures had been drawn and engraved. At a later time woodcuts were added, and the resemblance to an emblem-book rendered more complete.

Spenser's Works, folio edition, 1616.

Some of these *poesies* are from Italian, one is in English, six from the Latin, two from the Greek, and one in French. "*Diggons embleme,*" for September, "*Inopem me copia fecit,*" Plenty made me poor, is the saying of Narcissus, when he fell in love with his own shadow in the water; and one of Whitney's emblems is a picture of Narcissus gazing in a running stream, with the motto "*Amor sui,*" Self-love, and the lines:

Moxon's edition, p. 387.

Emblems, p. 149.

> "Narcissvs lou'de, and liked so his shape
> He died at lengthe with gazinge there vppon."

Spenser, Moxon's edition, p. 396.

Colins Embleme, that for December, "*Vivitur ingenio; caetera mortis erunt,*" *i.e.* Genius survives, other things are the prey of death, is also identical in spirit with one of Whitney's, "*Scripta manent,*" Writings are permanent; or with another, "*Pennæ gloria perennis,*" The glory of the pen never fades:

Emblems, pp. 131 and 196.

> "Then, what may laste, which time dothe not impeache,
> Since that wee see, theise monumentes are gone:
> Nothinge at all, but time doth ouer reache,
> It eates the steele, and weares the marble stone:
> But writinges laste, thoughe yt doe what it can
> And are preseru'd, euen since the worlde began."

and again:

> "——— no treasure can procure
> The palme that waites vpon the pen, which euer doth indure."

We are not so rash indeed as to attempt to place Whitney on a level with Spenser,—they can scarcely even be compared together; yet where a comparison is allowable, as in subjects which they both treat of, the Cheshire poet is no unworthy competitor. Spenser is diffuse, Whitney more compressed; the one most elaborate, the other strong by his very simplicity. Take as an example the description which both give of Envy. Spenser's certainly has a coarseness which does not belong to Whitney; his power of imagination may be greater, but not the fineness of his perceptions. Thus he describes the hag:

"Her handes were foule and durtie, never washt
In all her life, with long nayles over-raught,
Like puttocks clawes; with th'one of which she scratcht
Her cursed head, although it itched naught;
The other held a snake with venim fraught,
On which she fed and gnawed hungrily
As if that long she had not eaten ought:
That round about her iawes one might descry
The bloudie gore and poyson dropping lothsomely.

F. Queene, V. c. xii, s. 30.

Her name was Envie, knowen well thereby:
Whose nature is to grieve and grudge at all
That ever she sees doen prays-worthily:
Whose sight to her is greatest crosse may fall,
And vexeth so, that makes her eat her gall.
For when she wanteth other thing to eat
See feedes on her owne maw unnaturall,
And of her owne foule entrayles makes her meat;
Meat fit for such a Monsters monsterous dyeat."

Now mark how Whitney, with less force it may be, but with more simplicity and naturalness, describes the hateful monster:

"What hideous hagge with visage sterne appeares?
Whose feeble limmes, can scarce the bodie staie:
This, Enuie is: leane, pale, and full of yeares,
Who with the blisse of others pines awaie.
And what declares, her eating vipers broode?
That poysoned thoughtes, bee euer more her foode.

Emblems, p. 94.

What meanes her eies? so bleared, sore, and redd:
Her mourninge still to see an others gaine
And what is mente by snakes vpon her head?
The fruite that springes, of such a venomed braine.
But whie, her harte shee rentes within her brest?
It shewes her selfe, doth worke her owne vnrest.

Whie lookes shee wronge? bicause shee woulde not see,
An happie wight, which is to her a hell:
What other partes within this furie bee?
Her harte, with gall: her tonge, with stinges doth swell.
And laste of all, her staffe, with prickes aboundes:
Which showes her wordes, wherewith the good shee woundes."

But Whitney, it is said, had little originality; his ideas are many of them borrowed, and his stanzas are often translations only from Latin or French or Italian authors. True; "*The Choice of Emblemes*" is what it professes to be, "gathered out of sundrie writers;" but the good taste, the quaint elegance, the fullness and richness of tone which his translations and adaptations evince, show that he was no common genius: and the way in which he amplifies and often improves upon the original authors, betokens an innate power, had he put it forth, of equalling the best efforts of his contemporaries.

It was only in a few instances indeed that Whitney trusted to his own invention: from fifteen to twenty at the utmost are the emblems which may be claimed for him as entirely his own. He appears to have restricted his subjects to those for which illustrations could be supplied from the Plantinian printing office, and in treating these he naturally resorted to the other emblematists who had written to the same themes. Now and then, however, he "newly devised;" and an example or two will set forth his own mind, and strength or weakness of expression.

Plate VII. "*Constanter*," one of the words of his own motto, "*Constanter et syncere*," supplied him with promptings to such thoughts as these:

Emblems, p. 129 "THE raging Sea, that roares, with fearefull sounde,
And threateneth all the worlde to ouerflowe:
The shore sometimes, his billowes doth rebounde,
Though ofte it winnes, and giues the earthe a blowe.
Sometimes, where shippes did saile: it makes a lande.
Sometimes againe they saile: where townes did stande.
So, if the Lorde did not his rage restraine,
And set his boundes, so that it can not passe:
The worlde shoulde faile, and man coulde not remaine,
But all that is, shoulde soone be turn'd to was:
¶ By raging Sea, is ment our ghostlie foe,
By earthe, mans soule: he seekes to ouerthrowe.

And as the surge doth worke both daie and nighte,
And shakes the shore, and ragged rockes doth rente :
So Sathan stirres, with all his maine, and mighte,
Continuall siege, our soules to circumuente.
Then watchè, and praie, for feare wee sleepe in sinne,
For cease our crime : and hee can nothing winne."

The apostle's exhortation to avoid sinful anger is well paraphrased : Ephes. iv. 26.

"CASTE swordes awaye, take laurell in your handes, Emblems, p. 216.
Let not the Sonne goe downe vppon your ire.
Let hartes relente, and breake oulde rancors bandes,
And frendshippes force subdue your rashe desire.
Let desperate wightes, and ruffians, thirst for blood,
Winne foes, with loue ; and thinke your conquest good."

"*Veritas inuicta,*" Unconquered truth, and the Holy Book, the emblem of that truth, in the full light of the sun, with the brooding wings of God's spirit and the arm of his power supporting it in the heavens, form a device that the old Puritanism,* or rather the deep Christian religiousness of Whitney's mind delighted to contemplate. The book is open at the words, "ET VSQVE AD NUBES VERITAS TVA," Thy truth even to the clouds ; a chain is suspended to it, reaching to the earth ; and the great enemy of souls, to the manifest delight of demons looking on, is endeavouring to drag down the blessed volume. Such is the picture to which the fitting lines are devoted :

"THOVGHE Sathan striue, with all his maine, and mighte, Emblems, p. 166.
To hide the truthe, and dimme the lawe deuine:
Yet to his worde, the Lorde doth giue such lighte,
That to the East, and West, the same doth shine :
And those, that are so happie for to looke,
Saluation finde, within that blessed booke."

* The traces of Whitney's Puritanism are clear enough. His patron, from no high motive it is to be feared, countenanced that party, and is spoken of by our author as "*a zelous fauourer of the Gospell, and of the godlie preachers thereof.*" Several expressions, though in the broad sense properly applied to all truly religious men, were at that day appropriated to one section only of Christ's church, and Whitney appears so to employ them. A single instance will suffice to show this :

"THE pastors good, that doe gladd tidinges preache, Emblems, p. 8.
The godlie sorte, with reuerence do imbrace:
Though they be men, yet since Godds worde they teache,
Wee honor them, and giue them higheste place."

Emblems, p. 114.

Our last example of original verses by Whitney shall be, "*In diuitem indoctum*," On a rich man without learning; they certainly possess elegance as well as truth:

"A LEADEN sworde, within a goulden sheathe,
Is like a foole of natures finest moulde:
To whome, shee did her rarest giftes bequethe,
Or like a sheepe, within a fleece of goulde.
Or like a clothe, whome colours braue adorn,
When as the grounde, is patched, rente, and torne.

For, if the minde the chiefest treasures lacke,
Thoughe nature bothe, and fortune, bee our frende;
Thoughe goulde wee weare, and purple on our backe,
Yet are wee poore, and none will vs comende
But onlie fooles; and flatterers, for theire gaine:
For other men, will ride vs with disdaine."

The character of Whitney as a poet may be summed up briefly by saying that there is much of simple beauty and purity both of sentiment and of expression in most of his poems, whether original or translated. He shared however in the great fault of his age,* an excessive deference to classical authorities and an immoderate use of the pagan mythology. Hence, as in all writers who err in this way, there is to the modern reader, whose mind has not been so thoroughly imbued with the spirit of Greek and Roman literature, a frigidity and apparent want of

Rise of the Dutch Republic, vol. ii. pp. 484, 485.

* For a lively picture of the extent of the fault read Motley's account of the solemnities attending the inauguration, or rather consecration, of the university of Leyden on the 5th of February 1575. The procession is very graphically described, and then, "As it reached the Nun's Bridge, a barge of triumph, gorgeously decorated, came floating down the sluggish Rhine. Upon its deck, under a canopy enwreathed with laurels *and oranges*, and adorned with tapestry, sat Apollo, attended by the Nine Muses, all in classical costume; at the helm stood Neptune with his trident. The Muses executed some beautiful concerted pieces; Apollo twanged his lute. Having reached the landing-place, this deputation from Parnassus stepped on shore, and stood awaiting the arrival of the procession. Each professor, as he advanced, was gravely embraced and kissed by Apollo and all the Nine Muses in turn, who greeted their arrival besides with a recitation of an elegant Latin poem. This classical ceremony terminated, the whole procession marched together to the cloister of Saint Barbara, the place proposed for the new university, where they listened to an eloquent oration by the Rev. Caspar Kolhas, after which they partook of a magnificent banquet. With this memorable feast, in the place where famine so lately reigned, the ceremonies were concluded."

reality in many of his verses; as there ever must be, when a writer is rather the exponent of a painfully acquired learning than of a naturally flowing sympathy.

Yet a rich vein of beautiful simplicity, far different from the over refinement, I dare to name it in many instances the degeneracy, of some of our modern poetry, pervades Whitney's stanzas. True, he introduces Isis and Niobe, Actæon and Diana, Apollo and Daphne, Achilles and Ajax, and a whole host of Greek and Latin worthies; but they are seldom brought forward inappropriately to the occasion or the sentiment; his mind had been trained into intimacy with them; their deeds were the familiars of his thoughts; and so it was really natural for a scholar, educated as he had been, and accustomed to hear all around him continually speaking of the "Roman models and the Attic muse,"—natural to give forth of his stores and to array himself or his sentiment, now with the shield of Achilles, and now with the toga of Cicero.

The wonder is that this custom or habit of expressing his thoughts did not spoil "his well of English undefiled," and make it, like the speech of Cerberus, "a leash of languages at once." That it did not do this, among many instances, I appeal to the lines on Silence:

"And CATO sayeth: That man is next to GOD, Emblems, p. 60
Whoe squares his speeche, in reasons rightful frame:
For idle wordes, GOD threatneth with his rodde,
And sayeth, wee must give reckoninge for the same:
Sainct PAVLE likewise, this faulte doth sharplie tutche,
And oftentimes, condemneth bablinge muche."

And also to that stanza on the world which is above us, "*Superest quod supra est*:"

"This worlde must chaunge: That worlde, shall still indure. Emblems, p. 126.
Here, pleasures fade: There, shall they endlesse bee.
Here, man doth sinne: And there, hee shalbee pure.
Here, deathe he tastes: And there, shall neuer die.
Here, hathe hee griefe: and there shall ioyes possesse
As none hath seene, nor anie harte can guesse."

For pure, simple English, clothing very instructive thoughts, I would also name the fable of the Pine Tree and the Gourd to

Emblems, p. 34. the motto "*In momentaneam felicitatem,*" On momentary happiness. It has nearly every thing we can desire in a composition of the kind — clearness, a good conception well carried out, and an appropriate application of the imaginary tale:

"THE fruictfull gourde, was neighboure to the Pine,
And lowe at firste, abowte her roote did spread,
But yet, with dewes, and siluer droppes in fine,
It mounted vp, and almoste towch'de the head:
And with her fruicte, and leaues on euerie side,
Imbras'de the tree, and did the same deride.

To whome, the Pine with longe Experience wise,
And ofte had seene, suche peacockes loose theire plumes,
Thus aunswere made, thow owght'st not to despise,
My stocke at all, oh foole, thow much presumes.
In coulde, and heate, here longe hath bene my happe,
Yet am I sounde, and full of liuelie sappe.

But, when the froste, and coulde, shall thee assaie,
Thowghe nowe alofte, thow bragge, and freshlie bloome,
Yet, then thie roote, shall rotte, and fade awaie,
And shortlie, none shall knowe where was thy roome:
Thy fruicte, and leaues, that now so highe aspire
The passers by, shall treade within the mire.

Let them that stande, alofte on fortunes wheele,
And bragge, and boaste, with puffe of worldlie pride
Still beare in minde, howe soone the same maie reele,
And alwayes looke, for feare theire footinge slide:
And let not will, houlde vp theire heades for fame,
When inwarde wantes, maie not supporte the same."

The final characteristic and not the least is purity of thought and diction; not a single line in the whole book needs to be obliterated because of any impropriety of expression. And this merit is enhanced by the certainty that there is no affectation of prudery; the soul out of which Whitney spoke to his fellow men was one that feared God and loved truth, and clothed its thoughts in a poetic form only that it might with more fervour recommend the justice, the right-mindedness and the virtue which it prized and endeavoured to serve. All who know the grievous offensiveness of some of the writers of this age will esteem it no slight claim to praise that his mind, as Spenser describes Contemplation:

"His mind was full of spiritual repast."

And his themes, though confined by the narrow limits which ever attend proverbs and devices and emblems, were those which chasten and improve the intellectual and moral powers:

"Till oft converse with heavenly habitants
Begin to cast a beam on th' outward shape,
The unpolluted temple of the mind,
And turns it by degrees to the soul's essence
Till all be made immortal." Milton.

Most thankful am I that the enterprise which I dared to suggest has met with encouragement and is now near its desired end, and that Whitney's *Emblems* may again occupy a place of regard in his native county. Many have aided me by unlooked-for favour, good counsel and pleasant and most acceptable recognition; but in my own neighbourhood especially have I experienced sympathizing support, and cheering assistance,—all lending authority to the fine sentiment of our author:

"Not for our selues, alone wee are create, Emblems, p. 64.
But for our frendes, and for our countries good."

And good I am persuaded it is to listen to our worthies of old,—to glow with something of their inspiration,—to feel that life has an object, duties and motives, and that they live to the highest purposes who, besides seeking "under pleasaunte deuises" to commend "profitable moralles," carry on the chivalry of their age to progress and final triumph.

Good Reader! aid that work; and then will I say, as Whitney did, respecting the words and counsels of this old-world volume: "*Being abashed that my habillitie can not affoorde them suche, as are fit to be offred vp to so honorable a suruaighe: yet if it shall like your honour to allowe of anie of them, I shall thinke my pen set to the booke in happie houre; and it shall incourage mee, to assay some matter of more momente, as soone as leasure will further my desire in that behalfe.*" See Epistle Dedicatorie, p. xiii.

The excellencies of my author — his quaint, simple wisdom, and the deep under-current of devout thoughtfulness which everywhere pervade his writings — may not have been set forth in their proper light; and the natural beauties which belong to the subject may be marred by the unskilfulness with which they are arranged; yet truly can I say that in love and admiration I have wrought this framework for pictures of a by-gone age; they are apples of gold, I would they were set amid ornaments of silver.

Whitney to the Reader.

So I commend, as far as it is proper to be done, both Whitney's labours and my own to the candid judgment of the friends and lovers of the old literature, trusting, as our Geffrey of "*Cestreshir*" himself did, that "my good will shalbe waighed as well as the worke, and that a pearle shall not bee looked for in a poore mans purce, I submit my doings herein to their censures."

HENRY GREEN.

KNUTSFORD, CHESHIRE,
October 10th, 1865.

τὰ τρία ταῦτα·
1 COR. XIII. 13.

INDEX TO THE MOTTOES,

WITH

TRANSLATIONS; AND SOME PROVERBIAL EXPRESSIONS.

HAD regard only to be paid to the assistance which the learned require, nothing more would be given, by way of Index, than the arrangement of the Mottoes in alphabetical order, with references to the pages. The book however may chance to interest general readers; and for their use, to facilitate the understanding of the subjects which the stanzas treat of, and in compliance with an expressed wish, translations are subjoined.

Whitney's Mottoes, with Translations.

Page

CÆCUM odium; *blind hatred* 31
Cæcus amor prolis; *blind love of offspring* a 188
Calumniam contra calumniatorem virtus repellit; *virtue beats back slander against the slanderer* b 138
Captiuus, ob gulam; *a captive by gluttony* 128
Celsæ potestatis species; *a representation of exalted power* 116
Cœlum, non animum; *climate, not nature* 178
Concordia; *concord* a 76
Constanter; *steadfastly* 129
Constantia comes victoriæ; *steadfastness the companion of virtue* 137
Cùm laruis non luctandum; *we should not wrestle with phantoms* 127
Cum tempore mutamur; *we are changed with time* 167
Cuncta complecti velle, stultum; *'tis foolish to wish to compass all things* b 55
Curis tabescimus omnes; *from cares we all waste away* 25

DE inuido et auaro, iocosum; *of the envious and the greedy, a tale* 95
De morte, et amore: iocosum; *of death and love, a tale* 132
De paruis, grandis aceruus erit; *from little things a great heap will be* 88
Desiderium spe vacuum; *desire void of hope* 44
Desidiam abiiciendam; *sloth to be cast away* 85
Dicta septem sapientum; *sayings of the seven wise men* 130
Dissidia inter æquales, pessima; *dissensions among equals, the worst* 5
Dolor è medicina; *pain from medicine* a 156
Dolus in suos; *treachery to one's own* 27
Dominus viuit et videt; *the Lord lives and sees* 229
Dum ætatis ver agitur: consule brumæ; *while life's spring lasts, consult for winter* 159
Dum potes, viue; *live while thou canst* 97
Dum viuo, prosum; *while I live, I do good* b 77
Dura vsu molliora; *hard things become softer from use* b 156
Durum telum necessitas; *necessity a hard weapon* 36

Page

EI, qui semel sua prodegerit, aliena credi non oportere; *who has once squandered his own, ought not to be trusted with another's* 33
Ex bello, pax; *out of war, peace* a 138
Ex damno alterius, alterius vtilitas; *from loss of one, the advantage of another* 119
Ex maximo minimum; *from greatest least* b 229
Ex morbo medicina; *the cure from the disease* 209
Experientia docet; *experience teaches* 9

FATUIS leuia committito; *entrust trifles to fools* 81
Fel in melle; *gall in honey* 147
Ferè simile, in Hypocritas; *almost the like, on Hypocrites* 226
Ferè simile ex Theocrito; *almost the like from Theocritus* 148
(Cum quo conuenit aliud ex Anacreonte; *with which agrees another from Anacreon*) 148
Ferè simile præcedenti, ex Alciato; *almost like the foregoing, from Alciat* 170
Feriunt summos fulmina montes; *lightnings strike the highest mountains* 140
Festina lentè; *hasten slowly* 121
Fides non apparentium; *faith in things not seen* 71
Fortissima minimis interdum cedunt; *the strongest sometimes yield to the least* a 52
Fortiter et feliciter; *bravely and happily* 115
Fortuna virtutem superans; *fortune vanquishing virtue* 70
Fraus meretur fraudem; *guile merits guile* 210
Frontis nulla fides; *faith on the forehead, none* 100
Frustrà; *in vain* 12
Furor et rabies; *fury and madness* 45

GARRULITAS; *chattering* a 50
Gratiam referendam; *favour to be repaid* 73

HABET et bellum suas leges; *even war has its laws* 112
Homines voluptatibus transformantur; *men are transformed by pleasures*
Homo homini lupus; *man a wolf to man*

Page

Hosti etiam seruanda fides; *even to an enemy faith must be kept* 114

ILLICITUM non sperandum; *the unlawful must not be hoped for* b 139
Impar coniugium; *unequal marriage* 99
Imparilitas; *inequality* 207
Importunitas euitanda; *importunity must be avoided* 192
Impunitas ferociæ parens; *impunity the parent of cruelty* b 222
In amore tormentum; *in love torment* 219
Inanis impetus; *a vain attempt* 213
In astrologos; *on astrologers* 28
In auaros; *on the avaricious* 18
In colores; *on colours* 134
In copia minor error; *in exuberance less mistake* 142
In curiosos; *on the over-curious* 145
In desciscentes; *on those degenerating* b 189
In dies meliora; *better things daily* 53
In diuitem, indoctum; *on the rich man, unlearned* 214
Indulgentia parentum, filiorum pernicies; *indulgence in parents, of sons the destruction* 155
Industria naturam corrigit; *industry corrects nature* 92
In eos qui multa promittunt, et nihil præstant; *on those who promise much, and perform nothing* 162
In eos, qui, proximioribus spretis, remotiora sequuntur; *on those who despising the near, follow the distant* 157
In eum qui sibi ipsi damnum apparat; *on the man who prepares loss for himself* 49
In eum qui truculentiâ suorum perierit; *on him who will perish from his friend's harshness* 90
In fœcunditatem, sibi ipsi damnosam; *on fruitfulness injurious to its own self* 174
Infortunia nostra, alienis collata, leuiora; *our misfortunes, compared with other people's, made lighter* a 93
Ingenium superat vires; *genius excels strength* b 168
Inimicorum dona, infausta; *the gifts of enemies, unlucky* 37
Iniuriis, infirmitas subiecta; *to wrongs weakness is subjected* b 52
In iuuentam; *on youth* 146
In momentaneam felicitatem; *on happiness for a moment* 34

Page

In occasionem; *on occasion, or fortune* 181
In pace de bello; *in peace, for war* b 153
In pœnam sectatur et vmbra; *for punishment even a shadow is pursued* 32
In quatuor anni tempora; *on the four seasons of the year* b 54
Insignia poetarum; *the badge of poets* 126
In sinu alere serpentem; *in the bosom to nourish a serpent* a 189
In sortis suæ contemptores; *on despisers of their own lot* 102
Insperatum auxilium; *unlooked-for help* 113
In statuam Bacchi, *on the statue of Bacchus* 187
In studiosum captum amore; *on the student caught by love* 135
Interdum requiescendum; *sometimes we must rest* 103
Interiora vide; *look within* 69
Interminabilis humanæ vitæ labor; *endless the labour of human life* 215
Intestinæ simultates; *internal dissensions* 7
In victoriam dolo partam; *on victory gained by guile* 30
Inuidia integritatis assecla; *envy the attendant on integrity* 118
Inuidiæ descriptio; *description of envy* 94
In vitam humanam; *on human life* 14
In vtrumque paratus; *prepared for either part* 66
Iudicium Paridis; *the judgment of Paris* 83

LABOR irritus; *labour in vain* 48
Latet anguis in herba; *the snake lies hid in the grass* 24
Ludus, luctus, luxus; *gaming, grief, gluttony* 17
Luxuriosorum opes; *riches of prodigals* b 53

MALE parta malè dilabuntur; *badly gotten badly scattered* 169
Marte et arte; *by Mars and art* 47
Maturandum; *make good speed* b 188
Medici icon; *a physician's portrait* 212
Mediocribus vtere partis; *despise not moderate possessions* 39
Mens immota manet; *the mind unmoved remains* 43
Mihi pondera, luxus; *excess, a weight to me* 23
Minuit præsentia famam; *presence lessens fame* 20

Page

Mortui diuitiæ; *a dead man's riches* 86

Mulier vmbra viri; *woman man's shadow* b 218

Murus æneus, sana conscientia; *the wall of brass, a sound conscience* 67

Mutuum auxilium; *mutual help* 65

NEC sibi, nec alteri; *nor for himself, nor another* 184

Nec verbo, nec facto, quenquam lædendum; *nor in word, nor in deed, must we injure any one* 19

Neglecta virescunt; *neglected they flourish* a 222

Nemo potest duobus dominis seruire; *no man can serve two masters* 223

Nil penna, sed vsus; *the wing nothing, but the use* b 51

Nimium rebus ne fide secundis; *trust not prosperity too much* 59

Noli altum sapere; *aim not aloft* 78

Noli tuba canere eleemosynam; *not with a trumpet sound forth alms* b 224

Non dolo, sed vi; *not by craft, but force* 58

Non locus virum, sed vir locum ornat; *not place the man, but man the place adorns* 38

Non tibi, sed religioni; *not for thee, but religion* 8

Nullus dolus contra casum; *no craft against mischance* 22

Nusquam tuta fides; *faith never safe* 150

OMNIS caro fœnum; *all flesh is grass* 217

Orphei musica; *the music of Orpheus* 186

Otiosi semper egentes; *the idle ever destitute* 175

Otium sortem exspectat; *idleness awaits its destiny* 26

O vita, misero longa; *O life, long to the wretched* 75

PARUAM culinam, duobus ganeonibus non sufficere; *a small kitchen does not suffice two gluttons* a 55

Patria cuique chara; *native land to each one dear* 200

Paupertatem summis ingeniis obesse ne prouehantur; *poverty hinders the highest genius from gaining promotion* 152

Pennæ gloria perennis; *the pen's glory eternal* 196

Page

Perfidus familiaris; *a treacherous friend* 141

Peruersa iudicia; *perverse judgments* a 218

Petre, imitare petram; *Peter, imitate petre*, i.e. *rock* 96

Pietas filiorum in parentes; *piety of sons towards parents* 163

Pietas in patriam; *piety to one's country* 111

Pœna sequens; *punishment following* 41

Post amara dulcia; *after bitters sweets* 165

Post fata: vxor morosa, etiam discors; *after death: a cross wife still contrary* 158

Potentia amoris; *power of love* a 182

Potentissimus affectus, amor; *love, the most powerful passion* 63

Præcocia non diurturna; *precocious things not lasting* 173

Præpostera fides; *preposterous faith* 80

Pro bono, malum; *for good, evil* a 153

Prouidentia; *foresight* 3

Prudentes vino abstinent; *the wise refrain from wine* 133

Pulchritudo vincit; *beauty conquers* b 182

Pulchritudo sine fructu; *beauty without fruit* 205

QUA dij vocant, eundum; *where the gods call, we must go* 2

Quæ ante pedes; *things at our feet* 64

Quære adolescens, vtere senex; *young man seek, old man use* b 50

Quæ sequimur fugimus; *what we follow, we flee* 199

Qui me alit me extinguit; *who nourishes me, extinguishes me* 183

Qui se exaltat, humiliabitur; *whoso exalts himself, shall be humbled* a 216

Quod in te est, prome; *what is in thee, draw forth* 87

Quod non capit Christus, rapit fiscus; *what Christ takes not, the exchequer clutches* 151

Quod potes, tenta; *try, what thou canst* 16

REMEDIUM tempestiuum sit; *let there be a timely remedy* b 76

Res humanæ in summo declinant; *at their summit human affairs decline* 11

Respice, et prospice; *look behind, and before* 108

Ridicula ambitio; *foolish ambition* (76) 84

Page

SÆPIUS in auro bibitur venenum; *oftener in gold is poison drunk* 79
Scribit in marmore læsus; *being injured he writes on marble* *b* 183
Scripta manent; *writings remain* 131
Scripta non temerè edenda; *writings must not rashly be published* 185
Semper præsto esse infortunia; *ill luck is always at hand* 176
Serò sapiunt Phryges; *too late are Phrygians wise* 77
Sic ætas fugit; *so our age flees* 227
Sic discerne; *so winnow it* 68
Sic probantur; *so are they approved* *a* 224
Sic spectanda fides; *so fidelity is to be tested* *a* 139
Si Deus nobiscum, quis contra nos? *if God with us, who against us?* *b* 166
Silentium; *silence* 60
Sine iustitia, confusio; *without justice, confusion* 122
Si nihil attuleris, ibis Homere foras; *if you have brought nothing, Homer, you will go out of doors* *a* 168
Sirenes; *the Sirens* 10
Sobriè potandum; *we must drink soberly* 125
Soli Deo gloria; *to God alone the glory* 228
Sol non occidat super iracundiam vestram; *let not the sun set upon your wrath* *b* 216
Spes vana; *vain hope* *a* 191
Strenuorum immortale nomen; *of the brave immortal is the name* 193
Studiis inuigilandum; *we must be watchful at studies* 172
Stultitia sua seipsum saginari; *to glut oneself in one's own foolishness* *a* 98
Stultorum quantò status sublimior, tantò manifestior turpitudo; *the loftier the standing of fools, the plainer their dishonour* *a* 190
Superbiæ vltio; *vengeance on pride* 13
Superest quod suprà est; *what is above survives* 225

TECUM habita; *abide by thyself* 91
Temeritas; *rashness* 6

Page

Tempora cuncta mitiora; *with time all things more mellow* 206
Tempus omnia terminat; *time terminates all things* 230
Te stante, virebo; *thou standing, I shall flourish* 1
Tunc tua res agitur, paries cùm proximus ardet; *thine own is in question when the next wall is on fire* 208
Turpibus exitium; *destruction to the shameless* 21

VNICA semper auis; *the bird ever alone* 177
Vsus libri, non lectio prudentes facit; *the use of a book, not reading makes wise* 171
Vxoriæ virtutes; *the virtues of a wife* *b* 93

VARIJ hominum sensus; *various are the opinions of men* 46
Vel post mortem formidolosi; *even after death dreaded* 194
Venter, pluma, venus, laudem fugiunt; *gluttony, sloth, lust, put glory to flight* 42
Verbum emissum non est reuocabile; *the word uttered cannot be recalled* 180
Veritas inuicta; *truth unconquered* 166
Veritas temporis filia; *truth daughter of time* 4
Victoria cruenta; *a bloody victory* 195
Video, et taceo; *I see, and keep silence* 61
Vigilentia, et custodia; *watchfulness, and guardianship* 120
Vincit qui patitur; *who suffers conquers* 220
Vindice fato; *fate the avenger* 143
Virescit vulnere virtus; *virtue gains strength from wounds* *b* 98
Virtus vnita, valet; *virtue united, prevails* 72
Vitæ, aut morti; *for life, or for death* *a* 51
Vita irrequieta; *a restless life* 89
Voluptas ærumnosa; *sorrowful pleasure* 15

ZELOTYPIA; *jealousy* 211

fr...
Amico ...
feigned frie...

To the Reader, p. xiv, l. 39. A PEARLE shall not bee looked for in a poore mans purce.

p. xv, l. 5. Manie droppes pierce the stone, & with manie blowes the oke is ouerthrowen.

p. xv, l. 42. *So manie men, so manie mindes.*

Emb. p. 55, l. 2. One groaue, maie not two redbreastes serue.

p. 66, l. 2. The prouerbe saieth, one man is deemed none,
And life, is deathe, where men doo liue alone.

p. 77, l. 1. The prouerbe saieth, so longe the potte to water goes,
That at the lengthe it broke returnes.

p. 79, l. 7. Not euerie one, mighte to Corinthus goe.

p. 101, l. 9. The Prouerbe saithe, the bounde muste still obey,
And bondage bringes, the freest man in awe:
Whoe serues must please, and heare what other saye.

p. 103, l. 12. For ouermuch, dothe dull the finest wittes.

p. 107, l. 39. *Bicause, it is in vaine, to set a candell in the Sonne.*

p. 141, l. 13 All is not goulde that glittereth to the eye.

p. 147, l. 4. He founde that sweete, was sauced with the sower.

p. 164, l. 18. Then like, to like: or beste alone remaine.

p. 165, l. 11. None merites sweete, who tasted not the sower,
Who feares to climbe, deserues no fruicte, nor flower.

p. 170, l. 12. *That goodes ill got, awaie as ill will goe.*

p. 173, l. 9. Hereof the prouerbe comes: *Soon ripe, soon rotten turnes.*

p 191, l. 7. Heare much; but little speake; and flee from that is naught.

POSTSCRIPT TO THE INTRODUCTORY DISSERTATION.

(From Documents supplied by HENRY AUSTIN WHITNEY, *Esq., Boston, Mass., U.S.A.)*

REEMASONRY in literature surely exists, in virtue of which brotherhood is recognised among its votaries; and between men of similar pursuits there is a spiritualism which in an inexplicable manner draws them together, though continents and oceans divide. By an all-directing Wisdom they have been subjected to the same influences at almost the same time, and they feel and confess the bond by which they are united. Under such a persuasion, therefore, I follow only the simple and natural promptings of the mind, when by this Postscript I communicate to my readers the very valuable and interesting documents entrusted to my use by a fellow-labourer, in the purpose, if not in the actual enterprise, of bringing "The Choice of Emblemes" again before the world.

I do this the more readily because these documents at once confirm my conjecture that I had probably fallen into errors which further To the Reader, p. v. and vii. researches would rectify, and because also they display more fully the ramifications of the Whitney families which I had confined almost entirely to the counties of Hereford and Chester. Intr. Diss. pp. xxxv-lv. It appears that the branches spread from Bristol to York, and from Suffolk to Wales.

During the very time at which I was engaged on this fac-simile reprint, and even before, Mr. Samuel Austin Whitney of Glassboro', New Jersey, Horatio G. Somerby, esq., and Mr. Henry Austin Whitney were devoting themselves to the same object, and with the clearest right, if we do not term it, with direct obligation. Two of these gentlemen, I understand, are descendants from John Whitney of Islip, Document III. p. 9-12. See Pedigree opposite p. lxxxv. Oxfordshire, who in April 1635, with his wife Elinor and five sons, embarked from London for New England, and who in June of the same year "bought a sixteen-acre home-stall" at Watertown, where three other sons were born to him, making a goodly number for his quiver when he would "speak with the enemies in the gate." Some of the sons had a numerous offspring, — as John, with ten children, — Richard, with eight, — Thomas, with eleven, — Jonathan, with eleven, — Joshua, with eleven, — and Benjamin, with at least four. Thus the grandchildren of the emigrant John Whitney were not less than *fifty-five*. Whatever concerns the honour of the Whitney name may therefore justly be deemed the province and calling of their descendants.

And the more so, because of the common origin of the various families of Whitney; for Mr. H. A. Whitney testifies,—"From data in my possession, or at my command, the connection of families of the name in different parts of Herefordshire, in Radnor (Wales), Cheshire, Shropshire, Worcestershire, Yorkshire, and in Ireland, is readily traced to the parent stem,—the Whitneys of Whitney in Herefordshire." Again he says, "It is not unreasonable to suppose that all bearing the name had a common origin, and that they were descended from" Turstin the Fleming, "the son of the follower of William the Conqueror, who assumed the name of Whitney from his possessions" at Whitney in Herefordshire. A Fleming in 1086 founded the family, and after five hundred years his descendant Geffrey Whitney, in 1586, sought at Leyden the aid of a Fleming, Francis Rauelinghien, to imprint "The Choice of Emblemes." Three other centuries nearly have passed by, and the name which at first distinguished a border-chieftain is perpetuated to show how justice has greater triumphs than violence;

Document III. p. 11 *n* and p. 11.

Compare with Introd. Diss. p. xxxvi.

Essays, p. 269.

Emb. p. 123

> "That where this sacred Goddes is,
> That land doth florishe still, and gladnes, their doth growe:
> Bicause that all, to God, and Prince, by her their dewties knowe."

Feb 27, 1866.

The documents transmitted to me were: I° A manuscript copy of the Will of Geffrey Whitney the poet, lately extracted from the original, by Horatio G. Somerby; II° "Memoranda relating to families of the name of Whitney in England;" and III° "Wills relating to the name of Whitney in Buckinghamshire and Oxfordshire, England, 1549 to 1603; with a Pedigree."*

* Of the "Memoranda," ten copies were printed on royal 4to, pages 11, at Boston, U.S.A., April, 1859; and of "The Wills" twelve copies on royal 4to, pages 23, were privately printed at Boston, U.S.A., October 10th, 1865, — the very month and day and year on which at Knutsford in Cheshire I dated the Introduction to this Reprint, p. lxxiv.

I. Copy of the will of Geffrey Whitney, gentleman.

Document I.

From Her Majesty's Principal Registry of the Court of Probate, London.

"In the name of God, Amen. I Jeffery Whitney of Ryles Greene in the Countie of Chester, gent^{n}, being sick in bodie but of sounde and perfect memorie thancks be to god therefore make and sett downe with my owne hande this my last will and Testament in manner and fourme followinge. First I bequeath my sowle to Almightie god my Creator besechinge him for the merritts of Ihesus Christe my onlie Saviour and Redemer in his great mercie to receave the same into the congregac̃on of the faithefull to live with him forever. And for the buriall of my bodie to be at the appointement of my Executor. And for such smale worldlie goodes as the Lord hath blessed me withall my will ys they shalbe disposed as followethe. First, I bequeath to my brother Brooke Whitney the residue of yeares yet remaininge in my Farme or lease which I holde of Richard Cotton of Cambermere esquier together with the deede of the same Lease and all my severall parcells of howsholde stuff remaininge within my house there as allso eleven sylver spones a silver salte a tipple pot with silver and all other my goodes there and apparell whatsoever. Item I bequeath unto him my Dunne nag. Item I bequeath my Liberarie of Books whole without dim̃ishinge to Gefferie his sonne yf yt shall please God to indue him with learninge in the lattin tonge or else to anie other of his sonnes which shall attaine unto the same, yf none of them prove a scholler then I leave and bequeath them to my said brothers disposinge. Item I bequeath to him a trunck with Lynnen and apparell together with my plate remaininge in the safe custodie of my Cosen Jefferie Whitney of Draiton. Item I bequeath unto him all such debts as are due unto me by bond bill or otherwise. Out of which legacies so bequeathed to my brother as is remembred my will is that he shall pay unto Ioan Mills twentie pounds within one quarter of a yeare after my decease. Item to James Woodgate Tenne Poundes at his age of twentie yeares on this condic̃on that he applie himselfe to the gettinge of some arte or trade to live honestlie therewithall and not otherwise. Item I bequeath to my sister Eldershae five marks. Item to my sister Baron Fortie shillings. Item to my sister Evans Fortie shillings. Item to my sister Margerie twentie shillings. Item to Martha Colly ten shillings. Item to Charles Evance ten shillings. Item to Hellen Evance ten shillings. Item to Marie Eldershae Fortie shillings. Item I bequeath my best ringe to my Ladie Nedeham. The second Ringe in goodnes I bequeath to my sister in lawe Mawdlin Whitney. Item I bequeath my third Ringe to my Cosen Elizabethe Arnedell. My forth to my Cosen Mills. My seale Ringe to my Cosen Geffery Whitney. And my Brooche to my Cosen Walter Whitney. Item I bequeath to my brother Eldershae my gowne and fustian dublett. Item to Edmond Eldershae an other of my dubletts with a paire of best breeches and a paire of netherstocks. And for the performance of this my will I nominate and appointe my brother to be my sole executor. In witnes whereof I have subscribed to theise presents the eleventhe daie of September Anno Dni one thousand six hundred and in the two and fortethe yeare of the Raigne of our gracious soveraigne Ladie Queene Elizabeth. By me Geffery Whitney. Witnesses hereunto Angell Baron, Walter Whitney, John Browne."

Nantwich Hundred.

Br. Whitney, Emb. 88.

Richard Cotton, Emb. 200.

Geffrey Whitney, Emb. 181.

Mrs. A. Borron, p. xlvi. Emb. 191 *b*.

Mrs. D. Colley, p. xvii- xlvi. Emb. 93.

Emb. 181.

Date of Will Sept. 11, 1600.

John Browne, Emb. 212

"Probatum fuit hm̃di (*hujusmodi*) Testamentum apud London coram venerabili viro magr̃o (*magistro*) Jõhe (Johanne) Gibson Legum doctore Curie Prerogative Cant'

Probate, May 28, 1601.

(*Canterbury*) magr̃o (*magistro*) Custode sive Com̃issario ltime (*legitime*) constituto vicesimo octavo die men• (*mensis*) Maij Anno Domini millimo sexcentesimo primo Juramento mr̃i (*magistri*) Thome Browne nõ pub[cl] (*notarii publici*) procũris (*procuratoris*) Brokei Whitney fr̃s et ex[ris] (*fratris et executoris*) Cui etc (*et cetera*) de bene etc (*et cetera*) Jurat."

"Book Woodhall folio 33."

From the marginal references which I have added, it will be seen that to several persons remembered in the will devices were dedicated in "The Choice of Emblemes." Others who are named remain unknown; but the spelling antecedent to the seventeenth or even the eighteenth century was so unfixed that it is often nearly impossible to identify persons by their written names. Ioan Mills may have been of
Lyson's Cheshire, p. 387 and 837. the family of Meoles, which had representatives at Sluys in Flanders, near the end of the seventeenth century, and "my Ladie Nedeham" was of a family of great influence in South Cheshire and North Shropshire, who had and have estates as earls of Kilmorey, close to the birthplace* and residence of our author; but Woodgate, Eldershae, and Evans are undetermined.

Emb. 148. When we consider one of the Emblems, which follows up the thought
Emb. 147. that there is "*Fel in melle*," gall even in honey, and which is dedicated to a certain Lavra, with an intimation,

"Thy dartes do giue so great a wounde, they pierce the harte within;"

we are tempted to ask, was this Laura "Ioan Mills," to whom were bequeathed "twentie pounds," to be paid "within one quarter of a yeare," or was she "my Ladie Nedeham," who was honoured with "the best ringe"?

Teesdale's Map of Cheshire, 1830. "Ryles Greene," or as the name is now often given, Royals Green, in the parish of Dodcot-cum-Wilkesley, is in the extreme south of Nantwich hundred, where Cheshire points to the centre of Shropshire; it is near to the high-road from Audlem to Whitchurch, and if Plantin had set one leg of his compasses upon it, with a radius
Plate XI. *a.* of three miles the other leg would go round Coole Pilate, the probable
Emb. p. 172. place of the poet's birth, Audlem, "wheare," he says, "I my prime
Emb. p. 201. did spende," and "Cvmbermaire, that fame so farre commendes," and to which estate his own "farme or lease" belonged. A stretch

King's Vale Royal, p. 66. * Broomhall, within two miles of Coole Pilate, and not more than three miles from "Ryles Greene," is thus described, "a great Township, the greatest part whereof hath been the Lands of the Lord *Shavington* on the edge of *Shropshire*, now (A.D. 1621) Sir *Robert Needhams*, and near whereunto is scituate a Demean of the *Whitneys*, called the Mannour of *Coole Pilate*." A correspondent informs me "my Ladie Nedeham was only Lady by courtesy, and that her husband was Robert Nedeham esq.; she was the youngest daughter of Sir Edward Aston of Staffordshire."
T. W. Jones, esq. Nantwich, Mar. 2, 1866.

PEDIGREE OF WHITNEY, OF WHITNEY, IN HEREFORDSHIRE.

Sir BALDWIN WHITNEY, of Whitney in Herefordshire, Knt. = . . . daughter o. . . Pitchard.

Sir Eustace Whitney, of Whitney, Knt. = . . ., dau. of . . . [illegible]

Sir Robert Whitney, of Whitney, Knt. = . . ., dau. of . . . Russell.

Sir Eustace Whitney, of Whitney, Knt. = . . ., dau. of . . . Parree.

. . ., dau. of Thomas Rogers, of Herefordshire. = Robert Whitney, of Whitney = Constance, dau. of James Baron Audley, by . . ., dau. of . . . Holland, Earl of Kent.

James Whitney, of Whitney, Esq. = Blanche, dau. and coheir of Simon Melborne, of Tillington, co. Hereford; widow of Sir William Herbert, Knt.

Joan Whitney, mar. 1st, to Thomas Rogers; 2d, to . . Vaughan, of co. Hereford.

. . . married to William Harper of Wellington, co. Hereford.

Robert Whitney, of Whitney, Esq. = Margaret, dau. of Robert Wye, of Gloucestershire.

Watkins Whitney = Margaret, dau. and heir of Jenkin Ap Reece, of Clyron, co. Radnor.

- Jenkin Whitney.
- Katharine Whitney, wife of Robert Clough, of Shropshire.

James Whitney. Robert Whitney. Elizabeth Whitney, wife of Thomas Morgan, of Arkston.

Sir Robert Whitney, of Whitney, Knt. = Sibyl, dau. of Sir James Baskerville, Knt.

William Whitney, natural son.

James Whitney d. without issue. William Whitney, d. without issue. Elizabeth Whitney, wife of William Bastard, of Banbury. George Whitney =

George Whitney m. . . ., daughter of . . . Savage, of Worcestershire.

Sir James Whitney, of Whitney, Knt., died without issue.

Eustace Whitney, of Whitney, heir to his brother James; buried July 12, 1608. = Margaret, dau. and coheir of William Vaughan, of Glasbury, in co. Radnor; buried July 26, 1606.

Robert Whitney = Elizabeth, dau. of Morgan Ap Williams.

- Nicholas Whitney. Eustace Whitney. Richard Whitney.
- William Whitney. (Quære ?) bur. at Whitney, Jan. 4, 1659.
- Thomas Whitney, of Westminster.
- Margaret Whitney, wife of William Poell.
- Anne Whitney, wife of Thomas Robage, in the service of the Earl of Pembroke.

Robert Whitney, of Westminster. = Mary, dau. of John Towers.

John Whitney, aged 66, A. D. 1676, claimeth to be heir to the whole family.

Sir Robert Whitney, of Whitney, born Sept. 22, 1592; buried Sept. 13, 1658. = Anne, daughter of Sir Thomas Lucy, of Charlecote in Warwickshire, Kt.

Thomas Whitney born July 28, 1594.

Eleanor Whitney married to Sir Henry Williams, of Givarnevett, co. Brecknock, Knt.

Joan Whitney, wife of John Wigmore, of Lugton, in co. Hereford, Gent.

- Robert Whitney b. April 1, 1615.
- Constantine Whitney [Constance ?]. See Note below.*
- Richard Whitney baptized Jan. 6, 1620.
- Thomas Whitney bap. Jan. 6, 1622.
- Francis Whitney.
- William Whitney bap. Oct. 2, 1631.
- Lucy Whitney, wife of . . . Smallman, of Kinersley, co. Hereford, Gent.
- Anne Whitney, wife of Thomas Rodde, of Foxley in Herefordshire; born Feb 10, 1614; mar. Jan. 1, 1634.
- Bridget Whitney bap. Oct. 11, 1629; buried Feb. 9, 1629–30.
- Eleanor Whitney.
- Susan Whitney.
- Elizabeth Whitney.

---

* *Note.* — CONSTANCE WHITNEY. In Stowe's "Survey of London," folio, 1633, there is an inscription given, to be found on a monument in St. Giles Cripplegate Church, "on the South side of the quire," — the following account of which is taken from that work and the "New View of London," published in 1708.

"Above Mr. Fox's is a very spacious fine white Marble Monument, adorned with an entablature, Pediment; the figure of a young Lady rising (in a black coffin), with her winding-sheet about her (as an Emblem of the Resurrection); and two Cupids, one offering her a Crown, the other a Chaplet; with this Inscription, partly on the side of the Coffin, the rest under it [*the Inscription is given as printed in the 'Survey of London,' 1633*]: —

"'To the Memory

of CONSTANCE WHITNEY, eldest daughter to Sir ROBERT WHITNEY, of WHITNEY, the proper possession of him and his Ancestors, in Herefordshire, for above 500 yeres past. Her Mother was the fourth daughter of Sir THOMAS LUCY, of CHARLECOTTE, in Warwickshire, by CONSTANCE KINGSMILL, daughter and Heire of RICHARD KINGSMILL, Surveyor of the Court of Wards. This Lady LUCY, her grandmother, so bred her since she was eight yeares old,

[Thus farre written upon the figure in resemblance of a Coffin.]

As she excell'd in all noble qualities, becomming a Virgin of so sweet proportion of beauty and harmony of parts, she had all sweetnesse of manners answerable;
A delightfull sharpnesse of wit;
An offencelesse modesty of Conversation;
A singular respect and piety to her Parents; but Religious even to example.
She departed this Life most Christianly, at seventeene; dying, the griefe of all; but to her Grandmother an unrecoverable losse, save in her expectation shee shall not stay long after her, and the comfort of knowing whose she is, and where in the Resurrection to meet her.'"

The following is from the "New View of London:" —

"Under which Inscription are her Arms as a single woman, —

"'Sable a Cross Chequy Or and Gules, borne in a Lozenge.'

"There is no date to the Monument; but I have some reason to believe it about 100 years old. This is probably it that has given occasion to so many fabulous Relations of a Woman here, who, after she was Buried, was taken up alive, and had several Children afterward."

Note by H. O. S. - Some person has added, in ink, to the foregoing account, — "*two children*, there being two on the monument." (!) The monument was probably erected about 1622.

See p. LXXXVI.

WHITNEY OF CHINNOR AND ISLIP, OXFORDSHIRE.

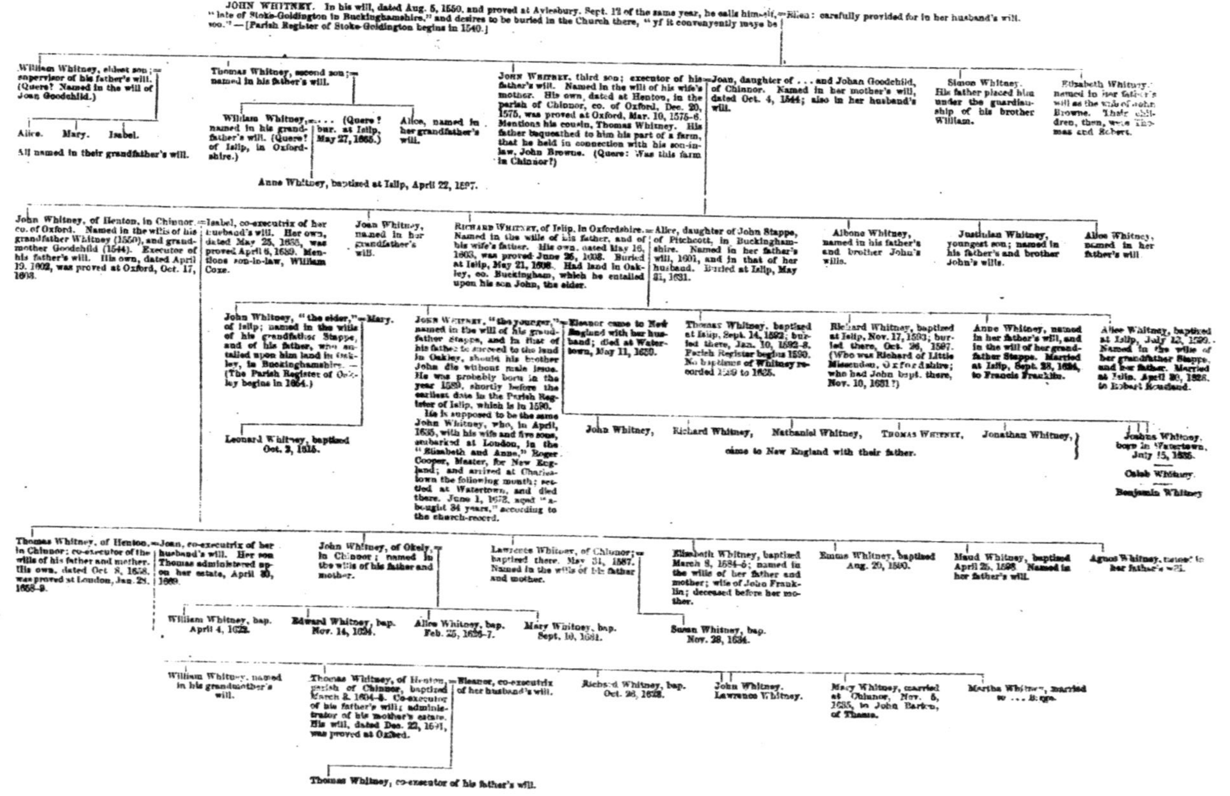

of eight miles would enclose Cholmondeley, and the "Hvghe Cholmeleys," father and son, — Woodhey, and Thomas Wilbraham, the Emb. 130 and 138. original of "the fine Old English gentleman, one of the olden time"— Emb. 199. Acton, the parish church of the Whitneys,—Shavington, the seat* of Plate XIII.*a*. the Needhams, in Adderley parish, near Market Drayton,—and Drayton- Emb. 181. in-Hales, where "Cosen Jefferie Whitney" dwelt, —also Ightfield, named as the residence of *sir* ARTHVRE MANWARINGE, *knight*, and Emb. 131. perhaps of his son "GEORGE MANWARINGE, *esquier*," "the worshipfull Emb. 139. and right vertuous yong Gentylman" to whom in 1573 Isabella Whitney Plate XI. wished "happy health with good succsesse in all his godly affayres." At Ryles Green there are three farms, of which the largest contains about 200 acres, and one of these would be the "farme or lease which," the testator declares, "I holde of Richard Cotton of Cambermere, esquier."

Thus in his latter days was the poet in the very midst of old friends. Tenderly, in a foreign land had he written the lines:

> "And as the bees, that farre and near doe straye, Emb. 201.
> And yet come home, when honie they haue founde:
> So, thoughe some men doe linger longe awaye,
> Yet loue they best their natiue countries grounde.
> And from the same, the more they absent bee,
> With more desire, they wishe the same to see;"

And again:

> "Wherefore, when happe, some goulden honie bringes? Emb. 201.
> I will retorne, and rest my wearie winges;"

And now, amid the bright scenes of his youth, with kindred near, full of faith and resignation the soul passed to his God.

II. "Memoranda *relating to families of the Name of Whitney, in England*." Document II.

These pages, their editor observes, "are, in part, the result of a Note by H. A. W. 1859. search made by Mr. SAMUEL AUSTIN WHITNEY of Glassboro', New Jersey, in 1856, and since continued by H. G. SOMERBY, esq., to ascertain the parentage of JOHN WHITNEY, who, with his wife ELINOR and five sons, embarked at London in the month of April 1635, for New England, and who settled in Watertown in the following June, where he continued to dwell until his death in 1673."

The pedigrees, *sixteen* in number, exhibit great labour and intelligent

* The Needhams, once of Cranage, co. Chester, are ancestors in a direct line of the present Francis Dod's Peerage. Jack Needham, earl of Kilmorey, whose seat is at Shavington. The first viscount, created in 1625, was son of a military commander in the Irish wars during the reign of Elizabeth.

research, but like most other pedigrees are defective in the early dates. They are compiled from various sources of undoubted authority, as the Public Record Office, London, the Prerogative Court of Canterbury, Parish Registers, and Family documents.

A brief recapitulation may be useful to some of our readers.

Compare with p. xxxvi.

Of these pedigrees we give the one which as far as England is concerned traces up the Whitney family to its early settlement in Herefordshire. Following page lxxxiv. is a photo-lithograph, being the Pedigree of Whitney, of Whitney in Herefordshire, from the "Memoranda," and at the head of it might be placed Turstin the Fleming, the son of Rolf, the father of Eustace who "assumed the name of Whitney, from his possessions, and thus established a family of that name, which was, for over six centuries, situated at Whitney in Herefordshire."

Document III. Wills, p. 11. *n.*

Document III. Oct. 10th, 1865.

III. "WILLS *relating to the name of Whitney in Buckinghamshire and Oxfordshire, England,* 1549 *to* 1603, *with a Pedigree.*" Edited by Henry Austin Whitney and dedicated to his "**Kinsman**, THOMAS HESTON WHITNEY, ESQUIRE, *of Glassboro', New Jersey.*"

The contents are:

Wills, p. 14.

From this IIIrd document, just before our page lxxxv, we extract in photo-lithograph, the pedigree of Whitney of Chinnor and Islip, to which are to be referred, "as is supposed," many of the Whitneys that for above two centuries have been settled in North America. To complete it there should be subjoined the pedigree of the Whitneys of Watertown, in New England, but we have already given notices of them sufficient to elucidate the subject. p. lxxxi. and lxxxv.

Many are the extracts we would make from the notes* to the Pedigrees and from the subject-matter of the Wills, but time and space both forbid. Of CONSTANCE WHITNEY, one of a family of twelve grandchildren of sir Thomas Lucy, of Charlecote in Warwickshire, Shakespeare's Mr. Justice Shallow, we must, however, give the record, which is sufficient of itself, if need were, to redeem the Lucy family from all the satirical inuendoes of the great dramatist. In St. Giles Cripplegate Church, London, there was erected to her "a very spacious fine white marble monument," described in Stowe's "Survey of London," folio, 1633, and bearing this inscription: Document II. p. I.

"'To the Memory
of CONSTANCE WHITNEY, eldest daughter to Sir ROBERT WHITNEY, of WHITNEY, the proper possession of him and his Ancestors, in Herefordshire, for above 500 yeeres past. Her Mother was the fourth daughter of Sir THOMAS LUCY, of CHARLECOITE, in Warwickshire, by CONSTANCE KINGSMELL, daughter and Heire of RICHARD KINGSMELL, Surveyor of the Court of Wards. This Lady LUCY, her grandmother, so bred her since she was eight years old,
As she excel'd in all noble qualities, becomming a Virgin of so sweet proportion of beauty and harmony of parts, she had all sweetnesse of manners answerable:
A delightfull sharpnesse of wit;
An offencelesse modesty of Conversation;
A singular respect and piety to her Parents: but Religious even to example.
She departed this Life most Christianly, at seventeene; dying, the griefe of all; but to her Grandmother an unrecoverable losse, save in her expectation shee shall not stay long after her, and the comfort of knowing whose she is, and where in the Resurrection to meet her.'"

See also Photo-lith. at p. lxxxiv.

So reverent a regard for the dead, as these documents manifest, betokens worthiness in the living. Fortunate do I esteem myself not

* One is a curious use of the word "world," as if it meant a period of time, the duration of a life, as well as a collected body of people; it is in the will of "Margret Whytnye," dated October 20th, 1568, "Item I do hereby confesse before God & the world that I have received of Edwarde Drax my servante a perfect acompte of all my rents and all other receipts which he have received from the beginninge of the world untill now." Document II. Memoranda, p. 3.

to have sent forth my volume until it was freighted with some memorials of John Whitney, the patriarch of Watertown in New England, and the immediate successor, if not companion, of those who sailed in the Mayflower, and were "the pilgrim fathers" of 1620. Of them almost prophetically did our Cheshire poet speak when he illustrated in verse the old saying "*Constantia comes victoriæ*," steadfastness is the companion of victory;

Emb. 137.

"THE shippe, that longe vppon the sea dothe saile,
And here, and there, with varrijng windes is toste:
On rockes, and sandes, in daunger ofte to quaile.
Yet at the lengthe, obtaines the wished coaste:
Which beinge wonne, the trompetts ratlinge blaste,
Dothe teare the skie, for ioye of perills paste.
Thoughe master reste, thoughe Pilotte take his ease,
Yet nighte, and day, the ship her course dothe keepe:
So, whilst that man dothe saile theise worldlie seas,
His voyage shortes: althoughe he wake, or sleepe.
And if he keepe his course directe, he winnes
That wished porte, where lastinge ioye beginnes."

Horace, Carm. I. 4.

"O NAVIS! referent in mare te novi
Fluctus? O! quid agis? fortiter occupa
Portum."

H. G.

March 10th, 1866.

A CHOICE OF EMBLEMES,

AND OTHER DEVISES,

For the moſte parte gathered out of ſundrie writers, Engliſhed and Moralized.

AND DIVERS NEWLY DEVISED,

by Geffrey Whitney.

A worke adorned with varietie of matter, both pleaſant and profitable: wherein thoſe that pleaſe, maye finde to fit their fancies: Bicauſe herein, by the office of the eie, and the eare, the minde maye reape dooble delighte throughe holſome preceptes, ſhadowed with pleaſant deuiſes: both fit for the vertuous, to their incoraging: and for the wicked, for their admoniſhing and amendment.

To the Reader.

Peruſe with heede, then frendlie iudge, and blaming raſhe refraine:
So maiſt thou reade unto thy good, and ſhalt requite my paine.

Jmprinted at LEYDEN,
In the houſe of Chriſtopher Plantyn,
by Francis Raphelengius.
M. D. LXXXVI.

HONI SOIT QVI MAL.Y.PENSE
DROIT ET LOYAL.

TO THE RIGHT HONO-RABLE, MY SINGVLER GOOD Lorde and Maiſter, ROBERT Earle of LEYCESTER, Baron of Denbighe, Knight of the moſte noble orders of the garter, and of ſaincte Michaël, Maiſter of her Maties horſe, one of her Highnes moſte honorable priuie Counſaile, and Lorde Lieutenant and Captaine Generall of her Maties forces in the lowe countries.

SOVLDIOR of Kinge PHILLIP, of MACEDONIA, (Righte honorable) ſuffering ſhipwracke, and languiſhinge throughe neceſſitie and extreme ſicknes, A Macedonian mooued with compaſſion, moſte louinglie entertayned, and longe cheriſhed and releeued him. Who being well recouered, promiſed at his departure if he might come to the preſence of his Soueraigne to requite his frendſhip. At the lengthe cominge to the courte, the ſouldior made reporte of the ſhipwracke, but not of the kindnes of the Macedonian: and contrariwiſe, ſo incenſed the Kinge againſt his louinge countryman, that he obtained a graunt of all his liuinges: But afterwarde his ingratitude and trecherous practiſe being diſcouered to this good prince, he reuoked his guifte, and in deteſtation of his dealinge cauſed him to bee marked with a hotte iron: The Emperor CLAVDIVS *reduced all thoſe to their former bondage, who neclecting the bountie and loue of their Lordes, in infranchiſinge them: requited them in the ende with anie vnkindnes. This foule vice Ingratitude hathe bin common in all ages, and yet ſo odious to the vertuous and*

Bruſonius lib. 3.

Idem.

best disposed, that they haue lefte behinde innumerable examples to the like effecte, for the rooting out thereof from all societies. If the former ages who knewe not the liuinge GOD, *nor his holie worde, haue bin so carefull herein: Then ought wee, muche more, who knowe not onlie howe odious it is, to man: but howe hatefull it is, cheeflie in the sighte of God. For we maie see in the holie scripture, howe often the children of Israel*
Exod. 14, 15, 16, 17. &c. *weare plagued for their vnthankefulnes. and howe the Lorde often complaineth therof, sayinge by the Prophet Isay,*
Isaie cap. 1. I haue nourished and exalted them and yet they dispised mee, the oxe knoweth his maister, and the asse his cribbe, but Israël knoweth not mee &c. *Also by the*
Ierem. cap. 8. *Prophet Ieremie*, The Storke, the Turtle, and the swallowe, doe obserue their time: but my people doe not knowe the iudgement of the Lorde. *In the newe Testament also, when Christe had clensed the ten lepers, and but*
Luc cap. 17. *one of them gaue thankes, our sauiour said,* Are not ten clen-
Mich. 6. Osee 13. sed? where bee the other nine? &c. *By whiche and manie other like places, it is manifest, howe ingratitude is vile bothe in the sighte of* GOD *and man.* W*herefore to cleare my selfe of the suspicion of my guilt herein, whiche your honor maye iustlie conceiue against mee, in deferring so longe before I present some testimonie of my bounden dutie to your good Lordship, (hauing so ofte, and so largelie tasted of your honourable bountie and fauor.) I haue therefore strained that small talent I haue, to pleade my cause in this behalfe to your honour: Most humblie beseeching the same, to pardon the wantes wherewith this my simple trauaile is blemisshed, throughe my lacke of leasure, and learninge. The first, denieth me to perfecte it, as I purposed: The other, to polishe it as it ought, that shoulde bee presented to so noble a personage. whose heroicall vertues so manie graue, and learned men haue eternised to all poste-*

all posterities. For leauinge your natiue countrie, where so manie godlie and vertuous are countenanced: So manie learned aduaunced, and so manie studious incoraged by your honour. What other countrie in Christendome, but knoweth that your lordship is a Noble, and moste faithfull counsellor to her excellent Matie, a zelous fauorer of the Gospell, and of the godlie Preachers thereof, a louinge patron of learninge, and a bountifull Mecœnas to all the professors of worthie artes, and sciences: whereof my selfe is a witnes, who haue often harde the same in other countries, to your euerlastinge memorie.

Learninge woulde be soone put to silence, without the aide and supporte of such noble Peeres as your Lordship: which was well considered by the Emperors, and Princes manie hundreth yeares since: whereof Artaxerxes the Kinge of Persia hath lefte behinde him this example, who wrat to a ruler of one of his dominions to this effecte. Kinge of Kinges great Artaxerxes to Hiscanus gouernor of Hellesponte greeting. The fame of Hippocrates a Phisition is come vnto mee, therfore see thou geue him as muche goulde as he desireth, and all other thinges he wanteth, and send him to me. He shalbee equall with anie Persian in honor, and if there be anie other famous man in Europe, spare no money to make him a frend to my courte. *Also Phillip of Macedonia fauored Aristotle, comitting his onlie sonne Alexander the great to his tutorship, reioysing that he had a sonne borne in suche a time, as he mighte haue such a famous Philosopher to be his instructor. The same Alexander so honored the poët Pindarus, that at the destruction of Thebes he gaue chardge that the familie and kinred of Pindarus shoulde bee spared. Hee loued so learninge that he vsed to laie the Iliades of Homer (which he learned of Aristotle)*

Suidas.

Aul. Gell. lib. 9 cap. 3.

Ælian. de Var Hist. lib. 13. ca.

Plutarchus in Alexand.

with his dagger vnder his beddes head. Also hauing learned certaine priuate instructions of his said Scoolemaister, after hauing knowledge that Aristotle had published the same to others, hee was highly offended: and althoughe hee weare busied in the great warres against Darius, yet in the middest of those waightie affaires, hee wrat vnto Aristotle, blaminge him for participating to others, that which hee desired to haue proper to him selfe. Sayinge, Howe can I excell others, in any thinges I haue learned of thee: if thou make the same common to all, for I had rather goe before them in learning, then in power and aboundance. *Gellius setteth downe the Epistle of the King to Aristotle, with the aunsweare thereunto, being worthie to bee imprinted in the mindes of the honorable, that they might bee for euer remembred. Scipio Africanus vsed the Poët Ennius as his companion in his greate affaires, and to shewe his griefe for the losse of such a one, caused the image of Ennius to bee laide with him in his owne tombe. Augustus countinanced Virgill, and so loued him: that after his death, hee carefullie preserued his workes from the fire to the which they weare adiudged. Mecœnas manie waies shewed his noble minde vnto Horace, and Plutarche was in highe estimation with the Emperor Traian. Yea famous citties and comon wealthes haue imbraced the learned, Smyrna and sixe other citties so loued Homer, that after his deathe, there grewe great controuersie amongst them, which of them should rightlie claime him to bee theirs. Athens honored a longe time Demosthenes: Rome reioysed for Tullie. And of later times Florence boasted of Petrarke, and Roterodam of Erasmus. with manye other citties that did the like to diuers famous men. And theise againe to requite their honorable regardes, made them famous throughe their worthie workes to all ages, that deathe to the which their bodies by nature weare subiect, coulde not extincte nor burie*

Aul. Gell. lib. 20. cap. 4.

Plinius lib. 7. cap. 30.
Idem, ibid.

Horatius.

Mossellanus super Gell. lib. 1. cap. 26.
Cicero in orat. pro Archia.

Sabellicus.

nor burie their memories: but that the ſame remaine ſo longe as the worlde ſhall indure. And to ſpeake of ſome of them, Ariſtotle, greatlie honored Phillip, and was no leſſe carefull for the education of Alexander. For when hee came to bee kinge, beſides the houlſome preceptes hee preſcribed vnto him of regiment, yet hauinge knowledge of his earneſt deſire, to vnderſtand the natures and qualities of all creatures, compyled almoſte fiftie bookes, intreatinge of the ſame: hauing by the commaundement of Alexander out of Greece and all Aſia, manie thowſandes of Hunters, Faulkeners, Fowlers, Fiſhers, Heardmen, and ſuche as kepte bees, birdes, or anie other liuinge thinge: to helpe and aide him, with theire knowledge and experiences, in ſearchinge the ſecrettes, natures and qualities of all creatures. Aul. Gell. lib. 1. cap. 7. *Ennius beinge mindfull of the noble inclination of Scipio, did highlie extoll his worthie actes, regiſtring them in his learned cronicles to all poſterities:* Petrus Crinitu. de poëtis Latini *Virgill to ſhewe him ſelfe thankefull to Auguſtus: ſpent manie yeares about his famous worke of Æneiads, to deriue the race of the Emperor from Æneas, and the noble Troians.* Idem. *Horace amongſt his rare & learned workes ſtuffed full of wiſe and graue preceptes, oftentimes enterlaceth the ſame with the birthe the bountie the learninge, and the noble qualities of Mecœnas, & hathe made him for euer famous, & renowmed.* Macrobius. *Plutarche beſides his priuate bookes he wratte to Traian, of counſell and gouernement: Hee framed that excellent worke of liues, and compariſons betwene the Romanes and the Grecians: giuing due commendation aſwell to the Romanes, as to his owne countrimen.* Suidas. *By which wee maie gather, that learning grounded vppon vertue hath bin alwaiſe enemie to ingratitude, and cannot lie hid, but is euermore workinge, & bewrayeth it ſelfe as the ſmoke bewrayeth the fire, And if anie thinge happen worthie memorie: by the benefit of the learned it is imparted, by their trauailes to future time. If there*

chaunce

chaunce nothinge in theire age famous, yet they set them selues a worke in handlinge suche accidentes, as haue bin done in times paste. Cornel. Nepos. *Dares Phrigius beinge a souldior at the battaile of Troye, made a large discourse thereof, yet like one too much affectioned, can scarce finde an ende of the praises of Hector. Homer finding small matter in his time to handle, attempted the same argument, being lothe that his countrymen shoulde lacke their due commendacion, and therefore almost as farre on the other side, extolleth the valour, and highe prowes, of Achilles: and the counsaile, and pollicie, of Vlisses.* Petr. Crinit. *Lucan seing nothing honorable in Nero to intreate of, fled to former times for matter, where he found to set his worthie muse a worke, and wratte in verse (equall with the haughtines of the argument) the battailes and bloodie conflicts, betwene Cesar, and Pompey. Seneca dispairinge of the nature and inclinacion of his vntowarde scholler the same Nero: wratte lamentable Tragedies, & bookes of great grauitie and wisedome. Moreouer learninge hath that secret workinge that tyrauntes haue bin mittigated therewith, and haue dissembled their affections for the time.* Plutarchus. *Dionysius the elder desired to heare Plato, and was contented a while to listen vnto him, after whome his sonne, hauing bothe his name and nature, did seeme ontwardlie to loue and reuerence Plato, and sente him great guiftes to Athens; and inuited him to his courte.* Suetonius. Petr. Crinit. *Nero for a time embraced Lucan and Seneca, althoughe naturallie he was wickedlie inclined: but hee soone did degenerate from their discipline, for there can bee no league betweene vertue and vice, nor perfecte vnion of meere contraries: And although time reuealed the bloodie mindes, of these cruell tirantes towardes those famous men, yet wee can not finde the like outrage, and crueltie done vnto the learned, by those that are honorable vertuous and noble minded: but by suche as bee of cruell vile and base natures, who are alwaies enemies to*

vertue.

vertue, and loue none, nor like anie, but such as are of their owne vglie stampe. For it is a rule that faileth not, that those that are moste honourable, are most vertuous: bicause honour alwaies followeth vertue, as the shaddowe doth the bodie: and it is as vnpossible that a bodie shoulde be without a shaddowe in the sonne, as the right honourable in this life shoulde be voyde of vertue. Thus it is manifest howe learninge hath bin embraced, and had in highe estimation, by great Princes and noble Peeres, and that worthelie: Bicause by the benefit thereof, The actes of mightie Monarches & great Princes, and the matters and thinges of former time worthie memorie, done by sage Gouernors, and valiant Captaines. The manners and Lawes of straunge nations, & customes of oulde time. The mutabillitie of worldly felicitie, and howe the wise haue behaued them selues in bothe fortunes: haue bin presented vnto them as in a glasse, for their instruction, from which they might drawe vnderstanding and good counsaile, to instruct and gouerne them selues in all their actions: and finde approoued examples for the whole course of their life, eyther to bee imitated, or eschewed. Of which singuler benefit, wee likewise are pertakers: For hereby, this present time behouldeth the accidentes of former times, as if they had bin done but yesterdaie. and wee maye behoulde the natures, & quallities, of our great grandfathers grandfathers, as if they yet liued before our eies. And as former time, and present time, haue reaped thereby, this inestimable Iuell; So likewise, future time so long as the worlde shall indure, shall taste of this blessing: For our succession, shall see what we haue seene, and behoulde hereby what famous thinges weare enterprised and done in our daies, as if they weare euen nowe standing at our elbowes. Yet howe greatlie learning hath bin impeached since the firste florishe thereof, when in stead of such louing and bountifull princes and patrons, the worlde broughte forthe, Licinius who tearmed learning a poyson and plague of the common wealthe. And Valentinianus his partner in that opinion, with the cursed crewe of their companions, As Caligula, Nero, Diocletian, with Machomet, Baiazet, and such like monsters of nature, being cruell persecutors, enemies of all humanitie, and distroyers of all discipline: who dispising God and all goodnes, did degenerate so farre from their forfathers, that they delighted whollie to spill the blood of the worthie men, to burne the famous libraries, and to rase and ouerthrowe the vniuersities, and schooles, of all artes and sciences: as in the tragicall Histories of former times is recorded, and can not bee but with great griefe remembred. And althoughe learning hath bin greatlie decaied in these later times, Yet wee must (with thankes vnto God therefore) confesse, That it hath pleased him alwaies, to raise vp some louers and fauorers therof, who haue tendered and embraced the same, and for the preseruinge it to their posterities, haue lefte behinde singuler monuments of their care, & zelous mindes in this behalfe: As Charles the great, Kinge of Fraunce, who erected two vniuersities, the one at Paris, the other at Pauia, placing therein many famous men: and Sigismundus Emperor, who highlie extolled the learned, and blamed the Princes of Germanie, for their small regarde vnto them: And vnderstanding by somme, that althoughe he cherished the learned, yet it was saied they were but pore and base persons, aunswered: I loue them who excell others for vertue, and learninge, out of the which I measure nobilitie. Also Ferdinandus gaue yearelie out of his treasurie, great sommes of money to the readers of diuinitie, Phisicke, Rethoricke, and Philosophie, to the great incouraginge of those that weare inclined to good studies: Likewise Alphonsus King of Naples, who vsed to saye, he had neuer greater pleasure, then when he was in the companie of those that weare singuler for knowledge

Bapt. Egnatius de Romanis principibus lib 1. & Pompon. Lætus in Rom. Histor. compendio.

Alexandriæ Bibliotheca omnium celeberrima, in qua Cccc. millia volumina librorum incensa, Frecul. Cron. tom. 1. lib. 7. cap. 9. Sed Plutarchus in Cæsare, & Aul. Gel. lib. 6. cap. vlt. & Sabel. Ennead. 6. libro 7. scribunt septingenta millia in eâdem consumpta. Vaticana Romæ Bibliotheca, sub Clemente 7. a militibus Germanis & Hispanis cremata. Æneas Syluius de Europa.

Instructiss. Budæ Bibliotheca per Solimannum incensa 1526. Aug. Cur. Athenæ deletæ, & funditus euersæ, per Machometum 8. Turcarum Imp. 1452. idem Curio.

Bapt. Egnat. de Rom. principibus lib. 3.

Idem ibi.

Pontanus de liberalitate.

ledge, and learninge: Laurentius Valla & Panormitanus, with diuers other tasted of his goodnes, and found him a rare example for princes, for his continual desire to aduance learninge. I mighte heere likewise bringe in diuers other, not inferior to them for their loue to the learned: As Fredericke Duke of Saxon Prince elector, and the Lorde Ernestus his brother, who erected the vniuersitie of Wittenberge, *and the said Duke noblie countinaunced and defended Martin Luther, against the furie of Pope Leo the tenthe, and all other his aduersaries. Also Laurentius Medices Duke of Florence honoured Picus Mirandula, and Hermolaus Barbarus: and Borsus Duke of Ferrara, reioysed in Titus Strozza. with many other Princes, who for their noble inclinations in this behalfe, amongst these mighte iustly haue their places.*

Crinitus lib. 1 cap. 9. Volaterranus Geog.

BVT *remembring I write to your good Lordship. I will therefore abridge of purpose, that which might bee more larglie amplified, knowing there needeth no Apologie to bee made vnto your honour, in the behalfe of learning: whose noble minde hath bin so addicted to the same these many yeares, that diuers, who are nowe famous men, had bin throughe pouertie, longe since discouraged from their studies: if they had not founde your honour, so prone to bee their patron. But I confesse, I haue thus largelie written therof to this ende, That if anie other happe to looke herevppon, in knowinge your zeale & honourable care of those that loue good letters: They might also knowe thereby, that you haue possession of that grounde from which true nobilitie florisheth: And likewise that you followe the good examples of manie Princes, and great personages, who are renowmed therefore, beyond anie other their desertes. And likewise, if anie be coulde, in countinancinge the learned, (as there are tootoo manie, whose frendship is (as I may saie) frozen, and starke towarde them.) This mighte a little thawe and mollifie them: and serue* as a spurre to pricke them forwarde, to follow the steppes of your good Lordship. There be three thinges greatlie desired in this life, that is healthe, wealthe, and fame. and some haue made question which of these is the chiefe: the sick, saieth health. the couetous, comendeth wealthe. and bothe these place good name laste of all. But they be bothe partiall iudges; for he that is of sincere and vprighte iudgement, is of contrarie opinion: Bicause that healthe, and wealthe, though they bee neuer so good, and so great, determine with the bodie, and are subiecte vnto time; But honour, fame, renowme, and good reporte, doe triumphe ouer deathe, and make men liue for euer: where otherwise the greatest Princes, in shorte time are worne out of memorie, and cleane forgotten. For, what is man in this worlde? without fame to leaue behinde him, but like a bubble of water, that now riseth, & anon is not knowne where it was. Which being wel cōsidered by your honour, you haue made choice of the best parte, and embraced throughe vertue, that which liueth, and neuer dieth. For vertue (as I said) alwaies goeth before honour, & giueth a perpetuitie of felicitie in this worlde, and in the worlde to come. And althoughe throughe the iniquitie of time (as is declared) such excellent learned men as haue bin, are not to bee exspected in this oulde age of the worlde, Yet as zelous care, and dewtifull affection as euer was to their Lordes and Patrons, there is no doubte dothe generallie florishe and is apparante: whereof your honour hath had tryall, by the learned labours of manie famous men. Farre behinde whome, my selfe, (although of all the meanest) yet beinge pricked forwarde by your good Lordshipps bountie, and incouraged by your great clemencie, moste humblie presente theise my gatheringes, and gleaninges out of other mens haruestes, vnto your honour: a worke both pleasaunte and pithie, which I haue garnished with manie histories, with the proper applica-

tions

tions and expositions of those Emblemes that I founde obscure: Offering it vp to your honour to looke vppon at some houres for your recreation. I hope it shalbee the more delightfull, bicause none to my knowledge, hathe assayed the same before: & for that diuers of the inuentiōs are of my owne slender workmanship. But chieflie, bicause vnder pleasaunte deuises, are profitable moralles, and no shaddowes, voide of substance: nor anie conceyte, without some cause worthie consideration: for the wounding of wickednes, and extoling of vertue. which maie serue, as a mirrour: to the lewde for their amendement. & to the godlie, for their better goinge forwarde in their course, that leades to euerlastinge glorie. Beinge abashed that my habillitie can not affoorde them suche, as are fit to be offred vp to so honorable a suruaighe: yet if it shall like your honour to allowe of anie of them, I shall thinke my pen set to the booke in happie houre; and it shall incourage mee, to assay some matter of more momente, as soone as leasure will further my desire in that behalfe.

THE *almightie God from whome all honour and true nobillitie doe proceede, who hathe manie yeares, moste louinglie and liberallie, indued your Lordship with the same, blesse and prolonge your daies here, that wee maie behoulde the consummatiō of happie ould age in your honour: before you shalbe summoned to the euerlasting honour, which is alwaies permanent without mutabilitie,* Amen. *At London the* XXVIII. *of Nouember, Anno* M. D. LXXXV.

Your Honours humble &
faithfull seruant

Geffrey Whitney.

TO THE READER.

VHEN I had finiſhed this my collection of Emblemes (gentle Reader,) and preſented the ſame in writinge vnto my Lorde, preſentlie before his Honour paſſed the ſeas into the lowe countries: I was after, earneſtlie required by ſomme that pervſed the ſame, to haue it imprinted: whoſe requeſte, when I had well conſidered, althoughe I did perceiue the charge was verie heauie for mee, (waighinge my owne weakenes) I meane my wante of learninge, and iudgement, to ſet forth any thinge vnto the viewe of this age, wherein ſo manie wiſe & learned doe floriſhe, and muſt haue the ſcanninge thereof. Yet knowinge their fauours to bee ſuch vnto mee, as in dewtie I mighte not denie them any thinge I can: I did rather chooſe to vndergoe any burthen, and almoſte fainte in forwardnes to ſatisfie them, then to ſhewe anie wante of good will, in denyinge their continuall deſires. wherefore, licence beinge obtained for the publiſhing thereof, I offer it heare (good Reader) to thy viewe, in the ſame ſorte as I preſented it before. Onelie this excepte: That I haue now in diuerſe places, quoted in the margent ſome ſentēces in Latin, & ſuch verſes as I thoughte did beſte fit the ſeuerall matters I wratte of. And alſo haue written ſomme of the Emblemes, to certaine of my frendes, to whome either in dutie or frendſhip, I am diuers waies bounde. which both weare wantinge in my firſte edition, and nowe added herevnto, for theſe reaſons inſuinge. Firſte I noted the ſame in Lattin, to helpe and further ſome of my acquaintaunce wheare this booke was imprinted, who hauinge no taſte in the Engliſhe tonge, yet weare earneſtly addicted to the vnderſtandinge hereof: and alſo, wheare I founde any verſe, or ſayinge agreable with the matter, I did gather the ſame of purpoſe for my owne memorie, not doubtinge but the ſame may bee alſo frutefull to others.

For my intitulinge them to ſome of my frendes, I hope it ſhall not bee miſliked, for that the offices of dewtie and frendſhip are alwaies to bee fauored: and herin as I followe my auctors in Engliſhinge their deuiſes, So I imitate them, in dedicatinge ſome, to ſuch perſons, as I thinke the Emblemes doe beſt fitte and pertaine vnto, which order, obſerued *Reuſnerus*, *Iunius*, *Sambucus*, and others: as by their workes are apparante, Confeſſinge my faulte to bee chiefly this, in preſentinge to famous and worthie men, meane mat er, farre to ſimple for their deſeruinges: yet truſtinge my good will ſhalbe waighed as well as the worke, and that a pearle ſhall not bee looked for in a poore mans purce, I ſubmit my doings herein to their cenſures.

Furthermore, wheare there are diuers Emblemes written of one matter, which may bee thoughte ſuperfluous. As againſt Pride, Enuie, Concupiſcence, Drunkennes, Couetouſnes, Vſurie, and ſuch like,

againſt

againste euery one of them seuerally, sondrie deuises: thereby the sondry inuentions of the auctours may bee decerned, which I haue collected against those vices especially, bycause they are growē so mightie that one bloe will not beate them downe, but newe headdes springe vp like *Hydra*, that *Hercules* weare not able to subdue them. But manie droppes pierce the stone, & with manie blowes tho oke is ouerthrowen, So with manie reprehencions, wickednes is wounded, and sinne ashamed and giueth place vnto vertue. It resteth now to shewe breeflie what this worde Embleme signifieth, and whereof it commeth, which thoughe it be borrowed of others, & not proper in the Englishe tonge, yet that which it signifieth: Is, and hathe bin alwaies in vse amongst vs, which worde being in Greeke ἐμβάλλεσθαι, vel ἐπιμβλῆσθαι is as muche to saye in Englishe as *To set in, or to put in:* properlie ment by suche figures, or workes, as are wroughte in plate, or in stones in the pauementes, or on the waulles, or suche like, for the adorning of the place: hauinge some wittie deuise expressed with cunning woorkemanship, somethinge obscure to be perceiued at the first, whereby, when with further consideration it is vnderstood, it maie the greater delighte the behoulder. And althoughe the worde dothe comprehende manie thinges, and diuers matters maie be therein contained; yet all Emblemes for the most parte, maie be reduced into these three kindes, which is *Historicall, Naturall, & Morall. Historicall*, as representing the actes of some noble persons, being matter of historie. *Naturall*, as in expressing the natures of creatures, for example, the loue of the yonge Storkes, to the oulde, or of suche like. *Morall*, pertaining to vertue and instruction of life, which is the chiefe of the three, and the other two maye bee in some sorte drawen into this head. For, all doe tende vnto discipline, and morall preceptes of liuing. I mighte write more at large hereof, and of the difference of *Emblema Symbolum, & Ænigma*, hauinge all (as it weare) some affinitie one with the other. But bicause my meaning is to write as briefely as I maie, for the auoiding of tediousnes, I referre them that would further inquire therof, to *And. Alciatus, Guiliel. Perrerius, Achilles Bocchius* & to diuers others that haue written thereof, wel knowne to the learned. For I purpose at this present, to write onelie of this worde Embleme: Bicause it chieflie doth pertaine vnto the matter I haue in hande, whereof I hope this muche, shall giue them some taste that weare ignoraunt of the same.

Pietas Ciconiæ erga parentes.

Lastlie if anie deuise herein shall delight thee, and if some other shall not please thee, yet in respect of that which doth like thee, passe ouer the same fauourably to others, with whome perhappes it maie be more agreable: For what one liketh, an other oftentimes doth not regarde: and what some dothe lothe, some other doth chieflie esteeme: whereof came the Prouerbe, *So manie men, so manie mindes.* But what? Shoulde I thinke that my simple trauaile herein should scape scot-free from the tonges of the enuious, who are alwaies readie with a preiudicate opinion

nion to condempne, before they vnderstande the cause. No? thoughe the verse weare (as I maye saye) written by the pen of *Apollo* him selfe? For in the former times, when the whole worlde was almoste ouershadowed with the mantle of ignoraunce, If then, the learned and excellent worke of *Homer*, could not shielde him from the stinge of *Zoilus*. If *Marcus Varro*, was taunted by *Remnius Palemon*. If *Cicero* had sixe bookes written againste him, by *Didymus Alexandrinus*. And if *Vergill* weare enuied by *Carbilius*, who wrat a booke *de Virgilianis erroribus*, which he intituled *Æneidomastix*: and diuers others whose workes weare most singuler; if they coulde not escape the bites of such Basiliskes broode: Then howe maye I thinke, in this time which is so blessed, generallie with most rare and exquisite perfection in all knowledge, and iudgement: that this slender assaye of my barren muse, should passe the pikes without pusshing at: where thousandes are so quicke sighted, they will at the first, behoulde the least iote, or tittle, that is not rightly placed. And althoughe, perhappes it maie bee embraced a while, for the newnes thereof, yet shortlie it shalbee cast aside as thinges that are vnsauerie & not esteemed. For the nature of man is alwaies delighted in nouelties, & too much corrupte with curiousnes and newfanglenes. The fairest garden, wherein is greate varietie bothe of goodlie coulors, and sweete smelles, can not like all mennes fancies: but some gallant coulours are misliked, and some pleasant smelles not regarded. No cooke, can fitte all mennes tastes, nor anie orator, please all mennes humors: but wheare the tasters are too daintie, his cookerie shalbe controlled: and wheare the auditors are to rashe and careles in regarding, his Rethoricke shalbe condempned: and no worke so absolute perfecte, but some are resolute to reprehende. Yet trustinge the learned, and those that are of good iudgemente (whome I doe chiefelie desire to bee the perusers hereof) with indifferencie will reade, and then fauorablie yeelde their verdicte. I offer this my worke, suche as it is, vnto them; wherein I hope the greater sorte shall finde somethinge to delighte them, and verie fewe of what age, or condition they bee, but may herin see some deuise, aunswerable to their inclinations; trusting they wil so frendly accept thereof, That I shalbe rather incouraged thereby, to assay some further matter, as soone as I shall haue leasure: then throughe their sinister interpreting of my good will, to discorage mee from the same, and to wishe I had not yet communicated this, vnto all: which I might haue kepte priuate to a fewe. Yet hereby I haue satisfied my frendes requestes, and haue in some parte discharged my dutie vnto them: Therfore if they shalbee well pleased with my paines, I shall the lesse care for anie others cauillinge. Thus wishing thee the fruition of thy good desires, I leaue thee vnto the same.

Martialis.

Textor in officin.

Petrus Crinitus de poëtis Latinis.

At Leyden in Hollande, the IIII. of Maye. M. D. LXXXVI.

G. Whitney.

IN GALFRIDI WHITNEI EMBLEMATA.

Illecebris scripti genus omne EMBLEMATA *vincunt,*
Vtile vbi dulci miscuit EVPHROSYNE.
Hoc præstant variis distincta Asarota figuris,
Apta tenere oculos, instruere apta animum.
SAMBVCVS *testis, testis mihi* IVNIVS, *& qui*
Omne tulit punctum hoc in genere ALCIATVS.
Sed scripti quantum genus omne EMBLEMATA *præstant*
Illecebris, doctâ vermiculata manu;
Tantum operis, WHITNÆE, *tui concedit honori,*
Quantum est SAMBVCVS, IVNIVS, ALCIATVS.

IANVS DOVSA à Noortwijck.

IN GALFRIDI WHITNEI EMBLEMATA,

MAGNI ILLIVS OLIM ANGLIÆ POETÆ GALFRIDI CHAVCERI, *cognominis.*

VNA duos genuit GALFRIDOS ANGLIA, Vates
Nomine, PHOEBÆO numine, & arte pares.
Vnum, Fama suæ patriæ indigitauit HOMERVM,
Anglicus hic meritò dicitur HESIODVS.
Ac veluti dubiis quondam victoria pennis
Inter MÆONIDEN HESIODVMque stetit:
Sic, quibus exultat modò læta Britannia alumnis,
GALFRIDOS palma est inter, in ambiguo.
CHAVCERI versant dudum aurea scripta Britanni:
Aurea WHITNÆVS sed sua pressit adhuc,
Nunc verò, auspiciis LEYCESTRI, EMBLEMATA lucem
Aspiciunt; & dant accipiuntque decus.
Qualis gemma micat fuluo redimita metallo
Indica, ab artificis vermiculata manu.
Perge tuæ WHITNEY titulos superaddere famæ,
Tollens astra super te patriamque tuam.

BONAVENTVRA VVLCANIVS Brugensis.

IN EMBLEMATA GALFRIDI WHITNEI.

QVALITER *insinuant oculis se Emblemata nostris,*
Quæ variè augusta vermiculata domo,
Artificique nitent opere exornata, modò illa,
Hac modò perdita mens dum stupet effigie:
Sic tu dum GALFRIDE *tuo hoc expressa libello*
Symbola cum variis edis imaginibus,
Nos legisse beat veterum dicta æmula dictis,
Carminibus variè vermiculata tuis,
Et modo priscorum Heroûm immortalia facta,
Virtutesque animo commeminisse iuuat.
Intrepidus dum CurtI animus, & Horatia corda,
Et tibi Fabricij cognita Pyrrhe, fides;
Dum fortes Decij, Iunij, Curij, atque Metelli,
Et Cunctatoris mens benesuada FabI,
Ac dum Scipiadæ belli duo fulmina, quosque
Est alios haud mens enumerare potis
Innumeros, per te virtutum hic clara suarum
Opponunt nostris lumina luminibus.
Quid! quod præcipuum, hæc meritò LEYCESTRIVS *heros*
Vindicat auspiciis edita scripta suis.
Vt qui hic cuncta simul laudata Heroica dona
Possidet, in magnis singula principibus
Quæ miramur. At olim etiam admirabitur ætas
Postuma, DVDLAEI *illustria facta ducis.*
Et simul agnoscet felici hunc alite librum
Olim per doctorum ora volare hominum.
Auguror. hinc etiam quondam tibi fama paratur,
Quæ WHYTNAEE *mori te quoque posse neget.*

PETRVS COLVIVS Brugensis.

IN GAL-

IN GALFRIDI WHITNEI EMBLEMATA, STEPHANI LIMBERTI ANGLI NORDOVICENSIS

Scholæ Magiſtri Decaſtichon.

VIRTVTIS formam ſplendentiaq́ue ora tueri,
Si Deus hic nobis, teſte Platone, daret:
Quantos pectoribus noſtris accenderet ignes
Cuius vel Phœbo pulchrius ora nitent?
Non Veneris, Triuiæ nec certet forma Dianæ,
Niſos hæc omnes vincit & Euryalos.
Huius at effigiem WHITNAEI Emblemata pingunt,
Zeuxide, vel docto dignus Apelle, labor.
Conſulet ergo boni multum ſpectabilis Heros
Et capiet facili talia dona manu.

ARTHVR BOVRCHIER TO THE READER.

PERFECTION needes no other foyles, ſuche helpes comme out of place:
For where it ſelfe, can grace it ſelfe, there needes no other grace.
Why ſhould I then my fruiteles praiſe on WHITNEYS *worke beſtowe,*
Where wiſdome, learninge, and deuiſe, ſo perfectly doe flowe.
Yet gentle Reader by thy leaue, thus muche I mente to wrighte,
As one that honours theſe his giftes, but ſeekes them not t'indighte.
No longe diſcourſe, no tedious tale, I purpoſ'de am to tell:
Leſt thou ſhouldſt ſaye, where is the nutte, you feede me with the ſhell.
Goe forwarde then in happie time, and thou ſhalt ſurely finde,
With coſte, and labour well ſet out, a banquet for thy minde.
A ſtorehouſe for thy wiſe conceiptes, a whetſtone for thy witte:
Where, eache man maye with daintie choice his fancies finely fitte.
Giue WHITNEY *then thy good report, ſince hee deſerues the ſame:*
Leſt that the wiſe that ſee thee coye, thy follie iuſtly blame.

D. O. M.

S INCE *man is fraile, and all his thoughtes are sinne,*
And of him selfe he can no good inuent,
Then euerie one, before they oughte beginne,
Should call on GOD, *from whome all grace is sent:*
So, I beseeche, that he the same will sende,
That, to his praise I maie beginne, and ende.

Faultes escaped in the Printing, (for the most parte already corrected,) yet in manie leaues ouerpassed as followeth.

Pag.	*Lin.*	*Faultes.*	*Reade.*
10	1	listen their	listen to their
56	4	the same	the man
77	12	false, to it	false, it
140	10	watcheman	watchemen
130	3	sapientem	sapientum
198	3 in margine	Chiliad. 42.	Chiliad. 1.
202	10 in margine	libro 6. de	libro de
217	3 in marg.	Esaie 42	Esaie 40
223	10	which	with

Te ſtante, virebo.

A MIGHTIE Spyre, whoſe toppe dothe pierce the ſkie,
An iuie greene imbraceth rounde about,
And while it ſtandes, the ſame doth bloome on highe,
But when it ſhrinkes, the iuie ſtandes in dowt:
The Piller great, our gratious Princes is:
The braunche, the Churche: whoe ſpeakes vnto hir this.

I, that of late with ſtormes was almoſte ſpent,
And bruſed ſore with Tirants bluddie bloes,
Whome fire, and ſworde, with perſecution rent,
Am nowe ſett free, and ouerlooke my foes,
And whiles thow raignſt, oh moſt renowmed Queene
By thie ſupporte my bloſſome ſhall bee greene.

Quà dij vocant, eundum.

THE trauaylinge man, vncertaine where to goe,
When diuers wayes before his face did lie,
Mercurius then, the perfect pathe did showe,
Which when he tooke, hee neuer went awrie,
But to his wishe, his iorneys ende did gaine
In happie howre, by his direction plaine.

This trauailinge man: doth tell our wandringe state,
Before whose face, and eeke on euerye side,
Bypathes, and wayes, appeare amidd our gate,
That if the Lorde bee not our onlie guide:
We stumble, fall, and dailie goe astraye,
Then happie those, whome God doth shew the waye.

SVCHE prouidence hathe nature secret wroughte
In creatures wilde, and eeke such knowledge straunge,
That man, by them in somme thinges maie be taughte,
As some foretell, when weather faire will chaunge,
    Of heate, of raine, of winde, and tempests rage,
    Some showe by signes, and with their songs presage.

But leauing theise, which almost all doe knowe,
The Crocodile, by whome th'Ægyptians watche,
Howe farre that yeare shall mightie Nilus flowe,
For theire shee likes to laie her egges, and hatche,
    Suche skill deuine, and science to foretell,
    Hath Nature lente vnto this Serpent fell.

Nic. Reusnerus.
Quò sacer excurret Nilus in arua
Praescius: adusua libera ponit
Oua: monens merito nos Crocodil
Quae fata imminenant, antè vider

Which showes, They should with due regarde foresee,
When anie one doth take in hande a cause,
The drifte, and ende, of that they doe decree,
And longe thereon to ponder, and to pause,
    For after witts, are like a shower of rayne
    Which moistes the soile, when withered is the graine.

Veritas temporis filia.

THREE furies fell, which turne the worlde to ruthe,
Both Enuie, Strife, and Slaunder, heare appeare,
In dungeon darke they longe inclosed truthe,
But Time at lengthe, did loose his daughter deare,
And setts alofte, that sacred ladie brighte,
Whoe things longe hidd, reueales, and bringes to lighte.

Thoughe strife make fier, thoughe Enuie eate hir harte,
The innocent though Slaunder rente, and spoile:
Yet Time will comme, and take this ladies parte,
And breake her bandes, and bring her foes to foile.
Dispaire not then, thoughe truthe be hidden ofte,
Bycause at lengthe, shee shall bee sett alofte.

Dissidia

Diſsidia inter æquales, peſsima.

THE Swallowe ſwifte, dothe beare vnto her neſte
The Graſshopper, that did no daunger feare,
For that ſhee thought, they loude togeather beſte,
Bycauſe they both, obſerude one time of yeare,
  And bothe, did ioye theire iarringe notes to ſounde,
  And neare the houſe they bothe, theire dwellings founde.

Alciatus.
Stridula ſtridentem, vernans verna, hoſpita lædis Hoſpitam, & aligeram penniger ales auem?

Yet time, and tune, and neighbourhood forgotte,
For perfect frende, a tyrant ſhee became,
Which taxeth thoſe, whome God dothe heare allotte.
Like gifts of grace, to winne a laſting name,
  Yet Enuie ſoe theire vertues doth deface,
  It makes them foes, to them theie ſhould imbrace.

Formicæ grata eſt formica, Cicada cicada
Et doctis doctus gaudet Apollo choris.

Nic. Reuſnerus.

Temeritas.

THE waggoner, behoulde, is hedlonge throwen,
And all in vaine doth take the raine in hande,
If he be dwrawen by horſes fierce vnknowen,
Whoſe ſtomacks ſtowte, no taming vnderſtande,
They praunce, and yerke, and out of order flinge,
Till all they breake, and vnto hauocke bringe.

That man, whoe hath affections fowle vntamde,
And forwarde runnes neglecting reaſons race;
Deſerues by right, of all men to bee blamde,
And headlonge falles at lengthe to his deface,
Then bridle will, and reaſon make thy guide,
So maiſte thow ſtande, when others doune doe ſlide.

Inteſtina

Inteſtinæ ſimultates.

WHEN ciuill ſworde is drawen out of the ſheathe,
And bluddie broiles, at home are ſet a broache,
Then furious Mars with ſworde doth rage beneathe,
And to the Toppe, deuowring flames incroache,
None helpes to quenche, but rather blowes the flame,
And oile doe adde, and powder to the ſame.

Inteſtine ſtrife, is fearefull moſte of all,
This, makes the Sonne, to cut his fathers throate,
This, parteth frendes, this, brothers makes to bralle,
This, robbes the good, and ſetts the theeues a floate,
This, Rome did feele, this, Germanie did taſte,
And often times, this noble Lande did waſte.

Now

Non tibi, sed Religioni.

THE pastors good, that doe gladd tidinges preache,
The godlie sorte, with reuerence do imbrace:
Though they be men, yet since Godds worde they teache,
Wee honor them, and giue them higheste place,
Imbassadors of princes of the earthe,
Haue royall Seates, thoughe base they are by birthe.

Yet, if throwghe pride they doe them selues forgett,
And make accompte that honor, to be theires:
And doe not marke with in whose place they sett,
Let them behowlde the asse, that ISIS beares,
Whoe thowghte the men to honor him, did kneele,
And staied therfore, till he the staffe did feele.

For, as he pass'd with ISIS throughe the streete,
And bare on backe, his holie rites about,
Th'Ægyptians downe fell prostrate at his feete,
Whereat, the Asse, grewe arrogante and stowte,
Then saide the guide: oh foole not vnto thee,
Theise people bowe, but vnto that they see?

Experien-

Experientia docet.

A YOVTHEFVLL Prince, in prime of luſtie yeares,
Woulde vnderſtande what weather ſhoulde betide,
For that hee thoughte, with manie noble Peares
To paſſe the time, on huntinge forth to ride:
  Th'Aſtronomer, did wiſhe hym ſtaie at courte,
  For preſent raine, ſhould hinder all their ſporte.

Which ſtaied the Prince, but raine did none diſcende,
Then, wente hee forth with manie Gallantes braue;
But when he thought the clowdes, did droppes portend,
Hee roade aſide, a plowghmans ſkill to craue,
  Whoe, looking ſtraighte vppon the varijng ſkie:
  Saide, twentie daies I thinke it will bee drie.

Proceedinge then, his iudgement true was founde,
Then, (quoth the Prince) weare thou the doctours Roabe,
And geeue to him, thy Harrowe on the grownde,
And in exchaunge, take thou his Spheare, and Gloabe:
  And further ſaied, henceforthe wee will allowe,
  That learninge ſhall vnto Experience bowe.

Sirenes.

Virg. Aeneid. lib. 5. & Ouidius lib. 5. Metamorph.

Nic. Reusnerus. *Illectos nautas dulci modulamine vocis, Mergebant auide fluctibus Ioniis.*

WITHE pleasaunte tunes, the SYRENES did allure
Vlisses wise, to listen theire songe:
But nothinge could his manlie harte procure,
Hee sailde awaie, and scap'd their charming stronge,
The face, he lik'de: the nether parte, did loathe:
For womans shape, and fishes had they bothe.

Which shewes to vs, when Bewtie seekes to snare
The carelesse man, whoe dothe no daunger dreede,
That he shoulde flie, and shoulde in time beware,
And not on lookes, his fickle fancie feede:
Suche Mairemaides liue, that promise onelie ioyes:
But hee that yeldes, at lengthe him selffe distroies.

Laertij tetrasticon sic per Claud. Minoëm conuersum.

Hæc Venus ad musas: Venerem exhorrescite Nimphæ,
In vos armatus aut amor insiliet.
Cui contrà musæ, verba hæc age dicito marti:
Aliger huc ad nos non volat ille puer.

Res hu-

Res humanæ in summo declinant.

THE gallante Shipp, that cutts the azure ſurge,
And hathe both tide, and wiſhed windes, at will:
Her tackle ſure, with ſhotte her foes to vrge,
With Captaines boulde, and marriners of ſkill,
With ſtreamers, flagges, topgallantes, pendantes braue,
When Seas do rage, is ſwallowed in the waue.

Periand. per Auſon.
Si fortuna iuuat: caueto tolli.
Si fortuna tonat: caueto mergi.

The ſnowe, that falles vppon the mountaines greate,
Though on the Alpes, which ſeeme the clowdes to reache.
Can not indure the force of Phœbus heate,
But waſtes awaie, Experience doth vs teache:
Which warneth all, on Fortunes wheele that clime
To beare in minde how they haue but a time.

Ouidius 4. pont. 3.
Tu quoque fac timeas, & quæ tibi læta videtur
Dum loqueris, fieri triſtia poſſe puta.

Paſſibus ambiguis fortuna volubilis errat,
Et manet in nullo certa, tenaxq́ue loco.
Sed modò læta manet, vultus modò ſumit acerbos
Et tantùm conſtans in leuitate ſua eſt.

Ouidius 5. Triſt. 9.

Frustra.

THE Poettes faine, that DANAVS daughters deare,
Inioyned are to fill the fatall tonne:
Where, thowghe they toile, yet are they not the neare,
But as they powre, the water forthe dothe runne:
No paine will serue, to fill it to the toppe,
For, still at holes the same doth runne, and droppe.

Which reprehendes, three sortes of wretches vaine,
The blabbe, th'ingrate; and those that couet still,
As first the blabbe, no secretts can retaine.
Th'ingrate, not knowes to vse his frendes good will.
The couetous man, thowghe he abounde with store
Is not suffis'de, but coueus more and more.

Superbia

Superbiæ vltio.

OF NIOBE, behoulde the ruthefull plighte,
Bicauſe ſhee did diſpiſe the powers deuine:
Her children all, weare ſlaine within her ſighte,
And, while her ſelfe with tricklinge teares did pine,
Shee was transformde, into a marble ſtone,
Which, yet with teares, dothe ſeeme to waile, and mone.

Fabula Niobes Ouid. 6. Metamorph.

De numero filiorum, vide Aul. Gellium lib. 20. cap. 6.

This tragedie, thoughe Poetts firſt did frame,
Yet maie it bee, to euerie one applide:
That mortall men, ſhoulde thinke from whence they came,
And not preſume, nor puffe them vp with pride,
Leſte that the Lorde, whoe haughty hartes doth hate, [ſtate.
Doth throwe them downe, when ſure they thinke theyr

Eſte procul læti; cernant mea funera triſtes;
Non ſimilis toto mæror in orbe fuit.
Bis ſeptem natos peperi, bis pignora ſeptem:
Me miſeram! Diuûm ſuſtulit ira mihi.
Dirigui demum lacrymis, & marmora manant.
Sic mihi mors dolor eſt; ſic mihi vita, dolor.
Diſcite, mortales, quid ſit turgeſcere faſtu,
Et quid ſit magnos poſthabuiſſe Deos.

Bapt. Gyraldus.

In vitam humanam.

THE wicked worlde, so false and full of crime,
Did alwaies mooue HERACLITVS to weepe,
The fadinge ioyes, and follies of that time,
DEMOCRITVS did driue to laughter deepe,
Thus heynous sinne, and follie did procure
Theise famous men, suche passions to indure.

De his, Seneca lib. De Tranquillitate vitæ.

What if they liude, and shoulde behoulde this age
Which ouerflowes, with swellinge seas of sinne:
Where fooles, by swarmes, doe presse vppon the stage,
With hellishe Impes, that like haue neuer binne:
I thinke this sighte, shoulde hasten their decaye
Then helpe vs God, and Sathans furie staie.

Horatius.

Damnosa quid non imminuit dies?
Ætas parentum peior auis tulit
Nos nequiores, mox daturos
Progeniem vitiosiorem.

Voluptas

Voluptas ærumnosa.

ACTÆON heare, vnhappie man behoulde,
When in the well, hee ſawe Diana brighte,
With greedie lookes, hee waxed ouer boulde,
That to a ſtagge hee was transformed righte,
　Whereat amaſde, hee thought to runne awaie,
　But ſtraighte his howndes did rente hym, for their praie.

Ouid. lib. 3. Metamorph.

By which is ment, That thoſe whoe do purſue
Theire fancies fonde, and thinges vnlawfull craue,
Like brutiſhe beaſtes appeare vnto the viewe,
And ſhall at lenghte, Actæons guerdon haue:
　And as his houndes, ſoe theire affections baſe,
　Shall them deuowre, and all their deedes deface.

Horatius 1. Epist. 12. *Sperne voluptates, nocet empta dolore voluptas.*

Cornibus in Ceruum mutatum Actæona ſumptis,
Membratim proprÿ diripuere canes.

Ita dis placitum, voluptati vt mœror comes conſequatur.

Anulus, in picta poesi.

Plautus in Amphit.

Quod

Quod potes, tenta.

WHILE, HERCVLES, with mightie clubbe in hande
In Lyons skinne did sleepe, and take his ease:
About him straighte approch'de the Pigmeis bande,
And for to kill this conquerour assaies,
But foolishe dwarffes? theire force was all to smalle,
For when he wak'de, like gnattes hee crush'd them all.

This warneth vs, that nothinge paste our strengthe
Wee shoulde attempte: nor anie worke pretende,
Aboue our power: lest that with shame at lengthe
Wee weakelinges prooue, and fainte before the ende.
The pore, that striue with mightie, this doth blame:
And sottes, that seeke the learned to defame.

Hi homunciones extremas Ægypti partes inhabitant agricolationi dediti, Subinde cum gruibus bellum gerunt. Plinius lib. 7. cap. 2. & Aul. Gellius lib. 9. cap. 4.

Propertius.

Turpe est quod nequeas capiti submittere pondus,
Et pressum inflexo mox dare terga genu.

Lucius

BEHOVLDE the fruites of dronkenneſſe, and plaie: — Propertius. *Vino forma perit, vino corrumpitur ætas*
Here corage, brawles with Cutthroate for a caſte,
And ofte in fine, if that they lacke to paie, — Horat. 1 Epiſt. 19 *Ludus enim genuit trepidum certamen, & iram:*
They ſweare it out, or blade it at the laſte:
This, frendſhippe breakes: this, makes vs laugh d to ſcorne, — *Ira truces inimicitias, & funebre bellum*
And beggerie giues, to thoſe that riche are borne.

The Lapithans, by drinke weare ouerthrowne, — Virgilius.
The wiſeſt men, with follie this inflames:
What ſhoulde I ſpeake, of father NOAH aloane, — Geneſ. 9.
Or bring in LOTT, or HOLOFERNES names: — Geneſ. 19. Iudic. 13.
This SIMON, and his ſonnes, did ouerthrowe, — 1 Machab. 15.
And BENEDAB, made flee before his foe. — 3 Regum 2.

And he that lik'd to ſpende his time at dice,
This lawe in Rome, SEVERVS did prouide:
That euerie man, ſhoulde deeme him as a vice,
And of his Landes, an other ſhoulde bee guide:
Like Lawes beſide, did diuers more deuiſe,
And wiſedome ſtill, againſte ſuche vnthriftes cries.

Tunc ſumus incauti, ſtudioq; aperimur ab ipſo,
Nudaq; per luſus pectora noſtra patent.
Ira ſubit deforme malum, lucriq; Cupido
Iurgiaq;, & rixæ, ſollicitusq; dolor, — Ouidius.
Crimina dicuntur, reſonat clamoribus æther,
Inuocat iratos & ſibi quiſque deos.

Nic. Reusnerus.
Frigoris impatiens: patiens operúmque, famisque:
Ecce rudes Asinus dat rudis ore sonos.

SEPTITIVS ritche, a miser moste of all,
Whose liuinges large, and treasure did exceede:
Yet to his goodes, he was so much in thrall,
That still he vsd on beetes, and rapes to feede:
So of his stoare, the sweete he neuer knewe,
And longe did robbe, his bellie of his due.

This Caitiffe wretche, with pined corpes so heare,
Compared right vnto the foolishe asse,
Whose backe is fraighte with cates, and daintie cheare,
But to his share commes neither corne, nor grasse,
Yet beares he that, which settes his teeth on edge:
And pines him selfe, with thistle and with sedge.

Plautus in Aulul.

Perditissimus ego sum omnium in terra,
Nam quid mihi opus vita est, qui tantum auri
Perdidi, quod custodiui sedulò? egomet me fraudaui
Animumq́; meum geniumq́; meum, &c.

Propertius 3. 13.

At nunc desertis cessant sacraria lucis,
Aurum omnes victa iam pietate, colunt.
Auro pulsa fides, auro venalia iura,
Aurum lex sequitur, mox sine lege pudor.

Nec ver.

HEARE, NEMESIS the Goddesse iuste dothe stande,
With bended arme, to measure all our waies,
A raine shee houldes, with in the other hande,
With biting bitte, where with the lewde shee staies:
And pulles them backe, when harme they doe intende,
Or when they take in wicked speeche delite,
And biddes them still beware for to offende,
And square theire deedes, in all thinges vnto righte:
But wicked Impes, that lewdlie runne their race,
Shee hales them backe, at lengthe to theire deface.

Est dea: quæ vacuo sublimis in aere pendens.
It nimbo succincta latus: sed candida palam:
Sed radiata comam: ac stridentibus insonat alis.
Hæc spes immodicas premit: hæc infesta superbis
Imminet: huic celsas hominum contundere mentes,
Successusq; datum: & nimios turbare paratus.
Quam veteres NEMESIM *&c.*
& paulò pòst:
Improba vota domans: ac summis ima reuoluens
Miscet: & alternâ nostros vice temperat actus, &c.

Politianus eleganter NEMESIM describit in Manto suo sic incipiens.

 Minuit

REPORTE, did ringe the ſnowe did hide the hilles,
And valleys lowe, there with alofte did riſe:
Which newes, with dowte the hartes of manie filles,
And Cowardes made, for feare at home to frieſe:
But thoſe that went, the truthe hereof to knowe,
When that they came, might ſafelie paſſe the ſnowe.

For-whie, the Sonne did make the ſame to waſte,
And all about, diſcouered had the grounde:
So, thoughe ofte times the ſimple bee agaſte,
When that reportes, of this, or that, doe ſounde,
Yet if they firſte, woulde ſeeke the truthe to knowe,
They ofte ſhoulde finde, the matter nothing ſoe.

Virg. lib. 4. Æneid. in deſcrip. famæ.

Mobilitate viget, vireſq; acquirit eundo,
Parua metu primo, mox ſeſe attollit in auras, &c.

Et Ouid. Metam, lib. 12. De domo famæ ſic,

Nocte dieq; patet: tota eſt ex ære ſonanti,
Tota fremit, voceſq; refert, iterátque quod audit, &c.

Turpibus

THE Scarabee, cannot indure the ſente
Of fragant roſe, moſte bewtifull to ſee:
But filthie ſmelles, hee alwaies doth frequent,
And roſes ſweete, doe make him pine and die:
His howſe, is donge: and wormes his neighbours are,
And for his meate, his manſion is his fare.

With theiſe hee liues, and doth reioice for aie,
And buzzeth freſhe, when night doth take her place,
From theiſe, he dies, and languiſſeth awaie:
So, whoſe delites are filthie, vile, and baſe,
Is ſicke to heare, when counſaile ſweete we giue,
And rather likes, with reprobates to liue.

Vos vbi contempti rupiſtis frena pudoris,
Neſcitis captæ mentis habere modum.
Flamma per incenſas citius ſedetur ariſtas,
Fluminaq; ad fontis ſint reditura caput. &c. Propert. 3. 19.
Quàm poſſit veſtros quiſquam reprehendere curſus,
Et rapidæ ſtimulos frangere nequitiæ.

BEHOWLDE the craftie foxe,
Vppon Danubius plaies,
What time through froste, both man, and beaste,
Thereon did make their waies.

At lengthe, with PHOEBVS beames,
The froste began to slake:
So that the yce with swelling streame,
To sundrie peeces brake.

Where, on a peece the foxe,
Doth to his tackling stande:
And in the sighte of Regenspurge,
Came driuing by the Lande.

At which, the townesmen laugh'de,
And saied, this foxe, on Ice:
Doth shewe, no subtill crafte will serue,
When Chaunce doth throwe the dice.

Seneca in Oed.

Regitur fatis mortale genus:
Nec sibi quisquam spondere potest
Firmum, & stabile: perq; casus
Voluitur varios semper nobis
Metuenda dies, &c.

Mihi

WHEN autumne ripes, the frutefull fieldes of graine,
And CERES doth in all her pompe appeare,
The heauie eare, doth breake the ſtalke in twaine,
Wherebie wee ſee, this by experience cleare:
Hir owne exceſſe, did cauſe her proper ſpoile,
And made her corne, to rotte vppon the ſoile.

Soe worldlie wealthe, and great aboundaunce, marres:
The ſharpenes of our ſences, and our wittes,
And oftentimes, our vnderſtanding barres,
And dulles the ſame, with manie carefull fittes:
Then ſince Exceſſe procures our ſpoile and paine,
The meane preferre, before immoderate gaine.

——nec te iucunda fronte fefellit
Luxuries prædulce malum, quæ dedita ſemper Claud. 2.
Corporis arbitriis, hebetat caligine ſenſus
Membraq; Circæis effeminat acrius herbis.

Latet

Of flattringe ſpeeche, with ſugred wordes beware,
Suſpect the harte, whoſe face doth fawne, and ſmile,
With truſting theiſe, the worlde is clog'de with care,
And fewe there bee can ſcape theiſe vipers vile:
With pleaſinge ſpeeche they promiſe, and proteſt,
When hatefull hartes lie hidd within their breſt.

The faithfull wight, dothe neede no collours braue,
But thoſe that truſte, in time his truthe ſhall trie,
Where fawning mates, can not theire credit ſaue,
Without a cloake, to flatter, faine, and lye:
No foe ſo fell, nor yet ſoe harde to ſcape,
As is the foe, that fawnes with freindlie ſhape.

Ouid.1.Art. *Tuta, frequensq; via eſt, per amici fallere nomen.*

Idem 1. Faſt. *Sic iterum, ſic ſæpe cadunt, vbi vincere aperte*
Non datur: inſidias, armaq; tecta parant.

Curio

IF griping greifes, haue harbour in thie breſte,
And pininge cares, laie ſeige vnto the ſame,
Or ſtraunge conceiptes, doe reaue thee of thie reſt,
And daie, and nighte, do bringe thee out of frame:
Then chooſe a freinde, and doe his counſaile craue,
Leaſt ſecret ſighes, doe bringe vntimelie graue.

Continuall care, did PLINIES harte poſſeſſe,
To knowe what cauſde VESEVVS hill to flame,
And ceaſed not, now this, nowe that, to geſſe:
Yet, when hee coulde not comprehende the ſame,
Suche was his fate, purſuing his deſier,
He headlonge fell into the flaming fier.

Veſeuus, ſecundum Seruium Virgil. lib. Georg. 2. mons eſt Liguriæ ſub Alpibus.

Non opibus mentes homini, curaq; leuantur, &c. — Tibul lib. 3. cap. 3.

O Curas hominum, ô quantum eſt in rebus inane. — Perſ. 1.

A Windmill faire, that all thinges had to grinde,
Which man coulde make, the father lefte his ſonne:
The corne was broughte, there nothing lack'd, but winde,
And Cuſtomers, did freſhlie to it ronne:
The ſonne repoaſ'de his truſte vppon the mill,
And dailie dream'de on plentie at his will.

Ouid. 1. Pont. 6.
Cernis vt ignauum corrumpant otia corpus?
Vt capiant vitium ni moueantur aquæ.

Thus he ſecure, a while his daies did paſſe,
And did not ſeeke, for other ſtaie at all:
And thoughe hee founde, howe coulde the profit was,
And that ſoe ſmall, vnto his ſhare did fall:
Yet ſtill he hoap'de, for better lucke at laſte,
And put his truſte, in eache vncertaine blaſte.

Plaut. Rud.
——vigilare decet hominem,
Qui vult ſua temperi conficere officia.
Nam qui dormiunt libenter, ſine lucro, & cum malo quieſcunt.

Vnto this foole, they maie compared bee,
Which idlie liue, and vainlie hoape for happe:
For while they hope, with wante they pine, wee ſee:
And verie fewe, are lul'de on fortunes lappe:
While graſſe doth growe, the courſer faire doth ſterue,
And fortune ſield, the wiſhers turne doth ſerue.

Dolus

WHILE nettes were ſette, the ſimple fowles to take,
Whoe kepte theire courſe alofte, and woulde not lighte,
A tamed ducke, her hoame did ſtraighte forſake,
And flewe alofte, with other duckes in flighte,
They dowtinge not, her traiterous harte at all,
Did flie with her, and downe with her did fall.

By this is mente, all ſuche as doe betraie,
Theire kindred neare, that doe on them depende,
And ofte doe make, the innocent a praie,
By ſubtill ſleighte, to them that ſeeke theire ende
Yea vnto thoſe, they ſhoulde moſte frendſhip ſhowe,
They lie in waite, to worke theire ouerthrowe.

Perfida cognato ſe ſanguine polluit ales,
Officioſa aliis, exitioſa ſuis.

And. Alciat.
De Anate.

HEARE, ICARVS with mountinge vp alofte,
Came headlonge downe, and fell into the Sea:
His waxed winges, the ſonne did make ſo ſofte,
They melted ſtraighte, and feathers fell awaie:
  So, whilſte he flewe, and of no dowbte did care,
  He mooude his armes, but loe, the ſame were bare.

Let ſuche beware, which paſte theire reache doe mounte,
Whoe ſeeke the thinges, to mortall men deny'de,
And ſearche the Heauens, and all the ſtarres accoumpte,
And tell therebie, what after ſhall betyde:
  With bluſſhinge nowe, theire weakeneſſe rightlie weye,
  Leaſt as they clime, they fall to theire decaye.

Martial. 1. *Illud quod medium eſt, atque inter vtrumque, probamus.*

Ouid. Triſt. 1. *Dum petit infirmis nimium ſublimia pennis*
Icarus, Icariis nomina fecit aquis.
Vitaret cælum Phaëton, ſi viueret, & quos
Optauit ſtultè tangere, nollet equos.

Amor

WHEN Boreas coulde, dothe bare both busshe, and tree,
Before the Springe, the Ringdoue makes her neste:
And that her yonge both softe, and warme, mighte bee,
Shee pulles her plumes, bothe from her backe, and breste:
And while shee stryues, her broode for to preserue,
Ofte times for coulde, the tender damme doth sterue.

MEDEA nowe, and PROGNE, blusshe for shame:
By whome, are ment yow dames of cruell kinde
Whose infantes yonge, vnto your endlesse blame,
For mothers deare, do tyrauntes of yow finde:
Oh serpentes seede, each birde, and sauage brute,
Will those condempne, that tender not theire frute.

WHAT dolefull dame is this in greate dispaire?
This prowes is, whoe mournes on AIAX toombe:
What is the cause, shee rentes her goulden haire?
Wronge sentence paste by AGAMEMNONS doombe:
But howe? declare, VLISSES filed tonge,
Allur'de the Iudge, to giue a Iudgement wronge.

For when, that dead ACHYLLIS was in graue,
For valiante harte, did AIAX winne the fame:
Whereby, he clamide ACHYLLIS armes to haue,
VLISSES yet, was honored with the same:
His suttle speeche, the iudges did preferre,
And AIAX wrong'de, the onelie man of warre.

Wherefore, the Knighte impatient of the same,
Did loose his wittes, and after wroughte his ende:
Loe, heare the cause that mooude this sacred dame,
On AIAX toombe, with griefe her time too spende:
Which warneth vs, and those that after liue,
To beare them righte, when iudgement they do giue.

Cacum

TH'Enuious man, when neighboures howſe dothe flame,
Whoſe chiefe delighte, is in an others harme,
Doth ſhutte his eies, and will nott ſee the ſame,
But pulles awaie, his ſellowe by the arme:
  And ſayeth, departe, wee care not for this ill,
  It is not ours, let others care that will.

Too manie liue, that euery wheare are founde
Whoe daye and nighte doe languiſhe in diſpite,
When that they ſee, an others wealthe abounde:
But, thoſe herein that moſte of all delighte,
  Let them repente, for God whoe knowes theire harts,
  Will them rewarde, accordinge to deſerts.

Vixq; tenet lacrymas quia nil lacrymabile cernit, &c.
Inuidus alterius rebus macreſcit opimis.
Inuidia Siculi non inuenere tyranni
Maius tormentum. ———

Ouid. 2. Metamorph. De inuidia sic.
Horatius 1. epist. 2.

In pæ-

THE wicked wretche, that mischiefe late hath wroughte,
By murther, thefte, or other heynous crimes,
With troubled minde, hee dowtes hee shalbe caughte,
And leaues the waie, and ouer hedges climes:
And standes in feare, of euerie busshe, and brake,
Yea oftentimes, his shaddowe makes him quake.

A conscience cleare, is like a wall of brasse,
That dothe not shake, with euerie shotte that hittes:
Eauen soe there by, our liues wee quiet passe,
When guiltie mindes, are rack'de with fearfull fittes:
Then keepe thee pure, and soile thee not with sinne,
For after guilte, thine inwarde greifes beginne.

Cato. *Conscius ipse sibi de se putat omnia dici.*

Ouid. Fast. 1. *Conscia mens vt cuique sua est, ita concipit intra*
Pectora, pro facto spemq;, metumq; suo.

Ei, qui

MEDEA loe with infante in her arme,
Whoe kil'de her babes, shee shoulde haue loued beste:
The swallowe yet, whoe did suspect no harme,
Hir Image likes, and hatch'd vppon her breste:
And lefte her younge, vnto this tirauntes guide,
Whoe, peecemeale did her proper fruicte deuide.

Ouid. lib. 7. Metamorp.

Oh foolishe birde, think'ste thow, shee will haue care,
Vppon thy yonge? Whoe hathe her owne destroy'de,
And maie it bee, that shee thie birdes should spare?
Whoe slue her ownes, in whome shee shoulde haue ioy'd
Thow arte deceauide, and arte a warninge good,
To put no truste, in them that hate theire blood.

MEDEÆ statua est: natos cui credis Hirundo?
Fer aliò: viden' hac mactet vt ipsa suos?

Borbonius.

E *In mo-*

Petrus Crinitus de honesta disciplina lib. 2. cap. 14.

THE fruictfull gourde, was neighboure to the Pine,
And lowe at firste, abowt her roote did ſpread,
But yet, with dewes, and ſiluer droppes in fine,
It mounted vp, and almoſte towch'de the head:
And with her fruicte, and leaues on euerie ſide,
Imbraſde the tree, and did the ſame deride.
To whome, the Pine with longe Experience wiſe,
And ofte had ſeene, ſuche peacockes looſe theire plumes,
Thus aunſwere made, thow owght'ſt not to deſpiſe,
My ſtocke at all, oh foole, thow much preſumes:
In coulde, and heate, here longe hath bene my happe,
Yet am I ſounde, and full of liuelie ſappe.
But, when the froſte, and coulde, ſhall thee aſſaie,
Thowghe nowe alofte, thow bragge, and freſhlie bloome,
Yet, then thie roote, ſhall rotte, and fade awaie,
And ſhortlie, none ſhall knowe where was thy roome
Thy fruicte, and leaues, that nowe ſo highe aſpire
The paſſers by, ſhall treade within the mire.

Nic. Reuſnerus.
Cæruleus cucumis, tumidáq. cucurbita ventre,
Cruda leuant, ſtomacho pernicioſa, ſimul.

Let

Let them that ſtande, alofte on fortunes wheele,
And bragge, and boaſte, with puffe of worldlie pride
Still beare in minde, howe ſoone the ſame maie reele,
And alwayes looke, for feare theire footinge ſlide:
And let not will, houlde vp theire heades for fame,
When inwarde wantes, maie not ſupporte the ſame.

Ære quandoque ſalutem redimendam.

THE Beauer ſlowe, that preſent daunger feares,
And ſees a farre, the eager howndes to haſte,
With grindinge teethe, his ſtoanes awaie he teares,
And throwes them downe, to thoſe that haue him chaſte:
Which beinge founde, the hunter dothe retire,
For that he hath, the fruicte of his deſire.

Nic. Reuſnerus.
Mordicus ipſe ſibi,
dicata virilia vellit
Inſidias vafer h
effugis arte fiber.

Theiſe, ſoueraigne are diſeaſes for to heale,
And for mannes healthe, from countries farre are broughte,
And if herein, the writers doe not faile,
This beaſte doth knowe, that he therefore is ſoughte:
And afterwarde, if anie doe him courſe,
He ſhewes his wante, to mooue them to remorſe.

Thus, to his paine he doth his life preserue:
Which teacheth vs, if foes doe vs pursue,
Wee showlde not care, if goodes for life maie serue,
Althoughe we giue, our treasure to a iewe:
  No ritches, maie with life of man compare,
  They are but drosse, and fortunes brittle ware.

...s Theba-
...im the-
...n spon-
...rderet,
ne abite, ait,
malæ diuitiæ:
...tius enim est
a me vos de-
mergi quam
ego à vobis
ipse.

Then life redeeme, althoughe with all thow haste,
Thoughe thow arte pore, yet seeke, and thow shalte finde,
Those ritches pure, that euermore shall laste,
Which are the goodes, and treasures, of the minde:
  Noe man so pore, but god can blesse his daies,
  Whoe patient IOB, did from the dunghill raise.

Ouid. lib. I. De Remed. amoris.

Vt corpus redimas, ferrum patieris & ignes,
  Arida nec sitiens ora lauabis aqua.
Vt valeas animo, quicquam tolerare negabis?
  At pretium pars hæc corpore maius habet.

Durum telum necessitas.

NECESSITIE doth vrge, the Popiniaye to prate,
And birdes, to drawe their bucketts vp, and picke theire meate through, grate:
Which warneth them, whoe needes must eyther serue, or pine:
With willing harte, no paines to shunne, and freedome to resigne.

Terent. in Adel. 4. 7.

Placet tibi factum Mitio? MI. non si queam
Mutare: nunc, cum nequeo, æquo animo fero.

In

IF of thy foe, thow doest a gifte receaue,
Esteeme it not, for feare the fates doe lower,
And with the gifte, ofte tyme thie life doe reaue,
Yea giftes wee reade, haue suche a secret power,
  That oftentimes, they LYNCEVS eies doe blinde,
  And he that giues, the taker faste doth binde.

To AIAX heare, a sworde did HECTOR sende,
A girdle stronge, to him did AIAX yeelde,
With HECTORS gifte, did AIAX woorke his ende,
And AIAX gifte, hal'de HECTOR throughe the fielde:
  Of mortall foes, then see noe gifte thow take,
  Althoughe a while, a truce with them thow make.

—— ——aut vlla putatis
Dona carere dolis Danaum, &c.

Lacoon apud Virgilium lib. Æneid. 2. sic de equo, loquitur Troianis.

Sic titulo obsequij, quæ mittunt hostibus hostes
Munera, venturi præscia fata ferunt.

Alciat.

To the Honorable Sir PHILLIP SIDNEY *Knight, Gouernour of the Garrison and towne of Vlißing.*

THE trampinge steede, that champes the burnish'd bitte,
Is mannag'd braue, with ryders for the nones:
But, when the foole vppon his backe doth sette,
He throwes him downe, and ofte doth bruse his bones:
His corage feirce, dothe craue a better guide,
And eke such horse, the foole shoulde not bestride.

Claud. 4. Honor. *Tu ciuem, patrémque geras, tu consule cunctis, Nec tibi, nec tua te moueant, sed publica vota.*

By which is ment, that men of iudgement graue,
Of learning, witte, and eeke of conscience cleare,
In highe estate, are fitte theire seates to haue,
And to be stall'd, in sacred iustice cheare:
Wherein they rule, vnto theire endlesse fame,
But fooles are foil'd, and throwne out of the same.

Horat. 1. Ser. 6.

——magnum hoc ego duco,
Quòd placuit tibi, qui turpi secernis honestum.

Medio

WHOME fortune heare allottes a meane estate,
Yet giues enowghe, eache wante for to suffise:
That wauering wighte, that hopes for better fate,
And not content, his cawlinge doth despise,
Maie vainlie clime, but likelie still to fall,
And liue at lengthe, with losse of maine, and all.

And he that poastes, to make awaie his landes,
And credittes all, that wandringe heades reporte:
Maye Tagus seeke, and Ganges goulden sandes,
Yet come at lengthe, with emptie purse to courte:
Let suche behoulde, the greedie dogge to moane,
By brooke deceau'd, with shaddow of his boane.

Hor. 2. Car. 16.
Viuitur paruo benè, paternum
Splendet in mensa salinum:
Nec leues somnos timor, aut Cupido
Sordidus aufert

Non minor est virtus, quàm quærere parta tueri,
Casus inest illic, hîc erit artis opus.

Ouid. lib. 2. Art.

Seruiet æternùm, quia paruo nesciat vti.
Cui non conueniet sua res, vt calceus olim,
Si pede maior erit, subuertet: si minor, vrget.
Lætus sorte tua viues, sapienter Aristi.

Horatius 1. Epist. 10.

Biuium

Virgil. in Fragm. de littera y.
Quisquis enim duros casus virtutis amore Vicerit, ille sibi laudémque decúsque parabit.
Atqui desidiã luxúmque sequetur inertem, Dum fugit oppositos incauta mente labores, Turpis, inópsque simul, miserabile transiget æuum.

WHEN HERCVLES, was dowtfull of his waie,
Inclosed rounde, with vertue, and with vice:
With reasons firste, did vertue him assaie,
The other, did with pleasures him entice:
They longe did striue, before he coulde be wonne,
Till at the lengthe, ALCIDES thus begonne

Oh pleasure, thoughe thie waie bee smoothe, and faire,
And sweete delightes in all thy courtes abounde:
Yet can I heare, of none that haue bene there,
That after life, with fame haue bene renoumde:
For honor hates, with pleasure to remaine,
Then houlde thy peace, thow wastes thie winde in vaine.

But heare, I yeelde oh vertue to thie will,
And vowe my selfe, all labour to indure,
For to ascende the steepe, and craggie hill,
The toppe whereof, whoe so attaines, is sure
For his rewarde, to haue a crowne of fame:
Thus HERCVLES, obey'd this sacred dame.

Pœna

WHEN ſilent nighte, did ſcepter take in hande,
And dim'de the daie, with ſhade of mantle blacke,
What time the theeues, in priuie corners ſtande,
And haue noe dowte, to robbe for what they lacke:
A greedie theefe, in ſhambles broke a ſhoppe,
And fil'de a ſacke, with fleſhe vp to the toppe.

Which done, with ſpeede he lifted vp the ſacke,
And bothe the endes, abowt his necke he knittes,
And ranne awaie, with burden on his backe
Till afterwardes, as hee at alehowſe ſittes:
The heauie loade, did weye ſo harde behinde,
That whiles he ſlept, the weighte did ſtoppe his winde.

Which truelie ſhowes, to them that doe offende,
Althowghe a while, they ſcape theire iuſt deſertes,
Yet puniſhment, dothe at theire backes attende,
And plagues them hoame, when they haue merieſt hartes:
And thoughe longe time, they doe eſcape the pikes,
Yet ſoone, or late, the Lorde in iuſtice ſtrikes.

Iuuenalis 13. de malis ſic ait.
Hi ſunt qui trepidant, & ad omnia fulgura pallent,
Cum tonat: exanimes primo quoque murmure cœli.
Senec. Troad.
Qui non vetat peccare, cum poſſit, iubet.

WHY fliest thow hence? and turn'ste awaie thie face:
Thow glorie brighte, that men with fame doest crowne:
GLO. Bycause, I haue noe likinge of that place,
Where slothfull men, doe sleepe in beddes of downe:
And fleshlie luste, doth dwell with fowle excesse,
This is no howse, for glorie to possesse.

But, if thow wilte my presence neuer lacke,
SARDANAPAL, and all his pleasures hate,
Driue VENVS hence, let BACCHVS further packe,
If not, behowlde I flie out of thie gate:
Yet, if from theise, thow turne thie face awaie,
I will returne, and dwell with thee for aie.

Propert. 4. 11. *Magnum iter ascendo, sed dat mihi gloria vires:*
Non iuuat ex facili lecta corona iugo.

Ouid. 1. Pont. 6. *Cernis vt ignauum corrumpant otia corpus?*
Vt capiant vitium, ni moueantur aquæ?

Men

To Sir ROBERT IERMYN *Knight.*

Psalm. 41.
Quemadmodu
desiderat Ceru
ad fontes aqua
Ita desiderat a
ma mea ad te
Deus, &c.

BY vertue hidde, behoulde, the Iron harde,
The loadestone drawes, to poynte vnto the starre:
Whereby, wee knowe the Seaman keepes his carde,
And rightlie shapes, his course to countries farre:
And on the pole, dothe euer keepe his eie,
And withe the same, his compasse makes agree.

Virg. in Ætna.
Est meritò pietas h
mini tutissima vi

Which shewes to vs, our inward vertues shoulde,
Still drawe our hartes, althoughe the iron weare:
The hauenlie starre, at all times to behoulde,
To shape our course, so right while wee bee heare:
That Scylla, and Charybdis, wee maie misse,
And winne at lengthe, the porte of endlesse blisse.

Conscia mens recti famæ mendacia ridet. Ouid. 4. Fast.

Sufficit & longum probitas perdurat in æuum,
Perq; suos annos hinc bene pendet amor. Ouid. de me faciei.

THE Lyon fierce, behoulde doth rente his praie,
The dogge lookes backe, in hope to haue a share,
And lick'd his lippes, and longe therefore did staie,
But all in vaine, the Lion none coulde spare:
And yet the sighte, with hope the dogge did feede,
As if he had, somme parte there of in deede.

This reprehendes, the sonnes, or greedie frendes,
That longe do hope, for deathe of aged Sires:
And on theire goodes, doe feede before theire endes,
For deathe ofte times, doth frustrate theire desires:
And takes awaie, the yonge before the oulde,
Let greedie heires, this looking glasse behoulde.

Ouid. 1. Metamorph.

Filius ante diem patrios inquirit in annos:
Victa iacet pietas, &c.

Furor

THE crewell kinges, that are inflam'de with ire:
With fier, and fworde, theire furious mindes fuffife:
And ofte to fhowe, what chiefelie they defire,
Within theire fheildes, they dreadefull fhapes deuife,
Some Griphins feirce, fome ramping Lions beare,
Some Tygers fell, or Dragons like to weare.

All which bewraye, theire inwarde bloodie thoughte,
Suche one, behoulde, kinge AGAMEMNON was:
Who had in fhielde, a ramping Lion wroughte
And eke this verfe, was grauen in the brafse:
Mannes terror this, to feare them that behoulde:
Which fhielde is borne, by AGAMEMNON *boulde.*

S ribit Claud. Minois fuper Alciatum, Agamemnoné Clypeum habuiffe, in quo Leo depictus erat, ad terrorem aliis incutiendum: quod quidem fcutum in Olympiæ fano per aliquot tempora pependit, cùm infcriptione adiecta.

Terror hic eft hominum, quique hanc geria... Agamemnonis

Dum furor in curfu eft, currenti cede furori:
Difficiles aditus impetus omnis habet.

Ouid. 1. Remed.

Varij

To Sir HENRY WOODHOWSE Knight.

AN aged dame, in reuerence of the dead,
With care did place, the sculles of men shee founde,
Vppon an hill, as in a sacred bed,
But as shee toil'de, shee stumbled to the grounde:
Whereat, downe fell the heades within her lappe,
And here, and there, they ranne abowt the hill:
With that, quoth shee, no maruaile is this happe,
Since men aliue, in myndes do differ still:
And like as theise, in sunder downe do fall,
So varried they, in their opinions all.

Persius 5.

Mille hominum species, & rerum discolor vsus.
Velle suum cuique est, nec voto viuitur vno.
Mercibus hic Italis, mutat sub sole recenti
Rugosum piper, & pallentis grana cumini:
Hic satur irriguo mauult turgescere somno:
Hic campo indulget, hunc alea decoquit: &c.

To Sir WILLIAM STANDLEY *Knight.*

WHERE courage great, and conſaile good doe goe,
With laſtinge fame, the victorie is wonne:
But ſeperate theiſe, then feare the ouerthrowe;
And ſtrengthe alone, dothe vnto ruine ronne:
Then Captaines good, muſt ioyne theiſe two, in one:
And not preſume with this, or that, alone.

As valiant hartes, and corage highe beſeeme,
The Captaines boulde, that enterpriſe for fame:
Soe muſte they ſtill, of pollicie eſteeme,
And wiſedomes rules, to bringe to paſſe the ſame:
While Cæſar great, ſubdude the countries farre:
In gowne at home, did TVLLIE helpe to warre.

Andr. Alciat.
Viribus hic præstat hic pollet acumine mi
Nec tamen alteri non eget alter ope.

VLISSES wiſe, and DIOMEDES forme,
Are heare ſet downe, for valiant wightes to viewe:
The one deuiſ'de, the other did performe,
Whereby, they did the Troiane force ſubdue:
The one, his foes with witte, and counſaile harm'de,
The other, ſtill him ſelfe againſte them arm'de.

Hor. 2. Carm. 10.
Rebus angustis animosus, atque Fortis appare: sapienter idem. Contrahes vento nimium secundo, Turgida ve

Labor

arte

HEARE, Ocnus ſtill the roape doth turne and winde,
Which he did make, of ruſſhes and of graſſe:
And when with toile, his worke was to his minde
He rol'de it vp, and lefte it to the aſſe:
Whoe quickelie ſpoil'de, that longe with paine was ſponne,
Which being kept, it might ſome good haue donne.

This Ocnus ſhewes, a man that workes and toiles,
The Aſſe declares, a wicked waſtfull wife:
Whoe if ſhee maie, ſhee quicklie ſpendes and ſpoiles
That he with care, was getting all his life,
And likewiſe thoſe, that lewdely doo beſtowe
Suche thinges, as ſhoulde vnto good vſes goe.

Iuuenalis 6. *Prodiga non ſentit pereuntem femina ſenſum:*
At, velut exhauſta rediuiuus pullulet arca
Nummus, & è pleno ſemper tollatur aceruo,
Non vnquam reputant quanti ſua gaudia constent.

In eum

THE rauening wolfe, by kinde my mortall foe,
Yet lo, inforſ'de, I foſter vp her whelpe:
Who afterwarde, as it did ſtronger growe,
Thoughe as my owne, I longe the ſame did helpe:
Yet, coulde I not contente it with my teate,
But that my ſelfe, hee rent to be his meate.

No willinge minde, to pleaſe him might ſuffiſe,
No dilligence, to geue the tyraunte ſucke,
Though whelpiſhe daies, his nature did diſguiſe,
Yet time at lengthe vnto my euell lucke,
Bewray'de his harte, a warninge good to thoſe,
Whoe in theire howſe, doe foſter vp theire foes.

For, thoughe throughe neede they frendlie ſeeme a while,
Or childiſhe yeares, do cloke their cancker'd minde,
Althoughe ſome doe, releeue them in exile,
And ſpend theire goodes, in hope to alter kinde:
Yet all theire loue, and care to doe them good,
Suche will forgett, and ſeeke to ſpill theire blood.

Nic. Reuſſierus.
Impaſtus ſtabulis ſæuit lupus: ubere raptos
Dilaniátque ferus miſeros cum matribus agnos.

Claudius Minois è Græco.
Nutritus per me, tandem fera ſæuiet in me.
Vertère naturam gratia nulla poteſt.

And. Alciat.
Improbitas nullo flectitur obſequio.

G *Carru-*

Garrulitas.

Ecclesiast. 20.
Qui multis vtitur verbis, lædet animam suam.

Paradisus poëticus.
Ver non vna dies, non vna reducit hirundo:
Multiplici vigilans prudentia surgit ab vsu.

Horat. 1. Epist. 8.
Sed tacitus pasci si posset coruus: haberet
Plus dapis, & rixæ multo minus, inuidiaque.

BETIME when sleepe is sweete, the chattringe swallowe cries,
And doth awake the wearied wighte, before he would arise:
Which carpes the pratinge crewe, whoe like of bablinge beste:
Whose tounges doe make him almoste deafe, that faine would take his rest.

Quære adolescens, vtere senex.

Ouid. 2. Art.
um vires annique sinunt tolerate labores,
veniet tacito curua senecta pede.

VVHILST youthe doth laste, with liuelie sappe, and strengthe,
With sweate of browe, see that for age thou toyle:
And when the same, arresteth thee at lengthe,
Then take thy rest, let younglinges worke, and moyle:
And vse thy goodes, which thou in yowthe haste wonne,
To cheare thy harte, whil'st that thy glasse shal ronne.

Vita

WITHIN one flower, two contraries remaine,
For proofe behoulde, the spider, and the bee,
One poison suckes, the bee doth honie draine:
The Scripture soe, hath two effectes we see:
Vnto the bad, it is a sworde that slaies,
Vnto the good, a shielde in ghostlie fraies.

De littera & spiritu,
S. Paulus Cor. 2.
cap. 3.
Paradisus poëticus.
Vsus abest nimium? di-
cens pede stamine texo;
Aluus lanigera fer-
tilitate scatet.

Non dulcem è quouis
apis ingeniosa liquorem
Flore: sed è lecto ger-
mine, mella legit.

Nil penna, sed vsus.

To. Pr. Dr.

THE Hippocrites, that make so great a showe,
Of Sanctitie, and of Religion founde,
Are shaddowes meere, and with out substance goe,
And beinge tri'de, are but dissemblers founde.
Theise are compar'de, vnto the Ostriche faire,
Whoe spreades her winges, yet sealdome tries the aire.

Martialis 2.
Decipies alios verbis,
vultuque benigno
Nam mihi iam notus
dissimulator eris.

Aelian. De varia hiſtoria lib 6 cap. 22.

Ouid. 2. Remed. Amoris.

Parua necat morſu ſpatioſum vipera taurum: A cane non magno ſæpe tenetur aper.

THE ſcarlet cloathe, dothe make the bull to feare.
The culler white, the Olephant dothe ſhunne.
The crowinge cocke, the Lion quakes to heare.
The ſmoke of cloathe, dothe make the ſtagge to runne.
All which doe ſhowe, wee no man ſhoulde diſpiſe,
But thinke howe harme, the ſimpleſt maie deuiſe.

Iniuriis, infirmitas ſubiecta.

And. Alciat.

…en iniuria manent …ndique debilitas.

THE mightie fiſhe, deuowres the little frie,
If in the deepe, they venture for to ſtaie,
If vp they ſwimme, newe foes with watchinge flie,
The caruoraunte, and Seamewe, for theire praie:
Betweene theſe two, the frie is ſtill deſtroi'de,
Ah feeble ſtate, on euerie ſide anoi'de.

In dies meliora.

THE greedie Sowe so longe as shee dothe finde,
Some scatteringes lefte, of haruest vnder foote
She forward goes and neuer lookes behinde,
While anie sweete remayneth for to roote,
Euen soe wee shoulde, to goodnes euerie daie
Still further passe, and not to turne nor staie.

Nic. Reusnerus.
Sylua iuuat capras: vnda tutúmque sub

Luxuriosorum opes.

ON craggie rockes, and haughtie mountaines toppe,
Vntimelie fruicte, one sower figtree growes:
Whereof, no good mankinde at all doth croppe,
But serues alone, the rauens, and the crowes:
So fooles, theire goodes vnto no goodnes vse,
But flatterers feede, or waste them on the stewes.

A Trompetter, the Captaines captiue leade,
Whoe pardon crau'de, and saide, he did no harme:
And for his life, with tremblinge longe did pleade,
Whereat, quoth they, and hal'de him by the arme:
Althoughe, thie hande did neuer strike a stroke,
Yet with thie winde, thou others did'st prouoke.

In quatuor anni tempora.

BY swallowes note, the Springe wee vnderstande,
The Cuckowe comes, ere Sommer doth beginne:
The vinefinche showes, that haruest is at hande:
The Chaffinche singes, when winter commeth in:
Which times they keepe, that man therebie maie knowe,
Howe Seasons chaunge, and tymes do come and goe.

Nic. Reusnerus de Ficedula.
Cum me ficus alat: cũ pascar dulcibus vuis:
Cur potius nomen non dedit vua mihi?

Paruam

IN smalle, and little thinges, there is no gaine at all,
One groaue, maie not two redbreastes serue, but euermore they brall.

Andr. Alciat.
Arbustum geminos non alit erithacos.

Cuncta complecti velle, stultum.

ET TVTTO ABBRACCIO
ET NVLLA STRINGO.

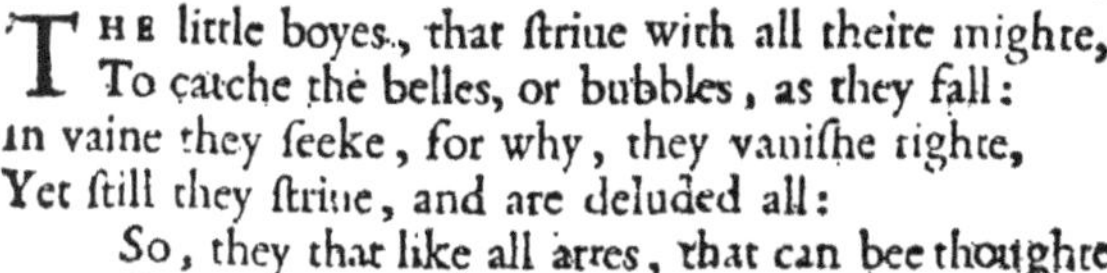

THE little boyes, that striue with all theire mighte,
To catche the belles, or bubbles, as they fall:
In vaine they seeke, for why, they vanishe righte,
Yet still they striue, and are deluded all:
So, they that like all artes, that can bee thoughte,
Doe comprehende not anie, as they oughte.

Alius

THE angrie dogge doth turne vnto the ſtone,
When it is caſte, and bytes the ſame for ire,
And not purſues, the ſame that hathe it throwne,
But with the ſame, fulfilleth his deſire:
Euen ſo, theyr are that doe bothe fighte, and brall,
With guiltleſſe men, when wrathe dothe them inflame,
And mortall foes, they deale not with at all;
But let them paſſe, to theire rebuke, and ſhame:
And in a rage, on innocentes do ronne,
And turne from them, that all the wronge haue donne.

And. Alciat. *Sic plerique ſinunt veros elabier hoſtes,*
Et quos nulla grauat noxia, dente petunt.

Æthio-

LEAVE of with paine, the blackamore to ſkowre,
With waſhinge ofte, and wipinge more then due:
For thou ſhalt ſinde, that Nature is of powre,
Doe what thou canſte, to keepe his former hue:
Thoughe with a forke, wee Nature thruſte awaie,
Shee turnes againe, if wee withdrawe our hande:
And thoughe, wee ofte to conquer her aſſaie,
Yet all in vaine, ſhee turnes if ſtill wee ſtande:
Then euermore, in what thou doeſt aſſaie,
Let reaſon rule, and doe the thinges thou maie.

Eraſmus ex Luciano.
Abluis Æthiopem fruſtrà: quin deſinis artē?
Haud unquā efficies nox ſit ut atra, dies.
Horat. 1. Epiſt. 10.
Naturam expellas furcā tamen uſque recurret.

—— —— equumq;
Nunquam ex degeneri fiet generoſus aſello,
Et nunquam ex ſtolido cordatus fiet ab arte.

Anulus in pict. poeti.

H *Non*

THE ape, did reache for Chestnuttes in the fire,
But fearinge muche, the burninge of his toes,
Perforce was bar'de, longe time from his desire:
But at the lengthe, he with a whelpe did close,
And thruste his foote, into the Embers quick,
Aelian. de var. Hist. lib. 5. ca. 26. And made him, pull the Chestnuttes out perforce:
Which shewes, when as ambition fowle doth prick,
The hartes of kinges, then there is no remorce,
But oftentimes, to aunswere theire desire,
The subiectes feele, both famine, sworde, and fire.

Horat. lib. 1. Epist. 2. *Quicquid delirant reges, plectuntur Achivi.*

Nimium

THE loftie Pine, that one the mountaine growes,
And spreades her armes, with braunches freshe, & greene,
The raginge windes, on sodaine ouerthrowes,
And makes her stoope, that longe a farre was seene:
So they, that truste to muche in fortunes smiles,
Thoughe worlde do laughe, and wealthe doe moste abounde,
When leste they thinke, are often snar'de with wyles,
And from alofte, doo hedlonge fall to grounde:
Then put no truste, in anie worldlie thinges,
For frowninge fate, throwes downe the mightie kinges.

Sæpius ventis agitatur ingens Hor. Carm. 2.
Pinus, & celsæ grauiore casu Od. 10.
Decidunt turres, feriúntque summos
Fulmina montes.

Vt cecidi, cunctiq; metu fugere ruinam, Ouid. 3. Trist. 5.
Versáque amicitiæ terga dedere meæ.

Ad D. T. C. M.

De laude ſilentij Aul. Gel. lib. 11. cap. 10. idem de vaniloquio lib. 1. cap. 15.

PYTHAGORAS, vnto his ſchollers gaue,
This leſſon firſte, that ſilence they ſhould keepe:
And this, wee reade Philoſophers moſte graue,
Yea in theire hartes, this Princes printed deepe:
VLISSES wordes weare ſpare, but rightlie plac'd:
This, NESTOR lik'de. LYCVRGVS this imbrac'de.

Epaminondas celebratur apud Pindarum qui, quanquam multa ſciret, pauca tamen loquebatur.

Locutū fuiſſe pœnituit, tacuiſſe verò nunquam.

This, famons made EPAMINONDAS boulde:
By this, great praiſe did DEMARATVS gaine:
This, Athens made to reuerence ZENO oulde:
SIMONIDES condemned ſpeaches vaine,
Whoſe ſayinge was, my wordes repentance had,
But Silence yet, did neuer make mee ſad.

Cato lib. 1. *Proximus ille deo, qui ſcit ratione tacere.*

Cor. 1. cap. 15. Corrumpunt mores bonos, colloquia praua.

De vaniloquio. *Paul. Timoth. 2. cap. 2.*

And CATO ſayeth: That man is next to GOD,
Whoe ſquares his ſpeache, in reaſons rightfull frame:
For idle wordes, GOD threatneth with his rodde,
And ſayeth, wee muſt giue reckoninge for the ſame:
Sainct PAVLE likewiſe, this faulte doth ſharplie tutche,
And oftentimes, condemneth bablinge mutche.

Guill. Lill. *Eſt vita ac pariter ſanua linguanecu.*

One calles the tounge, the gate of life, and deathe,
Which wiſelie vſ'd, extolleth men on earthe:
Which lewdlie vſ'de, depriueth men of breathe,

And

And makes them mourne, whoe might haue liu'de in mirthe:
For euell wordes, pierce sharper then a sworde,
Which ofte wee rue, thoughe they weare spoke in boorde.

Pet. 1. cap. 5. Qui enim vult vitam diligere, & dies videre bonos: coërceat linguã à malo.
Marc. 7. Nihil est extra hominem introiens in eum, quod possit eũ coinquinare, sed quæ de homine procedunt, &c.

Not that distroyes, into the mowthe that goes,
But that distroyes, that forthe thereof doth comme:
For wordes doe wounde, the inwarde man with woes,
Then wiselie speake, or better to bee domme
The tounge, althowghe it bee a member small,
Of man it is the best, or worste of all.

Hor. 1. Serm. 4. *Fingere qui non visa potest, cõmissa tacere Qui nequit: hic niger est, hunc tu Romane caueto.*

The foole, is thought with silence to be wise,
But when he prates, him selfe he dothe bewraye:
And wise men still, the babler doe dispise,
Then keepe a watche when thou haste owght to saie,
What labour lesse, then for to houlde thy peace,
Which aged daies, with quiet doth increase.

Ouid. 3. Amor. 2. *Quis minor est autem, quàm tacuisse labor?*

Horat. 1. Ep. 18. *Nec retinent patulæ cõmissa fideliter aures.*

Plutarch. in Moral.

Th'Ægyptians wise, and other nations farre,
Vnto this ende, HARPOCRATES deuis'de,
Whose finger, still did seeme his mouthe to barre,
To bid them speake, no more then that suffis'de,
Which signe thoughe oulde, wee may not yet detest,
But marke it well, if wee will liue in reste.

Written to the like effecte, vppon

Video, & taceo.

Her Maiesties poësie, at the great Lotterie in LONDON, *begon* M. D. LXVIII. *and ended* M. D. LXIX.

I See, and houlde my peace: a Princelie Poësie righte,
For euerie faulte, shoulde not prouoke, a Prince, or man of mighte.
For if that IOVE shoulde shoote, so ofte as men offende,
The Poëttes saie, his thunderboltes shoulde soone bee at an ende.
Then happie wee that haue, a Princesse so inclin'de.
That when as iustice drawes hir sworde, hath mercie in her minde,
And to declare the same, howe prone shee is to saue:
Her Maiestie did make her choice, this Poësie for to haue.

Ouid. 2. Trist. *Si quoties peccãt homines sua fulmina mittat Iupiter, exiguo tempore inermis erit.*

Sed piger ad pœnas princeps, ad præmia velox:
Cuique dolet, quoties cogitur esse ferox.

Ouid. 1. Pon.

To R. T. and M. C. *Esquiers.*

A Withered Elme, whose boughes weare bare of leaues
And sappe, was sunke with age into the roote:
A fruictefull vine, vnto her bodie cleaues,
Whose grapes did hange, from toppe vnto the foote:
And when the Elme, was rotten, drie, and dead,
His braunches still, the vine abowt it spread.

Which showes, wee shoulde be linck'de with such a frende,
That might reuiue, and helpe when wee bee oulde:
And when wee stoope, and drawe vnto our ende,
Our staggering state, to helpe for to vphoulde:
Yea, when wee shall be like a sencelesse block,
That for our sakes, will still imbrace our stock.

Virgil in Mœcenatis obitum.
Et decet, & certè viuã tibi semper amicus,
Nec tibi qui moritur, desinit esse tuus:
Ipse ego quicquid ero, cineres interq; fauillas,
Tunc quoque non potero non memor esse tui.

Ouid. 3. Pont. 2.

Ire iubet Pylades charum periturus Orestem:
Hic negat, inq; vicem pugnat vterque mori,
Extitit hoc vnum quod non conuenerat illis:
Cætera pars concors, & sine lite fuit.

Poten-

THE Lions grimme, behoulde, doe not resiste,
But yealde them selues, and Cupiddes chariot drawe,
And with one hande, he guydes them where he liste,
With th'other hande, he keepes them still in awe:
Theye couche, and drawe, and do the whippe abide,
And laie theire fierce and crewell mindes aside.

If Cupid then, bee of such mightie force,
That creatures fierce, and brutishe kinde he tames:
Oh mightie IOVE, vouchsafe to showe remorse,
Helpe feeble man, and pittie tender dames:
Let Africke wilde, this tyrauntes force indure,
If not alas, howe can poore man bee sure.

Quem non mille feræ, quem non Sthenelеius hostis,
Non potuit Iuno vincere, vincit amor. Ouid. Epist.

Quæ

To I. I. Esquier.

NOT for our selues, alone wee are create,
But for our frendes, and for our countries good:
And those, that are vnto theire frendes ingrate,
And not regarde theire offspringe, and theire blood,
Or hee, that wastes his substance till he begges,
Or selles his landes, whiche seruide his parentes well:
Is like the henne, when shee hathe lay'de her egges,
That suckes them vp and leaues the emptie shell,
Euen so theire spoile, to theire reproche, and shame,
Vndoeth theire heire, and quite decayeth theire name.

Ouid. 1. Art.
Sic ne perdiderit non cessat perdere lusor,
Et reuocat cupidas alea sæpe manus.

Sen. Hipp. 1.

Quisquis secundis rebus exultat nimis,
Fluitq́, luxu, semper insolita appetens,
Hunc illa magnæ dura fortunæ comes
Subit libido: non placent suetæ dapes.
Non tecta sani moris, aut vilis cibus: &c.

Mutuum

To R. COTTON *Eſquier.*

THE blynde, did beare the lame vppon his backe,
The burthen, did directe the bearers waies:
With mutuall helpe, they ſeru'd eche others lacke,
And euery one, their frendly league did praiſe:
The lame lente eies, the blynde did lend his feete,
And ſo they ſafe, did paſſe both feelde, and ſtreete.

Some lande aboundes, yet hathe the ſame her wante,
Some yeeldes her lacke, and wantes the others ſtore:
No man ſo ritche, but is in ſome thinge ſcante,
The greate eſtate, muſt not diſpiſe the pore:
Hee workes, and toyles, and makes his ſhowlders beare,
The ritche agayne, giues foode, and clothes, to weare.

So without poore, the ritche are like the lame:
And without ritche, the poore are like the blynde:
Let ritche lend eies, the poore his legges wil frame,
Thus ſhoulde yt bee. For ſo the Lorde aſſign'd,
Whoe at the firſte, for mutuall frendſhip ſake,
Not all gaue one, but did this difference make.

Whereby, with trade, and intercourſe, in ſpace,
And borrowinge heare, and lendinge there agayne:
Such loue, ſuch truthe, ſuch kyndnes, ſhoulde take place,

Quanta ſit mutui auxilij neceſſitas, cùm in cõmuni hac vitæ humanæ ſocietate multis modis intelligi poteſt: in qua homo hominis ope maximè indiget, adeo vt in prouerbium abierit, homo homini Deus: tum verò in ipſa corporis humani conſtitutione & fabrica luculentiſſimè apparet. Neque enim homo ſubſiſtere vlla ratione poſſit, niſi membra corporis mutuum ſibi auxilium præſtent. Quid enim futurum eſſet, niſi oculi pedes ad ingreſſum dirigerent: niſi rurſum pedes corpus mouerent; niſi manus ori cibũ, os ventriculo atq. hepati, hepar per venas vniuerſo corpori alimentum ſuggereret? Nihil itaque eſt quod per ſeipſum, ſine alterius auxilio, conſtare, aut vim ſuam & perpetuitatem conſeruare poſſit.

Hor. 1. ferm. 2. *Nam propriæ telluris herum natura neque illum, Nec me, nec quenquam statuit, &c.* Ausonius in Epig.

That frendshipp, with societie should raigne:
The prouerbe saieth, one man is deemed none,
And life, is deathe, where men doo liue alone.

Non est diues opum, diues: nec pauper inopsq;
Infelix: alio nec magis alter eget.
Diues eget gemmis; Cereali munere pauper.
Sed cùm egeant ambo, pauper egens minus est.

In vtrumque paratus.

To Iohn Payton *Esquier.*

2 Esd. cap. 4.

When Sanabal Hierusalem distrest,
With sharpe assaultes, in Nehemias tyme:
To warre, and worke, the Iewes them selues addrest,
And did repaire theire walles, with stone, and lime:
One hande the sworde, against the foe did shake,
The other hande, the trowell vp did take.

Ouid. 1. Pont. 4. *Nescio qua natale solum dulcedine cunctos Ducit, & immemores non finit esse sui.*

Of valiant mindes, loe here, a worthie parte,
That quailed not, with ruine of theire wall:
But Captaines boulde, did prooue the masons arte,
Which doth inferre, this lesson vnto all:
That to defende, our countrie deare from harme,
For warre, or worke, wee eyther hande should arme.

Murus

To Miles Hobart *Eſquier.*

BOTHE freſhe, and greene, the Laurell ſtandeth ſounde,
Thoughe lightninges flaſſhe, and thunderboltes do flie:
Where, other trees are blaſted to the grounde,
Yet, not one leafe of it, is withered drie:
Euen ſo, the man that hathe a conſcience cleare,
When wicked men, doe quake at euerie blaſte,
Doth conſtant ſtande, and dothe no perrilles feare,
When tempeſtes rage, doe make the worlde agaſte:
Suche men are like vnto the Laurell tree,
The others, like the blaſted boughes that die.

Nic. Reuſnerus.
Miſſa triumphalem nõ tangunt fulmina laurũ,
Cingunt hac vates tempora læta ſacri.

Integer vitæ, ſceleriſq; purus
Non eget Mauri iaculis nec arcu,
Nec venenatis grauida ſagittis,
Fuſce pharetra.

Siue per Syrtes iter æſtuoſas
Siue facturus per inhoſpitalem
Caucaſum, vel quæ loca fabuloſus
Lambit Hydaſpes.

Hor. 1. Carm. 22.

To Tho. Stutvile *Eſquier.*

IN fruictefull feilde amid the goodlie croppe,
The hurtfull tares, and dernell ofte doe growe,
And many times, doe mounte aboue the toppe
Of higheſt corne: But ſkilfull man doth knowe,
When graine is ripe, with ſiue to purge the ſeedes,
From chaffe, and duſte, and all the other weedes.

Ouid. 5. Triſt. 4. *Viue ſine inuidia, molliſque inglorius annos Exige, amicitias & tibi iunge pares.*

By which is ment, ſith wicked men abounde,
That harde it is, the good from bad to trie:
The prudent ſorte, ſhoulde haue ſuche iudgement ſounde,
That ſtill the good they ſhoulde from bad deſcrie:
And ſifte the good, and to diſcerne their deedes,
And weye the bad, noe better then the weedes.

Interiora

To George Brooke *Esquier.*

Though outwarde thinges, doe trimme, & braue, appeare,
And sightes at firste, doe aunswere thie desire,
Yet, inwarde partes, if that they shine not cleare,
Suspecte the same, and backe in time retire:
For inwardlie, such deadlie foes maie lurke,
As when wee trust, maie our destruction worke.

Though bewtie rare, bee farre and neare renoumde,
Though Natures giftes, and fortunes doe excell:
Yet, if the minde, with heinous crimes abounde,
And nothing good with in the same doe dwell:
Regarde it not, but shonne the outward showe,
Vntill, thou doe the inwarde vertues knowe.

Virtus omnia in se habet, omnia adsunt bona, quem Pene'st virtus, Plaut. in Amph.

To Fr. W. *Esquier.*

Simile de Aiace seipsum interficiente (super cuius tumulum virtus plorans pro falso iudicio) apparet antè, folio tricesimo. Nam cùm Achillis arma per Agamemnonis iudicium, Vlyssi adiudicabantur, Aiax illius iniuriæ impatiens, & postea insanus, seipsum interficiebat, sic inquiens vt Ouid habet 13. Metamorph.

Hectora qui solus, qui ferrum, ignémque, Iouémque,
Sustinuit toties, vnam non sustinet iram:
Inuictúmq. virū vicit dolor; arripit ensem:
Et meus hic certè est, an & hunc sibi poscit Vlysses?
Hoc ait, vtēdum est in me mihi, quiq. cruore
Sæpè Phrygum maduit, domini nunc cæde madebit,
Ne quisquam Aiacem possit superare, nisi Aiax,
Dixit, & in pectus, &c.

When Brutus knewe, Augustus parte preuail'de,
And sawe his frendes, lie bleedinge on the grounde,
Suche deadlie griefe, his noble harte assail'de,
That with his sworde, hee did him selfe confounde:
But firste, his frendes perswaded him to flee,
Whoe aunswer'd thus, my flighte with handes shalbee.

And bending then to blade, his bared breste,
Hee did pronounce, theise wordes with courage great:
Oh Prowes vaine, I longe did loue thee beste,
But nowe, I see, thou doest on fortune waite.
Wherefore with paine, I nowe doe prooue it true,
That fortunes force, maie valiant hartes subdue.

Fides.

To BARTHRAM CALTHORPE *Esquier.*

THE fisshermam, doth caste his nettes in sea,
In hope at lengthe. an happie hale to haue,
And is content, longe time to pause, and staie,
Thoughe, nothinge elles hee see, besides the waue:
Yet, onelie trust for thinges vnseene dothe serue,
Which feedes him ofte, till he doth almoste sterue.

If fisshermen, haue then suche constant hope,
For hidden thinges, and such as doe decaie,
Let Christians then, the eies of faithe houlde ope,
And thinke not longe, for that which lastes for aie,
And on GODS worde, theire hope to anchor faste,
Whereof eache iote, shalbee fulfil'de at laste.

Non boue mactato cœlestia numina gaudent,
Sed, quæ præstanda est & sine teste, fide. Ouid. Epist 18

Virtus

Ornatiss. iuuenibus nouem fratribus GEORGII BVRGOINE *armigeri F. F.*

THE surging Sea, doth salte, and sweete remaine,
And is preserude with working, to and froe:
And not corruptes, nor suffreth anie staine,
Whiles in his boundes, the same doth ebbe, and flowe:
But if it waste, and forth by sluses fall,
It soone corruptes, and hath no force at all.

The arrowes sharpe, that in one sheafe are bounde,
Are harde to breake, while they are ioined sure,
But seuer them, then feeble are they founde,
So where as loue, and concorde, doth indure:
A little force, doth mightilie preuaile,
Where Princes powers, with hate and discorde quaile.

Gratiam

SEE heare the ſtorke prouides with tender care,
And bringeth meate, vnto her hatched broode:
They like againe, for her they doe prepare,
When ſhee is oulde, and can not get her foode:
Which teacheth bothe, the parente and the childe,
Theire duties heare, which eche to other owe:
First, fathers muſt be prouident, and milde,
Vnto theire fruićte, till they of age doe growe:
And children, muſte with dutie ſtill proceede,
To reuerence them, and helpe them if they neede.

Aelianus lib. 10 cap. 16.

Idem libro 8. cap. 22. vbi de natura Ciconiæ mira fabula.

Defeſſum fertur portare Ciconia patrem,
Hinc illa pietas ſancta notatur aue.

Paradiſus poeticus.

Ouid. Metam. lib. 4.

HEARE TANTALVS, as Poëttes doe deuine,
This guerdon hathe, for his offence in hell:
The pleaſante fruite, dothe to his lippe decline,
A riuer faire vnto his chinne doth ſwell:
Yet, twixt theſe two, for foode the wretche dothe ſterue,
For bothe doe flee, when they his neede ſhoulde ſerue.

The couetons man, this fable reprehendes,
For chaunge his name, and TANTALVS hee is,
Hee dothe abounde, yet ſterues and nothing ſpendes,
But keepes his goulde, as if it weare not his:
With ſlender fare, he doth his hunger feede,
And dare not touche his ſtore, when hee doth neede.

Horat. Sermo. [illegible]
Sat. [illegible].

Tantalus à labris ſitiens fugientia captat
Flumina, quid rides? mutato nomine de te
Fabula narratur, congeſtis vndique ſaccis
Indormis inhians: & tanquam parcere ſacris
Congeris &c. ——— ———

O vita,

TO Cawcasus, behoulde PROMETHEVS chain'de, | De quo, Diodor Sicul. lib. 6.
Whose liuer still, a greedie gripe dothe rente:
He neuer dies, and yet is alwaies pain'de,
With tortures dire, by which the Poëttes ment,
That hee, that still amid missfortunes standes,
Is sorrowes slaue, and bounde in lastingo bandes.

For, when that griefe doth grate vppon our gall,
Or surging seas, of sorrowes moste doe swell,
That life is deathe, and is no life at all,
The liuer rente, it dothe the conscience tell: | Horat. 1. Epist. 1. --*hic murus ah neus esto, Nil conscire sibi, n pallescere culpa.*
Which being launch'de, and prick'd, with inward care,
Although wee liue, yet still wee dyinge are.

Qualiter in Scythica religatus rupe Prometheus,
Assiduam nimio pectore pauit auem, &c. | Martial. lib. 1.

And. Alciat.
Fœderis hæc species: id habet concordia signum, Vt quos iungit amor, iungat & ipsa manus.

OF kinges, and Princes greate, lo, Concorde ioynes the handes:
And knittes theire subiectes hartes in one, and wealthie makes theire Landes.
It bloodie broiles dothe hate, and Enuie doune dothe thruste,
And makes the Souldiour learne to plowghe, and let his armour ruste.

Remedium tempestiuum sit.

Ouid. 2. Pont. 6.
Cum poteram recto transire Ceraunia velo Vt fera vitarem saxa, monendus eram. Nunc mihi naufragio quid prodest dicere facto Qua mea debuerit currere cymba via?

THROVGHE rased wall, a serpente backwarde slydes,
And yet, before her poisoned head appeare,
The prudent man, for safetie that prouides,
Doth strike at firste, in dowte of further feare:
So all men shoulde, when they to daunger dreede,
With all their force, preuent the same with speede.

Sero

THE prouerbe ſaieth, ſo longe the potte to water goes,
That at the lengthe it broke returnes, which is appli'de to thoſe,
That longe with wyles, and ſhiftes, haue cloaked wicked partes,
Whoe haue, at lengthe bene paied home, and had theire iuſt deſertes.
Euen as the ſlymie eele, that ofte did ſlippe awaie,
Yet, with figge leaues at lengthe was catch'de, & made the fiſhers praie.

Tibul. 1. 9.
Ah miſer, & ſi quis primò periuria celat,
Sera tamen tacitis pœna venit pedibus.

Dum viuo, proſum.

AN aged tree, whoſe ſappe is almoſte ſpente,
Yet yeeldes her boughes, to warme vs in the coulde:
And while it growes, her offalles ſtill be lente,
But being falne, to it turneth into moulde,
And doth no good: ſoe ere to graue wee fall,
Wee maie do good, but after none at all.

Da tua, dum tua ſunt, poſt mortem tunc tua non ſunt.

K Noli

WITH, lime, and net, the Mauis, and the larke,
The fowler loe, deceaued by his arte:
But whilſte alofte, he leuel'd at his marke,
And did to highe exalte, his hawghtie harte,
An adder fell, that in the graſſe did lurke,
With poiſoned ſtinge, did his deſtruction worke.

Claud. 1. Ruf.
—iam non ad culmina rerum,
Iniuſtos creuiſſe queror: tollantur in altũ
Vt lapſu maiore ruant, &c.

Let mortall men, that are but earthe, and duſte,
Not looke to highe, with puffe of wordlie pride:
But ſometime, viewe the place wheretoo they muſte,
And not delighte, the pooreſt to deride:
Leſte when theire mindes, do mounte vnto the ſkies,
Their fall is wrought, by thinges they doe diſpiſe.

Cato.
Mitte arcana dei Cælúmque inquirere quid ſit.

& alius ſic.
Si Chriſtum bene ſcis, ſatis eſt ſi catera neſcis.

Some others are, that fitlie this applie,
To thoſe, whoe doe Aſtronomie profeſſe:
Whoe leaue the earthe, and ſtudie on the ſkie,
As if they coulde, all worldlie thinges expreſſe:
Yet, when to knowe the ſtarres they take in hande,
Of daungers neare, they doe not vnderſtande.

Sæpius

HEARE LAIS fine, doth braue it on the ſtage,
With muſkecattes ſweete, and all ſhee coulde deſire:
Her beauties beames, did make the youthe to rage,
And inwardlie Corinthus ſet on fire:
Bothe Princes; Peeres; with learned men, and graue,
With humble ſute, did LAIS fauour craue.

Not euerie one, mighte to Corinthus goe,
The meaninge was, not all mighte LAIS loue:
The manchet fine, on highe eſtates beſtowe,
The courſer cheate, the baſer ſorte muſt prooue:
Faire HELEN leaue for MENELAVS grace,
And CORIDON, let MABLIE ſtill imbrace.

And thoughe, the poore maie not preſume alofte,
It is no cauſe, they therefore ſhoulde diſpaire:
For with his choiſe, doth IRVS ioye as ofte,
As dothe the Prince, that hathe a VENVS faire:
No highe eſtate, can giue a quiet life,
But GOD it is, that bleſſeth man, and wife.

Then make thy choiſe, amongſte thy equalles ſtill,
If thou miſlike DIANAS ſteppes to trace:
Thoughe PARIS, had his HELEN at his will,
Thinke howe his facte, was ILIONS foule deface.
And hee, that moſte the houſe of LAIS hauntes,
The more he lookes, the more her face enchauntes.

De Laide Aul. Gel. lib 1. cap. 8.

Propertius Eleg. 2.
Non ita complebant Ephyræa Laidos ædes,
Ad cuius iacuit Græcia tota fores.

Horat. Epiſt. lib. 1. Epiſt. 18.
Non cuiuis homini contingit adire Corinthum.

Claud. 2. de volupt. Still. ſic,
Blanda quidem vultu, ſed qua non tetrior vllus,
Interius fucata genus, & amicta doloſis
Illecebris, &c.

Præpoſtera

ANELLVS, ſendes his corne vnto the mill,
Which beinge grounde, he tride it by the waighte:
And finding not the meaſure, to his will,
Hee ſtudied longe, to learne, the millers ſleighte:
For noe complaintes, coulde make him leaue to ſteale,
Or fill the ſacke, with fuſtie mixed meale.

Wherefore, to mill he ſente his deareſt wife,
That nighte, and daie, ſhee mighte the grindinge viewe:
Where ſhee, (kinde harte,) to ende al former ſtrife,
Did dubbe her Spouſe, one of VVLCANVS crewe:
Oh greedie foole Anellus, of thy graine,
And of thy wife, too prodigall, and plaine.

Fatuis

THE little childe, is pleaſde with cockhorſe gaie,
Althoughe he aſke a courſer of the beſte:
The ideot likes, with bables for to plaie,
And is diſgrac'de, when he is brauelie dreſte:
A motley coate, a cockeſcombe, or a bell,
Hee better likes, then Iewelles that excell.

Corn. Gall.
Diuerſos diuerſa iuuant: nō omnibus annis
Omnia conueniunt; &c.

So fondelinges vaine, that doe for honor ſue,
And ſeeke for roomes, that worthie men deſerue:
The prudent Prince, dothe giue hem ofte their due,
Whiche is faire wordes, that right their humors ſerue:
For infantes hande, the raſor is vnfitte,
And fooles vnmeete, in wiſedomes ſeate to ſitte.

L *Homi-*

Virgil. Aeneid. 7. Ouid. Metam. lib. 14.

SEE here VLISSES men, transformed ſtraunge to heare:
Some had the ſhape of Goates, and Hogges, ſome Apes, and Aſſes weare.
Who, when they might haue had their former ſhape againe,
They did refuſe, and rather wiſh'd, ſtill brutiſhe to remaine.
Which ſhowes thoſe fooliſhe ſorte, whome wicked loue dothe thrall,
Like brutiſhe beaſtes do paſſe theire time, and haue no ſence at all.
And thoughe that wiſedome woulde, they ſhoulde againe retire,
Yet, they had rather CIRCES ſerue, and burne in theire deſire.
Then, loue the onelie croſſe, that clogges the worlde with care,
Oh ſtoppe your eares, and ſhutte your eies, of CIRCES cuppes beware.

Horat. 1. Epiſt. 2.

Sirenum voces, & Circes pocula noſti:
Quæ ſi cum ſociis ſtultus, cupiduſq; bibiſſet,
Sub domina meretrice fuiſſet turpis, & excors,
Vixiſſet canis immundus, vel amica luto ſus.

Iudicium

TO PARIS, here the Goddeſſes doe pleade:
With kingdomes large, did IVNO make her ſute,
And PALLAS nexte, with wiſedome him aſſaide,
But VENVS faire, did winne the goulden fruite.
No princelie giftes, nor wiſedome he did wey,
For Bewtie, did comaunde him to obey.

The worldlie man, whoſe ſighte is alwaies dimme,
Whoſe fancie fonde eache pleaſure doth entice,
The ſhaddowes, are like ſubſtance vnto him,
And toyes more deare, them thinges of greateſt price:
But yet the wiſe this iudgement raſhe deride,
And ſentence giue on prudent PALLAS ſide.

Regna Iouis coniux; virtutem filia iactat.
Et poſtea ibidem.
Dulcè Venus riſit, Nec te Pari munera tangunt,
Vtraque ſuſpenſi plena timoris, ait.

Ouid. Epiſt. 15. De iudicio Paridis.

HEARE HANNO ſtandes, and lookes into the ſkye,
And feedes him ſelfe, with hope of future praiſe:
Vnto his birdes, he dothe his eare applie,
And truſtes in tyme, that they his name ſhould raiſe:
For they weare taughte, before they ſlewe abrode,
Longe tyme to ſaie, that HANNO was a God.

Aelian. de var. Hiſtor. lib. 14. cap. 30.

But, when the birdes from bondage weare releaſt,
And in the woodes, with other birdes weare ioin'de,
Then HANNOS name, theire woonted leſſon ceaſte,
For eache did ſinge, accordinge to his kinde:
Then flee this faulte, Ambition workes our ſhame,
And vertue loue, which dothe excell our name.

Deſidiam

VSE labour ſtill, and leaue thie ſlouthfull ſeate,
Flee Idleneſſe, which beggers ſtate dothe giue:
With ſweate of browe, ſee that thou get thy meate,
If thou be borne, with labouring hande to liue:
And get, to eate. and eate, to liue with praiſe:
Liue not to eate, to liue with wanton eaſe.

By DRACOES lawes, the idle men ſhoulde die,
*The Florentines, made baniſhement theire paine:
In Corinthe, thoſe that idlie they did ſee,
Weare warn'de at firſte, the ſeconde time were ſlaine:
And eke Sainct Paule, the ſlothfull thus doth threate,
Whoe laboreth not, denie him for to eate.

Queritur Ægiſtus quare ſit factus adulter:
In promptu cauſſa eſt, deſidioſus erat.

*Sabel.

Paul. Theſ. 2. ca. 3
Neque gratis panem manducauimus ab aliquo, ſed in labore, & in fatigatione, nocte, & die operantes &c.
& poſtea:
Quoniam ſi quis non vult operari, nec manducet.

Ouid. 1. Remed. Amoris.

Ad Reuerendum virum D**n.** ALEXANDRUM NOWELL *Paulinæ ecclesiæ Londini Decanum, doctrina & exemplo clarum.*

Horat. 1. Carm. 4.
Pallida mors æquo pulsat pede pauperum tabernas,
Regumq. turres, &c.

THE Princes greate, and Monarches of the earthe,
Whoe, while they liu'de, the worlde might not suffice:
Yet can they claime, by greatnesse of their birthe,
To beare from hence, when nature life denies,
Noe more then they, who for releife did pyne,
Which is but this, a shrouding sheete of twyne.

Propertius 2, 28.
Haud vllas portabis opes Acherontis ad vndas:
Nudus ab inferna stulte vehere rate.
Victor cum victis pariter miscebitur vmbris,
Consule cum Mario capte Iugurtha sedes.

Thoughe fewe there bee, while they doe flourishe heere,
That doe regarde the place whereto the muste:
Yet, thoughe theire pride like Lucifers appeere,
They shalbee sure at lengthe to turne to duste:
The Prince, the Poore, the Prisoner, and the slaue,
They all at lengthe, are summon'de to their graue.

But

But, hee that printes this deepelie in his minde,
Althoughe he set in mightie CÆSARS chaire,
Within this life, shall contentation finde,
When carelesse men, ofte die in great dispaire:
Then, let them blusshe that woulde be Christians thought,
And faile hereof, Sith Turkes the same haue taught.

As SALADINE, that was the Souldaine greate
Of Babilon, when deathe did him arreste,
His subiectes charg'd, when he shoulde leaue his seate,
And life resigne, to tyme, and natures heste:
They should prepare, his shyrte vppon a speare,
And all about forthwith the same shoulde beare.

Throughe ASCHALON, the place where he deceaste, Vrbs Palæstinæ.
With trumpet Sounde, and Heralte to declare,
Theise wordes alowde: *The Kinge of all the Easte*
Great SALADINE, *beboulde is stripped bare:*
Of kingdomes large, and lyes in house of claie,
And this is all, he bare with him awaie.

Quod in te est, prome.

Ad eundem.

THE Pellican, for to reuiue her younge,
Doth peirce her brest, and geue them of her blood:
Then searche your breste, and as yow haue with tonge,
With penne proceede to doe our countrie good:
Your zeale is great, your learning is profounde,
Then helpe our wantes, with that you doe abounde.

Parad. Poët.
Cur Pharium rostro figis
pelecanus amore,?
Et se pro natis [illegible]
[illegible]

To my brother M. BR. WHITNEY.

Ouid. 1. Remed. Amoris.
Flumina magna vides paruis de fontibus orta:
Plurima collectis multiplicantur aquis.

Vt huic vacuo ſpacio aliquid adiiciam, non facilè occurrit (mi frater) quod & tibi (iam patriſamilias) & huic Symbolo magis conueniat, quàm illud Horatianum ad Iccium.

ALTHOVGHE thy ſtore bee ſmall, for to beginne,
Yet guide it well, and ſoone it is increaſte,
For mightie men, in time theire wealthe did winne,
Whoe had at firſte, as little as the leſte:
Where GOD dothe bleſſe, in time aboundance ſpringes,
And heapes are made, of manie little thinges.

1. Epiſt. 12.

Fructibus Agrippæ Siculis, quos colligis Icci,
Si rectè frueris: non eſt vt copia maior
Ab Ioue donari poſſit tibi, tolle querelas.
Pauper enim non eſt, cui rerum ſuppetit vſus.

Vita

Ad Doctiss. virum W. M. *fortunæ telo ictum.*

THE Apodes, which doe in INDIA breede,
Still flie about, and seldome take theire ease:
They haue no feete, to reste them as wee reade,
But with theire flighte, do compasse lande, and seas:
Vnto this broode, those that about doe rome,
Wee maie compare: that haue no house, nor home.

Iuuen. Sat. 10.
Pauca licet portes argenti vascula puri,
Nocte iter ingressus gladium, contumque timebis,
Et mota ad lunam trepidabis arundinis umbram.
Cantabit vacuus coram latrone viator.

Bothe houses faire, and citties great, they veiwe,
But Riuers swifte, theire passage still do let,
They ofte looke backe, and doe theire fortune rue,
Since that therin, they haue no seate to set:
Thus, passe they throughe theire longe vnquiet life,
Till deathe dothe come, the ende of worldlie strife.

Omne solum forti patria est, vt piscibus æquor,
Vt volucri vacuo quicquid in orbe patet.

Ouid. 1. Fast.

Ad affinem ſuum, R. E. medicum inſignem.

Aelian. De Animalibus lib. 9. cap. 7. & lib. 12. cap. 12.

Alciatus.
Nam ſi nec propriis Neptunus parcit alumnis,
Quis tutos homines nauibus eſſe putat?

THE Dolphin ſwifte, vpon the ſhore is throwne,
Thoughe he was bred, and foſtered, in the flood:
If NEPTVNE ſhewe ſuch wronge, vnto his owne,
Then, howe maie man in ſhippes haue hope of good:
The raging Sea, our countrie doth declare;
The Dolphin fiſhe, thoſe that exiled are.

And thoughe this fiſhe, was mightie in the ſea,
Without regarde, yet was hee caſte on ſhore:
So famous men, that longe did beare the ſwaie,
Haue bene exil'd, and liud in habit pore:
This, SOCRATES: and MARCVS TVLLIVS tri'de:
DEMOSTHENES, and thouſandes moe beſide.

De his, Petrarcha lib. vtriuſq. fortunæ in titulo de morientibus extra patriam, luculenter ſcribit.

Auſonius Epigr. 135.

Fortuna nunquam ſiſtit in eodem ſtatu,
Semper mouetur, variat, & mutat vices,
Et ſumma in imum vertit, ac verſa erigit.

Tecum

Ad Agnatum suum R. W. *Coolensem.*

A Solemne feaste great IVPITER did make,
And warn'd all beastes, and creatures to be there:
The presse was muche, eache one his place did take:
At lengthe, when all weare in there cheifest cheare:
At seconde course, the snaile crepte slowlie in,
Whome IOVE did blame, cause hee so slacke had bin.

Who aunswered thus, oh kinge behoulde the cause?
I beare my house, wherefore my pace is slowe:
Which warneth all, in feasting for to pause,
And to the same, with pace of snaile to goe:
And further telles, no places maie compare,
Vnto our homes, where wee commaunders are.

Admonet hoc, sectanda gradu conuiuia tardo,
Atque domo propria dulcius esse nihil.

Ad D. H. Wh. patruelis mei F.

THE Lute, whose sounde doth most delighte the eare,
Was caste aside, and lack'de bothe stringes, and frettes:
Whereby, no worthe within it did appeare,
MERCVRIVS came, and it in order settes:
Which being tun'de, suche Harmonie did lende,
That Poëttes write, the trees theire toppes did bende.

Euen so, the man on whome dothe Nature froune,
Whereby, he liues dispis'd of euerie wighte,
Industrie yet, maie bringe him to renoume,
And diligence, maie make the crooked righte:
Then haue no doubt, for arte maie nature helpe.
Thinke howe the beare doth forme her vglye whelpe.

Ouid Epist. 1.

Si mihi difficilis formam natura negauit;
Ingenio formæ damna rependo meæ.

Info

Ad eundem.

THE Aſſe, and Ape complaine, and thought theire fortunes bad:
The Aſſe, for wante of hornes. the Ape, bycauſe no taile he had.
The Mole, then anſwere made: I haue no eyes to ſee,
Then wherefore can you nature blame, if that you looke on mee.
Which biddes vs bee contente, with lot that God doth ſende,
For if wee others wantes do wey, our happes wee maie commende.

Ouid. 9. Metam.
Quódque ego, vult genitor, vult ipſa ſocérque, futurum:
At non vult natura potentior omnibus iſtis

Vxoriæ virtutes.

To my Siſter, M. D. COLLEY.

THIS repreſentes the vertues of a wife,
Her finger, ſtaies her tonge to runne at large.
The modeſt lookes, doe ſhewe her honeſt life.
The keys, declare ſhee hathe a care, and chardge,
Of huſbandes goodes: let him goe where he pleaſe,
The Tortoyſe warnes, at home to ſpend her daies.

Plautus in Amph.
Non ego illam mihi dotem duco eſſe, quæ dos dicitur,
Sed pudicitiam & pudorem & ſedatum cupidinem,
Deum metum, parentum amorem, & cognatûm concordiam.

Inuidiæ descriptio.

Ad Ra. W.

Inuidiam Ouid. describit 2. Metamorph.

WHAT hideous hagge with visage sterne appeares?
Whose feeble limmes, can scarce the bodie staie:
This, Enuie is: leane, pale, and full of yeares,
Who with the blisse of other pines awaie.
And what declares, her eating vipers broode?
That poysoned thoughtes, bee euermore her foode.

Lucret. 3.
Macerat inuidia ante oculos illũ esse potentem, Illum adspectari, claro qui incedit honore: Ipsi se in tenebris volui, cœnoque queruntur.

What meanes her eies? so bleared, sore, and redd:
Her mourninge still, to see an others gaine.
And what is mente by snakes vpon her head?
The fruite that springes, of such a venomed braine.
But whie, her harte shee rentes within her brest?
It shewes her selfe, doth worke her owne vnrest.

Whie lookes shee wronge? bicause shee woulde not see,
An happie wight, which is to her a hell:
What other partes within this furie bee?
Her harte, with gall: her tonge, with stinges doth swell.
And laste of all, her staffe with prickes aboundes:
Which showes her wordes, wherewith the good shee woundes.

Ouid. lib. 1. De Arte Amandi.

Fertilior seges est alienis semper in agris,
Vicinumq; pecus grandius vber habet.

De In-

Auth. de Gueuara in Epistolis suis.

THE Goddes agreed, two men their wishe should haue:
And did decree, who firste demaunde did make,
Shoulde haue his wishe: and he that last did craue,
The others gifte shoulde double to him take.
The Couetous wretche, and the Enuious man:
Theise weare the two, that of this case did scanne.
They longe did striue, who shoulde the firste demaunde:
The Couetous man refus'de, bicause his mate,
Shoulde haue his gifte then doubled out of hande:
The thought whereof, vppon his harte did grate
Wherefore the Goddes, did plague him for his sinne,
And did commaunde, th'Enuious man beginne.
Who did not craue, what MIDAS cheife did choose,
Because his frende, the fruite thereof should finde:
But onelie wish'de, that he one eie might loose,
Vnto the ende, to haue the other blinde:
Which beinge say'd, he did his wishe obtaine:
So but one eye, was lefte vnto them twaine.
See heare how vile, theise caytiffes doe appeare,
To GOD, and man: but chieflie (as wee see)
The Couetous man, who hurteth farre, and neare.
Where spytefull men, theire owne tormentors bee.
But bothe be bad, and he that is the beste,
GOD keepe him thence, where honest men doe reste.

id orna-

Ad ornatiß. virum Dn. PETRUM WITHIPOLE.

Petre, imitare petram.

Hadrianus Iunius Harlemensis Medicus clariss. inter Emblemata sua, filio suo Petro hoc inscripsit.

WHAT IUNIUS sent his sonne, lo, here I send to thee:
Bycause his name, and Nature both, with thyne doe well agree.
Dispise all pleasures vayne, hould vertue by the hand,
And as in rage of wyndes, and Seas, the Rocke doth firmely stande.
So stand thou allwayes sure, that thou maist liue with fame,
Remembring how the Latins sounde a Rocke so like thy name.

Ouid. Epist. 15.

Permanet in voto mens mea firma suo.

Dum

Ad veterem suum amicum Dn. GEORGIVM SALMON, *qui maximo vitæ periculo Roma euasit.*

THE Cuttle fishe, that likes the muddie crickes,
To which, the sea dothe flowe at euerie tide:
For to escape the fishers ginnes, and trickes,
Dame nature did this straunge deuise prouide:
That when he seeth, his foe to lie in wayte,
Hee muddes the streame, and safelie scapes deceyte.

Then man: in whome doth sacred reason reste,
All waies, and meanes, shoulde vse to saue his life:
Not wilfullie, the same for to detest,
Nor rashlie runne, when tyrauntes rage with strife:
But constant stande, abyding sweete or sower,
Vntill the Lorde appoynte an happie hower.

Ouid. 3. Art. Amand.
Nec quæ præterijt, cur-su reuocabitur vnda:
Nec quæ præteriit hora redire potest.
Vtendum est ætate, cito pede labitur ætas,
Nec bona tam sequi-tur, quàm bona pri-ma fuit.

Obscuri latices me condunt: cernere tectam
Atramenta vetant: abdita, tuta nato.

Paradisus poët. de Sepia.

N *Celsa*

Stultitia ſua ſeipſum ſaginari.

Ad. H. S. communem viduarum procum.

The Foxe, that longe for grapes did leape in vayne,
With wearie limmes, at lengthe did ſad departe:
And to him ſelfe quoth hee, I doe diſdayne
Theſe grapes I ſee, bicauſe their taſte is tarte:
So thou, that hunt'ſt for that thou longe haſt miſt,
Still makes thy boaſt, thou maiſt if that thou liſt.

Vireſcit vulnere virtus.

The dockes (thoughe troden) growe, as it is dailie ſeene:
So vertue, thoughe it longe bee hid, with woundinge waxeth greene.

Impa

To Aphilus.

THE tyraunt vile MEZENTIVS, put in vre, Virg. 8. Æneid.
Amongst the plagues, wherewith hee murthered men: *Mortua quinetiã iũgebat corpora viuis Componens manibusq manus atque oribus o*
To binde the quicke, and dead, togeather sure,
And then, to throwe them both into a denne.
  Whereas the quicke, should still the dead imbrace,
  Vntill with pine, hee turn'd into that case.

Those wedding webbes, which some doe weaue with ruthe,
As when the one, with straunge disease doth pine:
Or when as age, bee coupled vnto youthe,
And those that hate, inforced are to ioyne,
  This represêntes: and doth those parentes showe,
  Are tyrauntes meere, who ioyne their children soe.

Yet manie are, who not the cause regarde,
The birthe, the yeares, nor vertues of the minde:
For goulde is first, with greedie men prefer'de,
And loue is laste, and likinge set behinde:
  But parentes harde, that matches make for goodes:
  Can not be free, from guilte of childrens bloodes.

Quàm malè inæquales veniunt ad aratra iuuenci,
Tam premitur magno coniuge nupta minor. Ouid. Epist. 9.

Frontis nulla fides.

Ad Lectiss. iuuenes Dn. Edm. Freake, & Dn. Anth. Alcock.

THE lions roare: the Bores theire tuſkes do whet.
The Griphins graſpe theire tallantes in theire ire:
The dogges do barke; the bulles, with hornes doe thret.
The Serpentes hiſſe, with eyes as redde as fire.

But man is made, of ſuche a ſeemelie ſhape,
That frende, or foe, is not diſcern'd by face:
Then harde it is the wickeds wiles to ſcape,
Since that the bad, doe maſke with honeſt grace.

And Hypocrites, haue Godlie wordes at will.
And rauening wolues, in ſkinnes of lambes doe lurke;
And CAIN doth ſeeke, his brother for to kill,
And ſainctes in ſhewe, with IVDAS hartes doe worke.

Nowe, ſince the good no cognizance doe beare,
To teache vs, whome wee chieflie ſhould imbrace:
But that the ſame the wicked ſorte doe weare,
And ſhewe them ſelues, like them in euerie caſe.

De vera Amicitia Pontius Paulinus, Auſon. ſcribit Epiſt. *Hoc noſtra ceruice iugum non ſæua reſoluit*

A table lo, herein to you I ſende,
Whereby you might remember ſtill to write,

His wor-

His wordes, and deedes, that beares the face of frende,
Before, you choose, suche one for your delite.

And if at lengthe, yow trye him by his tuche,
And finde him hault, whereby you stand in dout,
No harte, nor hand, see that you ioyne with suche
But at the first, bee bould to rase him out.
Yet if by proofe, my wordes, and deedes agree,
Then let mee still within your tables bee.

Fabula, non t
sermia longa dire
Nec perimet, tot
abstrahar orbe, vt
Nunquam anim
missus agam, prius
recedet
Corpore vita meo,
vester pectore vidi

Horat. 1. Serm.
At pater vt gna
nos debemus amici
Si quod sit vitium
fastidire, &c.

Animi scrinium seruitus.

Ad ornatum virum, D. Elisevm Gryphith.

THE Prouerbe saithe, the bounde muste still obey,
And bondage bringes, the freest man in awe:
Whoe serues must please, and heare what other saye,
And learne to keepe *Harpocrates his lawe:
Then bondage is the Prison of the minde:
And makes them mute, where wisedome is by kinde.

*Silentij deus apud Aegyptos.

The Nightingall, that chaunteth all the springe,
Whose warblinge notes, throughout the wooddes are harde,
Beinge kepte in cage, she ceaseth for to singe,
And mournes, bicause her libertie is barde:
Oh bondage vile, the worthie mans deface,
Bee farre from those, that learning doe imbrace.

 Multis

Cicero Tusc. 5. & Valer. Max. & Sidon. Apollinaris lib. 2. epist. 13.

Horat. Serm. 1. Satyra 1. *Qui fit Mæcenas, vt nemo, quam sibi sortē Seu ratio dederit, seu sors obiecerit, illa Contentus viuat: laudet diuersa sequentes? O fortunati mercatores, grauis annis Miles ait, &c.*

HERR DAMOCLES, desirous for to taste,
The princelie fare, of DIONYSIUS kinge,
In royall seate, was at the table plaste,
Where pages braue, all daintie cates did bringe:
His bed of goulde, with curious coueringes spred,
And cubbourdes ritche, with plate about his bed.

Horat. Carm. 3. Ode 1. *Districtus ensis cui super impia Ceruice pendet, non Siculæ dapes Dulcem elaborabunt saporem: Non auium, citharæque cantus Somnum reducent, &c.*

No where hee stay'de, but musique sweete did sounde;
No where hee went, but hee did odors smell;
Nowe in his pompe, when all thinges did abounde,
Being ask'd, if that this life did please him well:
Hee aunswere made, it was the heauen alone,
And that to it, all other liues weare none.

Seneca Oed. Act. 3. *Qui sceptra duro sæuus imperio regit, Timet timentes: metus in auctorem redit.*

Then, did the king comaunde a naked sworde,
Vnto the roofe, shoulde with a heare bee knit:
That right shoulde hange, when hee was plac'd at bourde,
Aboue his head, where he did vse to sit:
Which when hee sawe, as one distracte with care,
Hee had no ioye in mirthe, nor daintie fare.

But

But did beseech, the Tyraunt for to giue,
His former state, and take his pompe againe:
By which, wee learne, that those who meanely liue,
Haue ofte more ioye, them those who rule and raigne:
But cheifelye, if like him they doe appeare,
Who night, and daye, of subiectes stoode in feare.

Claud. 4. honor.
Qui terret, plus ipse timet: sors ista tyrannis
Conuenit, inuideant claris fortesque trucident,
Muniti gladiis viuant, septique venenis
Ancipites habeant arces, trepidiq. minentur.

Interdum requiescendum.

Ad Dn. PETRVM COLVIVM *Brugensem.*

Periander apud Ausonium.
Multis terribilis caueto multos.

Aelianus de tyrannis lib. 10. cap. 5. & lib. 6. cap. 13. De Var. Hist.

CONTINVAL toile, and labour, is not beste:
But sometimes cease, and rest thy wearie bones,
The daie to worke, the nighte was made to reste,
And studentes must haue pastimes for the nones:
Sometime the Lute, the Chesse, or Bowe by fittes,
For ouermuch, dothe dull the finest wittes.

For lacke of reste, the feilde dothe barren growe,
The winter coulde, not all the yeare doth raigne:
And dailie bent, doth weake the strongest bowe:
Yea our delightes still vs'd, wee doe disdaine.
Then rest by fittes, amongste your great affaires,
But not too muche, leste sloathe dothe set her snares.

——Nec enim facundia semper
Adducta cùm fronte placet: nec semper in armis
Bellica turba manet: nec tota classicus horror
Nocte dièque gemit: nec semper Cnoßius arcu
Destinat, exempto sed laxat cornua neruo.
Et galea miles caput, & latus ense resoluit.

Lucanus ad Pisonem.

THE SECOND PARTE

OF EMBLEMES,

AND OTHER DEVISES,

gathered, Engliſhed, and moralized,

And diuerſe newlie deuiſed, by

Geffrey Whitney.

IN PRAISE, OF THE TWO NOBLE EARLES, WARWICKE, AND LEYCESTER.

TWO Beares there are, the greater, and the lesse,
Well knowne to those that trauaile farre, and neare:
Without whose sighte, the shipman sailes by gesse,
If that the Sonne, or Moone, doe not appeare.
They both doe showe, to th'Equinoctiall line,
And one, vnto th'ANTIPODES doth shine.

Pes, vrsæ maioris ad Antipodes lucet.

These, haue their lighte from PHOEBVS goulden raies,
And all the worlde, by them receyueth good:
Without whose helpe, no man mighte passe the seas,
But euer stande in daunger of the flood;
Oh blessed lightes, the worke of heauenly hande,
You, millions saue from ruthe of rocke, and sande.

Two noble peeres, who both doe giue the beare,
Two famous Earles, whose praises pierce the skye:
Who both are plac'd in honours sacred cheare,
Whose worthie fame shall liue, and neuer dye:
In Englishe courte doe spende their blessed daies:
Of publique weale, two greate, and mightie staies.

And as those starres by PHOEBVS lighte are seene,
So, both these Earles haue honour, mighte, and power:
From PHOEBE brighte, our moste renowmed Queene,
Whose fame, no time, nor enuie can deuower:
And vnder her, they showe to others lighte,
And doe reioyce tenne thousand with their sighte.

But, since that all that haue bin borne, haue ende,
And nothinge can with natures lawes dispence:
Vowchsafe oh Lorde, longe time their liues to lende,
Before thou call these noble persons hence:
Whose fame, while that the Beares in skie shall showe,
Within this lande, all future times shall knowe.

In praise

In praise of the Righte Honorable my good Lorde, and Maister, the Earle of LEYCESTER.

HEE that desires to passe the surging Seas,
Bycause they are so wonderfull to see,
And without skill, doth venture wheare hee please,
While that the waues both caulme, and quiet bee,
Weare better farre, to keepe him on the lande,
Then for to take such enterprise in hande.
For, if hee lacke his compasse, and his carde,
And arte therfore, to shape his course arighte:
Or pylottes good, that daungers may regarde,
When surge doth swell, and windes doe showe their mighte,
Doth perrill life, throughe wanton wreckles will,
And doth to late lamente his lacke of skill.
So, hee that shoulde with will, bee stirr'd to wryte,
Your noble actes, your giftes and vertues rare:
If PALLAS ayde hee lacke, for to indite,
Hee should but haste his follie to declare.
And wronge your righte, deseruinge VIRGILS penne;
And HOMERS skill, if they weare here agayne.
Then, best for such to take a longer pause,
Then to attempte a thinge so farre vnfitte:
For, they may knowe to write of such a cause,
Beseemeth best, the fine, and rarest witte.
Yet those that woulde, I wishe their learninge sutche,
That as they shoulde, they mighte your vertues tutche.

An other of the same.

SINCE fame is wighte of winge, and throughe eche clymate flies,
And woorthy actes of noble peeres, doth raise vnto the skies.
And since shee hathe extoll'd your praises longe agoe,
That other countries farre, and neare, your noble name doe knowe.
Althoughe I houlde my peace, throughe wante of learned skill,
Yet shall your passinge fame bee knowne, and bee renowmed still.
And those that haue desire, vppon your praise to looke,
May finde it truly pen'd by fame, within her goulden booke.
Where, on the formost fronte of honours bautie stage,
Shee placeth you, in equall roome, with anie of your age.
Wherfore to fame I yeeld, and cease what I begonne:
Bicause, it is in vaine, to set a candell in the Sonne.

THE former parte, nowe paste, of this my booke,
The seconde parte in order doth insue:
Which, I beginne with IANVS double looke,
That as hee sees, the yeares both oulde, and newe,
So, with regarde, I may these partes behoulde,
Perusinge ofte, the newe, and eeke the oulde.

And if, that faulte within vs doe appeare,
Within the yeare, that is alreadie donne,
As IANVS biddes vs alter with the yeare,
And make amendes, within the yeare begonne,
Euen so, my selfe suruayghinge what is past,
With greater heede, may take in hande the laste.

This Image had his rites, and temple faire,
And call'd the GOD of warre, and peace, bicause
In warres, hee warn'de of peace not to dispaire:
And warn'de in peace, to practise martiall lawes:
And furthermore, his lookes did teache this somme;
To beare in minde, time past, and time to comme.

Quid per geminum Ianum significatur.
Plin. Natur. Hist. lib. 34. cap. 7.

SINCE

To the honorable Sir PHILIPPE SIDNEY *Knight, Gouuernour of the Garrison, and towne of Vlißinge.*

SINCE best deserte, for valour of the minde,
And prowes great, the Romanes did deserue;
And sithe, the worlde might not their matches finde,
In former times, as aucthors yet reserue:
A fewe of them I meane for to recite,
That valiaunt mindes maye haue therein delighte.

And but to tutche the naked names of some,
As *Romulus*, that first the wall did laye:
And so, from thence to nearer times to come,
To *Curtius* boulde, that did the gulfe assaye:
Or *Cocles* eeke, who did his foes withstande,
Till bridge was broke, and armed swamme to lande.

Romulus.
Marcus Cu
Horatius Co

Then *Posthumus*, I might with these repeate,
That did repulse the Latines, from the waules.
And *Manlius*, a man of courage greate,
Who did defende the Capitoll from Gaules:
And *Fabius* name, of whome this dothe remaine,
Three hundreth sixe, weare in one battaile slaine.

Aulus Posth
Manlius C linus.
Fabij.
Martius Co nus.

With these, by righte comes *Coriolanus* in,
Whose cruell minde did make his countrie smarte;
Till mothers teares, and wiues, did pittie winne:
Fabricius then, whome bribes coulde not peruerte.
And *Decij* eeke; and *Iunij* voide of dreede:
With *Curij*; and *Metelli*, doe succeede.

C. Fabriciu
De cuius fide, rbus apud Eu De bello Teren. Ille est Fabric difficilius ab state, quàm cursu suo au posset.
Decy.
Iunij.
Curij.
Metelli.

Dentatus nexte, that sixe score battailes foughte,
Who, Romanes call'de ACHILLES, for his force:
Vnto his graue no wounde behinde hee broughte,
But fortie fiue before, did carue his corse.
Torquatus eeke, his foe that ouercame,
And tooke his chaine, whereby he had his name.

Sicinius De Aul. Gell. li cap. 11. & Pli cap. 28.
Manlius To tus.

With *Claudius* blinde, and *Claudius Caudax* namde,
Two brothers boulde, for valour great renoumde;

Appius Cl Cæcus
Appius Cl Caudax.

Attilius Calatinus. And *Calatine*, that all SICILIA tam'de,
And one the Sea, Hamilcar did confounde:
Cornel. Nepos. *Luctatius Catulus.* *Luctatius* eeke, that Carthage fleete subdude,
Whereby, for peace they with submission sude.

Fabius Maximus. And *Fabius* greate, and *Marc Marcellus* boulde,
Marcus Marcellus That at the lengthe did SYRACVSA sacke:
Marcus Portius Cato. And eeke the actes of *Portius* wee behoulde,
Whose life thoughe longe, yet Rome to soone did lacke:
Cn. Duillius. *Duillius* yet, and *Liuius* wee doe knowe,
Liuius Salinator. Thoughe they weare turn'd to poulder longe agoe.

Claudius Nero. Eutrop. de secundo Bello Punico. What shoulde I speake of *Claudius Neros* harte,
When HANIBAL, did royall Rome dismaye:
And HASDRVBAL did hast to take his parte,
But *Claudius*, lo, did meete him by the waye,
And reau'd his life, and put his hoste to flighte,
And threwe his head to HANIBAL his sighte.

Scipio Africanus. *Quintius Flaminius.* Then *Scipio* comes, that CARTHAGE waules did race.
Fuluius Nobilior. A noble prince, the seconde vnto none:
Paulus Æmilius. *Sempronius Gracchus.* *Flaminius* then; and *Fuluius* haue their place
Æmilius actes, and *Gracchus*, yet are knowne:
Cornelius Sylla. With *Sylla* fierce, and *Caius Marius* stoute,
Caius Marius pater. Whose ciuill warres, made Rome tenne yeares in doubte.

Appianus De Bello Ciuil lib. 1. *Sertorius*, nexte, and eeke *Gabinius* name,
Quintus Sertorius *Aulus Gabinius.* With *Crassus*, and *Lucullus*, highe renoumde:
Licinius Crassus. And *Cæsar* great, that prince of endelesse fame,
Lucius Lucullus. *Iulius Cæsar.* Whose actes, all landes, while worlde dothe laste, shall sounde.
Octauius Augustus. *Augustus* eeke, that happie most did raigne,
The scourge to them, that had his vnkle slaine.

M. Antonius. *Anthonius* then, that fortune longe did frende,
Yet at the lengthe, the most vnhappie man:
Lepidus. And *Lepidus*, forsaken in the ende,
M. Brutus. With *Brutus* boulde, and *Cassius*, pale and wan:
Cassius. With manie more, whome authors doe reporte,
Whereof, ensue some tutch'd in larger sorte.

Mutius

Pietas in patriam.

This hande, and ſworde, within the furious flame, Cornelius Ne
Doth ſhewe his harte, that ſought PORSENNAS ende: pos.
Whoſe countries good, and eeke perpetuall fame,
Before his life did SCÆVOLA commende:
No paine, had power his courage highe to quaile,
But bouldlie ſpake, when fire did him aſſaile.

Which ſighte, abaſh'd the lookers on, but moſte
Amaz'de the kinge; who pardoned ſtraighte the knight:
And ceaſ'd the ſiege, and did remooue his hoſte,
When that hee ſawe one man ſo muche of mighte:
Oh noble minde, althoughe thy daies bee paſte;
Thy fame doth liue, and eeke, for aye ſhall laſte.

Habet

Forius Camillus.

CAMILLVS then, that did repulse the Gaules,
And vnto Rome her former state did giue:
When that her foes made spoile within her waules,
Lo here, amongst his actes that still shall liue.
I made my choice, of this example rare,
That shall for aye his noble minde declare.
Wherefore, in briefe then this his woorthie parte,
What time he did besiege FALERIA stronge:
A scoolemaster, that bare a IVDAS harte,
Vnto the place where he was fostred longe,
Ofte walk'd abrode with schollers that hee toughte,
Whiche cloke hee vsde, so that no harme was thoughte.
At lengthe, with sonnes of all the best, and moste,
Of noble peares, that kepte the towne by mighte:
Hee made his walke into the Romane hoste,
And, when hee came before CAMILLVS sighte,
Quoth hee, my Lorde, lo these thy prisoners bee,
Which beinge kepte, FALERIA yeeldes to thee.
Whereat, a while this noble captaine stay'd,
And pondering well the straungenes of the cause:
Vnto his frendes, this in effecte hee say'd.
Thoughe warres bee ill, yet good mens warres haue lawes,
And it behooues a Generall good to gaine
With valiant actes, and not with treacherous traine.

Verba Camilli apud Plutarchum, Xylandro interprete.
Grauis est inquit res bellum, vt quæ multis iniustis multisque violentis factis conficiatur. & tamen apud bonos viros, habentur etiam belli quædam leges, neque tantopere victoria expetenda est, vt non fugienda sint officia quæ per scelus ac malitiam offeruntur, magnum enim imperatorem suæ virtutis, nō alienæ improbitatis fiducia, conuenit bellum gerere.

Wit a.

With that, hee caus'de this *SINON to bee stripte,
And whippes, and roddes, vnto the schollers gaue:
Whome, backe againe, into the toune they whipte,
Which facte, once knowne vnto their fathers graue:
With ioyfull hartes, they yeelded vp their Toune:
An acte moste rare, and glasse of true renoume.

Virgil. lib. 1 Aeneid.

M. Valerius Coruinus.

Insperatum auxilium.

IF LIVIES pen haue written but the truthe,
And diuerse mo, that actes of ould declare.
Then knowe, when Gaules did dare the Roman youthe,
VALERIVS, lo, a Roman did prepare
By dinte of sword, the challenger to trye,
Who both in armes incountred by and by.
And whilst with force, they prooud their weapons brighte,
And made the sparkes to flie out of the steele,
A Rauen, straight, vppon VALERIVS lighte,
And made his foe a newe incounter feele:
Whome hee so sore did damage, and distresse,
That at the lengthe, the Roman had successe.
For, when his foe his forces at him bente,
With winges all spread the rauen dim'd his sighte:
At lengthe, his face hee scratch'd, and all to rente,
And peck'd his eies, hee coulde not see the lighte,
Which shewes, the Lorde in daunger doth preserue,
And rauens raise our wordlie wantes to serue.

Aul. Gell. l. cap. 11.

Eutropius re Romanarum lib. 2.

P Regulus

Hosti etiam seruanda fides.

THE Consull boulde ATTILIVS, here regarde,
That AFRICKE made to tremble at his name;
Who, for his faithe receyued this rewarde,
Cornelius Nepos. Two hundreth thousande men, hee ouercame.
And three score shippes, and eeke two hundreth townes,
Yet flattringe fate, in fine vppon him frownes.
For, after by XANTIPPVS ouerthrowne,
Eutropius lib. 2. De Bello punico. To CARTHAGE broughte, in dungeon deepe was caste;
Yet, with desire for to redeeme their owne,
Their messenger they made him, at the laste:
And in exchaunge, hee vnto Rome was sente,
For prisoners there, and on his worde he wente.
Silius Italicus lib. 6. Belli Punici, copiosissimè pulcherrimis elegantissimisq. versibus hanc historiam narrat. Who promis'd this, hee woulde retourne to bandes,
If that hee fail'd of that, they did require:
But when hee sawe so manie in their handes,
Thoughe Romanes glad, did graunt him his desire:
Yet coulde hee not theretoo, in harte agree,
Bycause for him, so manie shoulde bee free.
Thus, countries loue, was dearer then his life,
Who backe retourn'de, to keepe his promise true:
Where hee did taste longe time of tormentes rife,
But yet, his harte no tortures coulde subdue.
Aul. Gellius lib. 6. cap. 4. His mangled eies, the Sonne all daye assailes;
And in the ende, was thruste in tonne with nailes.

Marcus

Fortiter & feliciter.

MARC SERGIVS nowe, I maye recorde by righte,
A Romane boulde, whome foes coulde not dismaye:
Gainste HANNIBAL hee often shewde his mighte,
Whose righte hande loste, his lefte hee did assaye
Vntill at lengthe an iron hande hee proou'd:
And after that CREMONA siege remoou'd.

Plin. Nat. hi lib. 7. cap. 28.

Then, did defende PLACENTIA in distresse,
And wanne twelue houldes, by dinte of sworde in France,
What triumphes great? were made for his successe,
Vnto what state did fortune him aduance?
What speares? what crounes? what garlandes hee possest;
The honours due for them, that did the beste.

Celsæ potestatis species.

WHEN POMPEY great, with fortune longe was bleste,
And did subdue his foes, by lande, and sea,
And conquestes great obtained in the Easte,
And PARTHIANS, and ARABIANS, made obaye,
And seas, and Iles, did in subiection bringe,
Whose name with feare, did throughe IVDÆA ringe.

Primus in Hircanum, Rubrum, & Arabicum mare vsque peruenit, Cornelius Nepos.

And had restor'de kinge MASINISSAS righte,
And ouercame SERTORIVS with his power:
And made the Kinge of PONTVS knowe his mighte.
Yet, at the lengthe, hee had his haplesse hower:
For ouercome by CÆSAR, fled for aide,
To ÆGYPTE lande; wherein hee was betrai'd.

De cuius maximis victorijs & triumpho longè splendidissimo ætatis suæ, anno 35. Appianus libro De Bellis Mithridaticis.

Within whose ringe, this forme aboue was wroughte,
Whereby, his force, and noble minde appeares;
Which, with his head to CÆSAR being broughte,
For inwarde griefe, hee wash'd the same with teares,
And in a fire with odours, and perfumes:
This princes head with mourning hee consumes.

M.Otho

Audaces fortuna iuuat.

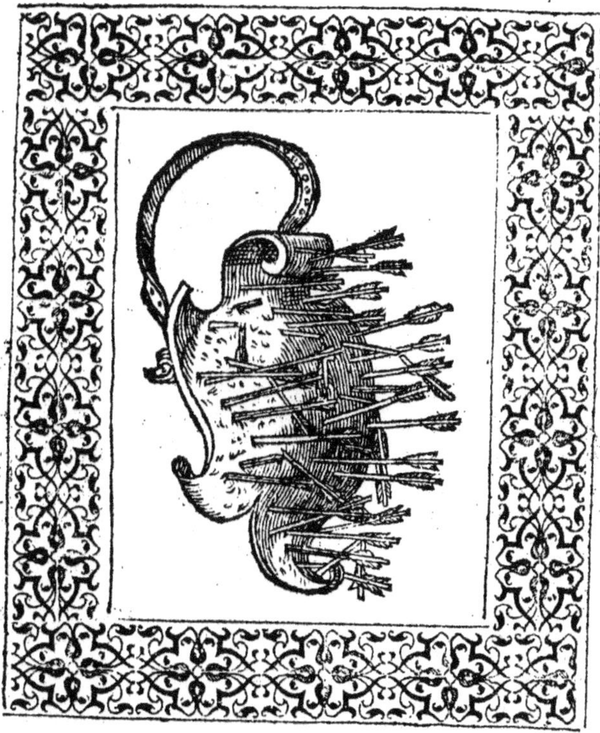

THIS monumente of manhoode, yet remaines, Suetonius.
A witnes true, of MARCVS SCÆVAS harte: Valerius Maximus.
Whose valliancie, did purchase him such gaines,
That deathe, nor time, can blemishe his deserte.
In battaile, boulde: no feare his harte coulde wounde,
When sixe-score shaftes within his shielde weare founde,

And in that fighte, one of his eies hee loste,
His thighe thrust throughe, and wounded sore beside:
Such souldiours, had greate CÆSAR in his hoste,
As by him selfe, and others, is discride.
But, those that would more of these Knightes behoulde,
Let them peruse the Roman Aucthours oulde.

Nic. Reusnerus.
Hæc, ramis tanquam dactylis, sublime renitens Ponderibus, superum molibus it ad astra via.

THE gallant Palme with bodie straighte, and tall,
That freshelie showes, with braunches sweete of smell:
Yet, at the foote the frogges, and serpentes crall,
With irckesome noise, and eke with poison fell:
Who, as it weare, the tree doe still annoye,
And do their worste, the same for to destroye.

When noble peeres, and men of highe estate,
By iuste deserte, doe liue in honor greate:
Yet, Enuie still dothe waite on them as mate,
And dothe her worste, to vndermine their seate:
And MOMVS broode dothe arme, with all their mighte,
To wounde their fame, whose life did geue them lighte.

Euseb. apud Stob.
[illegible] facientes per locum necessario comitatur umbra: [illegible] vero per [illegible]

Ex dum.

THE Lion fierce, and ſauage bore contende,
The one, his pawes: his tuſkes the other tries:
And ere the broile, with bloodie blowes had ende,
A vulture loe, attendes with watchinge eies:
And of their ſpoile, doth hope to præie his fill,
And ioyes, when they eche others blood doe ſpill.

When men of mighte, with deadlie rancor ſwell,
And mortall hate, twixte mightie Monarches raignes;
Some gripes doe watche, that like the matter well,
And of their loſſe, doe raiſe their priuate gaines:
So, SOLIMAN his Empire did increaſe,
When chriſtian kinges exiled loue, and peace.

Georgius Sabin
Sic modò dum fac
diſcordes prœlia re
Turcius Europa
rit hoſtis opes

Hic magnus ſedet Æneas ſecumq; volutat
Euentus belli varios, &c.

Virg. Aeneid

Et pendebat adhuc belli fortuna; diuq;
Inter vtrumque volat dubiis victoria pennis.

Ouid. Metam

Vigilan-

Ad reuerendiss. DN. D. GVLIELMVM CHATTERTONVM *Episcopum Cestrensem.*

THE Heraulte, that proclaimes the daie at hande,
The Cocke I meane, that wakes vs out of sleepe,
On steeple highe, doth like a watchman stande:
The gate beneath, a Lion still doth keepe.
And why? theise two, did alder time decree,
That at the Churche, theire places still should bee.

Aug. in Epist. 124. Episcopi munere ... in hac vita nihil difficilius, ita apud Deum nihil beatius.

That pastors, shoulde like watchman still be preste,
To wake the worlde, that sleepeth in his sinne,
And rouse them vp, that longe are rock'd in reste,
And shewe the daie of Christe, will straighte beginne:
And to foretell, and preache, that light deuine,
Euen as the Cocke doth singe, ere daie doth shine.

Quid per gallum & leonem significetur, Claud. Minos super Alciatum Emb. 15. oculêter scribit.

The Lion shewes, they shoulde of courage bee,
And able to defende, their flocke from foes:
If rauening wolfes, to lie in waite they see:
They shoulde be stronge, and boulde, with them to close;
And so be arm'de with learning, and with life,
As they might keepe, their charge, from either strife.

Festina

Ad Amplissimos viros Dn. FRANCISCVM WINDHAM, *& Dn.* EDWARDVM FLOWERDEWE *Iudices integerrimos.*

THIS figure, lo, AVGVSTVS did deuise,
A mirror good, for Iudges iuste to see,
And alwayes fitte, to bee before their eies,
When sentence they, of life, and deathe decree:
Then muste they haste, but verie slowe awaie,
Like butterflie, whome creepinge crabbe dothe staie.

The Prince, or Iudge, maie not with lighte reporte
In doubtfull thinges, giue iudgement touching life:
But trie, and learne the truthe in euerie sorte,
And mercie ioyne, with iustice bloodie knife:
This pleased well AVGVSTVS noble grace,
And Iudges all, within this tracke shoulde trace.

Consulere patriæ, parcere afflictis, fera
Cæde abstinere, tempus atque iræ dare,
Orbi quietem, seculo pacem suo
Hæc summa virtus, petitur hac cœlum via.

Cicero.
Est sapientia iudicis in hoc, vt non solùm quid possit, sed etiam quid debeat, ponderet: nec quantum sibi permissum meminerit, sed etiam quatenus commissum sit.

Idem 3 Offic.
Nec contra Remp. nec contra iusiurandum amici caussa vir bonus faciet: nec si iudex quidem erit de ipso amico: ponit enim personam amici, cùm induit iudicis: nam si omnia facienda sunt, quæ amici velint, non amicitiæ tales, sed coniurationes putandæ sunt.

Claud. Manl. Theodor.
...diis proximus ille est Quem ratio non ira mouet: qui facta rependens Consilio, punire potest mucrone pepercit.

Senec. Oct. act. 2.

Ad eosdem Iudices.

WHEN Fire, and Aire, and Earthe, and Water, all weare one:
Before that worke deuine was wroughte, which nowe wee
looke vppon.
There was no forme of thinges, but a confused masse:
A lumpe, which CHAOS men did call: wherin no order was.
The Coulde, and Heate, did striue: the Heauie thinges, and Lighte
The Harde, and Softe, the Wette, and Drye: for none had shape arighte
But when they weare dispos'd, eache one into his roome: [bloome.
The Fire, had Heate: the Aire, had Lighte: the Earthe, with fruites did
The Sea, had his increase: which thinges, to passe thus broughte:
Behoulde, of this vnperfecte masse, the goodly worlde was wroughte.
Then all thinges did abounde, that seru'd the vse of man:
The Riuers greate, with wyne, and oyle, and milke, and honie, ranne.
The Trees did yeeld their fruite: thoughe planting then vnknowne.
And CERES still was in her pompe, thoughe seede weare neuer sowne.
The season, Sommer was: the Groues weare alwayes greene,
And euery banke, did beare the badge, of fragrant FLORA Queene.
This

Ouid. in Metam: lib. 1.
...quia corpore in vno Frigida pugnabant calidis: humentia siccis: Mollia, cum duris: sine pondere, habentia pondus.

Tibul. 1. 3.
Non domus vlla fores habuit, non fixus in agris Qui regeret certis finibus arua lapis: Ipsa mella dabant quercus, vltroque ferebant Obuia securis vbera lactis oues: Non acies, non ira fuit, non bella, nec enses, Immiti saeuus duxerat arte faber, &c.

This was the goulden worlde, that Poëttes praised moste,
No hate, was harbor'd then at home: nor hatch'd, in forren coste.
But after, when the earthe, with people did increase:
Ambition, straighte began to springe: and pryde, did banishe peace.
For, as all tymes doe change: euen so, this age did passe.
Then did the siluer age insue, and then, the age of brasse.
The Iron age was laste, a fearefull cursed tyme:
Then, armies came of mischiefes in: and fil'd the worlde with cryme.
Then rigor, and reuenge, did springe in euell hower:
And men of mighte, did manadge all, and poore opprest with power.
And hee, that mightie was, his worde, did stand for lawe:
And what the poore did ploughe, and sowe: the riche away did drawe.
None mighte their wiues inioye, their daughters, or their goodes,
No, not their liues: such tyraunts broode, did seeke to spill their bloodes.
Then vertues weare defac'd, and dim'd with vices vile,
Then wronge, did maske in cloke of righte: then bad, did good exile
Then falshood, shadowed truthe: and hate, laugh'd loue to skorne:
Then pitie, and compassion died: and bloodshed fowle was borne.
So that no vertues then, their proper shapes did beare:
Nor coulde from vices bee decern'd, so straunge they mixed weare.
That nowe, into the worlde, an other CHAOS came:
But GOD, that of the former heape: the heauen and earthe did frame.
And all thinges plac'd therein, his glorye to declare:
Sente IVSTICE downe vnto the earthe: such loue to man hee bare
Who, so suruay'd the world, with such an heauenly vewe:
That quickley vertues shee aduanc'd: and vices did subdue.
And, of that worlde did make, a paradice, of blisse:
By which wee doo inferre: That where this sacred Goddes is.
That land doth florishe still, and gladnes, their doth growe:
Bicause that all, to God, and Prince, by her their dewties knowe.
And where her presence wantes, there ruine raignes, and wracke:
And kingdomes can not longe indure, that doe this ladie lacke.
Then happie England most, where IVSTICE is embrac'd:
And eeke so many famous men, within her chaire are plac'd.

Ouid. 1. Metam. *Iamque nocens ferr ferroq. nocentius au Prodierat, prodit lũ, quod pugnat vt Sanguineaq. manu pitantia concutit a Viuitur ex rapto, hospes ab hospite tu Non socer à genero: trum quoque gratia ra est, &c.*

Isidor. 2. Ethy. Factæ sunt leges, earum metu coër tur audacia, tuta inter improbos in centia, & in ipsis probis formidato s plicio refrænetur cendi facultas.

Anselmus de Iusti Iustitia est anim bertas, tribuens cuique suam propr dignitatem. maio reuerentiam, pari cordiam, minori di plinam, Deo ober tiam, sibi sancti niam, inimico pat tiam, egeno opere misericordiam.

Imago Iustitiæ vid tur apud Plutarch lib. De Iside & O ride, & apud Gell lib. 14. cap. 4.

——sed comprime motus,
Nec tibi quid liceat, sed quid fecisse licebit,
Occurrat, mentemq; domet respectus honesti.

De officio optimi I dicis, Claudian. Honorium &c.

Hor. Arte Poët. Nunquam te fallant animi sub vulpe latentes.

OF open foes, wee alwaies maie beware,
And arme our selues, theire Malice to withstande:
Yea, thoughe they smile; yet haue wee still a care,
Wee trust them not, althoughe they giue theire hande:
  Theire Foxes coate, theire fained harte bewraies,
  Wee neede not doubt, bicause wee knowe theire waies.

But those, of whome wee must in daunger bee,
Are deadlie foes, that doe in secret lurke,
Whoe lie in waite, when that wee can not see,
And vnawares, doe our destruction worke:
  No foe so fell, (as BIAS wise declares)
  As man to man, when mischeife hee prepares.

Bias. *Pernicies homini quæ maxima? solus homo alter.*

Sobriè

A Thirſtie dogge, to NILVS runnes to drinke,
A Crocodile, was readie in the flood:
Which made the dogge, to lappe harde by the brinke,
As one that much in feare of poiſoning ſtood:
And ſparingly, began to coole his heate,
When as hee ſawe, this Serpent lye in waite.

This carefull dogge, condemnes thoſe careles wightes,
Althoughe he bee of brutiſſhe kynde, bycauſe
Thoſe reaſon lacke, that ſpend both daies, and nightes,
Without regard, in keeping BACCHVS lawes:
And when throughe drinke, on feete they can not ſtande,
Yet as they lye, they haue their boales in hande

Cantharon hic retinet: cornu bibit alter adunco:
Concauat ille manus, palmaſq; in pocula vertit:
Pronus at ille lacu bibit, & crepitantibus haurit
Muſta labris, &c.

De Crocod. lian. de Anin lib. 8. cap. 15. lib. 9. cap. 3. præſcientia ei de qua, in pri parte huius lib fol. 3. idem A lib. 5. cap. 52. lib. 8. cap. 4.

Contra Ebrie tem.

Paul. { *Gal. ca* / *Eph. ca* }

Pytha. apud Sto Primum pocu ſanitatis eſt, al rum voluptati tertiũ contum liæ, vltimum ſaniæ.

Nemeſ. Eclog. contra potores

Ad Nobiliß. & doctiß. virum DN. IANVM DOVSAM A NOORTWIICK.

Ouid. Metam. 2.

Nic. Reusnerus.
Hunc volucrẽ Phœbo fertur sacrasse vetustas, Quod referat cantus, Delphica magne, tuos.

Hor. de arte poët.
Natura fieret laudabile carmen, an arte, Quæsitum est. ego nec studiũ sine diuite vena, Nec rude quid prosit video ingenium: alterius sic Altera poscit opem res, & coniurat amice.

Ouid. 3. Art. amandi.

THE Martiall Captaines ofte, do marche into the fielde,
With Egles, or with Griphins fierce, or Dragons, in theire shieldes.
But Phœbus sacred birde, let Poëttes moste commende.
Who, as it were by skill deuine, with songe forshowes his ende.
And as his tune delightes: for rarenes of the same.
So they with sweetenes of theire verse, shoulde winne a lasting name.
And as his colour white: Sincerenes doth declare.
So Poëttes must bee cleane, and pure, and must of crime beware.
For which respectes the Swanne, should in theire Ensigne stande.
No forren fowle, and once suppos'de kinge of LIGVRIA Lande.

Cura ducum fuerant olim, regumq́ poëtæ,
Præmiaq́ antiqui magna tulere chori.
Sanctaq́ maiestas, & erat venerabile nomen
Vatibus, & largæ sæpè dabantur opes.
Ennius emeruit Calabris in montibus ortus,
Contiguus poni Scipio magne tibi,
Nunc edera sine honore iacent: operataq́ doctis
Cura vigil Musis, nomen inertis habet.
Sed famam vigilare iuuat, quis nosset Homerum
Ilias æternum si latuisset opus.

Cum

WHEN Hectors force, throughe mortall wounde did faile,
And life beganne, to dreadefull deathe to yeelde:
The Greekes moste gladde, his dyinge corpes assaile,
Who late did flee before him in the fielde:
Which when he sawe, quothe hee nowe worke your spite,
For so, the hares the Lion dead doe byte.

Looke here vpon, you that doe wounde the dead,
With slaunders vile, and speeches of defame:
Or bookes procure, and libelles to be spread,
When they bee gone, for to deface theire name:
Who while they liude, did feare you with theire lookes,
And for theire skill, you might not beare their bookes.

Nullum cum victis certamen, & æthere cassis. Virg. Aeneid. r

Captiuus,

THE mouse, that longe did feede on daintie crommes,
And safelie search'd the cupborde and the shelfe:
At lengthe for chaunge, vnto an Oyster commes,
Felo de se. Where of his deathe, he guiltie was him selfe:
The Oyster gap'd, the Mouse put in his head,
Where he was catch'd, and crush'd till he was dead.

Isidorus lib. 1. de summo bono. Gulæ saturitas nimia aciē mentis obtundit ingeniumque euertere facit

The Gluttons fatte, that daintie fare deuoure,
And seeke about, to satisfie theire taste:
And what they like, into theire bellies poure,
This iustlie blames, for surfettes come in haste:
And biddes them feare, their sweete, and dulcet meates,
For oftentimes, the same are deadlie baites.

Lucanus 4.

——— O prodiga rerum
Luxuries nunquam paruo contenta paratu,
Et quæsitorum terra pelagóque ciborum
Ambitiosa fames, & lauta gloria mensæ.

Constan-

THE raging Sea, that roares, with fearefull sounde,
And threatneth all the worlde to ouerflowe:
The shore sometimes, his billowes doth rebounde,
Though ofte it winnes, and giues the earthe a blowe
Sometimes, where shippes did saile: it makes a lande.
Sometimes againe they saile: where townes did stande.

Cicer. 2. Offi. Praeclara est omni vita aeq bilitas, ide vultus, eade que frons.

So, if the Lorde did not his rage restraine,
And set his boundes, so that it can not passe:
The worlde shoulde faile, and man coulde not remaine,
But all that is, shoulde soone be turn'd to was:
By raging Sea, is ment our ghostlie foe,
By earthe, mans soule: he seekes to ouerthrowe.

And as the surge doth worke both daie, and nighte,
And shakes the shore, and ragged rockes doth rente:
So Sathan stirres, with all his maine, and mighte,
Continuall siege, our soules to circumuente.
Then watche, and praie, for feare wee sleepe in sinne,
For cease our crime: and hee can nothing winne.

Bern. in E Perseuera finis virtutu virtus sine nemo videt deum.

To Sir HVGHE CHOLMELEY *Knight.*

THE sages seuen, whose fame made Grecia glad,
 For wisedome greate, amongst theire sainges wise:
Eache one of them, a goulden sentence had,
And Alciat, did the pictures thus deuise,
  For to obserue the vse of Emblems righte,
  Which represent the meaning to our sighte.
Keepe still the meane, did CLEOBVLVS teache:
For measure, lo, the ballance ioyn'd thereto.
And *Knowe thy selfe*, did CHILON alwaies preache:
The glasse, behoulde, that thou the same maiste doe.
  Restraine thy wrathe, dothe PERIANDER tell:
  And shewes an hearbe, that choller dothe expell.
Nothinge too muche, did PITTACVS commende,
Thereto *a flowre, whereof too muche destroyes.
And SOLON sai'd, *Remember still thy ende*,
Before the which, none can haue perfect ioyes:
  A piller form'd, declininge downe he showes,
  Which telles that deathe, the strongest ouerthrowes.
Of wicked men the number dothe exceede:
This BIAS vs'd: and cause for foule defame,
SARDINIA mose is stained, as we reade,
On asses backe, behoulde one of the same.
  And THALES, laste of all the Sages, say'd:
  Flee suretiship, for feare thou be betray'd.
And vnderneathe, a birde vpon the net,
That dothe not feare, the craftie foulers call,
Hereby wee ofte, doe paie an others debte,
And free our frendes, and bringe our selues in thrall:
  Which sayinges wise, whoe keepe them in their brestes,
  By proofe shall finde, they harbour happie guestes.

*Semen quod dicitur gith, quod pharmacopolæ vocant Nigellam Romanam.

Plutarch. de lib. educand.
Cùm reliqua omnia tempore diminuantur, sapientia sola senectute augescit.

Bernard.
Sapientiæ otia negotia sunt: & quo otiosior est sapientia, eo exercitatior in suo genere.

Scripta

To Sir ARTHVRE MANWARINGE *Knight.*

IF mightie TROIE, with gates of steele, and brasse,
Bee worne awaie, with tracte of stealinge time:
If CARTHAGE, raste; if THEBES be growne with grasse.
If BABEL stoope: that to the cloudes did clime:
If ATHENS, and NVMANTIA suffered spoile:
If ÆGYPT spires, be euened with the soile.
Then, what maye laste, which time dothe not impeache,
Since that wee see, theise monumentes are gone:
Nothinge at all, but time doth ouer reache,
It eates the steele, and weares the marble stone:
But writinges laste, thoughe yt doe what it can,
And are preseru'd, euen since the worlde began.
And so they shall, while that they same dothe laste,
Which haue declar'd, and shall to future age:
What thinges before three thousande yeares haue paste,
What martiall knightes, haue march'd vppon this stage:
Whose actes, in bookes if writers did not saue,
Their fame had ceaste, and gone with them to graue.
Of SAMSONS strengthe, of worthie IOSVAS might.
Of DAVIDS actes, of ALEXANDERS force,
Of CÆSAR greate; and SCIPIO noble knight,
Howe shoulde we speake, but bookes thereof discourse:
Then fauour them, that learne within their youthe:
But loue them beste, that learne, and write the truthe.

Propertius.
Et Theba steterant, altaque Troia fuit.

Demosth. in Arg. lib. 1.
Clarissimæ olim vrbes, nunc nihil sunt, Quæ maximè nunc superbiunt eandem aliquando fortunam experientur.

Virg. in Mœcenatis obitu.
Marmora Mæonij vincunt monumenta libelli:
Viuitur ingenio, cætera mortis erunt. &
Ouid. 1. Amor. 10.
Scindentur vestes, gemmæ frangentur & aurũ.
Carmina quam tribuent, fama perennis erit.

TO EDWARD DYER *Esquier.*

WHILE furious Mors, from place, to place did flie,
And here, and there, her fatall dartes did throwe:
At lengthe shee mette, with Cupid passing by,
Who likewise had, bene busie with his bowe:
Within one Inne, they bothe togeather stay'd,
And for one nighte, awaie theire shooting lay'd.
The morrowe next, they bothe awaie doe haste,
And eache by chaunce, the others quiuer takes:
The frozen dartes, on Cupiddes backe weare plac'd,
The fierie dartes, the leane virago shakes:
Whereby ensued, suche alteration straunge,
As all the worlde, did wonder at the chaunge.
For gallant youthes, whome Cupid thoughte to wounde,
Of loue, and life, did make an ende at once.
And aged men, whome deathe woulde bringe to grounde:
Beganne againe to loue, with sighes, and grones;
Thus natures lawes, this chaunce infringed soe:
That age did loue, and youthe to graue did goe.
Till at the laste, as Cupid drewe his bowe,
Before he shotte: a younglinge thus did crye,
Oh Venus sonne, thy dartes thou doste not knowe,
They pierce too deepe: for all thou hittes, doe die:
Oh spare our age, who honored thee of oulde,
Theise dartes are bone, take thou the dartes of goulde.

Ioachim. Belleius.
Mutarunt arma inter
se Mors atque Cupido
Hic falcem gestat,
gestat at illa facem.
Afficit hac animum,
corpus sed conficit ille:
Sic moritur iuuenis,
sic moribundus amat.

Which

Which beinge ſaide, a while did Cupid ſtaye,
And ſawe, how youthe was almoſte cleane extinct:
And age did doate, with garlandes freſhe, and gaye,
And heades all balde, weare newe in wedlocke linckt:
Wherefore he ſhewed, this error vnto Mors,
Who miſcontent, did chaunge againe perforce.

Yet ſo, as bothe ſome dartes awaie conuay'd,
Which weare not theirs: yet vnto neither knowne,
Some bonie dartes, in Cupiddes quiuer ſtay'd,
Some goulden dartes, had Mors amongſt her owne.
Then, when wee ſee, vntimelie deathe appeare:
Or wanton age: it was this chaunce you heare.

Prudentes vino abstinent.

LOE here the vine dothe claſpe, to prudent Pallas tree,
The league is nought, for virgines wiſe, doe Bacchus frendſhip flee.

Max. lib. 6. Mulier quæ vini vſum immoderatè appetit, & virtutibus ianuam claudit, & delictis aperit.

Alciat. *Quid me vexatis rami? Sum Palladis arbor,*
Auferte hinc botros, virgo fugit Bromium.

Engliſhed ſo.

Why vexe yee mee yee boughes? ſince I am Pallas tree:
Remoue awaie your cluſters hence, the virgin wine doth flee.

To EDWARDE PASTON *Esquier.*

THE dier, loe, in ſmoke, and heate doth toile,
Mennes fickle mindes to pleaſe, with ſundrie hues:
And though hee learne newe collours ſtill to boile,
Yet varijng men, woulde faine ſome newer chooſe:
And ſeeke for that, which arte can not deuiſe,
When that the ould, mighte verie well ſuffiſe.

Ouid de Triſt.
Infœlix habitum temporis huius habe
Nec te purpureo velent vaccinia ſucco:
Non eſt conueniens luctibus ille color.

And ſome of them, here brieflie to recite,
And to declare, with whome they beſt agree:
For mourners, *blacke*, for the religious, *white*.
Which is a ſigne, of conſcience pure, and free.
The *greene*, agrees with them in hope that liue:
And eeke to youthe, this colour wee do giue.

Alciat.
Nos ſperare docet viridis, ſpes [illegible] eſſe
In viridis quoties irrita [illegible] cadit.

The *yelowe* next, vnto the couetous wighte.
And vnto thoſe, whome ielouſie doth fret.
The man refuſ'd, in *Taunye* doth delite.
The collour *Redde*, let martiall captaine, get.
And little boies, whome ſhamefaſtnes did grace,
The Romaines deck'd, in *Scarlet* like their face.

The marriners, the *Blewe* becometh well.
Bicauſe it ſhowes the colour of the ſea:
And Prophettes, that of thinges deuine foretell,
The men content, like *Violet* arraie.
And laſte, the poore and meaner ſorte prouide,
The *medley*, *graye*, and *ruſſet*, neuer dyde.

Loe here

Loe here, a fewe of colours plaine expreste,
And eeke the men, with whome they best agree:
Yet euerie one, doth thinke his hewe the beste,
And what one likes, an other lothes to see:
For Nature thoughe ten thousande colours haue,
Yet vnto man, more varijng mindes she gaue.
Nowe straungers, who their countries still commende,
And make vs muse, with colours they recite:
Maye thinke our lande, small choise of hues doth lende.
Bycause so fewe, of manie I doe write.
Yet let them knowe, my Author these presentes,
Inoughe for those, whome reason still contentes.
But saye wee lacke, their herbes, their wormes, their flies,
And want the meanes: their gallant hues to frame.
Yet Englande, hath her store of orient dies,
And eeke therein, a DYER *most of fame,*
Who, alwaies hathe so fine, and freshe, a hewe,
That in their landes, the like is not to vewe.

In studiosum captum amore.

A Reuerend sage, of wisedome most profounde,
Beganne to doate, and laye awaye his bookes:
For CVPID then, his tender harte did wounde,
That onlie nowe, he lik'de his ladies lookes:
Oh VENVS staie: since once the price was thine,
Thou oughtst not still, at PALLAS thus repine.

Omnes humanos sanat medicina dolores:
Solus amor morbi non amat artificem. Propert.

Abstinen-

Ad amplis. virum D^N^ CAROLVM CALTHORPE *Regiæ Ma^tis^ procuratorem in Hibernia, Dn. mihi omnibus modis colendissimum.*

WHO so are plac'd, in sacred Iustice roome,
And haue in charge, her statutes to obserue:
Let them with care, behoulde this garnish'd roome,
That suche a one, at lengthe they maie deserue:
Of marble harde, suppose the same to bee,
An Ewer eeke, vppon one corner standes,
At th'other ende, a bason wee maie see:
With Towell faire, to wipe theire washed handes:
Th'effecte whereof, let Iudges printe in minde,
That they maie leaue a lasting name behinde.
The marble showes: they must bee firme, and sure,
And not be pierc'd, nor mooued from the truthe:
The reste declare: they must bee cleane, and pure;
And not inclin'd to rigor, or to ruthe.
But, when a cause before them shalbee harde,
With conscience cleare, let them the same decide:
No Ritche, or Poore, or frend, or foe, regarde,
For feare, they doe throughe theire affections slide:
But let them washe, theire handes from euerie crime,
That GOD maye blesse, and here prolonge theire time.

Augusto super Psal. 37. Apud iustum Iudicem sola conscientia propria timenda est.

August. De comm. vit. Cler. Non vos iudicetis maleuolos esse, quādo alterius crimen iudicatis: magis quippe nocētes estis, si fratres vestros, quos iudicando corrigere potestis, tacēdo perire permittatis.

Stobæus ex Plutarchi Serm. 44. retulit imagines iudicum apud Thebas esse, sine manibus, at summi iudicis imaginem clausis oculis: Eò quòd iustitia nec muneribus capi, nec hominum vultu flecti debeat.

Auson. de viro bono Edyll. 18.

Non prius in dulcem declinat lumina somnum,
Omnia quàm longi reputauerit acta diei;
Quæ prætergressus? quid gestum in tempore? quid non?
Cur isti facto decus absuit, aut ratio illi?
Quid mihi præteritum: cur hæc sententia sedit,
Quam melius mutare fuit? miseratus egentem,
Cur aliquam fracta persensi mente dolorem?
Quid volui, quod nolle bonum foret? vtile honesto
Cur malus antetuli? num dicto, aut denique vultu
Perstrictus quisquam? cur me natura, magis quàm
Disciplina trahit? sic dicta & facta per omnia
Ingrediens, ortóque à vespere cuncta reuoluens,
Offensus prauis, dat palmam, & præmia rectis.

Constan-

To MILES CORBET *Esquier.*

THE shippe, that longe vppon the sea dothe saile,
And here, and there, with varrijng windes is toste:
On rockes, and sandes, in daunger ofte to quaile.
Yet at the lengthe, obtaines the wished coaste:
Which beinge wonne, the trompetts ratlinge blaste,
Dothe teare the skie, for ioye of perills paste.

Thoughe master reste, thoughe Pilotte take his ease,
Yet nighte, and day, the ship her course dothe keepe:
So, whilst that man dothe saile theise worldlie seas,
His voyage shortes: althoughe he wake, or sleepe.
And if he keepe his course directe, he winnes
That wished porte, where lastinge ioye beginnes.

Boni gubernatoris est, ventorũ flatibus accommodare: viri autem sapiẽtis, animi affectibus. Arist. apud Sto

Demetrius Phàler.

Tardè aggredere, quod aggressurus sis perseueranter prosequere. Nam vt inquit Greg. lib. 1. Mor. Incassum bonum agitur, si ante vitæ terminum deseratur: Quia frustra velociter currit, qui prius, quàm ad metas venerit, deficit.

To HVGHE CHOLMELEY *Esquier.*

THE helmet stronge, that did the head defende,
Beholde, for hyue, the bees in quiet seru'd:
And when that warres, with bloodie bloes, had ende.
They, hony wroughte, where souldiour was preseru'd:
Which doth declare, the blessed fruites of peace,
How sweete shee is, when mortall warres doe cease.

De Falce et ense, Martialis.

Pax me certa ducis placidos curuauit in vsus:
Agricola nunc sum, militis ante fui.

Calumniam contra calumniatorem virtus repellit.

WHO so with force against the marble wall,
Or piller stronge, doth shoote, to pierce the same:
It not preuailes, for doune the arrowes fall,
Or backe rebounde, to him from whence they came:
So slaunders foule, and wordes like arrowes keene,
Not vertue hurtes, but turnes her foes to teene.

Sic spe-

To George Manwaringe *Esquier.*

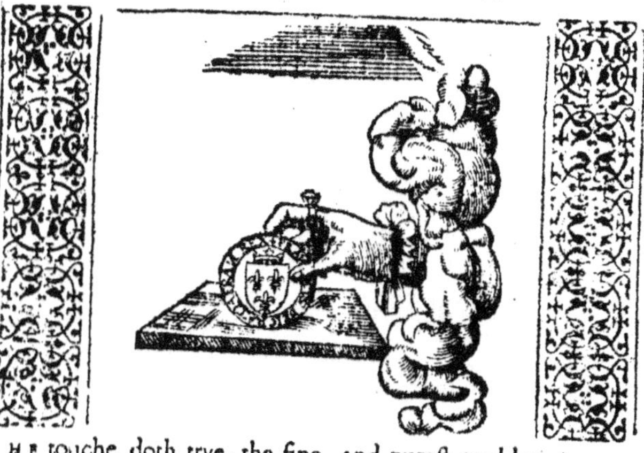

THE touche doth trye, the fine, and purest goulde:
And not the sound, or els the goodly showe.
So, if mennes wayes, and vertues, wee behoulde,
The worthy men, wee by their workes, shall knowe.
But gallant lookes, and outward showes beguile,
And ofte are clokes to cogitacions vile.

Claud. 2. Stil. de fide.
Hæc & amicitias, iungit, post tempore firmat, Mansuráque adamante ligat, nec mobile mutat Ingenium, paruo nec vincula rupta Dissolui patitur, nec fastidire priorem Allicitur veneranda nouum, &c.

Illicitum non sperandum.

HERE NEMESIS, and Hope: our deedes doe rightlie trie.
Which warnes vs, not to hope for that, which iustice doth denie.

Alciatus.
Spes simul & Nemesis, nostris altaribus adsunt:
Scilicet vt speres non nisi quod liceat.

To I. T. Esquier.

Gregor. in mor. Cùm quis positus in prosperitate diligitur, incertum est, vtrum prosperitas an persona diligatur. Amissio autē fœlicitatis interrogat vim di ectionis: nec prosperitas quidem amicum indicat, nec aduersitas inimicum celat.

THE bandogge, fitte to matche the bull, or beare,
With burthens greate, is loden euery daye:
Or drawes the carte, and forc'd the yoke to weare:
Where littell dogges doe passe their time in playe:
And ofte, are bould to barke, and eeke to bite,
When as before, they trembled at his sighte.

Yet, when in bondes they see his thrauled state,
Eache bragginge curre, beginnes to square, and brall:
The freër sorte, doe wonder at his fate,
And thinke them beste, that are of stature small:
For they maie sleepe vppon their mistris bedde,
And on their lappes, with daynties still bee fedde.

Eras. in Epist. Nihil aduersum, nisi quod nobis obstat ad æternam fœlicitatem properantibus: nihil prosperum, nisi quod deo conducit.

The loftie pine, with axe is ouerthrowne,
And is prepar'd, to serue the shipmans turne:
When bushes stande, till stormes bee ouerblowne.
And lightninges flashe, the mountaine toppes doth burne.
All which doe shewe: that pompe, and worldlie power,
Makes monarches, markes: when varrijnge fate doth lower.

Ouid. 2. Art. Amandi.

Luxuriant animi rebus plerumque secundis,
Nec facile est aqua commoda mente pati.

Perfidus

To G. B. Esquier.

WHILE throughe his foes, did boulde BRASIDAS thruste, *Lacedæmoniorum dux apud Plutarchum.*
And thought with force, their courage to confounde:
Throughe targat faire, wherein he put his truste,
His manlie corpes receau'd a mortall wounde.
Beinge ask'd the cause, before he yeelded ghoste:
Quoth hee, my shielde, wherein I trusted moste.

Euen so it happes, wee ofte our bayne doe brue,
When ere wee trie, wee trust the gallante showe:
When frendes suppoas'd, do prooue them selues vntrue,
When SINON false, in DAMONS shape dothe goe:
Then gulfes of griefe, doe swallowe vp our mirthe,
And thoughtes ofte times, doe shrow'd vs in the earthe.

Sæpe sub agnina latet hirtus pelle Lycaon: Súbque Catone pio, perfidus ille Nero.

All is not goulde that glittereth to the eye:
Some poison stronge, a sugred taste doth keepe;
The crabbe ofte times, is beautifull to see.
The Adder fell, within the flowers doth creepe:
The brauest tombe, hath stinking bones within:
So fawninge mates, haue alwaies faithlesse bin.

Yet, to preuent such harmes before they fall,
Thinke howe thy frende, maie liue to bee thy foe:
Then, when your loue exceedeth moste of all,

Looke that thy tonge, doe not at randonne goe:
    For feare thy speeche, doe turne vnto thy smarte,
    If that thy mate, doe beare a IVDAS harte.

Plaut. Capt.
Fac fidelis sis fideli: caue fluxam fidem geras.

But, if thou doe inioye a faithfull frende,
See that with care, thou keepe him as thy life:
And if perhappes he doe, that maye offende,
Yet waye thy frende: and shunne the cause of strife,
    Remembringe still, there is no greater crosse;
    Then of a frende, for, to sustaine the losse.

Cato.
Damnaris nunquã post longum tempus amicũ, Mutauit mores, sed pignora prima memento.

Yet, if this knotte of frendship be to knitte,
And SCIPIO yet, his LELIVS can not finde?
Content thy selfe, till some occasion fitte,
Allot thee one, according to thy minde:
    Then trie, and truste: so maiste thou liue in rest,
    But chieflie see, thou truste thy selfe the beste?

In copia minor error.

THE ape in tree, beganne at foxe beneath to raile:
    And said, hee was a shamelesse beast to weare so great a taile.
Then aunswere made the foxe, I maye thee more deride,
Bicause thou haste no taile at all, thy shamelesse partes to hide.
Which shewes the bitter fruite, that doth of mocking springe:
For scorners ofte, such mates doe meete, that worse then serpentes stinge.

Vindice

To G. B. sen. Esquier.

WHEN ſentence wronge, of will, and rigor vile,
Was framd, to pleaſe the Emperor VALENS minde:
Which ſhoulde condemne Sainct BASIL to exile:
And nothinge lack'd, but that it was not ſign'd:
Th'Emperor thoughte to take no longer pauſe,
But tooke his penne, for to confirme the cauſe.

But all in vayne, the quill would take no inke,
Yet ſtill herein, he lewdlie did perſiſte:
Vntill his hande beganne to ſhake, and ſhrinke,
Whereby, the penne did fall out of his fiſte:
Wherefore for feare, he rente the writte in twaine,
Then feare the Lorde, and raſhe attemptes reſtraine.

Valens Imper tor, Arrianæ ſ ctæ fautor, ta dem per Goth victus, in do muncula qua a ſconditus erat, combuſtus ann. Domini 380. Sabel. & Sex. Aur.

Homo

Sicut Rex in imagine sua honoratur: sic Deus in homine diligitur, & oditur. Non potest hominem odire, qui deū amat. nec potest deū amare qui hominem odit. Chrys. super Matth 22.

NO mortall foe so full of poysoned spite,
As man, to man, when mischiefe he pretendes:
The monsters huge, as diuers aucthors write,
Yea Lions wilde, and fishes weare his frendes:
And when their deathe, by frendes suppos'd was sought,
They kindnesse shew'd, and them from daunger brought.

Mira fabula de Androde & Leone. Aul. Gel. li. 5. ca. 14.

Idem de Arione lib. 16. cap 19.

ARION lo, who gained store of goulde,
In countries farre: with harpe, and pleasant voice:
Did shipping take, and to CORINTHVS woulde,
And to his wishe, of pilottes made his choise:
Who rob'd the man, and threwe him to the sea,
A Dolphin, lo, did beare him safe awaie.

Parad. poëticus.

Quis nescit vastas olim delphina per vndas,
Lesbida cum sacro vate tulisse lyram?

In Cu-

LET maidens sowe; let schollers: plie the schooles.
Giue PALINVRE: his compasse, and his carde.
Let MARS, haue armes: let VVLCANE, vse his tooles.
Giue CORYDON, the ploughe, and harrowe harde.
Giue PAN, the pipe: giue bilbowe blade, to swashe.
Let Grimme haue coales: and Iobbe his whippe to lashe.

Horat. Epist. lib. 2. cap. 1.
... Quod medicorum est Promittunt medici, tractant fabrilia fabri.

Let none presume an others arte to vse,
But trie the trade, to which he hath bene kept:
But those that like a skill vnknowne to choose,
Let them behoulde: while that the workeman slept,
The toying ape, was trempringe with his blockes,
Vntill his foote was crush'd within the stockes.

Nauita de ventis; de tauris narrat arator;
Enumerat miles vulnera; pastor oues.

Propert. 2. 1.

Two sonnes of Iove that best of man deserue,
Apollo great, and Bacchus, this impartes:
With diet good, the one doth healthe preserue,
With pleasante wine, the other cheares our hartes.
And theise, the worlde immortall Goddes would haue,
Bicause longe life, with sweete delighte, they gaue.

But if theise are so soueraigne vnto man,
That here, with ioye they doe increase his daies,
And freshe doe make the carefull colour wanne:
And keepe him longe from sicknes, and disease:
I graunte, they ought to be renowmed more,
Then all the Goddes, the Poëttes did adore.

Alciat. ad eosdem sic.

Tu vino curas, tu victu dilue morbos,
Vt lento accedat curua senecta pede.

Fel

LO CVPID here, the honie hyes to taste,
On whome, the bees did straight extende their power:
For whilst at will he did their labours waste,
He founde that sweete, was sauced with the sower:
And till that time hee thought no little thinges,
Weare of suche force: or armed so with stinges.

The hyues weare plac'd accordinge to his minde,
The weather warme, the honie did abounde.
And CVPID iudg'd the bees of harmelesse kinde,
But whilste he tri'de his naked corpes they wounde:
And then to late his rashe attempte hee ru'de,
When after sweete, so tarte a taste insu'de.

Paradis. poëticus.
Melle gerunt persusa, gerunt persusa veneno,
Et sua spicula apes, & sua spicula amor.

So ofte it happes, when wee our fancies feede,
And only ioye in outwarde gallant showes.
The inwarde man, if that wee doe not heede,
Wee ofte, doe plucke a nettle for a rose:
No baite so sweete as beautie, to the eie,
Yet ofte, it hathe worse poyson then the bee.

To LAVRA.

WHILST CVPID had desire to taste the honie sweete,
And thrust his hand into the tree, a bee with him did meete.
The boye no harme did doubt, vntill he felt the stinge:
But after to his mother ranne, and ofte his handes did wringe.
And cry'd to her for helpe, and toulde what hap befell:
Howe that a little beast with pricke, did make his finger swell.
Then VENVS smiling say'd, if that a little bee?
Doe hurte so sore: thinke howe thou hurt'st? that art a childe to see.
For where the bee can pierce no further then the skinne:
Thy dartes do giue so great a wounde, they pierce the harte within.

Cum quo conuenit aliud ex Anacreonte.

AS VENVS sonne within the roses play'd,
A busie bee that crept therein vnseene,
The wanton wagge with poysoned stinge assay'd:
Whereat, aloude he cri'de, throughe smarte, and teene.
And sought about, his mother for to finde:
To whome, with griefe he vttered all his minde.
And say'd, behoulde, a little creature wilde,
Whome husbandmen (I heare) doe call a bee,
Hath prick'd mee sore alas: whereat shee smil'de,
And say'd: my childe, if this be griefe to thee,
Remember then, althoughe thou little arte?
What greeuous wounde, thou makest with thy darte.

Arma

To D. E.

NARCISSVS loude, and liked so his shape,
He died at lengthe with gazinge there vppon:
Which shewes selfe loue, from which there fewe can scape,
A plague too rise: bewitcheth manie a one.
The ritche, the pore, the learned, and the sotte,
Offende therein: and yet they see it not.

This, makes vs iudge too well of our desertes,
When others smile, our ignorance to see:
And whie? Bicause selfe loue doth wounde our hartes,
And makes vs thinke, our deedes alone to bee.
Whiche secret sore, lies hidden from our eyes,
And yet the same, an other plainlie sees.

What follie more, what dotage like to this?
And doe we so our owne deuise esteeme?
Or can we see so soone an others misse?
And not our owne? Oh blindnes most extreme.
Affect not then, but trye, and prooue thy deedes,
For of selfe loue, reproche, and shame proceedes.

Ouid. Metam lib.

Anulus in pict. poës.
Narcissus liquidis formã speculatus in vnd Contemnens alios, ar amore sui, &c.

Terent. And. 2. &
Verum illud verbũ es vulgo quod dici solet Omnes sibi malle me lius esse, quàm alteri.

Suum cuique pulchrum est, adhuc neminem cognoui poëtam, qui sibi n optimus videretu sic res habet, me d lectant mea, te tua Cicer. 5. Tuscul.

Ælian. de Animal. lib. 13. cap. 8. scribit quod Elephāti sunt, altitudinis 9. cubitorum, latitud. 5. & lib. 17. ca. 7. quod viuunt ad ætatem 200. Annorum & nonnulli ad 300. & multa mira de illis, lib. 10. cap. 15.

NO state so sure, no seate within this life
But that maie fall, thoughe longe the same haue stoode:
Here fauninge foes, here fained frendes are rife.
With pickthankes, blabbes, and subtill Sinons broode,
Who when wee truste, they worke our ouerthrowe,
And vndermine the grounde, wheron wee goe.

Cato lib. 1.
Fistula dulce canit volucrem dum decipit auceps.

Numa Pompilius Roman. Rex 2.

The Olephant so huge, and stronge to see,
No perill fear'd: but thought a sleepe to gaine
But foes before had vndermin'de the tree,
And downe he falles; and so by them was slaine:
First trye, then truste: like goulde, the copper showes:
And NERO ofte, in NVMAS clothinge goes.

Silius 13.

Fœdera mortales ne sæuo rumpite ferro,
Sed castam seruate fidem: fulgentibus ostro
Hæc potior regnis, &c.

Quod

WHERE couetousnes the scepter doth supporte,
There, greedie gripes the Kinge dothe ofte extoll:
Bicause, he knowes they, doe but make a sporte,
His subiectes poore, to shaue, to pill, and poll?
And when he sees, that they are fatte, and full?
He cuttes them of, that he maye haue theire wolle?

Vnto a sponge, theise are resembled righte:
Which drie at firste, when it with water swelles,
The hande that late did wette it, being lighte:
The same againe, the moisture quite expelles.
And to the flood, from whence it latelie came,
It runnes againe, with wringinge of the same.

Orbem iam totum victor Romanus habebat,
Quà mare, quà terra, quà sidus currit vtrumque, Petrus Arbiter.
Nec satiatus erat, grauidis freta pulsa carinis,
Iam peragrabantur, si quis sinus abditus vltra,
Si qua foret tellus, qua fuluum mitteret aurum, &c.

Pauper-

Paupertatem summis ingeniis obesse ne prouehantur.

Ad Doctiss. virum Dn. W. MALIM.

ONE hande with winges, woulde flie vnto the starres,
And raise mee vp to winne immortall fame:
But my desire, necessitie still barres,
And in the duste doth burie vp my name:
  That hande woulde flie, th'other still is bounde,
  With heauie stone, which houldes it to the ground.

My wishe, and will, are still to mounte alofte.
My wante, and woe, denie me my desire:
I shewe theire state, whose witte, and learninge, ofte
Excell, and woulde to highe estate aspire:
  But pouertie, with heauie clogge of care,
  Still pulles them downe, when they ascending are.

Iuuenalis.
Haud facilè emergunt, quorum virtutibus obstat
Res angusta domi, &c.

Pro bono

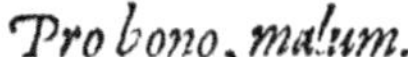

Pro bono, malum.

Duodecem hæc sequentia, ob elegantiam, & venustatem: è G. Faerni, selectis fabulis sumpta.

THE stagge, that hardly skap'd the hunters in the chase,
At lengthe, by shadowe of a tree, founde refuge for a space.
And when the eger houndes had lefte their wished praye,
Behoulde, with biting of the boughes, him selfe hee did bewraye.
Throughe which, the hunter straight did pierce him to the harte:
Wherear, (quoth hee) this wounde I haue, is iustly my deserte.
For where I good did finde, I ought not ill requite:
But lo, these boughes that sau'd my life, I did vnkindly bite.
Wherefore, althoughe the tree could not reuenge her wronge:
Yet nowe by fates, my fall is wrought, who mighte haue liued longe.

In pace de bello.

THE bore did whette his tuskes, the foxe demaunded why:
Since that he had no foes at hande, that should their sharpnes try.

To which, he answere made, when foes doe me beset,
They all aduantage gladlie take, and giue no leaue to whet.
Which teacheth vs, in peace, our force for warres to frame:
Whereby, we either shall subdue, or loose the field with fame.

Aliena pericula, cautiones nostræ.

The lyon, asse, and foxe, goe forthe to hunte for pray:
Which done: the lyon bad the asse, the spoile in partes to lay.
Then he with greate regarde, three partes alike did share:
Wherat, the lyon in a rage, the asse in peeces tare.
The foxe he charged then, for to performe the same:
Who, all the beste, vppon one heape, did for the lyon frame:
And littell of the worste, did for him selfe reserue:
Then beinge ask'd, what taughte him so vnequally to carue?
This spectacle (quoth hee) which I behoulde with care:
Which showes, those happie that can bee by others harmes beware.

Indul-

A Theefe, condemn'd to dye, to execution lead:
His wofull mother did beholde, for sorowe almoste dead.
And whilst she kiss'd her sonne, whome she did tender deare:
The towarde childe did kisse with teeth? and off her nose did teare:
Whereat, the standers by exclaymed at his acte:
Then quoth the theefe, my masters marke, I will defend the facte.
My mother, in my youthe, did with my faults dispence:
And euermore did like me best, when I did most offence.
So that, she was the cause that made me doe amisse:
For if shee had correction vs'de, I had not come to this.
Wherefore, I did reuenge my wronge, in what I mighte:
In hope my facte shall mothers warne, that doe behould this sighte.
For if the Children steale, and come vnto the rope:
It often is the parentes faulte, for giuing them such scope.

A Purblinde dame agreed with one to helpe her ſight;
Who, daylie when he home retorn'd, did ſteale what ſo he might.
At lengthe when all was gone, the pacient gan to ſee:
And then, the falſe Phiſition aſk'd the price, they did agree.
Whereat quoth ſhe, alas, no remedie I finde:
Bycauſe my ſences either faile, or ells my eies bee blinde.
For, where my houſe before was garniſh'd euerie nooke:
I, nowe can ſee no goodes at all, though rounde about I looke.

Dura vſu molliora.

WHEN firſt the foxe, the lyon did behoulde,
Hee quak'd for feare, and almoſt dead did fall:
The ſecond time, he waxed ſomewhat boulde;
But at the third, hee had no feare at all.
Which ſhewes, that artes at firſt moſte harde to ſee,
With triall oft, both playne, and eaſie bee.

In eos

THASTRONOMER, by night beheld the starres to shine:
And what should chaunce an other yeare, began for to deuine.
But while too longe in skyes, the curious foole did dwell,
As hee was marchinge through the shade, he slipt into a well.
Then crying out for helpe, had frendes at hand, by chaunce;
And nowe his perill being past; they thus at him doe glaunce.
What foolishe art is this? (quoth they) thou hould'st so deare,
That doth forshowe the perilles farre: but not the daungers neare.

Saturnus procul est, iámque olim cæcus, vt aiunt,
Nec propè discernens à puero lapidem: Morus in Epig.
Luna verecundis formosa incedit ocellis,
Nec nisi virgineum virgo videre potest:
Iupiter Europam, Martem Venus, & Venerem Mars,
Daphnen Sol, Hersen Mercurius recolit:
Hinc factum, Astrologe, est, tua cùm capit vxor amantes,
Sidera significent vt nihil inde tibi.

COLASMVS wiſe, in raging flood was drown'd?
Who longe did ſeeke her corpes, againſt the ſtreame:
His neigbours thought his ſences weare not ſound?
And did deride his madnes moſt extreme:
Who call'd aloude, thy wiſe beneath did fall?
Then dounwarde ſeeke, or ſeeke thou not at all.

To whome, quoth he, the place belowe I ſee,
Yet in her life, gainſt reaſon ſhe did ſtriue:
And contrarie to euerie one, woulde bee;
Wherefore, I knowe this way ſhe needes muſt driue?
Then leaue, quoth they, and let her ſtill be drown'd.
For ſuch a wiſe is better loſte then founde?

Dum

IN winter coulde, when tree, and bushe, was bare,
And frost had nip'd the rootes of tender grasse:
The antes, with ioye did feede vpon their fare,
Which they had stor'de, while sommers season was:
To whome, for foode the grashopper did crie,
And said she staru'd, if they did helpe denie.

Whereat, an ante, with longe experience wise?
And frost, and snowe, had manie winters seene:
Inquired, what in sommer was her guise.
Quoth she, I songe, and hop't in meadowes greene:
Then quoth the ante, content thee with thy chaunce,
For to thy songe, nowe art thou light to daunce?

Bilin-

A Satyre, and his hoste, in mid of winters rage,
At night, did hye them to the fire, the could for to aſſwage.
The man with could that quak'd, vpon his handes did blowe:
Which thinge the Satyre marked well, and crau'd the cauſe to knowe.
Who anſwere made, herewith my fingers I doe heate:
At lengthe when ſupper time was come, and bothe ſat downe to eate;
He likewiſe blewe his brothe, he tooke out of the potte:
Being likewiſe aſked why: (quoth hee) bicauſe it is to whotte.
To which the Satyre ſpake, and blow'ſt thou whotte, and coulde:
Hereafter, with ſuch double mouthes, I will no frendſhip houlde.
Which warneth all, to ſhonne a double tonged mate:
And let them neither ſuppe, nor dine, nor come within thy gate.

Aus de-

THE ſickly foxe, within her hole was hid,
Where, to the mouthe, the lion ſtraight did hye;
And did demaunde moſt frendly, how ſhee did,
And ſaide, his tonge woulde helpe her, by and by?
Bicauſe there was ſuch vertue hid therein,
That all he heal'd, if he did licke their ſkinne.

Then quoth the foxe, my Lorde? I doe not doubt,
But that your tonge is ſoueraigne, as I heare:
But yet, it hath ſuch neighbours round about?
It can not helpe, I iudge, while they be neare.
Wherefore, I wiſhe you woulde them baniſhe all?
Or ells, I thinke your pacients wilbee ſmall.

In malis promiſſis reſcinde fidẽ, in turpi voto muta decretũ, quod incautè vouiſti, non facias: impia eſt promiſſio, quæ ſcelere adimpletur Iſid. 2. Solilo.

THE crying babe, the mother ſharply threates,
Except he ceaſ'd, he ſhoulde to wolfe bee throwne:
Which being hard, the wolfe at windowe waites,
And made account that child ſhould bee his owne:
Till at the lengthe, agayne he hard her ſay
Feare not ſweete babe, thou ſhalt not bee his pray.

For, if he come in hope to ſucke thy blood,
Wee wil him kill, before he ſhall departe:
With that the wolfe retorned to the wood,
And did exclayme thus wiſe with heauie hart:
Oh Iupiter? what people now doe liue,
That promiſe much, and yet will nothing giue.

Pietas

AENEAS beares his father, out of Troye,
When that the Greekes, the ſame did ſpoile, and ſacke:
His father might of ſuche a ſonne haue ioye,
Who throughe his foes, did beare him on his backe:
No fier, nor ſworde, his valiaunt harte coulde feare,
To flee awaye, without his father deare.

Fœlix proles, quæ efficit vt g nuiſſe iuuet, generare libeat Max. lib 4.

Which ſhowes, that ſonnes muſt carefull bee, and kinde,
For to releeue their parentes in diſtreſſe:
And duringe life, that dutie ſhoulde them binde,
To reuerence them, that God their daies maie bleſſe:
And reprehendes tenne thowſande to their ſhame,
Who ofte diſpiſe the ſtocke whereof they came.

Hinc ſatus Æneas: pietas ſpectata per ignes:
Sacra patremq; humeris: altera ſacra, tulit.

Ouid. 4. Faſt.

To my Father M. GEFFREY WHITNEY.

Virgilius.
Mantua va misera nimium vicina Cremona.

Et Angel. Politianus in Manto sua.

Tu tamen ô, misera nimium vicina Cremona, Quid fles amissum: quid fles mea Mantua campum Pascentem niueos herboso flumine cycnas &c.

Et etiam apud Plautum, pauper Euclio recusat affinitatem cum diuite Megadoro. facetissime.

Ecclesiast. 13.
Et ditiori te ne socius fueris: Quid communicabit cacabus ad ollã? quando enim se colliserint, confringetur. Diues iniustè egit, & fremet: pauper autẽ læsus, tacebit. &c.

Ouid. 3. Trist. 4.
Viue sine inuidia, mollesque inglorius annos Exige, amicitias & tibi iunge pares.

TWO pottes, within a runninge streame weare toste,
The one of yearth, the other, was of brasse:
The brasen potte, who wish'd the other loste,
Did bid it staie, and neare her side to passe.
Whereby they might, togeather ioyned sure:
Without all doubt, the force of flood indure.

The earthen potte, then thus did answeare make,
This neighborhood doth put me much in feare?
I rather choose, my chaunce farre of to take,
Then to thy side, for to be ioyned neare,
For if wee hitte, my parte shalbe the wurste,
And thou shalt scape, when I am all to burste.

The running streame, this worldlie sea dothe shewe;
The pottes, present the mightie, and the pore:
Whoe here, a time are tossed too, and froe,
But if the meane, dwell nighe the mighties dore,
He maie be hurte, but cannot hurte againe,
Then like, to like: or beste alone remaine.

Past

TO M THOMAS MYNORS.

SHARPE prickes preserue the Rose, on euerie parte,
That who in haste to pull the same intendes,
Is like to pricke his fingers, till they smarte?
But being gotte, it makes him straight amendes
It is so freshe, and pleasant to the smell,
Thoughe he was prick'd, he thinkes he ventur'd well.
And he that faine woulde get the gallant rose,
And will not reache, for feare his fingers bleede;
A nettle, is more fitter for his nose?
Or hemblocke meete his appetite to feede?
None merites sweete, who tasted not the sower,
Who feares to climbe, deserues no fruicte, nor flower.
Which showes, we shoulde not fainte for anie paine,
For to atchieue the fruictes of our desire:
But still proceede, and hope at lengthe to gaine,
The thinges wee wishe, and craue with hartes entire:
Which all our toile, and labour, shal requite,
For after paine, comes pleasure, and delighte.
When winter endes, comes in the pleasant springe.
When nighte is done, the gladsome daye appeares.
When greifes be gone, then ioye doth make vs singe.
When stormes be paste, the varijng weather cleares.
So after paines, our pleasures make vs glad,
But without sower, the sweete is hardlie had.

Claud. in Rap[illegible] honor;
Non qu[illegible] fruitur veris odoribus.
Hyblaeos [illegible]
spoliat fauos,
Si fronti caueat, si ti-meat rubos.
Armat spina [illegible]
mella tegunt apes.

Dulcia non [illegible]
non gustauit a[illegible]

To my vncle GEFFREY CARTWRIGHTE.

THOVGHE Sathan striue, with all his maine, and mighte,
To hide the truthe; and dimme the lawe deuine:
Yet to his worde, the Lorde doth giue such lighte,
That to the East, and West, the same doth shine:
And those, that are so happie for to looke,
Saluation finde, within that blessed booke.

Si Deus nobiscum, quis contra nos?

De Vipera Aelian. lib. 15. ca. 16 & Plin. De natur. hist. lib. 8. ca. 39. & lib. 10. cap. 62.

Act. 28. Tremelius

HIS seruauntes GOD preserues, though they in danger fall:
Euen as from vipers deadlie*bite, he kept th'Appostle Paule.

Cuth

Ad Dn. IOHANNEM CROXTON.

TIMES chaunge, and wee doe alter in the same,
And in one staye, there nothing still maye bee:
What Monarches greate, that wanne the chiefest fame,
But stealinge time, their birthe, and deathe, did see:
Firste NESTOR suck'd, and HOMER first was taughte,
Bothe famous once, yet both to dust are broughte.

Wee first are younge, and then to age wee yeelde,
Then flit awaye, as we had not bene borne:
No wight so stronge, but time doth winne the feelde,
Yea wonders once, are out of memorie worne:
This Ægypte spires, and Babell, sawe in fine,
When they did mounte, and when they did decline.

Ouid. 6. Fast.
Tempora labuntur t citisq. senescimus ann Et fugiunt freno n remorante dies.

Fœlix qui propriis æuum transegit in aruis,
Ipsa domus puerum quem videt ipsa senem;
Qui baculo nitens, in qua reptauit arena,
Vnius numerat sæcula longa casæ:
Illum non vario traxit fortuna tumultu,
Nec bibit ignotas mobilis hospes aquas.

Claud. de Senec. Veronensi.

Et pauló póst.
Ingentem meminit par ue qui gramine quercũ Æquæuumque v consenuisse nemus.

Si nihil

To M. MATTHEW PATTENSON.

Ouid. 3. Amor. 7.
Ingenium quondã fuerat preciosius auro.
At nunc barbaria est grandis, habere nihil.

SOMETIME was witte esteem'de, of greater price then goulde:
But wisedome pore, maie nowe goe begge? and starue without for coulde.
Yea, thoughe that Homer come, with all the Muses guarde,
Yet if he nothinge bringe? must faste, and stande within the yarde?

Ingenium superat vires.

Ouid. 2. Pont.
Adde quod ingenuas didicisse fideliter artes,
Emollit mores, nec sinit esse feros.

MANS wisedome great, doth farre surpasse his strengthe,
For proofe, behoulde, no man could bende the bowe:
But yet, his witte deuised at the lengthe,
To winde the stringe so farre as it shoulde goe:
Then wisedome chiefe, and strengthe, must come behinde,
But bothe be good, and giftes from God assignde.

In fœneratores.

AN vſerer, whoſe Idol was his gouldе,
Within his houſe, a peeuiſhe ape retain'd:
A ſeruaunt fitte, for ſuche a miſer oulde,
Of whome both mockes, and apiſhe mowes, he gain'd.
Thus, euerie daie he made his maſter ſporte,
And to his clogge, was chained in the courte.
At lengthe it hap'd? while greedie graundſir din'de?
The ape got looſe, and founde a windowe ope:
Where in he leap'de, and all about did finde,
The GOD, wherein the Miſer put his hope?
Which ſoone he broch'd, and forthe with ſpeede did flinge,
And did delighte on ſtones to heare it ringe?
The ſighte, righte well the paſſers by did pleaſe,
Who did reioyce to finde theſe goulden crommes:
That all their life, their pouertie did eaſe.
Of goodes ill got, loe heere the fruicte that commes.
Looke herevppon, you that haue MIDAS minte,
And bee poſſeſte with hartes as harde as flinte.
Shut windowes cloſe, leſte apes doe enter in,
And doe diſperſe your goulde, you doe adore.
But woulde you learne to keepe, that you do winne?
Then get it well, and hourde it not in ſtore.
If not: no boultes, nor braſen barres will ſerue,
For GOD will waſte your ſtocke, and make your ſterue.

Si neceſſariis contenti eſſemus, minimè vſurariorum genus peſſimum inueniretur Plutarch. de vſur. vit.

Auaritia omnia in ſe vitia habet. Aul. Gell. lib. 11 cap. 2. Et idem lib. 3. cap. 1.

THE greedie kyte, so full his gorge had cloy'de,
He coulde not brooke his late deuoured praie:
Wherefore with griefe, vnto his damme hee cry'de,
My bowelles lo, alas doe waste awaie.
With that quoth shee, why doste thou make thy mone,
This losse thou haste is nothinge of thy owne.

Cato De re Rust. Peior ciuis existimatur fœnerator, quàm fur.

By which is mente, that they who liue by spoile,
By rapine, thefte, or grippinge goodes by mighte,
If that with losse they suffer anie foile,
They loose but that, wherein they had no righte?
Hereof, at firste the prouerbe oulde did growe:
That goodes ill got, awaie as ill will goe.

De malè quæsitis vix gaudet tertius hæres.

Vsus

Ad D. A. P.

THE volumes great, who so doth still peruse,
And dailie turnes, and gazeth on the same,
If that the fruicte thereof, he do not vse,
He reapes but toile, and neuer gaineth fame:
Firste reade, then marke, then practise that is good,
For without vse, we drinke but LETHE flood.

Of practise longe, experiense doth proceede;
And wisedome then, doth euermore ensue:
Then printe in minde, what wee in printe do reade,
Els loose wee time, and bookes in vaine do vewe:
Wee maie not haste, our talent to bestowe,
Nor hide it vp, whereby no good shall growe.

Lectio multorum voluminum, & omnis generis auctorum, habet aliquid vagum & instabile: certis* ingeniis immorari & innutriri oportet, si velis aliquid trahere, quod in animo fideliter sedeat. Senec. 1. Epist. 2.

melius fortè, certis ingenia [illegible]

Ad iuuentutem Scholæ Aldelemensis in Angliâ.

WHILES prime of youthe, is freshe within his flower,
Take houlde of time: for it doth haste awaye.
Watche, write, and reade, and spende no idle hower,
Inritche your mindes with some thinge, euerie daye:
For losse of time, all other losse exceedes,
And euermore it late repentaunce breedes.

Ouid. 3. Art.
Nec quæ præteriit cursu, reuocabitur vnda:
Nec quæ præterijt hora, redire potest.
Vtendũ est ætate, cito pede labitur ætas,
Nec bona tam sequitur quàm bona prima fuit.

The idle sorte, that ignoraunce doe taste,
Are not esteem'd, when they in yeares doe growe:
The studious, are with vnderstanding grac'd,
And still prefer'd, thoughe first their caulinge lowe.
Then haue regarde, to banishe idle fittes,
And in your youthe, with skill adorne your wittes.

Whereby, in time such hap maye you aduaunce,
As bothe your Towne, and countrie, you maye frende:
For, what I woulde vnto my selfe shoulde chaunce:
To you I wishe, wheare I my prime did spende.
Wherefore behoulde this candle, booke, and glasse:
To vse your time, and knowe how time dothe passe.

Studia, quæ sunt in adolescentia, tanquam in herbis significant, quæ virtutis maturitas, & quantæ fruges industriæ sint futuræ. Cicero pro Cœlio.

Præcocia

Doctissimo viro D. STEPHANO LIMBERTO *Nordouicensis Scholæ Magistro.*

THE fruicte that soonest ripes, doth soonest fade awaie.
And that which slowlie hath his time, will not so soone decaie.
Our writing in the duste, can not indure a blaste:
But that, which is in marble wroughte, from age, to age, doth laste.
Euen so it is of wittes, some quicke, to put in vre:
Some dull to learne, but oftentimes the slowe are sounde, and sure.
And thoughe the apte, and prompte: soone learne, and soone forget.
Yet ofte the dull doe beare in minde, what first therein was set.
Hereof the prouerbe comes: *Soone ripe, soone rotten turnes*:
And greenest wood, though kindlinge longe, yet whottest most it burnes.

Omnis profectus a lectione & meditatione procedit. quæ enim nescimus, lectione discimus: quæ didicimus, meditatione conseruamus. Isid. lib. 3. De summo bono.

O formose puer, nimium ne crede colori.
Alba ligustra cadunt, vaccinia nigra leguntur.

Virg. Eclog. 2

IF ſence I had, my owne eſtate to knowe,
Before all trees, my ſelfe hath cauſe to crie:
In euerie hedge, and common waye, I growe,
Where, I am made a praye, to paſſers by:
And when, they ſee my nuttes are ripe, and broune,
My bowghes are broke, my leaues are beaten doune.

Alciatus. *Quid sterili poſſet contingere turpius? eheu, Infelix, fructus in mea damna fero.*

Thus euerie yeare, when I doe yeelde increaſe,
My proper fruicte, my ruine doth procure:
If fruictleſſe I, then had I growen in peace,
Oh barrennes, of all moſt happie, ſure

Sueton. in vita Neronis.

Which wordes with griefe, did AGRIPPINA grone,
And mothers more, whoſe children made them mone.

Locus è nuce Ouidiana.

Certè ego ſi nunquam peperiſſem, tutior eſſem:
Iſta Clytemneſtra digna querela fuit.

Otioſi

HERE, Idlenes doth weepe amid her wantes,
Neare famished: whome, labour whippes for Ire:
Here, labour sittes in chariot drawen with antes:
And dothe abounde with all he can desire.
The grashopper, the toyling ante derides,
In Sommers heate, cause she for coulde prouides.

But when the coulde of winter did increase,
Out of her hill, the ante did looke for newes:
Whereas she harde the grashopper to cease,
And all her songes, shee nowe with sighing rues:
But all to late, for now for foode she staru'd,
Whereas the ante had store, she had preseru'd.

All which doe warne, while that our Sommer lastes,
Which is our youthe: with freshe, and liuelie strengthe.
Wee muste prouide, for winters bitter blastes.
Which is our age: that claimes his righte at lengthe.
Wherefore in youthe, let vs prouide for age;
For ere wee thinke he stealeth on the stage,

Semper

THREE carelesse dames, amongste their wanton toies,
Did throwe the dice, who firste of them shoulde die:
And shee that loste, did laughe with inwarde ioyes,
For that, shee thoughte her terme shoulde longer bee:
But loe, a tyle vppon her head did fall,
That deathe, with speede, this dame from dice did call

Cuiuis potest accidere, quod cuiquam potest. Senec. de tranquil. animi.

Euen so, it falles, while carelesse times wee spende:
That euell happes, vnlooked for doe comme.
But if wee hope, that GOD some good wil sende,
In earnest praier, then must wee not bee domme:
For blessinges good, come seild before our praier,
But euell thinges doe come before we feare.

Ouid. 4. Pont.

Ludit in humanis diuina potentia rebus,
Et certam præsens vix habet hora fidem.

Vnica

To my countrimen of the Namptwiche *in Cheshire.*

THE Phœnix rare, with fethers freshe of hewe,
ARABIAS righte, and sacred to the Sonne:
Whome, other birdes with wonder seeme to vewe,
Dothe liue vntill a thousande yeares bee ronne:
Then makes a pile: which, when with Sonne it burnes
Shee flies therein, and so to ashes turnes.
Whereof, behoulde, an other Phœnix rare,
With speede dothe rise most beautifull and faire:
And thoughe for truthe, this manie doe declare,
Yet thereunto, I meane not for to sweare:
Althoughe I knowe that Aucthors witnes true,
What here I write, bothe of the oulde, and newe.
Which when I wayed, the newe, and eke the oulde,
I thought vppon your towne destroyed with fire:
And did in minde, the newe NAMPWICHE behoulde,
A spectacle for anie mans desire:
Whose buildinges braue, where cinders weare but late,
Did represente (me thought) the Phœnix fate.
And as the oulde, was manie hundreth yeares,
A towne of fame, before it felt that crosse:
Euen so, (I hope) this WICHE, that nowe appeares,
A Phœnix age shall laste, and knowe no losse:
Which GOD vouchsafe, who make you thankfull, all:
That see this rise, and sawe the other fall.

Paradis. poët.
Solus in Eois ales [illegible] parabilis oris,
Igne suo vitam d[illegible] rapit, igne capit.

Mart. lib. 5. Epigr[illegible]
Qualiter Assyrios [illegible] nouant incendia nid[illegible]
Vna decem quoti[illegible] secula vixit auis.

Quæ quidem [illegible] iuxta Plinium, N[illegible] tural. histor. lib. [illegible] cap. 2. viuit ad se[illegible] centos sexaginta [illegible] nos. quo [illegible] alia quædam [illegible] giosa [illegible] rantur, quæ, [illegible] niam ad Emblem[illegible] tis sententiam nil [illegible] attinent, cui libet [illegible] legenda relinquo. & apud Ælian. [illegible] Anim. lib. 6. cap. [illegible]

Ouid. Met. lib [illegible]
Vna est quæ reparet [illegible]
[illegible]
Assy[illegible] [illegible]
[illegible]
Sed thuris lacrymis, [illegible]
succo viuit amomi, &c

Cælum, non animum.

To R. P.

WHY fleeſt thou throughe the worlde? in hope to alter kinde:
No forren ſoile, hath anie force to change the inward minde.
Thou doſte but alter aire, thou altereſt not thy thoughte:
No diſtance farre can wipe awaye, what Nature firſt hath wroughte.
The foole, that farre is ſente ſome wiſedome to attaine:
Returnes an Ideot, as he wente, and bringes the foole againe.
Propertius 3,7. *Natura ſequitur ſemina quiſque ſua.*
Where rancor firſte hathe roote, it growes, liue where wee ſhall:
And where as malice is by kinde, no abſence helpes at all.
The catte, in countries kepte, where are no myſe for praye,
Yet, being broughte where they doe breede, her ſelfe ſhee doth bewraye.
The beaſtes of crewell kinde, where hate, by nature growes,
Thoughe parted longe, yet when they meete, become moſt deadlie foes,
Which prooues, no trauaile farre, no coaſte, nor countrie ſtraunge:
Hath anie force to alter kinde, or Natures worke to chaunge.

Propert. 2, 30.

Quo fugis ah demens? nulla eſt fuga: tu licet vſque
Ad Tanaim fugias, vſque ſequetur amor.

DESIRE to haue, dothe make vs muche indure,
In trauaile, toile, and labour voide of reſte:
The marchant man is caried with this lure,
Throughe ſcorching heate, to regions of the Eaſte:
Oh thirſte of goulde, what not? but thou canſt do:
And make mens hartes for to conſent thereto.

The trauailer poore, when ſhippe doth ſuffer wracke,
Who hopes to ſwimme vnto the wiſhed lande,
Dothe venture life, with fardle on his backe,
That if he ſcape, the ſame in ſteede maye ſtande.
Thus, hope of life, and loue vnto his goods,
Houldes vp his chinne, with burthen in the floods.

Horat. lib. 1. Epiſt. *Impiger extremos cu mercator ad Indos, Per mare pauper fugiens per ſaxa pe ignes.*

WHO lookes, maye leape: and saue his shinnes from knockes.
Who tries, maye truste: els flattringe frendes shall finde.
He saues the steede, that keepes him vnder lockes.
Who speakes with heede, maye bouldlie speake his minde.
But hee, whose tonge before his witte, doth runne,
Ofte speakes to soone, and greeues when he hathe done.

> Praui sicut in sensu leues, ita sunt in locutione præcipites: Quia quod leuis cõscientia concipit, leuior protinus lingua prodit. Greg. Homil. 5.

A worde once spoke, it can retourne no more,
But flies awaie, and ofte thy bale doth breede:
A wise man then, settes hatche before the dore,
And while he maye, doth square his speeche with heede.
The birde in hande, wee maye at will restraine,
But beinge flowen, wee call her backe in vaine.

> Horat. Epist. 18. *Et semel emissum volat irreuocabile verbum.*

> Et si vtile est subitò sæpe dicere, tamen illud vtilius, sumpto spacio ad cogitandum paratius, atque accuratius dicere. Cicero 1 De Orator.

In o-

To my Kinſman M. GEFFREY WHITNEY.

WHAT creature thou? *Occaſion I doe ſhowe.*
On whirling wheele declare why doſte thou ſtande?
Bicauſe, I ſtill am toſſed too, and froe.
Why doeſt thou houlde a raſor in thy hande?
That men maie knowe I cut on euerie ſide,
And when I come, I armies can deuide.

Horat. lib. 1. Ep. ad Bullatium.
Tu quamcumque tibi fortunauerit h
Grata ſume manu dulcia differ in ann

But wherefore haſt thou winges vppon thy feete?
To ſhowe, how lighte I flie with little winde.
What meanes longe lockes before? *that ſuche as meete,*
Maye houlde at firſte, when they occaſion finde.
Thy head behinde all balde, what telles it more?
That none ſhoulde houlde, that let me ſlippe before.

Why doeſt thou ſtande within an open place?
That I maye warne all people not to ſtaye,
But at the firſte, occaſion to imbrace,
And when ſhee comes, to meete her by the waye.
Lyſippus ſo did thinke it beſt to bee,
Who did deuiſe mine image, as you ſee.

Palladius Soranus.
Omnia vincit amor, superum rex mugit in arvis,
Palluit & Titan, omnia vincit amor.
Omnia vincit amor, flexit Proserpina ditem,
Martē blanda Venus, omnia vincit amor.
Omnia vincit amor, barbam Polyphemus adornat,
Pan se vidit aquis, omnia vincit amor.
Omnia vincit amor, feruet Neptunus in undis,
Neuit & Alcides, omnia vincit amor.
Omnia vincit amor, Salomō, & Scipio victi,
Ilion euersum est, omnia vincit amor.
Omnia vincit amor cælos, & Tartara, & vrbes,
Et nemora, & pisces, omnia vincit amor.

HERE, naked loue doth sit, with smilinge cheare,
No bended bowe, nor quiuer he doth beare:
One hande, a fishe: the other houldes a flower:
Of Sea, and Lande, to shewe that he hath power.

Pulchritudo vincit.

To the fairest.

WHEN creatures firste weare form'd, they had by natures lawes,
The bulles, their hornes: the horses, hooses: the lions, teeth, and pawes.
To hares, shee swiftenes gaue: to fishes, finnes assign'de:
To birdes, their winges: so no defence was lefte for woman kinde.
But, to supplie that wante, shee gaue her suche a face:
Which makes the boulde, the fierce, the swifte, to stoope, and pleade for grace.

Quo

EVEN as the waxe dothe feede, and quenche the flame,
So, loue giues life; and loue, diſpaire doth giue:
The godlie loue, doth louers croune with fame:
The wicked loue, in ſhame dothe make them liue.
Then leaue to loue, or loue as reaſon will,
For, louers lewde doe vainlie languiſhe ſtill.

Scribit in marmore læſus.

IN marble harde our harmes wee alwayes graue,
Bicauſe, wee ſtill will beare the ſame in minde:
In duſte wee write the benifittes wee haue,
Where they are ſoone defaced with the winde.
So, wronges wee houlde, and neuer will forgiue,
And ſoone forget, that ſtill with vs ſhoulde liue.

To Aphilus.

A snarlinge curre, did in the manger lie,
Who rather steru'd? then made the haye, his meate,
Yet shew'd his fanges, and offred for to flie
Vppon the oxe, who hungred for to eate.
And there throughe spite, did keepe the oxe from foode:
Vntill for wante, hee faynted as hee stoode.

Inuidus alienas iacturas, suos quæstus existimat. Chrys. super Math. Homil. 41.

The couetous man enuious, here behoulde,
Who hath inowghe, yet vse thereof doth lacke:
And doth enuie his needie neighbour, shoulde
But get a groate, if he coulde houlde it backe?
Who, thoughe they doe possesse the diuill, and all?
Yet are they like the dogge, in oxes stall?

Scripta

Ad doctiß. virum D. St. Bullum.

LO, here Quinctilius sittes, a graue and reuerende sire:
And pulles a younglinge by the arme, that did for fame desire.
For, hee with pace of snayle, proceeded to his pen;
Lest haste shoulde make him wishe (too late) it weare to write againe.
And therfore still with care, woulde euerie thinge amende:
Yea, ofte eche worde, and line suruaye, before hee made an ende.
And, yf he any sawe, whose care to wryte was small:
To him, like wordes to these hee vs'd, which hee did meane to all.
My sonne, what worke thou writes, correcte, reforme, amende,
But if thou like thy first assaye, then not Quinctilius frende.
The fruicte at firste is sower, till time giue pleasante taste:
And verie rare is that attempte, that is not harm'd with haste.
Perfection comes in time, and forme and fashion giues:
And euer rashenes, yeeldes repente, and most dispised liues.
Then, alter ofte, and chaunge, peruse, and reade, and marke.
The man that softlie settes his steppes, goes safest in the darke.
But if that thirst of fame, doe pricke thee forthe too faste:
Thou shalt (when it is all to late) repente therefore at laste.

Quinctilij Var. censura de scriptis edendis Horat. Art. poet.

Ouid. 3. Fast. *Differ, habent parua commoda magna mora*

Senec. Agam. *Proinde quicquid est, da spacium & tempus tibi: Quod ratio nequit, sæpe sanauit mora.*

Ad eundem.

LO, ORPHEVS with his harpe, that sauage kinde did tame:
The Lions fierce, and Leopardes wilde, and birdes about him caine.
For, with his musicke sweete, their natures hee subdu'de:
But if wee thinke his playe so wroughte, our selues wee doe delude.
For why? besides his skill, hee learned was, and wise:
And coulde with sweetenes of his tonge, all sortes of men suffice.
And those that weare most rude, and knewe no good at all:
And weare of fierce, and cruell mindes, the worlde did brutishe call.
Yet with persuasions sounde, hee made their hartes relente,
That meeke, and milde they did become, and followed where he wente.
Lo these, the Lions fierce, these, Beares, and Tigers weare:
The trees, and rockes, that lefte their roomes, his musicke for to heare.
But, you are happie most, who in suche place doe staye:
You neede not THRACIA seeke, to heare some impe of ORPHEVS playe.
Since, that so neare your home, Apollos darlinge dwelles;
Who LINVS, & AMPHION staynes, and ORPHEVS farre excelles.
For, hartes like marble harde, his harmonie dothe pierce:
And makes them yeelding passions feele, that are by nature fierce.
But, if his musicke faile: his curtesie is suche,
That none so rude, and base of minde, but hee reclaimes them muche.
Nowe since you, by deserte, for both, commended are:
I choose you, for a Iudge herein, if truthe I doe declare.
And if you finde I doe, then ofte therefore reioyce:
And thinke, I woulde suche neighbour haue, if I might make my choice.

Horat. Art. poet.
Syluestres homines sacer interpresq. deorum, Cadibus & fœdo victu deterruit Orpheus; Dictus ob hoc lenire tigres, rapidosq. leones.

E. P. Esquier.

Propert. lib. 2. de Lino.
Tunc ego sim Inachio notior arte Lino.
De Amphione Horat. in Art. poet.
Dictus & Amphion Thebana conditor urbis Saxa mouere sono testudinis, & prece blanda Ducere quo vellet, &c.

In sta-

THE timelie birthe that SEMELE did beare,
See heere, in time howe monsterous he grewe:
With drinkinge muche, and dailie bellie cheare,
His eies weare dimme, and fierie was his hue:
His cuppe, still full: his head, with grapes was croun'de;
Thus time he spent with pipe, and tabret sounde.

Ouid. 3. Met.

Anac. apud Diog. Vitis tres vuas fert, primam voluptatis, secũdam ebrietatis, tertiam mœroris.

Which carpes all those, that loue to much the canne,
And dothe describe theire personage, and theire guise:
For like a beaste, this doth transforme a man,
And makes him speake that moste in secret lies;
Then, shunne the sorte that bragge of drinking muche,
Seeke other frendes, and ioyne not handes with suche.

Chrys. Hom. 46. Ebrietas, tempestas est tam in animo, quàm in corpore.

Iunge tibi socios pulchræ virtutis amore,
Nam Venere & Baccho iuncta repentè cadunt.

Iohan. Samb. in Epigr.

Vino forma perit, vino corrumpitur ætas,
Vino sæpè suum nescit amica virum?

Propertius.

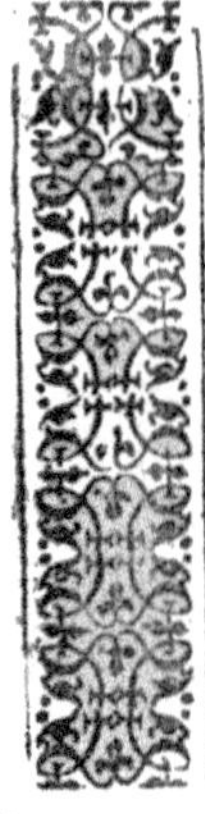

WITH kindenes, lo, the Ape doth kill her whelpe,
Throughe claſping harde, and lulling in her armes.
Euen ſo, the babes, whoſe nature, Arte ſhoulde helpe:
The parents fonde doe hazarde them with harmes,
And worke their ſpoile, and bringe them vnto naughte,
When fooliſhe loue forbiddes them to bee taughte.

In bello ferrum auro præſtat; in vita autem eruditio diuitiis. Socrat. apud Stob.

Admirata putat formoſum Simia fœtum:
Nempe ſolet pulchrum cuique placere ſuum.

Nic. Reuſnerus.

Maturandum.

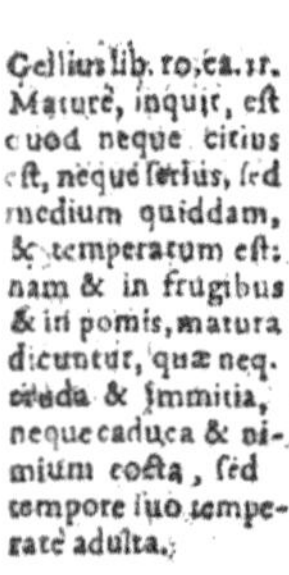

Gellius lib. 10. ca. 11. Maturè, inquit, eſt quod neque citius eſt, neque ſerius, ſed medium quiddam, & temperatum eſt: nam & in frugibus & in pomis, matura dicuntur, quæ neq. cruda & immitia, neque caduca & nimium cocta, ſed tempore ſuo temperatè adulta.

ABOVTE the arrowe ſwifte, ECHENEIS ſlowe doth foulde:
Which, biddes vs in our actions haſte, no more then reaſon woulde.

Ælian. de Animal. lib. 2. ca. 17. & Plin. lib. 9. cap. 25. & lib. 32. cap. 1. vbi multa mirabilia de Echeneid-piſce ſcribit. & quædam notatu digna quæ ſua memoria acciderũt.

In ſinu

In ſinu alere ſerpentem.

Ad Doctiſs. V. D. FRANCISCVM RAPHELENGIVM *in obſidione Antwerpiana periclitantem.*

THOVGHE, cittie ſtronge the cannons ſhotte diſpiſe,
And deadlie foes, beſéege the ſame in vaine:
Yet, in the walles if pining famine riſe,
Or elſe ſome impe of SINON, there remaine.
What can preuaile your bulwarkes? and your towers,
When, all your force, your inwarde foe deuoures.

In deſciſcentes.

WHEN that with milke, the goate had fil'd the pot,
Shee brake the ſame, that all about it ranne.
Wherat, the maide her pacience quite forgot,
And in a rage, the brutiſhe beaſte did banne?
Which toye, thoughe ſhorte, yet ſharply reprehendes
Beginnings good, that haue vnhappie endes.

Stultorum quantò ſtatus ſublimior, tantò manifeſtior turpitudo.

PROMOOTE the foole, his folly doth appeare,
And is a ſhame to them, that make him clime;
Whoſe faultes, before coulde not bee ſeene ſo cleare,
For lowe eſtate did ſhadowe euery crime:
But ſet him vp, his folly ſoone is harde,
Then keepe him doune, let wiſe men bee preſer'de.

Bis dat qui citò dat.

DOE not thine almes deferre, when neede doth bid thee haſte:
For why, one gifte is double thought, that in due time is plaſte.

Or ſo.

WHEN to the pore thou giu'ſt, make ſpeede the ſame to doe:
Bycauſe one gifte in time beſtowed, is worthe ſome other two.

Spes

THE eager haulke, with ſodaine ſighte of lure
Doth ſtoope, in hope to haue her wiſhed praye:
So, manie men do ſtoope to ſightes vnſure:
And curteous ſpeeche, dothe keepe them at the baye.
Let ſuche beware, leſt frendlie lookes be like,
The lure, to which the ſoaring haulke did ſtrike?

Ouid. Epiſt. 16.
Fallitur augurio ſpes bona ſæpe ſuo.

Audi, tace, fuge.

To my Nephew RO. BORRON.

HEARE much; but little ſpeake; and flee from that is naught:
Which leſſons, by theſe formes in briefe, to euery one are taught.

Vnworth-

WHO that with force, his burnish'd blade doth trie
On anuill harde, to prooue if it be sure:
Doth Hazarde muche, it shoulde in peeces flie,
Aduentring that, which else mighte well indure:
For, there with strengthe he strikes vppon the stithe,
That men maye knowe, his youthfull armes haue pithe.

Which warneth those, that louinge frendes inioye,
With care, to keepe, and frendlie them to treate,
And not to trye them still, with euerie toye,
Nor presse them doune, when causes be too greate,
Nor in requests importunate to bee:
For ouermuche, dothe tier the courser free.

Strenuo.

To the honorable Gentleman, Sir WILLIAM RVSSELL *Knight.*

ACHILLES tombe vpon SIGÆA ſhore,
This repreſentes: where THETIS ofte was ſeene:
And for his loſſe, did ſeeme for to deplore,
With gallant flower the ſame was alwaies greene:
And at the toppe, a palme did freſhelie bloome;
Whoſe braunches ſweete did ouerſpread the toombe.

Which ſhewes, thoughe deathe the valiaunt ouerthrowe,
Yet after fate, their fame remaines behinde:
And triumphes ſtill, and dothe no conqueſt knowe,
But is the badge of euerie noble minde;
And when in graue their corpes incloſed lye,
Their famous actes doe pierce the azure ſkye.

Aliij in Rhet littore: ſed ali Claud. Min. per Alciatũ, Emblem. 48. & Emblem. 135. & Plin. Natural Hiſtor. libro cap. 30.

Nunquam Stygias fertur ad vmbras
Inclyta virtus: viuite fortes
Nec Lethaos ſaua per amnes
Vos fata trahent: ſed cum ſummas
Exiget auras conſumpta dies,
Iter ad ſuperos gloria pandet.

Sen. Her. Fur Oet. act. 5.

b *Vel*

To the honorable Sir IOHN NORRIS *Knight, Lord preſident of Munſter in Irelande, and Colonell Generall of the Engliſhe Infanterie, in the lowe countries.*

A Secret cauſe, that none can comprehende,
In natures workes is often to bee ſeene;
As, deathe can not the ancient diſcorde ende,
Plin. De Nat. Hiſt. lib.17. cap.4. That raigneth ſtill, the wolfe, and ſheepe betweene:
The like, beſide in many thinges are knowne,
The cauſe reueal'd, to none, but GOD alone.

For, as the wolfe, the ſillye ſheepe did feare,
And made him ſtill to tremble, at his barke:
So beinge dead, which is moſte ſtraunge to heare,
This feare remaynes, as learned men did marke;
Claud. Min. ſuper Alciatum, Emb.117. For with their ſkinnes, if that two drommes bee bounde,
That, clad with ſheepe, doth iarre: and hathe no ſounde.

And, if that ſtringes bee of their intrailes wroughte,
And ioyned both, to make a ſiluer ſounde:
No cunninge eare can tune them as they oughte,
But one is harde, the other ſtill is droun'de:
Or diſcordes foule, the harmonie doe marre;
And nothinge can appeaſe this inward warre.

So, ZISCA thoughte when deathe did ſhorte his daies,
As with his voice, hee erſte did daunte his foes;

That after deathe hee shoulde newe terror raise,
And make them flee, as when they felte his bloes.
Wherefore, hee charg'd that they his skinne shoulde frame,
To fitte a dromme, and marche forth with the same.

Æneas Siluius 3. Comment. De rebus gestis Alphons.

So, HECTORS sighte greate feare in Greekes did worke,
When hee was showed on horsebacke, beeinge dead:
HVNIADES, the terrour of the Turke,
Thoughe layed in graue, yet at his name they fled:
And cryinge babes, they ceased with the same,
The like in FRANCE, sometime did TALBOTS name.

Cœlius Curio.

Fortes, & magnanimi habendi sunt, non qui faciunt, sed qui propulsant iniuriam Cic. 1. offic.

Victoria cruenta.

To Sir WILLIAM STANDLEY *Knight.*

THE Olephante with stinge of serpent fell,
That still about his legges, with winding cralles:
Throughe poison stronge, his bodie so did swell,
That doune he sinkes, and on the serpente falles:
Which creature huge, did fall vppon him soe,
That by his deathe, he also kill'd his foe.

Those sharpe conflictes, those broiles and battailes maine,
That are atchieude, with spoile on either parte:
Where streames of blood the hilles, and valleys staine,
And what is wonne, the price is deathe, and smarte:
This dothe importe: But those are captaines good,
That winne the fielde, with sheddinge leaste of blood.

Non est tanti gaudij excelsa tenere, quanti mœroris est, de excelsis corruere: nec tanta gloria sequi potest victoriam, quanta ignominia potest sequi ruinam. Ami.

To Edwarde Dier Esquier.

The Erle of Surrey, that wrat the booke of Songes and Sonettes.

When frowning fatall dame, that stoppes our course in fine,
The thred of noble Svrreys life, made hast for to vntwine.
Apollo chang'd his cheare, and lay'd awaie his lute,
And Pallas, and the Muses sad, did weare a mourninge sute.
And then, the goulden pen, in case of sables cladde,
Was lock'd in chiste of Ebonie, and to Parnassus had.
But, as all times do chaunge, so passions haue their space;
And cloudie skies at lengthe are clear'd, with Phœbus chearefull face.
For, when that barren verse made Muses voide of mirthe:
Behoulde, Lvsina sweetelie sounge, of Sidneys ioyfull birthe.

Sir Philip Sidney knighte.

Whome mightie Iove did blesse, with graces from aboue:
On whome, did fortune frendlie smile, and nature most did loue.
And then, behoulde, the pen, was by Mercvrivs sente,
Wherewith, hee also gaue to him, the gifte for to inuente.
That, when hee first began, his vayne in verse to showe.
More sweete then honie, was the stile, that from his penne did flowe.
Wherewith, in youthe hee vs'd to bannishe idle fittes;
That nowe, his workes of endlesse fame, delighte the worthie wittes.

No haul-

No haulting verse hee writes, but matcheth former times,
No*Cherillus, he can abide, nor Poëttes patched rimes.
What volumes hath hee writte, that rest among his frendes,
Which needes no other praise at all, eche worke it selfe comendes.
So, that hee famous liues, at home, and farre, and neare;
For those that liue in other landes, of SIDNEY'S giftes doe heare.
And suche as Muses serue, in darkenes meere doe dwell;
If that they haue not seene his workes, they doe so farre excell.
Wherefore, for to extoll his name in what I might,
This Embleme lo, I did present, vnto this woorthie Knight.
Who, did the same refuse, as not his proper due:
And at the first, his sentence was, it did belonge to you.
Wherefore, lo, fame with trompe, that mountes vnto the skye:
And, farre aboue the highest spire, from pole, to pole dothe flye.
Heere houereth at your will, with pen adorn'd with baies:
Which for you bothe, shee hath prepar'd, vnto your endlesse praise.
The laurell leafe for you, for him, the goulden pen;
The honours that the Muses giue, vnto the rarest men.
Wherefore, proceede I praye, vnto your lasting fame;
For writinges last when wee bee gonne, and doe preserue our name.
And whilst wee tarrye heere, no treasure can procure,
The palme that waites vpon the pen, which euer doth indure.
Two thousand yeares, and more, HOMERVS wrat his booke;
And yet, the same doth still remayne, and keepes his former looke.
Wheare Ægypte spires bee gonne, and ROME doth ruine feele,
Yet, both begonne since he was borne, thus time doth turne the wheele.
Yea, thoughe some Monarche greate some worke should take in hand,
Of marble, or of Adamant, that manie worldes shoulde stande,
Yet, should one only man, with labour of the braine,
Bequeathe the world a monument, that longer shoulde remaine,
And when that marble waules, with force of time should waste;
It should indure from age, to age, and yet no age should taste.
Oh happie you therfore, who spend your blessed daies
In seruing GOD, your Prince, your lande, vnto your endlesse praise.
And daily doe proceede, with trauaile of the minde,
To make you famous heere, and eeke, to leaue a fame behinde.
Which is the cheefest thinge, the greatest Prince can haue,
For, fame doth triumphe ouer deathe, when corpes are clos'd in graue.
Euen so, your worthie workes, when you in peace shall sleepe,
Shall make reporte of your desertes, and DIERS name shall keepe,
Whome, I doe reuerence still, as one of PALLAS peares:
And praye the Lorde, with ioyfull dayes for to prolonge your yeares.

*Horat. lib. Epist. 1. ad Augustum.

Homerus vixit Romam condi sed natus ante, Gell. lib. 17. ca

Sed Plinius sec qui ante Gelli tempore Vesp Imperatoris vi De Homeri ae lib. 7. ca. 16. N Histor: sic scri *Iam verò antè a propè mille, vat Homerus non ce &c.* Et Corn Nepos primo nicorum antè mam, Homer vixisse scribit.

De Pyramidu tate, incertum Natural. hist. li cap. 12. tamen dam post Hom conditas, prob De his, Herod

Animus

To EDWARD PASTON *Esquier.*

IN christall towers, and turrets richlie sette
With glittering gemmes, that shine against the sonne:
In regall roomes of Iasper, and of Iette,
Contente of minde, not alwaies likes to wonne:
  But oftentimes, it pleaseth her to staye
  In simple cotes, closde in with walles of claye.

Erasm. Chiliad. 61. Centuria 8. de Diogene, & quid per vitam doliatem: significatur.

DIOGENES, within a tonne did dwell,
No choice of place, nor store of pelfe he had;
And all his goodes, coulde BIAS beare right well,
And CODRVS had small cates, his harte to gladde:
  His meate was rootes: his table, was a stoole,
  Yet these for witte, did set the worlde to scoole.

Iuuenalis: *Tota domus Codri rheda componitur una.*

Horat. lib: 1. epist. 2. *Qui cupit, aut metuit, iuuat illum sic domus, aut res; Vt lippum picta tabula, fomenta podagram; Auriculas cithara collecta sorde dolentis.*

Who couettes still, or hee that liues in feare,
As much delighte is wealthe vnto his minde,
As musicke is to him, that can not heare,
Or pleasante showes, and pictures, to the blinde:
  Then sweete content, ofte likes the meane estate,
  Which is exempte, and free, from feare, and hate.

Quis diues? qui nil cupiat. quis pauper? auarus. Biantis dictum per Ausonium.

What man is ritche? not he that doth abounde.
What man is pore? not hee that hath no store.
But he is ritche, that makes content his grounde.
And he is pore, that couettes more and more.
  Which proues: the man was ritcher in the tonne,
  Then was the Kinge, that manie landes had wonne.

If then

If then, content the chiefest riches bee,
And greedie gripes, that doe abounde be pore,
Since that, inoughe allotted is to thee,
Embrace content, then CÆSAR hath no more.
Giue MIDAS, goulde: and let him pine with shame.
Vse you, your goodes, to liue, and die, with fame.

Claud. 1. Ruf.
-- Contentus honesta
Fabritius paruo spe
bat munera regum
Sudabatque graui c
sul Serranus aratro
Et casa pugnaces C
angusta tenebat.

Quæ sequimur fugimus.

To THOMAS WILBRAHAM *Esquier.*

WEE flee, from that wee seeke; & followe, that wee leaue: [weaue,
And, whilst wee thinke our webbe to skante, & larger still would
Lo, Time dothe cut vs of, amid our carke: and care.
Which warneth all, that haue enoughe, and not contented are.
For to inioye their goodes, their howses, and their landes:
Bicause the Lorde vnto that end, commits them to their handes.
Yet, those whose greedie mindes: enoughe, doe thinke too small:
Whilst that with care they seeke for more, oft times are reu'd of all,
Wherefore all such (I wishe) that spare, where is no neede:
To vse their goodes whilst that they may, for time apace doth speede.
And since, by proofe I knowe, you hourde not vp your store;
Whose gate, is open to your frende: and purce, vnto the pore:
And spend vnto your praise, what GOD dothe largely lende:
I chiefly made my choice of this, which I to you commende.
In hope, all those that see your name, aboue the head:
Will at your lampe, their owne come light; within your steppes to tread.
Whose daily studie is, your countrie to adorne:
And for to keepe a worthie house, in place where you weare borne.

Plautus Rud.
Boni quod bene fit haud perit.

Patria

To RICHARDE COTTON *Esquier.*

THE bees at lengthe retourne into their hiue,
When they haue suck'd the sweete of FLORAS bloomes;
And with one minde their worke they doe contriue,
And laden come with honie to their roomes:
  A worke of arte; and yet no arte of man,
  Can worke, this worke; these little creatures can.

Aelian. de animal. lib. 1. ca. 59. & 60. Et lib. 5. cap. 11. Et Plin. Natural. hist. lib. 11. cap. 5. & 16.

The maister bee, within the midst dothe liue,
In fairest roome, and most of stature is;
And euerie one to him dothe reuerence giue,
And in the hiue with him doe liue in blisse:
  Hee hath no stinge, yet none can doe him harme,
  For with their strengthe, the rest about him swarme.

Lo, natures force within these creatures small,
Some, all the daye the honie home doe beare.
And some, farre off on flowers freshe doe fall,
Yet all at nighte vnto their home repaire:
  And euerie one, her proper hiue doth knowe,
  Althoughe there stande a thousande on a rowe.

A comon

A Comon-wealthe, by this, is right expreste:
Bothe him, that rules, and those, that doe obaye:
Or suche, as are the heads aboue the rest,
Whome here, the Lorde in highe estate dothe staye:
By whose supporte, the meaner sorte doe liue,
And vnto them all reuerence dulie giue.

Plin. Natural. Hist. li.11.cap.5.

Which when I waied: I call'd vnto my minde
Your CVMBERMAIRE, that fame so farre commendes:
A stately seate, whose like is harde to finde,
Where mightie IOVE the horne of plentie lendes:
With fishe, and foule, and cattaile sondrie flockes,
Where christall springes doe gushe out of the rockes.

There, fertile fieldes; there, meadowes large extende:
There, store of grayne: with water, and with wood.
And, in this place, your goulden time you spende,
Vnto your praise, and to your countries good:
This is the hiue; your tennaunts, are the bees:
And in the same, haue places by degrees.

And as the bees, that farre and neare doe straye,
And yet come home, when honie they haue founde:
So, thoughe some men doe linger longe awaye,
Yet loue they best their natiue countries grounde.
And from the same, the more they absent bee,
With more desire, they wishe the same to see.

Ouid. 1. Pont. 4. *Rursus amor patria ratione valentior omni, &c.*

Euen so my selfe; throughe absence manie a yeare,
A straunger meere, where I did spend my prime.
Nowe, parentes loue dothe hale mee by the eare,
And sayeth, come home, deferre no longer time:
Wherefore, when happe, some goulden honie bringes?
I will retorne, and rest my wearie winges.

Primus gradus pietatis est iste, vt quos auctores tibi voluit esse deus, honores obsequiis, abstineas cõtumeliis, nec vultu lædenda est pietas parentum. *Amb.*

Ouid. 1. Pont. 4.

Quid melius Roma? Scythico quid frigore peius:
Huc tamen ex illa barbarus vrbe fugit.

Erasmus Chiliad. 1. Centur. 4. Adag. 25.

To G. M. Esquier.

Diogenes dicebat Aristippum (philosophum aulicum) aureis teneri compedibus ne posset exire.

IT better is (wee say) a cotage poore to houlde,
Then for to lye in prison stronge, with fetters made of goulde.
Which shewes, that bondage is the prison of the minde:
And libertie the happie life, that is to man assign'de,
And thoughe that some preferre their bondage, for their gaines:
And richely are adorn'd in silkes, and preste with massie chaines.
Yet manie others liue, that are accompted wise:
Who libertie doe chiefely choose, thoughe clad in gounes of Frise,
And waighe not POMPEYS porte, nor yet LVCVLLVS fare;
So that they may adorne their mindes, they well contented are.
Yea, rather doe accepte his dwelling in the tonne,
And for to liue with CODRVS cates; a roote, and barly bonne.
Where freedome they inioye, and vncontrolled liue:
Then with the chiefest fare of all, attendance for to geue.
And, if I should bee ask'd, which life doth please mee beste;
I like the goulden libertie, let goulden bondage reste.

Tertullianus lib. 6. De habitu muliebri cap. 4. Apud Barbaros quosdam (quia vernaculum est aurum) auro vinctos in ergastulis habent. idem narrat in lib. De cultu feminar. Plutarchus scribit autem in Erotico apud Aethiopas hoc in vsu esse. De quo etiam Aul. Gell. lib. 11. cap. 18.

Erasmus Chiliad. 1. Centuria 6. Adag. 76 de Codro.

Auxilio

To RICHARD DRAKE *Esquier, in praise of* Sir FRANCIS DRAKE *Knight.*

THROVGHE scorchinge heate, throughe coulde, in stormes, and tempests force,
By ragged rocks, by shelfes, & sandes: this Knighte did keepe his course.
By gapinge gulfes hee pass'd, by monsters of the flood,
By pirattes, theeues, and cruell foes, that long'd to spill his blood.
That wonder greate to scape: but, GOD was on his side,
And throughe them all, in spite of all, his shaken shippe did guide.
And, to requite his paines: *By helpe of power deuine.*
His happe, at lengthe did aunswere hope, to finde the goulden mine.
Let GRÆCIA then forbeare, to praise her IASON boulde?
Who throughe the watchfull dragons pass'd, to win the fleece of goulde.
Since by MEDEAS helpe, they weare inchaunted all,
And IASON without perrilles, pass'de: the conqueste therfore small? Ouid. Met. lib. 7.
But, hee, of whome I write, this noble minded DRAKE,
Did bringe away his goulden fleece, when thousand eies did wake.
Wherefore, yee woorthie wightes, that seeke for forreine landes:
Yf that you can, come alwaise home, by GANGES goulden sandes.
And you, that liue at home, and can not brooke the flood,
Geue praise to them, that passe the waues, to doe their countrie good.
Before which sorte, as chiefe: in tempeste, and in calme,
Sir FRANCIS DRAKE, by due deserte, may weare the goulden palme.

Auaritia huius sæculi.

To ARTHVRE BOVRCHIER *Esquier.*

WITH double dore this Pallace loe, doth ope;
The one, vnto the gallant roomes doth shewe,
Whereas the ritche with goulden giftes haue scope;
The other, to an emptie benche doth goe,
And there, the pore haue leaue for to resorte,
But not presume vnto the other porte.

For, alwaies that is shutte vnto the pore,
But ope to them, that haue the mines of goulde:
Then; thoughe the worlde of Poëttes haue no store,
No maruaile tho, sith bountie is so coulde;
For, if there did MECOENAS giftes abounde,
Newe HORACE soone, & VIRGIL should be founde.

Ouid. 2. Art. *Carmina laudantur sed munera magna petuntur,*
Dummodo sit diues barbarus, ille placet.

Martial. lib. 8. Epig. 55. ad Flaccum.

Ingenium sacri miraris abesse Maronis,
Nec quenquam tanta bella sonare tuba:
Sint Mæcenates, non deerunt Flacce, Marones;
Virgiliumq; tibi vel tua rura dabunt,

Pulchri-

To ARTHVRE STARKEY *Esquier.*

THE Cipresse tree is pleasinge to the sighte,
Straighte, tall, and greene, and sweete vnto the smell:
Yet, yeeldes no fruicte vnto the trauaylinge wighte,
But naughte, and bad, experience dothe vs tell:
Where, other trees that make not suche a showe,
Yeelde pleasante fruicte, and plentifullie growe.

This gallante tree that good, and fruictfull seemes,
In couerte sorte, a kinde of men doth checke:
Whose curtesie, no man but much esteemes,
Who promise muche, and faune about our necke:
But if wee trie, their deedes wee barren finde,
Or yeelde but fruicte, like to the Cipresse kinde.

Pulchra coma est, pulchro digestaq; ordine frondes;
Sed fructus nullos hæc coma pulchra gerit.

IANO DOVSÆ, *nobiliß. viri*, *Dn.* IANI DOVSÆ à *Noortwijck* F.

THE grapes not ripe, the trauailinge man dothwaste,
And vnder foote doth treade, as sower, and naughte:
Which, being ripe, had sweete, and pleasaunte taste
Whereby, wee maie this lesson true be taughte.
Howe simple men, doe simplie iudge of thinges.
And doe not waighe that time perfection bringes.

For in this worlde, the thinges most faire, and rare,
Are harde at firste, and seeme both harshe, and sower:
But yet in time, they sweete and easie are,
Then staie for time, which giues both fruite and flower:
And vse our time, and let vs still suppose
No greater losse, then time that wee doe lose.

Ouid. 1. Remed. *Nam mora dat vires, teneras mora percoquit vuas,*
Et validas segetes, quod fuit herba facit.

Impa-

To M. WILLIAM HAREBROWNE, *at Constantinople.*

THE faulcon mountes alofte vnto the skie,
And ouer hilles, and dales, dothe make her flighte;
The duckes, and geese, about the house doe flie,
And in eche diche, and muddie lake doe lighte,
They seeke their foode in puddles, and in pittes,
While that alofte, the princelie faulcon sittes.

Suche difference is in men, as maye appeare;
Some, throughe the worlde doe passe by lande, and sea:
And by deserte are famous farre, and neare,
So, all their life at home, some others staie:
And nothinge can to trauaile them prouoke,
Beyonde the smell of natiue countries smoke.

In sublime volans tenuem secat aëra falco:
Sed pascuntur humi graculus, anser, anas. Alciatus.

Tunc

Tunc tua res agitur, paries cùm proximus ardet

To M. THOMAS WHETELEY.

AWAKE from sleepe secure, when perrill doth appeare:
No wisedome then to take our ease, and not the worst to feare.
Still ARCHIMEDES wroughte, when foes had wonne the* towne,
And woulde not leaue his worke in hande, till he was beaten downe.
No suretie is within, when roofe alofte doth flame:
It is a madnes then to staye, till wee haue donne our game.
Yea, those that helpe deferre, when neighbours house doth burne:
Are like with griefe, to see their owne, with speede to cinders turne.
Then, cut of all delaies when daungers are begonne,
For if beginnings wee withstande, the conquest sooner wonne.

*Syracusa.

Plutarch. in vita Marcelli. Plin. lib 7. cap. 37.

Vegetius. Nunquam imperator ita paci credat, vt non se præparet bello. Et Bern. in Nat. Dom. Ser. 6. Ex consideratione remedij, periculi æstimatur quantitas.

Temporis officium est solatia dicere certi,
Dum dolor in cursu est, dum petit ager opem.

Ouid. 4. Pont. 11.

Ex morbo

To W. Ro.

WHEN that OPIMIVS ritche, had scraped manie a pounde;
And fil'd his baggs, & cofers full, that wealthe did most abounde.
Yet liu'd hee still in awe, as if it weare offence
To ope his purce, for any neede; hee spared so his pence.
At lengthe, this greedie carle the Lythergie posseste:
That vnneth hee could stere a foote, with sleepe so sore opprest.
And languishinge therein, not like for to escape:
His heire, was ioyfull of that sighte, who for his goodes did gape.
But, when that nothinge coulde OPIMIVS sleepinge let,
The quicke Phisition did commaunde, that tables shoulde bee set
About the misers bed; and budgettes forthe to bringe,
And poure the goulde vppon the bourde, that hee mighte heare it ringe.
And bad the heire to tell, and all the standers bye:
With that, hee to the sicke man call'de; what meane you thus to lye?
And will not haue regarde your treasure to preserue:
Behoulde your heire, and all the reste, howe largely nowe they carue?
With that, hee started vp; halfe dead, and halfe aliue;
And staringe on his heapes of goulde, longe time for life did striue.
So that, when nothinge coulde his drousie eies awake,
Such vertue, had the sighte of goulde, that sleepe did him forsake.
Which showes, when dreadfull deathe presentes the lastinge sleepe:
They hardly can departe in peace, whose goulde is rooted deepe.

Horat. Serm. lib. 2. Satyra 3.

Demosth. apud Volat.
Qui animum curat, seipsum curat: qui corpus, non se sed sua curat: qui pecuniam, non se, nec sua curat, sed valdè aliena curat.

Plut. de Polit.
Maiori odio diuitem populus persequi solet, nihil per benignitatē & gratiam depromentem, quàm inopem, qui bona subripiat publica. hoc enim necessitate domina stimulante, illud malignitate, atq. contemptu fieri arbitratur.

Gregor. in Homil.
Res suas, cum moreretur, diues secum tolleret, si ad petentis vocem, cùm viueret, tulisset: nam terrena omnia, quæ seruando amittimus, largiendo seruamus.

Effigiem Rex Crœse tuā ditissime Regum
Vidit apud Manes, Diogenes Cynicus.
Cōstitit vtq; procul solito maiore cachinno
Concussus, dixit. quid tibi diuitiæ
Nunc prosunt Regum Rex ô ditissime, cùm sis
Sicut ego solus, me quoque pauperior?
Nā quæcunq. habui, mecū fero, cùm nihil ipse
Ex tantis tecum Crœse feras opibus.

Auson. Epig 55.

Horat. Epist. lib. 1. Epist. 1.

THE Lion oulde that coulde not get his praye,
By swifte pursute, as he had done of late:
Did faigne him sicke, and in his denne did staye,
And præde on those, that came to see his state:
At lengthe, the foxe his dutie to declare,
Came to the dore, to knowe howe he did fare.

Who answered, sicke, my oulde beloued frende?
Come in, and see, and feele my pulses beate:
To whome, quoth he, I dare not now intende,
Bicause, these steppes some secret mischiefe threate:
For, all I see haue gone into thy denne,
But none I finde, that haue retorn'd againe.

Zeloty-

A Sicknes ſore, that dothe in ſecret wounde,
And gripes the harte, thoughe outward nothing ſhowe;
The force whereof, the paciente doth confounde,
That oftentimes, diſpaire therof doth growe:
And Ielouſie, this ſicknes hathe to name,
An helliſhe paine, that firſte from PLVTO came.

Which paſſion ſtraunge, is alwaies beauties foe,
And moſte of all, the married ſorte enuies:
Oh happie they, that liue in wedlocke ſoe,
That in their breſtes this furie neuer riſe:
For, when it once doth harbour in the harte,
It ſoiournes ſtill, and doth too late departe.

Lo PROCRIS heare, when wounded therwithall,
Did breede her bane, who mighte haue bath'de in bliſſe:
This corſie ſharpe ſo fedde vppon her gall,
That all to late ſhee mourn'd, for her amiſſe:
For, whilſt ſhee watch'd her huſbandes waies to knowe,
Shee vnawares, was praye vnto his bowe.

Ouid. Metam. lib. 7.

Similem de vxore Cyanippi, ſcribit Plutarchus in Moral.

Ad ornatiss. viros D. IOANNEM IAMES, *&* LANCELOTTVM BROWNE. *Medicos celeberrimos.*

THIS portrature, dothe ÆSCVLAPIVS tell.
The laurell crowne, the fame of phisike showes.
The bearde, declares his longe experience well:
And grauitie therewith that alwaie goes.
The scepter, tells he ruleth like a kinge
Amongst the sicke; commaunding euerie thinge.

Ouid.3. Pont.4. *Ad medicam dubius confugit ager opem.*

The knotted staffe, declares the crabbed skill
Moste harde t'attaine; that doth supporte his state:
His sittinge, shewes he must be setled still,
With constant minde, and rashe proceedinge hate:
The Dragon, tells he doth our age renewe,
And soone decerne, to giue the sicke his dewe.

Hier. in Epist. Corporis debilitas nimia, etiam animi vires frangit, mentis quoque ingenium marcescere facit: quicquid cum modo, & temperamento fit, salubre fit.

The cocke, dothe teache his watchinge, and his care,
To visite ofte his pacientes, in their paine:
The couchinge dogge, dothe laste of all declare,
That faithfulnes, and loue, shoulde still remaine:
Within their brestes, that Phisike doe professe.
Which partes, they all shoulde in their deedes expresse.

Inani-

Inanis impetus.

Clariß. omniq́; doctrina & virtutis laude ornatißimo viro D. IVSTO LIPSIO.

BY shininge lighte, of wannishe CYNTHIAS raies,
The dogge behouldes his shaddowe to appeare:
Wherefore, in vaine aloude he barkes, and baies,
And alwaies thoughte, an other dogge was there:
But yet the Moone, who did not heare his queste,
Hir woonted course, did keepe vnto the weste.

This reprehendes, those fooles which baule, and barke,
At learned men, that shine aboue the reste:
With due regarde, that they their deedes should marke,
And reuerence them, that are with wisedome bleste:
But if they striue, in vaine their winde they spende,
For woorthie men, the Lorde doth still defende.

Ouid. 1. Remed. *Ingenium magni liuor detrectat Homeri; Quisquis es, ex illo Zoile nomen habes.*

Esse quid hoc dicam, viuis quod fama negatur,
Et sua quod rarus tempora lector amat?
Hi sunt inuidiæ nimirum Regule mores;
Præferat antiquos semper vt illa nouis.

Martial. lib. 5. ad Regulum.

On goulden fleece, did Phryxus passe the waue,
And landed safe, within the wished baie:
By which is ment, the fooles that riches haue,
Supported are, and borne throughe Lande, and Sea:
And those enrich'de by wife, or seruauntes goodds,
Are borne by them like Phryxus through the floodds.

An other of the like argument.
To M. I. E.

Plaut. in pœn.
Pulcrum ornatum turpes mores peius cœno collinunt. Lepidi mores turpem ornatum facile factis comprobant.

A Leaden sworde, within a goulden sheathe,
Is like a foole of natures finest moulde:
To whome, shee did her rarest giftes bequethe.
Or like a sheepe, within a fleece of goulde.
Or like a clothe, whome colours braue adorne,
When as the grounde, is patched, rente, and torne.

Bern. in Epist.
Decor, qui cum veste induitur, & cum veste deponitur: vestimenti est, non vestiti.

For, if the minde the chiefest treasures lacke,
Thoughe nature bothe, and fortune, bee our frende;
Thoughe goulde wee weare, and purple on our backe,
Yet are wee poore, and none will vs comende
But onlie fooles; and flatterers, for theire gaine:
For other men, will ride vs with disdaine.

Inter-

To M. IOHN GOSTLINGE.

LOE SISYPHVS, that roles the reſtleſſe ſtone
To toppe of hill, with endleſſe toile, and paine:
Which beinge there, it tumbleth doune alone,
And then, the wretche muſt force it vp againe:
And as it falles, he makes it ſtill aſcende;
And yet, no toile can bringe this worke to ende.

Ouid. Metam. lib. 4.

This SISYPHVS: preſenteth Adams race.
The reſtleſſe ſtone: their trauaile, and their toile:
The hill, dothe ſhewe the daye, and eeke the ſpace,
Wherein they ſtill doe labour, worke, and moile.
And thoughe till nighte they ſtriue the hill to clime,
Yet vp againe, the morning nexte betime.

Plat. de proſper. Hanc rationem deus ſequitur in bonis viris, quàm in diſcipulis ſuis præceptores: qui plus laboris ab his exigunt, in quibus certior ſpes eſt.

Vita humana propriè vti ferrum eſt: Ferrum ſi exerceas, conteritur: ſi non exerceas, tamen rubigo interficit. Item homines exercendo videmus conteri. Si nihil exerceas, inertia atque torpedo plus detrimenti facit, quàm exercitatio.

Aul. Gell. lib. 11. ca. 2.

Qui

Qui se exaltat, humiliabitur.

THE boylinge brothe, aboue the brinke dothe swell,
And comes to naughte, with falling in the fire:
So reaching heads that thinke them neuer well,
Doe headlonge fall, for pride hathe ofte that hire:
And where before their frendes they did dispise,
Nowe beinge falne, none helpe them for to rise.

Ephes. cap. 4.

Sol non occidat super iracundiam vestram.

CASTE swordes awaye, take laurell in your handes.
Let not the Sonne goe downe vppon your ire.
Let hartes relente, and breake oulde rancors bandes,
And frendshippes force subdue your rashe desire.
Let desperate wightes, and ruffians, thirst for blood;
Winne foes, with loue; and thinke your conquest good.

Roman. 12.

Omnis

To M. ELGOCKE *Preacher.*

ALL fleshe, is grasse; and withereth like the haie:
To daie, man laughes, to morrowe, lies in claie.
Then, let him marke the frailtie of his kinde,
For here his tearme is like a puffe of winde,
Like bubbles smalle, that on the waters rise:
Or like the flowers, whome FLORA freshlie dies.
Yet, in one daie their glorie all is gone:
So, worldlie pompe, which here we gaze vppon.
Which warneth all, that here their pageantes plaie,
Howe, well to liue: but not how longe to waie.

Quis est, quamt
sit adolescens q
exploratum hab
se ad vesperum
victurum?

Sensim sine sen
ætas senescit, r
subitò frangitu
diuturnitate ex
guitur. Cicer. F
sip. 11.

Inter spem curamq;, timores inter & iras,
Omnem crede diem tibi diluxisse supremam.
Grata superueniet, quæ non sperabitur, hora.

Horat. 1. Epi

Ouid. Metam. lib. 11.

PRESVMPTVOVS PAN, did ſtriue APOLLOS ſkill to paſſe:
But MIDAS gaue the palme to PAN: wherefore the eares of aſſe
APOLLO gaue the Iudge: which doth all Iudges teache;
To iudge with knowledge, and aduiſe, in matters paſte their reache?

Mulier umbra viri.

OVR ſhadowe flies, if wee the ſame purſue:
But if wee flie, it followeth at the heele.
So, he throughe loue that moſte dothe ſerue, and ſue,
Is furtheſt off his miſtreſſe harte is ſteele.
But if hee flie, and turne awaie his face;
Shee followeth ſtraight, and grones to him for grace.

In amore

COSI DE BEN AMAR
PORTO TORMENTO

EVEN as the gnattes, that flie into the blaze,
Doe burne their winges and fall into the fire:
So, those too muche on gallant showes that gaze,
Are captiues caught, and burne in their desire:
And suche as once doe feele this inwarde warre,
Thoughe they bee cur'de, yet still appeares the scarre.

For wanton LOVE althoughe hee promise ioies,
Yet hee that yeeldes in hope to finde it true,
His pleasures shalbee mated with annoyes;
And sweetes suppos'de, bee mix'd, with bitter rue:
Bicause, his dartes not all alike, doe wounde:
For so the frendes of coye ASPASIA founde.

They lou'd; shee loth'de: they crau'd, shee still deni'de.
They sigh'd, shee songe: they spake, shee stopt her eare.
They walk'd, shee satte: they set, awaye shee hi'de.
Lo this their bale, which was her blisse, you heare.
O loue, a plague, thoughe grac'd with gallant glosse,
For in thy seates a snake is in the mosse.

Then stoppe your eares, and like VLISSES waulke,
The SYREENES tunes, the carelesse often heares:
*CROCVTA killes when shee doth frendly taulke:
The Crocodile, hathe treason in her teares.
In gallant fruicte, the core is ofte decay'd;
Yea poison ofte in cuppe of goulde assay'd.

*De malignitate Crocutæ feræ Æl. lib.7. cap. 21. & Plin. lib.8. cap.30.

 Then,

Then, in your waies let reaſon ſtrike the ſtroke,
ASPASIA ſhonne, althoughe her face doe ſhine:
But, if you like of HYMENÆVS yoke,
PENELOPE preferre, thoughe ſpinninge twine,
Yet if you like, how moſt to liue in reſt,
HIPPOLYTVS his life, ſuppoſe the beſt.

Vincit qui patitur.

THE mightie oke, that ſhrinkes not with a blaſte,
But ſtiflie ſtandes, when Boreas moſte doth blowe,
With rage thereof, is broken downe at laſte,
When bending reedes, that couche in tempeſtes lowe
With yeelding ſtill, doe ſafe, and ſounde appeare:
And looke alofte, when that the cloudes be cleare.

Eraſm. in Epiſt. Verè magni animi eſt, quaſdam iniurias negligere, nec ad quorundam conuitia aures, vel linguam habere.

When Enuie, Hate, Contempte, and Slaunder, rage:
Which are the ſtormes, and tempeſtes, of this life;
With patience then, wee muſt the combat wage,
And not with force reſiſt their deadlie ſtrife
But ſuffer ſtill, and then wee ſhall in fine,
Our foes ſubdue, when they with ſhame ſhall pine.

WHERE as the good, do liue amongst the bad:
And vertue growes, where seede of vices springes:
The wicked sorte to wounde the good, are glad:
And vices thrust at vertue, all their stinges:
The like, where witte, and learning doe remaine,
Where follie rules, and ignoraunce doth raigne.

Yet as wee see, the lillie freshlie bloomes,
Though thornes, and briers, enclose it round aboute:
So with the good, thoughe wicked haue their roomes,
They are preseru'd, in spite of all their route:
And learning liues, and vertue still doth shine,
When follie dies, and ignoraunce doth pine.

To M. RAWLINS *Preacher.*

THE Iuie greene that dothe diſpiſed growe,
And none doth plante, or trimme the ſame at all,
Althoughe a while it ſpreades it ſelfe belowe,
In time it mountes, with creepinge vp the wall.
So, thoughe the worlde the vertuous men diſpiſe,
Yet vp alofte in ſpite of them they riſe.

Impunitas ferociæ parens.

To M. STEEVENSON *Preacher.*

WHEN worthie men, for life, and learninge greate,
Who with their lookes, the wicked did appall,
If frowninge fates, with perſecution threate;
Or take them hence, or ſhut them vp in thrall:
The wicked ſorte reioice, and plaie their partes,
Thoughe longe before, they clok'd their fained hartes.

To M. KNEWSTVB *Preacher.*

HERE, man who firſt ſhould heauenlie thinges attaine,
And then, to world his ſences ſhould incline:
Firſt, vndergoes the worlde with might, and maine,
And then, at foote doth drawe the lawes deuine.
Thus GOD hee beares, and Mammon in his minde: *Matth. 6.*
But Mammon firſt, and GOD doth come behinde. Non poteſtis deo ſeruire & Mammonæ.

Oh worldlinges fonde, that ioyne theſe two ſo ill,
The league is nought, throwe doune the world which ſpeede:
Take vp the lawe, according to his will.
Firſt ſeeke for heauen, and then for wordly neede. Primùm quærite regnum dei, &c. *Ibidem.*
But thoſe that firſt their wordlie wiſhe doe ſerue,
Their gaine, is loſſe, and ſeeke their ſoules to ſterue.

Sic

Sic probantur.

To M. ANDREWES *Preacher.*

THROVGHE tormentes ſtraunge, and perſecutions dire,
The Chriſtians paſſe, with pacience in their paine:
And ende their courſe, ſometime with ſworde, and fire,
And conſtant ſtand, and like to lambes are ſlaine.
Bycauſe, when all their martirdome is paſt,
They hope to gaine a glorious croune at laſt.

Noli tuba canere Eleemoſynam.

WHEN that thou giu'ſt thy almes vnto the pore,
In ſecret giue, for GOD thy giftes doth ſee:
And openlie, will thee rewarde therfore.
But, if with trompe thy almes muſt publiſh'd bee,
Thou giu'ſt in vaine: ſith thou therby doſt ſhowe,
Thy chiefe deſire is, that the world maie knowe.

Supreſſ

A DVE *deceiptfull worlde, thy pleasures I detest:* Peregrinus Chri
Nowe, others with thy showes delude; my hope in heauen doth rest. stianus loquitur.

Inlarged as followeth.

EVEN as a flower, or like vnto the grasse, *Iacob. 1.*
Which now dothe stande, and straight with sithe dothe fall; *Ecclesiast. 14*
So is our state: now here, now hence wee passe: *Isaia 40.*
For, time attendes with shredding sithe for all.
And deathe at lengthe, both oulde, and yonge, doth strike:
And into dust dothe turne vs all alike.

Yet, if wee marke how swifte our race dothe ronne,
And waighe the cause, why wee created bee:
Then shall wee know, when that this life is donne,
Wee shall bee sure our countrie right to see.
For, here wee are but straungers, that must flitte: *2 Corinth. 5.*
The nearer home, the nearer to the pitte.

O happie they, that pondering this arighte,
Before that here their pilgrimage bee past,
Resigne this worlde; and marche with all their mighte
Within that pathe, that leades where ioyes shall last. Via veritas vi
And whilst they maye, there, treasure vp their store, *Ioan. 14.*
Where, without rust, it lastes for euermore. *Matth. 6*

f This

Apocal. 6. Apocal. 21. This worlde must chaunge: That worlde, shall still indure.
Here; pleasures fade: There, shall they endlesse bee.
Here, man doth sinne: And there, hee shalbee pure
1 Corinth. 15. Here, deathe hee tastes: And there, shall neuer die.
Apocal. 21. Here, hathe hee griefe: And there shall ioyes possesse,
1 Corinth. 2. As none hath seene, nor anie harte can gesse.

Amico ficto nulla fit iniuria.

SINCE fauninge lookes, and sugred speache preuaile,
Take heede betime: and linke thee not with theise.
The gallant clokes, doe hollowe hartes conceile,
And goodlie showes, are mistes before our eies:
But whome thou find'st with guile, disguised so:
No wronge thou doest, to vse him as thy foe.

Ferè simile, in Hypocritas.

A Face deform'de, a visor faire dothe hide,
That none can see his vglie shape within;
To Ipocrites, the same maie bee applide,
With outward showes, who all their credit winne:
Yet giue no heate, but like a painted fire;
And, all their zeale, is: as the times require.

TO M. IAMES IONSON.

Two horſes free, a thirde doe ſwiftlie chace,
The one, is white, the other, blacke of hewe:
None, bridles haue for to reſtraine their pace,
And thus, they bothe, the other ſtill purſue:
And, neuer ceaſe continuall courſe to make,
Vntill at lengthe, the firſt, they ouertake.

This formoſt horſe, that ronnes ſo faſt awaye,
It is our time; while heere, our race wee ronne:
The blacke, and white, preſenteth nighte, and daye:
Who after haſt, vntill the goale bee wonne,
And leaue vs not, but followe from our birthe, *Pſalm. 89.*
Vntill wee yeelde, and turne againe to earthe.

Labitur occultè; fallitq; volatilis ætas, Ouid. 1. Amo:
Et celer admiſsis labitur annus equis.

Soli Deo gloria.

To M. HOWLET *Preacher.*

HERE, man with axe doth cut the boughe in twaine,
And without him, the axe, coulde nothing doe
Within the toole, there doth no force remaine;
But man it is, that mighte doth put thereto:
  Like to this axe, is man, in all his deeds;
  Who hath no strength, but what from GOD proceedes.

Then, let him not make vaunt of his desert,
Nor bragge thereof, when hee good deedes hath donne
For, it is GOD that worketh in his harte,
And with his grace, to good, doth make him ronne:
  And of him selfe, hee weake thereto, doth liue;
Iud. Epist. And GOD giues power, to whome all glorie giue.

Dominus

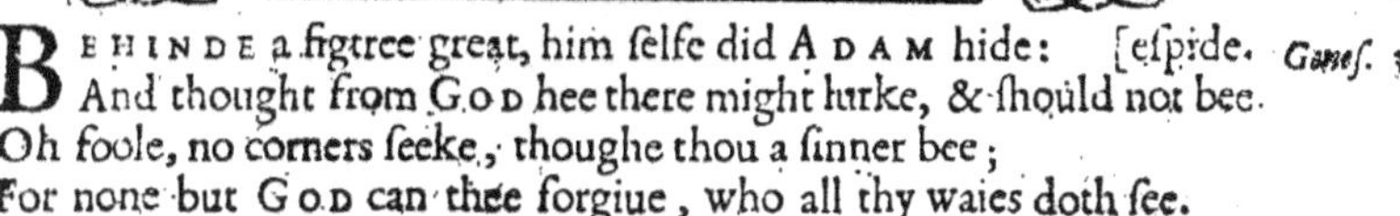

BEHINDE a figtree great, him selfe did ADAM hide: [espide. *Genes. 3*
And thought from GOD hee there might lurke, & should not bee.
Oh foole, no corners seeke, thoughe thou a sinner bee;
For none but GOD can thee forgiue, who all thy waies doth see.

Ex maximo minimum.

WHERE liuely once, GODS image was exprefte,
Wherin, sometime was sacred reason plac'de,
The head, I meane, that is so ritchly blefte,
With sighte, with smell, with hearinge, and with taste.
Lo, nowe a skull, both rotten, bare, and drye,
A relike meete in charnell house to lye,

Nic. Reusnerus,
Ut rosa manè viget, sæ-
ro mox vespere languet:
Sic modò qui summus,
cras levis umbra sumus.

Ad Illustrissimum Heroëm D. Robertum Dudlæum, Comitem Leicestriæ, *Baronem de Denbighe, &c. Dominum meum vnicè colendum.*

Tempus omnia terminat.

THE *longest daye, in time resignes to nighte.*
The greatest oke, in time to duste doth turne.
The Rauen dies, the Egle failes of flighte.
The Phœnix rare, in time her selfe doth burne.
The princelie stagge at lengthe his race doth ronne.
And all must ende, that euer was begonne.

Euen so, I, here doe ende this simple booke,
And offer it vnto your Lorshippes sighte:
Which, if you shall receiue with pleasinge looke,
I shall reioyce, and thinke my labour lighte.
And pray the Lorde your honour to preserue,
Our noble Queene, and countrie long to serue.

FINIS.

LABORE
ET
CONSTANTIA

Geffrey Whitney's Choice of Emblemes.

Photolithographed

by Alfred Brothers, Manchester.

M. DCCC. LXVI.

ESSAYS LITERARY AND BIBLIOGRAPHICAL

ILLUSTRATIVE OF

WHITNEY'S EMBLEMS

WITH

Explanatory Notes

BY

HENRY GREEN, M.A.

Thinking little of Socrates;
But much more of the Truth.

Nunquam procrastinandum.

ALCIATAE *gentis insignia sustinet alce;*
Vnguibus et μηδὲν *fert* ἀναβαλλομένος.
Constat Alexandrum sic respondisse roganti,
Qui tot obiuisset tempore gesta breui;
Nunquam, inquit, differre uolens, quod et indicat alce:
Fortior hæc dubites ocyor an ne siet.

Aldus, Venetiis M.D.XLVI.

ESSAY I.

SUBJECTS AND SOURCES OF THE MOTTOES AND DEVICES.

SECTION I. — General View — Devices not traced to other Emblematists — and those simply suggested by them.

HITNEY'S *Choice of Emblems* is most truly a representative book, — representative not of the entire emblem literature which preceded him, but of a very considerable portion. Either by way of reference, or by direct adoption, there is set before the reader a very full view, not to name it a complete one, of what had been ventured on and achieved by his fellow-labourers. Originality he does not claim, though for this he deserves more credit than is usually assigned to him; but what he does claim to have done, was done in a masterly way, which only a man of learning and of culture could have accomplished.

The word *motto* speaks for itself. By *device* is to be understood the pictorial illustration of the motto, excluding the *stanzas;* and by *emblem*, the whole combination of motto, device and stanzas into an artistic expression of thought. The motto gives the subject, the device pictures it, the stanzas clothe it in language more or less poetical, and Emblem furnishes a name for the results when the three are made one and the work is perfected.

"Choice of Emblemes" is the significant title which is prefixed to this book, and most accurately does that word "choice" describe the nature of what has been done. Whitney made a *selection* from the labours of earlier writers, and especially from those whose works had been imprinted "in the house of Christo- Whitney, "to the Reader," pp. xiv. and xv.

pher Plantyn." He had access to and made use of other books of emblems, and sometimes has accommodated their devices and explanatory stanzas to the collection which himself was forming; but these were the accessories to his plan, and not the principals by the express aid of which his purpose was carried out.

"Book of Roxburghe Ballads, 1592."

Collier informs us that in the sixteenth century it was the custom among printers to buy up the old wood-blocks which had been cut for other books, and, even without much coincidence of subject, to introduce them into their own publications. Of this practice he gives several amusing instances, but a better cannot be supplied than from the Great Folio Bible of Elizabeth's reign, to the expenses of which several of the nobility, as the earls of Leicester and Essex, contributed. Some of the large and highly-ornamented capitals belong properly to stories and anecdotes of the heathen mythology, but are heedlesly employed as embellishments of the sacred writings.

Latin edition, 1497. Plate IV.

French edition, 1498. Plate XXVIII.

Ed. 1539. Plate XXX.

Ed. 1540. Plate XXXII.

Ed. 1597. Plate XXXVIII.

The practice spoken of was very extensively adopted by emblem-printers and publishers, and without any blame to be attached. The highly graphic drawings in Locher's and Brant's "**Stultifera Nauis,**" *Fool-freighted Ship*, were introduced as illustrations for "**La grāt nef des folz du mōde,**" *The Great Ship of the Fools of the World.* Again, the borders round the devices of Perrière's "*Théâtre des bons Engins,*" are the same as those in Corrozet's "Hecatomgraphie," *The Hundred Engravings;* and copies of the same engravings as appear in Freitag's "*Mythologia Ethica,*" Ethical Mythology, are inserted in a work entitled "*Esbatiment moral des Animaux.*"

Plantin of Antwerp possessed abundant stores of pictorial embellishments* for books of many kinds; and when woodcuts or engravings had served for a work in Latin or French, he very freely employed them for a similar work in Flemish, Dutch, or English, and perchance in Spanish and Italian. The language was changed, and in emblem-books the stanzas also, to suit differences of thought or of customs, but, with a more or less ornamented border, the same woodcuts or engravings did service

* These stores, it is said, still remain in "*L'Imprimerie Plantinienne*" at Antwerp, and greatly is it to be desired that M. Edward Moretus should unveil the treasures of his inheritance and make them accessible to the literary world.

over and over again. It was no more considered strange to distribute the blocks than to distribute the type, and when either was wanted it assumed its fitting place on the compositor's table. The proofs of this are very distinctly to be traced, especially in the editions of Paradin or of Alciat from the year 1562 to 1608.

A writer of great authority maintains that Whitney's emblems were chiefly borrowed from Paradin's "*Heroical Devices.*" The analysis we are about to submit will show the inaccuracy of this statement, and that *Alciat* was the great source to which our author applied. Another writer, without entirely rectifying it, points out Dibdin's error, and affirms that some were taken from Paradin, others from Sambucus, Junius and Alciatus, and some also from the sacred emblems of Beza. Dibdin. Bibliog. Dec. vol. i. p. 275.

There are indeed a few coincidences between the emblems of Whitney and those of Beza, but not above two examples of direct and immediate borrowing. Of the emblematists of Whitney's era the greater part were either directly or indirectly laid under contribution by him: not many of them escaped, and that rather because of incongruity in their subjects than because the works were unknown.* One or two of these are simply referred to, as *Achilles Bocchius;* and others are alluded to among divers See Plates VIII and LIX. To the Reader. p. xv.

* Among emblem-books, neither used by Whitney nor alluded to by him, are to be included:

Gerard Leeu's "DIALOG. CREATUR. MORALI, Editio Primaria," or *Dialogues of the Creatures*, excellently moralized &c. to the praise of God and the edification of men. Gothic letter, large 4to, unpaged, 1480. Biblioth. Reg. the Hague.

Also "Een genoechlick boeck gheheten dyalogus der creaturen. Te Delf in Holland, 1488." The last edition.

A. Coelio Augustino's "HIEROGLYPHICA," or *Concerning the sacred things of the Egyptians and of other nations, &c.* In 70 bks. pp. 441. Folio. Basiliæ 1567.

Jeron. Ruscelli's "*Le Impresi illvstri,*" 4to, pp. 496. Venice 1584. Alluded to by sir Philip Sidney. Emb. Library of H. Y. Thompson

J. Keysersberg Geyler's "*Navicula, sive speculum fatuorum,*" *&c.* Small 4to. Argent. 1511.

Geyler's "*Navicula Pœnitentiæ,*" *&c.* Folio. Augsburg 1511.

J. P. Valerian's "HIEROGLYPHICA," or *Commentaries on the sacred characters of the Egyptians.* Folio. Basiliæ 1556.

Giovio's "*Dialogue des Devises d'armes et d'amour,*" *&c.* 4to. Lyon 1561.

Maerman's "*Apologi Creaturarum,*" *&c.* 4to. Antwerp 1584.

And perhaps we ought to name from the same library:

Holbein's "*Icones historiarum vet. Testamenti,*" *&c.* 4to. Lugduni 1547.

Bernard's "*Figure del Vecchio e del nuovo Test.*" *&c.* 8vo. Lione 1554.

persons "wel knowne to the learned." Of his own skill and invention, as far as the subjects and devices are concerned, very little was produced; in fact his aim was, not to strike out new paths, but to follow up the old.

Similar emblems to those of Whitney are to be found in many writers previous to the year 1586, when "the Choice of Emblemes" appeared; and in all probability, when not copied from other sources, they were suggested by the works of Sebastian Brant, William Perrière, Giles Corrozet, Horapollo, Bartholemew Aneau, Peter Coustau, Paolo Giovio, Gabriel Symeoni, Arnold Freitag, Theodore Beza and Nicholas Reusner. To these authors we may trace *like* thoughts and expressions and *like* devices.

But in the vast majority of instances there is an absolute *identity* between the mottoes and pictorial illustrations in *Whitney* and those in earlier or contemporary writers; and this identity extends to the employment of the very same wood-blocks for striking off the impressions. At various times, between 1562 and 1585, from Plantin's offices in Antwerp and Leyden, various editions had been published of emblems by Claude Paradin, Gabriel Faerni,* John Sambucus, Hadrian Junius and Andrew Alciat; these are the veritable originals of a large proportion of Whitney's stanzas, and supply his work with most of the pictorial devices which adorn it.

See Annales de l'Imp. Plantin. 1555-1589.

The devices *not hitherto traced to other emblematists* are these:

Page.	*Description of Device.*	*Page.*	*Description of Device.*
31	The house on fire and the envious man.	185	Quinctilian, the Author and Fame.
95	The envious and the covetous.	198	Alexander and Diogenes.
112	The schoolmaster of Faleria.	203	A ship drawn by Providence.
114	Regulus Attilius tortured.	216*a*	The broth boiling over.
129	An overwhelming sea.	*b*	Reconciliation at sunset.
133	The vine and the olive.	218*a*	Pan and Apollo, Midas being judge.
145	The ape caught in the stocks.	224*a*	A crown for the persecuted.
161	The sick fox and the lion.	*b*	Alms by sound of trumpet.
166*a*	A Bible in the heavens and the Enemy of souls.	225	The pilgrim looking heavenward.
167	The old man and the infant.	228	The axe wielded by the woodman.
168*a*	Homer and the Muses begging.	229*a*	Adam hiding behind a tree.
		230	The sun setting.

* Properly a book of Fables, like the editions of Æsop, printed by Plantin in 1565, 1567 and 1581.

We cannot however say with certainty that the whole of these 23 emblems are original; further researches may lessen the number, and two or three works, to which I have not obtained access, seem likely to supply some of the missing identifications; they are from Plantin's* press, and therefore Whitney probably had seen them. It is a point undetermined, though I should expect to find the emblems on pages 133, 145 and 161 derived from some book of fables. Annales de l'Imprimerie Plantinienne, pp. 88, 47 and 187.

For the other emblems the sources of the mottoes and devices may be arranged in two divisions:

I. Devices suggested only by those of other Emblematists, or *similar* to theirs:

II. Devices struck off from the same wood-blocks, and therefore *identical*.

I. Devices suggested only, or *similar* to those of other Emblematists.

Under this heading the emblems, with their description printed in *italic* letter, are alone really to be attributed to their respective authors as the sources from which Whitney took them; in other instances, with the description printed in *roman* letter, *similarity* exists,—little or nothing more. When a device is borrowed the motto belonging to it is generally borrowed also.

1°. Locher's translation into Latin of Sebastian Brant's "**Stultifera Nauis**," *Fool-freighted Ship*, quarto; with CLVI folios: there are 115 spirited though rather rough woodcuts, besides the title-page and the last page, ending with "In laudatissima Germaniæ vrbe Basiliensi: nup opa & pmotione Johãnis Bergman de Olpe Anno salutis nr̃e M.CCCCXCVII. Kl. Augusti."† See Plate IV.

* "Les Proverbes anciens Flamengs et François correspondans," &c., par M. François Goedthals. 8vo, pp. 143. Anvers 1568. Annales &c. p 88.

Estienne Perret, "XXV fables des animaux, vray miroir exemplaire," &c. Anvers 1578. Fol. de 26 feuillets. p 187.

"Fabulæ aliquot Æsopi, breves, faciles et jucundæ," &c. 8vo. Antverpiæ 1581. p. 225

† The German original was published in 1494, thus: "DAS NARRENSCHYFF Gedrucht zu Basil Im jar noch Christi geburt Tusant vier hundert vier und nüntzig. Jo. B. (Bergman) von Olpe." It is a quarto of 158 folios, or of 164 according to M. Graesse, with 114 figures in wood. For editions of Brant, consult Brunet's "Manuel du Libraire," 1860, vol. i. 1202-1209

See Plate XXVIII.

Geoffrey de Marnef's translation into French, "**La grãt nef des folz du mõde,**" *The Great Ship of the Fools of the World*, large quarto, with LXXXVIII feuillets in double columns, and an index; besides the title-page there are 116 woodcuts similar to those of the Latin edition, but not identical. The capital letters to each subject are ornamented. The ending is: "**Cy finist la nef des folz du monde. Premieremẽt cõposee en aleman par maistre Sebastien brant docteur es droitz. Consecutiuement daleman en latin redigee par maistre Jacques locher. Reueue et ornee de plusieurs belles concordances et additions par ledit brant. Et de nouuel translatee de latin en frãcoys et imprimee pour Geoffroy de marnef libraire de paris. Le viii iour du moys de Feburier. L an m.cccccxcix.**"

	Page.	Description of Device.		Page.	Description of Device.	
Plate XXIX Four wom	17	Drinking, gaming, throat cutting.	*fol.* XXVII.	176	*Three women gaming.*	French ed. *feuil.* LI.
	27	Fowlers and decoy bird.	XLIX.	181	Occasion or fortune.	*fol.* LXXXV.
Plate V. No man.	155	The thief and his mother.	XVI. and LVII.	223	*No man can serve two masters.*	XXIV.
	159	The ant and the grasshopper.	LXXX.			

See Plate XXX.

2°. William de la Perrière's "Le Théâtre DES BONS ENGINS," &c., *The Theatre of Good Contrivances, in which are contained one hundred Emblems,*" *&c.,* à Paris, Denys Ianot, 1539. Small octavo, unpaged, The work has 214 pages and CI emblems, with highly ornamented borders to nearly every page. Dedication: "A treshaulte & tresillustre princesse, Madame Marguerite de France, Royne de Nauarre, seur vnicque du treschrestien Roy de France. Guillaume de la Perriere son treshũble seruiteur." The mottoes on the title-page are, "AMOR DEI OMNIA VINCIT," and "AMOR UT FLOS TRÃSIET;" and the borders to the pages and emblems are the same with those in Corrozet's *Hecatomgraphie.*

Consult Brunet's "Manuel du Libraire," 1862, vol. iii. 829.

	Page.	Description of Device.		Page.	Description of Device.	
	27	Fowlers and decoy bird.	*Emb.* LIII.	180	*A fowler letting a bird fly.*	*Emb.* XC.
	53*a*	The sow and the gleanings.	XVII.	188*a*	*The ape and darling whelp.*	XLVII.
	60	Pythagoras enjoining silence.	VIII.	192	A sword tried on an anvil.	XXXI.
Plate XXX. Janus.	108	*Janus with sceptre and mirror.*	I.	205	*The cypress tree.*	LXV.
	165	*A man plucking roses.*	XXX.	208	*Playing at chess with the house on fire.*	LIX.
Plate XXXI. Diligence.	175	*Diligence drawn by ants.*	CI.			
	179	*Swimming with a burden.*	LXX.	221	*A lily among thorns.*	XIX.

See Plate XXXII.

3°. Giles Corrozet's "*Hecatomgraphie,*" *&c.,* "That is to say the descriptions of one hundred figures and histories, containing many Apophthegms, Proverbs, Sentences and Sayings, as well of the Ancients as of the Moderns, &c.;" Paris, by Denys Ianot, 1540, small octavo, pages 206, emblems 100; Dedication, "Gilles Corrozet Parisien avx bons espritz & amateurs des lettres."*

Page.	*Description of Device.*		*Page.*	*Description of Device.*	
19	The goddess Nemesis	*Emb.* 38	181	Occasion or fortune	*Emb.* 41, 34
28	Icarus falling into the sea	67	183*a*	The burning torch downwards	65
40	Virtue, Vice and Hercules	74	195	The elephant and the serpent	56
93*b*	A virtuous wife	96	210	The lion feigning sickness and the fox	55
156*b*	The fox and the lion	55			
157	The heedless astronomer	72	219	*The gnats round a candle*	76

Plate XXXII. The Gnats.

4°. Horapollo's "HIERÓGLYPHICA," &c., *Concerning the Sacred Signs and Sculptures, &c.;* Paris, Keruer, M.D.LI., small octavo, pages 20 for title &c. and 242. The plates are numerous. Plate II.

There were five editions of *Horapollo* previous to this—the first at Venice by Aldus in 1505, and the others in 1517, 1518, 1521 and 1548. For the manuscripts and editions of *Horapollo*, the best work to consult is that of Dr. Conrad Leemans of Leyden, whose own edition with a commentary may be named, on critical grounds, as the best of this author. See also Brunet's "*Manuel du Libraire*," vol. iii. col. 343. "Horapollinis Niloi Hieroglyphica." Amstelodami MDCCCXXXV.

Page.	*Description of Device.*		*Page.*	*Description of Device.*	
35	The hunted beaver	*p.* 162	131	*Buildings in ruins, books enduring*	*p.* 124
73	The stork feeding her young	155	159	The ant and the grasshopper	75
120	The cock, the lion and the church	55	177	The phœnix from the flames	52
126	*The swan, a poet's badge*	136	188*a*	The ape and her whelp	163
			200	Bees seeking their hive	87

Plate II. Swan.

5°. Bartholomew Aneau's "PICTA POESIS," &c., "*Pictured Poetry.* As a picture poetry will be." Motto "*From Labour, Glory;*" Lyons, Bonhomme, 1552, octavo, folios 119, containing 106 emblems. The woodcuts are small, but well executed. Plate XXXIII.

The same year and from the same printer appeared a French translation "L'IMAGINATION POËTIQUE, traduction en vers françois des latins et grecz par l'auteur mesme d'iceux." Brunet, 1860, vol. i. p. 283.

Page.	*Description of Device.*		*Page.*	*Description of Device.*	
15	Actæon seized by hounds	*fol.* 128	75	Prometheus and the vulture	*fol.* 90
29	A bird brooding	73	122	*Representation of Chaos*	49
74	Tantalus, water and fruit	108	141	Brasidas and his false shield	18

Plate XXXIII. Chaos.

* Consult Brunet's "*Manuel du Libraire,*" Paris 1861, tome ii. col. 299-308; and Dibdin's *Bibl. Dec.* i. 256.

Page.	*Description of Device.*		*Page.*	*Description of Device.*	
149	Narcissus and his shadow	*fol.* 48	215	Sisyphus rolling the stone	*fol.* 79
190*a*	*Urging a fool to climb a tree*	60	218*b*	The shadows	58
211	*The jealous wife*	77	229*b*	A human skull	53

Plate XXXIV. 6°. Peter Coustau's "PEGMA, *Cum narrationibus philosophicis,*" "Repository, with philosophical narrations;" Lyons, Bonhomme, 1555. The ornamented title-page has, like the *Picta Poesis,* a Mercury with the Gorgon's head, and the motto "ΕΚ ΠΟΝΟΥ ΚΛΕΟΣ," From Labour, Glory. The dedication is, "PETRVS COSTALIVS ANTONIO COSTALIO FRATRI S.D." Small octavo, pages 16, 336 and 8, or 360. The emblems count 92, with elaborate borders to each, but not well executed.

Plate XXXV. The French translation has every page highly embellished. "LE PEGME de Pierre Covstav," &c.; "from Latin into French by LANTEAVME de Romieu Gentleman of Arles;" Lyons, Molin, 1560. On the ornamented title-page is a figure of Minerva standing erect within a medallion having the motto around, "LITERAE ET ARMA PARANT (QVORVM DEA PALLAS) HONOREM." The woodcuts of the French translation are very similar to those of the Latin original, but the borders are not the same. Small octavo, pages 420. The emblems are 94.

	Page.	*Description of Device.*		*Page.*	*Description of Device.*	
	38	A warrior on a war-horse	*p.* 251	76*a*	Two warriors shaking hands	*p.* 162
Plate XXXIV. Ruins.	40	Virtue, Vice and Hercules	92	131	Ruins and writings	178
	60	Pythagoras enjoining silence	109	186	*Orpheus and the animals*	315
Plate XXXV. Time.	62	Withered elm and fruitful vine	62	230	The setting sun (Pegme)	374

Plate XXXVI. 7°. Paolo Giovio's and Gabriel Symeoni's "LE SENTENTIOSE IMPRESE," &c., *i.e. Devices for Sayings, &c.;* Lyons, Roville, 1562; quarto, pages 134, emblems 126. The devices of Gabriel Symeoni are 36 on pages 9-44; those of Vescovo Giovio are 90 on pages 45-134. The whole work is also named "TETRASTICHI MORALI," *Moral Four-lined Stanzas.* The clear woodcuts are the same as those which were used for the French translation of the "*Ragionamento di M. Paolo Giovio sopra i Motti & designi d'armi & d'amore,*" *&c.,* and which was printed at Lyons in 1561; the same blocks were used again for a reprint of the original Italian at Lyons in 1574. For an account of Giovio's works consult Brunet's "*Manuel du Libraire,*" iii. col. 582-584.

Manuel du Libraire, 1864, vol. v. col. 392. Brunet names a work of Symeoni's: it is "*Les Devises et Emblèmes héroïques et Morales, inventées par le seigneur Gabriel*

Symeon;" Lyons, Guil. Roville, 1559, quarto, in 50 pages, with very pretty woodcuts.

Page.	Description of Device.		Page.	Description of Device.	
35	The hunted beaver	p. 126	183*a*	Burning torch downwards	p. 35
98*b*	The trodden-down dock	32	183*b*	Wrongs cut on marble	24
110	A rampant lion with a sword	77	190*b*	Giving alms quickly	43
121	The crab and the butterfly	11	219	The gnats round a candle	25
168*b*	Bending the cross-bow	34	226	The cloak and mask	26
169	The ape and the miser's gold	40	227	Two horses chasing a third	30
177	The phœnix from the flames	14			

Plate XXXVII Wrongs.

8°. Arnold Freitag's "MYTHOLOGIA ETHICA," &c., "*Ethical Mythology*, that is, A very pleasant garden of Moral Philosophy, delivered through fables attributed to brute animals: In which, the labyrinth of human life being made clear, the path of virtue is taught in very beautiful precepts as by the thread of Theseus. With most artistic imitations of very noble sculptures by Arnold Freitag, explained in Latin, *and* engraved on brass. Antwerp M.D.LXXIX." Small quarto, pages 251, plates 125. Dedication: "CLARISSIMIS OPTIMISQVE VIRIS ABRAHAMO ORTELIO HISPANIARVM REGIS GEOGRAPHO, ET ANDREÆ XIMENIO LVSITANO, ARNOLDVS FREITAGHIVS S.D." Plate XXXVIII.

The above work is doubtless the same as that of which the title is given by M. A. A De Backer and Ch. Ruelens, with the addition "Philippo Gallæo Christophorus Plantinus excudebat;" thus fixing who the printer was. The copy used by me has written in it, by Mr. J. Brooks Yates, "The engravings by Gerard de Jode and others. The Rev. Thomas Corser has a work entitled *Esbatiment moral des Animaux*, with engravings from the same plates, but the explanations are in French sonnets." By whom the beautiful engravings were wrought is not exactly ascertained, for the *Plantinian Annals* say: "Pas de nom de graveur: mais les planches sortent évidemment de l'atelier de Galle, ce qui est constaté d'ailleurs par la mention faite au titre. Elles pourraient bien être l'œuvre de Gérard de Jode."

"Annales de l'Imprimerie Plantinienne," pp. 202, 203

Page 203.

Page.	Description of Device.		Page.	Description of Device.	
39	The dog and the shadow	p. 113	177	The phœnix from the flames	p. 249
58	The ape and the whelp's paw	129	184	*The ox and the cur*	69
73	The stork feeding her young	251	188*a*	The ape and her whelp	15
98*a*	The fox and the grapes	127	189	The snake warmed by the fire	177
128	The mouse and oyster	169	195	The elephant and the dragon	145
159	The ant and the grasshopper	29	210	The lion feigning sickness	5
160	A satyr and his host	167			

Plate XXXIX. Phœnix.

Plate XL. The Ant

Plate VIII. Beza. 9°. Theodore Beza's "ICONES *id est* VERÆ IMAGINES," &c., *Images, i.e. True Portraits of Men illustrious for learning and piety, &c.*, to which have been added some pictures which are named EMBLEMS; Geneva, Laonius, M.D.LXXX., quarto, unpaged, the emblems are 44. The dedication is, "SERENISSIMO PER DEI GRATIAM SCOTIÆ REGI IACOBO EIVS NOMINIS SEXTO, THEODORVS BEZA GRATIAM AC PACEM A DOMINO." The work is remarkable as containing the earliest known portrait of our James I. There was a French translation by Simon Goulart printed at Geneva in 1581, quarto.

Bibl. Decam. vol. i. p. 274. "These emblems," says Dibdin, "are of peculiar delicacy of execution, but being heavily printed on a thin and coarse-grained paper, they lose much of the merit of their execution. The borders are elaborate, and perhaps of rather too much importance for the subjects contained within them,—so as in some degree to impair the effect."

	Page.	Description of Device.		Page.	Description of Device.	
Plate XLI. Man.	32	Man and Shadow	Emb. 13	214	Phryxus on the golden fleece	Emb. 4
Plate LIX. Dog.	213	Dog barking at the moon	23	218*b*	Man, woman and shadows	14

Plate XLII 10°. Nicholas Reusner's "EMBLEMATA," &c., *Emblems, &c., partly ethical and physical, but partly historical and hieroglyphical, &c.*, to which is added a book of sacred images or emblems by Jeremiah Reusner; Franckfort, John Feyerabend, 1581, small quarto, pages 371.

The engravings on wood were by Virgil Solis and Jost Ammon. The emblems are comprised in four books of a general nature, and one book of sacred images; also three books of family pedigrees without any pictorial illustrations. Nearly all have dedications,—some of them very curious: as Emb. IIX. p. 210, "To Jesus Christ, God-man," entitled "Christ the ladder to heaven;" Emb. XXVI. p. 236, "To Jesus Christ, Pontifex and King, best and greatest," with the words "The stars shew the way to the king;" and Emb. XXXVI. p. 248, "To Peter an apostle of Jesus Christ." In the family pedigrees are celebrated "John Sambucus the learned physician," p. 297; "Christopher Plantin, the renowned printer," p. 328; and "Sigismund Feyerabend, the well-known bookseller," p. 329.

There is at the end of the volume a remarkable ornament, occupying the whole page; it is a figure of Fame, with a trumpet in each hand, one of which the goddess is sounding. The device is surrounded by the motto, "SI CVPIS VT CELEBRI STET TVA FAMA LOCO: PERVIGILES HABEAS OCVLOS, ANIMVMQVE SAGACEM" — *If thou desirest that thy fame should stand in a noble place, thou shouldst have the eyes watchful and the mind alert.*

There is also a poetical work by Reusner to which Whitney frequently refers; it is "POLYANTHIA, sive Paradisus poeticus," in VII books; Bâle 1579, octavo. Consult also Brunet's "*Manuel*," vol. iv. col. 1255.

Emblems, pp. 50, 51, 73, 87, 97, 144, 147, 177.

Page.	*Description of Device.*		*Page.*	*Description of Device.*	
39	The dog and his shadow	*p.* 82	127	We must not fight with ghosts	*p.* 87
47	Cæsar and Cicero	16	174	Arion and the dolphin	142
48	An ass eating grass ropes	88	177	The phœnix from the flames	98
63	Cupid drawn by lions	20	186	Orpheus and the animals	129
75	Prometheus and the vulture	37	188*a*	The ape and her whelp	70
87	The pelican feeding her young	73	189	The snake warmed by the fire	81
126	The poet's badge, the swan	91			

Plate XLIII. Arion.

Thus the devices in *Whitney*, which are *similar* to those of other emblem writers of his own era, and which might be *suggested* by them, are 103, — to be thus distributed: to Brant, 7; Perrière, 13, Corrozet, 11; Horapollo, 9; Aneau, 12; Coustau, 8; Giovio and Symeoni, 13; Freitag, 13; Beza, 4; and Reusner, 13. Probably, however, he did not borrow from these sources above 23 emblems.

SECTION II. — DEVICES STRUCK OFF FROM THE SAME WOOD-BLOCKS, AND THEREFORE *IDENTICAL*.

HOW far Devices and Mottoes that are similar to his own were really suggestive to Whitney of the subjects which he has chosen for illustration may be very questionable, but there can be no doubt with respect to those which are *identical.* In these the devices coincide stroke for stroke, line for line and figure for figure — the sole difference being a border of another pattern, which we know was easily effected, because the centre constituted a block by itself, and the framework in which it was set might be changed as propriety or fancy dictated.

The authors between whom and Whitney the *identity* existed of which we are speaking all found editors among the learned men whom Plantin gathered around him, and were sent forth from Antwerp or from Leyden. We shall arrange them rather in the order of their relative importance to Whitney's purpose than to their time or their merit. The names of the *ten* authors in Section I. who have similar emblems will be printed in *italic* letter.

Plate XXI. 1°. Andrew Alciat: "OMNIA ANDREÆ ALCIATI V.C. EMBLEMATA," &c., "All the Emblems of Andrew Alciat, with Commentaries, in which, the origin of every emblem being laid open, the meaning of the author is explained, and all obscurities and doubts cleared up, by Claude Mignault of Dijon. The third edition by far more richly stored than the others. Antwerp, from the office of Christopher Plantin,* chief printer to the king, M.D.LXXXI." Octavo, pages 782, emblems 197, trees 16, total 213. Each emblem has an ornamented border, and to each there are copious notes. The references are to this edition, unless an earlier be mentioned, but the arrangement and paging of it are very defective.

Plate VI. "ANDREÆ ALCIATI EMBLEMATVM LIBELLVS;" Paris, *Wechel* M.D.XXXIIII., small octavo, pages 120, emblems 112. On the title-page and at the end is the printer's symbol, with the motto "VNICVM ARBUSTŨ NÕ ALIT DVOS ERYTHACOS," *One tree does not support two Redbreasts.* The woodcuts are very curious and repeated from the same blocks in the Paris editions of 1536, 1540, 1542 and 1544.

J. B. Yates. Note.

Plate XVI "ANDREÆ ALCIATI EMBLEMATVM LIBELLVS," &c.; Aldus, Venice M.D.XLVI. "*With the privilege of Pope Paul III. and of the Senate of Venice for ten years.*" Small octavo, folios 47, emblems 84. The Aldine symbol is on the title-page and at the end, and the volume was printed by the sons of Aldus.

Plate XVII. "DIVERSE IMPRESE," &c., *Various Designs adapted to various Morals*, with verses which declare their significations, together with many others in the Italian language not often translated, *taken from the emblems of* ALCIAT; Lyons, Roville, 1551, octavo,

Annales, pp. 64, 152, 226, 258 and 266.

* The editions of Alciat which Plantin himself issued were in 1566, 1574, 1581, 1583 and 1584, all in Latin.

pages 191, emblems 180. Every page is richly ornamented with a border, and there are Italian stanzas to each emblem.

"EMBLEMATA D. A. ALCIATI," &c., "Emblems of A. Alciat, lately revised by the Author, and, what were desired, enriched with designs. Some new emblems by the Author remarkable for their designs are added." Lyons, Roville, 1551, octavo, pages 226, emblems 211. This Latin edition contains 31 more emblems than the Italian, but in each edition 180 of the emblems are from the same blocks, the borders being changed. Both editions are most profusely embellished. Plate XIX.

Page.	*Description of Device.*	
2	Mercury instructing the traveller, *ed.* 1551	*Emb.* 8, *p.* 14
5	The swallow and grasshopper	179, 617
6	A charioteer with fierce horses, *Corr.* 19	55, 223
8	An ass bearing Isis, *Faerni*	7, 48
10	Sirens and Ulysses	115, 410
13	Slaying of Niobe's children	67, 255
14	Heraclitus and Democritus	151, 535
16	Pigmies and Hercules	58, 232
18	Laden ass eating thistles	85, 313
19	The goddess Nemesis, *Corr.* E. 38	27, 128
27	Fowlers and decoy bird, *Brant.* ed. 1497, E. 49, *Perr.* E. 53	50, 209
28	Icarus falling into the sea, *Corr.* E. 67	103, 363
29	A bird brooding, *Aneau,* p. 73	193, 667
30	Prowess mourning for Ajax	48, 202
33	Swallow's nest and Medeia	54, 221
34	The gourd and the pine	124, 448
35	The hunted beaver, *Giovio,* 126, *Horap.* 162	152, 538
37	Hector and Ajax exchanging gifts	167, 579
38	A warrior on his war horse, *Coust.* p. 251	35, 160
45	Agamemnon, with sword and shield	57, 230
47	Cæsar and Cicero, *Reus. St.* i. 16	41, 181

Page.	*Description of Device.*	
48	An ass eating grass ropes, *Reus.* p. 88	*Emb.* 91, *p.* 328
49	She-goat and wolf's whelp	64, 247
50*a*	Weary man and swallows	70, 268
52*b*	Small fish and their enemies	169, 585
53*a*	The sow and the gleanings, *Perr.* E. 17	45, 196
b	Sour fig tree on the mountain	73, 276
54*a*	Trumpeter asking forgiveness	173, 596
b	Swallow, cuckoo, &c.	100, 352
55*a*	Two redbreasts fighting	93, 333
56	The dog biting the stone, *Italian ed.* 102	174, 599
57	Washing the Æthiop	59, 235
60	Pythagoras enjoining silence, *Lat. ed.* 1551, p. 17, *Perr.* E. 8, *Coust.* p. 109	
62	Withered elm and fruitful vine, *Coust.* p. 200	159, 556
63	Cupid drawn by lions, *Reus.* 15, i. 20	105, 370
65	The blind carrying the lame	160, 559
70	Brutus falling on his sword	119, 430
73	The stork feeding her young, *Horap.* p. 155, *Freit.* p. 251	30, 142
74	Tantalus, water and fruit, *Aneau,* p. 108	84, 310
75	Prometheus and the vulture, *Reus.* 27, i. 37, *Aneau,* p. 90	102, 358

Plate XVIII. Dog.

	Page.	*Description of Device.*	
	76*a*	Two warriors reconciled, *Coust.* p. 162, *Samb.* p. 16 *Emb.* 39, *p.* 175	
	77*a*	Fisherman and eel	21, 102
	78	Archer stung by an adder	104, 367
	79	Lais with her musk-cat	79, 294
	82	Transformation into swine, *Reus.* 24, iii. 134	76, 284
	85	To cast off sloth	81, 300
	90	The dolphin aground	166, 577
	94	Envy feeding on vipers	71, 271
	99	The tyrant Mezentius	197, 681
	119	Lion, boar and vulture	125, 452
	120	Cock, lion and church, *Horap.* p. 55	15, 78
	126	The poet's badge, a swan, *Horap.* p. 136, *Reus.* p. 91	183, 635
Plate XXII. Hares.	127	Hares and dead lion, *Reus.* p. 87	153, 542
	128	Mouse and oyster, *Freit.* p. 169	94, 335
	130	Emblems of the seven wise men	186, 646
	132	Love and Death exchanging arrows	155, 547
	134	A dyer at his cauldron	117, 420
Plate LVIII. Bees.	135	A sage, Cupid and the lady	108, 379
	136	Ewer &c. and tomb	31, 146
	137	Ship driven on its course	43, 188
	138*a*	Helmet becomes a hive	177, 608
Plate LIX. Dog.	139*b*	Nemesis and Hope	46, 198
	144	Arion and dolphin, *Reus.* p. 142	89, 323
	146	Apollo and Bacchus	99, 349
	147	Cupid and the bees *Emb.* 111, *p.* 391	
	148	Cupid complaining to Venus	112, 394
	149	Narcissus and his shadow, *Aneau* 48	69, 261
	151	The king and the sponge	147, 546
	152	The winged and weighted hands	120, 435
	163	Æneas rescuing Anchises	194, 670
	164	Brass and earthen pots, *Faerni* i. p. 7	165, 574
	170	Gorged kite and dam	128, 462
	174	The fruitful wayside tree	192, 665
	176	Three careless dames at dice, *Brant's St. Nav.* lxxxv.	129, 465
	181	Occasion or fortune, *Brant* xlvii, *Corr.* E. 41 and 84, *Perr.* E. 63	121, 438
	182*a*	Cupid's emblems	106, 374
	187	Bacchus and his emblems	25, 115
	188*b*	The lamprey and the arrow	20, 99
	189*b*	Goat overturning milk	140, 505
	193	Thetis at Achilles' tomb	135, 483
	194	The drum, terror after death	170, 587
	200	Bees seeking their hive, *Horap.* p. 87	148, 528
	202	Courtier in the stocks	86, 316
	207	Falcon, geese and ducks	139, 502
	213	Dog barking at the moon, *Beza* E. 23	164, 571
	214	Phryxus and golden fleece, *Beza* E. 4	189, 658

Thus there are 86 of Whitney's emblems, the sources of which are *identical* with those of Plantin's edition of *Alciat* in 1581.

Plate VII.

2º. Claude Paradin's "LES DEVISES HÉROÏQVES," &c., "The Heroical Devices of M. Claude Paradin, Canon of Beaujeau, of Signor Gabriel Symeon and of other authors." Antwerp, Plantin, M.D.LXII., in 16mo, folioed but not paged; with many well-executed woodcuts, and with notices of persons and events of much interest. The copy to which our references are made contains the autograph of our author Geffrey Whitney.

The earliest edition of *Paradin* was printed at Lyons in 1557,* thus: "Devises héroïques. Lyons, Ian de Tournes et Guill. Gazeau, 1557, in 8°, de 261 pp. avec 180 grav. sur bois." The printers, Plantin and Latius, issued several editions in Latin and French; there was in fact "une foule d'éditions, sortant de presses différentes;" as the Latin one,

Brunet, 1863, vol. iv. col 358.

"Annales," p. 75.

"SYMBOLA HEROÏCA M. Claudii Paradini Belliiocensis Canonici et D. Gabrielis Symeonis. Multo quam antea, fidelius de gallica lingua in latinam conversa. Antverpiæ, ex officina Christophori Plantini, 1567." In 16mo, pages 316; the figures are on wood, or rather "clichées en metal," stereotyped. The translator into Latin was "Jean le Gouverneur, de Gédinnes." This Latin edition was repeated in 1583.

"Annales de l'Imprimerie Plantinienne," 1865, pp. 32, 75, 76, 256.

"THE HEROICALL DEUISES of M. Claudius Paradin Canon of Beauieu. Whereunto are added the Lord Gabriel Symeons and others. Translated out of Latin into English by P. S. London. Imprinted by Will. Kearney dwelling in Adlin streete, 1591." 24mo. With devices neatly cut in wood.

Plate LVI.

We give a fac-simile of the title-page from a very rare copy lent for the purpose by the Rev. Thomas Corser. It is this English translation which Francis Douce supposes Shakespeare to have used when composing the triumph scene in *Pericles*. The dedication is curious: "To the renowmed Capteine Chr. Carleill Esq., chief Commander of her Maiesties forces in the prouince of Vlster, Ireland, and Seneschall there of the counties of Clandeboy, the Rowte, the Glens, the Duffre, and Kylultaugh."

Plate LVI.

Vol ii. p. 127.

Page.	*Description of Device.*		*Page.*	*Description of Device.*	
1	Ivy and obelisk, *H. Jun.* E. 14	*fol.* 43	86	A shroud on a spear	*fol.* 31
12	The tun pierced with holes	89	88	Ears of corn, handsful, and sheaf	126
21	The beetle on a rose	129	98*b*	The down trodden dock, *Giovio*, p. 32	167
23	Ears of corn breaking on a sheaf	144	102	A sword hanging by a thread	82
24	Snake and strawberry plant	41	111	Scævola's hand over the fire	73
51*b*	Ostrich with outspread wings	28	113	Valerius and the crow	63
66	Sword and trowel, *Reus. St.* i. 4	69	115	The garlands of Marcus Sergius	132
68	The sifting of corn	88	116	Rampant lion and sword, *Giovio*, p. 77	51

* Dibdin however has the following note: "In the collection of the marquis of Blandford the earliest edition of the devices of these authors is of the date of 1551, at Lyons, 18mo, in the French language."

Bibl. Decam. vol. i. pp. 264-266.

Page.	*Description of Device.*	
117	Arrows in the shield of M. Scæva	*fol.* 76
121	Crab and butterfly, *Giovio*, p. 11	153
138*b*	An arrow shot at marble	96
139*a*	Gold on the touchstone	101
143	The pen of Valens	93
166*b*	A snake shaken over the fire	112
168*b*	Bending the bow, *Giovio*, p. 34	169
169	Ape and miser's gold, *Giovio*, p. 40	174
177	The phœnix from the flames, *Horap.* p. 52, *Giovio*, p. 14, *Freit.* p. 249, *Reus.* p. 98	*fol.* 53
183*a*	The burning torch downwards, *Giovio*, p. 35, *Corr.* E. 65	169
b	Wrongs cut on marble, *Giovio*, p. 24	160
190*b*	Giving quickly, *Giovio*, p. 43	172
191*a*	The hawk's lure	93
217	Hay on a pole	135
226	Cloak and mask, *Giovio*, p. 26	161
227	Two horses chasing a third, *Giovio*, p. 30	163

Plantin's edition of *Paradin* for 1562 supplies 32 wood-blocks to illustrate *Whitney*.

Plate XXIV. 3°. John Sambucus: "EMBLEMATA," &c., "Emblems, with some coins of ancient work, by John Sambucus of Tornau in Hungary. Antwerp, from the office of Christopher Plantin, M.D.LXIV." Octavo, pages 240, emblems 166, and coins 23. The title is set in a framework representing the nine Muses, and the well-known compasses are wrought into the composition. There are fine borders to the engravings. Mr. J. Brooks Yates marked in his copy that the woodcuts were by Gérard de Jode. The monograms on some of the embellishments are an I inserted into a C, an A and a G; the first, it is said, denotes the work of Jean Croissant, the next that of Assuerus Van Londerzeel, and the third that of Hubert Goltzius. Sambucus dedicated his emblems to "Maximilian II. Emperor-Augustus, king of Bohemia, Dalmatia and Croatia, Archduke of Austria, Count of the Tyrol," &c. The symbolical device represents the emperor enthroned upon the temple of Janus, of which the gates are closed; at his feet is the wolf suckling Remus and Romulus; he is extending an olive branch to an eagle which presents him three crowns — one in each claw and one in its beak; on the left hand are three persons in attendance on the emperor: and the picture is followed by three pages of laudatory and descriptive verses. This work is certainly the most elegant of all the emblem-books of the age.

Liverpool Lit. and Phil. Society, 1849, No. V. p 28.

Annales de l'Imp. Plant p. 42.

From Plantin's press there issued in 1566 both a Latin and a Flemish edition; in 1567 a French translation by Jacques

Annales de l'Imp. Plant. 1865, pp. 64, 76, 95, 266.

Grevin; and in 1569 and 1584 also a Latin edition. We close the list with

"EMBLEMATA, et Aliqvot Nvmmi Antiqvi operis, Ioan. Sambvci, Timaviensis Pannonii *Qvarta Editio* Cum emendatione & auctario copioso ipsius auctoris *Ex Officina Plantiniana* Apvd Christophor. Raphel. Academiæ Lugduno-Bat. Typograp. cIↄ.Iↄ.ic." 16mo, pages 352, a portrait, emblems 206, coins 43.

Page.	*Description of Device.*	
7	Incendiary and assassin	*p.* 206
9	Prince, astronomer and husbandman	28
11	The gallant ship and the sun	46
15	Actæon seized by the hounds, *Alciat.* E. 52, p. 214, *Aneau*, p. 41	128
17	Drinking, gaming, throat cutting, *ed.* 1566, *Brant's Stult. Navis*, 1497, fol. 27	212
20	The sun over hills of snow	44
22	A fox on floating ice	98
25	Pliny over-curious	159
26	Miller sleeping under his mill	107
32	Murderer and his shadow, *ed.* 1566	241
36	Popinjay, bird and bucket	101
41	Thief strangled by his own cord	209
43	Astronomer and compass	84
46	Aged dame and skulls	65
52*a*	Bull, elephant, &c., *ed.* 1599	215
58	Ape using whelp's paw, *Freit.* 129	110
59	Whirlwind and trees, *ed.* 1569	279
64	Hen sucking her own eggs	30
67	Thunderbolt and the laurel	14
69	Well and curtained window	69
71	Casting nets into the sea	230
72	Sea-water through a sluice	70
76*b*	Killing the snake in the wall	47
77*b*	Old tree yielding fire-wood	*p.* 154
80	Anellus and his wife, *ed.* 1599	253
81	King, child and idiot, *ed.* 1599	258
83	Paris and the three goddesses	152
84 (76)	Hanno and his birds	60
89	The apodes of India flying	132
92	Mercury mending the lute	57
97	The cuttle fish escaping	76
100	Dog, bull and painter	177
103	Minerva watching and resting	137
124	Friendship in a fox's skin	198
125	Crocodile, dog and bacchanal	41
140	Ban-dog and lap-dog	183
142	The ape and the fox	19
150	Elephant and undermined tree	184
171	Reading and practising	62
173	Student and child gathering fruit	117
178	Lion &c. and travelled fool	104
182*b*	Bull, horse and fair woman	144
195	Poisoned elephant and serpent, *ed.* 1569, *Corr.* E. 56, *Freit.* p. 145	228
199	Time cutting off man and woman	23
204	Palace with two doors	197
206	Unripe grapes trodden down	104
209	Sick miser and his gold, *ed.* 1569	229
222*a*	The climbing ivy	140

Plate XXV. Actæon.

Forty-eight are the emblems in *Whitney* to be attributed to Sambucus.

4°. Hadrian Junius of Hoorn: "Hadriani Junii medici Emblemata," &c., "The Emblems of Hadrian Junius, physician, to M. Arnold Cobel. A book of his Enigmas to M. Arnold Rosen- Plate XXVI.

berg. Antwerp, from the office of Christopher Plantin, M.D.LXV." Octavo, pages 151, emblems 58 in 65 pages.

"Annales de l'Imp. Plant." pt. i. p. 48.

This volume is the most elegant that had hitherto issued from the presses of Plantin. Each page in the emblem part has a border, in the midst of which is a pleasing vignette, and the dedications are nearly all to persons eminent in politics or in literature. The engravings or woodcuts appear to be of Italian origin, and are of remarkable delicacy. The ornamented borders are the same as those used for Whitney's *Emblems.*

"Annales," pp. 60, 95, 279.

The edition of 1566 is less beautiful, and that of 1569 a repetition. The edition of 1585 is in 32mo.

"HADRIANI IUNII EMBLEMATA eivsdem ÆNIGMATVM LIBELLVS, *Cum noua & Emblematum & Ænigmatum Appendice.* Lvgdvni Batavorvm Ex Officina Plantiniana Apud Franciscum Raphelengium, cIↄ.Iↄ.XCVI." In 16mo, pages 167. The emblems are 62 on as many pages, with a Latin stanza of four lines to each; there are notes to the emblems pp. 69-151; of enigmas there are 53. The emblems are from the same blocks as former editions.

"Annales de l'Imp. Plant." 76, 87 and 166.

"EMBLESMES de Adrian le Jeune, faicts François et sommairent expliqués, Anvers, Christophe Plantin, 1567," is the title of a French translation attributed to Jacques Grevin. This edition was repeated in 1568 with Grevin's name as translator, and again in 1575.

"Annales," pp. 166 and 64.

"EMBLEMATA Adriani Junii Medici. Overgheset in nederlantsche talc, deur M. A. G. T'Antwerpen, ghedruct by Christoffel Plantyn, M.D.LXXV. Met privilegie." In 16mo, emblems pp. 5-62. There is an engraving on wood at the head of each emblem. The translator of *Junius* also translated *Sambucus* into Flemish: both versions were undertaken by the advice of the celebrated geographer Abraham Ortelius and at Plantin's expense.

Page.	*Description of Device.*		*Page.*	*Description of Device.*	
3	Crocodile and her eggs	*Emb.* 19	55*b*	Boys blowing bubbles	*Emb.* 16
4	Envy &c. imprison truth	53	87	Pelican feeding her young, *Reus.* p. 73	7
40	Virtue, Vice and Hercules, *Corr.* E. 74, *Coust.* p. 92	44	93*b*	The virtues of a wife, *Corr.* E. 96, *Perr.* E. 18	50
42	Glory fleeing the slothful	52	96	The rock and raging winds	59
44	The lion and dog	10	101	The caged nightingale	56
50*b*	Youth working, age feasting	35	118	Frogs, serpents and palm tree	9
51*a*	Spider and bee on one flower	33			

Page.	*Description of Device.*	
172	Candle, book and hour glass	*Emb.* 5
191*b*	Hear, be still, flee	62
196	Mercury armed with a pen	60
212	The insignia of Æsculapius, *Samb.* 89	25
219	The gnats round a candle, *Corr.* E. 76, *Parad.* fol. 161, *Giovio*, p. 25	*Emb.* 49
220	Reed, oak and tempest	43
222*b*	Cats in traps, rats at play	4

Whitney has to be debited with 20 emblems derived from *Junius.*

5°. Gabriel Faerni: "FABULÆ C. ex antiquis auctoribus delectæ et a Gabriele Faerno carminibus explicatæ (a Silvio Antoniano editæ) *Romæ Vin*-Luchinus, 1564." Quarto. "Les planches faites sur de bons dessins qu'on a attribués au Titien, sont gravées à l'eauforte." Brunet's Manuel du Libraire, vol. ii. pt. ii. col. 1160.

Plantin's first edition of Faerni's *Fables* appeared in 1563 in 16mo; a second edition in 12mo in 1567, and a third, also in 12mo, in 1585, with 100 plates on wood. The copy of the edition of 1585, belonging to William Stirling esq., of Keir, has the following title: "Annales," pp. 47, 70 and 279.

"CENTVM FABVLÆ ex Antiqvis Avctoribvs Delectæ, et a Gabriele Faerno *Cremonensi Carminibus explicatæ.* ANTVERPIÆ Apud Christophorum Plantinum, M.D.LXXXV." In 16mo, pages 173, emblems 100. Several traces of portions of the borders round Whitney's plates occur, as on pp. 16, 25, 34 and 44; also some of the ornaments are the same, as on pp. 27 and 118. The impressions in *Whitney*, even when from the same blocks, are on the whole clearer than those in this edition of *Faerni.* Plate XXVII.

Page.	*Description of Device.*	
39	The dog and his shadow, *ed.* 1585, *Freit.* p. 113, *Reus.* 23, ii. p. 82	*Emb.* 53, *p.* 90
91	Jupiter, the beasts and snail	57, 95
93*a*	Ass, ape and mole	43, 56
98	The fox and grapes, *Freit.* p. 127	19, 36
153*a*	The stag biting the boughs	70, 117
b	The fox and the boar	78, 132
154	Lion, ass and fox, hunting	3, 11
155	The thief and his mother, *Brant's Stult. Navis*, foll. 16 and 57	71, 119
156*a*	Lady and physician	68, 113
156*b*	Fox and lion, *Corr.* E. 55	*Emb.* 18, *p.* 35
157	The heedless astronomer, *Corr.* E. 72	73, 123
158	The drowning of Colasmus' wife	27, 49
159	The ant and the grasshopper, *Freit.* p. 29, *Brant's St. N.* fol. 80, *Horap.* p. 75	7, 17
160	Satyr and host, *Freit.* p. 167	58, 96
162	Wolf, mother and babe	76, 128
210	The lion feigning sickness, *Freit.* p. 5 *Corr.* E. 55	74, 124

So Whitney has borrowed from Faerni 16 emblems.

Now, ascertaining the results of inquiry after the devices in *Whitney*, struck off from the same wood-blocks, and therefore *identical* with those of other emblem writers, we count up — for Alciat 86 instances, Paradin 32, Sambucus 48, Junius 20, and Faerni 16; in all, 202.

Title-page of Whitney.

In Whitney's work there are 248 devices, and we have accounted for the whole; 23 were original, 23 suggested, and 202 are identical with those of the five emblematists last named. Thus in "The Choice of Emblemes" 225 have been "gathered out of sundrie writers," and 23 is the number of the "divers newly devised."

It is certainly an amount leaving little to the credit of the inventive or imaginative power bestowed on the mottoes and devices of a book often regarded, from its completeness, as the earliest work in the English language expressly on emblems. But this was of no great consequence, for the entire volume would be a novelty in England, except to the few who were versed in its mysteries. Whitney's fame rests on having so well executed what he undertook to accomplish, — to present to his nation a full and correct view of a species of literature which in a few years had grown into high favour and been the instruction and amusement of the monk in his cloister and of the pontiff in his chair of supremacy, engaged the talent of some of the foremost men in law, medicine and theology, and entertained alike Fleming, Frenchman and Spaniard,* the Hungarian on the Danube, and the Dutch by Utrecht, Leyden and the Zuyder Zee.

* A translation of Alciat's *Emblems* into Spanish was published about the middle of the sixteenth century. "Los Emblemas de Alciato traducidas en rhimas Españolas aña̅didas di figuras de nuovas emblemas &c., En Lyon por Girlielmo Rovillio 1549" — Francisco Guzman's "Trivmphas Morales," at Medina 1587 — Horosco Couaruvias' "Emblemas Morales," at Segovia 1589 — and Hernando de Soto's "Emblemas Moralezadas," at Madrid 1599, — attest that Spanish gravity was not slow to yield to the new infatuation as to emblems.

ESSAY II.

OBSOLETE WORDS IN WHITNEY, WITH PARALLELS CHIEFLY FROM CHAUCER, SPENSER AND SHAKESPEARE.

N collecting from the Emblems of Whitney the words that are *obsolete* we do not confound them with words that are *archaic*, of old forms but still in use though modernised in orthography. However strange the spelling may appear, as *caruoraunte* for cormorant, *condempne* for condemn, *ginnes* for gins, *inoughe* for enough, *randonne* for random, *shalbe* for shall be, *suruaighe* for survey, *varijnge* for varying, *wanne* for won, *whotte* for hot, and *yearthe* for earth, — still, if the words remain in use, they will not be admitted into the following list. Again, some words will be given which, though spelled in the same way with others now current, were made use of by Whitney with a meaning that has passed away.* Emblems 52, xvi, 97, 184, 34, 142, 86, xiii, 140, 167, 160 and 164.

ACCIDENTES: events, occurrences, deeds.

Such accidentes, as haue bin done in times paste. *Whit.* Ded. viii. l. 2.

This present time behouldeth the accidentes of former times. „ Ded. ix. l. 21.

* In the following references: —

Whit. Whitney; *E.* page of Emblems; *l.* line.

Chau. Chaucer (Moxon's edition, 1847); *p.* page and column; *l.* line; *without any other letter*, the Canterbury Tales; *B. K.* Complaint of Black Knight; *C. L.* Court of Love; *L. W.* Legend of Good Women; *P.* Persones Tale; *R.* Romaunt of the Rose; *T. C.* Troilus and Creseide.

Spen. Spenser (Moxon's edition, 1856); *p.* page and column; *without any other letter*, the book, canto, stanza and line of the Faerie Queene; *C.* Shepheardes Calender; *M. H.* Mother Hubbard's Tale; *V. G.* Virgil's Gnat.

Shak. Shakespeare (Cambridge and London edition, as far as published 1863-1865); act, scene and line.

Temp. v. i. 305. And the particular accidents gone by (*also l.* 250). *Shak.*
1 Hen. IV. I. ii. 199. And nothing pleaseth but rare accidents. ,,

AGASTE: terrified.

E. 20, l. 9. So, thoughe ofte times the simple bee agaste. *Whit.*
E. 67, l. 8. When tempestes rage, doe make the worlde agaste. ,,
p. 18, i. l. 2343. For which so sore agast was Emelie,
That she was wel neigh mad, and gan to crie. *Chau.*
p. 46, 2, i. 9, 21, 4. —— they gan espy
An armed Knight towards them gallop fast,
That seemed from some feared foe to fly,
Or other grisly thing, that him aghast. *Spen.*
Lear, II. i. Gasted by the noise I made. *Shak.*

AMISSE: misfortune, wrong.

E. 211, l. 16. That all too late shee mourn'd for her amisse. *Whit.*
p. 146, ii. l. 17226. O rakel hond, to do so foule a miss. *Chau.*
p. 67, 2, ii. 1. 19, l. 2. How that same Knight should doe so fowle amis. *Spen.*
Ham. IV. v. Each toy seems prologue to some great amiss. *Shak.*
Son. 151. Then, gentle cheater, urge not my amiss. ,,

ANNOY: trouble, hurt.

E. 219, l. 9. His pleasures shalbe mated with annoyes. *Whit.*
R. p. 243, i. 4404. Well more annoie is in me
Than is in thee of this mischaunce. *Chau.*
p. 32, 2, i 6, 17, 9. For griefe whereof the lad n'ould after ioy,
But pynd away in anguish and selfe-wild annoy. *Spen.*
Rich. III. v. iii. 156. Good angels guard thee from the boar's annoy. *Shak.*

BALE: poison, mischief, sorrow.

E. 180, l. 7. A worde once spoke, it can retourne no more,
But flies awaie, and ofte thy bale doth breede. *Whit.*
E. 219, 16. Lo this their bale, which was her blisse you heare. ,,
p. 144, i. l 16949. —— for ended is my tale
God send every good man bote of his bale. *Chau.*
p. 10. 1. l. 16, 7. For light she hated as the deadly bale. *Spen.*
1 Hen. VI. v. iv. 122. By sight of these our baleful enemies. *Shak.*
Cor. I. i. 156. The one side must have bale. ,,

BANDOGGE: the mastiff.

E. 140, l. 1. The bandogge, fitte to matche the bull, or beare. *Whit.*
Sir T. More, p. 586. And haue bandedogges to driue them out of the corne. ,,
V. G. p. 419, l. 540. Then greedie Scilla, under whom there bay
Manie great bandogs, which her gird about. *Spen.*

The time when screech-owls cry and ban-dogs howl. *Shak.* 2 Hen. VI. I. iv. 17.

BANE, or BAYNE: injury, destruction.

Euen so it happes, wee ofte our bayne doe brue. *Whit.* E. 141, l. 7.
Lo PROCRIS heare, when wounded therewith all,
Did breede her bane, who mighte haue bath'de in blisse. „ E. 211, l. 13.
But I was hurt right now thurghout min eye
Into min herte, that wol my bane be. *Chau.* p. 9, i. l. 1099.
—— it is all his joye and appetite
To ben himself the grete hartes bane. „ p. 13, l. 1682.
To bane thee when thou bite. *Tuberville.*
There caughte his bane (alas) to sonne. *Surrey.* Louer.
Lest Rome herself be bane unto herself. *Shak.* Titus v. iii. 73.
And I be pleased to give ten thousand ducats
To have it bain'd. „ Mer. V. IV. i. 45.

BANNE, or BAN: curse.

Whereat, the maide her pacience quite forgot,
And in a rage, the bruitishe beaste did banne. *Whit.* E. 189, l 9.
'Gan both envy, and bitterly to ban. *Spen.* p. 228, 2, iv. 9, 9, 7.
With Hecate's ban thrice blasted. *Shak.* Ham. III. ii.
Fell banning hag, enchantress, hold thy tongue! „ 1 Hen VI. v. iii. 42.
And ban thine enemies, both mine and thine! „ 2 Hen. VI. II. iv. 24.

BILBOWE: a rapier made at Bilboa, or one who uses it; the stocks.

Giue PAN, the pipe: giue bilbowe blade, to swashe. *Whit.* E. 145, l. 5.
I combat challenge of this latten bilbo. *Shak.* M.W.W. I. i. 146.
—— methought, I lay
Worse than the mutines in the bilboes. „ Ham. v. ii.
An honest bilbow-smith would make good blades. *Ben Jonson.*
—— our bilbows are as good,
As his,—our arms as strong. *Drayton.* Polyolbion.

BOORDE, or BOURD: jest, sport.

For euel wordes, pierce sharper than a sworde,
Which ofte wee rue, thoughe they weare spoke in boorde. *Whit.* E. 62, l. 2.
My wit is gret, though that I bourde and play. *Chau.* p. 97, i. l. 12710.
That that I spake, I sayd it in my bourde. „ 145, 17030.
They all agreed; so, turning all to game
And pleasaunt bord, they past forth on their way. *Spen.* p 206, 2, iv. 4, 13, 1.

BROACHE: break into, tap, spread abroad.

And bluddie broiles, at home are set a broache. *Whit.* E. 7, l. 2.

Rom.& J. I. i. 102. Who set this ancient quarrel new abroach. *Shak.*
1Hen. IV. IV. ii. 14. Alack what mischiefs might be set abroach. „
Right as who set a tonne a broche,
He perced the harde roche. *Gower.*
Broach a better tappe. *Gascoigne.*

CARKE: trouble, anxiety.
E. 199, l. 9. Lo, Time dothe cut vs of, amid our carke, and care. *Whit.*
p. 12, 1, i. 1, 44, 4. His heavie head, devoide of careful carke. *Spen.*
The wight, whose absence is our cark. „
In house, for wife and child, there is but cark and care. *Uncertain.*

CARLE: a hardy, country fellow, or churl.
E. 219, l. 5 At lengthe, this greedie carle the Lythergie possesste. *Whit.*
p. 5, i. l. 547. The MILLER was a stout carl for the nones. *Chau.*
p. 49, 2, i. 9, 54, 2. Which when the carle beheld, and saw his guest. *Spen.*
Cymb. v. ii. This carl, a very drudge of nature. *Shak.*

CARPES: blame, talk at or about.
E. 50, l. 3. Which carpes the pratinge crewe, who like of bablinge beste. *Whit.*
E. 137, l. 7. Which carpes all those, that loue to much the canne. „
p. 4. ii. l. 476. In felawship wel coude she laughe and carpe
Of remedies of loue she knew perchance. *Chau.*
Lear, I. iv. Do hourly carpe and quarrel. *Shak.*
—— shame not these woods
Timon, IV. iii. 206. By putting on the cunning of a carper.

CATES: delicacies, food.
E. 18, l. 9. Whose backe is fraughte with cates and daintie cheare. *Whit.*
E. 102, l. 4. Where pages braue, all daintie cates, did bringe. „
E. 198, l. 10. And CODRVS had small cates, his harte to gladde. (202, 12.) „
Com E. III. i. 28. But though my cates be mean, take them in good part. *Shak.*
1 Hen. IV. III i. 163. Than feed on cates and have him talk to me. „
1 Hen. VI. II. iii. 79. Taste of your wine and see what cates you haue.

CONTENTATION: content, contentment.
E. 87, l. 3. Within this life, shall contentation finde. *Whit.*
i. 236. To the great cōtentacion of the country. *Fabyan.*

CORSIE: bird of prey.
E. 211, l. 15. This corsie sharpe so fedde vppon her gall. *Whit.*

CREATE: created.

Not for our selues, alone wee are create. *Whit.* E. 64, l. 1.
And al be it so, that God hath create all thing in right ordre. *Chau.* P. p. 150, ii. l. 63.
And the issue there create,
Ever shall be fortunate. *Shak.* M.N.Dr. v. i. 394.
Being create for comfort. " John, iv. i. 107.
With hearts create of duty and of zeal. " Hen V. ii. ii. 31.

DEFACE: disfigurement, disgrace.

And headlonge falles at lengthe to his deface. *Whit.* E. 6, l. 10.
But wicked Impes, that lewdlie runne their race,
Shee hales them backe, at lengthe to theire deface. " E. 19, l. 10.
Think how his facte, was ILIONS foule deface. " E. 79, l. 22.
Oh bondage vile, the worthie mans deface. " E. 101, l. 19.
That heate might it not deface. *Chau.* H. of F. iii. l. 74.
Broke be my sword, my arms torn and defaced. *Shak.* 2 Hen.VI. iv. i. 42.

DEFAME: infamy.

With slaunders vile, and speeches of defame. *Whit.* E. 128, l. 8.
This BIAS vs'd: and cause for foule defame,
SARDINIA moste is stained. " E. 130, l. 20.
That to his body, when that he were ded,
Were no despit' ydon for his defame. *Chau.* p. 125, i, l. 14467.
It is a sinne, and eke a great folie
To apeiren any man, or him defame. " p 24, i. l. 3149.
In remembrance of thy defame. *Gower.*

ETERNISED: rendered eternal.

Learned men haue eternised to all posterities. *Whit.* Ded. iv. l. 32.
There his name who loue and prize
Stable stay shall eternize. *Sidney.*
But in them nature's copy not eterne. *Shak.* Macb. iii. ii. 38.

FACTE: deed, action.

Thinke howe his facte, was ILIONS foule deface. *Whit.* E 79, l. 22.
Then quoth the theife, my masters mark, I will defend the facte. " E. 155, l. 6.
In hope my facte shall mothers warne, that doe behould this sighte. " E. 155, l. 12.
As you were past all shame,
Those of your fact are so, — so past all truth. *Shak.* W.Tale, iii ii. 82.

FARDLE: a burden, a package.

E. 179, l. 9. Doth venture life with fardle on his backe. ***Whit.***

R. p. 254, i. l. 5686. Then goeth fardels for to beare,
With as good chere as he did eare. ***Chau.***

Ham. III. i. —— who would fardels bear? ***Shak.***

W. Tale, IV. iv. 734. The fardel there? what's i' the fardel? „

FEARE: terrify.

E. 45, l. 11. Mannes terror this, to feare them that behoulde. *Whit.*

E. 127, l. 11. Who while they liu'de, did feare you with theire lookes. „

E. 163, l. 5. No fier, nor sworde, his valiaunt harte coulde feare. „

p. 132, ii. l. 15392. Ran coward calf, and eke the veray hogges
So fered were for berking of the dogges. *Chau.*

1483. And thus he shall you with his wordes fere. „

p. 330, 2, vi. 8, 47, 4. Ne ought was feared of his certaine harmes. *Spen.*

Ant. & Cl. II. vi. Thou canst not fear us, Pompey, with thy sails. *Shak.*

M. for M. II. i. 1. We must not make a scarecrow of the law,
Setting it up to fear the birds of prey.

T. Shrew, I. ii. 202. Tush, tush! fear boys with bugs.

FONDE: foolish.

E. 223, l. 7. Oh worldlinges fonde, that ioyne these two so ill. *Whit.*

R. p. 250, i. l. 5370. The rich man full fond is ywis,
That weneth that he loved is. *Chau.*

p. 68, 2, ii. 1, 30, 1. Certes, said he, well mote I shame to tell
The fond encheason that me hither led. *Spen.*

p. 288, v. 11, 23, 9. The better to beguile whom she so fond did finde. „

M. for M. v. i. 104. By heaven, fond wretch, thou know'st not what thou speak'st. *Shak.*

M. N. Dr. III. ii. 317. You see how simple and how fond I am. „

3 Hen. VI. II. ii. 38. My careless father fondly gave away.

GATE: going, way.

E. 2, l. 9. Bypathes, and wayes, appeare amidd our gate. *Whit.*

R. p. 235, i. l. 3332. With that word, Reason went her gate. *Chau.*

Lear, IV. vi. Go your gait. *Shak.*

M. N. Dr. v. i. 404. With this field-dew consecrate,
Every fairy take her gait.

Hen. VIII. III. ii. 116. Springs out into fast gait; then stops again.

INGRATE: ungrateful.

E. 64, l. 3. And those, that are vnto theire frendes ingrate. ***Whit.***

p. 322, 1, vi. 7, 2, 5. Yet in his mind malitious and ingrate. ***Spen.***

T. Shrew, I. ii. 266. Will not so graceless be to be ingrate. ***Shak.***

LET: hinder, prevent.

But riuers swifte, their passage still do let. — *Whit.* E. 89, l. 8.
But when that nothinge coulde OPIMIVS sleepinge let. — „ E. 209, l. 9.
Now help, O Mars, thou with thy bloody cope,
For love of Cipria, thou me naught ne let. — *Chau.* T. C. p. 295, 2, III. l. 725.
Leave, ah! leave off, whatever wight thou bee,
To let a weary wretch from her dew rest. — *Spen.* p.70, 1, ii. 1, 47, 6.
I'll make a ghost of him that lets me. — *Shak.* Ham. I. iv.
What lets but one may enter at her window? — „ Two Gen. Ver. III. i. 113.
Therefore thy kinsmen are no let to me. — „ Rom & J. II. ii. 69.

LOBBE: a lazy, stupid person.

Let Grimme haue coales: and lobbe his whippe to lashe. — *Whit.* E. 145, l. 6.
Farewell, thou lob of spirits; I'll be gone. — *Shak.* M. N. Dr. II. i. 16.
—— and their poor jades
Lob down their heads, dropping the hides and hips. — „ Hen. V. IV. ii. 46.
But as the drone the honey hive doth rob:
With worthy books, so deals this idle lob. — *Gascoigne.*
Bion therefore was but a very lob and foole in saying this. — *P. Holland.*

MANCHET: fine bread, or flour.

The manchet fine, on highe estates bestowe. — *Whit.* E. 79, l. 9.
Thyrtie quarters of manchet floure. — *Bible. Ed.* 1555. 3 Kings iv.

MISLIKE: for dislike.

I hope it shall not bee misliked. — *Whit.* Ded. xiv. l. 31.
Some gallant coulours are misliked — „ Ded. xvi. 22.
She asketh him anon, what he misliketh. — *Chau.* Legacy of Dido.
Setting your scorns and your mislike aside. — *Shak.* 3 Hen. VI. IV. i. 24.

MOE: the old positive of more.

DEMOSTHENES, and thousandes moe beside. — *Whit.* E. 90, l. 12.
A manciple, and myself, ther n'ere no mo. — *Chau.* p. 5, i. l. 546.
To tell in short without words mo. — „ 234.
Sing no more ditties, sing no moe. — *Shak.* M. Ado, II. iii. 65.
If I court mo women, you'll couch with mo men. — „ Othel. IV. iii.

MOTLEY: a colour mixed or meddled, of various colours.

A motley coate, a cockescombe or a bell,
Hee better likes, then iewelles that excell. — *Whit.* E. 81, l. 5.
A motley fool.' Motley's the only wear. (*Sæpe.*) — *Shak.* Like it, II. vii. 34.
I wear not motley in my brain. — „ T. Night, I. v. 51.

MOWES: mouths.

E. 169, l. 4. Of whome both mockes, and apishe mowes, he gain'd. *Whit.*
T. C. p. 304, 2, iv. l. 7. Then laugheth she, and maketh him the mowe. *Chau.*
p. 326, 1, vi. 7, 49, 6. And other whiles with bitter mockes and mowes
He would him scorne. *Spen.*
Temp. II. ii. 9. Sometime like apes, that mow and chatter at me. *Shak.*
M. N. Dr. III. ii. 237. Ay, do, persever, counterfeit sad looks,
Make mows upon me when I turn my back.

MOYLE: defile, dirty with work and dust.

E. 50, l. 8. Then take thy rest, let younglinges worke and moyle. *Whit.*
E. 215, l. 10. Wherein they still doe labour, worke and moile. "
Hymn, p. 493, 2, l. 220. And doest thy mynd in durty pleasures moyle. *Spen.*
T. Shrew, IV. i. 66. How she was bemoiled. *Shak.*

MUSKE CATTES: an animal yielding musk.

E. 79, l. 1. Heare LAIS, fine, doth braue it on the stage,
With muske cattes sweete, and all shee coulde desire. *Whit.*
All's W. v. ii. 18. Fortune's cat, — but not a musk-cat. *Shak.*
M. W. W. III. iii. 18. How now, my eyas-musket! what news with you? "
What a coyle these musk-wormes take to. *Ben Jonson.*

NEWFANGLENES: attempt at something new.

Ded. xvi. l. 19. Too much corrupte with curiousnes and newfanglenes. *Whit.*
p. 83, ii. l. 10924. Men loven of proper kind newefangelnesse. *Chau.*
p. 83, ii. l. 10932. So newefangel ben they of her mete
And louen noueltees of proper kind.

NONES: occasions.

E. 38, l. 1. The trampinge steede, that champes the burnish'd bitte,
Is mannag'd braue, with ryders for the nones. *Whit.*
E. 103, l. 10. And studentes must haue pastimes for the nones. "
p. 4, i. l. 382. A COKE they hadden with hem for the nones,
To boile the chickenes and the marie bones. *Chau.*
Ham. IV. vii. A chalice for the nonce. *Shak.*
1 Hen. IV, I. ii. 172. I have cases of buckram for the nonce. "

PASSIONS: sufferings, commotions of mind.

E. 14, l. 5. Thus heynous sinne, and follie did procure
Theise famous men, such passions to indure. *Whit.*
Macb. III. iv. 57. You shall offend him and extend his passion. *Shak.*
3 Hen. VI. I. iv. 150. Beshrew me, but his passion moves me so. "
Timon, III. i. 53. —— O you gods,
I feel my master's passion.

PICK-THANKES: officious parasites.
With pick-thankes, blabbes, and subtill Sinons broode. *Whit.* E. 150, l. 4.
By smiling pick-thanks and base newsmongers. *Shak.* 1 Hen. IV III. ii. 25.
Base pick-thank flattery. *Daniel.* Civil Wars, ii.

PILL: rob, plunder.
His subiectes poor, to shaue, to pill, and poll. *Whit.* E 151, l. 4.
And pill the man, and let the wenche go. *Chau.* p 53, i. l. 6944.
So did he all the kingdome rob and pill. *Spen.* M. H. p. 430, 1, 1198.
Which pols and pils the poore in piteous wize. „ p 248, 2, v. 2, 6, 8.
The commons hath he pill'd with grievous taxes. *Shak.* Rich. II. II i. 245.
Large-handed robbers your grave masters are,
And pill by law. „ Timon, IV. i. 11.

PREIUDICATE: forejudging.
With a preiudicate opinion to condempne. *Whit.* Ded. xv. l. 44.
—— wherein our dearest friend
Prejudicates the business, and would seem
To have us make denial. *Shak.* All's W. I. ii. 7.

ROOME: place.
And shortlie, none shall knowe where was the roome. *Whit.* E. 34, l. 16.
She placeth you, in equall roome, with anie of your age. „ E. 107, l. 34.
The trees, and rockes, that lefte their roomes, his musicke for to heare. „ E. 186, l. 12.
—— and hath roume and eke space
To weld an axe or swerde, staffe, or knife. *Chau.* L. W. p. 425, i, l. 1997.
Hyest roumes. *Tyndal.* Luke xiv.

SCOT-FREE: free from scot, *i.e.* a reckoning, or payment.
My simple trauaile herein should scape scot-free. *Whit.* Ded. xv. l. 43.
He cannot scape yet scot-free, vncontrolled. *Mir. of Mag.*
That hot termagant Scot had paid me scot and lot too. *Shak.* 1 Hen. IV. v. iv. 114.

SHAMEFASTNES: modesty.
And little boies, whome shamefastnes did grace,
The Romaines deck'd, in Scarlet like their face. *Whit.* E. 134, l. 17.
Of hunting and of shamefast chastitee. *Chau.* p. 16, i. l. 2057.
And ye, sire clerk, let be your shamefastnesse. „ p. 7, ii. l. 841.
Shamefast she was in maidens shamefastnesse. „ p. 91, ii. l. 11989.
Uttered at last with impudency and unshamefastness. *H. Sidney.* May 18, 1566.
In like manner also, that women adorne themselues in modest apparell, with shamefastness and sobrietie. *Bible. Ed.* 1611. 1 Tim. ii. 9.

SIELD: happy.

E. 26, l. 18. And fortune sield, the wishers turne doth serue. *Whit.*
E. 176, l. 11. For blessinges good, come seild before our praier. ,,
T. C. p. 296, ii. l. 815. O God (quod she) so worldly seliness,
Which clerkes callen false felicite. *Chau.*
T. C. p. 296, ii. l. 827. That he hath very joy and selinesse. ,,
Arcadia, I. A seeled doue. *Sidney.*
Macb. III. ii. 46. Come, seeling night,
Scarf up the tender eye of pitiful day. *Shak.*

SILLYE: harmless, simple.

E. 194, l. 7. For, as the wolfe, the sillye sheep did fear,
And made him still to tremble, at his barke. *Whit.*
p. 31, i. l. 4088. These sely clerkes han ful fast gronne. *Chau.*
p. 31, i. l. 4106. Wery and wet as bestes in the rain
Cometh sely John, and with him cometh Alein. ,,
p. 46, i. l. 5952. But if a sely wif be on of tho. ,,
p. 168, 2, iii. 8, 27, 1. The silly Virgin stroue him to withstand. *Spen.*
W. Tale, IV. iii. 27. My revenue is the silly cheat. *Shak.*

SITHE: *since*, time.

E. 68, l. 7. By which is ment, sith wicked men abounde. *Whit.*
E. 109, l. 3. And sithe, the worlde might not their matches finde. ,,
E. 204, l. 10. No maruaile tho, sith bountie is so coulde &c. ,,
p. 14, ii. l. 1817. And therfore sith I know of loves peine. *Chau.*
p. 34, i. l. 4478. And sithen hath he spoke of everich on. ,,
p. 178, 1, iii. 10, 33, 3. And humbly thanked him a thousand sith. *Spen.*
C. Jan. p. 364, ii. l. 51. And eke tenne thousand sithes I bless the stoure. ,,
M for M. I. iii. 35. Sith 'twas my fault to give the people scope. *Shak.*
M. W. W. II. ii. 170. Sith you yourself know how easy it is to be such an offender.
Ham. IV. iv. Sith I have cause.

STITHE: anvil.

E. 192, l. 5. For there with strengthe he strikes vppon the stithe. *Whit.*
p. 16, i. l. 2027. Th'armerer, and the bowyer, and the smith
That forgeth sharpe swerdes on his stith. *Chau.*
Ham. III. ii. Vulcan's stithy. *Shak.*
Tr. & C. IV. v. The forge that stithied Mars his helm. ,,

TEENE: grief, vexation.

E. 138, l. 14. So slaunders foule, and wordes like arrowes keene,
Not vertue hurtes, but turnes her foes to teene. *Whit.*

That neuer was ther no word hem betweene
Of jalousie, ne of non other tene. — *Chau.* p. 23, ii. l. 3106.
'Gainst that proud Paynim king that works her teene. — *Spen.* p. 62, 2, i. 12, 18, 8.
To think o' the teen, that I have turn'd you to. — *Shak.* Temp. I. ii 64.
Of sighs, of groans, of sorrow and of teen! — ,, L.L.L. IV. iii. 160.

UNNETH: scarcely, not easily.
At lengthe, this greedie carle the Lethergie posseste:
That unneth hee could stere a foote, with sleepe, so sore oppreste. — *Whit.* E 209, l. 5.
So faint they woxe, and feeble in the folde,
That now unnethes their feete could them uphold. — *Spen.* C. Jan. p. 364, i. l. 5.
Uneath may she endure the flinty streets. — *Shak.* 2 Hen. VI. II. iv. 8.

UNREST: trouble.
It shewes her selfe, doth worke her owne vnrest. — *Whit.* E. 94, l. 12.
She shewed wel, for no worldly unrest. — *Chau.* p. 66, i. l. 8595.
Many vain fancies working her unrest. — *Spen.* p. 266, 2, v. 6, 7, 7.
Witnessing storms to come, woe and unrest. — *Shak.* Rich. II. II. iv. 22
Rest thy unrest on England's lawful earth. — ,, Rich. III. IV. iv. 29.
And so repose sweet gold for their unrest. — ,, Tit. A. II. iii. 8.
The more is my unrest. — ,, Rom. & J. I. v. 118.

UNTHRIFTES: wasters.
And wisedome still, againste such vnthriftes cries. — *Whit.* E. 17, l. 18.
Unmanly Murder, and unthrifty Scath. — *Spen.* p. 24, 2, i. 4, 35, 3.
Given away to upstart unthrifts. — *Shak.* Rich. II. II iii, 121.
And with an unthrift love did run from Venice. — ,, Mer. V. v. i. 16.
What man didst thou ever know unthrift that was beloved after his means? — ,, Timon, IV. iii. 308.

URE: use, destiny.
The tyrant vile MEZENTIVS, put in ure. — *Whit.* E. 99, l. 1.
Euen so it is of wittes, some quicke, to put in vre. — ,, E. 173, l. 5.
On his fortune, and on ure also. — *Chau.* B. K. p. 356, i. l. 152.
My goddesse bright, my fortune and my ure,
I yeve and yeeld my herte to thee full sure. — ,, C. L. p. 338, i. l. 634.

WHOTTE: hot.
Being likewise asked why: (quoth hee) bicause it is to whotte,
To which the satyre spake, and blow'st thou whotte, and coulde? — *Whit.* E. 160, l. 8, 9.

E. 173, l. 10. And greenest wood, though kindlinge longe, yet whottest most it burnes. *Whit.*

p. 71, 1, ii. 1, 58, 3. Nether to melt in pleasures whott desyre. *Spen.*

p 86, 1, ii. 5, 18, 5. Nath'lesse now quench thy whott emboyling wrath. ,,

Cæsar, 236. When then counter waxed somewhat to whot. *Goldinge.*

WONNE: dwell, dwelling.

E. 198, l. 3. In regall roomes of Iasper, and of Iette,
Contente of minde, not alwaies likes to wonne. *Whit.*

p. 59, i. l. 7745. Wher as ther woned a man of gret honour. *Chau.*

p. 5, ii. l. 608. His wonning was ful fayre upon a heth. ,,

p. 94, 2, ii. 7, 20, 3. Or where hast thou thy wonne, that so much gold
Thou canst preserve from wrong and robbery? *Spen.*

p. 129, 1, iii. 1, 3, 2. Where daungers dwelt, and perils most did wonne,
To hunt for glory and renowmed prayse. ,,

WORLDE: 1°. age; 2°. orbis terrarum, compass of the earth.

Ded. xii. l. 20. 1° A perpetuitie of felicitie in this worlde, and in the world to come. *Whit.*

E. 123, l. 1. This was the goulden worlde, that Poettes praised moste. ,,

E. 197, l. 27. Yea, thoughe some Monarche greate some worke should take in hand
Of marble, or of Adamant, that manie worldes shoulde stand. ,,

E. 222, l. 5. So thoughe the worlde, the vertuous men dispise, *&c.* ,,

Heb. i. 8. Thi throne is in to world of world. εἰς τὸν αἰωνα τοῦ αἰῶνου. *Wickliffe.*

Rev. xxii. 5. Thei schulen regne in to worldis of worldis. ,,

Matt. xii. 32. Neither in this world (αἰῶνι) nor in the world to come. *Auth. V.*

Heb. i. 2. —— made the worlds (αἰῶνας). *All Engl. V.*

Heb. xi. 3. The worlds (τοὺς αἰῶνας) were formed. ,,

E. 197, l. 29. 2° Yet, should one only man, with labour of the braine
Bequeathe the world a monument, that longer shoulde remaine. *Whit.*

E. 122, l. 10. Behoulde, of this vnperfecte masse, the goodly worlde was wroughte. ,,

p. 21, ii. l. 2841. That knew this worldes transmutation
As he had seen it chaungen up and doun. *Chau.*

p. 21, ii. l. 2849. This world n' is but a thurghfare ful of wo. ,,

Matt. iv. 8. Kingdomes of the world (τοῦ κόσμου). *Auth. V.*

YERKE: jerk.

E. 6, l. 5. They praunce, and yerke, and out of order flinge. *Whit.*

p. 325, 2, vi. 7, 44, 6. —— who, having in his hand a whip,
Her therewith yirks. *Spen.*

It is, we conceive, ever useful for the elucidation of our old words thus to bring together the phrases and expressions in which they agree, but which have passed out of the current language. The list might be extended without difficulty, if we included also words that are undergoing a change of meaning, or that may be regarded as old-fashioned, though still retained in use. We should however be pursuing too wide a field, if we ventured farther into this subject. They who enter upon it will not fail to perceive how pure was the English which Whitney wrote. He abounds indeed in Latin quotations in his marginal notes, and scarcely ever spares an opportunity of making classical allusions; but he never offends us by the intrusion of idioms or phrases foreign to our language. As his style is simple and unaffected, so his words are of native birth,—the English of the old time; they are rich in expressiveness, and they have strength in themselves.

Fortune Valour's Friend.

ESSAY III.

BIOGRAPHICAL NOTICES OF CHRISTOPHER PLANTIN AND OF FRANCIS RAPHELENG, AND OF THE EMBLEM WRITERS TO WHOM WHITNEY WAS INDEBTED.

TYPOGRAPHY in the sixteenth century boasts three celebrated names, in Venice, Paris and Antwerp. Aldo Manuzio printed his first work in 1490; Paolo Manuzio, his son, succeeded to the printing office in 1515, and continued it to 1574; and Aldo Manuzio for a time gave promise of excelling both his father and grandfather, but becoming negligent, he died in poverty at Rome in 1597. The earliest work printed by Henry Stephens of Paris was in 1502; his celebrated second son Robert, and more celebrated grandson Henry, extended the renown of the office until 1598; and other members of the family, as late as 1661, carried on the art with fame if not with profit.

Plate XLIV. It may not be that CHRISTOPHER PLANTIN excelled those who bore the names of Aldus and of Stephens, but he was no unworthy coadjutor; and to him at least emblem writers are especially indebted for bringing so completely into unison the arts of printing and engraving. From the time when he commenced his business at Antwerp in 1555, until his death in 1589, there issued from his press nearly *thirty* editions of the chief emblem-books of the day, all executed with care, some possessing great beauty of execution, and one or two equal if not superior to any similar work of that age. But for these editions, out of which chiefly Whitney made his choice, the English reader must have waited some years before seeing any adequate representation of the learning, wit and skill, which on the continent of

Europe had been bestowed upon emblem-books. It is therefore not inappropriately that these biographical notices begin with the name of the princely printer of Antwerp.

Christopher Plantyn, or Plantin, was born in 1514, at Mount Louis in Tourain, of poor and humble parents. He was very young when he came to Paris. There he worked for some time as a bookbinder; but afterwards, having learned the elements of printing with Robert Mace, of Caen in Normandy, he visited the chief printing offices of France, and more especially those in Lyons, where several emblem-books were printed. He now returned to Paris with the intention of establishing himself in business in that city. The religious troubles which prevailed decided him to go to the Netherlands. Soon after, about 1546, he married Joanna de la Rivière and fixed his abode in Antwerp, and the first book which issued from his press was "La institutione di una fanciulla nata nobilmente. L'institution d'une fille de noble maison, traduite de langue Tuscane en François. En Anvers, de l'Imprimerie de Christofle Plantin, avec privilege. 1555."*

Annales de l'Imp. Plant. Bruxelles, 1865, p. 5.

Here for forty-four years, except when he retired to Leyden in consequence of the war in the Netherlands, Plantin pursued his calling with an increasing reputation. The correctness and beauty of the works published by him spread abroad his fame, and in a little time he acquired a considerable fortune. Of that he made a very noble use; his house, like the house of the Aldi at Venice, or of the Stephens at Paris, became the asylum of the learned, of whom there were always several entertained at his table. Those who were in need received succour from him, and he sought to attach them to himself by offering them honourable maintenance. He had also constantly in his printing office, for correctors, men of rare merit, such as Cornelius Kilian, Theodore Pulman, Victor Goselin, Justus Lipsius and Francis Rapheleng; and to this day with pride are shown the desks and benches where these learned sat to aid in giving learning to mankind.

If we trust the testimony of Malinkrot, Plantin, after the example of Robert Stephens, exposed his proof-sheets at his gate,

De Ortu Typograph.

* Plantin is named as a master-printer in the registry of Saint Luc in 1550; but he was probably then in the office of John Bellerus, or in partnership with him. pp. 128, 135.

promising a reward to those who should discover in them any errata. Because of the account rendered to him of the talent and carefulness of Plantin, the king of Spain (Philip II.) named him his *Archi-typographus* or *Prototypographus*, *i.e.* Chief Printer, and charged him to bring out a new edition of the *Polyglott Bible* of Alcala, *that* of Cardinal Ximenes, the Complutensian, commenced in 1502 and finished in 1517, and of which the copies began to be rare. This edition, in Hebrew, Chaldaic, Greek and Latin, is justly regarded as Plantin's master-work; it was issued, the first volume in 1569 and the last in 1573, in 8 volumes folio, and, except some little carelessness in the paging, is a very splendid example of typographic art and labour.* The famous Guillaume Lebé was induced to come from Paris to cast the letters and characters intended for the impression, and Philip II. sent from Spain the learned Arias Montanus to direct the important enterprise. While however adding greatly to Plantin's reputation, this magnificent work was almost the cause of his ruin, for the Spanish ministers with excessive rigour demanded the repayment of the sums which, during the prosecution of the work, had been lent him from the royal treasury.

Annales de l'Imp. Plant. pp. 1-324.

The catalogue of Plantin's publications, compiled by MM. A. De Backer et Ch. Ruelens, gives the titles of nearly 1030 works which had their origin from his types and presses, and as some are known to be omitted, though unintentionally, future inquiries may increase their number.

The French historian, De Thou, on a journey to Flanders and Holland in 1576, visited the workshops of Plantin, and saw twenty-seven presses in action, although, as he remarks, this famous printer was embarrassed in his affairs; but carrying out his well known motto, "*Labore et Constantia*," By work and steadiness, he re-established his fortunes.†

Plantin died the 1st of July 1589, having bequeathed his library to his grandson, Balthasar Moretus, and was buried in the cathedral of Antwerp, where his gravestone is still pointed out.

* For an account of the eight volumes, "Annales de l'Imprimerie Plantinienne" may be consulted, published at Brussels 1865.

† To this day (1865) his descendants are among the wealthy families of Belgium, and the library and printing office are now the property of M. Edward Moretus.

Besides the printing office at Antwerp he possessed two others, one at Leyden, a second at Paris. These were assigned as portions to his three daughters, Margaret, Martine and Jane: the eldest, married to Rapheleng, had the Leyden printing office; that of Paris fell to the youngest, who had married Gilles Begs; and the Antwerp business devolved on the second daughter, married to John Moereturf or Moretus. Moretus carried on the office in partnership with his mother-in-law. She was placed in a large house, which Guicciardini, who died in Antwerp in 1589, regarded as one of the principal ornaments of the city, and which after nearly three centuries is still owned by a Moretus, and still possesses the very treasures of the olden time, besides a vine in full bearing which Plantin himself planted. There are stored his types and presses and all the appliances of his noble art, which in modern days queenly hands have not disdained to work.

See his Description of the Netherlands.

Conrad Zeltner says this printer had types of silver and implements of ivory, but the same thing had already been reported of Robert Stephens, and with as little foundation. We may however name with absolute certainty Plantin's typographic ensign,—it may not have braved a thousand years the battle and the breeze,—but it indicates, as long as man shall be upon the earth, what the elements of his success are. The ensign is a hand holding an open compass and striking a circle; and around the device we read the significant words "LABORE ET CONSTANTIA." A better could not have been chosen, and Rapheleng and Moereturf religiously preserved it, and it still stands over the old mansion in Antwerp.

See *Biographie Universelle*, à Paris 1823, vol. xxxv. p. 19; Timperley's *Dictionary of Printers and Printing*, pp. 408, 409; Aikin and Enfield's *Biog. Dict.*, vol. viii. p. 227; and Dibdin's *Bib. Decameron*, vol. ii. p. 151-57.

"In the house of Christopher Plantyn by Francis Raphelengius" were Whitney's *Emblems* "imprinted;" and we take for our second biographical notice, FRANCIS RAPHELENGIUS, or RAULENGHIEN, whose portrait is preserved in the university of Leyden.

He was born at Lanoy near Lille, the capital of the present department of the North, formerly French Flanders, February

27th 1539, and died July 20th 1597. He was from his boyhood intended for one of the learned professions, and was sent to school to Ghent, but his father's death compelled the interruption of his studies, and commerce seemed his destination. Business led him to Nuremberg, where he devoted his leisure hours to the ancient languages, and such rapid progress did he make that his mother no longer opposed his inclination, and literature became his pursuit. He went to Paris to perfect himself in Greek and Hebrew, but the civil wars, which desolated France about 1560-63, caused him to leave that country, and he passed over to England. Here, for some time, he taught Greek in the university of Cambridge, but his stay could not have been long; for on his return to the Netherlands he engaged as corrector of the press for Plantin, who was so charmed by his gentleness and ability as to offer him in marriage his eldest daughter Margaret, a most estimable woman; and the marriage took place in 1565.

Rapheleng rendered great services to his father-in-law, especially in the printing of the famous Polyglot Bible, issued between the years 1569 and 1573. Of this splendid work he corrected the proofs with great care; and besides, added to the sixth volume a Hebrew Grammar and an Epitome of Pagnini's Thesaurus of the Hebrew language; and in the seventh volume he assisted Montanus and the brothers Guido and Nicholas Fabricii in the Latin interpretation of the Hebrew Books, and gave the various readings and annotations by which the Chaldee paraphrase of the Book of Daniel was illustrated and amended.

Annales de l'Imp. Plant. Bruxelles, 1865, pp. 129, 130, 133.

During the civil wars of the Netherlands, or rather during part of them, Plantin retired to Leyden with his family. Rapheleng remained in Antwerp, charged with the direction of the printing office. During the famous seige, from July 1584 to August 17th 1585, Rapheleng was present, and shared its dangers. He then betook himself to Leyden to superintend and finally to own the printing office which his father-in-law had established there. He now learned Arabic and rendered himself a very able scholar in that language. John Dousa the elder, curator or rector of the university of Leyden, charged him in 1586 with the teaching of Hebrew, and in this employ he acquitted himself for some years with much distinction. Grief for the premature death of his wife, and a paralysis with which he was seized, rendered life almost

Whitney's Emblems, p. 189.

insupportable, and his career ended in 1597, with as fair a name as any in the republic of letters.*

See *Biographie Universelle*, vol. xxxvii. p. 89, Dibdin's *Bib. Decam.* vol. ii. p. 158, and Cooper's *Athenæ Cantabrigienses*, vol. ii. p. 126, where is a list of his works.

A worthy descendant from Rapheleng's only grand-child, Maryhe Christoffella, is now resident in Leyden, namely, M. John T. Bodel Nyenhuis, who from 1829 to 1850 was printer to the university of Leyden, and who among his ancestors reckons four others that held the same office. On the 27th of July 1865 I was enjoying his hospitality, and he then wrote out for me the genealogy of himself and his family traced back to Christopher Plantin, and also gave me an autograph of which the following is a copy:

—Van dese rekeninghe kenne ick onderschreven
—vernoecht te syn desen 22n April 1599
Christoffel van Ravelinghien

This Christopher Rapheleng was the second son of Francis, and appointed typographer to the university of Leyden in 1589; he was living in 1645. The other sons were Francis the eldest, eminent for early genius, who died in 1643, and Justus, named after Justus Lipsius; there was also a daughter Cornelia: but these do not appear to have left any descendants. M. John T. Bodel Nyenhuis is the author of a learned work, "Dissertatio Historico-Juridica, De Juribus Typographorum et Bibliopolarum in Regno Belgico. 8vo, pages 447, Leyden, M.D.CCCXIX." At the end of his book he quotes the famous words of Rénouard appended to his catalogue in 1819 of the library of an amateur: "*Otez-lui ses liens, et laissez-le aller;* c'est pour le commerce la plus facile et la plus efficace de toutes les protections."

According to the Genealogy by M. Bod Nyenhuis.

The portraits we are giving are from various sources: that of Plantin is from Dibdin; those of Brant, Giovio, Alciat, Junius

* One of the later books which issued from his press bears the title: "DEN LVST-HOF VAN Rethonia &c. GEDRVCT TOT LEYDEN. By Fransoys van Ravelengien. cIɔ.Iɔ.XCVI." 4to, pp. 155. The ornament on the title-page is a Dutch garden; in the centre is a lady holding in each hand two coats of arms; and below is the oft-repeated motto, "Labore et Constantia."

and Sambucus are from De Bry; Beza's is somewhat uncertain; and Reusner's is from the edition of his own emblems.

Plate XLV.

Plate XLVI.

Of THEODORE DE BRY we may remark that he was a celebrated portrait or miniature painter of the sixteenth century, who projected a work to contain the portraits of those illustrious for learning and erudition, with their lives written by J. J. Boissard. Of this work he lived to publish only Part I. in 1597 at Frankfort; but his heirs carried on his enterprise, and between 1598 and 1631 brought out *three* other parts, making *four* in all. The work is in quarto, and contains 198 portraits. A *fifth* part was added in 1632 by William Fitzer, but it comprises only 32 pages, with 20 portraits chiefly of English bishops and learned men.

Clement's Bibl. Curieuse, vol. v. pp. 18 &c.

In his Preface, De Bry affirms that the portraits were taken from the life, but this has been questioned and probably is not true in the full extent. The portraits are accompanied by biographical notices by John James Boissard, a highly esteemed antiquary, who was born at Besançon in 1528 and died at Metz in 1602. These notices are absent from some other editions, and render the first, which has besides the earliest proofs of the portraits, far superior to those which follow.

The work of Boissard and of De Bry and his heirs is the primary source from which the portraits and biographical notices of the emblem writers are derived, but not the only source, as the following pages will show.

MS. De Volucribus.

See p. 239 *ante*.

Cebes, the disciple of Socrates, B.C. 390, Horapollo, about A.D. 410, and Hugo de Foliato, prior of St. Lawrence near Amiens, in the thirteenth century, are among the earliest writers of emblematical works; but Whitney makes no allusion to them, though he appears to have been acquainted with the *Hieroglyphica*. We shall therefore begin our notices with

Plate II

Smith's Greek and Rom. Biog. and Conr. Leemans' Horap. ed. 1835, p. viii.

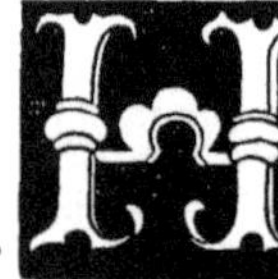

ORAPOLLO, who, according to the best authorities, was a distinguished Greek grammarian of Phenebethis in Egypt, flourishing in the reign of Theodosius, A.D. 408-50, and teaching first in Alexandria and then in Constantinople. The age at which he flourished does not appear to have been ascertained; and of his translator from the Egyptian tongue into Greek nothing is known beyond the name, Philippus. From the barbarous words introduced, and other marks of a corrupted Greek, the translation is of a comparatively late age, and some bring it down even to the fifteenth century. However this may be, the work enjoyed very considerable popularity in Whitney's time, and between the first Aldine edition in 1505 and that at Rome in 1599 there were at least eight editions. A separate French version was issued in 1543, a Latin in 1544, an Italian in 1548, and a German in 1554.* Leemans' Prolegomena, pp. xxv–xxxvi

Several of Whitney's emblems may be traced up to the *Hieroglyphica*,† not that they were adopted unchanged or immediately, but their sources were here, and they have been accommodated to suit modified thoughts and circumstances.

Champollion passes a disparaging judgment on Horapollo. He avers: "The study of this author has given birth only to vain theories, and the examination of the Egyptian inscriptions, book in hand, has produced only very feeble results. Would not that prove that the greater part of the symbols described and explained by Horapollo did not exclusively make part of what we call *hieroglyphic writing*, and belonged primitively to some other system of representing thought?" He then shows that the system is *anaglyphic* rather than *hieroglyphic*, — not sacred characters or sculptures, but allegorical representations, which abound on the Egyptian buildings. He afterwards admits, however, that he found on monuments information of many of the hieroglyphics of Horapollo, — indeed of a great part of those which are figured in Leemans' edition. Hieroglyph Egypt. p. 347. Leemans' Prolegomena, pp xii and xv.

An emblem writer is seldom very critical in judging the

* For a full account consult Dr. Conrad Leemans' Prolegomena to "HORAPOLLINIS NILOI HIEROGLYPHICA," 8vo, Amstelodami, 1835.

† The title "Hieroglyphica" was borne by other works of that age; as "HIEROGLYPHICA, sive De Sacris Ægyptiorum aliarumque Gentium &c. *A Cœlio Augustino.*" In 60 books, pages 441, folio, Basiliæ, M.D.LXVII. In a later age there was the most splendid work of Romein de Hooghe, "HIEROGLYPHICA of Merkbeilden Der oude Volkeren &c.," large 4to, Amsterdam, M.D.CCXXXV.; and another still more excellent for its fulness, learning and beauty of the printing and illustrations, Martinus Koning's "LEXICON HIEROGLYPHICUM SACRO-PROFANUM," &c., large folio, 6 vols., Amsterdam, 1722; also "*Science Hiéroglyphique*," small 4to, pages 128, with many plates, "à la Haye, M.D.CCXLVI."

sources of his devices, or their exact meaning; it is sufficient for his purpose if they are currently received and understood; he adopts them because they are known, and not because they are authoritative or authenticated expressions of human thought.

De Bry. Plate XLVII.

RANT, Sebastian, or Brandt, surnamed Titio, was born at Strasburg in 1458, and died at Bâle in 1520. The lines on his portrait say of him, that "he was equally skilled in law and in sacred poetry, noble in genius, but rude in art." His early studies were pursued in Bâle, where he enjoyed the titles of doctor and professor. His ability in business soon obtained for him a high reputation and the favour of many princes, especially of the emperor Maximilian I., who often consulted him and bestowed on him the title of imperial counsellor. Afterwards he was syndic and chancellor in his native land. He devoted his leisure to classic literature and poetic composition of various kinds. An edition of Virgil, ornamented with engravings, was published by him, and a translation into German verse of the *Disticha, or Catechism concerning Morals*, by Dionysius Cato. Indeed it has been said of Brant that he composed verses to infinity. The chief of his poems was in German iambics, a satirical work, entitled *The Ship of Fools*, which acquired great popularity, and was translated into Latin, French, Dutch and English. Of the Latin and of the French translation we present the title-pages and one of the emblems,—from which probably Whitney took the motto, "No man can serve two masters," though he has not treated it in the same way. Some idea may be gained of Brant's work from his lines

Biographie Universelle, Paris 1812, vol. v. p. 498.

Plates IV. and XXVIII.

See Plate V.

"*Concerning obedience to two Masters.*

"Two hares at one time may the swift hunter take
Whose single dog hunts the wild woods through;
But who aims to two masters his service to make,
And oft strives to please each,—'tis far harder to do.

Most foolish is he who would serve thundering Jove
And equally seek this bright world for his own;
Most rare 'tis accomplished,—two masters to love
With heart-service to each acceptable shown."

Between these stanzas the device is introduced, and at the side quotations chiefly from the Holy Scriptures, thus:

To serve two.

"No man can serve two masters: for either he will hate the one, and love the other; or else he will hold to the one, and despise the other. Ye cannot serve God and mammon." Matt. vi. 24. Luke xvi. 9.

"He who makes haste to each finisheth neither well. A thought for many things is less intent on each single one. The heart going two ways will have no successes."

In exemplification of Brant's work and of Whitney's adoption of similar thoughts we may refer to the French translation, **La grāt nef des folz du mōde,** where four women are playing at dice. Plates XXVIII. and XXIX. Whitney (p. 176) names only "three carelesse dames;" but in Brant we have the origin of the tale; and *there* may be seen in what spirit and in what way the *Stultifera Navis* has been furnished with its cargo.

Brant's object plainly was to turn into ridicule and also to reprove the vices, eccentricities and follies of the time; and we may accept this judgment passed upon his work: "It is a collection of pleasantries, sometimes whimsical, sometimes gross, which might be piquant in their day, but which at present have no other merit than that of having enjoyed much success three hundred years ago." Biographie Universelle, Paris 1812, vol. x. p. 498.

For the editions of Brant consult Brunet's "*Manuel du Libraire.*" Paris, 1860. Vol. i. col. 1202-9.

IOVIO, Paolo, bishop of Nocera, in order of time next takes precedence. He was born at Como in Italy April 19th 1483, and died at Florence December 11th 1552, his epitaph says aged 69 years, 7 months and 23 days. The lines beneath his portrait say of him: Plate XLVIII. Oettinger's Bibl. Biogr. col. 672.

"Thou art beloved of Cosmo, honoured also of Leo;
Thou wast a learned physician, thou wast a learned historian."

He was an accomplished scholar, of considerable eloquence, and of acute as well as refined intellect. His first profession was that of medicine, which he practised with happy success. Afterwards he applied himself to history and biography, and besides the lives of pontiffs and princes of Italy, especially of the viscounts of Milan, he collected the eulogies and the portraits of the illustrious men who had become famous, whether for arms or literature. He wrote also a history of his own time, embracing a period of fifty years, and narrating the chief events in Italy, Hungary, Asia, Africa, and other regions. At the storming and pillage of Rome by the Spaniards under Charles de Bourbon, May 6th 1527, Giovio suffered great losses of valuable silver vessels, but from a Spaniard who had taken possession of them he obtained the restoration of his books and manuscripts. As a reward for his learning and virtues the pontiff bestowed upon him the bishopric of Nocera,* and "the mighty Cosmo, prince of the Florentines," invited him to his court and made him one of his counsellors. On his death in 1552 he was buried in the church of St. Lawrence, and before a more illustrious monument was raised to his memory the somewhat boastful inscription was painted on the wall: "Of Paulus Jovius the most famous writer of histories, here are deposited the bones until a sepulchre be erected worthy of his eminent virtues." A later inscription recorded that he was the glory of the Latin tongue and the equal of Livy himself.

De Bry's Icones, pt. i. pp. 238-242.

As an emblematist his writings have already been mentioned. Of the work which Whitney sometimes follows the title and an illustration are given, which serve also for the next author whom we mention, Gabriel Symeoni. Brunet again may be consulted for an account of Giovio's writings.

See pp. xviii. and 240 *ante*.
Plates XXXVI. and XXXVII.
Manuel du Libraire, vol. v. pt. i. col. 392.

YMEONI, Gabriel, an Italian historian, was a Florentine, born in 1509. His emblems and those of Giovio are collected into one volume, of which the running title is, *Tetrastichi Morali*, Moral Stanzas. As a literary man, Symeoni possessed both powers and accomplishments, but he was of a haughty, capricious and exacting disposition. His early years were very precocious; at the age of six he was presented to Leo X. as a very extraordinary child; and his natural abilities were so well cultivated

Plate XXXVI.
Bibl. Biogr. col. 1681.

* Oettinger names another Paolo Giovio, as bishop of Nocera, who was born about 1530 and died in 1585. But Boissard's testimony to the contrary appears very decisive.

Bibl. Biogr. Bruxelles, 1854, col 672.

and improved that before reaching his twentieth year he was employed by the republic of Florence on a mission in which he had for colleague the celebrated Gianotti. Fêted at the court of Francis I. he endeavoured to gain that king's favour by flattering the vanity of the royal mistress, and his first verses, addressed to the duchess D'Etampes, were worth to him a pension of a thousand crowns. On his return to Florence he filled several employments, but after being imprisoned by the Inquisition he withdrew to Lyons in 1556, where and at Paris his *Devices and Emblems* were published in Italian, French and Spanish. He closed his career at Turin in 1570.

There was published by J. Burchard Mencke in Leipsic in 1727, *A Dissertation on the Life and Writings of G. Symeoni*, 4to, but I have not seen it.

As examples of Whitney's translations of Giovio and Symeoni we give their text to his emblems, p. 98 and p. 168*b*.

Virescit vulnere virtus.

Tetra. Morali, p. 32.

"Di Virtv oppresa.
Qual cespo verde per campagna o balza,
Che l'incanto villain col piede freme,
Tal (cosi forte & pretioso è il seme)
Virtute oppressa renunerdendo, inalza."

And again:

Ingenium superat vires.

Tetra. Morali, p. 34.

"Di Consalvo Fernando.
Come corrente lin dur' arco sforza,
Et l'altro teso nel curuo osso incocca,
Che poi con danno altrui souente scocca,
Cosi l'ingegno supera la forza."

ALCIATUS, Andreas, if not in priority of time, yet from superiority of genius, must be placed first in the ranks of emblem writers of the sixteenth century. He was born at Alzato in the duchy of Milan, May 8th 1492, or, according to Oettlinger, May 1st, the same year with our English printer Caxton, and died January 12th 1550. Boissard's estimate of his powers and attainments was most favourable, reflecting indeed the opinions of his contemporaries: "Not only was he the most noble jurisconsult, but in all liberal learning, and especially in poetry, so experienced that he could vie with the very highest geniuses." Whether he

See plate XLIX.

Bibl. Biogr. Universelle, col. 21.

De Bry's Icones, pt. ii. p. 134.

was the son of a merchant, or of more exalted birth, it is recorded of him that from early years he applied himself diligently and very successfully to the study of jurisprudence. In his fifteenth year he composed his "*Paradoxes of the Civil Law*," and in his twenty-second graduated as doctor of laws. It was not long before he became the most eminent in his profession. In 1521, when lecturer on law in the university of Avignon, his auditory numbered eight hundred persons; but his *honoraria* or fees were paid so inexactly that he returned to Milan. Here however he raised up enemies, and in 1529 found refuge in France. The king himself was one of his hearers, and bestowed on him a pension of six hundred crowns, which was increased the next year to one thousand two hundred. But Alciat was avaricious, and Francis Sforza, duke of Milan, used means to recall him to his native Italy. Sometimes at Pavia or Bologna, and sometimes at Ferrara, he pursued his profession, and his fame continued to increase. He enjoyed the favour of duke Hercules d'Este; the pope, Paul III., gave him the office of prothonotary; Charles V. created him count-palatine and senator; and wherever he might lecture numerous scholars crowded around him.

His writings are very numerous and extensive, embracing a great variety of subjects, from *Weights and Measures* up to *The most excellent Trinity.* The Lyons edition of 1560 occupies five folio volumes, and that of Bâle in 1571 the same number.

These we pass over for that particular species of literature of which he may be regarded, if not the founder, as the most successful cultivator, and which under the name of emblem writing, from the year 1522, when at Milan he published his *Book of Emblems,* to beyond the middle of the seventeenth century, for nearly one hundred and fifty years occupied so important a position in the estimation both of the learned and of that wider public who read "for delight and ornament."

Besides other instances in our illustrations of the text of *Alciat,* and which are referred to their proper place in *Whitney,* we append a short specimen of the stanzas of *Alciat* translated or adopted at page 138 of *Whitney:*

Alc. Emb. 177.

Ex bello, pax.

En galea, intrepidus quam miles gesserat, & quæ
Sæpius hostili sparsa cruore fuit:

Parta pace apibus tenuis concepit in vsum
Alueoli, atque fauos, grataq; mella gerit.
Arma procul iaceant: fas sit tunc sumere bellum,
Quando aliter pacis non potes arte frui.

Of the various editions, above fifty in number, we present the title-pages and illustrative plates from the editions of Wechel (Paris 1534), of Aldus (Venice 1546), of Roville (Lyons 1550 and 1551), and of Plantin (Antwerp 1581). Nearly all have a motto, a device or woodcut, and explanatory stanzas of Latin elegiac verse. Roville's editions of 1550 and 1551, in Latin and Italian, are the most ornate, and dedicated "To the most illustrious Maximilian duke of Milan." They present the text without comment or remark, but each page has a very elaborate border.

Plates VI. XVI. XVII XVIII. XIX. XX. XXI. XXII.

To the editions which included and followed that of Plantin in 1574, the very learned and abundant comments of Claude Mignault were often appended or interwoven. Mignault was born near Digon in 1536 and died March 3rd 1606. Like our king Alfred, he was twelve years of age before he began learning, but by great aptitude and diligence he soon surpassed his schoolfellows. In early manhood, successively at Rheims and in Paris he explained the Greek and Roman authors, and gained a very high reputation for erudition and skill; and to these it is recorded that he joined "a rare probity." His commentaries display great learning,—certainly needed to trace out, as he does, the numerous sources from which Alciat had derived his mottoes and devices, and to illustrate by references to classic and other authors the frequent allusions in Alciat's stanzas to the mythology and history of past ages. Indeed the praise which Mignault bestowed upon Alciat might be equally applied to himself: "Let us carefully note and fondly praise his ancient learning; let us wonder at his knowledge of law; let us emulate his eloquence; let us, with the common consent of learned men, approve his concise way of speaking; let us venerate his most dignified yet most pleasing variety; in these we possess a treasure to be matched neither with gold nor with gems;—and by so much the more admirable, if we compare the choice jewels of learning that were his own with the ornaments of many others."

Notæ Posteriores ad Alc. Emb. Leiden, 1614. p. 813.

Alciatus, however, had serious defects; vanity, avarice and

self-indulgence tarnished his moral reputation: but as a lawyer and a man of learning his glory was continually increasing. To his professional studies and pursuits he always added the culture of literature; and it is said "few men ever united so many branches of knowledge or carried them to higher perfection;" or, as it is noted on his portrait,

> "Andrew to their ancient splendor restored the laws,
> And thence made counsellors more learnedly to speak."

To the same purport is the record on his tomb in the church of the Holy Epiphany at Pavia: "*Qui omnium orbem absolvit, primus legum studia antiquo restituit decori,*" He completed the whole circle of learning, and was the first who replaced the study of the laws in its ancient dignity.

Bib. Biogr. Universelle. Bruxelles, 1854, vol. 21. Materials for a much fuller biography of Alciat are mentioned by Oettinger. We have chiefly made use of Claude Mignault's *Life*, Boissard's, and the *Biographie Universelle* of Paris; also Chambers's *Gen. Biog.* vol. i. p. 348.

ARADIN, Claude, from whom Whitney borrowed several of his emblems, was an ecclesiastic, a canon of Beaujeu, whose birth and death are alike unascertained. His brother William, however, was born in 1510 and died in 1590. Brunet. Paris, 1863, tome iv. col. 358. Claude published at Lyons in 1557 a *Selection of Emblems,* in French, from Gabriel Symeon and other authors. After several editions had appeared it was reprinted by Plantin in 1562, with Plate VII. the title "LES DEVISES HÉROÏQVES," which we have reproduced, because the copy used once belonged to Whitney, and contains both his autograph and his motto. Were the question gone into it might, perhaps, be ascertained with the same certainty as in Whitney's case which were the authors from whom Paradin's selection was made.

Paradin generally explains his devices by a prose narrative or remark; but to show his style we subjoin an example in which both prose and verse are combined, and which form the substance of Whitney's emblem, p. 88.

Paradin, fol. 126. "DE PARUIS, GRANDIS ACERUUS ERIT.

De l'Espic, à la Glenne, & de la Glenne, à la Gerbe. Ainsi le paure, bien auise, bien conseillé, & diligent, se peut aiser & moyener des biens. Esquels neantmoins Dieu lui faisant la grace de paruenir, faut qu'il s'arreste & mette son but, à la tres heureuse sufisance: qui est le comble de richesse. Se souuenant tousiours à ce propos d'vn beau huitain, qui s'enfuit: Duquel toute fois, si il sauoye le nom de l'Auteur, ne seroit cy non plus tem que partie du los qu'il merite.

De moins que rien, l'on peut à peu venir :
Et puis ce peu, n'a si peu de puissance,
Qu'assez ne face, à assez paruenir,
Celui qui veut auoir la sufisance.
Mais si au trop (de malheur) il s'auance,
Ne receuant d'assez contentement,
En danger est; par sa fole inconstance,
De retourner à son commencement."

CORROZET, Giles, a man of genius and learning, who was born in Paris January 4th 1510, and died July 4th 1568. He carried on the business of a bookseller, but seldom affixed his own name to his writings. In early youth he enjoyed few, if any, advantages from study; but, besides other attainments, he mastered the Latin, Italian and Spanish languages. Thirty-four works are said to have been composed or translated by him, of fourteen of which Brunet gives the titles and editions. As a French poet he was equal to any of his time, and his tale of the "*Rossignol*" possesses very considerable beauty. The *Tablet of Cebes* and the *Fables of Æsop* were rendered by him into French rhymes, and he compiled also a work of considerable repute on the *Antiquities of Paris*. He amassed a large fortune by his business, and his son and grandson sustained his reputation as booksellers. Manuel du Libraire, 1861, tome ii. col. 299-308.

The *Hecatomgraphie*, "an interesting little volume," says Dibdin, is a good specimen of his writings. By way of introduction he addresses an octain, "AVX BONS ESPRITZ & AMATEURS DES LETTRES." It is to the following effect: Plate XXXII.

"Whenever you shall be at your good leisure,
And neither care nor business longer find;
Whenever you shall wish to take some pleasure,
And give delight, by reading, to your mind:

When good examples you shall wish to know,
The morals sound of true philosophy,—
And what is needful in thy life to show;—
Read here, within this Hecatomgraphy."

Plate L.

UNIUS, Hadrian, who "conquered envy by study, uprightness and labour, and who at last had praise accorded to him worthy of his merit," was born at Hoorn in Holland in 1511. He pursued his studies at Haerlem, Louvain, Paris and Bologna, and in after life justified the titles bestowed upon him of being an able physician and a learned philologist. Whether he excelled as a poet may admit of a doubt, though, beside his emblems, he wrote verses on sacred subjects and an heroic poem on the marriage of Philip of Spain to Mary of England. He resided in England from 1543 to 1548, and dedicated to Edward VI. a Greek Lexicon, printed at Basle, to which he contributed above six thousand words. Holland was now his residence for a while, but he revisited England in 1553 or 1554 and remained only a short time. A few years afterwards he was appointed physician to the king of Denmark. Finally he settled at Haerlem, and received the appointment of "historian of the states of Holland." He presided over the college; but the loss of his library, consequent on the siege in 1573, greatly afflicted him, and he died in 1575. His works were numerous and on a variety of subjects, and the chief of them are enumerated by Boissard.

P. Hofmanni Peerlkamp Liber, &c. Harlemi, 1838, p. 112.

De Bry's Icones, pt. iv p. 171.

Plate XXVI

In addition to the specimen of the stanzas of Hadrian Junius given before, we present another, translated by Whitney, p. 96:

Had. Junius Emb. 59.

"Filio suo Petro Iunio.

En tibi quas, fili, genituræ consecro testes Ceras,
aucturas nomina amicitiæ.

Petram imitare iuuentus.

Sperne voluptates, iuuenis, constanter; vt iras
Ventorum, assultúsque maris Marpesiæ cautes.
Nate, tuo lepide ludens in nomine, dictas
Symbolico elogio, tu, Petram imitare Iuuentus."

ERRIÈRE, William de la, was a native of Toulouse. Of his birth and education we possess no information. His only literary monument appears to have been "*Le Théâtre des bons Engins*," published at Paris in 1539 by Denys Janot, the same printer as printed Corrozet's emblems. Both works "were composed in the quaint French verse of the time, and were accompanied by very beautiful woodcuts on a small scale. They were extremely popular." Plate XXX. J. B. Yates, 1849, p. 25.

The passages from Perrière are emblems I. and CI., from which a good idea may be gained of the work itself. The writer dedicates his work to the queen of Navarre, and speaks of himself "as a christian man writing to a christian princess." Of books like his own he declares: "It is not alone in our time that emblems are in renown, value and veneration, but from all antiquity, and almost from the beginning of the world." Several ancient authors are named by him (Chæremon, Horapollo and Lucan), and some modern (as Polyphilus, Celian Rogigien and Alciatus), thus: "In our time Alciatus has written out certain emblems and illustrated them with Latin verses," "and we, in imitation of the before-named, think we have well employed and appropriated our good leisure in the invention and illustration of our present emblems." Plate XXXI.

We may compare Whitney's, p. 205, with the following from Perrière:

"*Pulchritudo sine fructu.* Le Théâtre, &c. Emb. 65.

Le Cypres est arbre fort delectable,
Droict, bel, & hault, & plaisant en verdure:
Mais quãt au fruict, il est peu proffitable,
Car riẽ ne vault pour dõner nourriture.
Beaucoup de gens sont de telle nature:
Qui portẽt tiltre, & nõ de grand sciẽce:
Mais s'il aduient d'en faire experience:
L'õ ne cognoist ẽ eulx que le seul bruict.
C'est grand folie en arbre auoire fiance,
Dõt l'õ ne peult cuillir quelque bõ fruict."

OCCHIUS, Achilles, is simply named by Whitney in his Address to the Reader, and might be omitted from our notices, but our title-page and frontispiece are made up from his emblems; and therefore we Plate LII.

repeat what has been said of him by Joseph Brooks Yates:
Liverpool Lit. and Phil. Soc., 1849, p. 26. "Five years after the death of Alciato, a most beautiful book of emblems was presented to the world by another eminent Italian scholar, Achille Bocchi, commonly called Philerote. He was a native of Bologna, and sprung from a noble family of that city. Being equally distinguished for his scholarship and knowledge of public affairs, he served several Princes, and filled important offices in the court of Rome. In 1546 he instituted at Bologna an Academy, called after its founder Academia Bocchiana, and also (from the device of Mercury and Minerva, which it assumed) *Hermathena.* Bocchi's work, which was published in 1555, is entitled, '*Symbolicarum Questionum de universo genere quas serio ludebat, libri quinque.*' The copper-plates, comparatively of a large size, are engraved by the celebrated artist Guilio Bonasone, after designs partly by himself and partly by Bocchi, aided by Parmigiano and Prospero Fontana, many ideas being taken from Michael Angelo and Albert Durer. On the publication of the
Plate XXIII. second edition (1574) these plates, being much worn, were most of them retouched by a still more celebrated engraver, Augustino Caracci, then almost a boy. Both editions are scarce and much prized. The Latin verses of Bocchi are more remarkable for their beauty than their terseness."

The portrait of Bocchius is from his works, in which are emblems, pp. 91 and 183, dedicated, "To the best of friends, Andrew Alciat," and "To Paulo Jovio, bishop of Nocera." In Bocchius himself, it is said there is more to be understood than is expressed, and that while others could paint the features he could paint the mind, for that pure mind alone can comprehend mind.

OUSTAU, Peter, or Costalius, issued at Lyons in 1552, and again in 1555, his rare and curious book,
Plate XXXIV. entitled "PEGMA, *cum narrationibus philosophicis.*" The specimen given is "On the wretchedness of the human lot;" to which a few verses are added and then a dissertation, with each page elaborately ornamented, setting forth the nature of that wretchedness. Moral and religious reflections are interspersed.

In 1560 the *Pegma* was translated from Latin into French by
Plate XXXV. Lanteaume de Romieu, a gentleman of Arles. An emblem, p.

374, "*Time does all*," may have furnished Whitney with his last motto, "Tempus omnia terminat." One of the octains, addressed to the swan, and almost literally translated, possesses much simplicity:

"*Honour nourishes the arts.*
The swan melodious chants no lay,
Attempts no song of worth to sing,
Should zephyrs, breathing graciously
Over the fields, no sweetness bring:
And who desert from letters seeks,
Or undertakes some poet's theme,
If praise on learning never breathes,
Nor honours over labour beam?"

Whitney gave a very wide extension to his "*Music of Orpheus*," p. 186, but its substance is contained in Coustau's simpler lines:

"La force d'Eloquence. Le Pegme, p. 389.
De son gentil & fort melodieux
D'vn instrument, Orpheus feit mouuoir
Rocs & patiiz de leur places & lieux.
C'est eloquence ayant force & pouuoir
D'ebler les cueurs de tous part son scauoir
C'est l'orateur qui au fort d'eloquence
Premierement souz meme demourance.
Gens bestiaulx, & par ferocité
Les assembla: & qui à bienueillance
Les reuoqua de leur ferocité."

EZA, Theodore, occupies a large space in the literary and theological history of his times, and according to the religious bias of his early biographers is spoken of with bitter aversion or with high regard. There can be no doubt that at one period of his life he was guilty of excesses and immoralities, but that in after years he became distinguished for his indefatigable zeal and labours in behalf of the Reformation, and deserved the respect which he obtained when Balzec named him "the great minister of Geneva." Plate LI. Histoire sur la Vie &c. de T. de Bèze.

He was born at Vezelai in Burgundy June 24th 1519, and died 13th October 1605; and for above forty years occupied a high position among the Reformed in Switzerland. Nearly the whole of his works were of a religious and theological kind; and on these his renown rests, and not on the small volume of emblems contained in about 90 pages, though these are beautiful in execution and illustrated by verses of considerable neatness and piquancy.

Plates XLI. and LIX.

At a very early age he was brought to Paris, and the care of his education was undertaken by his uncle Nicholas de Bèze; and in his tenth year he was sent to Orleans to be instructed by Melchior Wolmar, an excellent Grecian, with whom he remained about seven years in Orleans and in the university of Bourges. Like some others, who in after life wrote emblems, his first studies were those of law, but he soon began chiefly to attend to classical literature. In 1539 at Paris he obtained his degree of licentiate of civil law, and passed several of the succeeding years amid the gaities of that capital, externally conforming to the Catholic church, in which he enjoyed some valuable benefices. A severe illness induced serious reflection; he fled from France, avowed his faith, and was married at Geneva in 1548. In 1549 he received the appointment to the Greek professorship at Lausanne, and here, by the addition of one hundred psalms, completed Marot's translation into French verse, and made the translation of the New Testament into Latin, which passes by his name; it was published at Paris in 1557. He was admitted as a Protestant minister in 1559, and soon after became Calvin's assistant in lecturing on theology; and in 1561 he was delegate from the university of Geneva to attend the conference of Poissy to effect, if possible, a reconciliation between the Catholic and Protestant churches of France. On Calvin's death in 1564 he succeeded to his important offices, and until 1597 continued to discharge them with eminent zeal and ability; the infirmities of age then came upon him, though to the very last his mind continued bright and clear. He died at the age of 86.

Manuel du Libraire, tome i. pp. 841-844.

His works are very numerous, though now almost forgotten. For the titles of these *Brunet* may be consulted; and for biographies of Beza, Oettinger's list, the Paris *Biographie Universelle*, or the article Beza in the *Penny Cyclopædia*.

Bib. Biogr. Univ. 1854, col. 149.

The twenty-four lines in *Whitney*, p. 165, appear founded on these four lines in *Beza:*

"POST AMARA DULCIA. Icones, Emb. 33.

In cauto quicunque rosas, collegerit vngue,
Vix vnquam illæso legerit vngue rosas.
Hoc sapite exemplo locupletes, plurima namque
Hisce latent vestris specula mixta rosis."

NEAU, Barthelemi, latinised into Anulus, whose device was a signet ring, was a Latin and French poet, a jurisconsult and an orator. He was born at Bourges at the beginning of the sixteenth century and died in 1565. In the year 1530 he was professor of rhetoric in Trinity College, Lyons, and principal of that institution in 1542.

Among his works are — "*The Mystery of the Nativity*," and "*The Merchant of Lyons*;" the latter is a French satirical drama, in which nine characters are introduced and the events of Europe narrated from 1524 to 1540. Aneau, in 1549, translated into French the emblems of Alciatus verse by verse, and also the *Utopia* of sir Thomas More. His own emblem-book, "PICTA POESIS," *Pictured Poetry*, was collected by him and published at Lyons in 1552. A French translation was set forth at Paris in the same year. The original has some Greek stanzas interspersed with the Latin. The first of his emblems bears the inscription, "DIVINI SPIRITVS INVOCATIO," *An Invocation to the Divine Spirit*, and may be accepted as a fair specimen of the author's power and method: Plate XXXIII.

"Every gift that is good, — perfect in blessedness,
From the Father of Light cometh down from the sky;
Let therefore the Poet who his work would set in order,
Invoke first of all divine help from on high.
We, verses adorning with pictures, most earnestly pray,
That God may shine on us, with fires of the heavenly day."

Aneau's death was very tragical. On the 21st of June 1565, being the Fête de Dieu, a stone had been thrown from one of the college windows as the Holy Sacrament was passing: it hit the priest who was carrying the Host, and the irritable populace broke into the college and massacred Aneau, believing him to be a Protestant and the author of the outrage.

Whitney's emblem, p. 141, shows how greatly on some occasions he amplified the text of his author. Whitney gives thirty-six lines, Anulus only four; but those four are correctly rendered in Whitney's first stanza:

Picta Poesis, p. 18.

"PERFIDUS FAMILIARIS.

PER medium Brasidas clypeum traiectus ab hoste;
Quoque foret læsus ciue rogante modum.
Cui fidebam (inquit) penetrabilis vmbo fefellit,
SIC AVI sæpe fides credita: proditor est."

Oettinger, col. 509.

AERNO, Gabriello, an Italian poet, was born at Cremona, and died 17th November 1561 in the prime of life. He was a man much beloved and admired. His scholarship was sound and extensive, and even the fastidious Bentley republished entire his notes on Terence. (Plate XXVII.) Though the name of *Emblems* is given to one of his works, it is, more properly, a book of very elegant Latin fables. They were written at the request of pope Pius IV., by whom the author was highly regarded. They are remarkable for correct Latinity, and for the power of invention which they display. Indeed the charge was made, though altogether groundless, that his fables "are written with such classic purity, as to have given rise to an opinion, that he had discovered and fraudulently availed himself of some of the unpublished works of Phædrus." (Roscoe's Leo X. Bohn's ed. vol. ii. p. 172.)

Emb. 72, p. 168. We subjoin one of his fables, with which the translation by Whitney, p. 157, may be compared:

"*Astrologus.*

OBSCURA astrologus graditur dum noctes in umbra
Intentus cœlo, & tacite labentibus astris,
Decidit in puteum: casuque afflictus iniquo
Implorabat opem, Divosque hominesque ciebat.
Excitus accessit pictei vicinus ad oras
Salsus homo: & Quæ nam hæc tua tam præpostera, dixit,
Dissita tam longe profiteris sidera nosse.
Quid rerum caussas, naturaeque abdita quaeris,
Ipse tui ipsius propriaeque oblite salutis."

AMBUCUS, John, "physician, antiquary and poet," "both stirs up the sound by his writings, and mighty in skill restores the sick by his medical art." He was born in the town of Tornau in Hungary in the year 1531. He studied with great credit to himself in several of the academies of Italy, France and Germany; and as in his special profession of medicine so in the knowledge of ancient philosophy and in the pursuit of literature generally he attained high repute. He was patronised by the emperors Maximilian II. and Rudolph II., and under them he held the offices of counsellor of state and of historian of the empire. After a life of usefulness and honour, he died at Vienna on the 13th of June "in the year of salvation M.D.LXXXIII." at the age of 53.

Plate LIII.

De Bry's Icones, pt. iii. ed. 1598, pp. 76-83.

The catalogue of his works, as prepared by himself and set forth in Boissard's life of him, is very extensive and of great variety,—from a simple exposition of the Lord's prayer to the harangues of Thucydides and Xenophon artistically explained. His principal or more important works were: *Lives of the Roman Emperors; A History of Hungary; Portraits of Physicians and Philosophers*, sixty-seven in number, with their lives; and translations into Latin of *Hesiod*, of the *Battle of the Frogs*, and of portions of *Plato*.

His emblems, of which there are at least five editions from Plantin's press, here chiefly demand our notice. They contain much that is original, but are not equal to those of Alciat in purity of style and in vigour of expression. With respect to Whitney's translations and appropriations from *Sambucus*, it is to be especially remarked they are very far from approaching the literal meaning; they are paraphrases, or accommodations—the carrying out of thoughts and hints which the Hungarian supplied. This may be illustrated from Whitney's emblem, p. 206, of which we give the original:

Brunet's Manuel, 1864, tome v. col. 104.

"TEMPORE CUNCTA MITIORA.

PRÆTERIENS quidam vites, nondumque calore
Maturum arripiens gustat, damnatque racemum.
Quinetiam pedibus contriuit, nullus vt inde
Austero imbueret saccõ sua labra viator.

Emb. J. Sambuci, ed. 1564, p. 104.

Iudicium prauum est hominum, nec tempora norunt
Expectare, minùs cupiunt subiisse labores.
Ardua sunt aditu primò, quæ pulchra fatemur
Tempore sed fiunt opera, & pòst mitia cuncta.
Sed refugit penitus botrum formosa puella,
Casta & ἄοινος enim, sidus nec palmiti amicum est."

Or, in reference to *Whitney*, p. 100, from

Emb. J. Sambuci, ed. 1564, p. 177.

"FRONTIS NULLA SIDAS.

CVNCTIS Deus creauit,
Quæcunque terra, & vndis,
Signum dedit, pateret,
Natura singulorum vt.
Latratibus canis sic
Suæ indicem dat iræ
Taurus monet furorem
Quòd cornuis petendo
Lædat, venena caudes
Serpens gerit, timendus
Et scorpius cauetur
Est nuda frons, sed index
Mortalibus negatus.
Vt nosse quis bonus sit,
Nequeas, tibi à malòque
Dum tempus est cauere
Dextra tenet tabellam
Rasam, notis nec vllis
Insignem, amicus vt sit
Quales tuus, colis quem
Tot sedulus per annos.
Scribas mihi potes si,
Num candidè, dolo ne
Tecum egit, at recusas."*

Plate XXXVIII.

FREITAG, Arnold, is a name to be recorded with honour, if we have respect to the beautiful work to which he contributed the descriptions and remarks in Latin, "MYTHOLOGIA ETHICA," or *Moral Philosophy taught in Fables;* but the notices of him with which we have met are very brief and unsatisfactory. There have been several distinguished physicians of the name Freitag, and Arnold seems to have been one of them. He was born at Emmerick, and, if a little before 1560, was very young when he wrote the Latin expositions of the engravings by Gerard de Jode and others which adorn his work. Foppens makes him professor of medicine at Groningen, but the university there was not founded until 1615, and the honour came to him therefore at a late period of his life. Among his works are mentioned some translations from Italian and Spanish treatises on *Food and Drink*, and *The Medicine for the Soul, or the Art of Dying.* He also translated Duplessis-Mornay's work, *On the Truth of the Christian Religion.*

Biog. Universelle, vol. xvi. p. 59.

* See Chambers's *General Biographical Dictionary*, vol. xxvii. p. 86.

Two plates set before the reader the nature of the illustrations in the *Ethical Mythology*: the one is the phœnix, applied as a type of Jesus Christ and as an emblem of the resurrection; and the other, in the fable of the Grasshopper and Ants, "the opposite rewards of industry and sloth," sets forth the proverb, "*The sluggard refused to plough by reason of the cold, therefore will he beg in harvest and it shall not be given him.*" (Prov. xx. 4.) Plates XXXIX. and XL.

EUSNER, Nicholas, like others of the emblem writers, was a man of extensive learning, a jurisconsult and a poet. He was born at Lemberg in Silesia February 2nd 1545, a little before Whitney, and he died at Jena April 12th 1602. He was a member of one of the most distinguished families of his native province. His law studies were pursued at Leipsic, and in 1565, at the age of 20, he lectured, or rather gave lessons, on Latin literature at Augsburg. The duke of Bavaria named him professor of Belles Lettres at the college of Launingen, of which afterwards Reusner became rector. He filled in succession several literary offices at Bâle, Spires and Strasburg; and in 1589 his reputation called him to Jena, a university founded in 1550, and to which he rendered important services. In a solemn assembly the emperor Rudolph II. decreed to him the poetic crown, and created him count-palatine. From the electorate of Saxony in 1595 he was deputy to that diet in Poland where the German princes formed a league against the Turks. He died during his second rectorate in 1602, and was buried in a tomb which he had caused to be constructed for himself, and of which the inscription gave little evidence of a humble, christian mind. His funeral sermon was preached by Mylius. Dominik Animæus and Thomas Sagittarius collected and published the facts of his parentage; and John Weitz set forth his life, in a quarto, at Jena in 1603. Plate LIV. Oettinger, 1854, col. 1515.

Reusner's works are fifty-eight in number; and we might say, more or less, for the number signifies little, when so many have passed away from observation. It is with his poetical works we have to do,—the first of which is entitled "POLYANTHIA, *sive Paradisus poeticus*," from which Whitney makes several quotations. These flowers of poetry are given in seven books, printed

Plate XLII. at Bâle, in octavo, 1579. The second poetical effusion was edited by his brother Jeremiah, and issued by the celebrated printer John Feyerabend of Frankfort in 1581. The emblem XXX., p. 142, "Man is a wolf to man," may have given Whitney his motto, p. 144, but supplies very few of the thoughts. Another emblem writer, whose name has escaped my memory, adopts the contrary sentiment, and heads his device, *Homo homini Deus*, Man is a God to man. A better instance is the following, which Whitney, p. 48, renders with some degree of accuracy:

Emb. Reusneri, p. 88.

"FIRMAMENTUM FAMILIÆ VXOR.

Cernis, vt obliquo funem vir torquet ocno:
Quo rabidem pascit turpis asella famem.
Sedulitas quorsum prodest, & cura mariti:
Prodiga si coniux est sine fruge domi?
Non minor est virtus, quam quærere, parta tueri:
Hoc opus est viri: coniugis istud opus.
Magnum vectigal, vxorem viuere parcè:
Semper habet, semper quæ sibi desse putat.
Seruat fida domum coniux, & censibus auget:
Paulatim magnas prodiga carpit opes:
Quodq' magis miserum est, vrit sine torre maritum:
O pereat, gaudet lædere si qua virum."

The number of emblem writers of the sixteenth century is by no means exhausted, but we are restricted by our subject to those who are supposed or proved to have contributed to Whitney's selection. Their biographies, brief though they are, suffice to show them as men of culture, of learning and of genius,—trusted and honoured in their respective countries, and still deserving of some record in the literature of modern times.

ESSAY IV.

SHAKESPEARE'S REFERENCES TO EMBLEM-BOOKS, AND TO WHITNEY'S EMBLEMS IN PARTICULAR.

OVELTIES respecting Shakespeare's genius may naturally expect to be looked upon with suspicion, and fresh NOTES upon his writings are a trouble to us,—we can scarcely endure them; yet, though seldom alluded to and never systematically carried out, his knowledge of emblem art, as applied in books, is a truth not to be questioned by any who have examined the evidence. His peculiar aptitude for the appreciation of art of every kind, even of the highest, is proved by his exquisite judgment of the supposed statue of Hermione, of the adornment of Imogen's chamber, of the pictures introduced into *The Taming of the Shrew*, and of the wonderful charms of melody and song when Lorenzo discourses to Jessica; and no man could have written the casket scene in *The Merchant of Venice*, nor the triumph scene as it is named in *Pericles*, who had not read and studied the emblem literature of the sixteenth century.

Winter's Tale, v. iii. 14-34. Cymbeline, II. iv. T. of Shrew, *Induction*, ii. 47-58. Mer. of Venice, III. ii. 114-128, v. i. 54. Pericles, II. ii.

To accomplish this two sources were open to him, for both of which, in the opinion of Douce, Drake and Capel Lofft, he possessed competent scholarship: the one was, to read for himself the emblem-books of France, Italy and Belgium; the other, to make use of our English *Whitney*, a work representative of the chief emblematists of those countries, and published at the very time when Shakespeare commenced his wonderful dramatic career. There were also open to him a translation into English by Daniell of the *Worthy Tract of Paulus Iovius*, printed in 1585, and by P. S. of Paradin's *Heroicall Devises*, printed in 1591.

Drake's Shakespeare and his Times, vol. i. pp. 32, 33 *note*, 54 *note*, 57, 58.

Act II. 7, 9. Act III. 2. It is also in the full spirit of emblematic art that the whole scenes are conceived and set forth in the *Merchant of Venice*, where are introduced the three caskets of gold, of silver, and of lead, by the choice of which the fate of Portia is to be determined:

"The first of gold, who this inscription bears,
'Who chooseth me shall gain what many men desire;'
The second silver, which this promise carries,
'Who chooseth me shall get as much as he deserves;'
This third, dull lead, with warning all as blunt,
'Who chooseth me must give and hazard all he hath.'"

And when the caskets are opened, the drawings and the inscription on the written scrolls, which are then taken out, examined and read, are exactly like the engravings or woodcuts and the verses by which the mottoes and emblems are set forth. Thus, on unlocking the golden casket, the prince of Morocco exclaims:

"O hell! what have we here?
A carrion Death, within whose empty eye
There is a written scroll! I'll read the writing.
All that glisters is not gold;
Often have you heard that told:
Many a man his life hath sold
But my outside to behold:
Gilded tombs do worms infold.
Had you been as wise as bold,
Young in limbs, in judgment old,
Your answer had not been inscroll'd;
Fare you well; your suit is cold."

The prince of Arragon also, on opening the silver casket, receives not merely a written scroll, as is represented in all Symeoni's DISTICHI MORALI, or *Moral Stanzas*, but corresponding to the device or woodcut, "the portrait of a blinking idiot," presenting him with the schedule or the explanatory rhymes:

For Example Plate XXXVII.

"The fire seven times tried this;
Seven times tried that judgment is,
That did neuer choose amiss.
Some there be that shadows kiss;
Such have but a shadow's bliss:

There be fools alive, I wis,
Silver'd o'er; and so was this.
Take what wife you will to bed,
I will ever be your head:
So begone: you are sped."

Shakespeare's emblems are thus complete in all their parts; there are the mottoes, the pictures, "a carrion Death," and "a blinking idiot," and the descriptive verses.

The words of Portia, when the prince of Arragon declares,

"I'll keep my oath,
Patiently to bear my wroth,"

are moreover a direct reference to the emblems which occur in *Giles Corrozet*, *Gabriel Symeoni*, *Claude Paradin* and *Geffrey Whitney*. The first adopts the motto, "La guerre doulce aux inexpérimentez," *War is sweet only to the inexperienced*, with a butterfly fluttering towards a lighted candle. The other three, with the same device, make use of Italian proverbs: Symeoni, of "COSI TROPPO PIACER CONDUCE À MORTE;" Paradin, of "Cosi viuo Piacer conduce à morte;" and Whitney, of "COSI DE DEN AMAR PORTO TORMENTO;"—*Too much, or too livèly a pleasure leads to death*, and *Thus love of happiness brings torment.* In close agreement with these devices are Portia's words: Plate XXXII. Emb. p. 219.

"Thus hath the candle singed the moth.
O, these deliberate fools! when they do choose
They have the wisdom by their wit to lose."

The opening of the third of the caskets, that of lead, is also as much an emblem delineation as the other two,—surpassing them indeed in the beauty of the language as well as in the excellence of the device. "What find I here?" demands Bassanio, and answers:

"Fair Portia's counterfeit! What demi-god
Hath come so near creation? Move those eyes?
Or whether, riding on the balls of mine
Seem they in motion? Here are sever'd lips,
Parted with sugar-breath: so sweet a bar
Should sunder such sweet friends. Here in her hairs
The painter plays the spider, and hath woven
A golden mesh to entrap the hearts of men,
Faster than gnats in cobwebs: but her eyes,—

How could he see to do them? having made one,
Methinks it should have power to steal both his
And leave itself unfurnish'd. Yet look, how far
The substance of my praise doth wrong this shadow
In under-prizing it, so far this shadow
Doth limp behind the substance. Here's a scroll,
The continent and summary of my fortune."
[*Reads:*] "You that choose not by the view,
Chance as fair, and choose as true!
Since this fortune falls to you,
'Be content and seek no new.
If you be well pleased with this,
And hold your fortune for your bliss,
Turn you where your lady is,
And claim her with a loving kiss.'"

In these scenes of the casket, therefore, Shakespeare himself is an emblematist, and only the woodcut or the engraving is needed to render those scenes as perfect examples of emblem writing as any that issued from the pens of Alciat or of Whitney. The dramatist may have been sparing in his employment of this tempting kind of illustration; yet, with the instances before us, we must conclude that he knew well what emblems were, and, most probably, had seen and was bearing in mind the emblem literature of that age.

Pict. Shakespeare, Vol. supplemental, pp. 13, 118 and 119.

But the probability rises to certainty when with Knight and other writers we believe that *Pericles* was, in the main, Shakespeare's composition, or, as Dryden expresses the fact,

"Shakespeare's own muse his Pericles first bore."

Books of emblems indeed are not mentioned by their titles and names, nor so quoted as we are accustomed to make quotations, by direct and specific references; but the allusions are so plain, the words so exactly alike, that they cannot be misunderstood. The author of *Pericles* was of a certainty acquainted with more than one emblem writer in more than one language, and very probably possessed greater familiarity with Geffrey Whitney's "Choice of Emblemes" than with any other. We may reasonably conclude that he had them before him, and copied from them, when he prepared the second scene of the second act of *Pericles.*

The whole of that second scene we will give, and then comment upon the parts. The dialogue is between Simonides, king of Pentapolis, and his daughter Thaisa, on occasion of the "triumph" or festive pageantry which did honour to her birthday: Pericles, II. ii.

"*Enter a Knight: he passes over the stage, and his Squire presents his shield to the Princess.*

Sim. Who is the first that doth present himself?
Thai. A knight of Sparta, my renowned father;
And the device he bears upon his shield
Is a black Æthiop, reaching at the sun:
The word, *Lux tua vita mihi.*
Sim. He loves you well that holds his life of you.
[*The second Knight passes.*
Who is the second that presents himself?
Thai. A prince of Macedon, my royal father;
And the device he bears upon his shield
Is an armed knight that's conquered by a lady:
The motto thus in Spanish, *Più per dulçura que per fuerça.*
[*The third Knight passes.*
Sim. And what o' the third?
Thai. The third of Antioch,
And his device a wreath of chivalry:
The word, *Me pompæ provexit apex.*
[*The fourth Knight passes.*
Sim. What is the fourth?
Thai. A burning torch, that's turned upside down:
The word, *Quod me alit, me extinguit.*
Sim. Which shows that beauty hath this power and will,
Which can as well inflame as it can kill.
[*The fifth Knight passes.*
Thai. The fifth, an hand environed with clouds,
Holding out gold that's by the touchstone tried:
The motto this, *Sic spectanda fides.*
[*The sixth Knight passes.*
Sim. And what's the sixth and last, which the knight himself
With such a graceful courtesy delivered?
Thai. He seems a stranger: but his present is
A wither'd branch, that's only green at top:
The motto, *In hac spe vivo.*

Sim. A pretty moral:
From the dejected state wherein he is,
He hopes by you his fortune yet may flourish."

It needs but a simple act of comparison between this dialogue in *Pericles* and the pages of an emblem writer to establish the indebtedness of the dramatist to those who, in setting forth their fables or other allegories, were aided by the skill of the designer and the art of the engraver. Take either page 138 of *Whitney* or page 35 of *Gabriel Symeoni:* the torch engraven and the motto displayed are identical — except in a single word, *qui* for *quod* — with those of the fourth knight in the triumph scene of *Pericles;* and the writer of that scene must have known them. The copying is so evident, that it does not even require an acknowledgment. Let us however pursue the subject in due order, and we shall see the fact brought out even more clearly.

Plate LVII. Paradin.

After considerable research, through above twenty different books of emblems preceding the time of *Pericles,* I have met with none containing the devices of the first and of the sixth knight; and we may assign these to Shakespeare's own invention. The motto of the old family of the Blounts, *Lux tua vita mea,* Thy light my life, is very close to that of the first knight; but their crest is an armed foot on the sun, not a black Æthiop reaching towards him. Emblems of Hope are found in great abundance;* but the source of the device and motto of the sixth knight also remains undiscovered. We may conjecture that Shakespeare, having read Spenser's "*Shepheard's Calender,*" published in 1579, did — from the line, January (l. 54),

Moxon's Spenser, p. 365.

"Ah, God! that love should breed both ioy and paine;"

and from the Italian emblem, as Spenser names it, "*Anchora speme,*" Hope is my anchor, — did compose for himself the sixth knight's device, "*In hac spe vivo,*" In this hope I live. The step from applying the emblems of other writers to the construction of new ones would be but small, and the dramatist would find

* In a little later age (1636) there issued "from the Plantinian office of Balthasar Moretus at Antwerp" a volume containing no less than thirty emblems of Hope alone the title is, "GVILIELMI HESI Antverpiensis, è Societate IESV EMBLEMATA SACRA DE FIDE, SPE, CHARITATE." 24mo, pages 404.

it no trouble to contrive for himself what was needed for the completion of his "triumph."

The case is different with respect to the other four emblems; for these we can trace to their sources. The second motto Shakespeare gives in Spanish, *More by gentleness than by force.* The Spanish emblem-books, by Francisco Guzman in 1587, by Hernando de Soto in 1599 and by Don Orozco in 1610, do not contain the motto in question, and could not be adduced as testimonies even if they did; but a near approach to it exists in "LOS EMBLEMAS DA ALCIATO traducidas en rhimas Españolas." "EN LYON *por Girlielmo Rovillio,* 1549," 8vo; The Emblems of Alciatus translated into Spanish Rhymes, &c. On page 124, corresponding with Alciat's 180th emblem, occurs the motto, Ed 1581, Antv. p. 621. "*Que mas puede la eloquençia que la fortaliza,*" Eloquence or persuasion rather than force prevails,—the very idea which the second knight expresses.

But, although I fail to discover Shakespeare's Spanish motto in a Spanish emblem-book, I meet with an exactly literal expression of it in a French work of extreme rarity, Corrozet's Plate XXXII. "HECATOMGRAPHIE," published at Paris in 1540. There, at emblem 28, "*Plus par doulceur que par force,*" More by gentleness than by force, is the saying which introduces the old fable of the sun and the wind, and of their contest with the traveller. A symbolical woodcut is appended, and the stanza—

> "Contre la froidure du vent,
> L' homme se tient clos & se serre,
> Mais le Soleil le plus souuent
> Luy faict mettre sa robe à terre;"

which may be pretty accurately translated thus:

> "Against the wind's cold blasts
> Man draws his cloak around;
> But while sweet sunshine lasts,
> He leaves it on the ground."

Now as the motto of the second knight existed in French so early as 1540, and as emblem-books were translated into Spanish nearly as early, it is very probable, though we have not been successful in tracing it out, that the author of *Pericles,*—Shakespeare if you will,—copied the words from some Spanish emblem-book that had come within his observation, and which applied the proverb to woman's gentleness subduing man's harsher nature. Future inquiries will, perhaps, clear up this mystery and name the very work in which the Spanish saying, "*Più per dulçura que per fuerça*," is original.

Three or four sources are open to which we may trace the mottoes and devices of the third, fourth and fifth knights. Shakespeare may have handled, probably did handle, some one of the various editions of Claude Paradin's and Gabriel Symeoni's "*Devises Hëroïqves*," which appeared at Lyons, at Paris and at Antwerp between the years 1557 and 1590; or, as Francis Dousa supposes, may have seen the English translation, published in London in 1591; or, with greater probability, may have used the emblems of his own countryman Geffrey Whitney, bearing the date 1586.*

Illustrations of Shakespeare, pp. 302, 393. Plate LVI.

The third knight, he of Antioch, has for his device "a wreath of chivalry,"

"The word, *ille pompæ provexit apex*,"

Fol. 146, or p. 292.

i.e. The crown at the triumph carried me onward. *Les Devises Hëroïqves* contains the wreath and the motto exactly as Shakespeare quotes them; but in *Paradin* a long account follows of the nature of the wreath and of the high value accorded to it in Roman estimation. "It was the grandest recompense or the greatest reward which the ancient Romans could think of, to confer on Chieftains over victorious armies, or Emperors, Captains, or victorious knights."

* We must not however forget another English source which was open to the dramatist, and which I have named in my account of *Early Emblem-books and their introduction into English Literature;* it is "THE worthy Tract of Paulus Iovius contayning a Discourse of rare inventions both Militarie and Amorous *called Imprese, whereunto is added a Preface contay*ning the Arte of composing them with *many other notable devises.* By Samuel Daniell late Student in Oxenforde. At London Printed for Simon Waterson 1585." In octavo, unpaged, 72 leaves in all including the title. This rare work, of which Mr. Stirling of Keir possesses a copy, and which is also in the British Museum, is without prints or cuts of any kind, except two or three initial letters of no great merit. It is therefore not so likely to have attracted the notice of Shakespeare as Paradin, Symeoni or Whitney. Indeed it is evident from Shakespeare's graphic lines, that he was describing from some picture or device actually before him. Nevertheless, as will be shown on pages 302 and 303, there is a very sound reason for concluding that Daniell's translation of *Jovius* was also known to the great dramatist.

Introductory Dissertation, p. 18.

Shakespeare does not add a single word of explanation or of amplification, which it is likely he would have done if he had used an English translation; but simply, without remark, he adopts the emblem and its motto, as is natural to a person who, though not unskilled in the language by which they are explained, is not perfectly at home in it.

But in the case of the fourth and fifth knights it is not the simple adoption of a device which we have to remark; the ideas, almost the very expressions in which those ideas are clothed, are also presented to us, pointing out that the dramatic poet had something more than stanzas or narratives in an unfamiliar tongue.

The fourth knight's device is thus described in *Pericles*: * Pericles, II. ii.

"A burning torch that's turned upside down,
The word, *Quod me alit, me extinguit;*
Which shows that beauty hath this power and will,
Which can as well inflame as it can kill."

Now the Italian stanza in the "TETRASTICHI MORALI" of Symeoni and Giovio is: Senten. Imprese, p. 35.

"*Nutrisce il fuoco à lui la cera intorno,*
Et la cera l' estingue, ô quanti sono, Qui me alit, me extinguit.
Che dopò vn riceuuto & largo dono,
Dal donator riceuon danno & scorno!"

To the following purport in English:

"The wax here within nourishes the flames,
And the wax stifles them; how many names,
Who after large gifts and kindness shown
Gain for the giver harm and scorn alone."

Reed's edition of *Shakespeare* presents the following note: Vol. xxi. p. 222.

"*A burning torch, &c.* This device and motto may have been taken from Daniel's translation of *Paulus Jovius*, in 1585, in which they are found."

The passage referred to is the following:

"An amorous gentleman of *Milan* bare in his standard a Torch Daniell's Worthy Tract of Jovius *in finem.*

* The idea of a torch extinguishing itself is also given in the lines: 1 Hen. VI. II. v. l. 122.

"Here dies the dusky torch of Mortimer,
Choked with ambition of the meaner sort."

figured burning, & turning downeward, whereby the melting wax falling in great aboundance, quencheth the flame. With this Poesie thereunto, *Quod me alit me extinguit.* Alluding to a Lady whose beautie did foster his loue & whose disdain did endamage his life."

Certainly if Daniell's translation had, like *Whitney*, presented a pictured emblem, there would scarcely be any way of escape from the conclusion that his work was the actual source of the fourth knight's device; but Shakespeare's description possesses so much apparent reality that we are upheld in supposing there was a pictorial model before him, and not simply a dead-letter narrative. His inventive power however was great, and Daniell's work may have taught him how to use it.

One fact decisively favours the conjecture that the motto, as quoted by Shakespeare, *Quod me alit me extinguit,* was derived from Daniell. The other emblematists, as Symeoni, Paradin, Paradin's translator, and Whitney, all read *Qui me alit &c.*, but Daniell gives *Quod me alit.* And therefore, as far as the motto is concerned, Daniell may be regarded as the source to Shakespeare of "the word" to his fourth knight's device.

Dev. Héroïq. fol. 169. Plate LVII. To the same motto, *Who nourishes me extinguishes me,* Paradin adds this little piece of history, amplifying Giovio:

"In the battle of the Swiss, defeated near Milan by the late King Francis, M. de Saint Valier, the old man, father of Madame Diana of Poictiers, Duchess of Valentinois, and Captain of a hundred Gentlemen, bore a standard whereon was a painting of a lighted torch turned downwards, and full of wax which kept flowing in order to stifle it, and the words, *Qui me alit, me extinguit.* Which device he feigned for love of a lady, wishing to show just in this way that her beauty nourished his thought, and also put him in danger of his life."

Douce's Illustrations, pp. 302 and 393. Paradin's translation of 1591, P. S., has been advanced as the source whence Shakespeare's torch-emblem was derived; but it is very note-worthy that the torch in the English translation is Plate LVII. not a torch "that's turned upside down," but one held uninverted, with the flame naturally ascending. This contrariety to Shakespeare's description seems therefore fatal to the translator's claim.

Whitney's Emb. p. 183. Let us next consider Whitney's stanza of six lines to the same motto and the same device, premising that Plantin has used for the *Whitney* in 1586 the identical woodcut which he inserted in the *Paradin* in 1562:

> "EUEN as the wax dothe feede, and quenche the flame,
> So loue giues life, and loue, despaire doth giue:
> The godlie loue, doth louers croune with fame:
> The wicked loue, in shame dothe make them liue.
> Then leaue to loue, or loue as reason will,
> For louers lewde doe vainlie languishe still."

Here placing in comparison Symeoni, Giovio's translator Daniell, Paradin, Paradin's English translator, and Whitney, as illustrative of the fourth knight's emblem, can we fail to perceive in *Pericles* a closer resemblance both of thought and expression to Whitney than to the others? Whitney wrote,

> "So loue giues life, and loue, despaire doth giue:"

and *Pericles* thus amplifies the line:

> "Which shows that beauty hath this power and will,
> Which can as well inflame as it can kill."

From this instance then we infer that Whitney's book was known to the author of *Pericles*, and that he has simply carried out the idea which had there been suggested to him.

But "the device" and "the word" of the fifth knight,

> "an hand environed with clouds,
> Holding out gold that's by the touchstone tried,
> The motto this, *Sic spectanda fides;*"

So fidelity is to be proved,—may be regarded as identical with the device and the word presented by Whitney, and which he copies from Paradin. This emblem is in fact that which was appropriated to Francis I. and Francis II., kings of France from 1515 to 1560, and which appears among the "HIEROGRAPHIA REGVM FRANCORVM,"* inscribed "Franciscus II. Valesius Rex Francorum XXV Christianissimus." The device then follows and the comment: "Coronatum aureum nummum ad Lydium lapidem dextra hæc explicat & sic, id est, duris in rebus fidem explo-

Emb. 139. Plate LVI.

Symbola Diuina, &c., vol. i. pp. 87 and 88.

* See "SYMBOLA DIUINA & HUMANA PONTIFICVM, IMPERATORVM, REGVM Accessit breuis & facilis Isagoge Iac. Typotii Fanckfvrti Apvd Godifridvm Schonwellervm, M.D.C.LII." Three volumes folio in one.

randam docet;" This right hand extends to the Lydian stone a coin of gold wreathed round (with an inscription) and so, that is, teaches that in times of difficulty fidelity is to be put to the proof. The coin applied to the touchstone in the "HIEROGRAPHIA" bears the inscription, "FRANCISCVS II. FRANCORVM REX;" but the engravings or woodcuts in *Paradin* and in
Plate LVI. *Whitney* have the inscription, "FRANCISCVS DEI GRATIA FRAN. REX."

Whitney, in which he is followed, though briefly, in *Pericles*, describes the emblem itself, and says:

Emb. p. 139.
"THE touche doth trye, the fine and purest goulde:
And not the sound, or els the goodly showe.
So, if mennes wayes and vertues, wee behoulde,
The worthy men, wee by their workes, shall knowe.
But gallant lookes, and outward showes beguile,
And ofte are clokes to cogitacions vile."

The comparison thus instituted between the authors who use the motto, "*Sic spectanda fides*," makes it appear, I think, that there is greater correspondence between Shakespeare and Whitney than between Shakespeare and Paradin, and therefore that Shakespeare did not derive his fifth knight's device either from the French emblem writer or from his English translator, but from the English *Whitney*, which had lately been published. Indeed if *Pericles* were written, as Knight conjectures, in Shakespeare's early manhood, previous to the year 1591, it could not be the English translation of *Paradin* which furnished him with the three mottoes and devices of the "triumph" scene.*

The fine frontispiece to Whitney's *Emblems* represents the arms of Robert Dudley: it is a drawing, remarkably graphic, of a bear grasping a ragged staff, with a collar and chain around him, and standing erect on the burgonet; a less elaborate drawing gives the same badge on the title-page of the second part of the *Emblems*. Most exactly, most artistically does Shakespeare ascribe the same crest, in the same attitude and on the same standing-place, to Richard Nevil, earl of Warwick, the king-

* Paradin in a great measure compiled his work from *Symeoni*, and therefore to old editions of *Giovio* we may look for further elucidation of this subject.

maker of history. Here is the dialogue between him and old Clifford, just after Warwick's taunting remark:

"*War.* You were best to go to bed and dream again, 2 Hen. VI. v. i. l. 196.
To keep thee from the tempest of the field.
Clif. I am resolved to bear a greater storm
Than any thou canst conjure up to-day,
And that I'll write upon thy burgonet,
Might I but know thee by thy household badge.
War. Now by my father's badge, old Nevil's crest,
The rampant bear, chain'd to the ragged staff,
This day I'll wear aloft my burgonet
(As on the mountain top the cedar shows
That keeps his leaves in spite of any storm)
Even to affright thee with the view thereof.
Clif. And from thy burgonet I'll rend thy bear,
And tread it under foot with all contempt,
Despite the bearward that protects the bear."

A closer correspondence between a picture and a description of it can scarcely be imagined. Shakespeare's lines and Whitney's frontispiece exactly coincide:

"like coats in heraldry, Mid. N. Dream, III. ii. l. 213.
Due but to one, and crowned with one crest."

A remarkable instance of similarity is found between Whitney and Shakespeare in the description which they both give of the commonwealth of bees. In this case Whitney's stanzas, dedicated "*To* RICHARD COTTON *Esquier*" of Combermere are original writing, not a translation, and the plea is inadmissible that Shakespeare went to the same fountain head, except in a single phrase; neither he nor Whitney follow Alciat,* who confines himself to four lines. The two accounts of the economy of these "creatures small" are almost equally excellent and offer several points of resemblance, not to name them imitations, by the more recent writer. Whitney speaks of the "Master bee"— Plate LVIII.

* Alciat's subject is "the mercifulness of a Prince," and, almost literally rendered, his expressions are in reference to his device of a bee-hive:

"That their ruler never will wound with the stings of the wasps,
And that greater he will be than others by a double-sized body;
He will make proof of mild empire and well ordered kingdoms
And that inviolable laws to good judges are entrusted."

Shakespeare of the king or "emperor;" both regard the head of the hive, not as a queen, but a "born king" or general, and hold forth the polity of the busy community as an admirable example of a well-ordered kingdom or government.

Emb. pp. 200, 201. Referring carefully to Whitney's verses, bearing the motto in mind which he uses, "*Patria cuique chara,*" Native land to each one dear,—by their side let us place what Shakespeare wrote on the same subject, the commonwealth of bees, and we shall perceive a close similarity in the thoughts, if not in the expressions. Hen. V. I. ii. l. 178. In *King Henry V.* the duke of Exeter and the archbishop of Canterbury enter upon an argument respecting a well-governed state; and the duke remarks:

"While that the armed hand doth fight abroad,
The advised head defends itself at home;
For government, though high and low and lower,
Put into parts, doth keep in one consent,
Congreeing in a full and natural close,
Like music.
Cant. Therefore doth heaven divide
The state of man in divers functions,
Setting endeavour in continual motion;
To which is fixed, as an aim or butt,
Obedience! for so work the honey-bees,
Creatures that by a rule in nature teach
The art of order to a peopled kingdom.
They have a king and officers of sorts;
Where some, like magistrates, correct at home,
Others, like merchants, venture trade abroad,
Others, like soldiers, armed in their stings,
Make boot upon the summer's velvet buds,
Which pillage they with merry march bring home
To the tent-royal of their emperor;
Who busied in his majesty surveys
The singing masons building roofs of gold,
The civil citizens kneading up the honey,
The poor mechanic porters crowding in
The heavy burdens at his narrow gate,
The sad-eyed justice, with his surly hum,
Delivering o'er to executors pale
The lazy yawning drone."

In a small way a strict correspondence exists between an expression in the quarrel scene of Brutus and Cassius and the emblems by Whitney and Beza of a dog barking at the moon. Whitney copied his motto and device and the first stanza from Alciatus, but his method of applying the fable from Theodore Beza. Alciat's lines are:

> "By night, as at a mirror, the dog looks at the lunar orb:
> And seeing himself, believes another dog to be there;
> And barks: but in vain is the angry voice driven by the winds,
> For Diana in silence pursues her course onward, — still on."

Ed. 1581, Antv. Emb. 164, p. 571.

But Beza's lines have the exact aim of Whitney's — to reprove detractors and to declare that cavillers at right and truth chiefly succeed in showing their own perverseness. Thus Beza:

> "The full orb'd moon, that views wide lands outspread,
> Despises barking dogs, — on high her zone:
> So who Christ's servants blame, or Christ their Head,
> Scorn's finger point to folly all their own."

Plate LIX.

Alciat's and Beza's thoughts are both united in *Whitney*, with additions of his own:

> "BY shininge lighte of wannishe CYNTHIAS raies,
> The dogge behouldes his shaddowe to appeare:
> Wherefore, in vaine aloude he barkes, and baies,
> And alwaies thoughte, an other dogge was there:
> But yet the Moone, who did not heare his queste,
> Hir woonted course, did keepe vnto the weste.
>
> This reprehendes, those fooles which baule, and barke,
> At learned men, that shine aboue the rest:
> With due regarde, that they their deedes should marke,
> And reuerence them, that are with wisedome bleste:
> But if they striue, in vaine their winde they spende,
> For woorthie men, the Lord doth still defende."

Emb. p. 213.

The variations or the agreements among the three emblematists as to the dog baying at the moon we need not determine; from one or from all of them Shakespeare probably took the expression which marks the hottest part of the contention of Brutus and Cassius. Brutus demands:

> "What shall one of us,
> That struck the foremost man of all this world,

Julius Cæsar, IV. iii. l. 21.

But for supporting robbers; shall we now
Contaminate our fingers with base bribes?
And sell the mighty space of our large honours,
For so much trash as may be grasped thus?"

and instantly exclaims, as if the device were before him,

"I had rather be a dog, and bay the moon
Than such a Roman."

Correspondences almost in scores might be given between Shakespeare and the emblem writers.* We close our account with one which we may trace through the English of *Whitney*, the French of *Paradin*, and the Italian of *Symeoni*. The device is a sculptor, with mallet and chisel, cutting a memorial of his wrongs into a block of marble, and above his head is the scroll and its motto, "*Scribit in marmore læsus*," Being wronged he writes on marble. The stanza from the Italian is:

Whitney, p. 183.

Symeoni. Plate XXXVII.

"Each one that lives may be swift passion's slave,
And though a powerful will at times delight
In causing others harm and terror's fright;
The injured doth those wrongs on marble grave."

In that scene of unparalleled beauty, tenderness and simplicity, in which there is related to queen Katherine the death of "the great child of honour," as she terms him, cardinal Wolsey, Griffith describes him as

Hen. VIII. VI. ii. l. 27.

"full of repentance,
Continual meditations, tears and sorrows,
He gave his honours to the world again,
His blessed part to heaven, and slept in peace."

And just afterwards, when the queen had been speaking with some asperity of the cardinal's greater faults, Griffith remonstrates:

* This assertion is not made unadvisedly. I went pretty thoroughly into the subject before announcing Whitney's *Emblems* for republication, and I have the results, illustrated by about 140 photographs from emblem writers, in a manuscript volume of nearly 400 pages, 4to, which I have entitled "THE EMBLEM WRITERS of the *Fifteenth* and *Sixteenth* Centuries, with the CORRESPONDENCES of Thought and Expression in SHAKESPEARE's Works." Were I a younger man I might hope to set this volume before the public in a manner worthy of the authors between whom so many similarities and identities can be established.

"Noble Madam,
Men's evil manners live in brass; their virtues
We write in water. May it please your highness
To hear me speak his good now."

Lavinia's deep wrongs were being written by her on the sand to inform Marcus and Titus what they were and who had inflicted them. Marcus was for instant revenge, but Titus counsels:

"You're a young huntsman, Marcus; let it alone, Titus And. IV. I.
And come, I will go get a leaf of brass,
And with a gad of steel will write those words,
And lay it by: the angry northern wind
Will blow these sands, like Sybil's leaves, abroad,
And where's your lesson then?"

How like the sentiments thus enunciated to the lines in *Whitney:*

"IN marble harde our harmes wee alwayes graue, Emb. p. 183.
Bicause, we still will beare the same in minde:
In duste wee write the benefittes wee haue,
Where they are soone defaced with the winde.
So, wronges wee houlde, and neuer will forgiue,
And soone forget, that still with vs shoulde liue."

"The famous Scenicke Poet, Master W. Shakespeare," may have been intimate with the Italian and French emblem-books, and from them have been supplied with the thought of "a leaf of brass," and of the records of "men's evil manners," and of "their virtues;" but there is a far closer similarity between him and Whitney: and allowing for the easy substitution of "brass" and "water" for "marble" and "dust," the parallelism of the ideas and words is very exact, and fully justifies the conclusion that Whitney's emblems were well known to Shakespeare.

For the sentiment of engraving our wrongs there may have been a common origin to which the emblematists and the dramatist had recourse, — it is a sentence written by sir Thomas More about the year 1516. Speaking of the ungrateful returns which Jane Shore experienced from those whom she had served in her Hist. of Rich. III. prosperity, More remarks: "Men use, if they haue an evil turne, to write in marble, and whoso doth us a good turne, we write it in duste."

The expressions are however of higher antiquity than any of

Jeremiah xvii. 1, 13. these quotations. The prophet Jeremiah sets forth most forcibly what Shakespeare names "men's evil manners living in brass," and Whitney, "harms grauen in marble hard." "The sin of Judah is written with a pen of iron, and with the point of a diamond: it is graven upon the table of their heart and upon the horns of your altar." And the writing in water or in the dust is in the exact spirit of the words, "they that depart from me shall be written in the earth," *i.e.* the first wind that blows over them shall efface their names, "because they have forsaken the LORD, the fountain of living waters."

It is but justice to Shakespeare to notice that at times his judgment of injuries rises to the full height of christian morals. The spirit Ariel avows that were he human his "affections would become tender" towards the shipwrecked captives, and Prospero enters into his feeling with a strong conviction:

Tempest v. i. l. 25.

> "Though with their high wrongs I am struck to the quick,
> Yet with my nobler reason 'gainst my fury
> Do I take part: the rarer action is
> In virtue than in vengeance: they being penitent
> The sole drift of my purpose doth extend
> Not a frown further."

And so I would end this subject by repeating those noble lines of a later writer, furnished me by a friend, the Rev. T. A. Walker, M.A., of Filey, late of Tabley, in which the sentiment of a free forgiveness of injuries is ascribed to the world's great and blessed Saviour:

> "Some write their wrongs on marble, He more just
> Stoop'd down serene, and wrote them in the dust,
> Trod under foot, the sport of every wind,
> Swept from the earth, quite banished from His mind,
> There secret in the grave He bade them lie,
> And grieved they could not 'scape the Almighty's eye."

The references and coincidences adduced, and which I know of a certainty may be very easily enlarged, cannot be regarded as entirely accidental. I would not urge them all with full confidence, and I do not pretend to say that my examples must of necessity carry conviction with them. Their conclusiveness is a matter of opinion only,—if you will, a dogma, and not a doctrine, of my Shakesperian and Whitneian faith,—yet what I have thus opened is a very curious and interesting subject of inquiry.* I am but a pioneer, or rather a miner digging for precious stones; and possibly I may verify the experience of the jet-seekers at Whitby, cast up a whole mountain of rubbish to bring to light two or three pieces of ornament, or a single specimen of crystallized charcoal.

* Were it necessary I might go into a fuller and more critical examination of the question to which emblem writer specially certain of Shakespeare's devices are to be traced. We may affirm generally that the ultimate resort must be to Symeoni, Giovio, or Alciat. From their stores and instructions, and from those of Girolamo Ruscelli Plate LXI. on the *Invention of Devices, Coats of Arms, Mottoes and Liveries,* and of Lodovico Domenichi "*on what are named Devices of Arms and of Love,*" emblem writers of a later date than 1556 very frequently borrowed or invented.

Indeed Ruscelli and, by implication, Giovio were the teachers to sir Philip Sidney See Note to Whitney's Emblem, p. 38. of the "Gentle Art" of attaching *pictorial illustrations* to *poesies*, and of making an emblem complete by motto, device and stanza; and what that noble cavalier commended and followed would find a ready entrance to his countrymen. Through him the *Imprese* of the Italians became known in England, and it is not unlikely were communicated to Spenser in 1579, and afterwards to his successors Daniell, Whitney and Abraham Fraunce.

Paolo Giovio's work on emblems bears the two titles of *Dialogo*, Dialogue, and Plate LXI. *Ragionamento*, Discourse; but they are essentially the same. The latter however, in the editions of 1556 and 1560 has seven or eight pages of additional matter. Pictorial illustrations appeared at a later time.

It was not from these fuller editions that Daniell executed his translation, but from Plate LX the Roman edition of 1555, or from some similar edition, to which the translator has appended "certaine notable deuises both militarie and amorous, *Collected by Samuel Daniell.*" It is in this additional part that the torch is named, "burning, and turning downeward," with the motto *QUOD me alit, &c.*

Of four editions of Giovio's *Dialogo* or *Ragionamento* — 1555 by Antonio Barre, Plate LX. and LXI. 1556 and 1560 by Giordano Ziletti, and another of 1556 by Gabriel Giolito — no one contains the motto which Daniell quotes. That motto appears in 1561 in Symeoni's Plate LXII. DEVISES OV EMBLEMES HÉROÏQVES ET MORALES, p. 244; in 1562 in SENTENTIOSE Plate XXXVI. IMPRESE, p. 35; and in 1574 in DIALOGO DEL L'IMPRESE MILITARI ET AMOROSE, Plate LXIII. p. 200: but, as in *Paradin* and *Whitney*, the motto reads, not *Quod*, but *Qui me alit.* Daniell seems therefore to have made the alteration without authority.

It could not however be from Daniell that Shakespeare derived any of his other emblems, for the burning torch is the only one which the translator of *Giovio* names. We return therefore to the conclusion, that Shakespeare read other emblem writers; and what work so likely to be read as one by his own countryman Whitney, selected and culled from the choice devices of French and Italian art?

For this note the reader is really indebted to William Stirling, esq., M.P. for Perthshire; for without the generous loan from his richly-stored library, of seven volumes bearing dates between 1555 and 1585, the editor would not have had the materials accessible for compiling what he has now put together.

However, I would have scholars work for every rational elucidation of "the sweet swan of Avon's" noble minstrelsy. If no other good be done, they who undertake such labours have their own spiritual perceptions enlarged ; further light enters the mind's dark chamber, and the beauteous images there impressed may take such fixure that they can be reproduced for other men's instruction. But seldom have literary labours so confined an influence: their ramifications are almost infinite, and, though begun in curiosity, may end in a more perfect development of the writings of the great masters of human thought. Our loved teachers and instructors God's providence calls away from earth, but the diligent learners in after ages reap the fruits of patient study, and thus the seeds of genius wisely scattered grow up a richer harvest for the world.

NOTES

LITERARY AND BIOGRAPHICAL, EXPLANATORY OF SOME OF WHITNEY'S EMBLEMS AND OF THE PERSONS TO WHOM THEY ARE DEDICATED.

SECTION I. — Containing Part I. from Title-page to Page 104.

MBLEMS, — some of them, — not all; for only a few possess any immediate historical interest, or are attached to names that can confer celebrity. In the preparation of this work the editor indeed has traced to their originals in Latin, Italian, French, or German, above *two hundred and twenty* of Whitney's woodcuts and mottoes, and has collected and transcribed an equal number of passages from their respective authors, whose stanzas Whitney translates or imitates; but these correspondences are useful chiefly to the thorough student of the emblem writers, and by far the greater part of them are altogether passed over in these notes without being presented to the reader. Sufficient however will be retained to set forth the nature of the subjects, and to give an adequate idea of the manner of growth which the "Choice of Emblemes" passed through.

See Essay I. Sections I. and II. pp. 237-252.

Though it would be a work of labour, it might not be very difficult to rival Claude Mignault in his very learned *Commentary on the Emblems of Andreas Alciatus*, the father of this kind of literature. In these literary and biographical notices on *Whitney*, we might explain each of his phrases and allusions, — fortify the text by numerous and full quotations from the poets, historians and orators of Greece and Rome, — bring in the Christian fathers as auxiliaries, — and occasionally press into the service the hieroglyphics of Egypt and the customs of Jews and Arabians; yet, in the present day, to do this would be to abuse the privilege of an editor, and to make the reading of our book a burden rather than a recreation.

We shall therefore endeavour to confine our elucidations to points of interest; not indeed entirely eschewing the curious, but at times contenting ourselves with simply indicating the sources of fuller information, and not attempting to compile memoirs and histories in the entire completeness to which each subject might lead. Besides, we presuppose that readers of education are sufficiently familiar with classic literature and general history not to need telling anything about heathen divinities and heroes, nor requiring special narratives carried out into particulars concerning persons who are famous in the annals of their respective countries.

Page [2].

THE FRONTISPIECE.—*Armorial bearings* of "Robert Earle of Leycester." These are said to have been the subject of eight Latin hexameters in Morel's *Commentary on Latin Verbs*, published in 1583. The crest, The bear and ragged staff, may be traced out in Dugdale's *Warwickshire* to Richard Beauchamp, earl of Warwick, who died in 1434, and to one of the Nevilles, also earl of Warwick, in 1438. Among the monuments in the Lady chapel at Warwick there is a full-length figure of "Ambrose Duddeley," who died in 1589 earl of Warwick, and a muzzled bear is crouching at his feet. His brother Robert Dudley, earl of Leicester, died in 1588, and on his magnificent tomb in the same chapel is also seen the cognizance of the bear and ragged staff. The arms however are a little different from those which Whitney figures. At an earlier date than 1586, the right-hand supporter, apparently a lioness, is represented with a single tail. If, as some say, the double tail be a mark of sovereignty, this frontispiece may lend support to the idea that Leicester really did make pretensions to supreme dignity in the Netherlands, and had even assumed one of its insignia. Motley, in his *History of the United Netherlands*, represents Deventer as urging that Leicester "might at once seize upon arbitrary power."

Ames' Typ. Ant. p. 988.

Dugdale, edit. 1730, pp. 400 and 410.

Vol. ii. pp. 115 and 231, also 16 and 349.

Page [3].

DEDICATION.—"ROBERT Earle of LEYCESTER, Baron of Denbighe," &c. A name of renown as the favourite of his queen, but rather of dishonour, because no ties, domestic or social, were allowed to stand in the way of his ambition. He was born in 1531, and died suddenly, it has been said of poison, September 4th 1588. His grandfather Edward Dudley, born in 1462, was one of the favourites of Henry VII., but through the fury of the people executed in 1510. John Dudley, the son of Edmund, was born in 1502, and his attainder in blood being removed he was created baron Malpas, viscount L'Isle, earl of Warwick, and finally duke of Northumberland, suffering death in 1553 for his disloyalty to Mary. Of his eight sons Guildford Dudley married the unfortunate lady Jane Grey, and the two were beheaded in 1554; Ambrose, Robert and Henry obtained distinction at the siege of St. Quentin in 1557, and for their services were received into Mary's favour.

When about nineteen years of age Robert Dudley married the ill-fated Amy Robsart, who died in 1560; in his twenty-first year he represented the county of Norfolk in parliament, and that same year, on the death of Edward VI., assisted to proclaim lady Jane Grey as queen, for which he was tried and received judgment of death, but was pardoned in October 1554. Soon after Elizabeth's accession in 1558 he obtained her favour, being constituted master of the horse, elected knight of the garter in 1559, and created baron of Denbigh and earl of Leicester in 1564. Many offices and honours were poured upon him. The university of Cambridge elected him high steward in 1563; the university of Oxford appointed him chancellor in 1564; the city of Chester made him their chamberlain in 1565; and the town of Great Yarmouth their high steward in 1572. The king of France conferred upon him the order of St. Michael in 1566. In July 1575 he entertained the queen for ten days at Kenilworth; and in 1578 he married the widow of Walter Devereux earl of Essex. In December 1585 he was sent as "Lorde Lieutenant and Captaine Generall of her Ma[ties] forces in the lowe countries." The nature of his administration is most graphically described in the pages of Motley's *History of the United Netherlands*. That See vol. ii. administration soon came to an end, for he surrendered his authority and was again in England at the end of November 1586; but in June 1587 he conducted a considerable force for the relief of Sluys in Zealand, but the town was lost and the queen recalled him November 9th 1587, and appointed lord Willoughby in his place. The year 1588 saw him named lieutenant-general of the forces assembled at Tilbury to resist the invasion threatened by the Spaniards; but the same year in September also witnessed his splendid funeral in our Lady's chapel at Warwick.

His character belongs to the historians of his time. His praise and his dispraise have employed many pens in his own day and
Succession of England's Monarchs, p. 889. 225.
ever since. As Speed records; "He had been a Peere of great estate, but lyable to the common destiny of most *Great ones*, whom all men magnifie in their life time, but few speake well of
A Paris, 1595. 8vo.
after their death." Against "*Discours de la vie abominable du*
Ultraj, 1582, 4to.
my lord de Leicestre," we may set "*Eulogium Rob. comitis Ley-*
London, 1658, 24mo.
cestrii," by Arnold Eickius; should we meet with "*Traditional Memoires in the reigns of Queen Elizabeth and king James*," and note how bitterly Robert Dudley is spoken of, — or take up
London, 1706.
Drake's "*Secret Memoirs*," we may correct their prejudicial con-
London, 1727, 8vo.
demnation by consulting "*The Life of Robert Earl of Leicester, the Favourite of Queen Elizabeth, drawn from Original Papers and Records.*" For a fair and just view of his life and actions
Cambridge, 1861, vol. ii. pp. 30-34. London, 1802, vol iii. p. 477.
the *Athenæ Cantabrigienses* may be read, or Aikin's *General Biography*.

Most of the events of his residence in Holland are set before us in the following works:

Retrospective Review, New Series, vol. i. p. 277.
"A briefe report of the militarie services done in the Low Countries by the erle of Leicester. Written by one who served in good place there, in a letter to a friend of his." 4to, 1587.

"Journal of Robert Earl of Leicester."

"Correspondence of Robert Dudley Earl of Leycester during his Government of the Low Countries in the years 1585 and 1586, edited
London, 1844.
by John Bruce F.S.A." Camden Society, 4to.

Leicester affected to be the patron of the fine arts, of literature, and of religion in the strict form of puritanism; and numerous and often curious, if not odd, are the books which asked favour from him. In the matter of Dedications there appears to have been a rivalry between himself and Essex, or rather between their respective partisans. If Whitney's praise of Robert Dudley seems to us excessive, that which Willet addressed to Devereux is scarcely under more restraint; for he speaks of him, as "noble, learned, the Mecænas and most excellent patron of all students, renowned not so much for the splendor of his race, as for the remarkable eminence of his own virtue." Willet's Sac. Emblematum, Centuria una.

An authentic portrait of Robert Dudley exists at Knole, the old seat of the Sackvilles, now the residence of the earl Amherst. It has been engraved, and occurs among Birch's "*Heads of Illustrious Persons of Great Britain.*" Vol. i. p. 43.

Thomas Newton, a Cheshire poet, celebrated the earl's return from Belgium, and likened him to Solon, Nestor, Numa and Cato. A dozen Latin lines conclude with invoking him as

> "Mighty count, of Britain's land the ornament immortal,
> Deservedly to be numbered among magnanimous powers."* Leland's Antiquaria, vol. v. p. 182.

As chancellor of Oxford or high steward of Cambridge, Leicester may have had Whitney's merits placed before him, for the poet was of both universities; but it is suggestive of the way in which the patron and the poet became acquainted that for twenty-three years, from 1565, the earl had been chamberlain of Chester. Ormerod's Cheshire, vol. i p. 56. During this time, about the year 1578 or 1579, Leicester's good offices had been sought in a dispute between several Cheshire gentlemen and the dean and chapter of Chester cathedral. After something very like bribery the quarrel was settled by both parties joining in a surrender of the estates to the queen, who regranted them to the fee farmers subject to certain rents to be paid to the dean and chapter. The Lysons, p. 573. Ormerod, vol. i. p. 241.

In 1583 the corporation of Chester received the earl of Leicester with almost regal honours. He was accompanied by the earls of Derby and Essex and lord North, and was met by most of the gentry of the county. There were fifteen hundred horse in his train, and the numerous cavalcade was welcomed at the High Cross in Chester by the mayor and the whole council of the city. The Lysons, p. 563. Ormerod, vol. i. p. 199. A present of forty angels of gold was made to the earl in a cup valued at 18*l*.

It is easy to see how Whitney, a Cheshire man, with near relatives among the gentry of the county, might gain introduction to Leicester; he might be admitted even as one of his retinue, and in his service make the acquaintance, and probably secure the friendship, of Sidney, Russell, Norris and Jermyn.

* "Magne Comes, terræ decus immortale Britannæ
Magnanimas inter merito numerande Dynastas."

Page [17].

VERSES CONGRATULATORY. — Of the five sets four are by persons to whom Whitney dedicated each an emblem, and of them a notice will be given in the proper place. BONAVENTURA VULCANIUS of Bruges is the only one whom we need here to mention. He was born in 1538 and died in 1614. "Whoever," says Peerlkamp, "has read the remarkable oration of Peter Curiaeus on the death of Bonaventura Vulcanius, of necessity will love him, as well for the choice virtues of his mind as for his attainments in literature of various kinds." After laying the foundation of learning at Ghent and Louvain, while yet a youth he went to Seville, and for eleven years was curator of cardinal Mendoza's library. Then he presided over the Gymnasium or Grammar school at Antwerp; and finally, about 1582, he was invited to the university of Leyden, and there taught Greek for the long space of thirty-two years. Here Whitney became acquainted with him, and was honoured by him with the complimentary stanzas in which the Geffrey of Elizabeth's reign is compared with the great poet of a former age, Geffrey Chaucer. In the library of the university there is a very fine portrait of Bonaventura Vulcanius, and also a manuscript by him of the *Hymns* of Callimachus. Among the *Poems* of James Dousa the younger are some Latin iambics on Bonaventura's publishing a work of Aristotle's and another of Apuleius. The *Hymns* of Callimachus and the *Idylls* of Moschus and Bion were printed at Antwerp by Plantin in 1584, — or rather at Leyden, where the great printer, fleeing before Farnese, had just established his office. An edition of Bonaventura's *Apuleius* was printed by Rapheleng at Leyden in 1594.

De Vita &c. Nederlandorum qui Carmina Latina composuerunt. Harlemi, 1838, pp. 239 and 240.

See Introductory Dissertation, pp. xxviii. and liii.

Poemata Roterodami, 1704, p. 135.

Annales de l'Imp. Plant. p. 264.

Page [20].

"D. O. M." Deo, Optimo, Maximo, *To God, best and greatest.*— In our modern times we shrink from such dedications; but it was with deepest reverence that the early emblem writers adopted them. There is a beautiful one by Willet, — his thirty-seventh emblem, — "Recte precanti praesto adest Christus," *Christ instantly is present to him who prays aright.* Of some Latin elegiacs on Exodus xxvi. 1, he adds this English translation, admirably expressing how we ought to pray:

Sacrorum Emblematum Centuria una.

> "The curtaines wrought with pictures were,
> hanging in holy place;

The Cherubs did with wings appeare,
 and gave a goodly grace.
The house of prayer Angels frequent,
 and Christ him selfe is there,
Then seeing these are alwayes present
 We ought to pray with feare."

EMBLEM, p. 1.—"*Te stante, virebo*," While thou standest I shall flourish. According to the purport of Whitney's stanzas, the name and titles of queen Elizabeth should head this emblem; but probably, as the entire work had been dedicated to a subject, it was not considered a courtly thing to devote simply a page to the sovereign.

The device is from Hadrian Junius, but the motto from Claude Paradin. The object of Junius is to illustrate the saying, that "the wealth of princes is the stay of the people," and he applies to that saying a four-lined stanza: Plate XXVI*b*.

"The pyramids of Pharaoh-kings are monuments lasting for ages,
 With wandering arms around them clasps the creeping ivy;
By the steadfast wealth of kings sustained are the needy people,
 And the mind's constant steadfastness secures age-lasting powers."

Paradin gives us the origin of the device of the pyramid and the ivy. The cardinal of Lorraine, on going to his abbey of Cluny, erected his device at the gate: it is a pyramid with a crescent on the top, and surrounded from the base to the summit by a beautiful verdant ivy. The whole was accompanied by the following inscription: Devises Héroiqves, Anvers, 1562.

"Quel Memphien miracle se haussant
Porte du ciel l'argentine lumière,
Laquelle va (tant qu'elle soit entiere
En sa rondeur) toujours croissãt?
 Quel sacre saint Lierre grauissant
Jusqu'au plus haut de cette sime fiere,
De son apui (ô nouuelle maniere)
Se fait l'apui, plus en plus verdissant!
 Soit notre Roi la grande Pyramide,
Dont la hauteur en sa force solide
Le terme au ciel plante de sa victoire:

M

Prince Prelat, tu sois le saint Lierre
Qui saintement abandonnant la terre
De ton soutien vas soutenant la gloire."

London, 1591, p. 87.

The English translation from *Paradin,* by P. S., gives the following version:

"O Readers tell what thing is ment
By tombes in Memphis towne,
Which on the top doth beare on high
The bright beames of the moone?
The moone which doth continually
Increase in light so bright,
Till that night come wherin her shine,
From world doth take her flight.
And what doth meane the sacred Iuy
Which creeps and binds about
This tomb, to whose high top he climbs,
Although it be full stout,
And what new fashion is this also
That leaning to it stickes,
Making his stay about the same,
That greenely ouer creepes.
This tombe it is that mightie king,
Whose maiestie honer craues,
For he in heauen triumphes for vs
To sathan that were slaues,
And the Iuie a bishop signifies
Euen thee most famous prince,
Who in a godly life doest yeeld
Not to the best an inch.
For though thy bodie lie in graue
Yet such thy vertue was,
That it beares vp our laud and praise
That neuer awaye shall passe." *

Frankfort, 1652, vol. ii. p. 6. Hierographia Cardinalium.

* Though restraining the application of this emblem, with the crescent moon, to the family of the Guises, namely to Claudius de Guise, cardinal deacon of S. Clement, and brother of Charles duke de Guise, the "*Symbols Divine and Human of Pontiffs, Emperors,*" *&c.* gives an account rather different from that of *Paradin,* but combining essentially the same sentiments and setting forth the sovereign as the source and support of the glory of the subject. Mention is also made of the crescent moon being a military standard of the Turks, but assumed both saucily and foolishly, "for the moon which increases also grows old," "*quæ crescit, senescit.*"

It will be seen that the ideas are adopted in some measure by Whitney; and this emblem of his supplies a good example of what is frequent with him, namely the accommodating of the thoughts of other writers to a subject not originally intended. Here he makes the device of the cardinal of Lorraine subservient to the praise of the English queen and of the Protestant church of England.

EMBLEM, p. 3.—*Prouidentia,* Providence. A motto and woodcut from Hadrian Junius, whose few lines simply inform us "Where the sacred Nile shall flow upon the fields, there the prescient Crocodile lays its eggs away from the flood, with good reason admonishing us to see beforehand what the fates may threaten." The monogram G is in the centre of the cut from *Junius,* and is said to mark the workmanship of Hubert Goltzius; but this is doubtful, though it certainly denotes an artist who frequently engraved for the printers of Antwerp. The reader will observe how the borders in this edition of *Junius* are the originals of those in *Whitney,* and also how Whitney amplifies and improves upon the Latin stanza.

Plate XXVI*d*.

Annales de l'Imp. Plantin. pp. 42 and 48.

EMBLEM, p. 4.—"*Veritas tempora filia,*" Truth the daughter of Time. A variation from the motto of Junius to the same device, "*Truth by time is revealed, by discord is buried.*" Whitney's lines bring out the meaning much more effectually than those of Junius—"Why, O winged Saturn, dost thou drag the naked maiden into the air? Why does the assembly of women overwhelm the furrow with piled up earth? Truth, daughter of Time, issuing forth from the cave, a three-fold plague appears to overwhelm,—Strife, Envy and Slander." This device was the badge of Mary Tudor when she succeeded to the throne.

Plate XXVI*c*.

EMBLEM, p. 15.—"*Voluptas ærumnosa,*" Sorrowful pleasure. The sad fate of Actæon furnishes a subject to at least three of the emblem writers previous to Whitney; namely to Alciat, Aneau and Sambucus. Alciat adopts for motto, "In receptatores sicariorum," *On the harbourers of assassins,* and thus carries out his thought:

Plates VI. XX. and XXV.

"Unlucky for thee a band of robbers and thieves through the city,
Goes as companion: and a troop girded with direful swords.
And so thou a prodigal judgest thyself generous in mind,
Because thy pot of meat entices many of the bad.
Behold a new Actæon, who after he took up the horns
Himself gave himself a prey to his own dogs."

Aneau applies the fable of Actæon to him who, "Ex domino servus," *From a master becomes a slave*, and proves his text in Latin elegiacs:

Picta Poesis, p. 41.

"CORNIBVS in ceruum mutatum Actæona sumptis,
Membratim proprij diripuere canes.
NAE, miser est Dominus, Parisitos quisquis edaces
Pascit, adulantum præda parata canum!
Se quibus irridendum suggerit, & comedendum,
Seruus & ex domino corniger efficitur."

Thus, if we please, to be rendered:

"Horns being assumed by Actæon changed into a stag,
Member from member his own hounds have torn him.
Verily, wretched is the master who feeds parasites voracious,
A prey is he made ready for those fawning dogs.
Himself he offers to whoever would mock and devour him,
And out of a master is he made a horn-bearing slave."

Plate XXV.

Sambucus however supplies the motto which Whitney follows, and seems himself to have borrowed some of his thoughts from the Greek of Palæphatus, *Concerning incredible Histories.** We give the sense of his stanzas:

"He, who follows the chase too eagerly, drains his paternal riches and lavishes them on dogs: so great the love of the vain sport, so great the infatuation continually becomes, that he puts on the double horns of the swift deer. Actæon's fate happens to thee, who having horns from thy birth hast by thine own dogs been torn in pieces. How many, whom the quick scented faculty of the dogs delights, does the passion for hunting finish and devour. Postpone not serious things for sports, advantages for losses, — regard whatever things remain as if thou wert destitute."

De Incr. Hist. Edition 1670, Cantab. p. 10.

* "To Actæon indeed, caring nothing about domestic affairs, and busied only with hunting, the means of livelihood failed; and when he had nothing left, people said: 'Poor Actæon! he has been eaten up by his own dogs.'"

It must be confessed that Whitney's treatment of the tale is superior to that of the other three; and the comparison thus carried out to some length may serve to vindicate for him greater clearness and unity of purpose. Emb. p. 15.

EMBLEM, p. 32.—"*In pœnam sectatur & vmbra*," Even a shadow is pursued for punishment. Beza's fourteenth emblem also treats of men pursuing shadows, but in a way considerably different from the method adopted by Whitney. The simple giving of Beza's meaning will make this apparent: Plate XLI.

"As a shadow flees those pursuing it and presses on those fleeing,—a shadow you know being added to bodies as their companion; So glory flees those coveting rewards of undeserved praise, and on the other hand is joined as companion to the humble in mind. And yet do these thoroughly prove by no false trial, what all this praise will be? Truly, but a worthless shadow."

On comparing the two the advantage will, I think, again be awarded to Whitney.

EMBLEM, p. 38.—"*To the Honorable Sir* PHILLIP SIDNEY *Knight*:" whom Spenser named—

—— "the President
Of Nobleness and Chevalree;"

Shepheard's Calender.

and whom, in his verses "To the Right Honourable and most vertuous Lady, the Countess of Pembroke," he lamented as—

—— "that most heroicke Spirit,
The hevens pride, the glory of our daies
Which now triumpheth (through immortall merit
Of his brave vertus) crown'd with lasting baies
Of hevenlie blis and everlasting praies;
Who first my Muse did lift out of the flore,
To sing his sweet delights in lowlie laies."

Spenser's Works, Moxon's Edition, p. 7.

The world-renowned and ever-worshipful Philip Sidney was the son of sir Henry Sidney and of his wife Mary, the eldest daughter of John Dudley, duke of Northumberland. At the time of his birth, November 29th 1554, his mother was wearing mourning for her father, her brother, and her sister-in-law the lady Jane Grey, who had all died on the scaffold. He was born

Pear's Memoirs, London, 1845.

at Penshurst in Kent, where still exist the ruins of the oak* planted at his birth. On Elizabeth's accession in 1558 sir Henry became lord president of the marches of Wales, and kept his court at Ludlow with much magnificence down to 1568. Hence his son Philip in 1566 was sent as a scholar to Shrewsbury school, and the very day, on which he and Fulke Greville (lord Broke) together entered, commenced the friendship between them which death alone terminated, and of which a loving memorial remains in Greville's *Life of Sidney*. At an early age, in 1569, when only fifteen, his student life began at Christ church college, Oxford, which he left in 1571 to travel for four years in France, Germany and Italy. It was only by taking refuge in the house of the English ambassador in Paris that he escaped the massacre on St. Bartholomew's day in 1572, when his friend and frequent correspondent Hubert Languet found shelter with Andrew Wechel the celebrated printer. A letter to Languet, written during this tour, shows that Sidney had made acquaintance with some of the emblem writers, for he mentions Girolamo Ruscelli's "*Imprese illustri, con esposizione e discorsi*," which was published in 1566;† and it may be that on his return to England he imparted his knowledge to Spenser, and to Whitney who was of the same university with himself.‡ In 1576 the queen appointed him her ambassador to the court of Rodolph, the new emperor of Germany. Spenser's acquaintance began about 1578, and probably

London, 1652; and again by Egerton Brydges, 1816.

The Correspondence of Sidney and Languet, p. 9

* Endeared to me especially as the centre of the scenes in which my boyhood was passed.

Virgils Ecl. vi. 27.

"Tum verò in numerum Faunósque ferásque videres
Ludere, tum rigidas motare cacumina quercus."

Plate LXI.

† Ziletti's edition of Giovio's *Ragionamento*, in Venetia, MDLVI., has appended to it Ruscelli's "DISCORSO, *intorno all' inuentioni dell' Imprese, dell' Insegne, de' Motti, & delle Liuree.*" 16mo, pp. 113-236.

‡ His acquaintance with and practice of emblem art appear also from his conduct when, in 1579, a son was born to the earl of Leicester by his wife Lettice, the widow of Walter, earl of Essex. Sidney had hitherto been reputed the heir of his uncle's large possessions; but "on the first tilt after the birth of this child he bore on his shield the word *speravi* scored through." In the *Arcadia* also the mottoes and devices on the shields of the knights show both rich fertility of invention and a full knowledge of emblem writers. Besides, to denote that he persisted in any course of action once decided on he adopted as his device "the Caspian sea, surrounded with its shores;" and, alluding to this body of water neither ebbing nor flowing, his motto was, "SINE REFLEXV," *Without an ebb*, *i.e.* No going back.

Pear's Correspondence, p. 183, *note*.

Gent. Magazine, 1819, vol. ii. p. 31.

in that year the poet of the *Faerie Queene* visited Sidney at Penshurst, and there wrote a portion of the *Shepheard's Calender*, dedicated "To the noble and vertuous Gentleman, most worthie of all titles both of learning and chivalry, Maister Philip Sidney." From 1579 he lived in retirement for two or three years either at Penshurst or at Wilton with his sister the countess of Pembroke. During this time he wrote what he entitled "*The Countess of Pembroke's Arcadia:*" it was not published until 1590, four years after his death; and it owes its fame rather to the great renown of its author than to any peculiar excellence of its own. In this poem under the name of "*Philoclea,*" and in his other poems under that of "*Stella,*" he celebrated the virtues and charms of the lady Penelope Devereux, to whom he was fondly attached. The year 1581 numbered him as one of the knights of the shire for his native county, and a manuscript in the British museum records: "Sir Philippe Sidney dubbed at Windesor on Sonday the 13 of January 1582, and was that day lykewise installed for Duke John Casimir counte Palatine and Duke of Bavaria." In 1583 Frances, only daughter of sir Francis Walsingham, became his bride, and in her arms his noble spirit was breathed forth on the 7th of October 1586, after the fatal wound at Zutphen which has immortalized his memory. One daughter was the issue of this marriage, born in 1585, and afterwards wife to Roger, earl of Rutland. Sidney's widow was married to Robert, earl of Essex, beheaded in 1600, and again to Richard, earl of Clanricarde and St. Albans. It seems that in 1584 he had been listening to a project by sir Francis Drake for engaging in an expedition against the Spaniards in the West Indies, but the queen herself forbad him, and conferred on him the office of "Gouernour of the Garrison and toune of Vlissing." Old Fuller's quaint, fond, admiring testimony might very excusably detain us, but we give only a single sentence:

Moxon's Spenser, pp. xi. and 360.

Bibl. Cotton. Claud. CIII. Plut. XXI.

Collier's Memoirs of the Sidneys.

> "This knight in relation to my book may be termed an ubiquitary, and appear among Statesmen, Soldiers, Lawyers, Writers, yea, Princes themselves, being (though not elected) in election to be king of Poland, which place he declined, preferring rather to be a subject to queen Elizabeth, than a sovereign beyond the seas."

Fuller's Worthies, vol. ii. pp. 142 and 143.

Whitney celebrates "the valour of the minde," "and prowes

Emb. pp. 109 and 110.

great," of a long array of Roman worthies, and to his stanzas affixes the title "*To the honourable Sir* PHILIPPE SIDNEY *Knight.*" He had intended to place the same name to the
Emb. p. 196. lines on "*Pennæ gloria perennis,*" The glory of the pen is everlasting, — but Sidney himself did not consider this renown as his due, and declined it in favour of "EDWARDE DIER;" for,

"At the firste, his sentence was, it did belonge to you."

The fancy is embodied in these verses, that on the death of the earl of Surrey —

"APOLLO chang'd his cheare, and lay'd awaie his lute,
And PALLAS, and the Muses sad, did weare a mourninge sute.
And then the goulden pen, in case of sables cladde
Was lock'd in chiste of Ebonie, and to Parnassus had."

Sidney however is born, gladness and brightness again pervade the seats of Apollo and the Muses, and to him —

—— "behoulde, the pen, was by MERCVRIVS sente,
Wherewith, hee also gaue to him, the gifte for to inuente,
That, when hee first began, his vayne in verse to showe,
More sweete than honie, was the stile that from his penne did flowe."

The profound grief for Sidney's untimely death may be judged of from the writings of his contemporaries and from the magnificent public funeral with which his remains were honoured. "His rare and never ending laudes" were the theme of many pens.* It will be enough in our brief notice to quote from Bamfield's epitaph printed in 1598:

"Here lyes the man; lyke to the swan, who knowing shee shall die
Doeth tune her voice unto the spheares, and scornes mortalitie."

London, 1747, vol. ii. p. 15. A portrait of him is given in Birch's *Heads of Illustrious Persons in Great Britain*, and also one from Diego Velasquez de

Bibl. Biog. Universelle, Édition 1676. * Oettinger may be consulted for the various memoirs and biographical notices of Sidney; to which we add a work published at Leyden in 1587: "Epithaphia in Mortem Nobilissimi et Fortissimi Viri D. Philippi Sidneji Equitis ex Illustrissima Waruicensium Familia, Qui incomparabili Damno Reip. Belgicæ Vulnere in proelio contra Hispanos
England's Monarchs, p. 883. 181. fortiter accepto paucis post diebus interiit." Speed's record of him testifies he was "that worthy Gentleman, in whom were compleat all vertues and valours that could
Amstelodami, 1621, vol. ii. p. 85. be required or residing in man;" and Baudart's *Polemographiæ Auriaco Nassovicæ* names him "the hero of thirty years, exceedingly well learned in languages and sciences" — "eloquent and courteous, one born for choicest honours."

Silva in Zouch's *Memoirs of his Life and Writings.* To form an estimate of his worth, two papers by J. Payne Collier should be consulted—"Sir Philip Sidney his Life and Death," and "Sir Philip Sidney and his Works." One of the most interesting and well-written memoirs of Sidney is by Steuart A. Pears, M.A., prefixed to *The Correspondence of Sir Philip Sidney and Hubert Languet.* I believe all Biographical Dictionaries, without exception, contain his history and praise.

York, 1808, 4to, pp. 389.

London, 1845.

EMBLEM, p. 43.*—"*To Sir* ROBERT JERMYN *Knight.*" He was the second son of sir Ambrose Jermyn, who was knighted "in the tyme of the reigne of Queene Mary." His university education commenced at Corpus Christi college, Cambridge, and was completed at the Middle Temple. He was sheriff of Suffolk in 1574, and again (according to Suckling, vol. i. p. xlii.) in 1579; and by the death of his father April 7th 1578, and of his elder brother John, "he succeeded to Rushbrooke and other estates in Suffolk." It was during one of Elizabeth's progresses that he "was dubbed at Bury St. Edmund on Saturday the first day of August Anno 1578." On a former progress in 1571 he entertained the French ambassadors who attended the queen "so exceedingly sumptuous," that it is said they "marvelled most exceedingly." He was knight of the shire on two occasions, in 1585 and 1586.

Athenæ Cantab. ii. p. 324.

Names and Arms of Knights from 1485 to 1624. Mus. Brit. MS.

Wodderspoon's Suffolk, p. 294.

Sir Robert was one of those who served under the earl of Leicester in 1585 and 1586, and is mentioned by him with high commendation. "I have founde him," writes the earl, "to be very wise and stowt, and most willing and ready to this service, and he hath come hither as well appointed as any that hathe commen ouer." And again: "Good Mr. secretary, this good

Leicester Correspondence, pp. 114 and 410.

* Whitney's version departs from the original, and is inferior to it:

"*DICITUR interna vi Magnes ferra mouere:*
Perpetuò nautas derigere inque viam,
Semper enim stellam fermè aspicit ille polarem.
Indicat hac horas, nos varieque monet.
Mens vtinam in cœlum nobis immota maneret,
Nec subito dubiis fluctuet illa malis.
Pax coëat tandem, Christe, vnum claudat ouile,
Lisque tui verbi iam dirimatur ope.
Da, sitiens anima excelsas sic appetat arces:
Fontis vt ortiui ceruus anhelus aquas."

Sambucus, Antv. 1564, p. 84.

N

gentleman, Sir Robert Jermin, one that hath declared euery way his hearty zeale and loue both to religion and to her majestie."

His zeal for religion indeed had before this caused Freake the bishop of Norwich to exhibit articles against him, and sir John Higham knt., and Robert Ashfield and Robert Badly esqs. .The complaint was that they favoured puritanism, to which in "A true answer," sent to lord Burghley, they replied that the charge was "old, weak, untrue, and malicious."

The family of the Jermyns was seated at Rushbrook at the beginning of the thirteenth century. Fuller speaks of Robert Jermyn as "a person of singular piety, a bountiful benefactor to Emanuel college, and a man of great command in this county (Suffolk). He was father to sir Thomas Jermin (privy councillor and vice-chamberlain to king Charles the First), grandfather to Thomas and Henry Jermin, esquires: the younger of these being lord chamberlain to our present queen Mary, and sharing in her majesty's sufferings during her long exile in France, was by king Charles the Second deservedly advanced Baron, and Earl of St. Albans." In the *Magna Britannia* it is asserted "there is hardly a man in England of the name of Jermyn."

Worthies, vol. iii. p. 195.

The only connected biography of sir Robert Jermyn that I have met with is in the *Athenæ Cantabrigienses*.

Vol. ii. pp. 323-325.

EMBLEM, p. 46.—*To Sir* HENRY WOODHOWSE *Knight.* The Woodhouses or Wodehouses of Kimberly in Norfolk "were Gentlemen of good Ranke, in and before the Time of King *John.*" Members of the family, either attended the Black Prince into Spain, or fought with Henry V. in 1415 at the battle of Agincourt, or served under Edward IV. at the fight of Tewkesbury;—and one was slain at Muselborough 10th September 1547. They were of a stock that bore very abundantly the honours of knighthood, when that dignity was almost a sure test of personal merit. By nearly twenty descents we arrive at "Sir William Woodhouse belonging to the shippes," who was knighted in the "triumphant reigne of Kinge Henry the eight" "on the 11 day of May Sunday after the destruction of Edenborouge and other townes;" he bore for his crest a woodman with a club. "In the happy reigne of Kinge Edward the sixt," sir Thomas Woodhouse received the same honour "by the handes of Edward

Blomfield's Norfolk, vol. i. pp. 752 and 761.

Names and Arms of Knights from 1485 to 1624.

Duke of Somersett Lord Protector." Sir Roger Woodhouse graces "the tyme of the reigne of Queene Mary;" and his second brother, the sir Henry Woodhouse of Whitney's *Emblems*, was "dubbed" "on tuesday the 26 of August 1578;" and "on the 27 of August 1578" another sir Roger Woodhouse, who died in 1588.

Sir Henry Woodhouse "was born 3 *Jan.* 1546." The time of his death is not ascertained. At his baptism "SIR JOHN ROBSART and his Lady answered for him; he was (as all his Ancestors for many Generations always were) Justice of the Peace, and twice Member for the County of NORFOLK, viz. in the 14 and 31 *Eliz.*" Blomfield, vol. i. p. 761.

A Mr. Ralph Woodhouse was one of the bailiffs of Great Yarmouth in 1580, and sir Roger Woodhouse, knt., in that year was one of "the respectable company" whom Whitney names as joining in the pic-nic to Scratby island. From Camden's *Elizabeth*, anno 1590, we learn that "Philip Woodhouse was very active at the taking of Cadiz, and for his good service was there knighted by the earl of Essex." Plates XII. and XIII.

This Philip, in 1611, was the first baronet of the family. The *fifth* baronet represented Norfolk in *five* parliaments, and the *sixth* was also the first peer, being created baron Wodehouse in 1797. His grandson is the present lord Wodehouse, educated like sir Philip Sidney at Christ Church, Oxford, and now representing her majesty queen Victoria as lord lieutenant of Ireland.

EMBLEM, p. 47.—"*To Sir* WILLIAM STANDLEY *Knight.*" The long renowned family of the Stanleys are descended from the ancient baronial family of Audley, and took their name from Stanleigh in Staffordshire, where they were sometime settled. The elder branch of the house has its direct representatives in the Stanleys of Great Storton and Hooton, Cheshire; and to a younger branch may be traced the Stanleys, earls of Derby, the Stanleys of Alderley park, Cheshire, and the Stanleys of Cumberland. Lysons' Cheshire, pp. 653, 367 and 481.

Sir Rowland Stanley of Storeton and Hooton, knt., who was sheriff of Cheshire in 1576, and who died April 5th 1613, in his ninety-sixth year, was the father of the sir William Stanley whom Whitney commemorates, and "lived to see his son's son's son settled at Hooton." Ormerod's Cheshire, vol ii. p. 229. Webb, p. 120.

In "*Names and Arms of Knights made from* 1485 *to* 1624" there are two sir William Stanleys, one knighted at Leith in the time of Henry VIII., and the other in the first year of Edward the Sixth's reign, but neither of these could be the sir William Stanley to whom Whitney offered two of his emblems; it is therefore uncertain where he obtained his knighthood, but "he was originally engaged in the service of the king of Spain," and afterwards in 1578 distinguished himself for his gallantry in reducing the rebellious province of Munster, and under either service may have received the honour. Heywood, however, says in 1579 "he was for his conduct knighted by Drury, at Waterford."

Ormerod's Cheshire, vol. ii. p. 231.

Heywood's Allen's Defence, p. v.

Under the earl of Leicester, who often mentions him in his letters, he was appointed to the command over the strong fortress of Deventer, very much to the discontent of the States General of Holland. This trust he betrayed in January 1587 into the hands of the Spaniards, and continued in their service for many years. He died March 6th 1630, being then governor of Mechlin or Malines for the Spanish king.

See Leicester Correspondence, 183, 250, 302, &c. &c.

Notes and Queries, vol. xii. p. 448.

From Watson's *History of Philip II.* we may learn some of the particulars of this dark treachery, but it is a subject we need not pursue here; the whole is set forth in one of the Chetham Society's publications, so well edited by Thomas Heywood esq. of Ledbury; it is "*Cardinal Allen's Defence of Sir William Stanley's Surrender of Deventer, January* 29, 1586-7." Here, too, we have in the INTRODUCTION the best account extant of Stanley's life and character, with most of the circumstances attending his career, from his birth in 1534 to his death.

See Ormerod's Cheshire, vol. ii. pp. 231 and 232.

Pages i-lxi.

Allen's *Defence* appeared in the form of a letter which was hastily printed by Joachim Trognæsius at Antwerp in 1587. The antidote or reply bears the title, "*A short admonition or warning vpon the detestable treason, wherewith sir William Standley, and Rowland Yorke haue betrayed and deliuered for monie, vnto the Spaniards, the towne of Deventer and the sconce of Zutphen.*" 4to. Licensed 1587.

His wife was Elizabeth, the eldest daughter of sir John Egerton of Egerton and Oulton knight, who died in 1590. Her monument, which was probably that of her husband also, was near the high altar of the church of Notre Dâme in Malines, and Thomas Heywood says, "the inscription is still to be seen." This last summer, 1865, I failed to find it there, and when I mentioned the circumstance to the librarian of the university of Louvain, M. Edm. Reusens D.D., he referred me to a book printed at Brussels in 1770, "*Provincie, Stad, ende District van Mechelen*," in which I found this inscription, very like the one given by Heywood:

Introduction to Allen's Defence, p. xxxvii.

"Ici gist la noble Dame
ELIZABETH EGERTON, jadis
Espeuse du tre prudent Chevallier
Messire GUILLAUME STANLEY
Coronel & du Conseil de guerre
de Sa Ma[te] d'Espaigne laquelle tres-
passa de ceste vie le 10 d'Avril 1614
priez Dieu pour son ame."

Page 170.

A note was added, stating that her body with many others* was removed from the church of Notre Dâme in Malines when it was repaired in 1762, and the inscription copied in the above book.

Page 56.—"*Alius peccat, alius plectitur*;" One sins, another is beaten. From Wechel's edition of *Alciat*, p. 74. The Latin text is here added:

Parisiis, 1534, Plate VI.

"*Arripit ut lapidem catulus morsu'q; fatigat*
Nec percussori mutua damna facit.
Sic plæriq; sinunt ueros elabier hosteis,
Et quos nulla grauat noxia, dente petunt."

With this may be compared the Italian version published by Roville at Lyons in 1551, and also Whitney's English version of 1586. It will be seen that Whitney's version combines expressions both of the Latin and of the Italian, and yet differs from them both.

Plate XVIII.
Emb. p. 56.

EMBLEM, p. 61.—*Her Maiesties poësie, at the great Lotterie in* LONDON. The badges and mottoes used by our sovereigns are of great variety. We will name only those of the Tudor race. Henry VII. sometimes adopted the white and red roses in union; at other times a crown in a bush, in allusion to Bosworth field.

See N. R. S. Gent. Magazine, 1826, pt. ii. pp. 203-205; also 1819, pt. ii. pp. 130-131.

* The margin says: "Met 8 Schilden sonder Namen ofte Wapens," *With 8 shields without names or arms.*

Henry VIII., among other devices, used an archer drawing his arrow to the head, and also a flame of fire. Edward VI. chose a sun shining, and a phœnix on the funeral pile, with the scroll, "*Nascatur ut alter*," That another may be born, &c. Mary, when princess, preferred the white and red rose and a pomegranate knotted together; when queen, Time drawing Truth out of a pit, and the words as in *Whitney*, p. 4, "*Veritas temporis filia*," Truth the daughter of Time. Elizabeth's badges were "her mother's falcon, or rather dove, crown and sceptre; and her devices were very numerous, most commonly a sieve without a motto."

From the same authority we learn that Elizabeth made use of several heroic devices and mottoes; among the latter are "*Semper eadem*," Always the same; and "*Video et taceo*," I see and am silent.

Gent. Magazine, 1821, pt. i. p. 531. "Lotteries were the inventions of the Romans during the Saturnalia. Augustus much relished them. Nero was the first who made a public lottery, of a thousand tickets a day, all prizes, some of which made the fortune of the holder. Elagabulus added blanks, *i.e.* ridiculous tickets of six flies, &c."

Emb p. 61. "The great Lotterie in London," to which Whitney alludes, is regarded as the first held in England. The proposals for it were published in 1567-8, and it was intended to be drawn at the house of Mr. Derricke, the queen's jeweller, in Cheapside, but was actually drawn at the west door of St. Paul's cathedral. "The drawing began on the 11th of January 1569, and continued incessantly drawing, *day and night*, 'till the 6th of May following." There were forty thousand chances or tickets at *ten* shillings each,—the prizes being articles of plate and probably jewellery. The profits were devoted "towards the reparation of the Havens and strength of the realme, and towards such other public good workes."

Bohn's Political Dictionary, vol. iii. p. 278.

Gent. Magazine, 1778, p. 470.

A Virginian state lottery is named in 1567, and when the Great Yarmouth corporation were in want of funds for the works of their harbour, they endeavoured to replenish them by subscriptions to the visionary scheme. The whole town was "elevated to the enthusiasm of poetry," and various doggerel lines were attached to the tickets which were purchased; thus "THE GENTLEMEN'S POSY" was,

Blomfield's Norfolk, vol. v. p. 1600.

"The fyrste, ne second lott I craue,
The thyrde yt ys that I wolde haue."

The LADIES' POSY was not quite so covetous; it read:

"A small stocke with good successe,
May shortly growe to good incresse."

Not daunted by failure the town again, in 1614, entrusted twenty-five pounds to the same lottery, and *bemotto'd* their adventure with some most pitiful rhymes, as— Blomfield, vol. v. p. 1601.

"Great Yarmouth haven, now in great distresse
Expects by lotterye some good successe."

For a fuller history consult "ARCHÆOLOGIA," vol. xix. pt. i. article x., "Account of the Lottery of 1567, being the first upon record. By Will. Bray Esq."

EMBLEM, p. 65.—"*To* RICHARDE COTTON *Esquier*" of Combermere. "The Cottons of Cumbermere Abbey," we are informed, "are descended from the ancient family of Cotton of Cotton in Shropshire,* and settled in Cheshire in the reign of Henry VIII.; they are the representatives in the female line of the Calveleys, Tattenhalls, Harthills and other ancient Cheshire families." Lysons' Cheshire, p. 399.

Collateral branches of the same stock, or *gens*, settled also in Huntingdonshire, Cambridgeshire, Sussex and Gloucestershire; those of Gloucestershire being represented by the earl of Derby. At the latter end of the sixteenth century, in 1596, a worthy of the race, Roger Cotton, published "*A Spirituall Song, containing an Historicall Discourse from the Infancie of the World untill this present Time*," and also "*An Armour of Proofe brought from the Tower of Dauid, to fight against the Spaniardes, and all the Enimies of the Trueth.*" Of another of the family, ROWLAND COTTON *Miles*, it is testified, "Incredible are the most true relations which many eye witnesses still alive do make of the valour and activity of this most accomplished knight; so strong, as if he had been nothing but bones; so nimble, as if he had been nothing but sinews." Lysons' Cheshire, p. 379. London, 4to. Fuller's Worthies, vol. iii. p. 82.

Sir Robert Bruce Cotton, of Cheshire descent, was born at Aikin's General Biography, vol. iii. p. 176.

* There were however Cottons in Cheshire as early as the reign of Henry III. (1216-72) and Edward III. (See Ormerod's *Cheshire*, vol. ii. p. 428; vol. iii. p. 372.)

Great Connington in Huntingdonshire, in 1570, and possessed estates also at Harley St. George, in Cambridgeshire. He was the founder of the celebrated collection of coins, manuscripts and books, now in the British museum, and known as the Cotton library. He died in 1631, almost from vexation and grief at being debarred from the free use of his literary treasures.

The sir George Cotton who was knighted "on Thursday the 19 day of Octobre Anno Dm. 1536," was the father of Richard Cotton named by Whitney, and received the grant of Combermere in the thirty-second year of Henry VIII.; and the uncle was the sir Richard Cotton,* one of the "Knightes of the carpett dubbed by the kinge (Edward the sixt) on tuesday the 22 day of ffebruary in the first year of his reigne." Richard Cotton, esq., the heir to Combermere, married for his first wife Mary the daughter of sir Arthur Mainwaring of Ightfield in Shropshire, Emb. p. 131. whom Whitney commemorates; and the descendants of this marriage in a direct line have well sustained and increased the Ormerod's Cheshire, vol. i. pp. 68 and 69; vol. iii. p. 212. honours of their family. Robert, the great grandson of Richard and Mary Cotton, born in 1635, was created a baronet in 1677, and with the exception of one parliament represented the county from the thirty-first of Charles II. to the death of William III. Sir Thomas Cotton, his son, was sheriff in 1713, and sir Robert Salusbury Cotton of Combermere, his grandson, was elected to the first parliament of George II.; and from 1780 to 1790 another sir Robert Salusbury Cotton, bart., was also the knight in parliament for the county of Chester. In the peninsular war sir Stapleton Cotton gained great distinction, and was created lord Combermere in 1814, an honour which he held for fifty years, attaining the rank of field marshal in the British army and viscount Combermere. He died in this present year, 1865. His sister Sophia was the mother of the present sir H. Mainwaring, bart., of Peover.

Emb. p. 201. The natural beauties of Combermere, and of the country around, Whitney celebrates with much tenderness and truth of feeling; they were those amidst which his youth was spent,

* This sir Richard Cotton was of Bedhampton in Hampshire and of Warblington in Sussex. He held under Edward VI. the offices of privy councillor and comptroller of the household; and in the first parliament of Philip and Mary was returned knight of the shire for Cheshire along with Richard Wilbraham of Woodhey, esq.

and time has by no means impaired them. The mansion is "a stately seate"—

> "With fishe, and foule, and cattaile sondrie flockes
> Where christall springes doe gushe out of the rockes."

One who knew the place in the generation which followed Whitney confirms to the full his testimony. "Upon the very Brow or Bank of the *Mere* is the Abby scituate, with the Park and all other parts for profit and pleasure surpassing, and environed on all sides to a large Extent, with such goodly Farms," "as that I know none for number and largenesse comparable to them in all these parts." "It is possessed by a branch of that renowned name of the *Cottons*, who have been of great accompt in many Shires, and of whom this Race hath now succeeded here unto the present owner thereof *George Cotton* Esquire,* a man of singular accompt for his wisdome, Integrity, gentlenesse, godlinesse, facility, and all generous dispositions." King's Vale Royal, pt. ii p. 65. Plate XIV.

A more stately mansion occupies the site where the old abbey stood; and the historian of Cheshire thus describes its locality: "On the banks of a natural lake, in a rich and well-wooded country, undulating sufficiently for picturesque effect in the immediate vicinity of the abbey, and rising at a short distance into elevations which command noble and extended prospects over Cheshire, Shropshire and North Wales." What the abbey was in Whitney's time may be judged of from a vignette which was drawn at the beginning of last century, and which is reproduced in this fac-simile reprint. Ormerod's Cheshire, vol. iii. p. 211. Plate XIV.

EMBLEM, p. 66.—*To* JOHN PAYTON *Esquier*. Very little more than conjectures can be made with respect to this gentleman. Payton and Peyton appear interchangeable names. There were Peytons of Isleham, Cambridgeshire, baronets of the first creation in 1611; and a sir Edward Peyton, knighted in 1610, who married a daughter of sir James Calthorp, knight. Gent. Magazine, 1854, pt. i. p. 421. Betham's Baronetage, vol. i. p. 46.

An estate in Norfolk, of which sir Thomas Mildmay was owner in 1567, was conveyed by him in 1581 to Francis Gawdy, afterwards chief justice of the common pleas; from him it passed to sir Robert Rich, who conveyed it to sir John Peyton, in whose Blomfield's Norfolk, vol. iv. p. 212.

* Who was in possession of Combermere in 1615, and died in 1649.

State Papers, Domestic Series, 1547-1580, p. 628.

family it remained in 1620. This sir John Peyton, may be the same with John Payton, esq., and against whom and the bishop of Ely in 1579 a memorial to the council was presented that they might be required to attend to the river of Wisbeach.

1849, pt. i. pp. 372 and 373; 1851, pt. ii. pp. 227-234 and 377-383.

EMBLEM, p. 67.—*To* MILES HOBART, *Esquier.* The writers in the *Gentleman's Magazine* have settled who the sir Miles Hobart was, the patriot member for Great Marlow, who died 29th June 1632; but do not appear to recognise the MILES HOBART, *Esquier*, whom Whitney honours, and who must have been a man of repute in 1586.

From the authorities quoted it appears the Hobarts were settled at Leyham in Norfolk A.D. 1488. James, the second son, became attorney-general to Henry VII., and died in 1525. "From him are descended the Hobarts of Blickling, represented by the earls of Buckinghamshire, those of Plumstead and those of Intwood." William, the eldest brother of the attorney-general James, inherited Leyham, and among his descendants are Miles Hobart of London, the father of sir Miles Hobart, knight, the renowned member for Great Marlow. As far as the time is concerned the former of these may have been our Miles Hobart, esq.

But the name was "already common in the more distinguished or legal branch of the family," and among them probably is to be identified Whitney's Miles Hobart.

Blomfield's Norfolk, vols. i. iv. and v.

EMBLEM, p. 68.—*To* THO. STVTVILE ESQUIER. With the enviable liberty of former times the name is written Stutteville, Stutevyle and Stutevil. It belonged to a Suffolk family, and had among its members a Roger in 1240, a sir Nicholas in 1291, a Robert in 1310, a John and a Richard in 1414, a William in 1495, and a Charles in 1574. A sir Martin Stutevile appears to have reigned over the manor of Kimberley from 1600 to 1644. There is room to insert Thomas between Charles in 1574 and Martin in 1600.

Vol. ii. pp. 359 and 360.

EMBLEM, p. 69.—*To* GEORGE BROOKE *Esquier.* The writers of the *Athenæ Cantabrigienses* make this George Brooke to have been the fourth and youngest son of William Brooke lord Cobham, K.G., and to have been "born at Cobham in Kent 17th

April 1568." When only twelve years of age "he was matriculated as a fellow-commoner of King's college in May 1580, and created M.A. 1586." He was mixed up with the supposed plot of sir Walter Raleigh, Henry lord Cobham &c., against James I. and his children, and was beheaded at Winchester December 5th 1603. A sir William Brooke, knight of the honourable Order of the Bath, was son to this George Brooke. Betham's Baronetage, vol. ii. p. 125.

Camden mentions a sir Robert Brooke, of Suffolk, who was lord chief justice of common pleas in 1554 and died in 1558, and George Brooke *may* have been of his family.

The Whitneys and the Brookes of Cheshire intermarried. Geffrey Whitney's brother was named Brooke, and we may therefore consider if it is not from Cheshire rather than from Kent that the *patron* of this emblem is to be sought, especially as lord Cobham's youngest son was only eighteen years of age when the *Choice of Emblemes* was published.

Adam, lord of Leighton, near Nantwich, in the reign of king John, was the common ancestor of the Brookes of Cheshire. His son took the name William DE LA BROOKE of Leighton, 33 Henry III.; for "under the said Manour-House in *Leighton* a Brook runneth,* from whence their Posterity assumed the Sirname del Brook." Sir P. Leycester's Historical Antiquities, p. 326.

The elder branch, the Brookes of Leighton, became extinct in the male line in or about the reign of queen Elizabeth; a younger branch settled at Norton in Cheshire, having purchased lands there from the king, 37 Henry VIII. An. Dom. 1545; and from this younger branch are descended the present Brookes of Norton and those of Mere. The Lysons, p. 363.

Richard Brook of Norton, the king's feoffee in 1545, was sheriff of Cheshire in 1563, and died in 1569; his son Thomas was twice sheriff, 1578 and 1592, and had a son George who was drowned in Warrington water. From relationship and from being of the same age and county this George Brook has some claim to be regarded as the person intended by Whitney. It is however only conjecture. Sir P. Leycester and Ormerod, vol. i. p. 501.

* Were it not for this express testimony we should derive the name from the old word, *Brock*, a badger, especially as a badger was and is the crest of the family. Brocklebank, Brocklehurst, &c., are also names of the same origin.

EMBLEM, p. 71.—*To* BARTHRAM CALTHORPE *Esquier.* The
Tymm's Camden. Calthorpes are a family of old standing in Norfolk, for in 1241 one of them, sir William de Calthorpe, aided in founding a
Names and Arms of Knights, 1485-1624. monastery of Whitefriars. Among "the knightes of the carpett dubbed by the kinge on tuesday the 22 day of ffebruary" 1547-8 is "sir Philippe Calthorpe;" and in the reign of queen Elizabeth 1566, "sir Willm Calthorpe." Barthram Calthorpe would probably be of this family, and brother to Charles Cal-
Emb. p. 136. thorpe whom Whitney afterwards mentions, and in connection with whom some other observations on the Calthorpes will be made.

EMBLEM, p. 72.—*To the very accomplished youths* nine brothers the sons of GEORGE BVRGOINE *Esquier.* That nine brothers should leave no impress *as nine* upon the history of their age is rather surprising, but as yet they have not been identified. The name has belonged to the county of Bedford for several cen-
Tymm's Camden, vol. iii. p. 21. turies. There is a tradition, not indeed to be implicitly believed, that the township of Sutton in Bedfordshire was bestowed on Roger Burgoyne by John of Gaunt, "time honour'd Lancaster," in terms as follow:

"I, John of Gaunt,
Do give and do graunt
Unto Roger Burgoyne
And the heirs of his loyne
Both Sutton and Potton
Until the world's rotten."

A Robert Burgoyne of Sutton, and of Wroxall in Warwickshire, was high sheriff of the county of Warwick 39 Elizabeth, An. Dom. 1597. There have been ten baronets of Sutton park, of whom the first was erected in 1641.

EMBLEM, pp. 86, 87.—*To the Reverend man Mr.* ALEXANDER NOWELL, *Dean of Saint Paul's Church, London, famous for learning and for character.* The first of the devices here assigned to Dr. Nowell was originally, as Whitney intimates, the standard which in view of death the renowned Saladin ordered to be borne throughout his army:

"With trumpet Sounde, and Heralte to declare,
Theise wordes alowde: *The Kinge of all the Easte*
Great SALADINE, *behoulde is stripped bare:*
Of kingdomes large, and lyes in house of claie,
And this is all, he bare with him awaie."

In *Symbols divine and human of Pontiffs, Emperors and Kings* Vol. i. p. 58.
this device is figured, as in Whitney, and named, "The Simple Hierograph of Mahometans." It is headed by the lines

"Saladin Sultan Ottoman of the Turks
Emperor, — of Babylon, Damascus, Egypt King."

A scroll bears the words, "*Restat ex Victore Orientis,*" What remains of the conqueror of the east. The explanation is added:

"Of Saladin, who destroyed our kingdom of Jerusalem, thou seest the equipment, even his banner or standard. For as he was dying he ordered to be proclaimed around, 'Let no one who worthily may stand up in our place, or who may rise in our Commonwealth, grow proud from the prosperity of his affairs.'"

A work of great research and authority worthily sets forth the biography and labours of this very excellent dean of St. Paul's. It is "THE LIFE OF ALEXANDER NOWELL," "chiefly compiled from Registers, Letters, and other authentic Evidences. By Ralph Churton, M.A." 8vo, Oxford, 1809. We cannot pretend to abridge it, and they who would fully appreciate what a man of worth and learning Nowell was must have recourse to Churton's volume.

Some few gleanings from other sources may be allowed; and first from old kind-hearted Isaak Walton, who as a fisherman The Complete Angler.
himself had a deep sympathy with Dr. Nowell. He speaks of him as "the good old man (though he was very learned, yet knowing that God leads us not to heaven by many nor by hard questions), like an honest angler, made that good, plain, unperplexed catechism which is printed with our good old Service Book."

Next we have the matchless Fuller to be our interpreter, and Worthies of England, vol. ii. pp. 204 and 205.
he tells us, "ALEXANDER NOWELL was born 1510 of a knightly family at Read," in the county of Lancaster, "and at thirteen years of age being admitted into Brazen-nose College in Oxford, studied thirteen years therein. Then he became schoolmaster

of Westminster. It happened in the first of queen Mary* he was fishing upon the Thames, an exercise wherein he much delighted, insomuch that his picture kept in Brazen-nose College is drawn with his lines, hooks and other tackling, lying in a round on one hand, and his angles of several sorts on the other. But, whilst Nowell was catching of fishes, Bonner was catching of Nowell; and understanding who he was, designed him to the shambles, whither he had certainly been sent, had not Mr. Francis Bowyer, then Merchant, afterwards sheriff of London, safely conveyed him beyond seas."

"Without offence it may be remembered, that leaving a bottle of ale, when fishing, in the grass, he found it some days after, no bottle, but a gun, such the sound at the opening thereof: and this is believed (casualty is mother of more inventions than industry) the original of bottled ale in England."

"Returning the first year of queen Elizabeth, he was made dean of St. Paul's; and for his meek spirit, deep learning, prudence and piety, the then parliament and convocation both chose enjoined and trusted him to be the man to make a catechism for public use, such a one as should stand as a rule for faith and manners to their posterity."

"He was confessor to queen Elizabeth, constantly preaching the first and last Lent sermons before her. He gave two hundred pounds per annum to maintain thirteen scholars in Brazen-nose College. He died, being ninety years of age, not decayed in sight, February 13, 1601."

There appear to have been three catechisms which owe their origin to his labour and countenance; *first*, the catechism in the Book of Common Prayer; *second*, "A Catechisme or Institution of Christian Religion to bee learn'd of all youth next after the little Catechisme appointed in the booke of common Prayer,"

Vol. ii. p. 391. * Bishop Burnet testifies that Nowell was elected to serve in the first parliament under queen Mary in 1553. On the second day of the session there was a debate, "whether he, being a prebendary of Westminster, could sit in the House? and the committee being appointed to search for precedents, it was reported, that he, being represented in the convocation house, could not be a member of that House, so he was cast out." The portrait, as described by Fuller, still exists at Brazen-nose. The engraving in Churton's *Life of Nowell* bears the inscription "Alexander Nowell D.D. Dean of St. Paul's Ob. Feb. 1601/2 An Æt 95 Piscator Hominum."

London, "with the grace and privilege of the queen's majesty, Anno 1572;" and *third*, "**ΚΑΤΗΧΙΣΜΟΣ**, *ἡ πρώτη παιδέυσις τῆς χριστιανῶν εισεβείας, τῇ Ελλήνων, καὶ τη Ρωμαίων διαλεκτῳ εκδοθεῖσα.* Catechismus Græce et Latine explicata." London, An. Dom. 1573. This catechism was translated into Greek by William Whittaker,* and dedicated to sir William Cecil. The catechism in Latin was written some years before it was printed, as appears from the *Calendar of State Papers*, 1547-1580; "June 16, 1570. Alexander Nowell, dean of St. Paul's, to sir Wm Cecil. The Latin catechism which he wrote about seven years since, and dedicated to him, is now at lengthe printed, by Appointment of the Archbishops of Canterbury and York." Domestic Series, p. 382.

Dr. William Cleaver, bishop of Chester from 1788 to 1799, republished, with notes, dean Nowell's "*Prima Institutio Disciplinæque Pietatis Christianæ*," and appointed to be used in his diocese by candidates in theology.

There is an engraving of Dr. Nowell in Holland's *Horoölogia;* and an excellent account of him in Bliss's edition of Wood's *Athenæ Oxonienses*. See also Chalmer's *Gen. Biog. Dict.* vol. xxiii. pp. 224-265. Vol. i. pp. 715-719.

EMBLEM, p. 93.—*To my sister M. D. Colley.* Generally in the biographical notices I have passed over the several members of the Whitney family, because they are treated of in the Introductory Dissertation. This name Colley however is suggestive of the fact that in Elizabeth's reign it was borne by the ancestors of the now world-wide celebrated Wellesley family. Sir Henry Colley was knighted in 1560, and his second son, also sir Henry, in 1576. "Cowley (or Colley as it has been more generally spelt) is well known to have been the original name of the family of Wellesley or Wesley. The latter name was assumed by the first lord Mornington." These Colleys were of English origin, at one time possessing "large property in Rutland." In Betham's *Baronetage* are named a Roger Colley and a Thomas Colley. Chap. II., Sect. II. p. xxxv. Gent. Magazine, 1822, pt. ii. p. 325; 1828, pt. i. p. 5. Gent. Magazine, 1822, pt. ii. p. 607. pt. iii. p. 19; pt. iv. p. 14.

* His father married a sister of dean Nowell's, and from that stock, through William's elder brother Robert, descended doctor Whitaker the historian, and from 1809 until his death in 1821 vicar of Whalley in Lancashire. Of William Whitaker, who died in 1595, bishop Hull said: "Never a man saw him without reverence, or heard him without wonder." Churton's Life of Nowell; and Gent. Magazine, 1810, pt. i. pp. 25 and 215.

Gent. Magazine, 1822, pt. ii. p. 416. The earliest notice in *Ormerod* of Cheshire Colleys is in the time of Charles II., when the township of Church-en-Heath, or Churton, "was purchased by Mr. Colley, a nonconformist minister, ancestor of Mr. Colley, the present proprietor of this little township, which contains only 120 statute acres, forming one farm."

See also The Lysons, p. 620.

It is however known that the Colleys were settled at Eccleston, near Chester, in the time of the civil war, and that of this family Whitney's sister was a member. Dr. Davies, a physician, now of the Whitefriars, Chester, is descended from M. D. Colley, and possesses a "safe conduct," granted December 1, 1643, to his ancestor, Mr. William Colley of Eccleston, by Arthur lord Capel, in which the "Lieutenant Generall of the fforces" charges all under his command "not to doe nor willingly permit or suffer to bee done any hurt, vyolence, damage, plunder, or detriment whatsoever unto the person, house, family, goods, chattels or estate of William Colley, of Eccleston in the Countie of Cheshire, gentleman." There were too Colleys of Audlem, for in the register of Acton church, the parish church of the Whitneys, under the date 1659, is the entry, "Thomas Colley of Audlem and Elizabeth Harrison of Poole were married 18th July," and 1662, "Samuell Colley & Maria Venables Septr 15."

Journal of the Arch. &c. Society of Chester, vol. ii. pp. 275 and 309.

EMBLEM, p. 95.— "*De Inuido et Auaro, iocosum,*" Of the envious and the greedy: a tale. This tale, as Whitney states in his margin, is from the epistles, *i.e.* "*The Golden Epistles*" of Guevara. Antony De Guevara was a Spaniard, bishop of Guadix in Granada, and known as the historiographer of the emperor Charles V., and for his "*Dial of Princes, or the Life of M. A. Antonius.*" He was the author of several other works; among which are "*The Golden Epistles,*" of which there was a translation into Italian—"*Delle Lettere Dell' ill^re Signore Don Antonio Di Guevara, &c. Nuouamente tradotto dal S. Alfonso Ulloa. In Venetia,* M.D.LXXV. *Appresse gli Heredi di Vincenzo Valgrisi,*" 4to,—in four books or volumes, containing respectively 230, 270, 181 and 187 pages. Guevara died in 1544.

EMBLEM, p. 96.— To the very accomplished Mr. PETER WITHIPOLE. The Coopers supply the following notice: "PETER

Athenæ Cantab. vol. ii. p. 13.

WITHYPOLL, son of a person residing at Ipswich, was educated in Trinity hall, where he was admitted a fellow 1st June 1572, proceeding LL.B. 1579. He was commissary of the bishop of Norwich for the archdeaconry of Suffolk 1580, and vacated his fellowship at Trinity hall on or shortly before 25th February 1582-3, and his commissaryship in 1586." Blomefield mentions "Sir William Wythypole of Christ Church in Ipswich in Suffolk descended from Robert Wythypole of Wythypole in Shropshire."

Norfolk, vol. iii. p. 458: also vol. i. p. 178.

Hadrian Junius by no means gives so complete a play upon the words as Whitney does, but very tamely says, "Petram imitare iuuentus," *Youth imitate the rock*, and thus addresses his son Peter: "*En tibi quas, fili, genituræ consecro testes Ceras, aucturas nomina amicitiæ*," "Behold what tablets as witnesses of thy natal hour I consecrate to thee, my son, which shall increase the renown of friendship." The stanzas of Junius may here be compared with those of Whitney:

Had. Ivnii Emblemata lix.

"*Sperne voluptates, iuuenis, constanter; vt iras*
Ventorum, assultúsque maris Marpesiæ cautes.
Nate, tuo lepidè ludens in nomine, dictas
Symbolico elogio, tu, Petram imitare Iuuentus."

EMBLEM, p. 97.—*To his old friend Mr.* GEORGE SALMON, *who escaped from Rome at the great peril of life.* As a Cheshire name Salmon boasts a considerable antiquity and a curious origin. It is the name of a Norman proprietor, Robert Salmon, who "remitted and quit-claimed" to Randle Blundeville, earl of Chester (*anno* 1181-1232) "all the lands which his father held in Normandy," and received in exchange the township of Lower Withington, near Macclesfield, and in addition "xx^{s} rent out of the mills of Macclesfield."* Robert's daughter Mary was married to Roger de Davenport.

Ormerod's Cheshire, vol. iii. p. 356.

* Ormerod adds in a note: "There is no regular descent of the SALMONS in the Cheshire collections, but their name occurs from a very early period among the marriages given in pedigrees of the families in the neighbourhood of Nantwich, and many respectable branches are yet in existence which, in all probability, derive their origin from this source." The Lysons name Mrs. Dighton Salmon, Messrs. Salmon, Margaret Salmon, the Rev. Richard Lowndes Salmon, &c.; and an obituary, "George Salmon Esq. of Nantwich, formerly Governor of Fort Marlborough in the East Indies."

See also The Lysons, pp. 624, 676, 711, 733, 768, and 831.

Gent. Magazine, 1848, pt. ii. p. 554.

British Museum MS. 1424, Plut. lvi. 1.

Ormerod's Cheshire, vol. iii. p. 243.

The *Visitation of Cheshire*, 1580, names a William Salmon among the freeholders in Nantwich hundred; and the occurrence of the name renders it probable that Whitney's old friend was from the same neighbourhood with himself. He was probably rector of Baddiley, near Nantwich, for on the list of rectors for that parish occurs the entry: "1605, 13 Ap. George Salmon," the patron, "Edmund Mainwaring."

In queen Mary's reign, on the accession of a new pope in 1555, the populace in Rome broke open the prisons of the inquisition, and set free the prisoners. Among the captives thus liberated were sir Thomas Wilson and Craig the Scottish reformer, who protested against the marriage of Mary and Bothwell in 1567. Might it not be that on occasion of the above named tumult George Salmon also escaped from Rome at the extreme peril of his life?

Plate XXVII.

EMBLEM, p. 98.—"*Stultitia sua seipsum saginari*," To glut one's self on one's own foolishness. This fable is translated from one of the fables of Gabriel Faerni, and should be compared with it.

Ath. Cantab. vol. ii. pp. 96 and 97.

EMBLEM, p. 100.*—*To the very learned youths Edm. Freake and Anth. Alcock.* The father of one of these youths was Edmund Freake, born in Essex about 1516, and successively bishop of Rochester 1571, of Norwich 1575, and of Worcester 1584, dying in 1590. His widow Cecily died full of days 15th July 1599. The bishop left three children, John, archdeacon of Norwich, born about 1545; Edmund, noticed here by Whitney;

Edit. Antv. 1564, p. 177.

* Compare Whitney's version with the original in *Sambucus:*

CVNCTIS Deus creauit
Quæcunque terra, et vndis,
Signum dedit, pateret
Natura singulorum vt.
Latratibus canis sic
Suæ indicem dat iræ
Taurus monet furorem
Quòd cornuis petendo
Lædat, venena caudis
Serpens gerit, timendus
Et scorpius cauetur.
Est nuda frons, sed index.
Mortalibus negatus,
Vt nosse quis bonus sit
Nequeas, tibi à maloque
Dum tempus est cauere.
Dextra tenet tabellam
Rasam, notis nec vllis
Insignem, amicus vt sit
Qualis tuus colis quem
Tot sedulus per annos.
Scribas mihi potes si,
Num candidè, dolo ne
Tecum egit, at recusas.

and "Martha, wife of Nathaniel Cole, sometime senior fellow of Trinity college." There were persons of the same name "of good repute in Somersetshire." Ralph Freake, esq., "was for many years auditor of the treasury in the reigns of King Henry VIII. and Queen Elizabeth, and died worth upwards of one hundred thousand pounds." His first son, sir Thomas Freake, was ancestor of the Freakes of Dorsetshire, and his second son, William, of the Freakes of Hampshire.

Blomefield's Norfolk, vol. iv. p. 482.

There were Alcocks of Cheshire and of Yorkshire, but I have not been fortunate enough to identify the very learned youth Anthony Alcock.

EMBLEM, p. 101.—*To the accomplished Mr.* ELLIS GRYPHITH. A name to be left undetermined. Were it allowed, from the transmission or repetition of the prænomen Ellis, to conclude that the Gryphith mentioned was of the same family as that which once bore both the names, we might decide to what stock this Ellis Gryphith should be assigned. We should then say that he was a Cheshire man of a Welsh origin, probably the Matthew Ellis, or Ellis Gryphith, of Overlegh, near Chester, gentleman, who died 31st July 1613. He was grandson to Matthew Ellis, one of the gentlemen of the body guard to king Henry VIII., the son of Ellis ap Dio, ap Griffith, lineally descended from Tudor Trevor earl of Hereford.

Ormerod's Cheshire, vol. i. p. 268.

See also The Lysons, pp. 628, 696 and 370.

EMBLEM, p. 103.—*To Mr.* PETER COLVIUS, *of Bruges.* Several learned men of Holland and the Netherlands have borne the name of Colvius, as Andrew Colvius, born at Dordrecht in 1549. Peter Colvius, whom Whitney addresses, was born at Bruges in 1567, and killed by a blow from a mule at Paris in 1594. His untimely fate was much lamented, and Dousa deplored it in an epitaph of considerable elegance, beginning with

Biog. Universelle, vol. ix.

Hofman Peerlkamp's Liber, 1838, pp. 159-161.

"Colvius hic situs est, Flandris generatus Athenis,
Illecebris pessum quem dedit aula suis,"

"Colvius here lies buried, born in the Athens of Flanders,
Whom by its allurements the court gave to perdition;"

but ending with a punning allusion both to his editing the *Golden Ass* of Apuleius and to the manner of his death:

"I nunc *Luci Asino* nativum redde nitorem,
Nata asino rumpat ut tibi mula caput,"

"Go now to Lucius Asinus the native splendor restore,
As a mule born from an Ass broke in pieces thy head."

For one so young he distinguished himself among the scholars of the sixteenth century. We owe to him, at Leyden in 1588, "*Ex officina Plantiniana Apud Franciscum Raphelengium*," an edition of all the works of APULEIUS, of Madaura, in Africa; an 8vo volume of 431 pages. He added to it from the same press and in the same year abundant notes, occupying 294 pages, to which are appended 38 elegiac verses by Janus Dousa the younger. Oudendorp and Ruhnken reprinted these notes at Leyden in 1786. The learned notes on Sidonius Apollinaris, published at Paris in 1598, were also written by Colvius. Of his Latin poetry, which he cultivated with some success, besides the ode to Whitney, there are specimens in the *Delitiae C. Poetarvm Belgicorvm:* but the choice of words is occasionally incorrect. Jöcher says he passed the year 1591 as a common soldier at the siege of Rouen, and was killed in his twenty-seventh year at Paris.

Page [18].
Francofvrti, M.DCXIV., tom i. pp. 798-983.
Allgemeines Gelehrten Lexicon, i. col. 1027.

Of the ode by Colvius, on the emblems of Geffrey Whitney, an English version is given in the Introductory Dissertation.

Page xxix.

"*Stans vno capit omnia puncto.*"

SECTION II. — CONTAINING PART II. FROM PAGE 105 TO THE END, PAGE 230.

OKED together as are the two parts of Whitney's *Emblems* in one continuous volume, no real necessity for separating them exists, but it is of some advantage to have a break in a long series of notes, and therefore we follow the division which the author himself adopted. There is no essential difference between the first and second parts, except it be that more references are made in the latter to the celebrated men of classical antiquity.

EMBLEM, p. 106. — "*In Praise of the two noble Earles,* WARWICKE *and* LEYCESTER." The badge of both earls is the bear and ragged staff, and therefore the allusion which Whitney makes to "TWO *Beares,* — *the greater, and the lesse*" is appropriate to

> "*Two noble peeres, who both doe giue the beare,*
> *Two famous Earles, whose praises pierce the skye.*"

We have already given a sketch of the life and character of one of the brothers, Robert Dudley, earl of Leicester, and rejoice that a much brighter picture may be given of his elder brother, Ambrose Dudley, earl of Warwick. The chivalry, the courtesy, the honour and the love of literature which distinguished the Sidneys, father and son, sir Henry and sir Philip, also eminently belonged to him. The respective qualities of the two brothers are very quaintly but very forcibly and truly drawn by our old friend Thomas Fuller: "John Dudley, duke of Northumberland, left two sons who succeeded to great honour; Ambrose earl of Warwick, heir to all that was good, and Robert earl of Leycester, heir to all that was great in their father."

See Page 315.

Worthies, vol iii p. 134.

There is so excellent a memoir of the "good earl" by the Coopers of Cambridge, that were their work as widely known and as accessible as it deserves to be, we should simply refer to its pages; but a brief account is required here. Ambrose was the fourth son, born about the year 1530, and knighted in 1549.

Ath. Cantab. vol. ii pp. 66-70.

He maintained a high place in king Edward's regards, but with the fortunes of his father and brother his own declined at the beginning of Mary's reign; in 1557 however he accompanied king Philip into Picardy, and in consideration of his faithful services his family was restored in blood. On Elizabeth's accession he early became one of the most distinguished at her court, and was created first baron L'Isle and then earl of Warwick, in 1562. The queen having determined to assist the Huguenots, Ambrose Dudley led the English forces, and received a severe and life-long troublesome wound at the siege of New-haven, or as now named Havre de Grace. He filled many high offices, and had many honours conferred upon him, but never joined in the intrigues of this busy reign. One historian says of him, "he was a man of great sweetness of temper and of unexceptionable character, so that he was beloved by all parties and hated by none."

Chalmers's Gen. Biogr. vol. xii. p. 405.

The wound which he had received in 1562 occasioned him at times great pain and inconvenience, and he died from the effects of amputation February 21st 1589-90, and a splendid tomb was erected over him in Our Lady's chapel at Warwick. He was married three times, but left no child. His portrait and the portraits of his father and of his brother Robert are at Knole, near Sevenoaks, Kent; his portrait is also at Woburn abbey and Hatfield house.* Many of his original letters exist, and sir Henry Ellis gives one, entitled, "Ambrose Earle of Warwick's Experience of Archers, penned with his owne hand."

Original Letters of Eminent Men, p. 55.

For particulars respecting him Bliss's edition of *Athenæ Oxonienses* may be consulted, and *Fasti Oxonienses*, 1566; also Chalmers's *General Biography*, London, 1813, vol. xii. p. 405.

EMBLEM, p. 115.—*Fortiter et feliciter.* This device, which Whitney assigns to the Roman Marcus Sergius, properly belongs to the dukes of Milan. With the motto, "ESTE DUCES," Be ye leaders, it was borne by John Galeas Sforza, who in some accounts is named the sixth duke.†

Symb. Div. et Hum. vol. iii. p. 19.

EMBLEM, p. 119.—"*Ex damno alterius, alterius vtilitas,*" From

* Also in Holland's *Heroölogia*.

† The duke Francis Sforza, according to Paolo Giovio, adopted for his device a greyhound seated under a pine-tree, yet on the watch, with the expressive motto, "QVIETVM NEMO IMPVNE LACESSET."

Dialogue, p. 36, à Lyon, 1561.

loss of one, the advantage of another. The George Sabine, to whom Whitney refers, was a Latin poet and man of learning in the sixteenth century. His principal poems are "*Res Gestæ Cæsarum Romanorum*," Exploits of the Roman emperors. He was born in Brandenburg in 1508, and died in Italy in 1560. His wife was Melancthon's eldest daughter.

EMBLEM, p. 120.—*To the* very reverend Dr. WILLIAM CHATTERTON *Bishop of Chester.* In reference to the device here given it may be mentioned that John Alcock, bishop of Ely, rejoicing probably in his name, published in 1498 a work in 4to, which bears the whimsical and punning title, "*Galli Cantus Johannis Alcock episcopi Eliensis ad fratros suos*," The crowing of the cock to his brethren. At the beginning is a print of the bishop preaching to his clergy, with a cock on each side; there is also a cock on the first page.*

In modern times there has been written an "*Alectrophonia Ecclesiastica*," or "The weathercock's Homily from the Church Steeple," but not to be compared to Whitney's, either for force of expression or for the quaint beauty of the sentiments. The opening lines however have considerable excellence: Gent. Magazine, 1842, pt. ii. p. 272

"The mimic Cock, that crests yon hallow'd spire,
What means he? well the churchman may inquire.
Deem not our pious ancestors would dare
Exalt a bauble on the House of Prayer!
If right we listen to the mystic bird,
'WAKE TO REPENTANCE,' is his watch-note heard,
'Repent!' within those walls the preacher cries;
'Repent!' the shrill-voic'd herald still replies,—
Perch'd high, and seen afar, that all may view
How free the general call, and hear it too."

Bishop Chatterton's name is usually written Chaderton, but the Cheshire historians scarcely touch on the origin of his family, which must be learned from other sources. Fuller supplies a brief notice: "William Chaderton, D.D. Here I solemnly Worthies, vol. i p. 269.

* The Italian emblematist Lodovico Dominichi adopted a watchdog, rather than the cock, as the symbol of vigilance and guardianship over the churches of Christ, and gave the motto "*Non dormit qvi cvstodit*," which will be mentioned again in the Addenda. Ragionamento, pp. 133 and 134, Venice, 1556.

tender deserved thanks to my manuscript author, charitably guiding me in the dark, assuring that this doctor was 'ex præclaro Chadertonorum Cestrensis comitatûs stemmate prognatus' (descended from the famous stem of Chadertons of the county of Chester). And although this doubtful direction doth not cleave the pen, it doth not hit the white; so that his nativity may with most probability (not prejudicing the right of Lancashire when produced) here be fixed. He was bred first fellow, then master of Queen's, and never of Magdalen College in Cambridge (as the Reverend Bishop Godwin mistaketh), and chosen first the Lady Margaret's, then the King's professor in divinity; and doctor Whitacre succeeded him immediately in his chair. He was, anno 1579, made bishop of Chester, then of Lincoln 1594; demeaning himself in both to his great commendation. He departed this life in April 1608."

An authority in every way competent, the Rev. F. R. Raines, of Milnrow parsonage, Rochdale, decides against Fuller's "manuscript author," thus: "There is little if any doubt that William Chaderton, Bishop of Lincoln, and Lawrence Chaderton, Master of Emanuel college, Cambridge, were of one family." "In 1605 there were only two families of heraldic rank of this name in Lancashire, represented by George Chaderton of Lees in Oldham, and Edmund Chaderton of Nuthurst in Manchester, the former the brother of Dr. Lawrence Chaderton and the latter the great-nephew of the Bishop of Lincoln. The precise degree of relationship between Dr. Lawrence Chaderton and the Bishop has not been discovered; but they are presumed to have been descended, one in the third and the other in the fourth degree, from the two sons of Edmund Chaderton of the Lees, living there in 1428, the Bishop being of the younger branch."

Gent. Magazine, 1854, pt. ii. p. 588.

The pedigree of bishop Chaderton's branch generally agrees with sir Peter Leycester's statement that "he had onely one Daughter and Heir, called *Jone*, the first Wife of Sir *Richard Brooke* of *Norton* in *Cheshire*;" and that their only daughter and heiress Mary, or Elizabeth, for this is uncertain, was married to Torrell Jocelyne esq., of Essex or Cambridgeshire, of which marriage also the only issue was a daughter Theodora.

Notes and Queries, vol. vi. p. 273. Historical Antiquities, p. 187.

Betham's Baronetage; vol. ii. p. 335.

To this Theodora was addressed that beautiful little book, beautiful for its spirit of deep love and devotion. "*The Mother's*

Legacy to her Unborn Child." With a sad presentiment it had been written; the daughter was born October 12th 1622, and the mother having thanked God that she had lived to see her child a Christian, in a few days, as the appendix to the work recites, "ended her Prayers, Speech and Life together, rendring her Soul into the Hand of her Redeemer." Mother'sLegacy, Appendix, p. 19

The bishop was a man of earnest mind and had a leaning towards puritanism in religion; to him Whitney's lines were very appropriate, for he was "arm'de with learning, and with life." During his abode in Cambridge he and Dr. Andrews, afterwards bishop of Ely, and Mr. Knewstubb, to whom Whitney devotes an emblem, and others united in the observance of weekly meetings for conference upon Scripture; and thus by nearly two centuries anticipated the small association of students formed by Charles Wesley in Oxford for setting apart Sunday evenings to the reading of divinity.* Emb. p. 223.

King's *Vale Royal* gives two instances of the bishop's wit or humour, of which one brought on him a severe rebuke. "This Doctor, while at *Cambridge* preacht a Wedding-Sermon, and used therein this merry Comparison: The choice of a Wife (said he) is full of hazard, not unlike to a man groping for one Fish in a barrel full of Serpents: if he scape harm of the Snakes, and light on the Fish, he may be thought fortunate, yet let him not boast, for perhaps it may be but an Eele." Chronicon Cestrense, p. 44.

Again, it is recorded: "He preached the Funeral Sermon of *Henry Stanley*, Earl of *Derby*, at *Orms-Church* in *Lancashire, An.* 1593; wherein having given large commendations of the deceased person, turned his Speech to *Ferdinando* the then present Earl. You (said he) noble Earl, that not onely inherit, but exceed your Father's virtues, learn to keep the love of your Countrey, as your Father did. You give in your Arms three Legs,† signi-

* From information furnished by the Rev. R. Brook Aspland.

† Arms very similar to those of the lords of Man were borne by the Signor Count Battista da Lodrone, who died at the taking of Casale in Monferrato. Lodovico Domenichi says that his special device was a caltrop, or *tribulus*, a ball armed with three projecting points of iron, one of which remains upright however the ball be thrown; the motto is, *In utraque fortuna*, Good luck on every side. So the motto to the Legs of Man, *Quocunque jacebis, stabit*, Whichever way you cast, it will stand, has the like meaning. Ragionamento, Venice, 1556, p. 95.

fying three Shires, *Cheshire*, *Derbyshire*, and *Lancashire:* stand fast on these three Legs, and you shall need fear none of their Arms. At which, the Earl somewhat moved, said in a heat, and sinfully sealed it with an Oath, This Priest, I believe, hopes one day, to make him three Courtesies;" *i.e.* three bendings of the knees on being appointed by the queen to higher dignities.

A more connected view of bishop Chaderton's life and character may be gathered from the *Athenæ Cantabrigienses*, where a list of his works is given, and his portrait and arms noticed. A considerable number of his letters are contained in Peck's *Desiderata Curiosa*.

Vol ii. pp. 482 and 483.

Vol. i. bk vi. 8.

In 1568 William Chaderton was appointed chaplain to the earl of Leicester, and there is a curious letter from the earl to his chaplain when the latter requested advice as to his own marriage. Baines's *History of Lancashire* may be consulted for many particulars respecting him.

Vol. ii. pp 356-360.

Plate XXXIII.

EMBLEM, pp. 121, 122.—*To the very honourable* FRANCIS WINDHAM, and EDWARD FLOWERDEWE, *most upright judges.*

In 1579 Francis Windham was appointed one of the justices of the common pleas, and Edward Flowerdewe in 1584 one of the barons of the exchequer.

Foss's Judges of England, vol. v. pp. 407, 409 and 421.

Sir Francis Windham, knt., married Jane, one of the daughters of sir Nicholas Bacon, lord keeper of the great seal in Elizabeth's reign, and thus was closely allied to the great philosophical writer, Francis Bacon, viscount St. Albans. The name has its origin, like so many others, from the possessions and residence of the family, whose estates were principally in Norfolk, and who in later times have been associated chiefly with Felbrigge, a portion of their property. The township name or the parish name and the family name were one, though variously written, as Winmuntham, Wimundhan, Wimondham, and Windham or Wyndham. In 1466 *John Windham*, the father, settled the manor of Banningham on *John* his son and *Margaret*, daughter of sir *John Howard*, knt., and their issue, from which time it has passed with Felbrigge.

Betham's Baronetage, vol. i. p. 16.

Blomefield's Norfolk, vol. i. p. 718.

Palmer's Manship's *Yarmouth* gives some account of Francis Wyndham; but a much more complete biography is to be found in the *Athenæ Cantabrigienses*, from which it appears that he was

Vol. i. p. 186

Vol. ii. p. 124.

the second son of sir Edmund Wyndham, of Felbrigg in Norfolk, represented his native county in parliament in 1572, and after filling several offices of importance, died at Norwich in July 1592.

Edward Flowerdewe succeeded to J. Clench as third baron of the exchequer October 23rd, 1584. He was one of the sons of John Flowerdew, esq., a large landed proprietor of Hethersett in Norfolk, entered at Cambridge without taking a degree, and was admitted a member of the Inner Temple October 11th 1552, and was very successful in his profession. His reputation as a lawyer is attested, as was that of lord keeper Egerton, by several annuities which his grateful clients, as Thomas Grimesdiche, Simon Harecourt, and sir Thomas Gresham, granted to him by way of rent charge on their estates "for his good and faithful counsel and advice." From Flowerdewe's friendship for Whitney we may mention that he was counsel to the town of Great Yarmouth in 1573, was chosen to settle their disputes with the Cinque Ports May 1575, and appointed under-steward in 1580. In the list of the pic-nic party which visited Scratby island Aug. 2nd 1580 he is named by Whitney, "Edm[d] Flowerdewe esq[r] Sergeant at law." At one time Whitney appears to have acted as Flowerdewe's deputy. Foss records that Flowerdewe was a correspondent of Lady Amye Dudley, the Amy Robsart of Scott's *Kenilworth.*

Foss's Judges, vol. v. p. 460.

Blomefield's Norfolk, vol. i. p. 721; vol v. p. 831.

Palmer's Manship's Great Yarmouth, vol. ii. pp. 337-339.

Plate 13.

Baron Flowerdewe's death was occasioned by the fearfully unhealthy state of Exeter gaol. A letter from Walsyngham to Leicester, 11th April 1586, testifies: "Sir Ant. Basset and Sir Jhon Chichester, and three justices more in Devonshire, are dead thorrowghe the infectyon of the gaole. Baron Flowerdewe, one of the justyces of that cyrcute, is also dead. The takyng awaye of well affected men in this corrupt tyme sheweth that God is angrye with us." See also Holinshed's *Chronicle,* vol. iv. p. 868.

Correspondence, Camden Society, p. 24.

These gatherings by the wayside may be supplemented from the ampler and better arranged stores of the *Athenæ Cantabrigienses,* or of Palmer's edition of *Manship's History of Great Yarmouth,* where a short life of the judge is given.

Vol. ii. p. 5.

Vol. ii. pp. 337-339.

EMBLEM, p. 126.—*To the very noble and learned* JAN DOUSA LORD OF NOORTWIICK.

The poet's badge derives its origin from Egyptian times, when

Plate 11

"an old man musical" was denoted by the bird fabled to sing the sweetest when power to sing is nearly over.* Through the whole course of Greek and Roman literature we find comparisons and illustrations taken from the supposed qualities of the swan, as in *Æschylus* and *Antipater* of Sidon; in *Virgil*, Æn. vii. 700; *Horace*, Carm. iv. 2, 25; and *Ovid*, Met. xiv. 430; but we will give only one instance in full, lest the lines should be applied,

Agamemnon, vv 1322, 1444. Anth. Gk. 76.

"Swans sing before they die; 'twere no bad thing,
Did certain persons die before they sing."

Plato's Works, Francofurti, 1602, p. 64A.

We refer to the conversation of Socrates as recorded by Plato. His friends were fearful of causing him trouble and vexation, but he reminds them that they should not think him inferior in foresight to the swans, for these "fall a singing as soon as they perceive that they are about to die, and sing far more sweetly than at any former time, being glad that they are about to go away to the God whose servants they are."

Both for his attainments and general excellence Whitney's friend deserved to wear this badge of fame. JAN DOUSA, or Van der Does, was a man of highest repute and patriotism in the war which achieved his country's independence. He was lord of Noordwijck, in Holland, a village domain situated between Leyden and the sea. Here he was born December 6th 1545. He passed his youth in study, chiefly at Louvain, but spent some time in England and France. In 1565 he married Elizabeth de Zwylen, by whom he had twelve children. Of these four were sons, all illustrious like their father for the love of literature and for worth of character. To estimate these it will be sufficient to read P. Hofmanni Peerlkamp's "*Liber De vita, doctrina et facultate Nederlandorum, qui Carmina Latina composuerunt*," and the Oration of Daniel Heinsius in commemoration of the virtues of the elder Dousa on his death in 1604.

Harlemi 1838, pp. 202, 178 and 406.

At the celebrated siege of Leyden in 1574 Jan Dousa devoted himself to his country's cause, and therefore was selected by William the Silent to be governor of the town and curator of

Amstelodami, 1685, pp. 619-659.

* It is singular that the bulky tome, "*Philosophia Imaginum*," 8vo, pp. 847, by C. F. Menestrerius, contains no reference to the swan. The eagle, the phœnix, the pelican, the ostrich, &c. are very frequently introduced, but Apollo's bird is unnoticed. No less than two hundred symbolical applications of the eagle are numbered and catalogued, besides seventy specially devoted to the bird of Jove.

the recently formed university, destined in a very few years to occupy a high station among the seats of learning and science. Van der Does distinguished himself as a philologist, an historian and a poet, as well as a magistrate.

He was the historian of his native land, and besides wrote very learned notes on Sallust, and critical remarks on Horace, Plautus, Tibullus, &c. Theodore De Bry presents his portrait to us as "poet and orator," and Boissard's brief notice of his character styles him "A man and a hero most worthy of memory as well from the merits of his ancestors as from his own virtues." Plate LV.

His sons will be named hereafter in the note to Whitney's emblem, p. 206. For other particulars consult Iöcher's *Allgemeines Gelehrten Lexicon*, vol ii. col. 205; also "*Biographie Universelle*," vol. ii. p. 619. Leipsig, 1750.

EMBLEM, p. 130.—*To Sir* HUGHE CHOLMELEY *Knight*. Bibl. Cotton. Claudius CIII. Plut. xxi. F. 4.

"Of those that were honoured with the order of knighthoode in the tyme of the triumphant reigne of Kinge Henry the eight," are numbered three Cholmeleys: sir Roger Cholmeley knighted anno Dom. 1536, sir Hugh Cholmeley of Cheshire, and sir Richard Cholmeley of Yorkshire."* These two are styled "Knightes made in Scotlande," "after the destruction of Edenborough and other townes" in the year 1544.

The knight to whom the emblem of the seven wise men is inscribed receives from Fuller a high meed of praise. "Sir HUGH CHOLMLEY, or CHOLMONDELEIGH. This worthy person bought his knighthood in the field at Leigh in Scotland. He was five times high sheriff of this county, *i.e.* Chester (and sometimes of Flintshire), and for many years one of the two sole deputies lieutenants thereof. For a good space he was vice-president of the marches of Wales under the Right Honourable Sir Henry Sidney, knight, I conceive it was during his absence in Ireland. For fifty years together he was esteemed a father of Worthies, vol. i. p. 289.

* Of the Yorkshire Cholmleys there was also a sir Hugh, distinguished as a royalist under Charles I. See "The Memoirs of sir Hugh Cholmley addressed to his two sons; in which he gives some account of his family, and the distress they underwent in the civil wars, and how far he himself was engaged in them; taken from an original manuscript in his own handwriting, now in the possession of Nathaniel Cholmley, of Whitby and Howsham, in the county of York." London, 1787, 4to.

his country, and dying anno 15— was buried in the church of Malpasse, under a tomb of alabaster, with great lamentation of all sorts of people, had it not mitigated their mourning, that he left a son of his own name, heir to his virtues and estates."

King's Vale Royal, pt. ii. pp. 55 and 56.

In the main features Fuller borrows his account from Webb's *Itinerary*, but does not speak of sir Hugh Cholmondeley's "admirable gifts of Wisdome, Temperance, Continency, Liberality, Hospitality, and many virtues of his life, and godly departure at his end," nor record the *Encomium* in his memory which Webb presented to sir Hugh the younger:

> "*Then for the last adieu to his pure Soul,*
> *Which leaves us gain for loss, and mirth for moan;*
> *I wish the Title might his Fame inroll,*
> *And be engrav'n with Gold upon his Stone.*
> *We have inter'd his reverend Body here,*
> *That was our Countries Father* 50. *Year.*"

Ormerod's Cheshire, vol. ii. pp. 356 and 78; vol. iii. pp. 198 and 199.

From his only surviving son are descended the noble families of Cholmondeley castle and of Vale Royal, in Cheshire; and from his only daughter Frances, the wife of Thomas Wilbraham, of Woodhey, celebrated by Whitney at p. 199, the excellent Lady Done, of Utkinton, and that branch of the Wilbrahams which finally became merged by the marriages of the coheiresses about 1680, into the families of Middleton, of Chirk castle, and of Lionel Tollemache, lord Huntingtour and earl of Dysart in Scotland.

Plate XXXIV.

EMBLEM, p. 131.—*To Sir* ARTHURE MANWARINGE Knight.

Bibl. Cotton. Claudius CIII. Plut. xxi. F.

Ormerod, vol. i. p. 373; vol. ii. p. 229; vol. iii. p. 325.

In the reign of Henry VIII. two "John Maynwaringes," each bearing for crest an ass's head, obtained the honour of knighthood, one in France in 1513, the other along with William Stanley, of Hooton, and John Stanley, of Hondford, natural son of the bishop of Ely, probably in the same year, though not on the same occasion. The first of the sir John Maynwaringes thus knighted was of Over Peover in Cheshire, the second of "Ichtfeild" in Shropshire. The fine and very curious **Chartularum Mainwaringianum**,"* compiled by William Dugdale, Norry King of Arms in 1669, and preserved at Over Peover hall, records:

* This Mainwaring Chartulary begins in the seventh year of William Rufus, A.D. 1093.

"Hereafter foloyn the names of the Captayns and pety Captayns wth the Bagges in ther standerts of the Aremy and vantgard of the Kigns Lefftenant enteryng into France the xvi^h^ day of Iune in the fift yere of the Reign of Kyng Henry the Eight. George Erle of Shrouesbury, the Kyngs Leftenant, Thomas Erle of Derby, Sr William Perpoynt;" and then follows "Sir John Maynwaryng of Eghtfeld, (Shropsh.) bayryth gold a Asse-hed haltered Sabul and a cresscent upon the same: And Rondell Maynwaryng hys pety Captayn. The said Sr John made Knyght at Lysk."

The Mainwarings of Over Peover, of Kermincham, and of Ightfield, as sir Peter Leycester assures us, were descended from a common ancestor in the reign of Richard II., "*Randle Manwaring* of *Over-Pever* Esquire," "stiled commonly *Honkyn Manwaring* in the Language of those times." "He was a Courtier, stiled *Armiger Regis, the King's Servant & Sagittarius de Corona*, 21 *Rich.* 2." Historical Antiquities, p. 34.

At a remote period of the Ightfield Mainwarings was Roger Mainwaring, bishop of Hereford, confessor to Henry IV.; and in later times, 1668, Arthur Mainwaring a poetical and political writer. Gent. Magazine, 1821, pt. i. p. 213.

"Sir John Maynweringe of Ichtfeild" was the father of the "Sir Arthure Manwaringe" whom Whitney celebrates, and whom "the handes of Edward Duke of Somersett Lord Protector" made a knight at Newcastle, October 1st 1547, on the return from the invasion of Scotland, as "Sir Arthure Manwerynge." Sir Arthur married Margaret, the eldest daughter of sir Randle Manwaring,* of Over Peover, knight. "The Lady Margaret" died in November 1574, and her husband at the end of August 1590. He had been sheriff of Shropshire in 1561 and 1575, and had served his native county in parliament in 1558-9. Bibl. Cotton. Claudius CIII. Plut. xxi. F. 4. Chart. Mainwar.

A daughter of sir Arthur Mainwaring, Mary, was married to the Richard Cotton of Combermere, to whom, as we have seen, Whitney dedicates two emblems. After a long descent, and after Emb. 65 and 200.

* This sir Randle died in 1557. His nephew, the second sir Randle, rebuilt the hall of Over Peover in 1585-6, at the very time when *The Choice of Emblemes* was a printing, and named his eighth child, born May 17th 1585, Arthur, the godfathers being "Sir Arthure Maynwaringe of Ightfelde," and "George Brereton of Ashley Esquier," and "Mystris Anne Tankarde of Burroe-brigge Godmother."

in fact the old line of the Mainwarings of Over Peover had become extinct in 1797, a Cotton of Combermere, Sophia, daughter of sir Robert S. Cotton, bart., in 1803, became the wife of sir Henry Mainwaring Mainwaring, bart., of the second creation, and thus their son, the present sir Harry Mainwaring, bart., re-enters into the blood of the old line, first through the Mainwarings of Ightfield, and then by a common ancestry in Randle Manwaring of the reign of Richard II. Thence sir Peter Leycester traces the pedigree to William Manwaring during the reign of Henry III., and sir Thomas Mainwaring, sir Peter's stout opponent, carries up the stream through Roger de Mesnilgarin (one of the old ways of spelling* Mainwaring) to Ranulphus, who held Warmincham and Over Peover &c. in fee from the Conqueror himself.

Historical Antiquities, p. 331.

The old feudal wars had ceased, but as exciting a contest raged from the year 1673 to 1679 as to Amicia, the daughter of Hugh Cyvelioc, earl of Chester, 1153-1181, and "wife of Raufe Manwaring, sometime judge of Chester," under Henry the Second, and Richard the First. Five hundred years after her birth no less than twelve books issued from the press on behalf of, or against her legitimacy. "Sir Thomas Mainwaring of Peover in Cheshire" claimed her to be in the line of his ancestry, and that she was born in wedlock; "Sir Peter Leycester, baronet," maintained the contrary. The whole controversy is summed up with great impartiality by Ormerod. "The essential question" "was long argued with great ability on the part of Sir Peter Leycester, but some of his arguments are ascertained to rest on the authority of incorrect transcripts, and it is probable that few will read the last book of his opponent" "without allowing the victory to Sir T. M. The opinions of the greater part of (if not all) the judges who were consulted, were given in favour of Amicia's legitimacy, and the authorities of the College of Arms have also been in her favour, under the express sanction of Sir William Dugdale."

History of Cheshire, vol. i. pp. 28-32, note.

Plate X.

EMBLEM, p. 132.—*To* EDWARDE DIER *Esquier.*

* Between the years 1093 and 1669 there have been established by autographs or valid legal documents *one hundred and thirty-one* ways of spelling the name; "to which are added," in a paper at Peover hall, "263 other variations," "making together the Number of 394 Diversifyings thereof."

In the reign of Elizabeth the name of Dier or Dyer was celebrated for eminence both in law and in literature. Sir Thomas Dyer and sir James Dyer had indeed been knighted at the beginning of Edward the Sixth's reign, and sir Richard Dyer, son and heir to sir James, was "dubbed 1585 the 4th of Aprill." Sir James is mentioned as "Sergeant at the Lawe" and speaker of the house of commons in 1552.

Names and Arms of Knights, Brit. Bibl. Cotton. Claudius CIII. Plut. xxi. F. 4.

Edward Dyer, so praised by Whitney, a poet and a courtier of the Elizabethan age, was born about 1540, and educated at Oxford. After travelling abroad he obtained considerable celebrity in Elizabeth's court, and was held in much respect. He was the friend of sir Philip Sidney, and if the little poetical narrative on Whitney's 197th page be true, as there is no reason to doubt, Sidney held Dyer in the highest esteem. This too is especially evidenced in Sidney's will, in which he bequeathed one-half of his books to sir Fulke Greville, and the other half to Mr. Edward Dyer.

Emb. p. 135.

Zouch's Memoirs of Sidney, p. 324.

In the emblem to Dyer, designated "The glory of the pen," our Cheshire poet declares his high admiration of Sidney:

Emb. p. 196.

"Wherefore, for to extoll his name in what I might,
This Emblem lo, I did present, vnto this woorthie Knight,
Who did the same refuse, as not his proper due:
And at the first, his sentence was, it did belonge to you."

"The laurell leafe," Whitney affirms, had been prepared for Dyer;—for Sidney,

"The goulden pen;
The honours that the Muses give, vnto the rarest men."

Sir Edward Dyer, who was knighted in 1596, was several times employed by his sovereign on embassies of importance, particularly to Denmark in 1589. The chancellorship of the order of the garter was conferred upon him, but like most of the courtiers he experienced some of Elizabeth's caprices. He partook of the credulity of the age, especially with respect to the power of chemistry to transmute the base into the noble metals. His death is said not to have taken place until 1610, but an extract from the burial register of St. Saviour's, Southwark, decides the point: "1607, May 11, Sr Edward Dyer, Knight, in the Chancel."

Gent. Magazine, 1850, pt. ii. p. 369.

His name as an English poet will never be forgotten while the beauty, force and simplicity are appreciated of the noble stanzas beginning

Notes and Queries, vol. ii. p. 335.

> "My mynde to me a kyngdome is,
> Such preasente joyes therein I fynde,
> That it excells all other blisse,
> That earth affordes or growes by kynde."

He was the author of certain pastoral odes and madrigals in "England's Helicon," and of other poems both printed and in manuscript. The *Athenæ Oxonienses* gives an account of these and of his life. See also *Gentleman's Magazine*, 1813, p. 525, and Chalmers's *Gen. Biog. Dict.* vol. xii. pp. 543, 534.

Bliss's Edition, vol. i, pp. 740-743.

EMBLEMS, pp. 134, 198.—*To* EDWARD PASTON *Esquier*. The family of the Pastons of Paston, in Norfolk, "is said by most historians to have come into England three years after the conquest," A.D. 1069. The name is of very frequent occurrence in Blomefield's voluminous *Norfolk*, in which there is a long account of the family. The Edward Paston whom Whitney celebrates appears to have been the grandson of sir William Paston, knt., of Oxnead in Norfolk, who was an eminent barrister and judge, and who, living to a great age, died in 1554. He had five sons, Erasmus, Henry, John, Clement and Thomas. Clement was a distinguished man under Henry, Edward, Mary and Elizabeth, and died February 18th 1599, appointing Edward Paston one of his executors. Thomas was knighted by king Henry VIII. in 1544 "at Bolleyne after the conquest of the towne," and he was father of sir Edward Paston who died in 1630. This Edward appears to have been the one whom Whitney distinguishes by devoting to him two of his emblems; and the conjecture is rendered very probable from the fact that Whitney held the office of under-steward in the town of Great Yarmouth, and consequently so become acquainted with the Norfolk Pastons.

Blomefield's Norfolk, vol. iii. p. 690.

Vol. iii. pp. 688-699.

Names and Arms of Knights.

Blomefield, vol. v. p. 788.

It was by this family, as is well known, that the celebrated "*Paston Letters*" were written;* and some brief information re-

* The doubts as to the authenticity of these letters have been entirely removed at a meeting of the Society of Antiquaries, recorded in *The Times*, and presided over by earl Stanhope. "The appearance of the originals of the fifth volume from custody beyond all suspicion virtually ended the controversy."

Dec. 1, 1865, p. 10.

specting their authors will reveal enough for us to know about the ancestors of Edward Paston. "The Paston Letters consist principally of the correspondence, from about 1440 to 1505, between the members and connexions of the respectable Norfolk family of that name, afterwards Earls of Yarmouth, of which the head, till his death in 1444, was Sir William Paston, Knight, one of the justices of the Common Pleas, and popularly called the 'Good Judge;' and afterwards, in succession, his eldest son, John Paston, Esq., who died in 1466; and the eldest and next eldest sons of the latter, Sir John Paston, a distinguished soldier, who died in 1479; and John Paston, Esq., also a military man, and eventually made a knight banneret by Henry VII., at the battle of Stoke in 1487, who survived till 1503." Pict. Hist. Eng. bk. v. ch. viii. p. 275.

EMBLEM, p. 136.—*To the very hon^ble^* CHARLES CALTHORPE, *Deputy of the Queen's Majesty in Ireland a gentleman in every way to be most highly respected by me.*

"Charles Calthorpe Esq., was a member of the Norfolk family of that name who had been seated at Calthorpe from the conquest. He was appointed steward of Yarmouth in 1573 and resigned in 1580, being employed by the Queen in Ireland." With Windham, Flowerdewe and Harbrowne he was, 31st May 1575, named on a commission to settle some disputes between Yarmouth and the Cinque Ports, and he was one of the company whom Whitney records as visiting Scratby island August 2nd 1580. Manship's Yarmouth, vol. i. p. 295. Plate XIII.

It is from sir William Calthorpe, knight, born in 1404 and dying in 1494, and from his four sons, that "several distinct branches are derived of this honourable and knyghtly family." Among the knights of Edward the Sixth's and of Elizabeth's creation were "Sir Philippe Calthorpe," and "Sir Willm Calthorpe;" there was also in 1589 a sir Martin Calthorpe, knight, lord-mayor of London. Gent. Magazine, 1839, pt. ii. p. 238.

Whitney's emblem is evidence of the high office which Charles Calthorpe held in Ireland under the queen; and sir John Perrot's *Government of Ireland*, a work published in 1624, records the same fact.* The name appears as the author of "*The Relation between a Lord of the Manor and the Copyholder his Tenant*" in

* The name however is not recorded in sir Peter Leycester's *Catalogue of the Chief Governors of Ireland*, p. 82.

1635, and is printed with Sir Edward Coke's *Copyholder* in 1650, but probably it is not the same person as the "Deputy of the Queen's Majesty in Ireland."

EMBLEM, p. 137.—*To* MILES CORBET *Esquier.*

From Henry III. 1247 to Elizabeth 1592 the office of sheriff of Shropshire was held by a Corbet on twenty occasions, and from the time of the conquest, when Roger Corbet held lands under the earl of Shrewsbury, their possessions descended to sir Andrew Corbet, bart., by twenty-three generations. It is far from unlikely that Miles Corbet was of the Shropshire family, and a schoolfellow of Whitney's at Audlem, just on the borders of Cheshire and Shropshire. Among the Corbets mentioned by Ormerod however there is not one bearing the name Miles; neither, as far as appears from Burke's *Extinct Baronetage*, is there among the Corbets of Stoke, of Moreton Corbet, or of Stoke and Adderley.

Phillip's Shrewsbury, pp. 239-244.

Hubert's Salop, p. 141.

Cheshire, vol. ii. p. 98; vol. iii. pp. 174-175.

The knightage under Henry VIII. furnishes "Sir Richard Corbett, 1523;" and under Edward VI. sir Andrew Corbet and sir Richard Corbet, 1547.

The heir of John Corbet of Sprowston, in Norfolk, living in the reign of Henry VII., was sir Miles Corbet, knight, and he left a son, sir Thomas Corbet, whose second son was Miles Corbet, of Lincoln's Inn, one of the registrars of chancery, but he lived at too recent a period to be Whitney's *Miles*, for he was one of the judges of the ill-fated Charles I., and suffered death as a regicide April 19th, 1662. He was of an ancient Norfolk family, as appears from Blomefield's *Norfolk*, vol. v. p. 1372.

Burke's Extinct Baronetage.

Notes and Queries, vol. xi. p. 423.

EMBLEM, p. 138.—*To* HVGHE CHOLMELEY *Esquier.*

Lysons' Cheshire, p. 364.

Historians tell us, "The Cholmondeleys and Egertons are descended from the same stock; Robert, ancestor of the Cholmondeleys, being a younger brother, and Philip, ancestor of the Egertons, a younger son of David, Baron of Malpas, who, in or about the reign of Henry III., took their family names from the places of their respective residences. Robert de Cholmondeley was the lineal ancestor of Sir Hugh Cholmondeley, Knight" (*i.e.* of Whitney's "HVGHE CHOLMELEY *Esquier*"), who died in 1601. From Hugh the third son of this sir Hugh the present marquis of Cholmondeley is descended, and from the fourth son, the lord Delamere of Vale Royal. Of the daughters, Mary, married sir George Calveley of Lea, knight; Lettice, sir Richard Grosvenor of Eaton, bart.; and Frances, Peter Venables, baron of Kinderton. Leycester's Historical Antiquities, p. 345.

The helmet which here enters into Whitney's emblem is doubly symbolical. It appears from "*Armes in Cheshire after the maner of the Alphabeth,*" that the squire's helmet, the badge of war, was borne generally by the warlike race of the Cholmondeleys, and was appropriated by the various families of that ancient house.* King's Vale Royal, p. 103.

Cheshire was not represented in the parliament of England until the year 1546, when Thomas Holcroft was elected. "Hvghe Cholmeley Esquier" was chosen to serve as one of the knights for the county, along with Thomas Egerton, then solicitor-general to the queen. This was in the year 1585, the year when Whitney presented his emblems to the earl of Leicester. His descendants since then have represented Cheshire in no less than twelve parliaments, and, with one short interval, the office of lord-lieutenant of the county was held from 1708 to 1783 by four earls of Cholmondeley in succession. Ormerod's Cheshire, vol. i. pp. 67-69.

Our Hugh Cholmondeley was born in 1552, and obtained his knighthood at the Spanish invasion in 1588. He was sheriff of Cheshire in 1589, and died in 1601. His wife was "*Mary,* Daughter and sole Heir of *Christopher Holford* of *Holford,*" near Ormerod's Cheshire, vol. ii. p. 78.

* The Italian version of *Alciat* gives the following stanzas: Edit. Lyons, 1551, p. 165.

CHE DALLA GUERRA PROCEDE LA PACE.

Ecco, chel' elmo, onde l' soldato armato
Spargendolo di sangue altrui feria,
Hora de l'Api è fatto albergo grato.
E dentro il mel si patorisce e cria.
Pongansi l'arme, fuor che alhor che giace
Morto il riposo, e non si gode pace.

The original Latin was, according to Wechel's edition, p. 49, Parisiis, 1534. Plate VI.

EX BELLO PAX.

En galea intrepidus quam miles gesserat, et quæ
Sæpius hostile sparsa cruore fuit.
Parta pace apibus tenuis concessit in usum,
Alueoli atque fauos grataq; mella gerit.
Arma procul iaceant, fas sit tunc sumere bellum,
Quandò aliter pacis non potes arte frui.

It may be noticed that the Italian version, as was to be expected, is closer to the original than the English.

Leycester's Hist. Antiq. p. 345.

Knutsford. "The Lady *Mary Cholmondley* survived her Husband, and lived at her Manor-House of *Holford*, which she builded new, repaired, and enlarged, and where she died about 1625, aged 63 Years, or thereabouts. King *James* termed her *The Bold Lady of Cheshire.*" Webb styles her "a Lady of great worth, dignity and revenue," and records that in the church of Malpas are memorials of the two sir Hughs and of the lady Mary, "erected of Alabaster, cut and richly adorned, according to the degrees and deserts of these worthy persons."

King's Vale Royal, vol. ii. pp. 85 and 54.

EMBLEM, p. 139.—*To* GEORGE MANWARINGE *Esquier.*

Plate XI.

Geffrey Whitney's sister Isabella, in 1573, addresses her **Sweet Nosgay** to this same **"worshipfull and right vertuous yong Gentylman;"** and after sundry disparagements to herself, in which she avers that she is "*like the pore man, which hauing no goods, came with his handsful of water to meete the Persian Prince withal;*" she concludes: "*I also haue good hope that you will accept this my labour for recompence of al that which you are unrecompenced for, as knoweth god: who I beseeche giue vnto you a longe and a lucky lyfe with encrease of all your vertuous studies.*" **"By your welwillyng Countriwoman"** IS. W.

Chart. Mainwaringianum.

In Dugdale's splendid Peover manuscript, under the date 23rd of Elizabeth, *i.e.* 1581, the names of "Sr Arth^r^ Maynwar. of Ightfield, knt.," and of "George Maÿwaringe Esq." his son and heir, occur in the same document. There too we find the record that he was knight of the shire for Salop in 1572, and that his wife was Anna, daughter of Edward Mare of Loseley. The wife was buried in the church of Ightfield in 1624, and the husband in 1628. According to Betham he had become sir George Manwaring, knt.; and his daughter Anna bore ten sons and ten daughters to John Corbet of Shropshire, who was created a baronet in 1627.

Vol. iv. p. 173.

Plate LVI.

This emblem has a remarkable history; it was adopted from 1515 to 1560, by Francis I. and Francis II., kings of France, as their device, teaching, "*duris in rebus fidem explorandam,*" That fidelity must be put to the proof in times of difficulty. It is, moreover, one of the emblems to which Shakespeare expressly refers, for he represents "the device" and "the word" of a certain knight as almost identical with those of Whitney; thus

Hierog. Regum Francorum I. pp. 87 and 88.

Pericles, vol. ii. p. 2.

Essay, p. 303.

"an hand environed with clouds,
Holding out gold that's by the touchstone tried,
The motto this, *Sic spectanda fides.*"

EMBLEM, p. 144.—*Homo homini lupus,* Man a wolf to man.

The motto is the same with that of Reusner, but the device altogether different. Plate XLIII.

EMBLEM, p. 152.—*To the very learned* W. MALIM.

In emblem p. 89 the initials W. M. probably belong to the same name.* From the Coopers of Cambridge we learn that William Malim was born in 1533 at Staplehurst in Kent, and that after having studied at Eton he was admitted a scholar of King's college in 1548, and a fellow in 1551. "During the time he held his fellowship he travelled into various countries of Europe and Asia. He himself states that he had seen Antioch, Constantinople, Jerusalem, and other eastern cities." In 1561 he was appointed master of Eton school and discharged the duties of it for ten years, and from 1573 to 1580 or 1581 he was head-master of St. Paul's school. His death occurred, it is said, about August 15th, 1594. Athen. Cantab. vol. ii. p. 175.

Respecting his works, of which a list is given in the *Athenæ Cantabrigienses,* it may be said that Ames marks the *Famagosta* as printed at Antwerp, and notes six Latin verses on sir Thomas Chaloner *de Republicâ Anglorum instaurandâ.* Typ. Antiq. pp. 653 and 1070.

EMBLEM, p. 159.—*The Grasshopper and the Ants.*

Freitag's beautiful illustration of *the opposite rewards of industry and sloth* may be compared with this; Whitney's ideas here have their source. Plate XL.

EMBLEM, p. 164.—ANGELO POLITIANO, quoted in the margin, was a native of Tuscany, born in 1454, a man of great learning, and for a time tutor to the children of Lorenzo de' Medici. He is the author of one "of the most celebrated Italian poems of the fifteenth century, the *Giostra of Giuliano de' Medici.* The character of his Latin poetry is thus given by

* The *Athenæ Cantab.* however assigns this emblem to William Master, LL.D., born 1532 and died 1589. Vol. ii. p. 65.

Roscoe, when speaking of the reputation acquired by the Florentines in the cultivation of that branch of Roman literature:—"Though some possess a considerable share of merit, not one of them can contend in point of poetical excellence with Politiano, who in his composition approaches nearer to the standard of the ancients than any man of his time." Of his character, erudition and misfortunes, a most interesting account is presented by the historian of Lorenzo de' Medici, and to that history we refer our readers. His death took place in 1494, in the fortieth year of his age. An edition of his works in folio was printed at Brixia, Brescia, M.CCCC.LXXXVI, and at Bâle, 8vo, 3 vols. 1550, folio 1553. Of course the Biographical Dictionaries do not omit to mention so eminent a scholar.

Life of Lorenzo de' M., Bohn's Edition, p. 266.

EMBLEM, p. 165.—*To* M. THOMAS MYNORS.

The name belongs both to Gloucestershire and Hertfordshire. Rudder, in his *Gloucestershire*, mentions a Gilbert de Myners about the end of the reign of king Stephen, and Henry de Myners of Westbury under king John purchasing a licence to enclose a park. Clutterbuck records how "Ralph Minors of Hertford, Gent., schoolmaster, gave to the Parish of All Saints £10, the interest to be yearly disposed of, half in the purchase of three pairs of white gloves for the Mayor, Justice of the Peace, and Minister of All Saints, if they come to the breaking up of the scholars of the said school at Christmas, and the other half to the best deserving scholars there."

Rudder's Glouc. pp. 315, 79 and 2

Hertfordshire, vol. i. p. 173.

Of Thomas Mynors however I have gleaned no certain information. One of the name, the Rev. Willoughby Mynors, M.A., curate of St. Leonard, Shoreditch, preached a seditious sermon June 10th 1716, and was committed to custody to answer for it, but whether of the same family no evidence is adduced to show.

Notes and Queries, Series ii. vol. iv. p. 108.

EMBLEM, p. 166.—*To my vncle* Geffrey Cartwrighte.

The conjecture has been made that Whitney's mother was of the family of Cartwright. It is a great puritan name, Thomas Cartwright, born in 1535, and dying in 1603, having borne it with high honour through much persecution. There appears however no real evidence to determine that Geffrey Cartwright was of this stock; it is most probable that he was of the same

Intr. Dissert. p. xlviii.

neighbourhood with the Whitneys, for Sheppenhall, in the township of Newhall, a few miles from Nantwich, was owned by the Cartwrights before the year 1600. In the registry of marriages at Acton church we find, 1662, "Inter Thomam Cartwright et Ann Roe Decembris 23." Sir Peter Leycester records, in 1666, among the landowners of *Sale*, "*Geffrey Cartwright* Gentleman. His lands in *Sale* were formerly bought from *Massy* of *Sale*." Ralph Churton supposes that Geffrey Cartwright belonged to "a branch of the Cartwrights of Aynho, Northamptonshire, some of whom were seated at Wrenbury (Bridges' *Northamptonshire*, vol. i. p. 137), and are recorded among the benefactors of the church." Whalley, in his *History and Antiquities of Northamptonshire*, gives the pedigree of Hugh Cartwright, from which it appears that of his descendants one was John Cartwright of Aston in Wrenbury, whose son Richard, that died in 1637 at the age of 74, married Mary, the daughter of sir John Egerton of Egerton, and was contemporary with, if not a relative of, Geffrey Whitney.

The Lysons, p. 399. Hist Antiq. p. 352. Life of Nowell. Vol. i. p. 137.

EMBLEM, p. 167. — *To Mr.* JOHN CROXTON.

The manor of Ravenscroft, a small township about one mile from Middlewich, passed by the marriage of Margery Ravenscroft with Roger Croxton to the Croxtons, and after five generations was vested with other lands in William Croxton, who died June 21st 1579. His son and heir, "John Croxton, of Ravenscroft, gent., who died April 24, 1599, leaving a son George fourteen years of age," was probably the friend to whom Whitney in 1586 devoted the emblem of a child in the cradle and of an infirm man on crutches. This John Croxton owned a third part of the manor of Bexton, near Knutsford, which he sold "to the lady *Mary Cholmondley* of *Holford;*" the Cholmondeleys sold their share, and the whole manor vested in the Daniel family, passed to the Duckenfields and Astleys. From John Astley, the painter, "it was purchased by dame Catherine Leicester, for her son sir J. F. Leicester bart.," and it is now the property of lord de Tabley.

Ormerod's Cheshire, vol. iii. pp 110 and 111. Sir P. Leycester, p. 222. Ormerod's Cheshire, vol. i. p. 390.

John Croxton's grandson Thomas was colonel Croxton, "a distinguished political and military character in Cheshire during the civil disturbances of the seventeenth century. He had for a time the office of governor of Chester castle on the part of the

Ormerod's Cheshire, vol. iii. p. 110.

parliament; and in 1650, when four regiments were raised in the county, he had the colonelcy of one of the regiments, composed of the men of Northwich hundred, and part of Nantwich. The castle of Chester was also under his care at the time of sir George Booth's attempt in 1659, and was summoned by sir George Booth and sir Thomas Middleton; to which the governor replied, 'That as perfidiousness in him was detestable, so the castle which he kept for the parliament of England was disputable; and if they would have it, they must fight for it; for the best blood that ran in his veins, in defence thereof, should be as a sluice to fill up the castle trenches.'" The consequence of Croxton's steadiness was the division of the forces of the insurgent royalists, which led to the defeat of Middleton at Prees heath, and of Booth at Winnington.

Colonel Croxton's wife was Elizabeth, daughter of Edward Holland of Denton, Lancashire.

EMBLEM, p. 168. — *To* M. MATTHEW PATTENSON.

I am informed that a notice of Matthew Pattenson will appear in the forthcoming volume, vol. iii. of the *Athenæ Cantabrigienses*, which is now in the printer's hands; and to that I refer the reader.

Did the distance of time between 1586 and 1623 allow we should suppose that Whitney's Pattenson was the author of

Tournay, 1623, 16mo. "*The Image of Bothe Chvrches, Hierusalem and Babel, vnitie and Confvsion, obedience and sedition;*" but it is by no means clear that the Pattensons of 1586 and of 1623 were the same person.

EMBLEM, p. 172.—*To the youth at the school of* AUDLEM *in England.*

AUDLEM, or as it was anciently written, Aldelime or Adelym, is a small market town, with a fine old church on the crest of a hill, about six miles from Nantwich on the line of railway from Nantwich to Market Drayton. The whole parish comprises an area of above 12,000 acres, bounded on the south by Shropshire, on the north by Acton, to the east by Wybunbury, and to the west by Wrenbury.

Plates XIa and XIIIa. Though Whitney's birth-place was in the parish of Acton, yet that homestead on the banks of the Weaver is nearly six miles from Acton church, and under two miles from Audlem church and school. We have in this fact the reason why his earliest instruction was obtained at Audlem; that town was near his home, and by pleasant Weaver's banks he would morning and evening pursue his way for the learning which in after life he used so well. Taking Whitney's home or Audlem's church of St. James as centres, there are spreading round them the various places with which the poet would be chiefly familiar,—Combermere, Woodhay, Shippenhall, Wrenbury, Nantwich, Acton, Wybunbury, and perchance Ightfield and Cholmondeley. Here dwelt his friends and relatives, or those whom his youth had been taught to hold in honour.

The present grammar school of Audlem was founded or rather endowed in 1655 by sir William Bolton and Mr. Gamull, citizens of London; but it is evident from this emblem that the school existed for at least a century before; and not unlikely is it from its central situation that here the schoolboy Geffrey Whitney formed acquaintance if not friendship with R. Cotton, G. Salmon, Hugh Cholmeley, George Manwaring, John Croxton, Arthur Starkey, and others of the country round. Ormerod's Cheshire, vol. iii. p. 248.

The venerable church of St. James, when Ralph Sandford was vicar, 1557-1582, doubtless often heard the tread of young Geffrey's feet; and there rests one, a scholar of the same school, whose gravestone records as "the Modest Charitable and Dutifull Daniel Evans, Son to Mr. Evans School Master. He departed aged 14. 1712. God's Will be done." The father's grave is close by, and were it but to show that men of worth and learning have presided over the school where Whitney was trained, we add his epitaph, in Latin, as becomes a scholar's fame:

"GULIELMUS EVANS A.M. eruditus Theologus
Ecclesiæ de *Barthomley* per sex Annos
Pastor fidus et sedulus
Scholæ prius *Audlemensis* per Annos xxxv.
Moderator Præstantissimus
Mira in illo emicuit Urbanitas, Comitas, Lepos
Vultus tamen Hilantatem, vitæ Severitate,
Colloquiorum Facetias, morum Simplicitate
Temperavit
{Pauperum Fautor, Divitum monitor
Optimis charus, Pessimis venerabilis}
Animam, puram, probam, piam
Deo reddidit, Aprilis xv
Anno Sal[tis] M.DCCXXXIX. Æ[tis] LXXIII."

Sir P. Leycester, p. 371: Ormerod, vol. iii. pp. 246-248.

The Masseys, who held Tatton, near Knutsford, from the reign of Henry III. to 1475, possessed lands in Audlem down to 1457, when "Sir *Geffrey Massy* of *Tatton*, Knight," settled his lands in Audlem and Denfield on his illegitimate son John Massy, with whose descendants they remained until 1666 or later. Hugh Massey, the fifth in a direct line from John, married Elizabeth, sister of Hugh Whitney of Cool-lane in Wrenbury, near Audlem, and she in all probability was one of the same family with Geffrey Whitney. This Hugh Massey died in 1646, and was buried at Audlem.

EMBLEM, p. 173.—*To the very learned* STEPHAN LIMBERT *Master of the School at Norwich.*

Ormerod, vol. iii. p. 230.

On the supposition that "*Nordovicensis*" was Northwich in Cheshire it has been conjectured that Limbert had been Whitney's tutor, first at Audlem and next at Northwich, before the poet went to Oxford. The Latin name means Norwich in Norfolk, and through the courtesy of the Rev. Augustus Jessopp, head master of king Edward VI. school in that city, I have been informed that for thirty-two years, from 1570 to 1602, Stephen Limbert was master of that school. As to dates this account differs very materially from the epitaph which Blomefield and the Coopers give, namely, thirty-five years of service, and dying in 1589. But thirty-five years make the service commence in 1554, some years before his matriculation at Cambridge as a sizar of Magdalen college. We stay not to reconcile the dates; certain it is he was head master of Norwich school, and on one of Elizabeth's progresses, in August 1578, made an oration in Latin "to the most illustrious Princess Elizabeth, Queen of England, France and Ireland." Little is known of his success as a teacher, but "a grateful and eminent pupil," Robert de Naunton, "many years afterwards" set up a memorial of one whom he names "an excellent Master and a most beloved Preceptor," and averred that he died "full of Dayes and of Comfort in the Multitude and Proficiency of his Scholars."

Blomefield's Norfolk, vol. ii. p. 531. Athen. Cantab. vol. ii. p. 61.

His power of writing Latin verses may be judged of by the ten elegiac lines which are prefixed to Whitney's emblems, and of which the translation in the Introductory Dissertation is a free approximation.

Intr. Dissert. ch. ii. sect i. p. xxx.

EMBLEM, p. 175.—"*Otiose semper egentes,*" The idle ever destitute.

A very fine amplification of a similar subject in "*Le Théâtre des bons Engins.*" Whitney's power and genius will appear by comparing together the simple beauty of the French verses with the no less simple and beautiful lines of the English, in which the thoughts are carried out, rounded and polished without losing anything of natural grace. In the French the reader may notice the contrivance for indicating *e* silent.

Plate XXXI.

EMBLEM, p. 176.—"*Semper præsto esse infortunia,*" Ill luck is always at hand.

The subject treated of by Whitney is undoubtedly the same with that of Brant, namely, the gamblers, the difference being that the Englishman speaks of "three carelesse dames," the German, in his French translation, folio 50, of four. It is merely as suggestive to Whitney of his subject that Brant's emblem is adduced; the devices agree, but not the methods of illustration.

Plate XXIX.

The woodcut of the gamblers is at folio 85 of the **Stultifera Nauis,** but at folio 50 of "**La grāt nef des folz du mōde.**"

EMBLEM, p. 177.—*To my countrimen of the* Namptwiche *in Chesshire.*

Ch. ii. sect. ii. pp. 41 and 43.

As we have seen in the Introductory Dissertation, it was in the parish of Acton, by which Nantwich is nearly surrounded, that Whitney was born, yet "the Namptwiche" is a term which comprehends the district round, and the people truly were the poet's "countrimen."

The Register of the Church.

The fearful calamity with which the town was visited is thus described by an eye-witness. On the 10th of December 1583, "chaunced a most terrible and vehement fyre, beginninge at the Water-lode, aboute six of the clock at nighte, in a kitchen, by brewinge. The wynde being very boysterouse, increased the said fyre, whiche verie vehementlie burned and consumed in the space of fifteen houres six hundred bayes of buyldinges and could not be stayed neither by laboure nor pollice, which I thoughte good to commende unto the posteritie as a favoureable punishment of the Almightie in destroying the buildings and goodes onlie, but sparinge the lyves of manye people, which, consideringe the tyme, space, and perill, were in great jopardie, yet by God's mercie, but onlie two persones that perished by fyre."

One who not long after the fire in sober prose described "the newe NAMPWICHE," scarcely departed from Whitney's fond eulogium,

"A spectacle for anie man's desire."

King's Vale Royal, pt. ii. p. 68.

That writer says: "The Buildings within the same Town are very fair and neat, and every street adorned with some speciall mansions of Gentlemen of good worth, the middle and the principal parts of the Town being all new buildings, by reason of a lamentable fire which happened there in *Anno* 1583, that consumed in one night all the dwellings from the River side, to the other side of the Church, which Church it self by the great mercy of God escaped, and was left standing naked without neighbours, saving onely the school-house, in a few hours; yet such were the estates of many the Inhabitants, and so graciously did Queen *Elizabeth* of blessed memory favour them, with her own earnest farthering of a Collection through the whole Kingdom, and the businesse so well managed by the care and industry of Sir *Hugh Cholmly*, Mr. *John Masterton*, and other chief agents in the same, that the whole scite and frame of the Town so suddenly ruined, was with great speed re-edified in that beautifull manner that now it is."

Our author adds: "The Church is very large, and of so beautifull a structure composed in form of a crosse, like the great Minsters or Cathedrals, and the Steeple erected in the middle Juncture of the Crosse, with fair Iles on each side." Plates XV. and XV*a*.

To all its original beauty that fair church has lately been restored by the munificence and zealous love of many hearts, the widow's mite vying with the rich man's offering; and to all who have contributed to this worthy work there cannot be a better thought, that the veneration and regard of the present day have re-established and renewed the temple which the piety of a past age had founded. The poet's words are again fulfilled:

> "an other Phœnix rare
> With speede dothe rise most beautifull and faire."

That fable of the phœnix indeed is one with which all ages and many nations have been familiar. Herodotus, Pliny, Horapollo, among the ancients; Gabriel Symeoni, Claude Paradin, Arnold Freitag, Reusner, and Whitney, with some others among the emblematists, serve to swell the wonder and the praise. We are told, "in honour of Queen Jane, who died willingly to save her child, Edward VI., a phœnix was represented on a funeral fire, with this motto, NASCATUR UT ALTER, *That another may be born*." As the phœnix is always alone, and the only bird of its kind in the world, so are excellent things that are of marvellous rarity; hence it was somewhat proudly borne as the device of Madame Elenor of Austria, queen dowager of France. Also, "My Lady Bona of Savoy, the mother of John Galeaz, Duke of Milan, in her widowed state, took the phœnix for her emblem, with the words,* 'being made lonely I follow God alone.'" The Plate XXXIX., Freitag. Gent. Magazine, 1819, pt. ii.

* The original text, as given in Symeoni's *Devises ov Emblemes Heroiqves et morales*, *à Lyon* 1561, *p.* 238, is: "*Madame Bone de Sauoye mere de Iean Galeaz, Duc de Milan, se trouuant vefue, feit faire vne deuise en ses Testons d'vne Fenix au milieu d'vn feu auec ces paroles:* SOLA FACTA SOLVM DEVM SEQVOR. *Voulant signifier que comme il n'y a au monde qu'vne Fenix, tout ainsi estant demeuree seulette, ne vouloit aymer sinô le seul Dieu, pour viure en apres eternellement.*" Plate LXII.

phœnix too is typical of long duration for the soul, and of the resurrection of Christ and of all mankind.*

The Lay of the Phœnix, translated by G. Stephens, 1844.

An Anglo-Saxon poem of the eleventh century embodies both the legends and the applications of this ancient fable. After describing the process by which

"As from round eggs he
Eagerly crept him
Sheer from the shell,"

the author goes on to narrate the final production of the marvellous creature:

As in Plate XXXIX.

"Soon then thereafter,
With feathers rich fretted,
He soars as at first—all
Blooming and brightsome,
Bird waxing quickly
Fresh as to-fore, and
Fitly in all things
Sunder'd from sin."

It is then nothing wonderful that, on hearing of the town of his "countrimen" rising from its ashes to a glory it had never before attained, Whitney should assume as its device,

"The Phœnix rare, with fethers freshe of hewe."

EMBLEM, p. 183.—*The inverted torch.*

This device is found in Symeoni and Giovio's *Tetrastichi Morali*, and also in Paradin's *Devises Héroïques*, but the plate in illustration is from the English translation of Paradin, published in 1591, which curiously enough differs from the original as well as from Whitney, in presenting the torch nearly upright instead of inverted. The invention of the device is thus accounted for: "In the exile or banishment of the Helvetians neer Millan, after the decease of Francis their king, the Lord of Saint Valier, the father of the Ladie Diana of Poitiers Dutchesse of Valentinois, and gouernour ouer an hundreth noble knights carried a standard about, wherein was pictured a burning Torch turned vpside downe, the waxe melting and quenching the same with this sentence, *Qui me alit me extinguit*, that is, He that feedeth me, killeth me. Which simbole was framed for a certain noble woman's sake,

Plate LVII

Heroicall Devises, London, 1591, pp. 357 and 358.

Plate LXI.

* So in the device on the title-page of Giovio's *Dialogo*, printed by *Giolito* at Venice in 1556, the phœnix appears rising above the world; the mottoes being "SEMPER EADEM," *Always the same*, and "DE LA MIA MORTE ETERNA VITA," *From my death I live eternal life.*

willing to insinuate thereby that as her beautie and comelines did please his minde, so might it cast him into danger of his life."

On pages 301, 302 and 311 of the *Essays Literary and Bibliographical* the subject of the inverted torch and its motto is treated of; and we now refer to Symeoni's text to show that Daniell is far from accurate in the information he professes to give as to the origin of the device; and that Paradin omits the not unimportant fact that Saint Valier's motto was but an imitation of that of the king his master,—"NVTRISCO ET EXTINGVO." Plates LXII. and LXIII.

EMBLEM, p. 183.—*Engraving wrongs on marble.*

Whitney's device is *identical* with that of Paradin's, but may be compared with the similar *Impresa* in the *Tetrastichi Morali*, or rather in the *Devises Héroïqves et Morales*, from which Paradin copied, without however taking the highly ornamented border. The Italian stanza is to the following effect: Plates XXXVII. and LXII.

> "Each one that lives may be swift passion's slave,
> And through a powerful will at times delight
> In causing others harm and terrors fright:
> The injured doth those wrongs in marble grave."

If comment be required we may resort to Symeon's *Emblemes Héroïqves et Morales*, p. 230, "Povr vn homme inivstement offense." Plate LXII.

EMBLEMS, pp. 185, 186.—*To the very learned* STEPHEN BULL.

A name the echoes of which have sounded through the chief libraries of Holland and Belgium without obtaining any reply. St. or Stephen Bull seems to have been one that has left no mark on Whitney's century. The name however is not unknown to history. On the expedition into France in April 1513 it is mentioned that the admiral Howard, among other persons of note, was accompanied by sir *Stephen Bull.* And of Flodden field, September 9th 1513, it is recorded: "In this Battle the Vanguard was led by the Lord Thomas Howard, who had with him," along with several lords and knights who are named, "Sir *Stephen Bull.*" Whitney's Stephen Bull may have been this knight's son or grandson. In Elizabeth's reign there were also Bulls in Hertfordshire, for Clutterbuck registers among the bailiffs of Hertford "In 1578 Richard Bull, Gent." Tindal's Rapin, Edit. 1743, vol. i. p. 721 Hertford, vol. ii. p. 147.

If we might resort to the last refuge of a discomfited critic, we would suggest a misprint. In conformity with the subject of the second emblem devoted to this learned man, namely, *the Music of Orpheus*, he should be one who was skilful, learned and wise, and

"if his musicke faile, his curtesie is suche
That none so rude, and base of minde, but hee reclaimes them muche."

Now there was an Englishman of Whitney's century, one JOHN BULL, in whom these qualities were united, and to whom there was great propriety in dedicating as well the Quinctilian emblem as that which celebrates the praise of Orpheus. He was a native of Somersetshire,* born about the year 1565, and in 1586 admitted bachelor of music at Oxford, and doctor at Cambridge. He possessed remarkable skill and power, and filled the offices of organist in the Queen's chapel and professor of music in Gresham college. He died in the year 1615. The memoir of him may be consulted in Chalmers.

Biog Dict. vol. ii. pp. 271 and 273.

EMBLEM, p. 189.—*To the very learned* FRANCIS RAPHELENG, *famous at the siege of Antwerp.*

Essay iii. p. 269.

A notice of Rapheleng has been given in connection with Plantin in a former part of this work. We shall therefore simply confirm the truth of Whitney's testimony to the internal treachery in Antwerp, at the famous siege of 1585, by an extract from Schiller's history, "Die Regierung dieser Stadt war in allzuviele Hände vortheilt, und der stürmischen Menge ein viel zu grossen Antheil daran gegeben, als dasz man mit Ruhe hätte überlegen mit Einsiecht wählen und mit Festigkeit ausführen können." "The government of this town was shared among too many hands, and too strongly influenced by a disorderly populace to allow any one to consider with calmness, to decide with judgment, or to execute with fairness." As we have observed Plantin retired to Leyden during the siege of Antwerp, but Rapheleng remained, and won at least the admiration of Whitney by his conduct.

Werke, Band viii pp. 426-427.

* George Bull, bishop of St. David's, born March 25th 1634, and so celebrated in the controversy on the Trinity, was also a native of the same county. "He was," says Fosbrooke, "descended from an ancient and genteel family, seated at Shapwich."

Fosbrooke's Gloucester, p. 229.

EMBLEM, p. 191.—*To my Nephew*, RO. BORRON.

The Introductory Dissertation shows that Ro. Borron was one of the "prety Boyes" of Whitney's sister Ann. The name belongs to Cheshire, but is not met with in the county histories. Ch. ii. Sect. ii. p. xlvii.

EMBLEM, p. 193.—*To the honorable Gentleman Sir* WILLIAM RVSSELL *Knight*.

Sir William Russell, from whom the dukes of Bedford are descended, was the fourth son of Francis Russell, the first earl of Bedford, whom Henry VIII. favoured, and Mary sent ambassador to Spain to conduct king Philip to England. He was educated with his brothers at Magdalen college Oxford, "at the feet," it is said, "of that excellent divine Dr. Humphreys." From travels through France, Germany, Hungary and Italy he returned, "not merely accomplished in languages and improved in his address and range of knowledge, but uninjured by the affectation of foreign fashions, and uncorrupted in his moral and religious principles." His first campaign was served with reputation in the Netherlands, where he obtained the honour of knighthood. In 1583 he married Elizabeth, the daughter and heiress of sir Henry Long of Cambridgeshire. Wiffen's House of Russell, vol. i. p. 506.

Again in the Netherlands he served under Leicester, and a letter from the captain-general to Walsingham thus testifies to his character: "This gentleman is worthy to be cherished, for he is a rare man of courage and government: it were pitty but he should be encouraged in this service, where he is like to learne that knowledge which three yeres perhaps in other places wold not yeld to him. In few words, there canot be to much good said of him." Leicester Correspondence, p. 225.

He was afterwards, in 1594, lord-deputy of Ireland. In 1602, a few months only before her death, he was visited by queen Elizabeth at Chiswick; and on the 21st July 1603 he was created by James I. baron Russell of Thornhaugh. He died in 1613, soon after prince Henry. There is a portrait of him at Woburn abbey. His brother Edward, earl of Bedford, was succeeded in his style and honours by Francis, "the only son of the heroic William, baron of Thornhaugh," and Francis was the father of lord William Russell, beheaded in 1683. Leycester's Hist. Ant. p. 82. Wiffen's House of Russell, vol. ii. pp. 73, 93 and 124.

Thomas Newton, a Cheshire poet, contemporary with Whitney, inscribed in 1589 one of his ENCOMIA of illustrious English- Leland's Antiquarii, vol. v. p. 174. men "to the very valiant and magnificent knight, William Russell." He speaks of his talent, his comeliness, eloquence, industry, bravery and warlike prowess, and concludes with the exhortation, in Latin not altogether classical,

> "Opergas rutilam Bedfordis addere lucem
> Francisci patris facta imitando tui;"

"Add to Bedford's red golden light, by imitating the deeds of Francis thy father."

EMBLEM, p. 194—*To the honorable Sir* JOHN NORRIS *Knight, Lord president of Munster in Irelande, and Colonell Generall of the English infanterie, in the lowe countries.*

Briefly are his character and services sketched by the editor of London, 1845, p. 169. *Sidney and Languet's Correspondence:* "Sir John Norris, second son of Henry, first lord Norris, an excellent soldier, who had served under Coligny in France and Essex in Ireland. He was continually employed on foreign service, and was Commander in Chief of the English forces sent afterwards to relieve Antwerp, and still later of the troops sent by Elizabeth to assist Henry IV. in Bretagne."

So brave a leader deserves for himself as well as his ancestry more than this passing notice. He was descended from that Henry Norris, groom of the bedchamber, present at the private marriage of Henry VIII. with Anne Boleyn. The absurd jealousy of the king charged him and four others with familiarities with the queen; but when pardon was offered on condition of confessing to the supposed truth of the charge, he answered with Pict. Hist Eng. vol. iii. p. 392. utmost honour of mind, "and as it became the progenitor of so many valiant heroes, that in his conscience he thought her guiltless of the objected crime, and that he had rather undergo a thousand deaths than betray the innocent." *

Worthies of Eng. vol. iii. pp 17 and 18. The portrait of sir John Norris is at Knole, and his character is painted by Fuller with great truth and fervour: "He was a most accomplished general, both for a charge, which is the sword, and a retreat, which is the shield, of war. By the latter he purchased to himself immortal praise, when in France he brought off

* From so honourable a stock is descended the earl of Abington.

a small handful of English from a great armful of enemies; fighting, as he retreated, and retreating as he fought; so that always his rear affronted the enemy; a retreat worth ten victories got by surprise, which speak rather the fortune than either the valour or discretion of a general.

"He was afterwards sent over with a great command into Ireland, where his success neither answered his own care, nor others' expectations. Indeed hitherto Sir John had fought with right-handed enemies in France and the Netherlands; who was now to fight with left-handed foes, for so may the wild Irish well be termed (so that this great master of defence was now to seek a new guard), who could lie on the coldest earth, swim through the deepest water, run over what was neither earth nor water, I mean bogs and marshes. He found it far harder to find out than to fight his enemies, they so secured themselves in fastnesses. Supplies, sown thick in promises, came up thin in performances, so slowly were succours sent to him.

"At last a great lord was made lieutenant of Ireland, of an opposite party to Sir John; there being animosities in the court of queen Elizabeth (as well as of later princes), though her general good success rendered them the less to the public notice of posterity. It grieved Sir John to the heart, to see one of an opposite faction should be brought over his head, insomuch that some conceive his working soul broke the cask of his body, as wanting a vent for his grief and anger; for, going up into his chamber, at the first hearing of the news, he suddenly died, anno Domini 1597."

So burst the mighty heart that could not brook undeserved disfavour from his queen.

A writer of that day, on "The Gouernment of Ireland vnder the Honorable Ivst and wise Gouernour Sir John Perrot Knight &c. beginning 1584 and ending 1588," speaks of "Generall *Norreys* Lord President of *Mounster* &c." as "braue hearted Norreys," "neuer enough praysed Norreys;" and thus is Spenser's eulogium justified:

London, sm. 4to, 1626, pp. 19 and 22.

Moxon's Edition, p. 7.

"*To the Right Noble Lord and most valiaunt Captaine* Sir JOHN NORRIS, *Knight, Lord President of Mounster.*

Who ever gave more honourable prize
To the sweet Muse then did the Martiall crew,

That their brave deeds she might immortalize
In her shril tromp, and sound their praises dew!
Who then ought more to favour her then you,
Most Noble Lord, the honor of this age,
And Precedent of all that armes ensue!
Whose warlike prowesse and manly courâge,
Tempred with reason and advizement sage,
Hath fild sad Belgicke with victorious spoile;
In Fraunce and Ireland left a famous gage;
And lately shakt the Lusitanian soile.
Sith then each where thou hast dispre̊dd thy fame,
Love him that hath eternized your Name."

Vol. ii. pp 180 and 193.

Some letters from sir John Norris are printed in Wright's *Queen Elizabeth and her Times.*

EMBLEM, p. 199.—*To* THOMAS WILBRAHAM *Esquier.*

History of Cheshire, vol. iii. p. 196.

"Sir Richard Wilburgham, or Wilbraham," says Ormerod, "the earliest known ancestor of the family, is supposed to have derived his name from the manor of Wilbraham in Cambridgeshire, where a family, bearing the local name, was settled about the time of Henry II."

King's Vale Royal, p. 57.

Thomas Wilbraham, or Wilbram, of Woodhey, near Nantwich, was sheriff of Cheshire in 1585, the year of the dedication of Whitney's emblems. He ranked third in the list of the gentry of his hundred, and appears well to have deserved the respect universally accorded to him by his contemporaries. William Webbe, who knew him intimately, pays a warm tribute to his worth in the *Itinerary of the Hundred of Namptwiche:*

King's Vale Royal, p. 73.

"And so we come to *Faddiley*, another member, or rather entire Lordship of it self, divided between the houses of *Peever* and *Handford;* and hereunto lyeth adjoyning the Demain and Hall of *Woodhey*, which as it was the first place where my feet had some rest after the variable courses of my youth, so I could here long dwell upon the remembrances of that ever worthy honoured owner of it, and of me his most unworthy servant, *Thomas Wilbraham* Esquire, if even here my Ink were not forced to give place to the tears that fall from my eyes. But what need I think upon the commending of him, the world takes knowledge of his worth. The God whom he served is the God of his Seed, the blessing of Heaven is upon his house, and so I hope and pray it may long continue."

Need we wonder, since Geffrey Whitney was born in the same parish of Acton in which Woodhey is situated, that he should make its owner the model of the English gentleman,

"Whose daily study is, your country to adorne,
And for to keepe a worthie house, in place where you weare borne."

But alas! of that Cheshire-renowned Woodhey, except the extensive stabling, and the garden wall and the façade of the chapel, not a brick remains. The entire structure has been cast down and removed. The green sward, in this very spring of 1865 as beautiful as the rich-hued emerald, alone is spread over the foundations of hall and bower; yet still out of that green sward springs the remembrance of one,

"Whose gate, was open to his frende: and purce, vnto the poor." *

And at the distance of about two centuries another of our great Cheshire writers speaks almost as lovingly as did Whitney and Webb, the one of his neighbour, the other of his "old master:" "The memory of private worth seldom survives the contemporaries of its possessors, but this is not the case with the Wilbrahams of Woodhey. Wherever it is possible to glance beyond genealogical deductions, and obtain a knowledge of the individual representatives of the family, they appear to have been graced with every social virtue that could render rank endearing to their equals, and venerated by their dependants, and their family is rarely noticed in the Cheshire collections, without evident expressions of respect and affection." Ormerod, vol. iii. p. 198.

Thomas Wilbraham's first wife was Frances, daughter of one sir Hugh Cholmondeley, and sister of the other. His second wife was Mary, eldest daughter and coheiress of Peter Warburton esq. of Arley, Cheshire. From the first marriage were born his heir sir Richard Wilbraham of Woodhey bart., and among other daughters Dorothy, who was married to sir John Done of

* In the spirit of the roundel of Elizabeth's time—

"Content thy selfe withe thyne estat,
And sende no poore wight from thy gate:
For why this councell I the giue,
To learne to dye, and dye to lyue."

Journey from Chester to London. Utkinton knt., and of whom, according to Pennant, "when a Cheshire man would express excellency in the fair sex, he will say, 'there is a lady Done for you.'"

Ormerod's Cheshire, vol. ii. p. 136; vol. iii. pp. 196-199. Thomas Wilbraham died in 1610 at his seat of Tilston Fearnall, in Edisbury hundred, and his numerous estates descended in his family in a direct line until, in 1692, a coheiress conveyed them to her husband, Lionel Tollemache earl of Dysart, in whose family they still remain, the present owner being John Tollemache esq. of Peckforton castle.

Gent. Magazine, 1821, p. i. pp. 275 279. Like the name Mainwaring, this name Tollemache sets all rules of orthography at defiance. It is Talmash, Tollmash, Tallemache, Tollemache, and in the Domesday book Toedmag. The family possessed lands at Bentley in Suffolk long before the Norman conquest, and there, until very lately, was to be seen in the old manor house the following inscription:

"When William the Conqueror reign'd with great fame
Bentley was my seat and Tollemache was my name."

For the ramifications of the Wilbrahams of Cheshire and Lancashire, *i.e.* of Wilbrahams of Woodhey, of Townend, of Dorfold, of Delamere, of Rode and of Latham, where they bear the title of the lords Skelmersdale, see *The Lysons*, p. 369, and *Ormerod* in various places. George Fortescue Wilbraham esq. of Delamere house is the present head of the *gens* Wilbraham.

EMBLEM, p. 200.—*To* RICHARD COTTON *Esquier.*

For the account of the Cotton family refer back to p. 333. The device of the bee-hive is traceable to Horapollo or to Alciatus, from the latter of whom we present the emblem as given in the edition of 1551. Combermere is mentioned in Whitney's stanzas, and is represented in its old form in one of the illustrations.

Plate LVIII.

Plate XIV.

EMBLEM, p. 203.—*To* RICHARD DRAKE *Esquier, in praise of Sir* FRANCIS DRAKE *Knight.*

A manuscript note to Mr. Swinnerton's copy of Whitney's emblems supplies the following information: "This is the Crest of the Drake's family, viz.: a Ship under reeff drawn round a Globe with a Cable Rope by an hand out of the Clouds. It shou'd have this motto over it, *Auxilio divino,* & under it, *Sic*

See Collins's Baronetage, vol. i. p. 533.

parvis magna." Also, "Sir F. Drake after his great voyage took for his device the Globe of the world with this motto, *Tu primus circumdedisti me.* But not excluding his former motto, '*Divino Auxilio.*'" Prince's Worthies of Devon, p. 240 and 245.

This voyage round the world was accomplished between the 15th of November 1577, when Plymouth was left, and the 26th of September 1580, when Plymouth harbour again was entered. An account of the voyage was published by the nephew of the circumnavigator, with the significant title, "THE WORLD ENCOMPASSED," and doubtless gave origin to Whitney's device and stanzas. The preface declares that the work itself was compiled "out of the notes of Master Francis Fletcher, Preacher in this employment, and divers others his fellows in the same: Offered now, at last, to publique view, both for the honour of the actor, but especially for the stirring up of heroick spirits to benefit their countrie and eternize their names by like noble attempts."

Whitney's stanzas and some of the sentiments and expressions in "*The World Encompassed*" are in close accord. Thus the narrator of the voyage declares: "We safely, with joyful minds and thankful hearts to God, arrived at Plimouth, the place of our first setting forth, after we had spent two years ten months and some odd days besides, in seeing the wonders of the Lord in the deep, in discerning so many admirable things, in going through with so many strange adventures, in escaping out of so many dangers, and overcoming so many difficulties in this our encompassing of this nether globe, and passing round about the world which we have related."

"To the sole worker of great things,
To the sole governor of the whole world,
To the sole preserver of his saints,
To God alone be ever glory."

The Richard Drake named by Whitney was a cousin of sir Francis the navigator, being the brother of sir Bernard Drake, who was knighted in 1585. Richard was born in 1534, and was equery to queen Elizabeth. The Cheshire Drakes of Malpas and Shardeloes "are descended from Richard Drake of Esher in Surrey, a younger son of the ancient family of Drake of Ash in Devonshire." Emblems, p. 203. Ormerod's Cheshire, vol ii. p. 382.

Prince's Worthies of Devon, Ed. 1701, p. 245.

There is an anecdote of sir Bernard and sir Francis Drake, which may find a not inappropriate place in connection with Whitney's adoption of the circumnavigator's badge and device. Sir Bernard's crest was a naked arm grasping a sword, which sir Francis had unduly assumed. A quarrel on the subject arose between them, and was carried to such a height that sir Bernard boxed the ears of sir Francis within the verge itself of the royal court. "The displeasure of the queen was shown in a grant of a crest to Sir Francis, wherein the coat of the Ash family was suspended inverted in the rigging of a ship." "Unto all which sir Bernard coolly replied, that though her majesty could give a nobler, yet she could not give him an ancienter coat than his." The coat in question is a dragon, or as it called in heraldry a *wyvern*, which with the battle axe is also borne by the Drakes of Malpas in Cheshire. The family name therefore is not from *drake*, a male bird, but from *draco*, a dragon. The contrary supposition however is made in the epigram, written in 1581, on occasion of queen Elizabeth going on board "the Golden Hind," at Deptford, and there knighting the now famous captain:

> "O Nature, to old England still
> Continue these mistakes,
> Give us for all our *Kings* such Queens,
> And for our *Dux* such Drakes."

Hayman (*Epigrams*, published in 1628) takes the other derivation and avers,

> "Drake like a dragon through the world did flie,
> And every coast thereof he did descrie;
> Should envious men be dumbe the spheres will shew,
> And the two poles, his journey which they saw,
> Beyond Cades pillars far he steered his way,
> Great *Hercules* ashore, but *Drake* by sea."

Of course Drake's glories were in his own time sung in Latin as well as in English. Our Cheshire poet, Thomas Newton, in 1589, published *sixty-one* Latin verses addressed to John Ælmer, bishop of London, "concerning the return of the magnanimous knight Francis Drake after his three years' voyage;" and H. Holland has some elegiacs to his memory. Camden's *Annals* and Stowe's *Chronicle* give accounts of his exploits: "RICHARD

Herωologia Anglica, p. 110. London, 3 vols. 4to, 1599 and 1600.

HAKLVYT *Preacher, and sometime* student of Christ-Church, Oxford," in his "PRINCIPAL NAVIGATIONS, VOYAGES, TRAFFIQVES AND DISCOVERIES of the *English Nation*," records for us "The famous voyage of Sir *Francis Drake* into the South Sea, and therehence about the whole Globe of the earth, begun in the yeere of our Lord, 1577." Thomas Fuller in his "*Holy State*" wrote his life at large; Dr. Johnson compiled that life for the *Gentleman's Magazine;* and passing by other lives of the circumnavigator, it will be sufficient to refer to the long biography in Betham's *Baronetage*, and to "*The Life, Voyages and Exploits of Admiral Sir Francis Drake, Knt. &c.*, by John Barrow Esq." London, Murray, 1843.

Vol. iii. pp. 730-742.

Gent. Magazine, vol. x. and xi.

Vol. i. p. 260.

Portraits of the admiral exist at Knole, the seat of earl Amherst, and at Knowsley, the equally well-known seat of the earl of Derby. Among the "penny sights and exhibitions in the reign of James I." was the good ship "The Golden Hind," in which the encompassing of the world was performed, and which for a long time was preserved at Deptford as an object of admiration. A portion of this ship was made into a chair for the Bodleian library, to which in 1662 Cowley attached some verses, and a friend, George E. Thorley esq. of Wadham college, informs me the heart of oak is still in its sanctuary, "with Cowley's stanzas attached, but the metal plate* on which the stanzas are engraved is worn almost smooth by age." The astrolabe which Drake used came into the possession of Bigsby, the author of

Letter, May 23, 1865.

* Cowley's verses in fact are undecipherable, but were engraved "in an old-fashioned sort of italic hand, with a good many flourishes and capital letters." They are thus given in a *Life of Drake:*

"To this great Ship which round the Globe has run,
And match'd in race the chariot of the Sun;
This Pythagorean Ship (for it may claim
Without presumption, so deserv'd a name)
By knowledge once, and transformation now,
In her new shape this sacred port allow.
Drake and his Ship could not have wish'd from Fate
An happier station, or more blest estate;
For, lo! a seat of endless rest is given,
To her in Oxford, and to him in Heaven."

ABRAHAM COWLEY, 1662.

Sent to the University of Oxford
by order of John Davis Esq[r] the King's Commissioner at Deptford."

"*The Triumph of Drake,*" and the walking cane, "a bamboo, discoloured by time, 2 feet 10 inches long, with an ivory head and a hole in it," remained in the possession of Drake's family from 1581 to 1821, or 240 years, and was then given to Captain William Henry Smith, R.N.

Penny Cyclopædia.

Sir Francis Drake, the eldest of twelve sons of a poor yeoman, was born on the banks of the Tavy in Devonshire in 1545, and died at sea in 1595. His body was buried in the ocean, and one of his contemporaries wrote of the funeral the rough expressive lines:

"The waves became his winding sheet
The waters were his tomb;
But for his fame the ocean sea
Was not sufficient room."

EMBLEM, p. 204.—*To* ARTHVRE BOVRCHIER *Esquier.*

This was the author of the commendatory verses "*To the Reader*" prefixed to the emblems, and ending with the lines:

"*Giue* WHITNEY *then thy good report, since hee deserues the same:*
Lest that the wise that see thee coye, thy follie iustly blame."

But it is uncertain to what family he belonged. The name was one of renown, for Thomas Bourchier, cardinal-archbishop of Canterbury, is said to have introduced printing into England, and John Bourchier, who was chancellor of the exchequer to Henry VIII., translated *La Chronique* of Froissart.

Biogr. Univ. vol v. p. 354.

Arthur Bourchier published a fable of Æsop versified, and is the writer of a poem which appeared in the edition of *The Paradise of Dayntie Deuises* in 1600. It is entitled "Golden Precepts," of which the following are two of the stanzas:

Farr's Select Poetry of Elizabeth's reign, vol. i. p. xxv.; vol ii. p. 297.

"Perhaps you thinke me bolde
That dare presume to teach,
As one that runs beyond his race,
And rowes beyond his reach,
Sometime the blind doo goe,
Where perfect sights do fall;
The simple may sometimes instruct
The wisest heads of all."

EMBLEM, p. 205.—*To* ARTHVRE STARKEY *Esquier.*

We may naturally look for some of the persons to whom Whitney devotes his power of song in the neighbourhood where he was himself born and brought up. The Starkeys, bearing for their crest a stork, as a Cheshire family were settled at Stretton in Budworth at least as early as the reign of Henry II. A.D. 1154, and at Over about 1287, and on April 4th 1382, under the seal *Galfridi De Warburton*, a release was granted to *Thomas Starkey* of *Stretton*. Two Starkeys in Richard II.'s reign married two coheiresses of the Oultons of Oulton and Wrenbury; of the one was descended sir Humphrey Starkey, chief baron of the exchequer, and members of this family may be traced to 1728; of the other are derived the Starkeys of Wrenbury, who became extinct in 1803.

Sir P. Leycester, p. 355.

The Lysons, pp. 391 and 719.

Now Wrenbury is very near to the place of Whitney's birth, and to Audlem where he went to school. Contemporary with him was Arthur Starkey of Wrenbury, who was buried there in October 1622. His father Thomas Starkey died in 1566, and his mother was Katherine, daughter of sir Richard Mainwaring of Ightfield in Shropshire. In the three generations preceding his father the Starkeys of Wrenbury became allied with the Egertons of Oulton, the Mainwarings of Peover, and the Warburtons of Arley.

Ormerod's Cheshire, vol. iii. pp. 204 and 205.

EMBLEM, p. 206.—*To* JAN DOVSA, *son of the very noble* JAN DOVSA, *lord of Noortwijck.*

Janus Dousa, or John Vanderdoes the elder, and John Vanderdoes the younger, were among the most celebrated of the literary men of Holland in an age which abounded in famous Dutchmen. John Vanderdoes the younger, born January 16th 1571, and dying 21st December 1598, was the most renowned of four brothers—himself, George, Francis and Theodore. George was an accomplished linguist, and undertook a journey to Constantinople, of which he published an account, and added to it various ancient inscriptions from different parts of Greece. Francis, like his eldest brother, was a poet and a man of considerable learning; and Theodore, born in 1580 and dying in 1663, a man of knightly rank and judge of the supreme court, was recognised among the Latin poets of his country, and known also for his edition of Logotheta's *Chronicon* and other learned

Leyden, clↄ.iↄ.ic. (1599.)

Peerlkamp's Latin Poets, pp. 406-408.

Francf. 1598.

works. It was however John Dousa the younger, on whose untimely death Joseph Scaliger composed a long poem, an "*Epicedium*" or funeral dirge, and to whose memory, in modern times, Mattby's *Sigenbeek* has presented a warm "*Laudatio*," or offering of praise.

Leyden, 1812.

At the time when Whitney dedicated this emblem to him he had not reached his fourteenth year, but his extraordinary acquirements at a very early age gave him a place among those who were remarkable for learning even in their childhood. The Latin stanzas bearing the name "JANVS DOVSA à Noortwijck" prefixed to the emblems, and attributed to the father, were really the composition of the son.* In his sixteenth year he wrote commentaries on Plautus, and at the age of nineteen he had made annotations on several learned works. He was in fact even then a poet, critic, mathematician and philosopher. His moral character was not less excellent than his intellectual faculties were admirable. He had been preceptor to Henry Frederic prince of Orange, and was cut off in his twenty-sixth year, leaving a name still fondly remembered in his native land, and highly estimated in the annals of learning.

Intr. Dissert. p. xxvii.

Considering his youth Whitney's emblem to him is very appropriate. It represents a man gathering grapes, treading the unripe bunches under his feet, but presenting the ripe fruit to a woman standing by his side. In the distance appears the bow of promise and Iris, the messenger of the gods, seated in expectation at its feet.

In the university library of Leyden is a curious relic, regarded as having belonged to John Dousa from his fourth year to his death in 1598, and then continued by some other member of the family down to February 14th 1628. It is a quarto manuscript, bearing on the binding the date 1575, with borders to the pages of which more than one-half are not written on. Among the entries one is, "A memorial relating to the marriage of Ysbrandt van der Does, when he married, whom he married, and the birth of his children by his wife."

A good account of John Dousa the son, is given in Peerlkamp's

* As appears in the edition of the poems of John Dousa, the son, "JANI DOUSAE FILII POEMATA" Roterodami CIↃ IↃCCIV. 8vo pp. 212; where, at p. 205, occur these very stanzas, "In Gulfridi Whitnei Emblemata nomine Patris."

"*Book, concerning the Life, Learning and Genius of the Latin poets of the Netherlands.*" Harlem, M.DCCCXXXVII. 8vo, pp. 575. pp. 178-282.

EMBLEM, p. 207.—*To* M. WILLIAM HAREBROWNE, *at Constantinople.*

In connection with the county of Norfolk, and with Yarmouth, one of its towns, we find this name variously written, as Harborne, Harbrown, Hareborne, Harbrowne, Harbourne, but all referring to persons of the same family. Were there not numberless instances of similar variations we should doubt whether Whitney's "William Harebrowne at Constantinople" was Hakluyt's "master *William* Hareborne," "her maiesties Ambassadour or Agent, in the partes of Turkie" from 1582 to 1588. Manship's *History of Great Yarmouth* however removes all uncertainty, for that work says expressly, "William Harborne of Mundham was sent Ambassador by Queen Elizabeth to the Grand Seignior in 1582."* The name of this William Hareborne is among the names of those who joined in the pic-nic to Scratby island August 2nd 1580. Hakluyt, vol. ii. pp. 157 and 289. Palmer's Edition, vol. ii. p. 283.

Sir Anthony Harborne, a knight in the army of Edward III., is regarded as the ancestor of the Yarmouth family of this name, and the arms which he bore were granted in 1582 to "William Harborne of Yarmouth and London, son of William Harborne of Yarmouth, who married Joan Piers," cousin of John, archbishop of York. Palmer's Manship, vol. ii. p. 283.

William Harebrowne, the father, was one of the bailiffs of Yarmouth in 1556, and in 1571 and 1572, and one of the burgesses in parliament in 1575. William Harebrowne the son is first mentioned in 1580 and 1582. Palmer's Manship, vol. i. pp. 36, 73 and 186; vol. ii. pp. 199 and 302.

The revival of the interrupted trade of England with the Levant is attributed "*to the speciall industrie of the worshipfull and worthy Citizens, Sir* Edward Osborne, *Knight, M.* Richard Staper, *and M.* William Hareborne." In the "Queenes Commission under her great seale" it is recited, "that wee thinking well, and hauing good confidence in the singular trustinesse, obedience, wisedome, and disposition of our welbeloued seruante Hakluyt, vol. ii. p. 158.

* "His great-grand-daughter married Edward Ward of Bexley. She was created a baroness in 1660. This was an elder branch of the family of Lord Ward."

William Hareborne, one of the Esquiers of our body, towards vs, and our seruices, doe by these presents, make, ordaine and constitute him our true and vndoubted Orator, Messenger, Deputie, and Agent." The sovereign to whom Harebrowne was accredited was "the most renowned, and most inuincible Prince Zuldan Murad Can," the same with Amurath III., who reigned from 1575 to 1595.

Hakluyt, vol. ii. p. 165.

"The voyage of the *Susan* of *London* to *Constantinople*, wherein the worshipfull M. *William Harborne* was sent first Ambassadour vnto *Sultan Murad Can*, the great Turke," is an account well worth the reading. The ship left Blackwall the 14th of November 1582, and arrived at Constantinople on the 29th of March 1583, and on "the 11 day of April came to the Key of the Custom house."

From his mansion, "Rapamat in Pera," Mr. Harebrowne dates several letters and consular documents. He remained in charge of English trade and English interests until his return "from *Constantinople* ouerland to *London*, 1588." In a brief but interesting narrative of his journey we are told that he left the city of the sultan "with thirty persons of his suit and family" the 3rd August 1588, passing through Romania, Wallachia and Moldavia, and by the middle of September entering Poland, with the chancellor of which he had an interview on the 27th of September. The exact date of his arrival in England is not noted down, but he was at Hamburg the 19th of November, "and at Stoad the ninth of December."

Blomefield, vol. i. p. 339.

It appears that soon after his return, 16th September 1589, he was married to Elizabeth Drury of Besthorp, in Norfolk. He now joined with sir Edward Osborne knt. and others in setting open "a trade of merchandize and trafficke into the landes, Ilandes, Dominions and territories of the great Turke," and is several times named in "the second letters Patents graunted by the Queenes Maiestie to the Right worshipfull companie of the English Marchants for the Leuant, the seventh of Januarie 1592."

Hakluyt, vol. ii. p. 295.

Pict. Hist. England, bk. vi. c. iv. vol. iii. p. 790.

The Turkey company was incorporated in 1581, and it was to promote its interests chiefly that Mr. Harebrowne had been sent to Constantinople; and by that same company various attempts were made to open a direct English trade with India, until on the 22nd of September 1599 about a hundred of the merchants of London united themselves into an association known as "The Governor and Company of the Merchants of London trading into the East Indies."

EMBLEM, p. 208.— *To* M. THOMAS WHETELEY.

The name Whitley, or Wheteley, exists among Cheshire names;* but no identification of Thomas Wheteley with any family in the county has been made. There was a puritan vicar of Banbury in Oxfordshire, William Whateley, during the greater part of the reign of James I.; and an interesting account of him, with a portrait, is given in Clarke's *Marrow of Ecclesiastical History.* In 1570 the *Domestic Series of State Papers,* p. 381, mentions a Mr. Wheteley of Norwich as one who might "well be charged with the whole or part of the loan assessed on him by Privy Seal." This may have been Mr. Thomas Wheteley, or of his family.

Edition 1634, p. 929.

EMBLEM, p. 212.—*To the very accomplished and very celebrated physicians,* JOHN, JAMES *and* LANCELOT BROWNE.

Doubtless a most celebrated name among physicians; but Benjamin Hutchinson's *Biographia Medici, or Lives and Writings of the most eminent Medical Characters &c. from earliest account of time to the present period,* contains no mention of John, James and Lancelot. Sir Thomas Browne, the author of *Religio Medici,* though born in London in 1605,† was of a family long settled at Upton, near Chester, and if the three physicians whom Whitney distinguishes were not brothers, one or two of them might have been of the same family; but as to Lancelot Browne, the Coopers decide that he was a native of York, "matriculated as a pensioner of St. John's college in May 1559, proceeded B.A. 1562-3, and commenced M.A. 1566." In 1570 he received his licence to practise physic, was created M.D. in 1576, and "on 10 June 1584 was admitted a fellow of the college of physicians."

2 vols. 8vo, London, 1799.

Ormerod, vol. ii. p. 444.

Athen. Cantab. vol. ii. p. 421.

* Peele hall, near Tarporley, was the residence of that zealous royalist, colonel Roger Whitley, who accompanied Charles II. in his exile, and who entertained William III. here on his passage to Ireland. An heiress of the Whitleys in 1706 brought the estate to Other Windsor, second earl of Plymouth.

Ormerod, vol. ii. p. 180. The Lysons, p. 797.

† "Hic situs est Thomas Browne M.D. Miles A° 1605, LONDINI natus, Generosâ, Familiâ apud Upton in Agro Cestriensi oriundus," &c.

Blomefield, vol. ii. p. 264.

"He was principal physician to queen Elizabeth, king James I. and his queen. It appears that he died shortly before 11 Dec. 1605." He was the author of an Epistle prefixed to Gerard's *Herbal, or General History of Plants*, 1597.*

Smith's Gr. and Rom. Biog. vol. i. pp. 45 and 46.

The emblems which Whitney assigns to Æsculapius are very correct. The sanctuary of the god, at Epidaurus, "contained a magnificent statue of ivory and gold, the work of Thrasymedes, in which he was represented as a handsome and manly figure, resembling that of Zeus. He was seated on a throne, holding in one hand a staff, and with the other resting upon the head of a dragon (serpent) and by his side lay a dog." A cock was sacrificed to him by those who had experienced healing.

EMBLEM, p. 213.—*To the very famous* JUSTUS LIPSIUS, *adorned with all the glory of learning and worth.*

Poemata, pp. 49-203,

About the time that Whitney penned this dedication, the youthful Latinist John Dousa had strung together above a dozen elegies, odes and juvenile epigrams on the illness, or the garden, or the image, or the various praises of Justus Lipsius, who then filled a very large space in the affection and admiration of literary men. The emblem assigned to him, taken from Beza's *Portraits &c.*, represents a dog barking at the moon and stars, and figures in the dog those who attacked the great luminary of the university of Leyden. In learning indeed he had few, if any, equals,—it was both extensive and profound; and at this date (1586) he was at the very height of his reputation, not having manifested the inordinate vanity, mixed with narrowness of mind, which in 1591 induced him to dedicate a silver pen to the Virgin of Hall in a copy of verses filled with his own praises. In spite however of his errors and weaknesses he must be regarded as a man of great literary powers.

Plate LIX.

Oettinger's Bib. Biog. p. 376.

Biog. Universelle, vol. xxiv, pp. 551-557.

Lipsius was born at Isch near Brussels 18th October 1547, and died at Louvain 24th March 1607. His school learning was acquired at Brussels, Aeth and the Jesuits' college of Cologne: in 1567 he went to Rome and then passed to Louvain and Vienna. Soon after, in 1572, he accepted the professorship of history in

Dyer's Cambridge, vol. i. p. 257.

* A Lancelot Brown, who died in 1783, rendered himself famous for his skill in landscape gardening.

the Lutheran university of Jena, and acknowledged the Lutheran faith. In 1574 he was again a Roman Catholic in the retirement of his native place, but about 1577 he filled with great renown the chair of history at Leyden, where for thirteen years his external religion was Calvinistic. At the end of this period he returned to Louvain, and publicly abjured the Protestant religion. So many changes of course exposed him to the charges of inconsistency and want of conscientiousness, and doubtless he is to be censured for teaching in a Protestant college that no state ought to allow a plurality of religions, and for manifesting such extreme credulity when he re-adopted the profession of his youth. He was however a great scholar and a sound critic, as his works testify.*

An entire edition of his works was published at the Plantin press in Antwerp, four vols. in folio, in 1637, and justifies Oettinger in naming him "philologue belge du premier ordre." For a fuller account of his life and writings the reader may consult Chalmers's *Gen. Biog. Dict.* vol. xx. pp. 314-319, and *Biographie Universelle*, vol. xxiv. pp. 551-557. Bib. Biog. p. 376.

EMBLEM, p. 215.—*To* M. JOHN GOSLINGE.

Whitney had established friendships with several persons of

* Several of his works issued from the Plantin press at Antwerp, as

"Justi Lipsii variarum lectionum libri iiii. Ad illustrissimum et amplissimum Antonium Perrenotum, S. R. E. cardinalem." CIↃ.IↃ.LXIX., —the first work which Lipsius published. Ann de l'Imp. Plantinienne, p. 96.

"Corn. Taciti opera cum notis Justi Lipsii." 8vo. 1574. p. 149.

"Justi Lipsii antiquarum lectionum commentarius, tributus in libros quinque," &c. "Plauti præcipue," &c. 8vo. M.D.LXXV. p. 165.

"Justi Lipsii epistolicarum quæstionum libri v." &c. "Pleræque ad T. Livium notæ." 8vo. M.D.LXXVII. p. 182.

"Titi Livii Historiarum liber primus ex recensione Justi Lipsii." 8vo. 1579. p. 199.

"C. Cornelii Taciti opera omnia quæ exstant. Quorum index pagina sequenti J. Lipsius denuo castigavit et recensuit." 8vo. M.D.LXXXI.; also CIↃ.IↃ.LXXXV. pp. 224 and 177.

"Justi Lipsii Saturnalium sermonum libri duo qui de Gladiatoribus." 4to. 1582; also 1585. pp. 242 and 282.

"Justi Lipsii Electorum libri duo." 4to. 1582. p. 242.

"Justi Lipsii de Constantia libri duo," &c. 4to and 8vo. 1584; also CIↃ.IↃ.LXXXV. pp. 265 and 282.

And from the Plantin press at Leyden.

"Justi Lipsii antiquariæ lectiones. Epist. quæst. Electa variæ lect. Satyra Menipp. De amphitheatro in et de eo extra Romam." 1585. p. 288.

"Justi Lipsii politicorum sive civiles doctrinæ libri sex." 4to. 1589. p. 323.

repute in East Anglia. This Mr. John Gostlinge, or Gostlin, was a native of Norwich, and chosen *Fellow* of Gonvile and Caius college, Cambridge, in 1591. He was appointed *Proctor* in 1600, graduated as *Doctor* of *Physic* in 1602, and became *Warden* February 16th 1618. On that same day and year he was also elected *Vice-chancellor.* "This learned and excellent Gouernor of the College," records Blomefield, "died October 21, 1626, and is still commemorated on that day." There is this inscription to the memory of Dr. Tomas Legge,* in which he is named,

Blomefield's Norfolk, vol. ii. pp. 216 and 214.

"JVNXIT AMOR VIVOS, SIC JVNGAT TERRA SEPVLTOS
GOSTLINI RELIQVVM COR TIBI LEGGUS HABES
MORIENDO VIVIT."

Dr. Gostlin was one of the executors to his old friend and predecessor in office.

EMBLEM, p. 217.—*To* M. ELCOCKE, *Preacher.*

At Poole, a township in the parish of Acton, about two and a quarter miles N.N.W. from Nantwich, a family of the name of Elcocke possessed the estate of White Poole in the reign of Edward VI., and resided there for more than two centuries and a half, until the death of Mrs. Ann Elcocke in 1812, when under her will the property passed to her nephew William Massey, and is now enjoyed by Francis Elcock Massey esq.

The Lysons, pp. 381, 403 and 475.

The Elcockes were originally of Stockport. Alexander Elcocke, who died November 15th 1550, left four sons, of whom the eldest, Francis, died October 14th 1591, and the fourth son was named Thomas. A Thomas Elcocke occurs as rector of Barthomley in Cheshire before 1605, and this is the Mr. Elcocke, *preacher,* whom Whitney commemorates.

Ormerod, vol. iii. pp. 188 and 164. Lanc. MSS. vol. xii.

"Preacher," says the Rev. Canon Raines in a communication with which he favoured me, "would be the highest style of commendation and address in an age when there were very few of the sacred calling able to preach." He also supplies me with the following facts: "1576-7, March 24. Mr. Thomas Elcocke presented to the Rectory of Barthomley by Robert Fullerhurst of Crewe on the death of Robert Kinsey, Clerk, the last Parson. He afterwards gave bond to the Bishop of Chester on being in-

June 15, 1865.

Lanc. MSS. vol. xxxii. pp. 53 and 42.

* See *Athenæ Cantabrigienses*, vol. ii. pp. 454-457.

stituted." Elcocke's ministry at Barthomley probably terminated about 1617.

In that age, as we learn from Shakespeare's sir Hugh Evans, it was not unusual to give the title *sir* to clergymen who had not proceeded to the Master of Arts' degree. The Rev. Edward Hinchliffe names Thomas Elcocke, clericus, but records a little bit of gossip respecting him, the very year in which Whitney's emblem is dedicated to him, "1586." In this year the parishioners of Barthomley preferred numerous complaints against their parson, sir Thomas Elcocke (inter alia), "That he greatly abused his Parishioners, and patron of the church, and that his curate, sir Robert Andrew, was a brawler and a drunkard, and was so drunk returning from Nantwich that had it not been for Robert Lant and Robert Yardley drawing him out of the water, he had been in danger of his life." The tenor of the narrative shows that if there was truth there was no less malice in some of the witnesses.

Notes and Queries, vol. i. pp. 234, 299 and 401.

History of Barthomley, Edit. 1856, pp. 43, 44 and 353.

EMBLEM, p. 219. — "*In amore tormentum*," In love torment.

The gnats round the candle are favourites with the emblem writers. Whitney borrows the device from Corrozet's *Hecatomgraphie*, printed at Paris in 1540, and it occurs also in *Le Sententiose Imprese* of Symeoni and Giovio; but neither of these writers gives more than a stanza of four lines, and Whitney, according to his wont, extends the subject thirty lines, with many examples by way of warning to the inexperienced.

Plate XXXII.

Essay i. p. 241.

The device and the Italian motto are both claimed by Symeoni as his own invention, for he says, "*Vn gentilhomme mien amy estant amoureax, me pria de luy trouuer vne deuise, pourquoy ie luy feis pourtraire vn Papillon à l'entovr d' vne chandelle allumée auec ces paroles:* "COSI VIVO PIACER CONDVCE A MORTE."

Dev. Her. et Morales, Edit. 1561, p. 231.

EMBLEM, p. 222. — *To* MR. RAWLINS, *Preacher.*

As there is no Christian name added, and there were in Mary's and Elizabeth's reigns many preachers of the name of Rawlins, or Rawlinges, we have some license in considering whom Whitney intended. "A brief discours off the troubles begonne at Franckford in Germany Anno Domini 1554; abowte the Booke off common prayer and ceremonies," published in 1575, contains the names "off such as subscribed" to "the Discipline reformed and confirmed by the authorities off the churche and Magistrate," and among the names is *William Raulinges*, elsewhere in the same book spelt *Rawlinges*. The date of the subscription is about 1557.

Erkinald Rawlins and Dorothy his wife, Mr. Raines informs me, were friends of Bradford the martyr, and there is an interesting letter from Bradford addressed to them, and also a letter from Rawlins to Bradford, dated Antwerp, July 31st 1554. The two Rawlins and others were sent to the Tower by queen Mary 18th March 1555-6.

Parker Society, vol. i. pp. 221 and 97.

Martyn's Diary, p. 102.

Ormerod, vol. i. p. 261.

Edit. 1749, p. 1358.

Among the vicars of St. Peter, Chester, is entered, "1570 January 9, Edward Rawlins," who remained vicar unto March 14th 1573, when he resigned; and in the "*Typographical Antiquities of Joseph Ames*" is mentioned "1591 R. Rawlins consort of the creatures with the creator, and with themselves."

Blomefield, vol. i. pp. 355 and 237.

But not one of these is the Rawlins of Whitney's emblem; that was a Norfolk friend of the poet's, John Rawlyns, who on the 8th March 1581 was presented by the earl of Sussex and Henry Gurney esq. to the united rectory of Atleburgh. In Mortimer's chapel against the east wall of the church is or was a mural monument, with the Rawlins' arms, and beginning

"Fui Johannes Rawlyns, Northamptoniensis."

From the inscription we learn that he was born at Paston, and educated at Spalding in Lincolnshire; that he was a scholar of St. John's college, Cambridge, and that he was rector of Atleburgh for thirty-three years, dying May 2nd 1614, in the 67th year of his age.

"Caelum mihi iam Domicilium."

His eulogy is set forth in two elegiac stanzas, it being premised that he had only one wife, by name Mary, dear, prudent, frugal, faithful, buried here beside him, and that he left four sons and two daughters, well brought up:

"If, Reader, thou seekest why this stone should speak,
Here are entombed the vast riches of his genius;
The praises of Rawlings living, living tongues did praise,
His duties of life discharged, the rocks cannot be silent."

EMBLEM, p. 222.—*To* MR. STEEVENSON, *Preacher.*

There was a Mr. William Stevenson, prebendary of Durham, 1561–1575, a friend of bishop Pilkington; whether he left a son also a preacher is not known, but himself died in 1575. I do not find the name either in the *Athenæ Oxonienses* or the *Athenæ Cantabrigienses*, at the time in question, 1586. Ormerod's *Cheshire* is silent, and so is Blomefield's *Norfolk*.

The device from Hadrian Junius, edition 1564, is noteworthy Plate XXVI*a*. for the spirited execution of it; the rats indeed are triumphant, and the cats very subdued. To the beautiful border there is nothing superior in the whole compass of emblem literature. Note also the border of the plates XXVI*b*, XXVI*c*, and XXVI*d*. These, as we have before remarked, p. 250, are the sources of the borders for Whitney's devices.

EMBLEM, p. 223.—*To* MR. KNEWSTVB, *Preacher*.

Were Whitney addicted to satire, we might conjecture that Plate V. both the device and the stanzas were an indirect reproof of the preacher whom he names. This was John Knewstub, B.D., at the time of the emblems being published chaplain to the earl of Leicester, and frequently mentioned in the histories of the day. He was born at Kirby Stephen, Westmoreland, in 1540, and probably educated there until he entered at Cambridge. Like many from the north of England he was chosen fellow of St. John's college, and afterwards ranked among its benefactors. During his residence in the university he united with Dr. Andrews and Dr. Chadderton in the observance of weekly meetings for conference upon Scripture. There is "A Sermon preached at Paules Crosse the Fryday before Easter, 1576, by I. Knewstub;" and a work, which passed through several editions, 1577–1600, authorized by the bishop of London, and dedicated "to the Lady Anne, Countesse of Warwick," the wife of Ambrose Dudley; "The LECTVRES of John Knewstub, vpon the twentieth Chapter of Exodus, and certeine other places of Scripture." 4to.

On his removing from Cambridge, in 1579, Knewstub became rector at Cockfield in Suffolk, and gained distinction as the leader of the Puritan and Nonconformist clergy in the counties of Norfolk, Suffolk, and Cambridge. When the earl of Leicester was sent into the Netherlands, Knewstub accompanied him as

Leycester Correspondence, Bruce's Edit. 1844. chaplain, and a note on a letter from Walsyngham to Leicester, 25th April 1586, narrates the celebration of St. George's day in the earl's court at Utrecht, and informs us "then began prayers and a sermon by master Knewstubs my lords chaplaine, after which my lord proceeded to the offering, first for her majesty and then for himself, &c."

Neale's Puritans, Edit. 1822, vol. ii. p. 15. In 1603 Knewstub was one of the Puritan divines who took part in the Hampton court conference before James I., and maintained that "rites and ceremonies were at best but indifferent, and therefore doubted, whether the power of the church could bind the conscience without impeaching Christian liberty."

He died May 29th 1624, at the age of 84.*

EMBLEM, p. 224. — *To* M. ANDREWES, *Preacher.*

Fain would we make out that this was the celebrated Lancelot Andrews, in succession bishop of Chichester, Ely and Winchester; but as he was only born in 1565, he would be only a student, not a preacher, in 1586. As far as name and locality are concerned, the Andrewes of the emblem may have been in 1586 Elcocke's curate at Barthomley, not far from Nantwich, and whom Hinchliffe names "a brawler and a drunkard," "Sir Robert Andrew." The *History of Great Yarmouth* however shows very decisively who was Whitney's Andrewes the preacher: In "1585 Mr. Andrews, a learned and godly preacher, was appointed by the corporation, with a salary of £50 a year, and a house was built for his residence." Bartimæus Andrewes was his name, and he was the author of *A Catechism with Prayers*, 8vo, London, 1591.

Palmer's Manship, vol. ii. p. 151.

This Mr. Andrewes seems to have been a very pains-taking and deserving clergyman, for in 1591 the corporation agreed to give him £50 a year "if he be not put to silence;" but if he were silenced they mark their sense of his merit by still promising to pay him £25 a year. In 1600 they paid him £32 10s. "for his pains and labour, he giving the town a general acquittance."

Notes and Queries, vol. xii. p. 253.

* To those desirous of pursuing this subject the references by C. H. Cooper may be useful: Brook's *Lives of the Puritans*, vol. ii. p. 308; Strype's *Life of Whitgift*, pp. 328, 572, 575; Strype's *Annals*, vol. i. p. 625, vol. ii. p. 608, Append. p. 160, vol. iii. p. 471, Append. p. 188; Page's *Supplement to Suffolk Traveller*, pp. 9, 35; Peck's *Desiderata Curiosa*, lib. vi. numb. 8.

EMBLEM, p. 227.—*To* M. IAMES IONSON.

Previous to 1593 there was a Mr. Hamnet Johnson, merchant of Chester, and a fair tomb existed to another of the same name "untimely deceased, and thus writ upon": King's Vale Royal, p. 48.

> "*Here lieth the Body of* William Johnson, *Merchant; sometime Alderman of this City, who died the* 12th day of *January* Anno Dom. 1607.
>
> Vivit post funera virtus."

Among the rectors of Church Coppenhall, which is about five miles N.E. from Nantwich, Ormerod places Anthony Johnson, who occupied the rectory from 1583 to 1621. History of Cheshire, vol. iii. p. 176.

Whether James Jonson was of either of these families remains altogether uncertain, but the vicinity of Coppenhall to Nantwich suggests that he may have been allied to Anthony Johnson.

EMBLEM, p. 228.—*To* M. HOWLTE, *Preacher.*

The name Holt is of high antiquity in Cheshire. The manor of Wimbersley, or Wimbaldesley, near Middlewich, with Lea hall, belonged to the family of Holt for several generations; and the manor of Sale, once "the property of Geffrey, son of Adam Dutton, ancestor of the Warburtons," was bestowed by him "in year 1187 on two of his gentlemen, Richard Mascie and Thomas Holte," and "their descendants continued to hold it in moities in the reign of Queen Elizabeth." From this family of Holts therefore might be Mr. Howlte the preacher. The Lysons, pp. 485 and 694.

But the name Holt is not unfrequent in Lancashire, and a Mr. William Holte, second son of Robert Holte of Ashworth hall, is mentioned in the 1st of Elizabeth. In 1589 he is described as brother of Holte of Ashworth, a *Jesuit*, and in league with cardinal Allen and others against queen Elizabeth. It is not however probable that Whitney, himself of puritan leanings, would entitle such a man a *preacher.* Lanc. MSS. vol. xiv. p. 50.

A curious old book, before quoted p. 396, in the library of Mr. Toulmin Smith of Highgate, near London, among the names "off such as subscribed," in 1557 at Francfort, "The Discipline reformed and confirmed by the authorities of the churche and Magistrate," records "*John Olde;*" not very like indeed to Holte, but opposite is marked in pencil by some one who made Letter, Oct. 23, 1865.

inquiry into the fact the name *Howlte*, and thus, one of the confessors under Mary's reign, may claim to be Whitney's "Howlte the Preacher" in 1586.

EMBLEM, p. 230.—"Tempus omnia terminat," *Time terminates all things.*

With the final device of Whitney's emblems we place by way
Plate XXXV. of contrast the device from Coustau to the motto "Le Temps fait tout," *Time accomplishes every thing.* It is a quaint and curious ditty, that old French of his:

"The man well advised plucks hair after hair
At his leisure from tail of his horse;
Be it good, be it bad, the foolish by force
At one jerk leaves the animal bare.
Time and labour conjoined, together work well;—
All things they bestow, as all people must know
Whom despair never grieves here below;
Time and labour together, they ever excell."

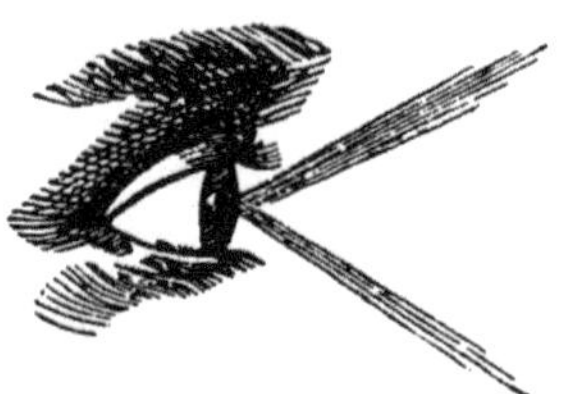

Per cæcum videt omnia punctum.

ADDENDA.

UESTIONS still remain unconsidered; but here, in the Addenda, only a few of them will be introduced.

INTRODUCTORY DISSERTATION, p. xiv.—"Gerard Leeu." An earlier work from Leeu's press is dated 22nd April 1472, but I have not seen it: the title, as given by M. Bodel Nyenhuis, is, *Spiegel der Sassen*. Diss. Hist. Jurid. Leyden, 1819, p. 439.

WHITNEY'S AUTOGRAPHS, p. xl. (note †).—Since this note was written, the courtesy of George W. Napier esq. of Alderley Edge, Cheshire, has supplied me with the means of giving a photo-lithograph impression Plate XLIII*a*.
of the title-page of the very book mentioned in *Notes and Queries*, and of which he has lately become the purchaser; it is Ocland's *Battles of the English*,* a Latin hexameter poem of about 3420 lines, dedicated "AD ILLVSTRISSIMAM, POTENTISSIMAMQVE PRINCIPEM, D. ELIZABETHAM, ANGLIÆ, *Franciæ, & Hiberniæ Reginam, fidei propugnatricem*," and preceded by her arms. A comparison between the autographs on Plate XLIII*b*.
Plate VII. and Plate XLIII*a* will justify the conclusion that they were written by the same hand. Whitney's writing also appears, I think, on Plate XIII. in the words "*Soli dei honor et gloria in æua sempiterna. Amen.*"

* "The Tenour of the Letters," "from the Court at *Greenewich*, the 21 of Aprill. 1582," "directed by the Lords of hir highnesse priuie Counsell to her Maiesties high cōmissioners in causes Ecclesiasticall," enjoins, "the publike receyuing and teaching of *Ch. Ocklandes* Booke in all Grammer and freeschooles within this Realme." The letters are signed by Ambrose Warwicke, Robert Leicester, and others, and assign as a reason that "in common schooles, where diuers heathen Poets are ordinarily read and taught," "the youthe of the realme doth rather receiue infection in manners than aduauncement in vertue." Bound up in the same volume is Ocland's "ΕΙΡΗΝΑΡΧΙΑ," on the peaceful state of England under Elizabeth, a Latin poem of 1096 lines; and Alexander Neville's KETTVS, a history in Latin prose of Kett's insurrection in Norfolk.

Plates XI*a*. and XIII*a*. INTROD. DISSER. pp. xli-xlii.—"Coole Pilate, in the parish of Acton." A drawing of the house which tradition assigns as Whitney's birthplace is presented among the illustrations, and also of the church of the parish of Acton in which "the Mannour of *Cole Pilate*" is situated. The old portion of the house has most of the characteristics of a Cheshire home of Elizabeth's time, and the tradition therefore possesses some of the elements of authenticity; yet as Whitney writes of the phœnix,

> "And thoughe for truthe, this manie do declare,
> Yet thereunto, I meane not for to sweare."

Plates XII. and XIII. INTROD. DISSER. p. lv.—"Account in Latin of a visit to Scratby Island," from Whitney's entry on the rolls in the archives of Great Yarmouth, August 2nd 1580.

Anno 1580. Plate XII. **Porro Secundo die mensis Augusti Anno** presenti, Domini Ballivi cum venerabili consortio tam Millitum quam generosorum et aliorum expertorum hominum associati, unâcum quibusdam Burgensibus prudentissimis et maxime discretis, In insulam quandam novam, Tria milliaria de villâ distantem, nuper ex borialiali parte e contra Scrotbie crescentem, Et continuis ventorum motibus ex arenâ conglomeratam et exaggeratam, transfretabant. **ubi omnes** insimull prandebant **Et** postea super eandem globulabantur, Et nomen de **Yermouth** Ilande eidem imposuerunt. **Et** quia speraverunt eandem, tempore futuro ventorum continuis flatibus auctam fore, Et idcirco piscatoribus, nautis et omnibus per eundem cursum navigantibus maximo adiumento et sublevamini esse: **Ideo** superiorem eiusdem partem cum Sepe cinxerunt, per quam, arenâ tardatâ, citius acervus et congeries eiusdem in molem accumulatus esset, et paulatim in firmam terram cresceret et corroboraretur, **vt deo Auspicante** parvo Temporis spatio ab vehementissimis Tempestatum incursionibus, naves cum quaque eandem commorantes, quasi in tuto portu ab omni periculo preservati[*æ*] essent, et custodirentur. **Cuiusquidam** Insulæ Longitudo tunc per estimationem continebat ferme unum milliarium, Et latitudo idem [?]

Plate XIII. **Nomina eorum Tam Generosorum** quam Burgensium et Nautarum, qui prædicta Insula tunc ingrediebantur, sequuntur; viz.

Nomina militum:	Arthurus Heuiningham Radulphus Shelton Rogerus Wudhowse	milites.
Nomina Armigerorum:	Edwardus ffowerdewe sergentus ad legem.	
	Thomas Tasberowe Thomas Blowerhasset Philippus Wudhowse	Armigeri.

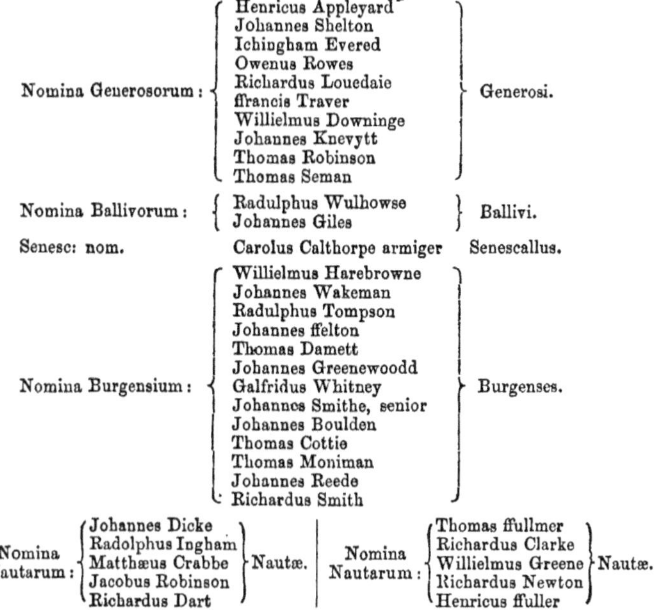

Nomina Generosorum:	Henricus Appleyard* Johannes Shelton Ichingham Evered Owenus Rowes Richardus Louedaie ffrancis Traver Willielmus Downinge Johannes Knevytt Thomas Robinson Thomas Seman	Generosi.
Nomina Ballivorum:	Radulphus Wulhowse Johannes Giles	Ballivi.
Senesc: nom.	Carolus Calthorpe armiger	Senescallus.
Nomina Burgensium:	Willielmus Harebrowne Johannes Wakeman Radulphus Tompson Johannes ffelton Thomas Damett Johannes Greenewoodd Galfridus Whitney Johannes Smithe, senior Johannes Boulden Thomas Cottie Thomas Moniman Johannes Reede Richardus Smith	Burgenses.

Nomina Nautarum:	Johannes Dicke Radolphus Ingham Matthæus Crabbe Jacobus Robinson Richardus Dart	Nautæ.	Nomina Nautarum:	Thomas ffullmer Richardus Clarke Willielmus Greene Richardus Newton Henricus ffuller	Nautæ.

Soli dei honor et gloria in æua sempiterna. Amen.

Note.—The last line, "*Soli dei*" *&c.*, appears to be in Whitney's own handwriting,—the rest to have been copied upon the roll by his clerk, who certainly was not a perfect Latin grammarian, or he would not have written *naves, preservati essent.*

A translation of Whitney's "Account" is printed in Palmer's *Manship's History of Great Yarmouth*, but as the exact designations of the original Latin are not given, nor the order and spelling of the names observed,* I here append another version: Vol. i. p. 105-6.

Furthermore, on the second day of the month of August in the A.D. 1580.
Year (*now*) present, the Master Bailiffs associated with a worshipfull company as well of knights as of gentlemen and other men of experience, together with certain most prudent and highly discreet Burgesses,

* The original has forty-three names: Manship's translation gives forty-five, two additional being inserted—"John Bladded gent.," and "Mr. Henry Manship." The probability is that Whitney's clerk had inadvertently omitted these two names, and that Manship, who wrote his history not later than 1614, knowing of their presence at the corporation's *gipseying*, therefore placed them on his list. Introd. Diss. p. 52.

crossed over the channel to a certain new island, Three miles distant from the town, lately growing up on the northern part opposite to Scrotbie, And by the constant movements of the winds gathered out of the sand and heaped up. **Where all** at the same time dined **And** afterwards played at bowls upon the same, And to the same gave the name of **Yermouth** Island. **And** because they hoped that the same in future time would be increased by the constant blowing of the winds, and so be of the greatest help and succour to fishermen, sailors and all persons sailing by the same course, **Therefore** they girded the higher part of the same with a Hedge by which the sand being retarded, the heap and gathering together of the same might be the sooner accumulated into a huge mass, and by little and little might grow and be strengthened into firm ground, **that, by God's favour,** in a small space of time, ships, whenever tarrying at the same, might be kept and guarded from the most violent assaults of Tempests, as in a harbour safe from every danger. **Of which Island** the Length by estimation then contained almost a mile and the breadth about the same.

The names of the knights, esquires, gentlemen, bailiffs, burgesses and sailors may easily be made out from the Latin original, to which readers are referred.

INTROD. DISSER. p. lxxiv. — "τὰ τρία ταῦτα." Faith, Hope and Charity, here symbolized by the cross, the anchor and the dove, were also symbolized, though in a different manner, by Lorenzo the Magni-
Plate LXX. ficent. Giovio's *Dialogo*, pp. 42, 43, as translated by Daniell, gives us the following account: "*Iou.* I cãnot go beyond the three Diamãts which the great *Cosimo* did beare, which you see engrauen in the chamber wherein I lye. But to tell you the trueth, although with all diligẽce I haue searched, yet canot I find precisely what they signifie, & thereof also doubted Pope Clemẽt, who in his meaner fortune lay also in the selfe same chamber. And trueth it is that he sayd, the *Magnifico Lorenzo* vsed one of them with greate brauerie, inserting it betweene three feathers of three sundrie colours, greene, white, and red: which betokened three vertues, Faith, Hope and Charitie, appropriate to those three colours: Hope, greene: Faith, white: Charitie, red, with this worde, *Semper*, belowe it. Which *Impresa* hath bene vsed of all the successors of his house, yea, and of the Pope: who did beare it imbrodered on the vpper garments of the horsmen of his garde, vnder that of the yoke."

WHITNEY'S MOTTOES, pp. lxxv-lxxx. — In general, Whitney has given the same mottoes as the authors whose devices he has appropriated, but in several instances—probably in upwards of sixty—while imitating and adopting the devices, he made some changes in the mottoes; thus:

Page.	*Motto.*	*Author.*
184	Æstuans inuidiæ nocendi libido.	*Myth. Eth.* 69
93	Aliena si aestimaris infortunia, Tunc aequiore mente perferes tua.	*Faerni*, p. 56
211	A matrimonio absit svspicio.	*P. Poesis*, 77
29	Amor filiorum.	*Alc.* 193, 667
190*b*.	Bis dat qui tempestivè donat.	*Dev. Her.* 172
140	Canis queritur nimium nocere.	*Samb.* p. 183
82	Cauendum a meretricibus	*Alc.* 76, 284
102	Cœlitus impendet.	*Dev. Her.* 82
178	Cœlum, non animum mutant.	*Samb.* p. 104
67	Conscientia integra, laurus.	*Samb.* p. 14
98	Consueuere homines, euentu si qua sinistro Vota cadunt, iis sese &c.	*Faerni*, p. 36
156	Corrumpunt multi, atque hominum de pectore dolent Offensis sua sæpe novis &c.	*Faerni*, p. 114
214	Dives indoctus.	*Alc.* 189, 658
153*a*.	Divina ingratos homines vlciscitur ira.	*Faerni*, p. 118
5	Doctos doctis obloqui nefas esse.	*Alc.* 179, 617
147	Dulcia quandoque amara fieri.	*Alc.* 111, 391
68	Ecquis discernit utrumque.	*Dev. Her.* 88
115	Etiam Fortunam.	*Dev. Her.* 132
111	Et pati fortia.	*Dev. Her.* 73
37	Ἐχθρῶν ἄδωρα δῶρα.	*Alc.* 167, 579
155	Exitium natis parit indulgentia patrum.	*Faerni*, 120
124	Fictus amicus.	*Samb.* p. 198
12	Hac illac perfluo.	*Dev. Her.* 89
57	Impossibile.	*Alc.* 59, 235
38	In adulari nescientem.	*Alc.* 35, 160
202	In aulicos.	*Alc.* 86, 316
144	In avaros, vel quibus melior conditio ab extraneis offertur.	*Alc.* 89, 323
77*a*.	In deprehensum.	*Alc.* 21, 102
94	Invidia.	*Alc.* 71, 271
16	In eos qui supra vires quiquam audent.	*Alc.* 58, 232
79	Lascivia.	*Alc.* 79, 294
162	Lupus et Mulier.	*Faerni*, p. 128
210	Magna mala ex leuibus vitat mens prouida signis.	*Faerni*, p. 125
189	Maleficio beneficium compensatum.	*Myth. Eth.* 177
170	Malè parta, malè dilabuntur.	*Alc.* 128, 462
158	Morosa, & discors vel mortua litigat uxor.	*Faerni*, p. 49
39	Ne incerta certis anteponantur, veto.	*Faerni*, p. 91
58	Non dolo, sed vertute.	*Samb.* p 110
99	Nupta contagioso.	*Alc.* 197, 681
52*b*.	Obnoxia infirmitas.	*Alc.* 169, 585
48	Ocni effigies de iis qui meretricibus donent quod in bonos usus verti debent.	*Alc.* 91, 328
153*b*.	Paratus animo contra iniqua casuum, Aut vincet illa, aut &c.	*Faerni*, p. 133
54*a*.	Parem delinquentis et suasoris culpam esse.	*Alc.* 173, 596
117	Parce Imperator.	*Dev. Her.* 76
196	Pennæ gloria immortalis.	*Jun.* 60, 66
96	Petram imitare iuuentus.	*Jun.* 59, 65
149	Φιλαυτία.	*Alc.* 69, 261
9	Plusquâm Diomedis & Glauci permutatio.	*Samb.* p. 28
200	Principis clementia.	*Alc.* 148, 528
108	Prudentes.	*Alc.* 18, 92
75	Quæ supra nos, nihil ad nos.	*Alc.* 102, 358
160	Quem bilinguem nosti; amicum ne tibi hunc adsciscito.	*Faerni*, p. 97
78	Qui alta contemplantur, cadere.	*Alc.* 104, 367
157	Quid rerum causas, naturæque abdita quæris, &c.	*Faerni*, p. 123
86	Restat ex victore Orientis.	*Dev. Her.* 31
227	Solus pro meretis.	*Dev. Her.* 161
191	Spe allectat inani.	*Dev. Her.* 93
137	Spes proxima.	*Alc.* 43, 188
186	Sur la Harpe d'Orpheus.	*Pegme*, 389
143	Ulterius ne tende odijs.	*Dev. Her.* 93
47	Unum nihil, duos plurimam posse.	*Alc.* 41, 185
171	Vsus, non lectio prudentes facit.	*Samb.* p. 62
4	Veritas tempore reuelatur, dissidio obruitur.	*Jun.* 53, 59
91	Vicinitas mala instar infortunii est.	*Faerni*, p. 95
172	Vita mortalium vigilia.	*Jun.* 5, 11

THE FRONTISPIECE. p. 232.—*Armorial Bearings* of Andreas Alciatus,
Plate XVI. emblazoned in 1546, from the edition of his emblems by Aldus:

"NEVER PROCRASTINATE.
Of Alciat's race the elk the motto bears,
'Procrastination every moment shun.'
The conqueror answered one who longed to know
How he so much in time so short had done;
'Never of will defer;' the elk declares,
That swift as strong his course shall onward go."

ESSAY I., p. 233.—Whitney made a *selection* from the labours of earlier writers, and especially from those whose works had been imprinted "in the house of Christopher Plantyn."

This statement furnishes the reason why there should be so very many correspondences and resemblances between Whitney and his predecessors for nearly a century in the same art, and yet that absolute identities should be confined to the circle of writers that were patronized at Antwerp and Leyden. Looking at his work, and
Pages 3-16. particularly at the "Epistle Dedicatorie" and the address "to the Reader," we can scarcely admit that he was unaware of the *Treatises on Devices of Arms and Love*, by Giovio, Ruscelli and Dominicho. In the *Choice of Emblemes* so many counterparts exist, set forth with word, device and stanza, to the descriptions and mottoes of these three Italian writers, that it is only reasonable to infer Whitney's knowledge of them, and unconscious if not direct use of the materials which they supply.

We will therefore, so far as relates to Whitney, trace out some correspondences and resemblances, and the more so because the principles, history and construction of emblems which Giovio's *Treatise* develops possess high value in themselves, and present many points of interest in connection with emblem art. Besides this plan will afford a suitable opportunity for introducing some of the historical anecdotes with which certain devices and mottoes are accompanied.

For this purpose we take the seven emblems from Whitney, on pages 111, 121, 139*a*, 140, 153*a*, 166 and 195, which correspond in their
Plate LX. mottoes or general nature with seven others in Giovio's *Dialogo*, edition *in Roma* M.D.LV.*

Emb. p. 111. Whitney's motto, "*pietas in patriam*," and the device of Scævola's
Dialogo, p. 64. hand thrust into the flame, correspond with Giovio's "*fortia facere et pati Romanvm est*," To do braue deeds and to suffer belongs to a Roman.

* We give the references to the Italian of Giovio, Ed. 1555, and the translation by Daniell, 1585.

This motto was placed by S. Mutio Colonna on the "vpper Armour and Ensignes" of his "companie of an hundred Launces," with the device of "an hande burning in the fire vpon an Aulter of Sacrifice." The allusion is to Mutius Scævola, who burned his hand because it had failed to strike Porsenna dead, — thus expressed by Paradin: "*Tel regret & desplaisir reçeut M. Scæuola Rommain, d'auoir failli à occire le Tirant, qui opprimoit sa patrie, que lui mesmes dans vn feu, en voulut punir sa main propre.*" Devises Héroïqves, fol. 73.

The next motto, "*Festina lentè*," with its appropriate device of a butterfly held captive by a crab, is expressed in Giovio by the synonymes "*propera tarde*," Hasten slowly. Giovio takes this as an example of *Impresas* known to the ancients, and records among others how "*Plutarch* reporteth that Pompey the great did beare for his Enseigne a *Lyō* with a sword clasped in his claw. We find also in the remaynes of old antiquities many to haue like signification to our moderne *Impreses*, as appeareth in that of *Vespasianus*, which was a *Dolphin* intangled with an Anchore, with this posie: *Festina lentè*, Make soft speede." Daniell adds to the text of Giovio, "A sentence which *Octavianus Augustus* was wont often to vse."* Giovio and Symeoni's *Sententiosi Imprese* gives the following Italian version: Emb. p. 121. Dialogo, p. 5. For example, see Whitney, p. 116. Edit. 1562, p. 11.

"Di Cesare Avgvsto

Augusto pria col Granchio & la Farfalla
Fece in oro scolpire il bel concetto,
Quasi dicisse in cosi vario obietta,
Chi bien pensa, & fa tosto, mai non falla."

Festina lenté.

"*Sic spectanda fides*," and gold on the touchstone, find their counterpart in Giovio's "*Fides hoc vno, virtvsqve probantur*," Fidelity and valour are proved by this one thing; where the allusion is to *Fabritio Colonna* who took for his *Impresa* a touchstone, "to importe that his vertue & faith should of al men bee knowne by touch and triall. This did he weare at the cōflict of *Rauenna*, where his valiant courage was manfully shewen, albeit he was there wounded and taken prisoner." Emb. p. 139*a*. Dialogo, p. 61.

Previous notices at pp. 303, 304 and 364 show that other persons

* The addition to Giovio's text is probably from Symeoni's *Devises Héroïqves et Morales*, p. 218, edition à Lyon 1561, which is also the source of Paradin's and of Whitney's emblem. We there read of the "*bon Prince et Empereur Auguste*," that wishing to show that the first reports and informations are not lightly to be believed, "*feit frapper entre plusieurs autres en vne sienne medaille d'or vn Papillon et vne Escreuisse, signifiant la vistesse par le Papillon, et par l'Escreuisse, la paresse, lesquelles deux choses font vn temperement necessaire à vn Prince.*" Plate LXII.

Edit. 1553, fol. 101. also adopted the same device. Paradin, from whom Whitney borrowed it, merely remarks: "*Si pour esprouuer le fin Or, ou autre metaus, lon les raporte sus la Touche, sans qu'on se confie de leurs tintemens, ou de leurs sons, aussi pour connoitre les gens de bien, & vertueus personnages, se faut prendre garde à la splendeur de leurs œuures, sans s'arrester au babìl.*"

Emb. p. 140. Dialogo, p. 10. The motto, "*Feriunt summos fulmina montes,*" was adopted by Cæsar Borgia's brother *Don Francisco* duke of *Candia*, "who had for his *Impresa* the Mountaine *Chimera*, or *Acroceraunes* strikê with the lightning of heauen." "Which likewise was verified in his vnhappie end, being strangled and throwne into *Tiber* by *Cæsar* his brother." Whitney has nothing in common with Giovio but the motto, and the last of his three stanzas. The device in the *Choice of Emblemes* is identical with one in Sambucus, and the first two stanzas are founded on the ten elegiac lines of the same author, whose motto, "Canis queritur nimium nocere," is far more suitable to the subject than the one adopted through Giovio from Horace.

Edit. Antv. 1564, p. 183.

Emb. p. 153*a*. Dialogo, p. 135. Again in the motto only, *Pro bono malum*, is there a correspondence between Whitney and Giovio. The illustrations given are widely different, though both appropriate: "Master *Lodouico Aristo,*" says Giovio, as translated by Daniell, "inuented a notable *Impresa*, figuring a Hiue of Bees with their home, whom the vngratfull peasant doth stiffle with smoke, bereauing them of life, to recouer their honie and waxe: with this mot, *Pro bono malum*: signifying thereby as it is thought how he had beene ill intreated of a certaine Nobleman, which may also bee gessed by his *Satyrs.*"

Fable 70 Whitney's device is from Faerni's *Fables*, and pictures the hind that injured the branches which concealed her, and thus returned evil for good, and brought vengeance on herself; for

"*Divina ingratos homines ulciscitur ira.*"

Emb. p. 166*b*. Dialogo, p. 26. Whitney applies the motto, "*Si Deus nobiscum, quis contra nos,*" so as to suit a device for the apostle Paul;* but Giovio, in a passage which Daniell omits, appropriates it to one of the kings of France. After describing the device of Louis XII., a hedgehog crowned, Giovio says: "I have passed by the *Impresa* of Charles VIII., because it had neither shape nor subject, though it had a motto very beautiful in spirit, '*If God be for us, who against us.*' On the standards and the coats of the

Devises Héroïques, fol. 112. * Thus given by Paradin: "*Saint Paul, en l'isle de Malte fut mordu d'vn Vipere: ce neantmoins (quoique les Barbares du lieu le euitasse autrement) ne valut pis de la morsure, secouant de sa main la Beste dans le feu: car veritablement à qui Dieu veut aider il n'y a rien qui puisse nuire.*"

archers of the guard there was nothing but the letter K surmounted by the crown, which indicated Charles's own name."

Our last instance is of similarity of devices between Whitney and Emb. p. 195. Giovio, but of dissimilarity of mottoes. The device was invented by Dialogo, p. 79. Giovio himself, — an elephant crushing a dragon. The mottoes are, in the dialogue, a Spanish one, "NON VOS ALABEREIS," You need not boast; and in the *Choice of Emblemes*, "*Victoria cruenta*," A bloody victory, from Plantin's edition of Sambucus, 1569, p. 228. Giovio is rehearsing three *Impresas* of his own, which he made "at the request of two Gentlemen of the house of *Flisca*, *Sinibaldo & Ottobuono*, whereof one was to signifie the revenge, which they had of the death of their Brother *Girolamo*, cruelly murdered by the *Fregosi* cõpetitors of the state: for the which these lost their liues, *Zaccaria Fregoso*, *S. Fregosino*, *Lvdouvico* and *Guido:* which reuenge did something recomforte them for the losse of their Brother." "I therfore figured an Elephant assalted of a Dragõ, who twinding about the legges of his enemie, is wont by his venomous byting to empoyson him, wherewith he dieth. But the Elephant by nature knowing the daunger, trayleth him along the grounde till he come to some stone or blocke, whereunto leaning himself he rubbeth there against the Dragon that he dieth."

Ruscelli's *Discourse* furnishes little, if anything, to be remarked upon Plate LXI. in immediate connection with Whitney: the case is somewhat different with regard to the "*Ragionamento*," or *Treatise*, by Lodovico Domenichi, edition *Venice* 1556. Here we find the germs at least of several of Whitney's emblems. I name two for example's sake: one, the withered elm and the fruitful vine supported by it* — illustrating Emb. pp. 62 and 120. the motto, "*Amicitia post mortem dvratvra*;" the other, a wakeful dog Ragionamento, (Whitney says a lion) keeping guard over a flock, or at the gate of a pp. 102 and 134. church† — a device suiting the motto, *Non dormit qvi cvstodit*, He sleeps

* Domenichi's text is: "*Questo m'ha fatto ricordare una Impresa dell' Alciato ne* Plate LXI. *suoi Embleme, laquale è una Vite fresca & uiua abbracciata sopra uno Olmo secco, con* p. 102. *un motto*, AMICITIA POST MORTEM DVRATVRA; *ilche si potrebbe appropriare a Donna ualorosa & pudica, la quale si come in uita ha di continuo amato, & mantenuta fede al marito, cosi lama & honora ancho dopo morte, con fermo proponimento di non douersi mai piu scordar di lui, & della sede promessagli.*"

† "*Per li Cani anchora*," says Domenichi, "*sono interpretati i prelati del le sacre* pp. 133 and 134. *Chiese di Christo; iquali si proueggono per difendere le greggie dalle insidie de gli auuersari & per custodir sicure le pecorelle da ogni ingiuria de lupi. È attribuita ancho al Cane la memoria, la fede, & lamicitia. Però mi parue conuenirsi questa Impresa si honorato personaggio, col motto* NON DORMIT QVI CVSTODIT."

not who watches, or "*Vigilantia et custodia*," Watchfulness and guardianship. A comparison of the two writers, and an investigation into the two emblems, will reveal how close the relations are between emblem writers generally, and how we may often trace out their resemblances and imitations.

Edit. 1581, Emb. 159. The first example we have in Alciat's lines, followed by Whitney, p. 62:

"ARENTEM *senio, nudam quoq; frondibus vlmum,*
Complexa est viridi vitis opaca coma:
Agnoscitq; vices naturæ, & gratæ parenti
Officij reddit mutua iura suo.
Exemploq; monet, tales nos quærere amicos,
Quos neque disiungat fædere summa dies."

Edit. 1581, Emb. 15. The second also from the same author, Whitney, p. 120:

"INSTANTIS *quòd signa canens det gallus Eoi,*
Et reuocet famulas ad noua pensa manus:
Turribus in sacris effingitur ærea peluis,
Ad superos mentem quòd reuocet vigilem.
Est leo: sed custos oculis quia dormit apertis,
Templorum idcirco ponitur ante fores."

"PAOLO GIOVIO'S AND GABRIEL SYMEONI'S SENTENTIOSE IMPRESE," p. 240.

This joint work is the only one of theirs to which we have given special references for devices copied by Whitney; but if the inquiry had not been limited to such books as were the probable or the undoubted sources of his emblems, a much fuller notice of Giovio and of Symeoni would have been given. The omission might in part be supplied by references to the titles of some of the earliest editions both of the "*Dialogo*," and of the "*Devises Héroïques*," to which first Paradin and then Whitney were largely indebted. (Plates LX. LXI. and LXII.)

Essays, p. 275. From the records of Giovio's death, December 11th 1552, and the date of Antonio Barre's Roman edition of the *Dialogo*, October 8th 1555, it appears that nearly three years elapsed between the one event and the other; and Ruscelli, writing in February 1556, in some degree confirms this by speaking of the bishop of Nocera as "the very reverend Paolo Giovio of happy memory."

Plates LX. and LXI. To the want of the author's own supervision it is to be attributed that, between the editions of Antonio Barre in 1555 and of Gabriel Giolito in 1556 and the editions of Giordano Ziletti in 1556 and 1560, there should be a difference amounting to eight or nine pages. The pages thus added are however omitted from Roville's French edition of 1561, and from his Italian edition of 1574, which agree with Barre's and Giolito's. The titles of Roville's French and Italian editions have not been given, and are here subjoined, because, through Paradin, they are the undoubted originals of many of Whitney's devices.

DIALOGVE DES DEVISES D'ARMES ET D'AMOVRS DV S. PAOLO IOVIO, *Auec vn Discours de M. Loys Dominique sur le mesme subiet.* Traduit d'Italien par S.ʳ Vasquin Philieul. *Auquel auons adiousté les Deuises Héroïques & Morales du Seigneur* GABRIEL SYMEON. *A LYON,* PAR GVILLAVME ROVILLE. 1561. *Auec Priuilegio du Roy.*" 4to, pp. 255, devices 136, ovals with highly ornamented borders.

DIALOGO DELL' IMPRESE MILITARIA *et Amorose* di Monsignor Giouio Vescouo di Nocera, *Et del S. Gabriel Symeoni Fiorentino.* Con vn ragionamento di M. Lodouico Domenichi, nel medesimo sogetto. *Con la Tauola. IN LYONI* Appresso Guglielmo Rouillio, 1574." 8vo, pages 280, besides the tables. The devices are 136, also ovals, but without borders, yet evidently from the same blocks with the French edition of 1561, though considerably worn by use.*

We will just add, respecting "the Worthy Tract of Paulus Iouius" "*by Samuell Daniell late Student* in Oxenforde," that it is dedicated "TO THE RIGHT WORSHIPFVL SIR EDWARD Dimmock, Champion to her Maiestie," to whom "SAMVEL DANIEL wisheth happie health with increase of Worship." In 10 pages "To his Good Frend Samvel Daniel N. W. Wisheth health;" and in 14 pages S. D. makes an address "TO THE FRENDLY READER;" then writes the translator, "HERE BEGIN THE Discovrses of Pavlvs Jovivs Bishop of Nocera, in the forme of a Dialogue had betweene him and *Lodouicus Dominicus. Dedicated to S. Cosimo Duke of Florence.*" The translation comprises 99 pages; and then in 12 pages "HERE FOLLOW tovching the Former subiect, certaine notable deuises both militarie and amorous, *Collected by Samuel Daniel.*" Plate LX.

The rarity of these editions almost demands the notice which has been given of them; but that notice is the more required because the works themselves opened up the principles on which devices and emblems are formed, and furnished the students and scholars of the latter half of the sixteenth century with examples of emblem art to guide as well as to instruct. Indeed any general history of the subject

* "LE SENTENTIOSE IMPRESE," also published by Roville in 1562, makes use of 126 of the same blocks, with an ornamented but different border. Discarding the borders altogether, Plantin's artist, in executing the devices for the Antwerp edition of Paradin, followed Roville's woodcuts very closely; and thus, as we have shown, 32 of Whitney's emblems are, for the designing at least, to be ascribed to the artists of Lyons or of Italy. Plate XXXVI. Essays, p. 240. Essays, p. 248.

would bestow marked attention on the Italian writers who, in discoursing of *Imprints military and amorous*, have collected and preserved information full of interest and value.

And now, having brought my labours as editor to a close, I may be allowed to say that I feel far less confident than I did when I began them, of having sufficiently prepared myself by reading and study for the work. With every research that I have made, the extent, and I may add the worth, of emblem literature has grown upon me; and if I had known as much then as I do at this time, probably I should have retired from the enterprise, deeming myself unequal to it: but having once in earnest put my hand to the plough I determined not to look back: the fallow ground has been upturned, and such seed cast in as research and opportunity supplied. His task accomplished is of course a creation of joy to the writer; much more would he have it, for his readers, a creation of regard in behalf of a class of authors long neglected, and especially of interest in those combinations of artistic skill and poetic imagery which at the revival of learning in Europe contributed so much both to amuse and instruct the literary world.

Knutsford,
January xiiith, m.dccc.lxvi.

SOLIDEO HONOR ET GLORIA

INDEX TO THE ILLUSTRATIVE PLATES.

INDEX TO SOME OTHER ILLUSTRATIONS.

Plate 1

TABULA CEBETIS

Græce, Arabice, Latine.

Item

AUREA CARMINA PYTHAGORÆ,

Cum paraphrasi Arabica,

AUCTORE

IOHANNE ELICHMANNO M. D.

Cum Præfatione

CL. SALMASII.

LUGDUNI BATAVORUM,

Typis IOHANNIS MAIRE,

cIↄ Iↄ c•xL.

Plate 7

ΩΡΟΥ Α-
ΠΟΛΛΩΝΟΣ ΝΕΙΛΩΟΥ
ἱερογλυφικά.

ORI APOLLINIS
NILIACI, DE SACRIS
notis & sculpturis libri duo, vbi ad
fidem vetusti codicis manu scripti restituta sunt loca permul-
ta, corrupta ante ac
deplorata.

Quibus accessit uersio recens, per Io. Mercerum Vticesem concinnata, & obseruationes non infrugiferæ.

PARISIIS
Apud Iacobum Keruer, via Iacobæa,
sub duobus Gallis.
M. D. LI.

Πῶς γέροντα μουσικόν. 39.

Γέροντα μουσικὸν βουλόμενοι σημῆναι, κύκνον ζωγραφοῦσιν. οὗτος γὰρ ἥδιστον μέλος ᾄδει γηράσκων.

Quo modo senem Musicum.

Senem musicum volentes cómonstrare, cygnum pingunt: quod hic senescens suauissimũ edat concentum.

Plate 3.

Emblematical Tableau of Human Life, from Cebes the Theban, B.C. 390.

Plate 4.

I

Stultifera Nauis.

Narragonice ꝑfectionis nunq̄

ſatis laudata Nauis: per Sebaſtianu̅ Brant: vernaculo vul=
garicq̧ ſermone & rhythmo / ꝓ cu̅ctorum mortaliu̅ fatuitatis
ſemitas effugere cupie̅tiu̅ directione / ſpeculo / co̅modoq̧ &
ſalute: proq̧ inertis ignaueq̧ ſtultitie ꝑpetua inſamia̅ / exe=
cratione / & confutatione / nuꝑ fabricata: Atq̧ iampridem
per Iacobum Locher / cognome̅to Philomuſum: Sueuu̅: in
latinu̅ traducta eloquiu̅: & per Sebaſtianu̅ Brant: denuo
ſeduloq̧ reuiſa / & noua q̄da̅ exactaq̧ emendato̅e elimata:
atq̧ ſuꝑadditis ꝗbuſda̅ nouis / admira̅diſq̧ fatuorum generi=
bus ſuppleta: fœlici exorditur principio.

·1497·

Nihil ſine cauſa.

Io. de. Olpe.

XXIX

De obsequio duoꝝ dn̄orum

Ille duos lepores venator captat in vno
Tempore: per syluas quos canis vnus agit
Qui cupit ardenter dominis seruire duobus:
Hic plusq̄ poterit: sepe agitare volet.

Seruire duobus.

Nemo p̄t duob⁹ dn̄is seruire: aut enī vnū odiet & alterū diliget aut vni adherebit & alterū cōtemnet. Nō potestis deo seruire & mamō/ne. Qui ad vtrū= ꝗ festinat neutrū bene peragit. pluribus intentus minor est ad singu= la sensus Cor igre diēs duas vias nō habebit successus

Stultus & is sumo qui vult magnoq; tonanti:
Et mundo pariter querit seruire ꝓphano.
Nam veluti dominis qui seruire duobus
Raro fit: vt talis semper sit gratus vtriq;.

Math.vi.
Luce.xvi.
Eccle.iii.

Brant's Ship of Fools. Ed. 1497.

ANDREAE ALCIATI EMBLEMATVM LIBELLVS.

PARISIIS,
Excudebat Christianus Wechelus,
sub scuto Basiliensi, in uico
Iacobeo. Anno
M. D. XXXIIII.

In receptatores sicariorum.

Latronum furumq; manus tibi Scæua per urbem
It comes, & diris cincta cohors gladijs.
Atque ita te mentis generosum prodige censes,
Quod tua complureis allicit olla malos.
En nouus Actæon, qui postquàm cornua sumpsit,
In prædam canibus se dedit ipse suis.

G ij

Plate 6.

Whitney p. 15.

Plate 7.

Constanier LES et synsere
DEVISES
HEROIQVES,
De M. Claude Paradin, Chanoine
de Beaujeu,
Du Seigneur Gabriel Symeon & autres Aucteurs.

A ANVERS,
De l'Imprimerie de Christophle
Plantin,
M. D. LXII.
AVEC PRIVILEGE.

Gulfridus Whytney: Cestreshir

Me pompæ provexit apex.

La plus grande recompense, ou plus grãd loyer que les antiques Rommains estimassent faire aux Chefz d'armee, Empereurs, Capitaines, et Cheualiers victorieus, c'estoit de les gratifier & honnorer

T 2

Plate 18.

ICONES,

id est

VERAE IMAGINES

VIRORVM DOCTRINA SIMVL ET PIETATE ILLVSTRIVM, QVORVM PRÆcipuè ministerio partim bonarum literarum studia sunt restituta, partim vera Religio in variis orbis Christiani regionibus, nostra patrúmque memoria fuit instaurata: additis eorundem vitæ & operæ descriptionibus, quibus adiectæ sunt nonnullæ picturæ quas EMBLEMATA vocant.

Theodoro Beza Auctore.

GENEVÆ,

APVD IOANNEM LAONIVM.

M. D. LXXX.

Plate 9.

MINERVA BRITANNA: *THE SECOND PART* OR A GARDEN OF HEROYCAL Devices: furnished, and adorned with Emblemes, and *Impresa's* of sundry natures. Newly devised, *moralized, and published,*

BY HENRY PEACHAM, Mr. of Artes.

PRINCEPS
TIBI
CRESCIT
VTRVMQUE

P 3.

Date 1612.

DEATH meeting once, with *CVPID* in an Inne,
Where roome was scant, togeither both they lay.
Both wearie, (for they roving both had beene,)
Now on the morrow when they should away,
CVPID Death's quiver at his back had throwne,
And *DEATH* tooke *CVPIDS*, thinking it his owne.

Hoc [illegible] habet Whitnæus in [illegible] Embl: quod bona cum illius venia ab Authore etiam mutuatur [illegible].

By this o're-sight, it shortly came to passe,
That young men died, who readie were to wed:
And age did revell with his bonny-lasse,
Composing girlonds for his hoarie head:
Invert not Nature, oh ye Powers twaine,
Giue *CVPID'S* dartes, and *DEATH* take thine againe.

Later

Peacham's Min. Brit.

Plate 11

A sweet Nosgay,

Or pleasant Posye: contayning a hundred and ten Phylosophicall Flowers. &c.

¶ The I. Flower.

Such freendes as haue ben absent
more ioyful be at meeting (long
Then those which euer presẽt are
and dayly haue their greetyng.

¶ The II

¶ When peryls they are present, then
doth absence keepe thee free:
Whereas, if that thou present were
might dangers light on thee.

The III.

¶ The presence of the mynd must be
preferd, if we do well:
Aboue the bodyes presence; for
it farre doth it excell.

B.ii.

To the worship-

full and right vertuous yong Gentylman, GEORGE MAINVVARING Esquier: IS. VV. wissheth happye health with good successe in all his godly affayres.

When I (good M. MAINVVARING) had made this simple Nosegaye: I was in minde to haue to the same on sonderie frind, of which number I haue good occasion to accompt you chiefe: But waying with my selfe, that although the Flowers bound in the same were good: yet so little of my labour was in them that they were not (as I wysht they should) to bee esteemed as recompence for the least of a great number of benefits, which I haue frõ time to time (euen from our Childhod hetherto) receaued of you: yet least by me, you m be occasioned to say, as ANTIPATER said DEMADES of Athens, that he should neuer fill him with geuing, I woulde to shew my selfe satisfied, gratifye your Guifts, and also by the same, make a confession that by deedes you haue deserued benefits: which as DIOGENES saith)

A.iii.

Isabella Whitney, 1573.

Plate 11a

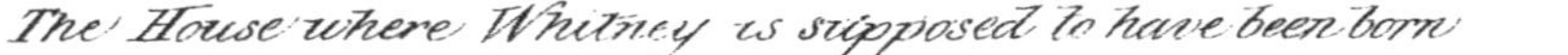

The House where Whitney is supposed to have been born

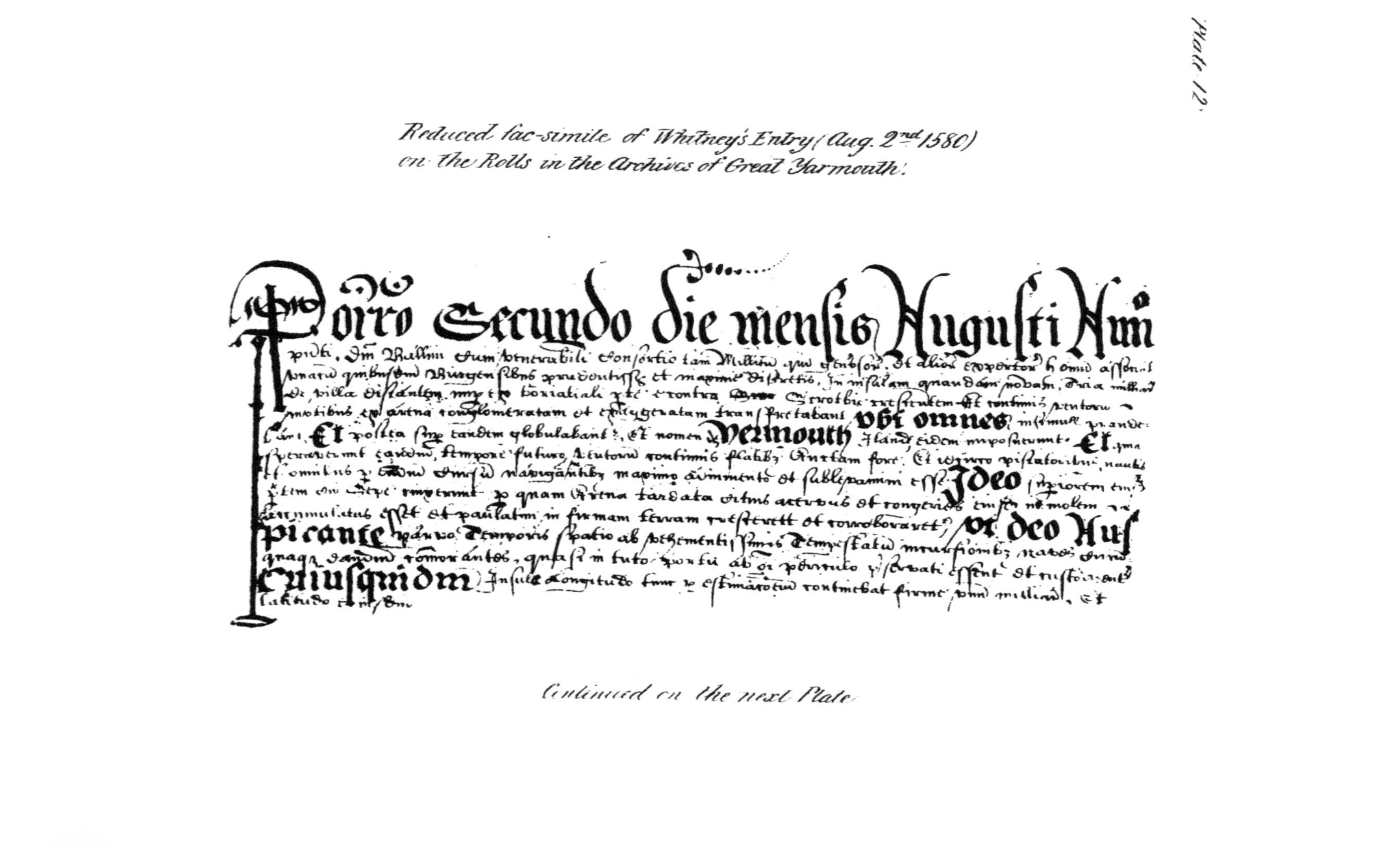

Reduced fac-simile of Whitney's Entry (Aug. 2nd 1580) on the Rolls in the Archives of Great Yarmouth.

Continued on the next Plate

Nōia eorum tam Generosorum

quam Burgensium et Rusticanorum qui [illegible] insula tunc [illegible] sequent. viz.

Nōia militum

- Arthurus Heumarkham
- Radus Shelton
- Rogerus Woodhouse

— militis

Nōia Armigerorum

- Edwardus Flowerdewe Justiciarius ad legem
- Thomas Gasbrowne
- Thomas Westerhassett
- Johannes Woodhouse
- Henricus Appleyard

— Armigeri

Nōia generosorum

- Johannes Shelton
- Franciscus Calthorpe
- Edmundus Rowes
- Petrus Lovedaie
- Franciscus Traver
- Willelmus Downinge
- Johannes Kettyll
- Thomas Robinson
- Thomas Aleman

— generosi

Nōia Burgensium

- Radus Penthorne et Johannes Giles
- Davidus Calthorpe ar.
- Willelmus Harthrowne
- Johannes Wakeman
- Radus Tompson
- Johannes Fulton
- Thomas Damett
- Johannes Greenewood
- Galfridus Whitney
- Johannes Smithe sen.
- Johannes Woulden
- Thomas Collins
- Thomas Wimman
- Johannes Pelde
- Petrus Smithe

— Burgenses

Nōia Rusticanorum

- Johannes Ort
- Radus Jyngam
- Michael Walbe
- Jacobus Robinson

- Petrus Dart
- Thomas Mullins
- Petrus Starker

- Willelmus Greene
- Petrus Newton
- Henricus Miller

Soli deo honor et gloria in aeua sempiterna. Amen

Plate

The Church of Acton, near Nantwich.

Plate 14.

Combermere about 1725.

Plate 15

NANTWICH CHURCH.

Plate 15[a]

NANTWICH CHURCH.

Plate 16

ANDREAE AL-
CIATI EMBLEMATVM LI-
BELLVS, NVPER IN LV-
CEM EDITVS.

VENETIIS, M. D. XLVI.

Cum priuilegio Pauli III. Pont. Max. & Senatus Veneti, ad annos decem.

EMBLEMATVM LIBELLVS.

Terminus.

Quadratum infoditur firmissima tessera saxum,
Stat cirrata super pectore imago tenus,
Et sese nulli profitetur cedere. talis
Terminus est, homines qui scopus unus agit.
Est immota dies, præfixaq; tempora fatis,
Deq; ferunt primis ultima iudicium.

E

Plate 11

DIVERSE IMPRE
SE ACCOMMODATE A
diuerse moralità, con versi
che i loro significati dichia
rano insieme con molte al-
tre nella lingua Italiana
non piu tradotte.
Tratte da gli Emblemi
dell' ALCIATO.

IN LIONE DA GVLIELMO
ROVILLIO. 1551.

CON PRIVILEG

40

Plate 18

Che Altro pecca, & altro n' ha la punitione.

Il cane il sasso ond' è percosso, prendre,
Ne pur riuolge a chi'l percote, i denti,
Cosi alcun lascia gir quei che'l onfede,
E fa portar le pene a gli innocenti.

Whitney p. 56

Plate 19

EMBLEMATA
D. A. ALCIATI,
denuo ab ipso Autore
recognita, ac, quæ desi-
derabantur, imagini
bus locupletata.
*Accesserunt noua aliquot ab
Autore Emblemata suis quoq;
eiconibus insignita.*

LVGD. APVD GVLIEL.
ROVILIVM. 155[illegible]

CVM PRIVILEG

Plate 20

60 PERFIDIA.

In receptatores sicariorum.

Latronum furumq; manus tibi Scæua per vrbem
It comes: & diris cincta cohors gladijs.
Atque ita te mentis generosum prodige censes,
Quòd tua complures allicit olla malos.
En nouus Actæon, qui postquàm cornua sumpsit,
In prædam canibus se dedit ipse suis.

Whitney p. 15.

Plate 21

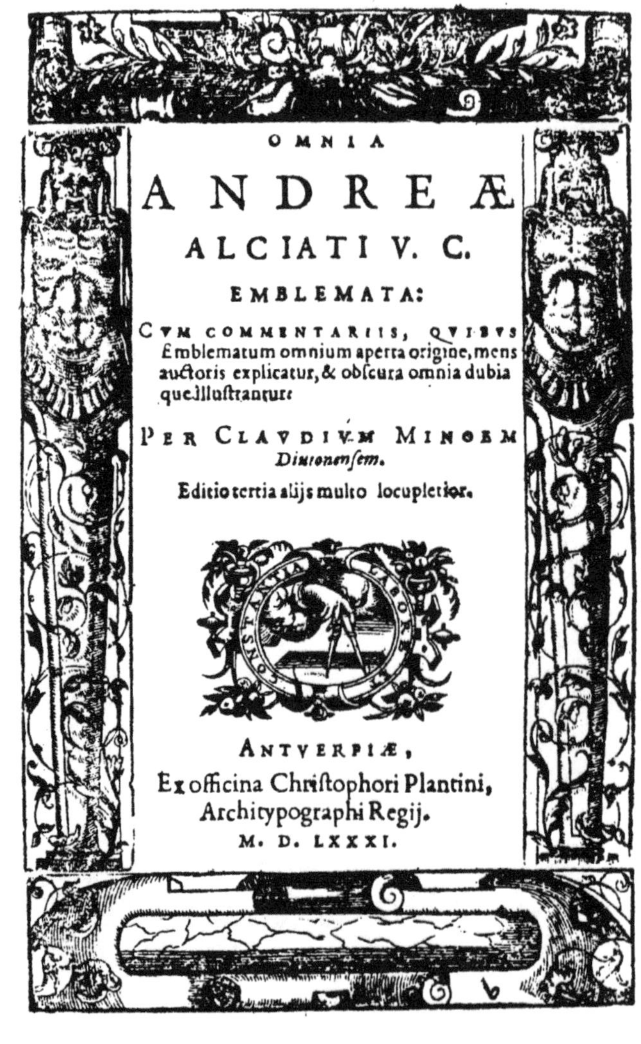

OMNIA

ANDREÆ

ALCIATI V. C.

EMBLEMATA:

CVM COMMENTARIIS, QVIBVS Emblematum omnium aperta origine, mens auctoris explicatur, & obscura omnia dubiaque illustrantur.

PER CLAVDIVM MINOEM *Diuionensem.*

Editio tertia alijs multo locupletior.

ANTVERPIÆ,
Ex officina Christophori Plantini,
Architypographi Regij.
M. D. LXXXI.

Cum laruis non luctandum.

EMBLEMA CLIII.

AEACIDAE moriens percussu cuspidis Hector,
Qui toties hosteis vicerat ante suos;
Comprimere haud potuit vocem, insultantibus illis,
Dum curru & pedibus nectere vincla parant.
Distrahite ut libitum est: sic cassi luce leonis
Conuellunt barbam vel timidi lepores.

ID sumptum esse liquet ex Homericae Iliados χ. Graeci Hectorem ab Achille iam interfectum circumstantes impetebant, & mortuo insultabant, nec erat quisquam qui extincto vulnus non infligeret. Sic enim Homerus:

Locus Homeri.

— ἄλλοι

Whitney p 127

Plate 23

ACHILLIS BOCCHII BONON. SYMBOLICARVM QVAESTIONVM,

De vniuerſo genere, quas ſerio ludebat,

LIBRI QVINQVE.

BONONIAE,

Apud Societatem Typographiae Bononienſis.

MDLXXIIII.

Curiae Epiſc. & S. Inquiſit. conceſſu.

Plate 24

EMBLEMATA,
CVM ALIQVOT
NVMMIS ANTIQVI
OPERIS, IOANNIS
SAMBVCI TIRNAVI-
ENSIS PANNONII.

ANTVERPIAE,
EX OFFICINA CHRI-
STOPHORI PLANTINI.

M. D. LXIV.

CVM PRIVILEGIO.

Voluptas ærumnoſa.

QVI nimis exercet venatus, ac ſine fine
Haurit opes patrias, prodigit inque canes:
Tantus amor vani, tantus furor vſque recurſat,
Induat vt celeris cornua bina feræ.
Accidit Actæon tibi, qui cornutus ab ortu,
A canibus proprijs dilaceratus eras.
Quàm multos hodie, quos paſcit odora canum vis,
Venandi ſtudium conficit, atque vorat.
Seria ne ludis poſtponas, commoda damnis,
Quod ſupereſt rerum ſic vt egenus habe.
Sæpe etiam propria qui interdum vxore relicta
Deperit externas corniger iſta luit.

Conſue-

Whitney p. 15

Plate 26

HADRIANI

IVNII MEDICI

EMBLEMATA,

AD

D. ARNOLDVM COBELIVM.

EIVSDEM

AENIGMATVM LIBELLVS,

AD

D. ARNOLDVM ROSENBERGVM.

ANTVERPIÆ,

Ex officina Christophori Plantini.

M. D. LXV.

CVM PRIVILEGIO.

Plate 26a

Impunitas ferociæ parens.

Insultant pauida hic natio musculi
Clausis muscipulæ carcere felibus.
Sublató que metu fortè periculi
Crescit tunc animus degeneri insolens.

Vita

Whitney p 222

Plate 26 b

Principum opes, plebis adminicula.

Pyramides Phariûm monumēta perennia Regū,
Errātibus circūligat hedera sequax brachiis.
Regum opibus firmis plebs sustentatur egena:
Mentisq; constans firmitas viret perenniter.

Seipsum

Whitney p 1

Plate 26 c

Veritas tempore reuelatur, dissidio obruitur.

Quid penniger Saturne in auras virginem nu-
dam rapis?
Quid fœminarum cœtus aggesta obruit terra
scrobem?
Specu emicãtem veritatẽ, temporis natã, triplex
Obruere pestis apparat; Lis, Inuidia, Calumnia.

Discor-

Whitney p. 4.

Plate 20 d

Prouidentia.

Ad Iacobum Endium reipub. Holl. caussarum vindicem.

Quò sacer excurret Nilus in arua,
Præscius, alluuie libera ponit
Oua, monens meritò nos Crocodilus
Quæ fata immineant antè videre.

Whitney p 3

CENTVM

FABVLÆ
EX
ANTIQVIS
AVCTORIBVS
DELECTÆ,

ET

A GABRIELE FAERNO
Cremonensi Carminibus explicatæ.

ANTVERPIÆ,
Apud Christophorum Plantinum.
M. D. LXXXV.

VVLPES *esuriens, alta de vite racemos*
Pendentes nulla cum prensare arte valeret,
Nec pedibus tantum, aut agili se tollere saltu,
Re infecta abscedens, hæc secum, Age desine, dixit,
Inmatura uva est, gustuq́; insuauis acerbo.

Consueuere homines, euentu si qua sinistro
Vota cadunt, iis sese alienos velle videri.

INSE-

La grãt nef des folz du mõde

En ce liure trouuer pourrõt les ſaiges
Les folz auſſi ſe par bonne memoire
Prenrẽt plaiſir a lire les paſſaiges
De la lettre et le ſens de liſtoire
Expoſee ſans long prolocutoire

Pluſieurs grans biens: car dedãs ceſte nef
Qui de ſalut eſt la porte et la clef
Chaſcun peult veoir q̃ vault vertu ou vice
Par ce liuret et petit ediffice
Que trouuerez chez gieffroy de marnef.

Plate 29

En iterum nostris ⁊c.

Mon commencemēt de ceste satyre est vne quarte furie adiou
stee a troys qui est. le ieu dit
ie andoubteray icy mes folz.
Et ainsi a noz chansons de
rechief se offre la tourbe ⁊ cōpaignie sordide
des ieux Car aucuns sont tellement abra-
sez du debat du ieu ⁊ hōnorent les ieux p si
grāde seduite ⁊ haste qlz se reputent ioyes
souueraines tourner les dez ⁊ ainsi troys
dez bien courās sur table leur appareillent
leurs seules ioyes tant que les estrifz de
leurs ieux tournēt ⁊ passent les iours ⁊ les
nuictz Car tousiours le decourt et deman
de les gaingz sordides ou infames ⁊ mal
acqs Aduiēt aucunesfoys q̄ le de enrichist

Nunc sendo ditat ⁊c.

aucun p le frequēter Mais la chiēne faulse
⁊ dōmaigeuse le mort Cest a dire luxure q̄
incōtinent le rase et luy oste tout a la fin et
voulentiers voyt on cōmunement q̄ ce q̄
vng iouer d dez y gaigne sil ne le repert il
le despend auecqs quelque paillar de q̄ ainsi
q̄ vne chiēne le mort Et sil en est tant soit
pou abuse ne fait point difference de luy
donner tout ce q̄ elle demande / car il luy
semble bien q̄ cest argēt la ne couste rien Le
ieu est mauuais / car il fait lhōme vile et

La v⁹ agit vilem ⁊c.

iracundieux relasche les secretz de la pēsee
gaste et infait lentendement et lengin de
lhomme et nuyst aux sens Il fait les hō
mes courroussez quant ilz perdent et
froisse les precordes si que par le de les
hommes sont tousiours sollicites en peine trauail et soucy Car combien que on
ny vse point les souliers ⁊ q̄ la peine des
membres ne soit pas grande les esperitz
sont tousiours en trauail ⁊ sans quelque
repos. Rien aultre chose ne curent les

Nil curant aliud. ⁊c.

ioueurs que le ieu Toute leur volupte
et plaisance est fichee aux sors et aux ad
uentures du de ou de la carte si quil leur
semble que ce soit vne grace de dieu quāt
le de leur dit bien. Et par nuict sans repos veillent crient iurent souuent / et ne
les esmeut aucune fain ou aucune soif.
Et le grant mal est q̄ souuēt par griefue

Sepe furore grau ⁊c.

fureur ilz diffament les playes de Iesu
crist en iurant par le sang par la mort
ou par la vertu et tournent leurs ordes
et nephandes parolles aux dieux souue-
rains et blasphement dieu et les sainctz ain-
que se le conditeur du monde eust la cure ou
garde des ioueurs pestiferes et ql ployast
a leurs laydes parolles Une chose plus
spurcide et orde toutesfoys est que la fēme
meslee auecques les mauuais hōmes ioue
⁊ vacque tousiours a la table Et ont acou
stume le noble / le clerc / le citoyen / le ieune /
lancien iouer souuent auecques les petis
vulgaires et tendre peuple auquel il est de-
cent et appartient quil ioue peu / quil pren-
ne temps conuenables et quil eslise person
nes pareilles a luy Cest assauoir que quāt
vng simple homme de mestier veult iouer
par quelque maniere de recreation il le doit
faire brief non pas y vser les nuictz de peu
de chose et en temps quil ne perde point a
faire son labeur ordinaire Auecques gens
aussi qui ne soyent point plus grans mai-
stres que luy ou aultrement il se destruit.

Whitney p 176

Le Theatre
DES BONS EN-
gins, auquel sont con-
tenus cent Emble-
mes.

Auec priuilege.

On les vend à Paris en la rue neufue nostre
Dame à l'enseigne sainct Iehan Baptiste, pres
saincte Geneuiefue des Ardens.

CI.

EN ce pourtraict pouuez veoir diligence,
Tenant en main le cornet de copie:
Elle triumphe en grand magnificence:
Car de paresse onc ne fut assoupie:
Dessoubz ses piedz tiẽt faininę acroupie
Et attachée en grand captiuité:
Puis les formys par leur hastiuité
Diligemment tirent le tout ensemble:
Pour demonstrer qu'auec oysiuité,
Impossible est que grãdz biẽs l'õ assẽble.

O iii

Whitney p 175

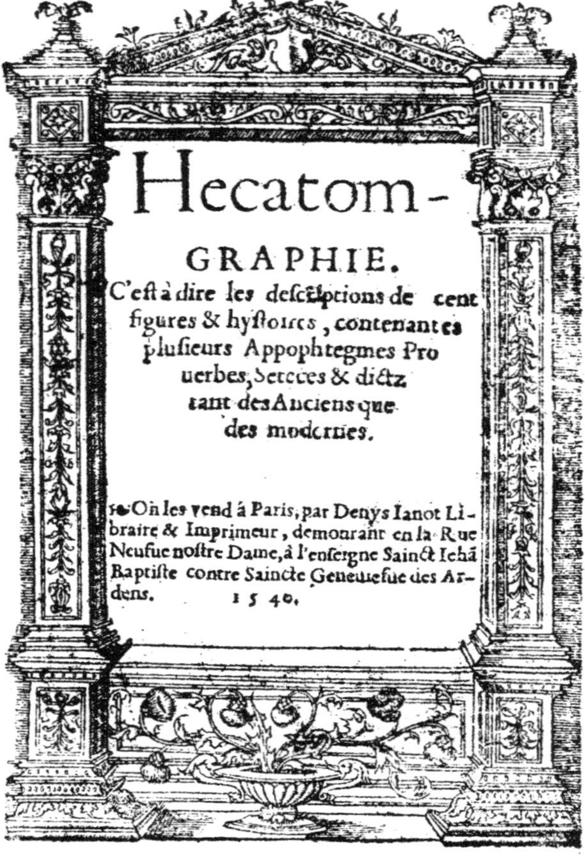
Hecatom-
GRAPHIE.
C'est à dire les descriptions de cent
figures & hystoires, contenantes
plusieurs Appophtegmes Pro
uerbes, Sentences & dictz
tant des Anciens que
des modernes.
On les vend à Paris, par Denys Ianot Libraire & Imprimeur, demourant en la Rue
Neufue nostre Dame, à l'enseigne Sainct Iehā
Baptiste contre Saincte Geneuiefue des Ardens. 1540.

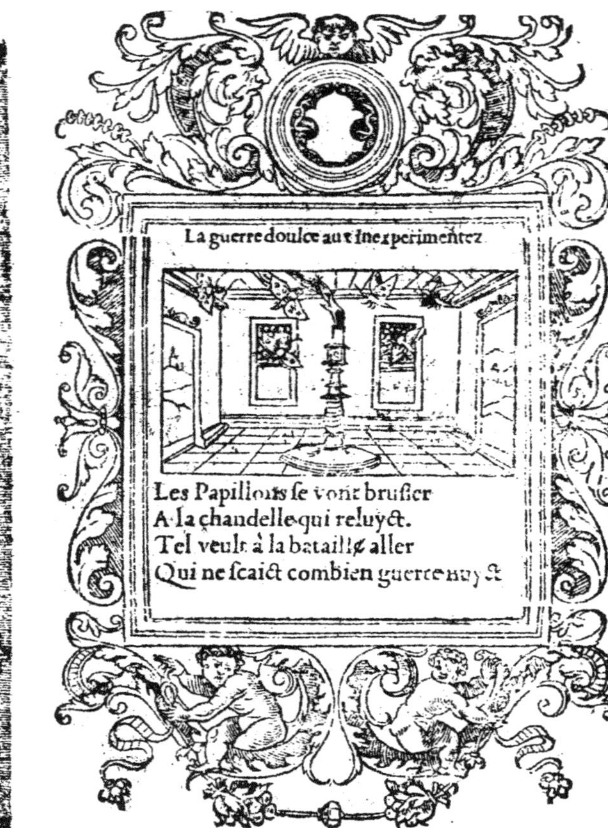
La guerre doulce aux inexperimentez
Les Papillons se vont brusler
A la chandelle qui reluyct.
Tel veult à la bataille aller
Qui ne scaict combien guerre nuyct

Plate 33

PICTA POESIS.

VT PICTVRA POESIS ERIT.

LVGDVNI,

Apud Mathiam Bonhomme.

1552

CVM PRIVILEGIO.

SINE IVSTTIA, CONFVSIO.

Si TERRAE Cœlum se misceat: & mare cœlo.
Sol Erebo. Tenebris lumina, Terra Polo.
Quattuor & Mundi mixtim primordia pugnent.
Arida cum siccis, algida cum calidis.
In Chaos antiquum omnia denique confundantur:
Vt cùm ignotus adhuc mens Deus orbis erat.
Est Mundanarum talis confusio rerum.
Quo Regina latet Tempore Iustitia:

D

PETRI COSTALII
PEGMA,
Cum narrationibus philosophicis.

LVGDVNI,
Apud Matthiam Bonhomme.

1555
CVM PRIVILEGIO REGIS.

Plate 34

Ferrum.

In miseriam humanæ sortis.

Cladibus in multis hominum traducitur
Sed stat in accessu mortis inempta
Hoc duce uel miseris subitò licet esse beatis:
Quem qui obiit, credo ne superesse uelit.

Whitney p 131

LE
PEGME DE PIERRE
COVSTAV, auec les NARRATIONS
PHILOSOPHIQVES,
Mis de Latin en Françoys par LANTEAVME de Romieu Gentilhome d'Arles.

A LYON, Par Barthelemy Molin.
M. D. LX.
Auec Priuilege du Roy.

Sur l'exemple d'un fol & d'un sage.

Le temps fait tout.

L'homme auisé poil apres poil arrache
A son loysir la queuë du cheual:
Mais l'imprudēt d'un effort, biē ou mal,
De l'emporter par violence tache.
Tems & labeur cōioints & mis ensemble.
Conferent tout: n'y a rien que ne sache
Celuy auquel l'esperance ne fache,
Si le labeur auec le tems assemble.

LE SENTENTIOSE IMPRESE DI MONSIGNOR PAVLO GIOVIO, ET DEL SIGNOR GABRIEL SYMEONI, RIDOTTE IN RIMA PER IL DETTO SYMEONI.

Al sereniſsi. Duca di Sauoia.

IN LYONE,
APRESSO GVLIELMO ROVIGLIO.
1562.
Con Priuilegio del Rè.

DI POVERTA OFFESA.

Scribit in marmore læsus.

Tempri l'ira veloce ogniun, che viue,
Et per esser potente non ha cura,
Di far' altrui talhor danno o paura,
Che l'offeso l'ingiuria in marmo scriue.

Whitney p. 183

Plate 38

MYTHOLOGIA
ETHICA,

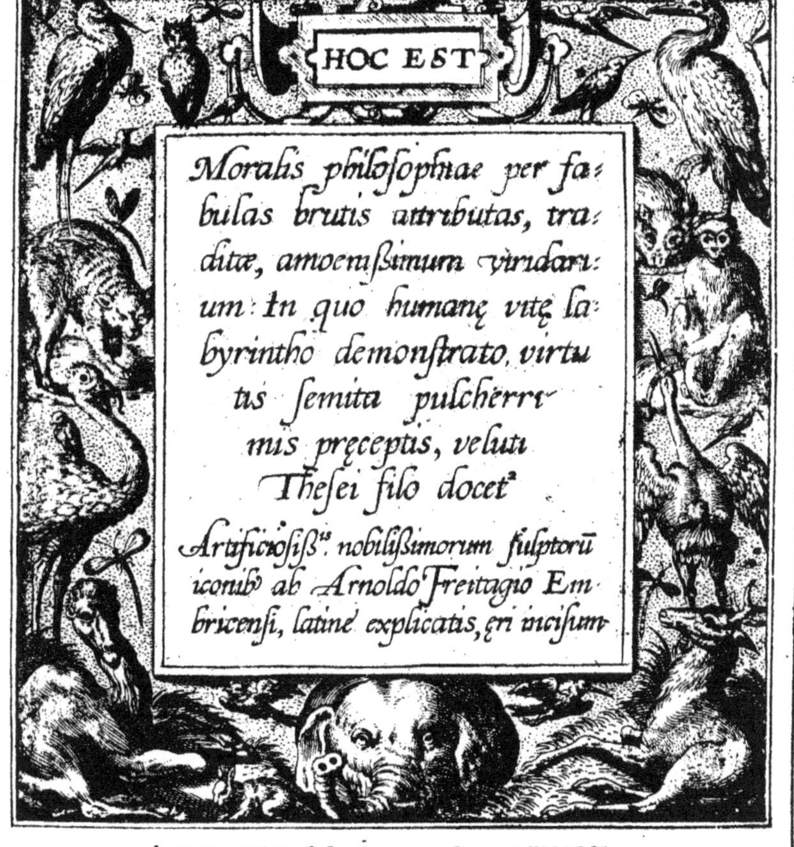

HOC EST

Moralis philosophiae per fa-
bulas brutis attributas, tra-
ditæ, amoenißimum viridari-
um: In quo humanę vitę la-
byrintho demonstrato, virtutis semita pulcherri-
mis pręceptis, veluti
Thesei filo docet.

Artificiosiss. nobilißimorum sculptorū
iconib. ab Arnoldo Freitagio Em-
bricensi, latine explicatis, æri incisum.

ANTVERPIÆ, M. D. LXXIX.

Iuuenilia ſtudia cum prouectiori ætate permutata.

Deponite vos, ſecundum priſtinam conuerſationem, veterem hominem, qui corrumpitur ſecundum deſideria erroris. Epheſ. 4, 22.

PHOE-

Contraria induſtriæ ac deſidiæ præmia.

Propter frigus piger arare noluit: mendicabit ergo æstate, & non dabitur illi.
Prouerb. 20, 4.

LV

The Grasshopper and the Ants *Whitney p 159*

EMBLEMA. XIIII.

Sectantes velut umbra fugit, fugientibus instat,
Addita corporibus scilicet umbra comes,
Sic fugit immeritæ captantes præmia laudis,
Demissis contra gloria iuncta comes.
Et tamen haud falso trutinata examine, quidnam
Laus hæc omnis erit? scilicet umbra leuis.

Whitney p 32

Plate 42

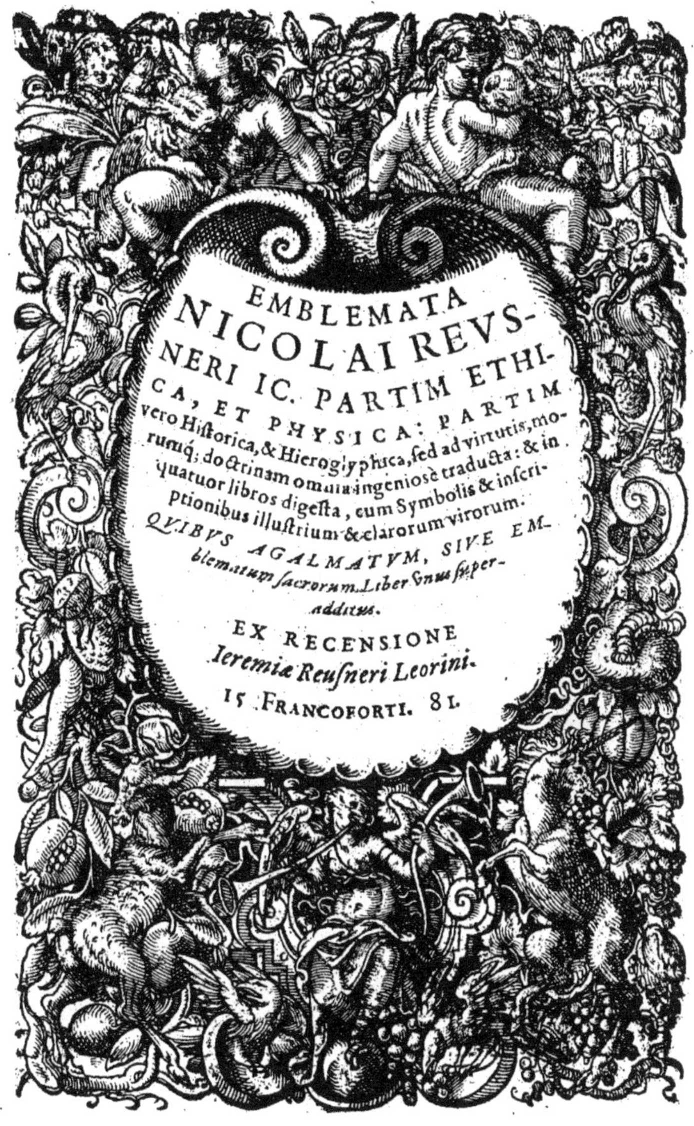

EMBLEMATA
NICOLAI REVS-
NERI IC. PARTIM ETHI-
CA, ET PHYSICA: PARTIM
vero Hiſtorica, & Hieroglyphica, ſed ad virtutis, mo-
rumq; doctrinam omnia ingenioſè traducta: & in
quatuor libros digeſta, cum Symbolis & inſcri-
ptionibus illuſtrium & clarorum virorum.
*QVIBVS AGALMATVM, SIVE EM-
blematum ſacrorum Liber Vnus ſuper-
additus.*

EX RECENSIONE
Ieremiæ Reuſneri Leorini.

15 FRANCOFORTI. 81.

Plate 43

Sed benè, Palladiæ quod seruor numine dextra:
Perdicem me sicillico fecit auem.

Homo homini lupus.

EMBLEMA XXX.

Ad Hieronymum Reusnerum Leorinum.

LYncus rex Scythiæ ferus, Arcadiæq́; Lycaon,
Quàm benè nomen habet, sæuus vterq́;, lupi.
Pœna fit hæc sceleris: namq́; hospes, vt hostis, vterq́;
Dum parat hospitibus damna, fit inde lupus.
Aut homini Deus est homo; si bonus: aut lupus hercle,
Si malus: ô quantum est esse hominem, atq́; Deum.

Quid

Whitney p 144

ANGLORVM PRÆLIA

ab anno Domini. 1327. anno nimirùm primo inclytissimi Principis Eduardi eius nominis tertij, vsque ad annũ Domini. 1558. Carmine summatim perstricta.

ITEM.

De pacatissimo Angliæ statu, imperante Elizabetha, compendiosa Narratio.

Authore CHRISTOPHORO OCLANDO, primò Scholæ Southwarkiensis propè Londinum, dein Cheltennamensis, quæ sunt à serenissima sua Maiestate fundatæ, Moderatore.

Hæc duo Poemata, tàm ob argumenti grauitatem, quàm Carminis facilitatem, Nobilissimi Regiæ Maiestatis Consiliarij in omnibus huius regni Scholis prælegenda pueris præscripserunt.

Hijs Alexandri Neuilli KETTVM: tùm propter argumenti similitudinem, tùm propter orationis elegantiam adiunximus.

LONDINI:
Apud Radulphum Nubery, ex assignatione Henrici Bynneman Typographi. ANNO. 1582.
Cum priuilegio Regiæ Maiestatis.

From Ocland's Anglorum Prœlia — Londini, 1582

Plate 44

CHRISTOPHORVS PLANTINVS

Plate 45

ICONES
QVINQVAGINTA VIRORVM
illustrium doctrina & erudi-
tione præstantium ad vivum
effictæ, cum eorum vitis
descriptis
a
Ian. Iac. Boissardo Vesunti:
Omnia recens in æs artificiosè
incisa, & demum foras data
per
Theodorum de Bry Leodien
civem francofurti
Anno M.D.XCVII.

Plate I

III. PARS
ICONVM
VIRORVM ILLVS-
TRIVM,
QVORVM ALII QVIDEM INTER VIVOS ESSE, IAM OLIM
desierunt, aliȷ vero nunc quoq; vitali aura, honorumq;
suorum beati per fruuntur gloria.
Natalium eorundem succincta notatio, singulis Iconibus adiuncta:
Disticha passim addita singulis, opera et studio
Omnia in ære recens scite facta, et edita per Hæredes Theodori de Bry.
Francofurdi ad Moenum Anno MDIIC.

Plate 47

SEBASTIANVS BRANDVS QVI ET TITIO
Nascitur Argent.
Anno 1458.
Obijt ibid. An. 1520.
Tractavit Leges pariter, sacramque Poesin,
Nobilis ingenio Brandus, at arte rudis.

Plate 48.

PAVLVS IOVIVS NOVOCOMENSIS.
Diligeris Cosmæ, coleris quoque Paule, Leoni:
Doctus eras medicus, doctus es historicus.

Plate 49

ANDREAS ALCIATUS IURECONSULTUS
Nascitur Mediolani
Anno
Obijt anno 1550
Andreas prisco reddit sua jura nitori,
Consultosque facit doctius inde loqui

HADRIANUS IUNIUS HORNANUS Medicus.
Invidiam uincis studio, probitate laborç.
Gratia nunc meritis reddita digna tuis.

Plate 51

THEODORVS BEZA VEZELIVS
Qui tibi seruiuit tot CHRISTE fideliter annos,
Ipse tua BEZAM quæso tuere manu
Viuat qui viuit nulli grauis, omnibus vsu;
Viuat qui viuit, maxime Christe, tibi.
nat. 1519. den. 1605

Plate 52

Plate 53.

IOANNES SAMBUCUS MED ET HISTORIC
Nascitur in Vngaria an 1531
Obijt Vienna an 1583
Excitat et sanos scriptis Sambucus, et ægros
Restituit medica maximus arte manu

Plate 51

IMAGO NICOLAI REVSNERI IVRISCONSVLTI.

TAlis eram, septem lustris sine labe peractis:
Quod superest, aeuum tu rege, CHRISTE, meum.

IV. Non. Febr. M. D. XXC.
Aet. XXXV.

NICO-

I. 1

Whitney p 126 & 206.

Plate 56

THE HEROICALL DEVISES OF M. CLAVDIVS PARADIN

Canon of Beaulieu.

Whereunto are added the Lord Gabriel Symeans, and others.

Translated out of Latin into English by P. S.

LONDON,
Imprinted by William Kearney dwelling in Adlingst-
1591.

Sic spectanda fides,

So is faith to be tried.

The goodnes of gold is not onely tryed by ringing, but also by the touchstone: so the triall of godlines and faith is to bee made not of wordes onely, but also by the action & performance of the deedes.

Whitney p 139

Plate 57

Me pompæ prouexit apex.

The desire of renowne hath promoted me, or set me forward.

The Romaines supposed it the chiefest reward of famous deedes, if they adorned their Emperors, captaines, knights, & other cōmon soldiers, euery one notwithstāding according to their dignity, degree & place, with crownes

farre from fearing least his pollicie which hee vsed should be espied, that he gaue for his simbole a bow which was wont to bee bent with strings or cordes, this apothegme being added thereto, *Ingenium superat vires*, Pollicie is of greater force then strength.

Qui me alit, me extinguit.

He that nourisheth me, killeth me.

In the exile or barnishment of the Heueti-

Whitney p 183

Plate 58

Principis clementia.

Vesparũ quòd nulla vnquam Rex spicula figet:
Quodq; aliis duplo corpore maior erit.
Arguet imperium clemens, moderataq; regna,
Sanctaq; iudicibus credita iura bonis.

T.

Whitney p 200

EMBLEMA XXII.

Luna velut toto collustrans lumine terras,
Frustra allatrantes despicit alta canes:
Sic quisquis Christum allatrat Christive ministros,
Index stultitiæ spernitor vsque suæ.

Whitney p. 213. From Theodore Beza

DIALOGO

DELL'IMPRESE MILITA-
RI ET AMOROSE DI
Monsignor Paolo Giouio *Ve-
scouo di* Nucera

Con Gratia & Priuilegio.

IN ROMA APPRESSO
ANTONIO BARRE
M D L V.

THE

Worthy tract of

Paulus Iouius, contayning a
Discourse of rare inuentions, both
Militarie and Amorous
called Imprese.

VVhereunto is added a Preface contay-
ning the Arte of composing them, with
many other notable deuises.

By Samuell Daniell late Student
in Oxenforde.

AT LONDON,
Printed for Simon Waterson.
1585.

DI MONS. PAOLO GIOVIO
ſoprai motti, & diſegni d'arme,
& d'amore, che commu-
nemente chiamano
IMPRESE.

CON VN DISCORSO DI
Girolamo Ruſcelli, intorno allo
ſteſſo ſoggetto.

Con Priuilegio.

IN VENETIA, MDLVI.
Appreſſo Giordano Ziletti, all'Inſegna della Stella.

DELL'IMPRESE MILITARI ET AMOROSE,

DI MONSIGNOR GIOVIO
VESCOVO DI NOCERA.

CON VN RAGIONAMENTO DI
MESSER LODOVICO DOMENICHI,
NEL MEDESIMO SOGGETTO.

CON LA TAVOLA.

IN VINEGIA APPRESSO GABRIEL
GIOLITO DE' FERRARI.
M D L V I.

Plate 62

LES
DEVISES, OV
EMBLEMES HEROI-QVES ET MORALES,

INVENTEES PAR LE S. GABRIEL SYMEON,

A MONSEIGNEVR LE Conestable de France.

A LYON,

PAR GVILLAVME ROVILLE,

1561.

Auec Priuilege du Roy.

Plate 63

SAINT VALIER.

En la iournee des Suisses desfaicts pres de Milan par le feu Roy François, Monsieur de Saint Valier le vieil, pere de Madame Diane de Poitiers, Duchesse de Valentinois, & Capitaine de cent Gentilshommes, porta vn Estendard, là ou estoit en peincture vne torche allumee contre bas, & tout plein de cire qui couloit pour l'esteindre, auec ces paroles: QVI ME ALIT, ME EXTINGVIT. *Suyuant la deuise du Roy son maistre, à sauoir,* NVTRISCO ET EXTINGVO. *Et la nature de la cire qui nourrit le feu, & l'esteint, quand elle coule dessus par trop grande abondance. Laquelle deuise il feit pour amour d'vne Dame, voulant signifier que tout ainsi que sa beauté nourrissoit sa pensee, ainsi le mettoit en danger de sa vie.*

PAT

Whitney p 183

GENERAL INDEX.

Roman numerals refer to the Introductory Dissertation; *Arabic* with [ ] to Whitney's Dedication &c., and without a bracket to the Emblems, Essays and Notes; *O. L.*, ornamented letter; *Ed.* edition; *Emb.*, emblem; *Pl.*, plate.

Fools, p. xiv, 237; Locher's Stultifera Nauis, 1497, Title, Pl. 4, xiv; specimen of, Pl. 5, Emb. 223, p. 274; Marnef's Grat nef des folz du monde, 1499, title, Pl. 28, xv, 238; specimen of, Pl. 29, Emb. 176, 275; Barclay's Shyp of Folys of the Worlde, 1509; *see* Barclay.

Brant, Sebastian, 1458–1520; Portrait, Pl. 47; notice of, and works 274, 5.

Britain,—its interest in emblem literature, xxii, xxiii.

Brooke, George, *Esquier*, 1568–1603, Emb. 69, son of lord Cobham, beheaded at Winchester, 337; or one of the Cheshire Brookes, 337; who intermarried with the Whitneys; branches of the family,—Brookes of Norton, 337.

Browne, John, James *and* Lancelot, *eminent physicians*, Emb. 212,—name celebrated among physicians; Brownes of Cheshire; Lancelot a native of Yorkshire, 391; landscape Brown, 392 *n.*

Bry, Theodore De,—his Icones or Portraits, title, Ed. 1597 Pl. 45; Ed. 1598, Pl. 46, p. 272. Account of the work;—source of several of the portraits, p. 272.

Brydges, Samuel Egerton,—notice of Willet, xx; Retrospective Review on Whitney's emblems, p. xxxii and xxxiii.

Brydges, sir Egerton,—account of Isabella Whitney, p. lix.

Bull, St., *the very learned*, Emb. 185 and 186, no certain information of, p. 375. A sir Stephen Bull,—Bulls in Hertfordshire, p. 375; Conjecture of a misprint, and John Bull,—1565–1615, the musician, suggested, p. 376.

Bvrgoine, George, *Esquier*,—his Nine Sons, Emb. 72; not identified, 338;—Name belongs to Bedfordshire,—tradition in the township of Sutton,—ten baronets of the family, 338.

Butterfly and crab, the device of Augustus, Emb. 121, p. 407 and 407 *n.*

C. *O. L.* 281, Alciat's Emblems, [p. 38] *Antverpiæ* 1581.

O. L. 284, of uncertain origin.

Calthorpe, Barthram, *Esquier*, Emb. 71. The Calthorpes of old standing in Norfolk,—Barthram probably a brother to Charles, Emb. 136, p. 338.

Calthorpe, Charles, *the very hon^{ble}*, Emb. 136, brief notice of, 361; at Scratby island, Pl. 13, p. 403; Members of this "knyghtly family;" Charles in high office in Ireland, 361.

Candia, duke of, his *Impresa*, 408.

Caracci, Augustino,—in 1574 retouched the device of Bocchius, 284.

Cartwrighte, Geffrey,—Whitney's uncle, Emb. 166; may be brother of Whitney's mother, xliii, xlviii, 366; in 1666 a Geffrey Cartwright of Sale; Churton's conjecture; Richard Cartwright (1563–1637) married a daughter of sir John Egerton, and was a relative of Whitney, 367.

Catz, Jacob,—1577–1660,—"Vader Catz," xxiii. Moral Emblems from,—*London* 1862, xxiii *n.*

Cebes, Tablet of, B.C. 390, p. 272; title, Ed. 1640 Pl. 1, numerous editions since 1497, p. xi. Delineation of the Tablet by de Hooghe, Pl. 3, p. xi; character of Cebes, p. xi.

Champollion's judgment of Horapollo, p. 273.

Charles VIII., his Impresa and motto, 408.

Chater, Rev. Andrew F., rector of Nantwich, xlv.

Chartvlarvm Mainwaringianvm, 1093–1669, compiled by Dugdale, 356. Extracts from, 357, 364; records, 364; diversifyings of the name Mainwaring, 358 *n.*

Chatterton or Chaderton, *Bishop of Chester*, died 1608, Emb. 120. Remarks on the device, 349; Fuller's notice, 349; that by the Rev. F. R. Raines; pedigree, daughter and grand-daughter, 350; the bishop's character; instances of his wit, 351; Chaplain to Leicester in 1568; Sources for information, 352.

Cheshire gentlemen and the dean and chapter of Chester,—Leicester's good offices between them, 317.

Chester,—Robert Dudley, entertained there, p. 317.

Choice of Emblemes, Ed. 1586; *see* Whitney.

Cholmeley, *Sir* Hvghe, *Knight*, Emb. 130. Knighted with others; how named in Fuller's Worthies, 355; Webb's encomium; descendants, 356.

Cholmley, sir Hugh, of Yorkshire, 355 *n.*

Cholmeley, Hvghe, *Esquier*, 1552–1601, Emb. 138; descent of the family, 362; arms, 363; member for Cheshire; wife, the bold Ladye of Cheshire, 364; lords-lieutenant, 363; tomb, 364.

Cholmondeleys and Egertons of the same stock, 362.

Clemens on Egyptian writing, xii *n.*

Colley, *Mrs.* D., Whitney's sister, xvii, xlvi, Emb. 91, 341; name borne by the Wellesley family, 341; Colley of Audlem, 342.

Collier, J. Payne,—"Sir Philip Sidney his Life and Death," 327.

F. *O. L.* xix, and 290, Corrozet's HECATOMGRAPHIE. f. 51, *Paris* 1540.
O. L. xxiii and 288, Nef des Folz, f. xxv, *Paris* 1499.
Fables and Epigrams, a work by Whitney,—no trace of it known, lvi, conjecture respecting it, lvii.
Fables by Perret, *Anvers*, 1578; of Æsop, *Antverpiæ* 1581, p. 237.
Faerni's "FABULÆ C." &c., *Romæ* 1564,—designs from Titian, p. 251; Plantin's editions 1563–1585, p. 251; "CENTUM FABVLÆ" &c., *Antverpiæ* 1585, Pl. 27, p. 251; Fox and Grapes, Pl. 27, Emb. 98, p. 344; Whitney has *sixteen* identical devices,—some of his borders from this edition, 251. The hind injuring the leaves, 408.
Faerno, Gabriello, died 1561; his fables written at the request of Pius IV.—correct Latinity; notice of the author, 288.
Feriunt summos fulmina montes Emb. 140,—adopted by Francisco duke of Candia, p. 408.
Festina lentè Emb. 122,—the motto of Augustus and of Vespasian, 407.
Flemish emblem books; translations from Sambucus, 1566, 248; and Junius, 1575, 250; also Goedthal's Proverbs, 1568, p. 237.
Flisca, S., O., and G.,—their device and motto, 409.
FLOWERDEWE, EDWARD, *an eminent judge* died 1586, Emb. 121 and 122. Under steward of Great Yarmouth in 1580, p. li, Pl. 13, p. 402; Notice of; other sources of information, 353.
Foliato, Hugo de,—his Emblems, "De Volucribus" of the thirteenth century, xxxii *n*, 272.
Fontana, Prospero, a contributor to the devices in Bocchius, Ed. 1555. p. 284.
Fortiter et feliciter, Emb. 115,—the device of the dukes of Milan, 348.
Fraunce, Abraham, *London* 1588, his work rather a book of heraldry, xxi.
FREAKE, EDM., *an excellent youth*, Emb. 100, son of bishop Freake, 344,—the name in Devonshire and Hampshire, 345.
Freitag's "MYTHOLOGIA ETHICA," Ed. 1579, Title Pl. 38, p. 241; specimen devices, Pl. 39, The Phœnix Emb. 179, 291; Pl. 40, the ants and grasshopper, Emb. 159, p. 291, 365: *twelve* devices similar to those in Whitney,—one of the same origin, 241; Engravings by Gérard de Jode, 241, 290.
Freitag, Arnold, born about 1560,—Notice of him, 290, 1.
French Emblem-books; *original*,—Corrozet's Hecatomgraphie, *Paris* 1540, Pl. 32, p. 239; Paradin's Devises Héroïques, Ed. *à Lyons* 1557, 247,—also Ed. *Anvers* 1562, Pl. 7, p. 246; Perret's "XXV. fables des animaux," *Anvers* 1578, p. 237; Perriere's "Théâtre des bons Engins," *Paris* 1539, Pl. 30, p. 238; Symeoni's Devises ou Emblemes Héroïques &c., *à Lyon* 1561, Pl. 62, 240, 410: *translations*,—Aneau's Alciat, Ed. 1549, p. 287; Aneau's "Imagination Poëtique, *Paris* 1552, p. 239, 287; Filleul's or Philieul's,—Giovio, 1561, p. xviii, 411; Grevin's Emblesmes de Adrian le Jeune, 1567, p. 250; Grevin's Sambucus, 1567, p. 248; Goedthal's Proverbes anciens &c. 1568, p. 237; Goulart's Beza, 1581, p. 242; Horapollo, 1543, p. 273; Lanteaume's Pegme, 1560, Pl. 35, p. 240; Marnef's "Grand Nef des Folz du Monde," 1499, Pl. 28, p. xv and 238; Symeoni's Devices and Emblems, 1565, p. 277; 1561 p. 411.
Frontis nulla fides, Emb. 100, the stanzas to be compared with Sambucus, p. 344.
Frontispieces,—Whitney's arms, p. iv, xxxix; Leicester's, p. [2] 105, 314; Alciat's, p. 232, 406; queen Elizabeth's, Pl. 43 *a*, p. 401.

G. *O. L.* ix, Linacre's GALEN, f. 1, C. altered, *Paris* 1538.
O. L. 275, Corrozet's HECATOMGR. f. 61, *Paris* 1540.
GALLI CANTUS Johannis Alcock, &c., 1498, p. 349.
German Emblem-books: Brant's "Narrenschyff," Ed. 1494, p. xiv, xxxi, 237; Horapollo, 1554, p. 273.
Giovio and Symeoni's "SENTENTIOSE IMPRESE," or "Tetrastichi Morali," Ed. 1562, Pl. 36, p. 240 and 410; probable source of *thirteen* of Whitney's emblems, p. 241; Wrongs on marble, Pl. 37, p. 241, 276; correspondence in Shakespeare, 308; device of Augustus, 407; through Paradin, the original of many of Whitney's devices, p, 410.
Giovio's *Dialogo &c.*: Ed. *Rome* 1555, Pl. 60, p. 406; *Venice* 1556, Pl. 61, p. 311 *n*; *Lyons* 1574, p. 411, or Ragionamento &c., Ed. *Venice* 1556, Pl. 61, p. xviii and 311 *n*, 406. Daniell's version, p. xviii, *London* 1585, Pl. 60, 311 *n*.
Giovio Paolo, 1483–1552, Portrait, Pl. 48, biographical notice, 275, 6, and 410; Oettinger names another bishop of

Nocera, 276 *n*; Device of his invention, p. 409.
Goltzius Hubert, an engraver, his monogram on some of the devices of Sambucus and Junius, as Pl. 20 *d*, p. 248, 321.
GOSLINGE, *Mr.* JOHN, Emb. 215, p. 393, of Norwich, educated at Cambridge, p. 394; named in an inscription to Dr. Legge, 394.
Grasshopper and Ants, Emb. 159, Pl. 40, p. 291, 365.
Greek Emblem-books,—Tablet of Cebes, B.C. 390, p. 272, Pl. 1 and 3, Ed. 1640, p. xi; Hieroglyphics of Horapollo, A.D. 408–450, Pl. 2, p. xi, xii, 272, 3. Some Greek stanzas in the Picta Poesis, p. 287.
Greville, Fulke, lord Broke,—Sidney's friend, p. 324, 359;—his Life of Sidney, 324.
GRYPHITH, ELLIS, Emb. 101, conjectures respecting him, 345.
"*Guerre doulce aux inexperimentez*," Pl. 32, Emb. 219,—Portia's words agree with this device and motto, p. 295.
Guevara, Antony de, died 1544, author of the Golden Epistles, Emb. 94, p. 342.

H. *O. L.* 243, 372, Nef des Folz, xv *b*, *Paris* 1499.
Hadrian Junius;—*see* Junius.
Hakluyt's Voyages,—quoted 389, 390.
HAREBROWNE, M. WILLIAM, *at Constantinople*, Emb. 207; of a Norfolk family, 389; variations in spelling the name, 389; Elizabeth's ambassador to the Sultan, 1582–1588, p. 389; Journey to and from Constantinople, 390: the Turkey company, 390.
Hermann's PIA DESIDERIA &c., *Antwerp* 1628, englished by Arwaker 1686, p. xxii.
HEROICALL DEVISES &c., translated by P. S. 1591, Pl. 56, p. xviii and 247; testing Gold, Pl. 56, Whitney's Emb. 139,—remarkable history, 303, 364, 407,—applied by Shakespeare in Pericles, 304,—also the wreath of chivalry, and burning torch, Pl. 57; questionable whether from this translation, 304.
Hesius Guilielmus,—EMBLEMATA, &c., *Antwerp* 1636,—p. 298—Emblems of Hope, 298.
Heywood, Thomas, esq.—information respecting the Herefordshire Whitneys, p. xxxvii; edition of Cardinal Allen's Defence of Sir W. Stanley, p. 330.
HIEROGLYPHICA,—title of various works; by Cœlius Augustinus, Ed. 1567, p. 273; by Valerian, Ed. 1556 and 1567, p. xxi; Horapollo, Pl. 2, Ed. 1551, p. xi, 239; Romein de Hooghe, p. 273.
"HIEROGRAPHIA REGVM FRANCORVM," p. 303.
Historical Anecdotes connected with certain devices, 406–409.
Hive of bees, Emb. 200, Pl. 58, p. 305; with their home destroyed, 408.
HOBART, MILES, *Esquier*, Emb. 67, p. xxxiii, not the patriot member of Great Marlow; several Hobarts named;—who this Miles was undetermined, p. 336.
Holland's HEROÖLOGIA, *not* Horoölogia, p. 341.
Homo homini lupus, Emb. 144;—same motto, but not same device in Reusner, Pl. 43, 292, 365;—better, Homo homini deus, 292.
Hooghe, Romyn de, engraver of the Tablet of Cebes, Pl. 3, p. xi; splendid work,—HIEROGLYPHICA of Merkbeilden Der oude Volkeren &c., 1735, p. 273.
Hope, numerous emblems of, p. 298 *n*.
Horace, imitated by Whitney, lxi.
Horapollo's HIEROGLYPHICA, Ed. 1551, Pl. 2, a book of emblems, p. xi; early editions 1505–1548,—Dr. Conrad Leeman's edition, 1835; Whitney has *nine* similar devices, p. 239, 273, as the Swan, Pl. 2, Emb. 126, the poet's badge, p. 353, 4.
Horapollo, A.D. 408–450,—contrary opinions respecting him, xii; some account of, 272: various versions; Champollion's judgment of, 273.
HOWLTE, M., *Preacher*, Emb. 228; an old Cheshire and Lancashire name,—conjectured to be one of the Frankfort divines in 1557, p. 399.

I. *O. L.* 253, Alciat's DIVERSE IMPRESE, p. 2, *Lyons* 1551.
O. L. 282, Coustau's PEGME, *Lyons* 1560.
ICONES, *id est* Veræ Imagines &c., Pl. 8; Beza.
ICONES QUINQUAGINTA VIRORUM &c., Pl. 45 and 46; *see* De Bry.
Identical Devices in Whitney to those in earlier emblem writers, p. 243–252; to the number of 202, p. 252; confined to Plantin's editions, p. 244, 406.
Ille pompæ prouexit apex; in Paradin, Pl. 57; motto of the third knight in Pericles, 297 and 300.
IMPRESE, Imprints, p. xvii,—known to sir P. Sidney, 311 *n*; also to the ancients, 407.
IMPRESE ILLUSTRI &c., Ed. 1566; *see* Ruscelli.
In amore tormentum, Emb. 219, Device

from Corrozet, Pl. 32, 395; also in Giovio and Symeoni, 395.
Index,—to Mottoes in Whitney, lxxv–lxxix; to Proverbial Expressions, lxxx; to Mottoes in Whitney different to those in other emblem writers, 405; to the Illustrative Plates, 413–414, and other Illustrations, 414; *General Index*, 415.
Indices,—of Devices, similar in Whitney to those in other writers, 238–243;—identical, 245–251.
In pœnam sectatur & vmbra, Emb. 32, Pl. 41 from Beza, p. 323.
INSIGNIUM ARMORUM &c., Ed. 1588; *see* Fraunce.
Invocation to the Divine Spirit, p. 287.
Italian Emblem books;—Alciat,—Diverse Imprese &c., 1551, Pl. 17, p. 244; Domenichi's Ragionamento &c., 1556, Pl. 61, p. 311, 349, 351; Giovio's Dialogo, Ed. 1555 Pl. 60, Ed. 1556 Pl. 61, p. 311 *n*, 406, Ed. 1574, p. 411; Ragionamento, Ed. 1556, Pl. 61, p. 311 *n*; Giovio and Symeoni's Sententiose Imprese &c., 1562, Pl. 36, p. 240, 410; Horapollo, Ed. 1548, p. 273; Ruscelli's Discorso, Ed. 1556, p. 311 *n*; furnishes little to Whitney, 409.
Italian origin of devices to Junius, p. 250, to Bocchius p. 284; to Whitney 411 *n*.

JACOBS, Lucas, of Leyden, a celebrated engraver, p. xvi.
James I. of England, earliest known portrait of, in Beza's Emblems, p. xvii and 242.
JERMYN, *Sir* ROBERT, *Knight*, Emb. 43, Account of,—commended by Leicester, 327; of puritan principles,—Fuller's testimony; rarity of the name, 328.
Jocelyne, Mary, granddaughter of bishop Chaderton,—daughter of sir Richard Brooke, 350; author of the Mother's Legacy, 351.
JONSON, M. JAMES, Emb. 227; uncertain, 399.
Junius, Hadrian,—"EMBLEMATA" &c. Ed. 1565, Pl. 26, p. 249; most elegant devices of Italian origin, 250; specimens of this edition,—the cats entrapped, the rats at play, Pl. 26 *a* Emb. p. 222, 397; ivy and obelisk, Pl. 26 *b* Emb. 1, p. 319; truth from the well, Pl. 26*c*, Emb. p. 4, 321; the provident crocodile, Pl. 26 *d* Emb. p. 3, 321; from this edition Whitney has *twenty* identical devices, 250, 1:—"EMBLEMATA" &c. Ed. 1596; "EMBLESMES DE ADRIAN LE JEUNE" &c. Ed. 1567; "EMBLEMATA" "IN NEDERLANTSCHE TALC" &c. Ed. 1575, p. 250.
Junius, Hadrian, physician, 1511–1575, Portrait, Pl. 50; biographical notice, 282; works, 249; stanzas to his son Peter, p. 282 and 343.

KENRICK'S EGYPT,—modern discoveries in hieroglyphics, xii.
KNEWSTVB, M. *Preacher*, Emb. 223, *Nemo potest duobis dominis seruire*, Pl. 5, p. 397. A friend of bishop Chaderton and Dr. Andrews, p. 351; chaplain to the earl of Leicester; his works; rector of Cockfield, 397: further information where to be found, 398 *n*.
Koning's "LEXICON HIEROGLYPHICUM SACRO-PROFANUM," &c., 6 vols. large folio, *Amsterdam* 1722, p. 273.

LANGUET, Hubert, a friend of sir P. Sidney,—his correspondence, p. 324, 327.
Lanteavme de Romieu,—PEGME de Pierre Covstav, &c., Ed. 1560, Pl. 35, p. 240; Device, Le temps fait tout, Pl. 35,—to compare with Whitney's Emb. p. 230. *Eight* similar devices in Whitney, p. 240.
Latin Emblem books;—*original*, Alciat's Ed. 1534, Pl. 6; Ed. 1546, Pl. 16; Ed. 1551, Pl. 19; Ed. 1581, Pl. 21, p. 244, 245:—Aneau's "Picta Poesis," Ed. 1552, Pl. 33, p. 239; Beza's "Icones, id est Veræ Imagines," &c., Ed. 1580, p. 242; Bocchius "SymbolicarvmQvaestionvm," &c, Ed. 1574, Pl. 23, p. 284; Costalius,—"Pegma," &c., Ed. 1555, Pl. 34, p. 240; Faerni's "Centvm Fabvlæ," &c., Ed. 1585, p. 251; Freitag's "Mythologia Ethica," &c., Ed. 1579, Pl. 38, p. 241; Junius',—"Emblemata," &c., Ed. 1565, Pl. 26, p. 249; Reusner's "EMBLEMATA," &c., Ed. 1581, Pl. 42, p. 242; Sambucus, "EMBLEMATA," &c., Ed. 1564, Pl. 24, p. 248.
Latin Emblem books;—*translations;* Æsop,—"Fabulæ aliquot," &c., Ed. 1581, p. 237; Geyler's "Navicula, sive speculum fatuorum," &c., Ed. 1511, p. 235; Gouverneur, Jean le,—"Symbola Heroica M. Claudii Paradini," &c., Ed. 1567, p. 247; Horapollo, Ed. 1544, p. 273; Locher's "Stultifera Nauis," Ed. 1597, Pl. 4, p. 237; Maerman's "Apologi Creaturarum," &c., Ed. 1584, p. 235.
Leemans' Dr. Conrad,—edition of Horapollo's HIEROGLYPHICA, *Amstelodami*, 1835,—the best on critical grounds, 239, 273.
Leeu's "Dyalogus spraeck der creaturen,"

Ed. 1481, p. xiii., xiv.; "DIALOG. CREATUR. MORALI," Ed. 1480, p. 235; "*Spiegel der Sassen*," Ed. 1472, p. 401.
Leeu, Gheraert,—a printer of Gouda, p. xiii., xiv., 235 and 401.
Le Grys, a friend of Whitney, li.
Leicester, sir J. F., 367.
Leigh, major Egerton,—his copy of Whitney, xxvii.; probably a presentation copy to J. Allen, xxxi. *n.*
"Letter by a yonge Gentilwoman," &c., by Is. Whitney, p. lix.
Leycester, Robert earle of, *see* Dudley, Robert.
Leycester sir Peter; Historical Antiquities, Ed. 1673; quoted xli., xlii., 337, 357, 358, 361, 363, 364, 367, 370, 387; contest with sir Thomas Mainwaring, as to Amicia, daughter of Hugh Cyvelioc, p. 358.
Leyden—Catalogue of Students—1575–1616—,—Whitney's name, p. vii.
LEXICON HIEROGLYPHICUM SACRO-PROFANUM, &c., p. 273.
LIMBERT, STEPHAN, *the very learned*, for 32 years master of Norwich school, Emb. 173; p. 370, 1; his stanzas on Whitney, p. (19) xxx.;—Whitney's tutor, 370; memorial by a pupil, 371.
LIPSIUS JUSTUS, *the very famous*, Emb. 213, p. 392, a friend of Whitney, liv.; his learning, brief biography, 392; works from the Plantin press, 393 *n*; sources of information, p. 393.
Locher's "Stultifera Nauis," p. xiv., Ed. 1497, Pl. 4, p. 237; Device, Pl. 5, Emb. 223; of Whitney's devices *five* similar, *two* derived, p 238.
Londerzeel, Assuerus Van, an engraver,—some of his work in Sambucus, p. 248.
"*Lotterie in* LONDON," p. xlix., l., "*Her Maiesties poësie at*," Emb. p. 61, 331–333: Lotteries invented by the Romans;—Virginian state-lottery, in 1567, p. 332; "Gentlemen's Posy," and "Ladies' Posy," on tickets purchased for Gt. Yarmouth, p. 333; where a fuller history of Lotteries is given, p. 333.
"LVSTHOF VAN Rethonia," Ed. 1596, one of the later books from Rapheleng's press, p. 271 *n*.

M. *O. L.* p. v—from Linacre's GALEN, f. 35, *Paris* 1538.
Mainwarings,—branches of, p. 356, 357; crest, 356; rebuild the hall of Over Peover in 1585–6, p. 357 *n*; sir Thomas, in 1673–1679, carries on a controversy with sir Peter Leycester, p. 358; the Chartvlarium, 356; "diversifyings" of the name, 358 *n*.
MALIM, W., *the very learned*, 1533–1594, Emb. 89, q? and 152, p. 365; a great traveller,—notice of him,—Source of information,—his Famagosta, printed at Antwerp, 365.
Manship's History of Yarmouth, p. li., lv., 361, 389, 398.
Manuzio, Aldo, printer of Venice, in 1490; Paolo, in 1515, Ed. of Alciat, 1546, Pl. 16; and Aldo 1574–1597, p. 266.
MANWARINGE, *Sir* ARTHVRE, *Knight*, Emb. 131, p. 356, of Ightfield, in Shropshire,—his father sir John,—himself, his wife, and daughter, 357. Roger, bishop of Hereford (Hen. IV.), of this family,—and Arthur Mainwaring, in 1668, p. 357. Sir Arthur's daughter Mary, married to Richard Cotton 357,—descent of the present Mainwarings from this stock, 357, 8, and upward from Roger Mesnilgarin in the Conqueror's time, 358.
MANWARINGE, GEORGE, *Esquier*, Emb. 139, p. 364; Dedication to, by Is. Whitney, Pl. 11, p. lviii, and 364; Account of by Dugdale,—knighted,—daughter Anna bore *ten* sons and *ten* daughters to sir John Corbet, 364. Remarkable history of the emblem, 364.
Marnef Geffrey, Le grat nef des Folz du mode, Ed. 1499, Pl. 28, p. xv., 238; of the emblems *six* similar to Whitney's, *one* the original, p. 238; the women gaming, Pl. 29, Emb. 176; the devices from Stultifera nauis, 234.
Masseys allied to the Whitneys, p. xli. and 370,
MEMOIR AND WRITINGS OF GEFFREY WHITNEY, xxvi.–lxxiv.; Sect. 1, Estimation in which he was held,—Notices and Criticisms, xxvi.–xxxv.; Sect. 2, the Whitneys of Herefordshire and Cheshire, xxxv.–lv.; Sect. 3, the Writings of Whitney—some estimate of their worth, lv.–lxxiv,
Mens immota manet, Emb. 43, Whitney's stanzas inferior to the original in Sambucus, p. 327.
Merchant of Venice,—Shakespeare's casket scenes in the spirit of emblem-art, p. 294–296.
Mere Thomas, before 1600, mentions in "Wit's Commonwealth," Whitney, Combe, and Willet, xxx.
Mignault, Claude, or Minoïs, 1536–1606. his distinction between emblems and symbols, p. x.; COMMENTARIES ON ALCIAT, Ed. 1581, Pl. 21, p. 244,—some account of, and of the author, p. 279; great learning, 279.
MINERVA BRITANNA, 1612,—*see* Peacham.

Minoïs, *see* Mignault.
MIRROUR OF MAJESTIE, Ed. 1618,—the only perfect copy is Mr. Corser's, p. xxi.
MORAL EMBLEMS, from Catz and Farlie, Ed. 1862, p. xxiii. *n.*
Moretus, or Moereturf, John, was Plantin's son-in-law, 269,—Balthazar, the grandson, inherited Plantin's library, 268; the family, in 1865, still wealthy, 268 *n*; Edward,—the present owner of the library and printing office, 268 *n*, 234 *n*.
Mother's LEGACY to her unborn child, 351.
Motto, meaning of, p. 233; Whitney's "Constanter et syncere," p. lxviii.
Mottoes, Index to, and translation of, lxxv.-lxxix. Mottoes of emblems as well as devices by Whitney, generally borrowed, p. 237;—instances to the contrary, 405, 406.
Mottoes of historical and other personages quoted; Alciat,—*Never procrastinate*, 232, 406; Aristo, *Pro bono malum*, 408; Augustus and Vespasian, *Festina lentè*, 407; Bona of Savoy, *Sola facta solum Deum sequor*, 373; Fabritio Colonna, *Fides hoc uno virtusque probantur*, 407; Mutio Colonna, *Fortia facere et pati Romanum est*, 406; *Cosi vivo piacer conduce a morte*, 219, 395; Drake, *Auxilio divino,—sic parvis magna*, 382; Edward VI., *Nascatur ut alter*, 332, 373; Elizabeth, *Semper eadem*, and *Video et taceo*, 332; Flisca, *Non vos alabereis*, 409; Francis I., *Nutrisco et extinguo*, 375; Francis I. and II., *Sic spectanda fides*, 303, 407; Leycester, *Droit et loyal* (2); Battista da Lodrone, *In utraque fortuna*, 351; Cardinal of Lorraine, *Te stante, virebo*, 319; Dukes of Milan, *Este duces*, 348; Lorenzo di Medici, *Semper*, 404; the Pope, *Semper*, 404; Saladin, *Restat ex victore Orientis*, 339; Sir P. Sidney, *Sine refluxu*, 324; Mary Tudor, *Veritas temporis filia*, p. 321, 332; S. Valier, *Qui me alit me extinguit*, 302, 374.
Mottoes of Printers;—Bonhomme, Ed. 1552, Pl. 33, ΕΚ ΠΟΝΟΥ Ο ΚΛΕΟΣ, p. 239; Ed. 1555, Pl. 34, ΕΚ ΠΟΝΟΥ ΚΛΕΟΣ, p. 240; *Bononiæ*, Ed. 1574, Pl. 23, Libertas, p. 284; Giolito, Ed. 1556, Pl. 61, De la mia morte eterna vita vivo, and, Semper eadem, p. 374 *n*; Denys Ianot, Ed. 1539, Pl. 30, Amor Dei omnia vincit, and, Amor ut flos trãsiet, p. 238; Maire, Ed. 1640, Pl. 1, Fac et spera, p. xi.; Molin, Ed. 1560, Pl. 35, Literæ et arma parant (quorum dea Pallas) nonoremp. 240; Peacham Ed. 1612, Pl. 9, Princeps tibi crescit vtrvmque, p. xxi.; Plantin, Ed. 1562, Pl. 7; 1564, Pl. 24; 1565, Pl. 26; 1581, Pl. 21; 1585, Pl. 27; Labore et constantia, p. 268; Wechel, Ed. 1534, Pl. 6; Unicum arbustũ non alit duos erythacos, p. 244.
MYNORS, *Mr.* THOMAS, Emb. 165, name unidentified,—belongs to Gloucestershire and Hertfordshire, p. 366.
"MYTHOLOGIA ETHICA," Ed. 1579, Pl. 35, p. 241,—*see* Freitag.
Mythology, pagan, immoderate use of it in Whitney's time,—instance, p. lxx.

N. *O. L.* 293, Nef des Folz, lxxiii. *Paris*, 1499.
Names and Arms of Knights made from 1485 to 1624,—a manuscript in the British Museum, p. xxxviii, xl, 327, 328, 355.
Names, proper, variously spelled; Chatterton, 349; Cholmondeley, 355; Colley, 341; Dier, 359; Gryphith, 345; Harebrowne, 389; Leycester (3), 314; Manwaring, 357-358; Mynors, 366; Peyton, 335; Standley, 329; Stutvile, 336; Tollemache, 382; Whitney, iv. Pl. 43*a*, xli, xlii; Wilbraham, 380; Windham, 352; Withipole, 342; Woodhouse, 328, 9.
NAMPTWICHE, to my countrimen of the, Emb. 177,—neighbourhood of Whitney's birth-place, xliv,—name used for the district, 372; Register of the parish from 1572, p. xlv. The Great Fire; restoration of the town, 372; the Church, Pl. 15 and 15*a*—lately restored, p. 373. Fable of the Phœnix, 373, 374.
Napier, George W., esq., has a photograph of Whitney, Pl. 43*a*, p. 401.
NARRENSCHYFF,—Ed. 1494, *see* Brant.
Nef des folz du Monde, Ed. 1499, Pl. 28 and 29, *see* Marnef.
Nemo potest duobus dominis seruire, Emb. 223,—the illustration Pl. 5, p. 274 and 397.
Neville, Alexander, his KETTVS, p. 401*n*.
Newton, Thomas, Latin stanzas by him on Robert Dudley, p. 317; sir William Russell, 378; sir Francis Drake, 384.
Ninety English verses by Whitney, lvii.
NORRIS, *Sir* IOHN, *Knight, Lord President of Munster*, Emb. 194, p. 378. Character and services; noble character of Henry Norris; portrait at Knole of sir John, 378; Fuller's testimony; Spencer's lines, p. 379; some letters of, where printed, 380.
Nosgay, Swett, by Is. Whitney, Pl. 11, *see* Is. Whitney.

Scribit in marmore læsus, Emb. 183 *b*, from Sententiose Imprese, Ed. 1561, Pl. 37, p. 308 and 375; alluded to by Shakespeare, who probably saw it in Whitney, p. 309; origin of the sentiment, 309; a nobler thought, 310. Whitney's device identical with Paradin's;—for comment consult Symeoni, p. 375.

Semper eadem, one of Elizabeth's mottoes, p. 332; used by the printer Giolito, p. 374. Lorenzo the Magnificent, 404,—the Popes, 404.

Semper præsto esse infortunia, the dames gambling, Emb. 176,—the device adopted from Brant, Pl. 29, p. 238 and 371.

"SENTENTIOSE IMPRESE," &c., Ed. 1562, Pl. 36, p, 240,—*see* Giovio and Symeoni.

SHAKESPEARE'S REFERENCES TO EMBLEM-BOOKS, and to Whitney's emblems in particular, Essay IV., p. 293–312. His excellent judgment of art, 293; English emblematists open to him, 293. Emblems in the Merchant of Venice, from Corrozet, Pl. 32. Symeoni, Paradin, or Whitney, Emb. 219; p. 294–296; Emblems in the Pericles, 296–298,—*see* Pericles. Various Emblems, 304–110,—*see* Bear and ragged staff,—the beehive; dog barking at the moon, and *scribit in marmore læsus*.

"SHEPHEARD'S CALENDER;" *see* Spenser.

Shields with Emblems,—of Achilles, Hercules and Æneas, p. xi.

Shyp of Folys of the Worlde, 1509; *see* Barclay.

Sic spectanda fides, Emb. 139, Pl. 56; *see* Pericles; remarkable history of, 364.

Si Deus nobiscum &c., Emb. 166 *b*, a motto of Charles VIII., 408.

Sidney, sir Henry, father of sir Philip, 323, lord president of the marches of Wales, 324.

SIDNEY, *sir* PHILIP, *knight* &c., 1554–1586, Emb. 38 and 109; Spenser's lines to, p. 323; acquaintance with emblem art, 311, 324 *n*; sketch of his life, 323-325; Fuller's eulogy, 325; Whitney's, 326; profound grief for his death, 326; his portraits, and memoirs &c. to be consulted, 326; Speed's record, 326 *n*.

Silence, lines on, Emb. 60, p. lxxi.

Similar devices in Whitney to those in other authors, p. 236 and 237–243,—the number about 103, p. 243.

Sinful anger, to avoid, stanzas, Emb. 216, p. lxix.

Sir, a title applied to clergymen, 395.

Soli deo honor et gloria in æua sempiterna, Pl. 13, probably written by Whitney, 403.

Sources of Whitney's emblems; many from Plantin's editions, l and liv; Dibdin's conjecture and J. B. Yates', xxxiv, xxxv; researches, xxxv *n*; of *similar* devices, 237–243; of *identical*, 244–252.

Sources remoter of Whitney's emblems, 406–410.

Spanish emblem books; *original*,—Couaruvia's "Emblemas Morales," *Segovia* 1589, p. 252 *n*; Guzman's "Triumphas Morales," *Medina* 1587, p. 252 *n*, 299; De Soto's "Emblemas Moralezadas," *Madrid* 1599, p. 252 *n*; Don Orozco, 1610, p. 299; *translations*, Roville's "Los Emblemas da Alciate" &c., 1549, p. 252 and 299; Symeoni, p. 277.

Specimens from emblem writers for comparison with Whitney: *see* original stanzas.

Spenser, Edmund,—emblems in the Shepheard's Calender, and in Visions of Bellay, xvi, xvii and lxvi; not equal to Whitney in translating, lxiv; corresponding expressions, lxv; Description of Envy, Emb. 94, p. lxvii; Lines on Sidney, 323 and Norris 379.

SPIEGEL DER SASSEN, Ed. 1472; *see* Leeu.

STANDLEY, *sir* William, *knight*, died 1630; Emb. 47 and 195; Family and branches, 329; Services and defection, 330; Allen's defence of, Heywood's edition, 330; Dame Elizabeth Egerton his wife,—inscription on the tomb, 331.

Stanzas on Whitney, p. xxvii–xxxi.

STARKEY, ARTHVRE, *Esquier*, Emb. 205; a Cheshire family, 387; alliances, 387.

STEEVENSON, Mr. *Preacher*, Emb. 222, unidentified,—the device from Junius, Pl. 26 *a*, p. 397.

Stephens Henry and Robert, celebrated printers, 266.

Stirling Wm., Esqr.,—his fragment of Perrière, xvii.; Combe unknown, xix.; copy of Faerni, 251; copy of Daniell's Jovius, Title Pl. 60, p. 300 and 311; also copies of Giovio, Ruscelli, Domenichi, and Symeon, Pl. 60, 61, and 62, p. 311.

Stirry's Satire against Laud, Ed. 1641, p. xxii.

Stultifera Nauis, Ed. 1497, Pl. 4,—*see* Brant and Locher.

"*Stultitia sua seipsum saginari*," Emb. 98, from Faerni, Pl. 27, p. 344.

STVTVILE, THO., *Esquier*, Emb. 68; belonged to a Suffolk family, p. 336.

SUBJECTS AND SOURCES OF THE MOTTOES AND DEVICES IN WHITNEY, Essay I., p. 233–252.

Surrey, earl of, xvi.

THIS anchor stout, nor fails in calm, nor storm,
That holy cross doth weary pilgrims guide;
On either hand a dove, of peace the form,
By cross and anchor, ever will abide:
So hope, and faith, and love these symbols give,
The very way of truth by which to live.

In worldly strife our souls are tost and torn,
They have no rest who seize ambition's lure,
Round rugged deserts wander they forlorn,
Nor health nor healing comes their wounds to cure;
But own the cross, the anchor and the dove,—
Then beams around our lives eternal love.

SUBSCRIBERS TO THE REPRINT OF WHITNEY'S EMBLEMS.

Of this Edition 50 copies on large paper have been printed and issued to subscribers; 450 have been printed on small paper, and 314 subscribed for. *The negatives of the emblem plates have been destroyed, and cannot be re-produced without fresh photographs being taken.*

ADAMS, Rupert, esq., Birmingham.
Adams, William, esq., the Oaks, near Burslem.
Addis, John, jun., esq., Rustington, Littlehampton, Sussex.
Ainsworth, Ralph Fawsett, M.D., Manchester (*large paper*).
Ainsworth, Thomas, esq., the Flosh, Whitehaven (*large paper*).
Alexander, Walter, esq., 29, St. Vincent Street, Glasgow.
Allen, Mr. Josiah, sen., Birmingham.
Alliott, Rev. R., B.A., Knutsford.
Allwork, C. L., esq., Maidstone.
Ashton, F. W., esq., Stockport.
Ashton, Thomas, esq., Ford Bank, near Manchester.
Aspden, Mr. Robert Henry, Manchester.
Aspland, Alfred, esq., Dukinfield, Cheshire.
Aspland, Sidney, esq., barrister-at-law.
Atkinson, Rev. Arthur, M.A., Vicarage, Audlem, Cheshire (*two copies*).
Avison, Thomas, esq., F.S.A., Liverpool.

BAGEHOT, Edward Watson, esq., Langport.
Baker, Charles, esq., F.S.A., 11, Sackville Street, London.
Baker, Rev. Franklin, M.A., near Lancaster.
Barmby, Rev. Goodwyn, Wakefield.
Barnacle, Rev. Henry, M.A., Knutsford.
Barnes, Thomas, esq., M.P., Bolton-le-Moors.
Barratt, John, esq., Malling House, Southport.
Barry, A. H. Smith, esq., Marbury Hall, Cheshire (*large paper*).
Barton, Richard, esq., Caldy Manor, Birkenhead.
Bates, Henry, esq., the Vintage House, Yardley.
Bates, William, esq., B.A., 19, the Crescent, Birmingham.
Beard, James esq., the Grange, near Manchester.
Beard, Joseph, esq., Alderley Edge, Cheshire (*large paper*).
Belcher, lady, Regent's Park, London.
Bellot, Wm. Henry, gent., Moreton Lodge, Leamington Priors, late First Royal Cheshire Militia.
Betteley, Joseph, esq., Oakfield, Nantwich.
Beyer, C. F., esq., Stanley Grove, Manchester.
Binning, the lord, Eaton Banks, Tarporley (*large paper*).
Bird, W. F. W., esq., Dartford, Kent.
Blackie, John Stuart, M.A., professor of Greek, Edinburgh.
Blackman, Frederick, esq., 4, York Road, London S.
Bolton, T. F., esq., Liverpool.
Booth, Benjamin W., esq., Swinton, near Manchester.
Booth, John, esq., Monton, near Manchester.
Bright, H. A., esq., M.A., Fairfield, Liverpool.
Brooke, Henry, esq., Forest Hill, Northwich.
Brooks, James Howard, esq., 40, Brown Street, Manchester.
Brothers, Mr. Alfred, F.R.A.S., St. Ann's Square, Manchester (*four copies*).
Brough, Mr., bookseller, Birmingham.
Buckton, Frederick, esq., Leeds.
Bulkeley, sir R. Williams, bart., M.P., Baron Hill, Beaumaris.
Bulmer, Martin, esq., C.E., Maidstone.

CADBY, Mr., 83, New Street, Birmingham.
Caldwell, Mr. W. G., Knutsford.
Campbell, James Ashburner, esq., Edgbaston, Birmingham.
Carlton, James, esq., Norbury Booths, Knutsford (*large paper*).
Carlyle, J. A., M.D., the Hill, Dumfries.
Carter, William, esq., Pall Mall, Manchester.
Cheetham, George, esq., Fernside, Upper Norwood S.
Cholmondeley, the most hon. the marquess of, Cholmondeley Castle (*large paper*).
Christie, Richard C., esq., barrister-at-law, 7, St. James' Square, Manchester.

Clarke, Miss, Knutsford.
Clay, Charles, M.D., Manchester.
Clement, William J., esq., M.P., the Council House, Shrewsbury.
Coleridge, John Duke, esq., Q.C, 6, Southwick Crescent, W. (*large paper*).
Colley, T. Davies, M.D., White Friars, Chester.
Collie, John, esq., Thornfield, Alderley Edge, Cheshire.
Collier, John Payne, esq., Riverside, Maidenhead.
Combermere, field-marshal the viscount (deceased), Combermere Abbey.
Congreve, William, esq., Burton Hall, Neston, Cheshire.
Coppock, Henry, esq., Stockport (*large paper*).
Cornish Brothers, Messrs., Birmingham (*two copies*).
Corser, Rev. Thomas, M.A., F.S.A., Stand, near Manchester (*large paper*).
Cottam, Mr., 28, Brazenose Street, Manchester.
Crompton, Mrs., 89, Oxford Terrace, Hyde Park, London.
Cropper, Rev. John, M.A., Stand, near Manchester.
Crossley, James, esq., F.S.A., president of the Chetham Society, Manchester.
Croston, Mr. J., King Street, Manchester.
Crouch, Walter, jun., esq., 20, Coborn Street, Bow.
Cunliffe, sir Robert, bart., 9, Holles Street, Cavendish Square, London.

DARBISHIRE, S. D., esq., Pendyffryn, near Conway (*one large and one small paper copy*).
Darbishire, James, esq., Dunowen, Belfast.
David's (St.), the right Rev. the bishop of, Abergwili Palace, Carmarthen.
Davis, J. Barnard, M.D., F.S.A., Shelton, Staffordshire.
Deane, Mrs., Knutsford.
Deane, Charles, esq., Cambridge, Mass., U. S. A.
Dendy, John, esq., B.A., Worsley, near Manchester.
Devonshire, his grace the duke of, Devonshire House, London (*large paper*).
Doeg, Mr. W. Henry, Manchester.

ECKERSLEY, Thomas, Esq., Wigan.
Eddleston, Dickenson, esq., Sowerby Bridge, Halifax.
Egerton of Tatton, the r[t] hon. the lord, Tatton Park, Cheshire (*large paper*).
Egerton, sir Philip de Malpas Grey, bart., M.P., Oulton Park, Cheshire.
Egerton, the hon. Wilbraham, M.P., Rostherne Manor, Cheshire.
Ellis, Charles, sen., esq., Maidstone, Kent.

FAIRBAIRN, William, esq., C.E., LL.D. &c., Manchester (*one large, and one small copy*).
Fairbairn, George, esq., the Polygon, Manchester (*two copies*).
Falcon, Charles, esq., Forest Hey, Northwich (*two copies*).
Falcon, captain Maxwell, R.N. (*two copies*).
Falconer, Thomas, esq., judge of the county court, Glamorganshire.
Fawdington, Arthur E., esq., 43, Chancery Lane, London.
Fergusson, sir James, bart., M.P., Ayrshire.
Ffoulkes, W. W., esq., barrister-at-law, Chester.
Field, E. W., esq., Hampstead, London.
Fielden, Samuel, esq., Centre Vale, Todmorden.
Fowle, W. F., esq., Boston, Mass., U. S. A.
Fryer, Mr. George Henry, Bowdon, Cheshire.

GASKELL, Daniel, esq., Lupset Hall, Wakefield (*large paper*).
Gaskell, J. Milnes, esq., M.P., Thornes House, Wakefield.
Gaskell, John Upton, esq., Ingersley Hall, Macclesfield.
Gaskell, Samuel, esq., Latchford, Warrington (*large paper*).
Gibson, Rev. Matthew, Dudley.
Gladstone, Thomas, esq., Edgbaston, Birmingham.
Gray, W., esq., M.P., Darcy Lever Hall, Bolton-le-Moors.
Green, Charles, esq., Winnington, Northwich.
Green, Mr. Charles Notcutt, Winnington, Northwich.
Green, Mr. Frank, 60, Watling Street, London.
Green, J. Philip, esq., LL.B., barrister-at-law, Bombay (*one large and one small copy*).
Green, Thomas, esq., Stapeley, Nantwich.
Greene, J. S. Turner, esq., Adlington Hall, Lancashire.
Greg, Robert Hyde, esq., Norcliffe, Cheshire.
Griffith, Rev. David, Tavistock, Devon.
Griffiths, Mr. E. H., bookseller, Nantwich (*two copies*).
Grundy, Frederick Leigh, esq., 6th Royal Regiment, Jamaica.
Grundy, J. A., esq., 4, Clarence Street, Manchester.
Grundy, R. E., esq., 4, Clarence Street, Manchester.

Grundy, William, esq., Bury, Lancashire.
Guild, J. Wylie. esq., 3, Park Circus, Glasgow.

HADFIELD, George, esq., M.P., Victoria Park, Manchester.
Harland, Mr. John, F.S.A., Manchester.
Harrison, William, esq., F.S.A., Galligreaves Hall, Blackburn (*large paper*).
Harrison, Mr. George, Cross Street, Manchester.
Harwood, John, jun., esq., Mayfield, Bolton-le-Moors.
Hatton, James, esq., Richmond House, near Manchester.
Hawkins, Edward, esq., F.R.S., 6, Lower Berkeley Street, London.
Hawkshaw, John, esq., F.R.S., 43, Eaton Place, London (*two copies*).
Heaton, Charles, esq., Leek, Staffordshire.
Hessels, J. H. esq., 6, Union Road, Cambridge.
Heywood, Arthur H., esq., Bank, Manchester (*large paper*).
Heywood, Mr., John, Deansgate, Manchester.
Heywood, Thomas, esq., F.S.A., Ledbury, Hereford.
Hibbert, John, esq., Hyde, near Manchester.
Hill, Rev. George, Queen's College, Belfast.
Hill, Henry, esq., Knutsford.
Hodgetts, Alfred, esq., Whitehaven.
Holden, Mr. A., 48, Church Street, Liverpool (*two copies*).
Holland, sir Henry, bart., 25, Brook Street, London.
Holland, Miss, Church House, Knutsford.
Holland, Robert, esq., Mobberley, Cheshire.
Holt, Mrs., Rake Lane, Edge Hill, Liverpool.
Holt, William D., esq., Edge Lane, Liverpool (*large paper*).
Holt, Alfred, esq., Fairfield, Liverpool.
Holt, Philip H., esq., Prince's Park, Liverpool.
Holt, James, esq., Chorley, Lancashire.
Howard, Thomas, esq., Brookfield, Nantwich (*two copies*).
Hughes, Mr. Thomas, Grove Terrace, Chester (*large paper*).
Humberston, Miss, Newton Hall, Chester.
Humberston, Philip S., esq., M.P., Mollington, Chester.
Humble, Miss Susan, Vicar's Cross, Chester.
Hunter, Rev. Stephenson, The Parade, Carmarthen.

JACKSON, Francis M., esq., Portland Street, Manchester.
Jackson, Henry M. esq., barrister-at-law, 7, Oxford Square, London.
Jackson, William, esq., M.P., The Manor House, Birkenhead.
James, W. M., esq., Q.C., Vice-Chancellor of Lancaster, London.
Jesus College Library, Cambridge.
Jewitt, Llewellyn, esq., F.S.A., Derby.
Johnson, W. R., esq., The Cliffe, Wybunbury, near Nantwich.
Jones, C. W., esq., Gateacre, near Liverpool.
Jones, Thomas, esq., Cheetham Library, Manchester.
Jones, T. W., esq., Nantwich.
Jordan, Joseph, esq., Bridge Street, Manchester.

KENRICK, Rev. John, M.A., F.S.A., Monkgate, York.
Kershaw, the Rev. Canon, Barton, near Manchester.
Kershaw, John, esq., Cross Gate, Audenshaw, Manchester.

LAIRD, John, esq., M.P., Birkenhead.
Latham, Mrs., Liverpool (*large paper*).
Ledgard, E. A. esq., Ashton-under-Lyne.
Lees, Harold, esq., Saddleworth (*one large paper, one small*).
Legh, George Cornwall, esq., M.P., High Legh Hall, Cheshire.
Leigh, Egerton, esq., The West Hall, High Leigh, Cheshire (*large paper*).
Leigh, Henry, esq., Patricroft, near Manchester.
Leigh, John, esq., 26, St. John's Street, Manchester.
Leppoc, Henry J., esq., The Kersal Crag, Manchester (*large paper*).
L'Isle, right hon. lord de, Penshurst, Kent.
Long, John, esq., Grove House, Knutsford.
Long, Henry, esq., Woodlands, Knutsford.
Long, J. Brandreth, esq., Grove House, Knutsford.
Long, Peter, esq., The Elms, Hale, Cheshire.
Lumb, R. Kershaw, esq., The Park, Cheltenham.

M'CONNEL, James, esq., Prestwich, near Manchester.
Mackenzie, John Whitefoord, esq., F.S.A., Sc., Edinburgh.
Mackie, Ivie, esq., Auchencairn House, Castle Douglas (*one large paper and two small*).
M'Vicar, Duncan, esq., Abercromby Square, Liverpool.

Mainwaring, Sir H., bart., Peover Hall, Cheshire.
Mainwaring, Townshend, esq., M.P., Galltfaenan, Rhyl.
Manchester Free Library (*large paper*).
Marcus, H. J., Ph.D., Manchester.
Marsden, Rev. John Howard, canon of the Cathedral, Manchester.
Marsh, John F., esq., Fairfield House, Warrington.
Mart, M. Joseph Foveaux, Salford, Manchester.
Mather, lieutenant-colonel, Coed Mawr, near Conway (*large paper*).
Minshull and Hughes Messrs., booksellers, Chester (*two copies*).
Moorhouse, Christopher, esq., Congleton.
Morrall, Michael T., esq., F.S.A., Balmoral House, Matlock.
Morton, Mr. William, artist, 2, Essex Street, Manchester.
Mosley, sir Oswald, bart., Rolleston Hall, Burton-on-Trent.
Moss, Rev. J. J., East Lydford, Somerton,
Mott, Charles Grey, esq., Birkenhead.
Muller, M. Fred., bookseller, Amsterdam (*two copies*).
Munroe, Henry Whitney, esq., Paris.
Murdoch, James Barclay, esq., 33, Lynedoch Street, Glasgow.
Murland, Robert, esq., Woodlawn, Castlewellan, Ireland (*one large paper and one small*).

NAPIER, George W., esq., Alderley Edge, Cheshire.
Naylor, Benjamin Dennison, esq., F.R.S A. Dunham Massey, Cheshire.
Nichols, John Gough, esq., F.S.A., 25, Eaton Place, Brighton.
Nichols, Rev. W. L., M.A., F.S.A., Keynsham House, near Bath (*large paper*).
Nicholson, Robert, esq., Chesham Place, Bowdon, Cheshire.
Nijhoff, M. Martinus, bookseller, The Hague, Holland.
Norton, Charles Eliot, esq., Cambridge, Mass., U.S.A.

OPENSHAW, Thomas Lomax, esq., Bury, Lancashire.
Ormerod, George, esq., D.C.L., Sedbury Park, near Chepstow.
Ouvry, Frederic, esq., Tr.S.A., London (*large paper*).

PALMER, Charles John, esq., F.S.A., Great Yarmouth.
Panton, Rev. George A., Crown Circus, Dowan Hill, Glasgow.
Parker, Mrs., Kirkdale Road, Liverpool (*large paper*).
Peacock, Richard, esq., Gorton Hall, near Manchester (*large paper*).
Pearson, Mrs. William, Borderside, Newton-in-Cartmel.
Peel, George, esq., Brookfield, near Manchester (*large paper*).
Pemberton, Oliver, esq., 17, Temple Row, Birmingham.
Philips, R. N., esq., M.P., the Park, Manchester (*large paper*).
Pilkington, Mr. Joseph Mills, Newcastle-on-Tyne.
Plant, John, esq., F.G.S., Peel Park Library, Manchester.
Portico Library, the, Manchester.
Procter, Charles Edward, esq., Ashfield House, near Macclesfield.
Pyne, Mr. Joseph J., 63, Piccadilly, Manchester.

QUARITCH, Mr. Bernard, 15, Piccadilly, London (*two copies*).

RAINES, the Rev. Canon, M.A., F.S.A., Milnrow Parsonage, Rochdale.
Reade, George, esq., Congleton (deceased).
Read, John William, esq., Woodhouse Cliff, Leeds.
Redfern, Rev. Robert, M.A., Vicarage, Acton, Nantwich.
Robberds, Rev. John, B.A., High Park Street, Liverpool.
Roberts, Mr. William, Foregate-st., Chester.
Robinson, George, esq., the Cedars, Bowdon, Cheshire.
Robinson, Samuel, esq., Blackbrook Cottage, Wilmslow, Cheshire.
Roscoe, Mrs., Bath (*large paper*).
Roscoe, Miss Laura, Knutsford
Ruskin, John, esq., M.A., Denmark Hill, London.

SACKETT, Mr. W. J., 11, Bull Street, Birmingham (*two copies*).
Satterfield, Joshua, esq., Alderley Edge, Cheshire.
Siddeley, Mr. John, Knutsford.
Sidebotham, Joseph, esq., 12, George Street, Manchester.
Simms, Mr. Charles, King Street, Manchester (*two copies*).
Slater, Mr. Edwin, St. Ann's Square, Manchester (*one large paper and one small*).
Slater, Mr. E., Sankey Street, Warrington.
Smith, Brooke, esq., Edgbaston, Birmingham.
Spark, H. King, esq., Greenbank, Darlington (*large paper*).

Stanley of Alderley, the right hon. the lord, Alderley Park, Cheshire.
Steinthal, Rev. S. Alfred, Manchester.
Stirling, William, esq., M.P., Keir, Dunblane (*one large paper and one small*).
Strathern, Alexander, esq., sherif-substitute of Lanarkshire, Glasgow.
Sudlow, John, esq., 18, Princess Street, Manchester.
Swanwick, John, esq., 18, Booth Street, Manchester.
Swanwick, the Misses, 23, Cumberland Terrace, Regent's Park, London.
Swinnerton, Mr. James, Macclesfield (*six copies*).
Swinburne, J. W., esq., solicitor, Gateshead.

TABLEY, the right hon. the lord de, Tabley House, Cheshire (*large paper*).
Tate, William James, esq., Woodlands, Altrincham, Cheshire.
Taylor, George I., esq., 74, George Street, Manchester.
Taylor, Mrs., Knutsford (*large paper*).
Teacher, Mr. W., St. Enoch Square, Glasgow,
Templar, Mr. B., Cheetham Hill, Manchester.
Temple, Rev. Robert, the Lache Hall, Chester.
Thom, Rev. John H., Oakfield, Liverpool.
Thompson, S. H., esq., Thingwall Hall, Liverpool (*one large paper and one small*).
Thompson, Henry Yates, esq., Thingwall Hall, Liverpool (*large paper*).
Thorley, George, esq., M.A., Wadham College, Oxford.
Thornely, John, esq., barrister-at-law, 68, Chancery Lane, London.
Thornely, Alfred, esq., Liverpool.
Thornely, Edward, esq., 5, Fenwick Street, Liverpool.
Thorp, Mr. Henry, Piccadilly, Manchester (*large paper*).
Timmins, Samuel, esq., Elvetham Lodge, Birmingham.
Townshend, Lee P., esq., Wincham Hall, Cheshire.
Twyford, Edward P. M.D., St. Helens, Lancashire (*large paper*).

VAN WART, Mrs. William, Hagley Road, Birmingham.
Vawdrey, Benjamin Ll., esq., Middlewich.

WADSWORTH, George, esq., 96, Cross Street, Manchester (*large paper*).
Wales, George W., esq., Boston, Mass., U. S. A.
Walker, Rev. Thomas Andrew, M.A., Filey, Yorkshire.
Warburton, R. E. Egerton, esq., Arley Hall, Cheshire (*two copies*).
Ward, Frederick, esq., 21, George Street, Sheffield.
Ware, T. Hibbert, esq., Hale Barns, Altrincham, Cheshire.
Watts, Sir James, Abney Hall, near Manchester.
Wedgwood, Clement F., esq., Barlaston, Stone.
Wellings, John, esq., Wotton-under-Edge, Gloucestershire.
Westmacott, J. V. L., esq., Ardwick Green, Manchester.
Whalley, Mr. John Edward, Eccles, near Manchester.
Wheatley, Henry B., esq., 53, Berners' Street, London W.
Wheeler, Benjamin, esq., Exchange Arcade, Manchester.
White, George H., esq., 8, Bishopsgate Street within, London.
Whitney, Henry Austin, esq., Boston, Mass., U. S A. (*two large and nine small paper*).
Whitney, Joseph, esq., Boston, Mass., U. S. A.
Whitney, Henry Lawrence, esq., Boston, Mass., U. S. A.
Whitney, Joseph Cutler, esq., Boston, Mass., U. S. A.
Whitney, Ellerton Pratt, esq., Boston, Mass., U. S. A.
Whitney, Miss Elizabeth, Boston, Mass., U. S. A.
Whitney, Miss Constance, Boston, Mass., U. S. A.
Whitney, Thomas Heston, esq., Glassboro', New Jersey, U. S. A.
Whittard, Rev. T. Middlemore, The College, Cheltenham.
Wilbraham, Randle, esq., Rode Hall, Cheshire.
Williams, Ignatius, esq., The Grove, near Denbigh.
Williams, Mr. S. 14, Henrietta Street, Covent Garden, London.
Williams, Samuel De la Grange, esq., Birmingham.
Wilson, Mr. John, 93, Great Russell Street, London, W.C.
Wood, John, esq., Wellington Terrace, Rochdale (*large paper*).
Wood, R. H., esq., Crumpsall, near Manchester.
Wood, William Rayner, esq., Singleton, near Manchester.
Woodcock, J., esq., Knutsford.
Worthington, Rev. A. W., B.A., Mansfield.

Worthington, Andrew I., esq., Leek, Staffordshire.
Worthington, James, esq., Sale Hall, Cheshire (*large paper*).
Worthington, Rev. Jeffrey, Bolton-le-Moors.
Wright, J. Harvey, esq., Boston, Mass., U. S. A.

YATÈS, James, esq., M.A., F.R.S., Lauderdale House, Highgate.
Yates, Miss Jane Ellen, The Dingle, Liverpool.
Yates, Mrs. Richard, Maryland Street, Liverpool.
Young, Alexander, Esq., 138, Hope Street, Glasgow.

CORRIGENDA.

Page xxxvi,	line 35.	Drew *should be* Dew.
„ xxxix,	„ 20.	
„ 234,	„ 22.	Edition 1498 *should be* 1499.
„ 321,	„ 20.	*tempora filia should be temporis filia.*
„ 324,	„ 10 of note ‡.	REFLEXV *should be* REFLVXV.
„ 341,	„ 17.	*Horoölogia should be Heroölogia.*
„ 370,	„ 13.	Hilantatem *should be* Hilaritatem.
„ 371,	„ 21.	*Otiose should be Otiosi.*
„ 394,	„ 9.	Tomas Legge *should be* Thomas Legge.
„ 401,	„ 20.	*Soli dei honor should be Soli deo honor.*
„ 403,	„ 32,3.	
„ 404,		Plate LXX *should be* Plate LX.

MANCHESTER:
PRINTED BY CHARLES SIMMS AND CO., KING STREET.